GMAT® PREP PLUS 2022-2023

Our 80 years' expertise = Your competitive advantage

6 PRACTICE TESTS + PROVEN STRATEGIES + ONLINE

Editor, 2022–2023 Edition

Paula L. Fleming, MA, MBA

Contributing Editor

Ethan A. Weber

Special thanks to our faculty authors and reviewers

Steve Bartley; Harry Broome; James Carney; Chris Cosci; Amy T. Craddock; Thomas Darragh; Aisa Diaz; Emily Graves; Jack Hayes, MBA; Alexandre Khan; Katarina Kurtz; Jo L'Abbate; Gordon Spector; Chris Sun; Caroline Sykes; Mary Toro

Additional special thanks to

Brian Carlidge, MBA; M. Dominic Eggert; Robin Garmise; Rita Garthaffner; Joanna Graham; Craig Harman; Jaimie Lazare; M. L. Liu; Mandy Luk; Jennifer Moore; Camellia Mukherjee, MFA; Denise Pangia; Anne Pennick; Stevonnie Ross; Carly Schnur; Sascha Strelka, MA; Oscar Velazquez; Michael Wolff; Amy Zarkos; Boo; Fifteen Thousand; Scooby; and the countless others who have contributed to this and past editions.

GMAT is a registered trademark of the Graduate Management Admission Council™. Kaplan materials do not contain actual GMAT items and are neither endorsed by nor affiliated in any way with GMAC.

Published by Kaplan Publishing, a division of Kaplan, Inc.
1515 W. Cypress Creek Road
Fort Lauderdale, FL 33309

ISBN: 978-1-5062-7723-3

10 9 8 7 6 5 4 3 2 1

Kaplan Publishing print books are available at special quantity discounts to use for sales promotions, employee premiums, or educational purposes. For more information or to purchase books, please call the Simon & Schuster special sales department at 866-506-1949.

TABLE OF CONTENTS

HOW TO USE THIS BOOK

Welcome to Kaplan's GMAT Prep Plus 2022

Congratulations on your decision to pursue an MBA or other graduate management degree and thank you for choosing Kaplan for your GMAT preparation.

You've made the right choice in acquiring this book—you're now armed with a comprehensive GMAT program that is the result of decades of researching the GMAT and teaching many thousands of students the skills they need to succeed. You have what you need to score higher; the next step is to make the commitment to your study plan.

Let's walk through everything you need to know to take advantage of this book and your online resources.

LEARNING OBJECTIVES

In this section, you will learn how to:

- Identify the types of study resources included with this book
- Explain how to register and access this book's online resources
- Create a study plan so you can prepare for the GMAT with confidence

---

Your Book

There are two main components of your *GMAT Prep Plus* study package: your book and your online resources. This book contains:

- Detailed instruction covering the essential verbal, math, integrated reasoning, and writing concepts
- Student-tested, highly effective Kaplan Methods and strategies for every question type
- More than 350 practice questions, followed by detailed answer explanations

Your Online Resources

Your Kaplan online resources give you access to additional materials to reinforce key concepts and sharpen your GMAT skills. These include:

- Six full-length computer-adaptive practice tests (CATs)
- Analysis of your performance on each practice test, including detailed answer explanations
- The GMAT Strategy Sheet
- In-depth analyses of how the GMAT generates your score and what this means for taking and retaking the test

Getting Started

Studying for the GMAT can be daunting, and with so many resources available to you, it may not be clear where to begin. Don't worry; we'll break it down one step at a time, just as we'll do with the GMAT questions that you will soon be on your way to mastering.

Getting Started

STEP 1 Register your online resources.

STEP 2 Take a computer-adaptive GMAT practice test to identify your strengths and opportunities for improvement.

STEP 3 Create a study plan.

STEP 4 Learn and practice using this book and your online resources.

STEP 5 Take more computer-adaptive practice tests to gauge your progress.

Step 1: Register Your Online Resources

Register your online resources using these simple steps:

1. Go to **kaptest.com/moreonline**.
2. Follow the on-screen instructions. Please have a copy of this book available.

Access to the online resources is limited to the original owner of this book and is nontransferable. Kaplan is not responsible for providing access to the online resources to customers who purchase or borrow used copies of this book. Access to the online resources expires one year after you register.

Step 2: Take a GMAT Practice Test

It's essential to take a practice test early on. Doing so will give you the initial feedback and diagnostic information that you will need to achieve your maximum score. Taking a full-length test right at the start can be intimidating, but remember: your practice test scores don't count. During your first practice test—and any practice test you take—turn off your cell phone, give the test your full attention, and learn from your performance.

All of Kaplan's online full-length tests are computer-adaptive tests (CATs), meaning they have the same format as the actual GMAT. You will learn more about CATs in **Part One** of this book. The computer-adaptive format presents distinct challenges for time management, because you can only move forward through the test. Because you can't skip a question and come back to it later, you need to decide for each question how much time to spend trying to get it right and when you should just guess and move on. This ability to triage questions as you meet them is key to maximizing your GMAT score, and you can only practice it in an adaptive online test.

After taking your first practice test, review the detailed answer explanations to better understand your performance. Our explanations label each question according to its question type and topic. Look for patterns in the questions you answered correctly and incorrectly. Were you stronger in some areas than others? This analysis will help you target your practice time to specific concepts.

Step 3: Create a Study Plan

Use what you've learned from your initial practice test to identify areas for closer study and practice. Take time to familiarize yourself with the key components of your book and online resources. Think about how many hours you can consistently devote to GMAT study. We have found that most students realize success by putting in about 100 hours of study over about three months.

Schedule time for study, practice, and review. Many people find it works best to block out short, frequent periods of study time throughout the week. Also, keep a log of questions you find challenging or simply interesting. Come back to these questions every week or two until you feel you've learned all you can from them. Then check them off or cross them out and focus on the new questions you've added to your log. Check in with yourself often to make sure you're not falling behind your plan.

Step 4: Learn and Practice

Your book and online resources come with many opportunities to develop and practice the skills you'll need on Test Day. Read each chapter of this book and complete the practice questions. Depending on how much time you have to study, you can do this work methodically, covering every chapter, or you can focus on those question types and content areas that are most challenging for you. You will inevitably need more work in some areas than in others, but know that the more thoroughly you prepare, the better your score will be.

Initially, your practice should focus on mastering the needed skills and not on speed. As you become more proficient, begin pushing yourself to answer questions more efficiently.

Step 5: Take More Practice Tests

Once you feel you have addressed the areas that gave you trouble on your diagnostic test, take another full-length practice test, also available in your online resources. The Kaplan CATs are realistic practice tests, and taking the full-length tests that come with this book is one of the best ways to prepare fully for what you will face on the real GMAT.

Always review your practice test results thoroughly to make sure you are addressing the areas that are most important to your score. Allot time to review the explanations so that you can learn from your mistakes and not make these errors when it actually matters, on Test Day. After your second practice test, you'll probably find that some of your initial weaknesses aren't weaknesses anymore. Now, to continue to build your score, you'll probably want to adjust your study plan to focus on some different areas. Continue taking full-length practice tests every week or two leading up to Test Day.

Thanks for choosing Kaplan. We wish you the best of luck on your journey to business school.

Changes and Corrections

The material in this book is accurate and up-to-date at the time of printing. However, the Graduate Management Admission Council may have instituted changes in the tests or test registration process after this book was published. Be sure to read carefully the materials you receive when you register for the test.

If there are changes or corrections to the materials in this book, these can be found at **kaptest.com/publishing**.

The test maker's website, the source for all official information about test registration and policies, is **mba.com**.

[PART ONE]

GMAT ESSENTIALS

CHAPTER 1

GMAT FORMAT AND SCORING

LEARNING OBJECTIVES

- List the four sections of the GMAT and recognize the options for the order in which you can take them
- Describe the 200–800 point scoring scale, including which sections contribute to it, and describe the scoring scales for the other sections
- Describe the resources you will use when taking the GMAT
- Explain when and how to register for the GMAT

Let's start with the basics. The GMAT is, among other things, an endurance test. It consists of 127 minutes of multiple-choice math and verbal questions, a 30-minute reasoning section, and a 30-minute essay. Add in the administrative details, plus two 8-minute breaks, and the testing experience takes about 3.5 hours.

It's a grueling journey, and if you don't approach it with confidence, you can easily get tired and lose your composure. That's why it's important that you take control of the test, just as you take control of the rest of your business school application process.

COVID-19 AND THE GMAT

As this book goes to press, the COVID-19 pandemic remains a significant feature of the environment in many countries. The virus has impacted test administration and education more generally, and it may continue to do so. For the most up-to-date details about test format and administration, check the test maker's website at **mba.com**.

GMAT Format

The GMAT consists of four sections, and you can choose your section order on Test Day. Before you begin your test, you'll be presented with three orders and asked to select one:

- Analytical Writing Assessment (AWA), Integrated Reasoning (IR), Quantitative, Verbal
- Quantitative, Verbal, Integrated Reasoning, Analytical Writing Assessment
- Verbal, Quantitative, Integrated Reasoning, Analytical Writing Assessment

If you do not choose an order, then after 2 minutes, the first order—beginning with Analytical Writing—will be chosen for you.

The order you take the sections in will not appear on your score report, and the test maker's research has not shown that section order gives one test taker a statistical advantage over another. If you are especially concerned about a section and want to take it when you are mentally freshest, then choose the order that puts that section first. If you want to build confidence by completing other sections first, then choose an order that puts that section later. And if you don't care what order you take the sections in, that's perfectly okay—just choose whichever order you have practiced most.

The Quantitative section contains 31 questions in two formats, Problem Solving and Data Sufficiency, which are mixed together throughout the section.

The Verbal section contains 36 questions in three formats, Reading Comprehension, Sentence Correction, and Critical Reasoning, which are also mixed throughout the section.

The Integrated Reasoning section is 30 minutes long. This section has 12 questions, each of which may require more than one response. The questions in this section ask you to draw conclusions based on information in tables, interpret graphs, understand information presented across different layouts, and find two answers that fit given information in a complementary way.

The Analytical Writing Assessment (AWA) requires you to complete an essay, typing it into the computer using a simple word processing program. You are given 30 minutes for this essay, during which you have to analyze the flawed reasoning behind a given argument and recommend how to improve the argument.

GMAT EXAM SECTION	QUESTIONS	TIME
Analytical Writing Assessment	1	30 minutes
Integrated Reasoning	12	30 minutes
Quantitative	31	62 minutes
Verbal	36	65 minutes
Total Testing Time		**3 hours, 7 minutes**

Length of Sections on the GMAT

You will also get two optional 8-minute breaks between sections. Kaplan recommends that you take these breaks.

ORDER A	ORDER B	ORDER C
Analytical Writing Assessment	Verbal	Quantitative
Integrated Reasoning		
8-minute break (optional)		
Quantitative	Quantitative	Verbal
8-minute break (optional)		
Verbal	Integrated Reasoning	Integrated Reasoning
	Analytical Writing Assessment	Analytical Writing Assessment

Breaks on the GMAT by Section Order

We'll talk more about each of the question types in later chapters. For now, note the following: you'll be answering 79 multiple-choice questions in about 2.5 hours. Clearly, you'll have to move fast. But you can't let yourself get careless. Taking control of the GMAT means increasing the speed of your work without sacrificing accuracy.

If You Take the GMAT Online

Instead of registering to take the GMAT at a test center, you might prefer to take the exam on your own device. Some test takers appreciate the convenience and comfort of taking the test at home. If you go this route, ensure that your equipment meets the test maker's technical requirements and that you can comply with the security protocols for online testing.

Be aware that as of this writing, you may take the test online only twice; if you've already taken the GMAT online twice and wish to take it again, you'll need to take it at a test center. Both online and test center administrations count toward the annual and lifetime limits on how many times you can take the test.

One key difference between the two test settings is the tools you're given for your scratchwork. At the test center, you'll use a laminated notepad and unerasable black pen. Online, you'll use an onscreen whiteboard and/or a physical erasable whiteboard and markers that meet the test maker's specifications. Most students find either set of tools easy to use and trouble-free.

The test maker has changed registration, score-reporting, and test format details for the online GMAT administration several times and may make further changes. Get the most up-to-date information about taking the GMAT at a test center or online from **mba.com**.

Overview of the GMAT Sections

Following are previews of each of the four sections of the GMAT.

Quantitative Section Overview

Slightly less than half of the multiple-choice questions that count toward your overall score appear in the Quantitative (math) section. You'll have 62 minutes to answer 31 Quantitative questions in two formats: Problem Solving and Data Sufficiency. These two types of questions are mingled throughout the Quantitative section, so you never know what's coming next.

Here's what you can expect to see:

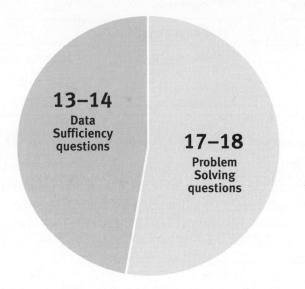

The Approximate Mix of Questions on the GMAT Quantitative Section

You may see more of one question type and fewer of the other due to the test's somewhat random selection of questions.

Pacing on the Quantitative Section

Since you'll have 62 minutes to answer 31 questions, you should spend about 2 minutes per question. Problem Solving and Data Sufficiency questions take, on average, about the same amount of time, so you don't need to worry about different timing for different question types on this section.

The tidy timing also makes section management straightforward. When there are about 40 minutes remaining, you should have answered about 10 questions. When there are about 20 minutes remaining, you should have answered about 20 or 21 questions. And when time runs out, you'll have answered all 31 questions.

Math Content Knowledge

Naturally, the Quantitative section tests your math skills, so you will have to work with concepts that you may not have used for a few years. You are not allowed to use a calculator on the Quantitative section, and even if you use math all the time on the job or in college, it's probably been a while since you were unable to use a calculator or computer to perform computations. So refreshing your fundamental math skills is definitely a crucial part of your prep.

Fortunately, the range of math topics tested is fairly limited. The GMAT covers only the math that US students have usually seen by the second year of high school. No trigonometry, no advanced algebra, no calculus. As you progress in your GMAT prep, you'll see that the same concepts are tested again and again in remarkably similar ways.

Areas of math content tested on the GMAT include arithmetic, number properties, algebra, ratios in various forms, basic statistics, and geometry. Arithmetic and algebra are the most commonly tested topics—they are tested either directly or indirectly on a majority of GMAT Quantitative questions.

Quantitative Analysis

Often the most difficult part of a GMAT Quantitative problem is figuring out which math skills to use in the first place. In fact, the GMAT's hardest Quantitative problems are about 95 percent analysis, 5 percent calculation. You'll have to do the following:

- Understand complicated or awkward phrasing
- Process information presented out of order
- Analyze incomplete information
- Simplify complicated information

To make questions more challenging, the test maker combines different areas of math. Rare is the question that tests a single concept; more commonly, you will be asked to integrate multiple skills to solve. For instance, a question that asks you about triangles could also require you to solve a formula algebraically and apply your understanding of ratios to find the correct answer.

In Part Three of this book, you'll learn how to approach Quant problems strategically and review all the math content you need so you can solve these questions efficiently and earn a high score.

Verbal Section Overview

A little more than half of the multiple-choice questions that count toward your overall score appear in the Verbal section. You have 65 minutes to answer 36 Verbal questions in three formats: Reading Comprehension, Sentence Correction, and Critical Reasoning. These three types of questions are mingled throughout the Verbal section, so you never know what's coming next.

Here's what you can expect to see:

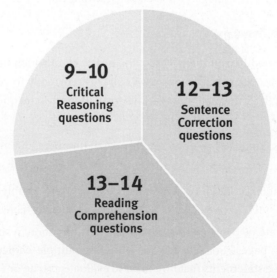

The Approximate Mix of Questions on the GMAT Verbal Section

You may see more of one question type and fewer of another. However, the GMAT is a standardized test, so the number of each kind of question won't vary too much from what you expect and have studied for.

Pacing on the Verbal Section

The GMAT will give you about four Reading Comprehension passages. With less than 2 minutes per question on the Verbal section, where will you find the time to read those passages?

The Reading Comprehension chapters of this book will give you great tips about how to read the passages efficiently. However, a big part of pacing yourself well is how you handle Sentence Correction questions. Follow the Kaplan Method for Sentence Correction, which you will see in the chapters devoted to that question type, and through practice, you will bring your average time down to 60 seconds per Sentence Correction question. Moving through Sentence Correction questions efficiently will allow you the time you'll need to read long Reading Comprehension passages and take apart complex arguments in Critical Reasoning.

Here are Kaplan's timing recommendations for the Verbal section of the GMAT. While it's far more important at first that you practice to build mastery of the strategies, it's also a good idea to keep these timing recommendations in mind. Then, by incorporating more timed practice as you progress in your GMAT prep, you will grow comfortable reading and answering questions at the suggested pace, setting yourself up for success on Test Day.

VERBAL SECTION TIMING	
QUESTION TYPE	**AVERAGE TIME YOU SHOULD SPEND**
Sentence Correction	1 minute per question
Critical Reasoning	2 minutes per question
Reading Comprehension	4 minutes per passage and a little less than 1.5 minutes per question

In Part Four of this book, you'll learn strategies for each of these question types.

Integrated Reasoning Section Overview

There are 12 items in the Integrated Reasoning (IR) section, nearly all of which include multiple parts. There is no partial credit on the multi-part items; you must answer all parts correctly to get credit for the item. These questions require you to synthesize information in various formats, and some questions will have both verbal and quantitative elements.

There are four types of IR items. You'll see these in roughly equal numbers, but you might see two of one kind and four of another.

1. Graphics Interpretation items contain two statements that must be completed using drop-down menus. Information will be presented in one or more visual formats, such as tables or graphs.

2. Multi-Source Reasoning items come in a set of several questions about a shared stimulus that is divided up across several tabbed "pages." Some of the questions are multiple-choice with one correct answer, while others present three statements that you need to evaluate as true or false, or something similar. You need to evaluate all three statements correctly to get credit.

3. Table Analysis items present information in a spreadsheet with basic sorting functionality. Table Analysis questions also feature the multi-part true/false format.

4. Two-Part Analysis items give you some information and ask you to choose answers to two related questions about that information from a common pool of choices.

Fortunately, Integrated Reasoning questions draw on many of the same skills you need for the Verbal and Quantitative sections, so improving your performance on these sections, along with getting familiar with the different IR question formats, should improve your IR score as well.

Pacing on the Integrated Reasoning Section

You have 30 minutes for this section's 12 items, with all their parts. Many students find the timing of the Integrated Reasoning section challenging. You'll need to decide when to give an item your best effort and when to make a guess, conserving time for items later in the section. You can only move forward through the section, so you cannot peek ahead at all the items and decide which ones you will give the most attention. You'll need to continuously weigh the risk of guessing against the opportunity cost of taking too much time.

Because the questions are of such varied format and content, there are no rules of thumb for timing by item type. One student might solve a Two-Part Analysis question that hinges on a math formula in under a minute but need several minutes to read through a Two-Part Analysis question that requires understanding an argument; another student might experience the opposite timing. Through practice, however, you will be able to determine your personal timing for these questions and then, on Test Day, pace yourself confidently.

The chapter on Integrated Reasoning in this book will introduce you to each IR question type and walk you through several examples of each. There's more IR practice in your online resources; for example, each practice test comes with an IR section, just like the actual GMAT.

Analytical Writing Assessment Section Overview

The Analytical Writing Assessment (AWA) section gives you 30 minutes to write one essay in response to an argument. Your job is to analyze the logic of the argument, identifying its weaknesses and suggesting evidence that would improve it. You'll use the same approach to analyze the argument here as you use to analyze arguments to answer many of the Critical Reasoning questions on the Verbal section. Planning your essay before you begin writing, as explained in the chapter on the Analytical Writing Assessment in this book, will allow you to write a solid essay within the time allowed.

GMAT Scoring

The most important score on the GMAT is the total score, which ranges from 200 to 800. Schools primarily look at this number. Over two-thirds of all GMAT test takers score within 120 points of the approximate mean, which is about 560. Pulling yourself out of that cluster is an important part of distinguishing your application.

PERCENTILE	SCORE
99%	760–800
91%	710
80%	670
64%	630
49%	590

Some GMAT Percentiles vs. Total Scores

The total score is calculated from "scaled scores" from the Quantitative section and Verbal section. These scores are meant to provide a timeless, absolute measure of skill. For example, a Quant score of 40 in 2011 represents the same level of ability as does a Quant score of 40 in 2021.

While the scaled scores haven't changed over time, the population of test takers has. Quant performance has gone up, and Verbal performance has gone down. While Verbal section scores still follow a fairly even distribution, Quantitative scaled scores now skew high. Thus, percentiles have shifted.

Schools view your percentile performance (which is the same thing as a "percent ranking") overall and on each section of the GMAT. The relationship between the section percentiles and the overall percentile is not simple. We're frequently asked, "One of my scaled scores is 82nd percentile and the other is 85th percentile. How can my overall score be 87th percentile?" An example shows how this works. Imagine that of 100 students taking the test, 50 people got a 51 Quant and an 11 Verbal, while the other 50 people got an 11 Quant and a 51 Verbal. You take the same test and get 40 Quant and 40 Verbal. You'd be 50th percentile on each section, because 50 percent of test takers in this sample group scored worse than you. However, your total score would put you higher than anyone else on the test—99th percentile.

QUANTITATIVE	
PERCENTILE	SCORE
97%	51
87%	50
74%	49
67%	48
59%	47
56%	46
53%	45
47%	44

VERBAL	
PERCENTILE	SCORE
99%	45–51
96%	42
90%	40
84%	38
80%	36
70%	34
60%	31
50%	28

Some Percentiles vs. Scaled Scores for the Quantitative and Verbal Sections

Let's note two key takeaways about percentiles. The first is that your overall score is about balanced performance on the two sections. Generally, you will not win on the GMAT by nailing one section and hoping your performance will overcome a deficit on the other. The second key point is that admissions officers often look at Quant and Verbal percentiles separately and may reject a candidate who does not meet a certain threshold for either subscore. This is especially true for Quantitative percentiles, particularly at programs with a strong analytical focus.

You'll receive a separate score for the Integrated Reasoning (IR) section, which has its own scoring scale, independent of the 200 to 800 scale. You'll receive a score from 1 to 8, in whole-point increments. The magic number this time is 6, as this is the score at which you beat the median. You'll see your IR score at the same time as your Quantitative and Verbal scores.

INTEGRATED REASONING	
PERCENTILE	SCORE
90%	8
79%	7
64%	6
48%	5
31%	4
18%	3
8%	2
0%	1

Percentiles vs. Scaled Scores for the
Integrated Reasoning Section

You will want to show schools that you're in the better half of the Integrated Reasoning field. At the same time, an exceptional 200–800 score will do more for your application than will an exceptional IR score, so you should prioritize your study time accordingly.

The 1–8 score is derived from 12 items, nearly all of which have multiple parts, and there is no partial credit. Integrated Reasoning items come in four types, described in more detail in the Integrated Reasoning chapter of this book: Graphics Interpretation, Multi-Source Reasoning, Table Analysis, and Two-Part Analysis.

Unlike the Quantitative and Verbal sections of the GMAT, the Integrated Reasoning section isn't adaptive: you'll see a predetermined sequence of 12 questions no matter how many you get right and wrong as you go along. However, despite not being adaptive, the Integrated Reasoning section does not let test takers skip questions or return to previously answered questions. As a result, it's often advantageous to guess quickly on a tough question early in the section to make sure you get to easier questions toward the end of the section with enough time to do them.

The Analytical Writing Assessment (AWA), which is administered if you take the exam at a test center, is also scored separately from the rest of the GMAT. AWA scores aren't available on Test Day but show up in your score report within three weeks. Your AWA score will be a number from 1 to 6 in increments of 0.5 (you get a zero if you write off-topic or in a foreign language). The magic number here is 4. Although you should strive for the best score possible, an essay graded 4 is considered "satisfactory" according to the grading rubric, while an essay graded 3 is not.

ANALYTICAL WRITING ASSESSMENT	
PERCENTILE	SCORE
88%	6
81%	5.5
57%	5
47%	4.5
18%	4
12%	3.5
4%	3

Some Percentiles vs. Scaled Scores for the AWA

Percentiles give a different perspective on the AWA. An AWA score of 4 ranks at a only the 18th percentile. To break the median, you have to score a 5.0 or higher. The good news is that few programs, in our experience, use the AWA score to differentiate candidates' competitiveness. It's more of a reality check against the writing skills that you demonstrate in your application essays. Here's a little-noticed fact: business schools receive the actual text of your AWA essay in the official score report.

Experimental Questions

A few experimental questions will be scattered throughout the Quantitative, Verbal, and Integrated Reasoning sections. They look just like the other questions but won't contribute to your score. The test maker is evaluating these questions for possible use on future tests.

To get good data, the test maker has to test each question against the whole range of test takers—that is, high and low scorers. Therefore, on the adaptive Quantitative or Verbal sections, you could be on your way to an 800 and getting tougher and tougher questions—and suddenly come across a question that seems pretty easy.

Bottom line: Don't worry about what the adaptive algorithm is doing and what that might, or might not, say about your performance. The test will take care of itself. You take care of *yourself* and focus on doing your best on the question in front of you.

Score Reports

You'll see your unofficial scores for the Quantitative, Verbal, and Integrated Reasoning sections right away, as well as your overall 200–800 score. Within a few weeks after your test date, your official score report, including your AWA score, will be available online. You'll receive an email when yours is ready.

GMAT Strategies and Attitude

In the chapters that follow, we'll cover techniques for answering the GMAT questions. But you'll also need to go into the test with a certain attitude and approach. Here are some strategies.

Make Scratchwork Work for You

Depending on whether you take the exam at a test center or online, you'll use different tools for your scratchwork. The good news is that they all work! Most test takers experience no problems. However, you will want to get used to using the tools you'll have available on Test Day. We suggest that you use a dry-erase board (or anything with a similar surface) and a nonpermanent marker while taking the practice tests. If you'll be taking the test online, use an onscreen whiteboard tool.

Be Systematic

Use your scratchwork to organize your thinking. To facilitate eliminating choices, especially on the Verbal section and for Data Sufficiency questions on the Quant section, draw an answer choice grid and cross off choices as you rule them out. This process will minimize any tendency to re-read choices you've already determined are wrong and keep you advancing toward the correct answer.

If You Take the Exam at a Test Center

The administrator will give you a notepad to use. This is a spiral-bound booklet of five sheets of legal-sized or A4 laminated paper. You can write on the front and back of the sheets. You'll also be given a black wet-erase pen. You will not be given materials to erase the pen.

The administrator will replace your used notepad with a clean one upon request. Many students find a single notepad provides more than enough space for all their scratchwork for the entire test. But if you're concerned about running out of space, a good strategy is to raise your hand with the notepad in it during your first break; the administrator will know what you need and bring you a new notepad to replace your used one. You may not remove the notepad from the test room during or after the exam.

Cap your pen when not using it so it doesn't dry out. If your pen does begin to dry out, or leak, you can request a new one. Hold the pen up as you raise your hand for assistance so the proctor knows what you need and can bring it to you right away.

You can't erase marks you make on the notepad with your pen. Say you make a mistake during a calculation or you smudge your work with your hand. If you try to write on top of the smudge or error, you'll just be left with a blob of ink that you can't read. So what should you do? Just start over. Seriously. Starting fresh will take much less time than trying to rescue a lost cause.

If You Take the Exam Online

You may use your own portable dry-erase whiteboard and marker or use the provided onscreen whiteboard, or use both (recommended). Your own whiteboard may be a maximum of 12 by 20 inches (30 by 50 centimeters). You may have two dry-erase markers and an eraser with you.

Our colleagues at Manhattan Prep have posted an excellent video that demonstrates how to use the onscreen whiteboard tools to maximum advantage: **manhattanprep.com/gmat/blog/online-whiteboard**.

Pace Yourself

The last thing you want is to run out of time before you've answered all the questions in a section. Not only would you not earn points for the questions you left unanswered, but you'd actually get a penalty for each question you didn't get to.

Pace yourself so that this doesn't happen. We're not saying you have to spend exactly 2 minutes, for instance, on every Critical Reasoning question. But you should have in mind how much time to spend on each type of question, on average, and have a good sense of whether you are ahead, behind, or on pace in the section. We'll talk about timing guidelines for each question type later in this book.

Most importantly, if a question is taking too long, don't hesitate to make your best guess and move on. It can be tempting to think, "I'm nearly there. If I spend just a little longer, I might be able to get this!" However, the opportunity cost of not having enough time for questions toward the end of the section is simply too high. Being willing to guess on questions becomes easier as you become more confident in your ability. It's easier to think, "Looks like I'll have to guess on this one, but I know I'll be able to answer lots of the remaining questions."

We'll go into more depth about this in Chapter 2 , where we talk about how the GMAT's computer-adaptive test format works. For now, rest assured that most top scorers on the GMAT make some strategic guesses as they go through the test.

Remain Calm

It's imperative that you remain calm during the test. You can't let yourself get rattled by a hard question to the degree that it throws off your performance on the rest of the section.

When you face a tough question, remember that you're surely not the only one finding it difficult. The test is designed to challenge everyone who takes it. Having trouble with a difficult question isn't going to ruin your score, but getting upset and letting it throw you off track will. When you understand that part of the test maker's goal is to reward those who keep their composure, you'll recognize the importance of keeping your cool when you run into challenging material.

GMAT Checklist

The GMAT is offered by appointment, at your convenience, almost every day of the year. You will be required to register online before making an appointment.

Decide Where You Will Take the Test

Consider whether taking the test at home or in a test center will be more convenient and comfortable for you. Perhaps not having to travel to a test center would be a significant benefit for you. On the other hand, maybe finding an uncluttered space that will be distraction-free for several hours would be a real challenge, or maybe you'd have trouble meeting the test maker's technical requirements for an online administration. There's no "right answer" to the question of where to take the test. Just do what will work best for you.

Test appointment slots are available around the clock for an online administration and nearly every day of the year at a test center. If you want to take the test at a center, make sure to register at least a few weeks in advance, since the more popular slots (e.g., evenings and weekends) fill up quickly.

You are allowed to retake the exam either way; you may retake an online administration once, and you may take the test five times in a rolling 12-month period if you do so at a test center.

There are various fees for rescheduling or canceling a test you've registered for, with the exact amount of the fees depending on whether you've registered for an online or test center administration and your location.

Register and Schedule Your Appointment

Available time slots change continuously as people register for the test. You will find out what times are available for an online administration or at your chosen testing center when you register.

Admissions deadlines for business schools vary. Check with the schools to which you plan to apply and make your test appointment early enough to allow your scores to be reported before the schools' application deadlines.

The easiest way to register and schedule your appointment is to do so online. Start by going to **mba.com** and creating an account.

As this book goes to press, the fee to take the GMAT Online exam is US$250 worldwide, and the fee to take the GMAT at a test center is US$275 in the United States and may vary elsewhere. If you have questions about GMAT registration, visit **mba.com** to consult the FAQ, fill out a form with your question, or submit your question using the correct email address or phone number for your region.

When scheduling your test appointment, be sure that the spelling of your name and your stated date of birth match the ID you will present before your test. If those do not match, you will not be permitted to take the test, and your test fee will be forfeited.

The Day of the Test

You should arrive at the testing center or log in to your device 30 minutes before your scheduled appointment. Whether you are taking the exam at a center or online, you will have to complete a number of security measures before you will be allowed to take the exam. A late arrival may result in not being allowed to take the test and forfeiting your test fee.

Proper Identification

You will be asked to present ID—no exceptions. The following are the only acceptable forms:

- Passport book
- Government-issued driver's license or (US only) laminated learner's permit
- Government-issued national/state/province identity card (including European ID card)
- Military ID card
- Permanent resident/green card (US only)

If you aren't a citizen of the country in which you take your test, you'll need your passport. In some countries, even if you are a citizen, a passport is required. Visit **mba.com** for the current requirements.

The ID must be current (not expired) and legible, and it should contain all four of the elements listed below. If you do not have one ID with all four of these elements, you will need to bring a second ID (also from the list above) that shows the missing elements.

1. Your name in the Roman alphabet. It must be exactly the same as what you provided when you made your appointment, including the order and placement of the names.
2. Your date of birth. The date of birth must also exactly match the date provided when you made your appointment.
3. A recent, recognizable photograph
4. Your signature

If these elements do not match what the test administrator has on file for you, you will not be allowed to take the GMAT, and your test fee will be forfeited.

Before you schedule your test appointment, make sure you understand all the requirements that are particular to your situation and have acquired or renewed the ID you will use. Also, note that if your ID is found to be fraudulent or invalid after you take the exam, your scores will be canceled and your test fee forfeited.

Palm Scan, Signature, and Photograph

If you are taking the exam at a test center, the administrator will take your palm scan, signature, and photograph using digital equipment. The testing rooms are also equipped with audio and video recorders, which are active during the exam. If you do not complete the entire check-in process or refuse to be recorded, you will not be allowed to take the GMAT, and your test fee will be forfeited.

At a test center, each time you leave and return to the testing room during a break, your palm will be scanned. If you exceed the allotted break time, the excess time will be deducted from the next section of your exam.

The GMAT Online exam is administered with comparable security protocols.

Agreements

You will be asked to agree to the GMAT Test Taker Rules & Agreement. You will electronically confirm that you agree to the GMAT Non-Disclosure Agreement and General Terms of Use statement. If you do not agree, you will not be allowed to take the GMAT, and your test fee will be forfeited. If you are caught violating the agreement, the business schools that you're applying to will be informed of this fact.

Prohibited Items

The following items cannot be in the room where you take your exam:

- Electronics of any kind, including cell phones, media players, cameras, radios, and photographic devices (If you test online, your cell phone should be retrievable in case the proctor needs to call you, but it should not be within immediate reach or within your line of sight.)
- Any timepieces, including wristwatches, stopwatches, and watch alarms
- Notes, scratch paper, books, pamphlets, dictionaries, translators, and thesauruses
- Measuring tools such as rulers
- Calculators and watch calculators

If you are taking the exam online, no one else may be in the room or pass through the room during the test. You may have water in a clear container.

Essentially, you can't bring anything that may cause distractions, provide aid during testing, or be used to remove exam content from the testing area. (Note that you are not permitted to use a calculator for the Quantitative section, though there is an onscreen calculator available for the Integrated Reasoning section.)

Prohibited Behavior

You will not be allowed to smoke, eat, or use a cell phone in the testing room. In fact, you won't be allowed to use a phone or send a text message at all once the test has begun, even during breaks.

You cannot leave the testing room without the administrator's permission. Should you have any questions or problems during the exam, raise your hand—or, if online, click the chat button or raise your hand via the software—and wait for the administrator to respond.

CHAPTER 2

A CLOSER LOOK AT THE CAT

LEARNING OBJECTIVES

- Describe how the adaptive format of the CAT is designed to be more accurate than a linear test and explain why it will always feel difficult
- Articulate strategies for approaching the first 10 questions, the questions in the middle of a section, and the last 10 questions
- Explain why pacing matters on the GMAT and how you are penalized for not finishing

The GMAT is a computer-adaptive test, or CAT. The test is called "adaptive" because, in the course of a Quantitative or Verbal section, the test notices whether you answered the previous question correctly or incorrectly and "adapts" in its selection of the next question.

A few basic rules make the adaptive format possible:

- You're presented with one question at a time, and you must answer it to move on to the next question.
- You can't return to previously answered questions within a section.
- You can't skip questions—or rather, the only questions that can be skipped or omitted are any questions at the end of a section that you leave unanswered.
- Within a section (Quantitative or Verbal), the questions are not grouped by topic or type. You don't, for example, finish Reading Comprehension and then move on to Sentence Correction and then to Critical Reasoning; those three question types are interspersed with one another throughout the section.

The CAT Explained

Here's how the adapting works. You start the section (Quantitative or Verbal) with questions of about medium difficulty; about half of test takers get them right, and half get them wrong. Those who answer correctly begin to get harder questions, and those who answer incorrectly get easier items. This pattern continues: Throughout the section, if you got the previous question right, generally you'll get a harder question next. Conversely, if you got the previous question wrong, generally you'll get an easier one next. In this way, you'll follow a generally upward, downward, or flat trajectory through the questions. The test homes in on the difficulty level that is best matched to your performance; at that difficulty level, generally, you'll be getting about half the questions correct and half incorrect. Your score is determined by how high on the difficulty scale you end up, along with how many questions you answer. There is a significant penalty for leaving questions unanswered at the end of a section.

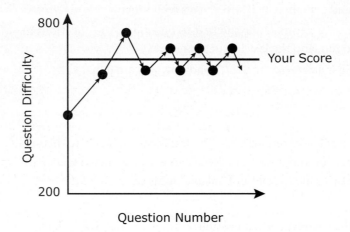

A Rough Schematic of How Adaptive Scoring Works on a CAT

The adaptive design of the test has two purposes:

1. **Accuracy:** A CAT is allegedly more accurate than a "linear" (i.e., nonadaptive) test because it zeroes in on a test taker's ability level. Lucky guesses cause the GMAT to give lucky testers harder questions that they cannot answer correctly, thus eliminating any gains resulting from chance. Conversely, unlucky arithmetic errors on tough problems give unlucky testers easier problems, and these unlucky testers should be able to get the easier questions right, thus correcting the nonrepresentative drop in score.

2. **Time:** CATs can be made shorter than comparable linear tests, and the shorter duration is a benefit to both you and the test maker. The reason for this efficiency is that a CAT does not waste questions. If you get most of the questions right, you pretty much never see an easy one, and if you get most of the questions wrong, you pretty much never see a hard one. On a linear test, on the other hand, everyone gets the same mix of easy and hard questions. On such a test, students struggling on the easy questions will do little better than chance on the challenging problems, while high-scoring students will get close to 100 percent of the easy questions correct. Thus, giving low-scoring questions to high-scoring students (and vice versa) doesn't actually provide much useful statistical data. In this respect, many questions are "wasted," whereas the CAT can afford to be a shorter test at equal accuracy.

Those points define the basic pattern of the CAT, but there are additional bells and whistles in the algorithm. One of the most important details to be aware of is that the test does not always adjust difficulty level question by question. Therefore, avoid the temptation to assess the difficulty level of a question you're on or to infer whether you got the previous question correct. Even if you could precisely assess a question's difficulty level (and even GMAT experts can't do this without looking at psychometric data on the question), you wouldn't be able to draw any conclusions, since the test doesn't always adapt immediately.

The experimental questions are another refinement to the CAT formula. Some of the questions in each section do not count toward your score. The test maker must try future questions on people who do not know that they are experimental in order to determine the validity and difficulty of the questions. Trying to guess which questions are experimental is just a waste of mental bandwidth.

For a more technical look at how a CAT works, check out the appendixes in the online resources: "How Much Can a GMAT Score Change?" and "A Closer Look at GMAT Scoring." Here, we'll talk about the practical implications of the format for your test-taking strategy.

Are the First Questions More Important?

One of the most frequently asked questions about GMAT scoring is "Are the first 10 or so questions more important than the rest?"

As we've discussed, the GMAT adaptive algorithm starts with medium-difficulty questions. If you get questions right, your next questions are harder, and if you get questions wrong, your next questions are easier. The swings are relatively large at first but become smaller as the test zeroes in on an estimate of your performance. For that reason, you may find it tempting to spend lots of extra time at the beginning of the test.

The short word on that idea: don't.

The test maker concedes that the computer-adaptive testing algorithm uses the first 10 questions to obtain an initial estimate of your ability. The key word, though, is *initial*. As you continue to answer questions, the algorithm self-corrects by computing an updated estimate on the basis of how many questions you have answered, and then it administers items that are closely matched to this new estimate of your ability. Your final score is based on your responses, the difficulty of all the questions you answered, and the number of questions left unanswered. Taking additional time on the first 10 questions will not "game the system" and can hurt your ability to finish the test.

The reason you can't outsmart the GMAT by spending extra time at the beginning is timing: if you answer more questions correctly than you should in more time than you should, then you will face much harder questions, under more time pressure, in the rest of the section. Your short-term gains will be erased.

However, you still want to adjust your test prep strategy to account for those early swings. Specifically, remember that even when your test-taking skills have become so strong that most of your test will be made up of challenging, high-reward problems, you'll still have to go through some simpler problems to get there—don't rush or become overconfident just because those first few questions are easier.

A good comparison is to a sporting event. Are the first innings of a baseball game more important than the following ones? Perhaps, since the early part of the game sets the tone for the game and gives the leading team options. But doing well during the first part of a game does not guarantee a win; you need to start strong *and* finish strong.

The cost of not finishing strong on the GMAT is substantial. If you don't answer all the questions, a penalty is assessed that will precipitously lower your score. In fact, this effect is more exaggerated in the case of high scorers. As an example, provided by GMAC, if you are at the 91st percentile but then fail to answer five questions, your score could drop to the 77th percentile. A score difference of that magnitude is substantial.

The Importance of Pacing

The GMAT is a test of both accuracy and speed. There is a substantial penalty for not finishing a section, as we've seen. But there is no need to think of the GMAT as a race. In fact, according to the test maker, the GMAT is created to be optimally timed so that most test takers finish the first time they sit for the test. Those who don't finish the GMAT the first time often retake the test, and almost all finish the second time.

You want to be in the group that finishes the test on the first try. Also, while you don't want to rush or make sloppy guesses, you do need to finish the test on time in order to maximize your score.

The graph below is an illustration of the penalty incurred by test takers who leave a string of unanswered questions at the end of a CAT section. Even if you had previously been performing well on questions at a high level of difficulty, running out of time will lead to a severe drop in your score. Fortunately, pacing can be improved through practicing some key principles of time management.

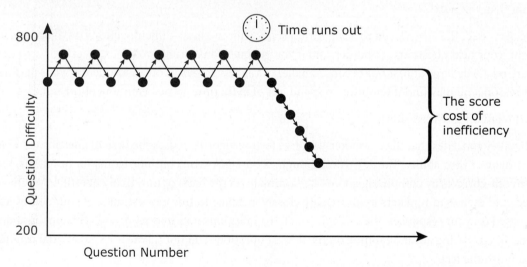

Spending Extra Time at the Beginning of a Section Can Lead to Failure at the End of the Section

You can pace yourself on both the Quantitative and Verbal sections, broadly speaking, by dividing each section into three parts:

1. The first 10 questions
2. The last 10 questions
3. Everything in between

Each part has its own strategy.

- **The first 10 questions:** Given what we've covered above, you now have an idea of how to pace yourself on the first 10 questions. To recap: the first questions are likely to produce some large swings in your score, but it's important to finish just as strong as you start. The theme of these 10 questions: proceed diligently, keep an eye out for pitfalls, and avoid preventable errors.

- **The middle segment:** Regardless of how the first 10 questions go, you're almost certain to find some challenges in this segment. Most test takers will "top out." Topping out means that you will be unable to solve any more difficult problems and you will begin to hover around your skill level, getting about half of the questions right and half of them wrong. The great danger at this point in the test is that you will feel you ought to be able to "get" every problem and you will spend too much time on some of them. Since time spent here takes away from the time you have for the later questions in the section, you may need to guess on a few questions to stay on pace. Fortunately, if you've budgeted your minutes well, you will have some time to give your guesses a little thought. The theme of the middle segment: stay on pace, keep your morale high, and make strategic guesses where necessary.

- **The final 10 questions** are the home stretch. You're trying to finish before the bell rings. Here you must pick your battles. Make an effort not to guess on more than one or two questions in a row. As the end draws nigh, alternate any guesses that you need to make, rather than saving them for a series at the end. Doing so will increase your options to solve without guessing, decrease the odds of accidentally running out of time, and most likely reduce the score drop from questions answered incorrectly. The theme of this segment: choose your questions and finish on time.

Now you're done. You've maximized your payoff. It can be exciting to set a pace and stick to it, and giving yourself permission to guess on the trickiest questions can reduce your anxiety and frustration.

Other CAT Strategies

In addition to the strategies mentioned earlier about pacing, keep in mind other CAT-specific strategies that will have a direct, positive impact on your score:

- Because each right or wrong answer affects the next question you get, the CAT does not allow you to return to questions you've already answered. In other words, you cannot go back to double-check your work. So be as sure as you can be about your answer before moving on.

- If you're given a question you cannot answer, you'll have to guess. Guess intelligently and strategically by eliminating any answer choices that you know are wrong and guessing among those remaining. The faster you can determine that you can't answer a question, the more time you'll save by guessing; that's more time to spend on other questions that you *can* get right.

- Don't get nervous if the questions seem easy. They may be tough questions that only seem easy to you because you're well prepared.

- Don't get rattled if you keep seeing really tough questions. It can mean you're doing very well. Keep it up—you're on your way to a great GMAT score!

Practice these strategies each time you take a CAT in your online resources, and you'll have the right mindset for success on Test Day.

GO ONLINE

kaptest.com/login

K   **23**

CHAPTER 3

THE FOUR CORE COMPETENCIES AND THE GMAT

LEARNING OBJECTIVES

- Articulate how the GMAT tests key reasoning skills

Unlike most subject-specific tests you have taken throughout your academic career, the scope of knowledge that the GMAT requires of you is fairly limited. In fact, you don't need any background knowledge or expertise beyond fundamental math and verbal skills. While mastering those fundamentals is essential to your success on the GMAT—and this book is concerned in part with helping you develop or refresh those skills—the GMAT does *not* primarily seek to reward test takers for content-specific knowledge. Rather, the GMAT uses math and verbal questions as a platform to test your critical-thinking and problem-solving capabilities—the reasoning skills you will use in your business career. As you prepare for the GMAT, you will notice that similar analytical skills come into play across the various question types and sections of the test.

Kaplan has adopted the term *Core Competencies* to refer to the four bedrock thinking skills rewarded by the GMAT: Critical Thinking, Pattern Recognition, Paraphrasing, and Attention to the Right Detail. The Kaplan Methods and strategies presented throughout this book will help you apply these skills to get GMAT questions of all kinds right.

Critical Thinking

Most potential MBA students are adept at creative problem solving, and the GMAT offers many opportunities to demonstrate this skill. From work, school, and volunteer projects, you probably already have experience assessing situations to see when data are inadequate, synthesizing information into valid deductions, finding creative solutions to complex problems, and avoiding unnecessary, inefficient work.

In GMAT terms, a critical thinker is a creative problem solver who engages in critical inquiry. One of the hallmarks of successful test takers is their skill at asking the right questions. GMAT critical thinkers first consider what they're being asked to do, then study the given information and ask the right questions, especially, "How can I get the answer in the most direct way?" and "How can I use the question format to my advantage?"

For instance, as you examine a Reading Comprehension passage, you'll interrogate the author: "Why are you writing about Walt Whitman?" or "Why have you included this detail about elephants in paragraph 2?" For Critical Reasoning, you'll ask the author "What's your main point?" or "What evidence have you presented to convince me to agree with you?" For Sentence Correction questions, you'll ask: "Why do three of the five answer choices share the same grammatical construction?" or "Is there a better way to express the idea?"

As you analyze a Problem Solving question, you'll ask the test maker: "What are you really telling me with this equation or scenario?" "What are you really looking for in this math problem?" and "Why are the answer choices set up this way?" Likewise, as you examine a Data Sufficiency question, you'll learn to ask: "What information will I need to answer this question?" or "How can I determine whether more than one solution is possible?"

Those test takers who learn to ask the right questions become creative problem solvers and GMAT champs. And they go on to thrive in groundbreaking careers as they ask the right questions about complex business challenges.

Pattern Recognition

Many people fail to appreciate the level of constraint that standardization places on test makers. Because the test makers must give reliable, valid, and comparable scores to many thousands of students each year, they're forced to reward the same skills on every test. They do so by repeating the same kinds of questions with the same pitfalls for the unwary, which are susceptible to the same strategic solutions.

Inexperienced test takers treat every problem as if it were a brand-new task, whereas the GMAT rewards those who spot the patterns and use them to their advantage. Of course, the test makers don't want their patterns to be too obvious, so they disguise them by varying the details or the way information is arranged in the question. Train yourself to see through these superficial differences, and you'll begin to recognize the same finite set of skills being tested over and over—skills you'll learn in this book.

The rewards don't stop when you take the GMAT. Pattern Recognition is a key business skill: executives who recognize familiar situations and apply proven solutions to them will outperform those who need to reinvent the wheel every time.

Paraphrasing

Yet another Core Competency is Paraphrasing: the GMAT rewards those who can reduce abstract, complex, or polysyllabic information to simple terms. Habitually putting complex ideas and convoluted wording into your own simple, accurate terms will ensure that you "get it"—that you understand the information well enough to drive to the correct answer. For example, you won't be overwhelmed by the complicated prose of Critical Reasoning or Reading Comprehension questions if you make your own straightforward mental translations. Likewise, the ability to mentally strip a sentence down to its essentials will help you spot Sentence Correction errors the test maker tries to hide between a lot of lengthy phrases.

In the Quantitative section of the GMAT, you will often need to paraphrase a word problem as "math sentences" (equations or inequalities) so you can solve. Some questions will give you information already written "in math," but you'll need to use arithmetic or algebra to simplify and rearrange the information so it's easier to work with.

Thoughout this book, the Kaplan Methods will emphasize Paraphrasing as one of the first steps to answer any GMAT question, whether that's by mapping a Reading Comprehension passage or by analyzing a question stem. After the test, you'll continue to use Paraphrasing in business school and beyond. In today's world of "big data" and a seemingly infinite stream of information—news articles, social media posts, podcasts, video webinars, and on and on—executives can feel as though they're drowning in details. Those who can astutely filter this deluge of information and reduce complicated requirements to clear tasks will be able to set goals at a strategic level and execute bold plans.

Attention to the Right Detail

Details present a dilemma: missing them can cost you points. But if you try to absorb every fact in a Reading Comprehension passage or Critical Reasoning stimulus, you will find yourself overwhelmed, behind time, and still unready for the questions that follow because the relevant and irrelevant details are all mixed together in your mind. Even short question stems require discernment: there are words and phrases in Sentence Correction questions that have no bearing on the errors (or lack thereof) in the sentence, and there are details in math problems that having nothing to do with the underlying pattern or with the rules or formulas you'll apply to solve.

Throughout this book, you will learn how to discern the essential details from those that can slow you down or confuse you. The GMAT test maker rewards examinees for paying attention to the right details—the ones that make the difference between right and wrong answers. Attention to the Right Detail distinguishes great administrators from poor ones in the business world as well. Just ask anyone with a boss who has the wrong priorities or who is so bogged down in minutiae that the department has stopped functioning.

PART TWO

DIAGNOSTIC TEST

CHAPTER 4

GMAT DIAGNOSTIC TEST

LEARNING OBJECTIVES

- Complete a GMAT practice test in a test-like environment
- Self-assess your strengths and opportunities after gaining familiarity with GMAT test questions
- Create a goal-oriented study plan

How to Take This Test

To take Practice Test 1 (Diagnostic Test), log in to your online resources at **kaptest.com/login**. (If you have not yet registered your book, follow the instructions in the "How to Use This Book" section found before Chapter 1.)

GO ONLINE

kaptest.com/login

Before taking the diagnostic test, find a quiet place where you can work without interruptions for a little over 3 hours. If you cannot set aside this much time in a block, you can take the test in multiple sessions by using the Suspend button. However, this button will not be available during the actual test, so your experience will be more test-like—and you'll build more mental endurance—if you take the entire test in one sitting.

Make sure you have a comfortable desk, scratch paper or an erasable noteboard, and something to write with. To avoid a frustrating experience, use a strong internet connection; a weak connection can cause the test to think you've quit. Close all other apps on your device and all other tabs in your browser to avoid distracting content. If your device has a calculator app, do not use it during the Quantitative section, as you will not be permitted to use a calculator of any kind during this section on the actual GMAT.

The diagnostic test accurately reflects the question types and content of the GMAT Analytical Writing Assessment, Integrated Reasoning, Quantitative, and Verbal sections. The number of questions and timing of each section are also just like those of the real exam. And you'll be able to choose in which order you want to take the sections, just like on Test Day.

You'll gain several important benefits from taking this test. One is familiarity with the test format and content. This will give you context for the studying you're about to embark on, because you'll be able to relate what you learn to the hands-on experience of taking the test. Another benefit is an assessment of your strengths and areas of opportunity. This will provide important guidance as you plan your studying, allowing you to invest your time where it will yield the biggest score payoff.

If you have not already done so, read Chapters 1 and 2 about the GMAT and the nature of computer-adaptive tests. The information in these chapters will prepare you to get the most out of your diagnostic test experience.

Review and Reflect

Taking a practice test is useful, but even more valuable is your review of the test—if you do it right.

How to Interpret Your Results

The most important thing to remember about your practice test results is that *they don't count*. They represent your skill at the test right now, but they don't reflect the scores you will earn on Test Day after you have put in many hours of practice.

More than your overall 200–800 score, pay attention to what types of questions you were most and least likely to get correct. First, did you perform better on the Verbal section or the Quantitative section, or did you do about the same on both? As shown in "GMAT Scoring" in Chapter 1, the same subscore means very different things on these two sections. For example, a subscore of 40 on the Verbal section represents quite strong performance, but a subscore of 40 on the Quant section is well below the 50th percentile. So when comparing your performance on these sections, use percentiles rather than subscores in order to compare "apples to apples." Both these sections are important for your overall score, and business schools look at the scores on both sections, so if you are much weaker on one than the other, you should plan to spend proportionally more time practicing for your weaker section.

Then within each section, look for patterns in which questions you got right and wrong. Did you struggle with Critical Reasoning, for example, but do pretty well on Reading Comprehension and Sentence Correction? Or did you find Data Sufficiency questions challenging? Or are there certain areas of math that you don't remember well from whenever you last had a math class? Once you've identified the questions that give you the most trouble, plan to study the related book chapters early in your prep. That way, you'll be able to spiral back and review them several times before Test Day; this spiral approach is a proven technique for boosting your learning and your score.

How to Review the Test

The explanations themselves are valuable learning tools. Review all the explanations, both for the questions you answered incorrectly *and* those you got right. For the questions you missed, once you understand how to arrive at the correct answer, hide the explanation and redo the question. By actually doing the question correctly, you'll build "mental muscle memory" of doing it right. This is much more powerful than simply reading about how you could have done it right. Now, having successfully worked from the information given to the correct answer, you'll be more likely to be able to do it again on a similar question—on Test Day.

For the questions you got correct, first confirm that you answered correctly for the right reasons and not just based on a lucky hunch. Then consider whether the explanation offers a more efficient path to the right answer that you can add to your toolbox. If so, then practice redoing the question the same as if you'd missed it, in order to master the alternative approach. Or maybe you aced the question! Even in this case, reviewing the explanation will reinforce your successful approach, helping you be even more confident and efficient the next time you see a similar question.

As you review these explanations, you may not understand everything they say. Don't worry! The GMAT tests many concepts, and you haven't yet begun to learn all the valuable Kaplan Methods and strategies contained in this book. You may find it useful to return to these explanations later in your studies, once you've read and practiced with this book and your online resources. It's likely that by that point, things that were confusing at first will have become much clearer. It will also be a great confidence booster to see how far you've come in your mastery of the GMAT!

How to Plan Your Practice

No matter what your performance is on the diagnostic test, you can and will improve if you set aside time to study for the GMAT. Block out study time on your calendar, just as you would write down any other appointment. These blocks of time are appointments with yourself, so keep them!

Research shows that people learn better in shorter, more frequent study sessions. Therefore, plan to study at least three days a week for one to three hours, rather than one or two days a week for four or more hours. Sometimes students avoid studying because they feel too tired at the end of a long day at work, but that's often because they think "studying" means spending several hours focusing on tough academic material. Remember that putting in even 30 minutes—perhaps reading one section in your book, doing a handful of questions, or even reviewing questions you've done before—moves you forward toward your goal. Plus, it's much better to do a little and feel good about it than to feel overwhelmed from falling behind. Making time to study will help you feel motivated to study even more.

Every time you sit down to study, set a specific goal for each chunk of study time that addresses a skill you need to develop to score higher. Here are some examples of goals:

- Study the "Averages and Weighted Averages" section in the Math Content Review, complete the accompanying practice set, and review the explanations, noting challenging questions in my question log.
- Review again the Reading Comprehension Strategy chapter to reinforce my understanding of strategic reading. Then try a passage set under timed conditions, reviewing the explanations thoroughly.
- Complete five Problem Solving and five Data Sufficiency questions from the Quantitative Reasoning—Advanced Practice chapter. Review the explanations, noting challenging questions in my question log.

How you put together your study plan will depend on three factors:

1. How much improvement you want to achieve
2. When you want to take your test
3. How much time you have each week for GMAT practice

Clearly, these factors are interdependent. If you want to see a big score increase and you need to take your test in four weeks to meet an application deadline, then you'll probably need to put in at least 25 hours each week to meet your goal. In this case, if you weren't able to study that much in the next month, this would be a good time to reconsider how you will travel your path toward business school. By thinking through these three factors now, you will set yourself up for success and avoid frustration.

If you have ample time before Test Day, you will benefit from working through each chapter in this book, taking full advantage of the strategic explanations, and using your online resources at **kaptest.com/login** for further practice. If, however, you have more limited time to prepare, you may need to prioritize your studies to make sure you address the areas in which you are struggling the most—thereby making the most of your opportunities for score improvement.

And again, don't concern yourself with how many questions you got right on this test or how you scored. You've still got a lot to learn about the GMAT, but you have good tools to help you on your journey—and taking and reviewing your diagnostic test is a great first step. Just remember to be patient with yourself as you make mistakes. Everyone does—making mistakes is an essential part of learning. But consider this: every wrong answer you choose, *and then learn from*, reduces the chance that you'll get a similar question wrong on the one and only day when wrong answers matter. So make mistakes willingly and even happily now, while they don't count. Just resolve to learn from every one of them.

Happy studying!

PART THREE

QUANTITATIVE REASONING SECTION: STRATEGIES, CONTENT, AND PRACTICE

CHAPTER 5

QUANTITATIVE REASONING STRATEGY: PROBLEM SOLVING QUESTIONS

LEARNING OBJECTIVES

- Describe the format and content of Problem Solving questions
- Apply the steps of the Kaplan Method for Problem Solving
- Apply various strategic approaches to answer Problem Solving questions
- Recognize how the four Core Competencies apply to Problem Solving questions

You'll encounter about 17 Problem Solving questions in the GMAT Quantitative section, so these questions comprise just over half the problems in the 31-question section. Since you have 62 minutes for the Quantitative section, to stay on pace, you'll want to spend an average of 2 minutes on each question.

Each Problem Solving question consists of the question stem—which gives you information and defines your task—and five answer choices. One choice is the correct answer to the question. Although the choices aren't labeled with letters on the test, for ease of reading, we denote them with the five letters **(A)**, **(B)**, **(C)**, **(D)**, and **(E)** in this book.

The instructions for the Problem Solving questions look like this:

Directions: Solve the problems and choose the best answer.

Note: Unless otherwise indicated, the figures accompanying questions have been drawn as accurately as possible and may be used as sources of information for answering the questions.

All figures lie in a plane except where noted.

All numbers used are real numbers.

The directions indicate that some diagrams on the GMAT are drawn to scale, which means that you can use them to estimate measurements and size relationships. Other diagrams are labeled "Not drawn to scale," so you can't eyeball them. In fact, when a diagram says "Not drawn to scale," working past the confusing picture is often a key to the problem.

The directions also let you know that you won't have to deal with imaginary numbers, such as $\sqrt{-1}$, and that you'll be dealing with flat figures, such as squares and circles, unless a particular question says otherwise.

Problem Solving questions may deal with any of the math topics tested on the GMAT, covered in the "Math Content Review" chapters in this part of the book.

The Kaplan Method for Problem Solving

Kaplan has developed a Method for Problem Solving based on our study of the approach of students who do well on these questions. You'll notice that the Kaplan Method front-loads critical thinking so it happens before any math. That's because it's your critical thinking skills that the test makers are really trying to evaluate, much more than your ability to factor a quadratic, identify prime factors, or find the volume of a cylinder—all interesting skills but not ones commonly used in business management. You can use this four-step Method to efficiently solve every Problem Solving question you see on Test Day.

THE KAPLAN METHOD FOR PROBLEM SOLVING

STEP 1 Analyze the question.

STEP 2 State the task.

STEP 3 Approach strategically.

STEP 4 Confirm your answer.

Step 1: Analyze the Question

Begin your analysis of the problem by getting an overview. If it's a word problem, what's the basic situation? Or is this an algebra problem? A ratios problem? A permutations problem? Getting a general idea of what's going on will help you to organize your thinking and identify which rules or formulas you'll need to use.

If there's anything that can be quickly simplified, do so—but don't start solving yet. For example, if a question stem gives you the classic quadratic $x^2 - y^2 = 64$, it would be fine to rewrite it immediately in your scratchwork as $(x + y)(x - y) = 64$ in case you need to refer to it in that form. But you wouldn't want to start solving for values just yet; doing so would likely cause you to miss an important aspect of the problem or overlook an efficient solution.

Also, make sure to glance at the answer choices. Can they help you choose an approach? If they are variable expressions, you might substitute numbers for the variables to avoid complicated algebra. If they are numerical values, you might be able to plug them back into the question, a strategy known as backsolving. If they are numerical values that are far apart, you can often estimate. Looking at the choices may trigger an important strategic insight for you.

Step 2: State the Task

Before you choose your approach, make sure you know what you're solving for. The most common wrong answer in Problem Solving is the right answer to the wrong question. And perhaps you won't have to do as much work as you might think—for example, you may be able to solve for what you need without calculating the value of every variable involved in the problem.

Step 3: Approach Strategically

The operative word here is *strategically*. Resist the temptation to hammer away at the problem, hoping for something to work. Use your analysis from steps 1 and 2 to find the most straightforward path to the answer.

There is rarely a single "right approach" to a GMAT Problem Solving question. Choose the easiest one for you given your preferences and the question. Broadly speaking, there are three approaches:

Approach 1: A Kaplan strategy. Frequently, there will be a more efficient approach than straight-ahead math. Consider picking numbers or backsolving, which you will learn about later in this chapter. These approaches can simplify some tough problems and should always be on your mind as possible alternatives. Sometimes estimation or the application of a bit of logic will get you the answer, or at least eliminate some wrong answers. Keep these options in your toolkit, too—they will often be faster than doing the math.

Approach 2: Straightforward math. Sometimes simply doing the math is the most efficient approach. But remember, only do math that feels straightforward. Almost always, the hardest problems will make you sweat during the *analysis*, but you should never find yourself performing extremely complicated calculations.

Remember, the only thing that matters is that you select the correct answer. There is no GMAT grader out there who's going to give you extra points for working out a math problem the hard way.

Approach 3: Guess. You only have an average of 2 minutes per question, so you need to keep moving. Making a guess is better for your score than spending too much time on a question. If you have spent 60 to 90 seconds analyzing the problem and haven't figured it out, make a guess. Even better, recognize within 20–30 seconds that you won't be able to solve this one and make a guess. That banks a little extra time for a question later in the section that you'll actually be able to solve. Don't wait until you fall so far behind that you are forced to guess on questions that you could otherwise have easily solved.

When you can, make your guess a strategic one. That is, eliminate one or more choices based on logic (e.g., "The machine can't possibly make fewer than 20 items a minute" or "The answer definitely needs to have 100 in the denominator").

Step 4: Confirm Your Answer

Because the GMAT is adaptive, you aren't able to return to questions you've already seen to check your work, so you need to build that step into your process on each question. The most efficient way to do this is to re-read the question stem as you select your answer. If you notice a wrinkle in the problem that you missed earlier, redo the problem (if you have time) or change your answer. If you took into account all the information in the question stem and are answering the question that is asked, move on to the next problem with confidence.

Applying the Kaplan Method

Below is a typical Problem Solving question for you to try. As you answer the question, note the features of its format and the math concepts it's testing. Also consider what you do and don't already know about how to solve. The explanation that follows the question demonstrates how a GMAT expert uses Kaplan's four-step Method for Problem Solving to solve this question efficiently.

In a certain town, there are four times as many people who were born in the town's state as there are people who were born outside the state. The ratio of those residents born in the town's state to the town's total population is

○   1 to 4

○   1 to 3

○   1 to 2

○   3 to 4

○   4 to 5

Step 1: Analyze the Question

You're given a part-to-part ratio of people born in-state to people born elsewhere, and the question asks for the part-to-whole ratio of people born in-state to the "total population."

Step 2: State the Task

Use the given ratio of those born in-state to those born out-of-state to determine the ratio of those born in-state to the total population.

Step 3: Approach Strategically

This question doesn't provide any actual numbers of people, nor does it ask for actual numbers. You can use one ratio to solve for another. Having four times as many people born in-state as out-of-state means a ratio of 4:1. Thus, the number that would represent the town's whole population in a ratio is $4 + 1 = 5$. So, the ratio of townsfolk born out of state to all townsfolk is 4 to 5, choice **(E)**.

If thinking in terms of ratios feels awkward, you could pick numbers. If there is 1 person in the town who was born out of state, then since there are four times as many people born in-state, that would be 4 people born in-state. Now there are 5 total people living in the town, and 4 of them were born in-state, so the ratio of in-state to total is 4 to 5.

Step 4: Confirm Your Answer

Confirm that you found the ratio the question asks for. Incorrect choices in ratio questions often provide ratios between different values in the question. Here, for example, **(A)** just repeats numbers used in the original part-to-part ratio.

CONCEPT CHECK

- On average, you should spend _____ minutes on a Problem Solving question.
- Why is step 1—analyze the question—important to success on Problem Solving?

  _____

- What are the three general ways you can execute step 3 and approach the problem strategically?

  _____

Example answers are in your book's online resources (**kaptest.com/login**).

Next, and throughout the rest of this chapter, you'll find in-format Problem Solving questions so you can practice using the Kaplan Method.

Practice Set: The Kaplan Method for Problem Solving

(Answers and explanations are at the end of the chapter.)

1. A machine manufactures notebooks in a series of 5 colors: red, blue, black, white, and yellow. After producing a notebook of 1 color from that series, it produces a notebook of the next color. Once 5 are produced, the machine repeats the same pattern. If the machine began a day producing a red notebook and completed the day by producing a black notebook, how many notebooks could have been produced that day?

    ○   27

    ○   34

    ○   50

    ○   61

    ○   78

2. Youssef lives x blocks from his office. It takes him 1 minute per block to walk to work and 20 seconds per block to ride his bicycle to work. If it takes him exactly 10 minutes more to walk to work than to ride his bicycle, what is the value of x?

    ○   4

    ○   7

    ○   10

    ○   15

    ○   20

3. A book club rented the party room of a local restaurant to meet and discuss a novel over dinner. The total charge, including food and service, was $867.50. If each member of the club paid at least $42, then what is the greatest possible number of members in the club?

    ○   19
    ○   20
    ○   21
    ○   23
    ○   25

4. A team won 50 percent of its first 60 games in a particular season and 80 percent of its remaining games. If the team won a total of 60 percent of its games that season, what was the total number of games that the team played?

    ○   180
    ○   120
    ○   90
    ○   85
    ○   30

5. A convention center recently renovated its banquet space, purchasing new tables and chairs to use in addition to the original tables and chairs. The new tables each seat 6 people, while the original tables each seat 4 people. Altogether, the banquet room now has 40 tables and is capable of seating 220 people. How many more new tables than original tables does the banquet room have?

    ○   10
    ○   20
    ○   30
    ○   34
    ○   36

Step 3: Approach Strategically—Picking Numbers

LEARNING OBJECTIVES

- Pick numbers to solve problems with unknown values and percents
- Pick numbers to solve must be/cannot be/could be problems

There's a belief that all great GMAT test takers share: there must be a straightforward way to problem solve, and there's no need to panic if you don't find it right away. Even if you don't use the algebra-based approach that your high school math teacher would have preferred, you will get the right answer and you will raise your score.

Identifying a more efficient alternative approach involves staying open to possibilities that might not occur to you immediately. Two such approaches—picking numbers and backsolving—can eliminate a lot of math and can be used so often that they deserve special mention.

Picking numbers is a powerful alternative to solving problems by brute force. Rather than trying to work with unknown variables, you pick concrete values for them. In essence, you're transforming algebra or abstract math processes into basic arithmetic, often giving yourself a much simpler task.

How does picking numbers work?

- Pick **permissible** numbers. Some problems have explicit rules such as "x is odd." Other problems have implicit rules. For example, if a word problem says, "Betty is 5 years older than Tim," don't pick $b = -2$ and $t = -7$; these numbers might not work in the problem because age is always a positive number.

- Pick **manageable** numbers. Some numbers are simply easier to work with than others. For example, $d = 2$ will probably be a more successful choice than $d = 492 \sqrt{\pi}$ would be. The problems themselves will tell you what's manageable. For instance, $d = 2$ wouldn't be a great pick if an answer choice were $\frac{d}{12}$. (The number 12, 24, or even 120 would be much better in that case, since each is divisible by 12.)

- Once you've picked numbers to substitute for unknowns, approach the problem as arithmetic instead of algebra or number properties.

- When choices include variables, test every choice. Sometimes the numbers you pick will happen to make more than one choice work. If you get more than one "right answer," pick a new set of numbers and retest only the choices that worked for the first set. The correct answer will work for all permissible numbers.

When a question has variables in the answer choices, the special properties of 0 and 1 mean that picking these numbers, if they are permissible, is more likely to lead to the "false positive" noted in the last bullet point above. However, they are the most manageable numbers in all of math, so keep them in mind if other numbers would make the calculations unreasonable. Imagine picking numbers for the following problem with anything other than $b = 0$ or $b = 1$.

$7^b + 7^b + 7^b + 7^b + 7^b + 7^b + 7^b =$

○ $7b$

○ 7^{b+1}

○ 7^{7b}

○ 8^b

○ 49^b

Picking $b = 0$ makes short work of this exponents question:

$$7^b + 7^b + 7^b + 7^b + 7^b + 7^b + 7^b$$

$$= 7^0 + 7^0 + 7^0 + 7^0 + 7^0 + 7^0 + 7^0$$

$$= 1 + 1 + 1 + 1 + 1 + 1 + 1$$

$$= 7$$

Your target result is 7. See which choices yield 7 when you plug in zero for b:

(A) $7^b = 7^0 = 1$

(B) $7^{b+1} = 7^{0+1} = 7^1 = 7$

(C) $7^{7b} = 7^{7 \times 0} = 7^0 = 1$

(D) $8^b = 8^0 = 1$

(E) $49^b = 49^0 = 1$

The correct choice is **(B)**.

CONCEPT CHECK

- What criteria should you follow when selecting values in place of unknowns?

- When evaluating choices that contain variables, you must

Example answers are in your book's online resources (**kaptest.com/login**).

You'll see opportunities to pick numbers sprinkled throughout the Quantitative Reasoning section on Test Day. They follow certain patterns, which makes them easy to spot once you've gotten familiar with the patterns. The following sections discuss these patterns and give examples.

Picking Numbers with Unknown Values in the Question Stem

Unknowns in Problem Solving questions may be represented by variables (n, x, t, etc.) or just be unspecified values (e.g., "a factory produces some number of units" or "a grocer sells one-fifth of the canned goods in stock"). If you see a question that has unknown values in the question stem, consider picking numbers to represent the unknown(s). Doing so converts the question from algebra to arithmetic, which is often easier and faster. Look in the question stem and the answer choices for clues about the most manageable numbers to pick.

Example:

> Carol spends $\frac{1}{4}$ of her savings on a stereo and $\frac{1}{3}$ less than she spent on the stereo for a television. What fraction of her savings did she spend on the stereo and television?
>
> ○ $\frac{1}{4}$
>
> ○ $\frac{2}{7}$
>
> ○ $\frac{5}{12}$
>
> ○ $\frac{1}{2}$
>
> ○ $\frac{7}{12}$

Common denominators of fractions in the question stem are good choices for numbers to pick. So are numbers that appear frequently as denominators in the answer choices. In this case, a common denominator of the fractions in the stem is $4 \times 3 = 12$, and 12 is also a multiple of most of the denominators in the answer choices, so let Carol's total savings be $12.

That means she spends $\frac{1}{4} \times \$12 = \$3$ on her stereo and a third less than that, or $\frac{2}{3} \times \$3 = \$2$, on her television. That comes out to $\$3 + \$2 = \$5$ spent on the stereo and television combined. You're asked what *fraction* of her savings she spent. Because her total savings was $12, she spent $\frac{5}{12}$ of her savings; **(C)** is correct. Notice that picking a common denominator for the unknown (Carol's savings) made it easy to convert each of the fractions $\left(\frac{1}{4} \text{ and } \frac{2}{3} \times \frac{1}{4} \text{ of her savings} \right)$ to a simple integer.

A tricky part of this question for many students is understanding how to determine the price of the television. The television does not cost $\frac{1}{3}$ of her savings. It costs $\frac{1}{3}$ *less* than the stereo; that is, it costs $\frac{2}{3}$ as much as the stereo.

By the way, some of these choices could have been eliminated quickly using logic. **(A)** is too small, since the stereo alone costs $\frac{1}{4}$ of her savings. **(D)** and **(E)** are too large. The television costs *less* than the stereo, so the two together must cost less than $2 \times \frac{1}{4}$, or half, of Carol's savings. We'll look more at using logic to eliminate answers later in this chapter.

CONCEPT CHECK

- When a question includes one or more unknown values in the stem but numerical answer choices, what should you do when you find a choice that works for the numbers you have picked?

  _____

- If there are fractions in the question, what is usually a good choice for a number to pick?

  _____

Example answers are in your book's online resources (**kaptest.com/login**).

Applying the Kaplan Method: Picking Numbers with Unknown Values in the Question Stem

Now see how a GMAT expert using the Kaplan Method picks numbers to answer a Problem Solving question with unknown values in the question stem.

> If $w > x > y > z$ on the number line, y is halfway between x and z, and x is halfway between w and z, then $\dfrac{y - x}{y - w} =$

- ○ $\dfrac{1}{4}$

- ○ $\dfrac{1}{3}$

- ○ $\dfrac{1}{2}$

- ○ $\dfrac{3}{4}$

- ○ 1

Step 1: Analyze the Question

This question presents a relationship among four variables. The math seems like it would be difficult and time-consuming. You'd have to translate each rule that states a relationship between variables into a separate algebraic equation and then combine them to solve for the fraction in the question stem. Picking numbers, on the other hand, will be much more straightforward. Since the question refers to a number line, you may want to draw a number line to help visualize the situation.

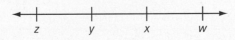

Step 2: State the Task

The question asks you to evaluate a fraction with three variables: $\dfrac{y - x}{y - w}$. The question stem gives no values for the variables, but the answer choices are numbers. This means that the value of the fractional expression must always be the same, as long as the values of the variables follow the rules described in the question stem.

Step 3: Approach Strategically

Pick numbers one at a time, making sure the numbers you pick are permissible (follow the rules) and manageable (easy to work with). The variables x and z each appear twice in the rules, so starting with those two numbers would seem to make sense.

Try $z = 1$ and $x = 3$ to leave room for y.

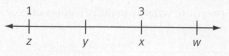

Then y is halfway between 3 and 1, so $y = 2$.

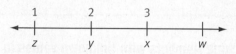

Finally x, or 3, is halfway between w and 1, so $w = 5$.

Once you've picked a set of permissible numbers, it's time to plug these numbers into the expression you're solving for:

$$\frac{y - x}{y - w} = \frac{2 - 3}{2 - 5} = \frac{-1}{-3} = \frac{1}{3}$$

The answer is (**B**).

Step 4: Confirm Your Answer

Look back at the question stem and make sure you understood all the rules and picked permissible numbers. Did you get "y is halfway between x and z"? Check. Did you get "x is halfway between w and z"? Check. Another potential error would have been to make w the smallest value instead of the largest. (Did you notice that the question stem puts w on the left of the inequality statement, even though it belongs on the right-hand side of the number line?) That's another potential mistake you could catch in this step.

Next, you'll find in-format questions with unknowns in the question stem that can be solved efficiently by picking numbers.

Practice Set: Picking Numbers with Unknown Values in the Question Stem

(Answers and explanations are at the end of the chapter.)

6. If $\dfrac{4y - 4x}{z - x} = 2$, then $\dfrac{2(z - x)}{z - y} =$

    ○   −1

    ○   1

    ○   2

    ○   3

    ○   4

7. DeShawn set aside some of his savings to make charitable donations. If he gives $\dfrac{1}{8}$ of the money to Charity A and $\dfrac{1}{5}$ of the remainder to Charity B, what fraction of the original amount that he set aside does DeShawn have left to distribute to other charities?

    ○ $\dfrac{3}{10}$

    ○ $\dfrac{3}{5}$

    ○ $\dfrac{27}{40}$

    ○ $\dfrac{7}{10}$

    ○ $\dfrac{11}{13}$

8. During a sale, a store sells 20 percent of its remaining stock each day, without replenishment. After 4 days, what fraction of its original stock has it sold?

    ○ $\dfrac{1}{625}$

    ○ $\dfrac{256}{625}$

    ○ $\dfrac{61}{125}$

    ○ $\dfrac{64}{125}$

    ○ $\dfrac{369}{625}$

Picking Numbers with Percents in the Answer Choices

Picking numbers also works well on Problem Solving questions for which the answer choices are percentages and the baseline value for the percentage calculations is not given. When the question concerns percents, 100 will almost always be the most manageable number to pick. Using 100 not only makes your calculations easier but also simplifies the task of expressing the final value as a percent of the original.

Example:

The manufacturer of Sleep-EZ mattresses is offering a 10 percent discount on the price of its king-size mattress. Some retailers are offering additional discounts. If a retailer offers an additional 20 percent discount, then what is the total discount available at that retailer?

- O   10%
- O   25%
- O   28%
- O   30%
- O   35%

Since the answers are in percents, pick $100 as the original price of the mattress. (Remember, realism is irrelevant—only permissibility and manageability matter.) The manufacturer offers a 10% discount: 10% of $100 is $10. So now the mattress costs $90.

Then the retailer offers an additional 20% discount. Since the price has already fallen to $90, that 20% is taken off the $90 price. A 20% discount is a reduction of $90 × 0.20 = $18. The final price of the mattress is $90 – $18, or $72.

The mattress has been reduced to $72 from an original price of $100. That's a $28 reduction. Since you started with $100, you can easily calculate that $28 is 28% of the original price. Choice (**C**) is correct.

Notice that (**D**) commits the error of simply adding the two percents given in the question stem. A choice like (**D**) will never be correct on a question that gives you information about multiple percent changes.

CONCEPT CHECK

- What is a good number to pick when the answer choices are given in percents?

_____

An example answer is in your book's online resources (**kaptest.com/login**).

Applying the Kaplan Method: Picking Numbers with Percents in the Answer Choices

Now see how a GMAT expert using the Kaplan Method picks numbers to answer a Problem Solving question with percents in the answer choices.

> In 2018, the profits of Company N were 10 percent of revenues. In 2019, the revenues of Company N fell by 20 percent, but profits were 15 percent of revenues. The profits in 2019 were what percent of the profits in 2018?
>
> ○   80%
>
> ○   105%
>
> ○   120%
>
> ○   124.2%
>
> ○   138%

Step 1: Analyze the Question

Profits and revenues are both changing over time. Since the question provides several changes as percents and the answer choices are percents, picking 100 as a baseline will be a good idea.

Step 2: State the Task

Compare the profits of the two years and express the relationship as a percent. Note that you're not solving for the percent increase or decrease but for the relative amount year over year. The year 2018 is the basis of the comparison. In other words, you want this fraction, $\frac{2019\ profits}{2018\ profits}$, expressed as a percent.

Step 3: Approach Strategically

Start with the earlier year. In 2018, the profits of Company N were 10 percent of revenues. You're given no information about revenues. Instead of calling 2018 revenues R, pick $100 for these revenues. Now 2018 profits are $0.10 \times \$100 = \$10$.

In 2019, the revenues of Company N fell by 20 percent. You decided that revenues in 2018 were $100, so they fell $0.20 \times \$100 = \$20$ to $80. Profits were 15% of revenues that year, so profits were 15% of $80, or $0.15 \times \$80 = \$12$.

Plugging your results back into the question yields $\frac{2019\ profits}{2018\ profits} = \frac{12}{10} = 1.2$.

Multiply by 100% to convert the decimal to a percent: $1.2 \times 100\% = 120\%$. Choice (**C**) is correct.

Step 4: Confirm Your Answer

Re-read the question stem to confirm that you interpreted the relationships correctly.

Next, you'll find in-format questions with percents in the answer choices that can be solved efficiently by picking numbers.

Practice Set: Picking Numbers with Percents in the Answer Choices

(Answers and explanations are at the end of the chapter.)

9. If bicyclists in motion increase their speed by 30 percent and then increase this speed by 10 percent, what percent of the original speed is the total increase in speed?

    ○   10%

    ○   40%

    ○   43%

    ○   64%

    ○   140%

10. A driver delivered food from a restaurant to a customer's home by way of a certain route. If the driver then completed 20 percent of the return trip by way of the same route before the delivery vehicle broke down, what percent of the round trip did the driver complete?

    ○   10%

    ○   20%

    ○   60%

    ○   70%

    ○   80%

11. Sofia runs a business delivering boxes of frequently used household supplies to monthly subscribers. After hiring a workflow manager, she delivered 20 percent more boxes per month while working 20 percent fewer hours herself each month. Hiring a workflow manager increased Sofia's personal productivity per hour by what percent?

    ○   40%

    ○   50%

    ○   60%

    ○   140%

    ○   150%

Picking Numbers with Variables in the Answer Choices

When answer choices contain variables, consider whether algebra or picking numbers will be the more efficient approach. You'll solve the question using the number(s) you pick and get an answer. The correct choice is the one that yields the same answer when you plug in the same number(s). Make sure that you test each choice, just in case more than one produces the desired result. If that happens, you will need to pick a new set of numbers and repeat the process, but only for the choices that worked out the first time.

Example:

If $a > 1$, which of the following is equal to $\dfrac{2a + 6}{a^2 + 2a - 3}$?

- ○ a
- ○ $a + 3$
- ○ $\dfrac{2}{a - 1}$
- ○ $\dfrac{2a}{a - 3}$
- ○ $\dfrac{a - 1}{2}$

The question says that $a > 1$, so the most manageable permissible number is probably 2. Substitute that for a to get $\dfrac{2(2) + 6}{2^2 + 2(2) - 3} = \dfrac{4 + 6}{4 + 4 - 3} = \dfrac{10}{5} = 2$.

Now substitute 2 for a in each answer choice, looking for choices that equal 2 when $a = 2$. Eliminate choices that do not equal 2 when $a = 2$.

(A) $a = 2$. Possibly correct.

(B) $a + 3 = 2 + 3 = 5$. This is not 2. Discard.

(C) $\dfrac{2}{a - 1} = \dfrac{2}{2 - 1} = \dfrac{2}{1} = 2$. Possibly correct.

(D) $\dfrac{2a}{a - 3} = \dfrac{2(2)}{2 - 3} = \dfrac{4}{-1} = -4$. This is not 2. Discard.

(E) $\dfrac{a - 1}{2} = \dfrac{2 - 1}{2} = \dfrac{1}{2}$. This is not 2. Discard.

You're down to **(A)** and **(C)**. Pick another number. Try $a = 3$. Then $\dfrac{2(3) + 6}{3^2 + 2(3) - 3} = \dfrac{6 + 6}{9 + 6 - 3} = \dfrac{12}{12} = 1$.

Now work with the *remaining* choices.

(A) $a = 3$. This is not 1. Discard.

Now that all four incorrect choices have been eliminated, you know that **(C)** must be correct. If time permits, check whether it equals 1 when $a = 3$.

(C) $\dfrac{2}{a - 1} = \dfrac{2}{3 - 1} = \dfrac{2}{2} = 1$. **(C)** does equal 1 when $a = 3$.

This approach to picking numbers also applies to many word problems on the GMAT. Picking numbers can resolve a lot of that confusion. The key to picking numbers in word problems is to re-read the question stem after you've picked numbers, substituting the numbers in place of the variables.

Example:

A car rental company charges for mileage as follows: x dollars per mile for the first n miles and $x + 1$ dollars per mile for each mile over n miles. How much will the mileage charge be, in dollars, for a journey of d miles, where $d > n$?

○ $d(x + 1) - n$

○ $xn + d$

○ $xn + d(x + 1)$

○ $x(n + d) - d$

○ $(x + 1)(d - n)$

Suppose that you pick $x = 4$, $n = 3$, and $d = 5$. (Note that the question stem says that d must be greater than n.) Now the problem would read like this:

A car rental company charges for mileage as follows: $4 per mile for each of the first 3 miles and $5 per mile for each mile over 3 miles. How much will the mileage charge be, in dollars, for a journey of 5 miles?

All of a sudden, the problem has gotten much more straightforward. The first 3 miles are charged at $4/mile. So that's $4 + $4 + $4, or $12. There are 2 miles remaining, and each one costs $5. So that's $5 + $5, for a total of $10. If the first 3 miles cost $12 and the next 2 cost $10, then the total charge is $12 + $10, which is $22.

Plugging $x = 4$, $n = 3$, and $d = 5$ into the answer choices, you get ...

(A) $d(x + 1) - n = 5(4 + 1) - 3 = 22$

(B) $xn + d = 4 \times 3 + 5 = 17$

(C) $xn + d(x + 1) = 4 \times 3 + 5(4 + 1) = 37$

(D) $x(n + d) - d = 4(3 + 5) - 5 = 27$

(E) $(x + 1)(d - n) = (4 + 1)(5 - 3) = 10$

Only **(A)** yields the same number you got when you plugged these numbers into the question stem, so **(A)** is the answer. No need for algebra at all.

CONCEPT CHECK

- How does your approach to a question with variables in the answer choices differ from one with numbers in the choices?

_____

An example answer is in your book's online resources (**kaptest.com/login**).

Applying the Kaplan Method: Picking Numbers with Variables in the Answer Choices

Now see how a GMAT expert using the Kaplan Method picks numbers to answer a Problem Solving question with variables in the answer choices.

> Cindy paddles her kayak upstream at m kilometers per hour and then returns downstream the same distance at n kilometers per hour. How many kilometers upstream did she travel if the round trip took her a total of p hours?

> ○ mnp
>
> ○ $\dfrac{mn}{p}$
>
> ○ $\dfrac{m+n}{p}$
>
> ○ $\dfrac{mnp}{m+n}$
>
> ○ $\dfrac{pm}{n} - \dfrac{pn}{m}$

Step 1: Analyze the Question

Cindy is going upstream and then the same unknown distance back downstream. You're told only that she traveled the two legs of the trip at the rates of m and n, respectively, and that the trip took p hours—and you're not even given a variable for the distance she paddles. The answer choices are expressed with variables. There are many unknowns and no numbers here. Picking numbers could be an efficient strategy.

Step 2: State the Task

Solve for the distance traveled upstream, expressed in terms of m, n, and p. Note that you're not solving for the total distance of the round trip, just the first part of it.

Step 3: Approach Strategically

If you start by picking two manageable numbers for m and n—for example, $m = 2$ and $n = 3$—then the question becomes this:

> Cindy paddles her kayak upstream at 2 kilometers per hour and then returns downstream the same distance at 3 kilometers per hour. How many kilometers upstream did she travel if she spent a total of p hours for the round trip?

To solve for time, you'll need a distance. Since the speeds are now 2 kilometers per hour and 3 kilometers per hour, picking a distance of 6 kilometers for each leg of the trip will work nicely. Now the question is this:

> Cindy paddles her kayak 6 kilometers upstream at 2 kilometers per hour and then returns 6 kilometers downstream at 3 kilometers per hour. How many kilometers upstream did she travel if she spent a total of p hours for the round trip?

Now the time, p, is straightforward to calculate. Six kilometers upstream at 2 kilometers per hour means a total of $6 \div 2 = 3$ hours. Six kilometers downstream at 3 kilometers per hour means a total of $6 \div 3 = 2$ hours. That's $3 + 2 = 5$ hours for the round trip.

Now plug $m = 2$, $n = 3$, and $p = 5$ into the answer choices to see which yields 6—the distance you picked—for the number of kilometers traveled upstream.

(A) $mnp = 2 \times 3 \times 5 = 30$. Eliminate.

(B) $\dfrac{mn}{p} = \dfrac{2 \times 3}{5} = \dfrac{6}{5}$. Eliminate.

(C) $\dfrac{m + n}{p} = \dfrac{3 + 2}{5} = \dfrac{5}{5} = 1$. Eliminate.

(D) $\dfrac{mnp}{m + n} = \dfrac{2 \times 3 \times 5}{2 + 3} = \dfrac{2 \times 3 \times 5}{5} = 2 \times 3 = 6$. (D) could be right, but you need to test (E) to make sure.

(E) $\dfrac{pm}{n} - \dfrac{pn}{m} = \dfrac{5 \times 2}{3} - \dfrac{5 \times 3}{2} = \dfrac{10}{3} - \dfrac{15}{2} = \dfrac{20}{6} - \dfrac{45}{6} = -\dfrac{25}{6}$. Eliminate.

Only choice (D) remains, so it is correct.

Step 4: Confirm Your Answer

Re-read the question stem to confirm that you interpreted the information correctly.

Next, you'll find in-format questions involving picking numbers with variables in the answer choices.

Practice Set: Picking Numbers with Variables in the Answer Choices

(Answers and explanations are at the end of the chapter.)

12. If $n \neq 1, j \neq 0, k \neq 0$, and $m \neq 0$ and if $n = \dfrac{jkm}{jk + jm + km}$, then $\dfrac{1}{n-1} =$

   ○ $\dfrac{1}{j} + \dfrac{1}{k} + \dfrac{1}{m}$

   ○ $\dfrac{jk + jm + km}{jkm - jk - jm - km}$

   ○ $\dfrac{jk + jm + km}{jkm}$

   ○ $\dfrac{jkm - jk - jm - km}{jk + jm + km}$

   ○ $j + k + m$

13. In 15 minutes, Jyoti can read p pages of her economics book. How many minutes will it take her to read r pages of her marketing book, if she reads both books at the same rate?

   ○ $\dfrac{r}{15p}$

   ○ $\dfrac{15r}{p}$

   ○ $\dfrac{15}{rp}$

   ○ $\dfrac{15p}{r}$

   ○ $\dfrac{p}{15r}$

14. To raise money for a charity, v volunteers each pledge to contribute an equal portion of the total goal of d dollars. If r more volunteers join the fund-raising campaign and agree with the original volunteers to contribute equally to the goal, how much less must each original donor give?

   ○ $\dfrac{d}{2v + r}$

   ○ $\dfrac{dv}{2v + r^2}$

   ○ $\dfrac{dr}{v^2 + vr}$

   ○ $\dfrac{dv}{r^2 + vr}$

   ○ $\dfrac{d(v + r)}{2\,(vr)^2}$

Picking Numbers on Must Be/Cannot Be/Could Be Questions

This is a slightly different style of question that asks things like "Which of the following must be an even integer?" or "Which of the following CANNOT be true?" These questions are usually based not on algebra or arithmetic but rather on the properties of the numbers themselves. Some of these questions can be very abstract, so picking numbers really helps. Just as with word problems, making a number properties question concrete helps you to understand it.

Example:

If a and b are odd integers, which of the following must be an even integer?

- ○ $a(b - 2)$
- ○ $ab + 4$
- ○ $(a + 2)(b - 4)$
- ○ $3a + 5b$
- ○ $a(a + 6)$

You can run through the answer choices quite quickly using the picking numbers strategy. Try $a = 1$ and $b = 3$. For **(A)**, $1(3 - 2) = 1$. For **(B)**, $1(3) + 4 = 7$. For **(C)**, $(1 + 2)(3 - 4) = -3$. For **(D)**, $3(1) + 5(3) = 18$, is even—keep this one. For **(E)**, $1(1 + 6) = 7$. Only **(D)** produces an even integer, so it's correct.

Knowing how to test the answer choices on "must be/cannot be/could be" questions is essential to your success on these questions. On a "must be" question, it's usually not enough to stop when you reach the first option that works with the numbers you picked. If a choice works, that only proves that it *could* be true, not that it *must* be true every time. The same logic applies to "cannot be" questions.

To be sure you're choosing the right answer to a "must be" or "cannot be" question, pick numbers with a goal of *eliminating* all four incorrect answers. If none of the choices using the numbers you picked eliminate the four incorrect choices, you will need to pick another set of numbers and test the remaining choices again. Always think critically about what the question stem is asking and how to pick numbers to find the answer most efficiently.

The logic is different for a "could be" question (e.g., "Which of the following could be odd?"). You can safely choose the first answer choice that works because that satisfies the "could be" condition.

Roman numeral questions often feature "must be/cannot be/could be" language in their question stems. Here's an example.

Example:

If integers x and y are distinct factors of 24, then which of the following CANNOT be a factor of 24?

   I. $(x + y)^2$

   II. $x^2 - y^2$

   III. $xy + y^2$

  ○ I only

  ○ I and II

  ○ II and III

  ○ II only

  ○ III only

Work methodically, evaluating the statements one at a time and eliminating answer choices as you go. You can start with the statement that appears most frequently in the choices or simply with the statement that looks easiest to evaluate.

This question asks you to figure out which statement or statements can *never* be a factor of 24. That means you should eliminate a statement if it could possibly equal a factor of 24. If you pick some numbers that don't yield a factor of 24, that means the statement *might* be part of the right answer. But if you pick numbers that do yield a factor of 24, you know that any choice that includes that statement can be eliminated. It's much more straightforward, therefore, to prove choices wrong than to prove them right.

Since the question involves factors of 24, it's a good idea to list these factors out.

$$1, 2, 3, 4, 6, 8, 12, 24$$

Statement II appears three times among the choices, so if you can eliminate it, you'll be down to two choices right away. Squaring something large like 24 or 12 is going to produce a large number, which wouldn't be a factor of 24. So choose smaller numbers; try $x = 4$ and $y = 2$. Then $x^2 - y^2$ would equal $16 - 4$, or 12. Because 12 is a factor of 24, you can eliminate any choice containing Statement II. That leaves only (**A**) and (**E**).

Look at Statement III next. Not only are you squaring and multiplying, but you're also adding, so this number is going to get big fast. To keep it in your target range, pick the smallest numbers on your list, $x = 1$ and $y = 2$. Then $xy + y^2$ would equal $1(2) + 4$, or 6. That's a factor of 24, so (**E**) is eliminated. You know that (**A**) is the correct answer without ever having to evaluate Statement I.

CONCEPT CHECK

- Describe how to pick numbers to solve "must be/cannot be" problems.

  _____

- Describe how to pick numbers to solve "could be" problems.

  _____

Example answers are in your book's online resources (**kaptest.com/login**).

Applying the Kaplan Method: Picking Numbers on Must Be/Cannot Be/Could Be Questions

Now see how a GMAT expert using the Kaplan Method picks numbers to answer a "must be" Problem Solving question.

If j and k are integers, and $2j + k = 15$, which of the following must be true?

○ $j + k$ is odd.

○ $j + k$ is even.

○ j is odd.

○ k is odd.

○ $k > j$

Step 1: Analyze the Question

You're given the equation $2j + k = 15$ and are told that j and k are integers. Those two variables also show up in the answer choices, which speak to odd and even number properties. You may be able to solve this question efficiently by applying your knowledge of number properties, but if you feel uncertain about that approach, consider picking numbers.

Step 2: State the Task

You're looking for an answer that *must* be true. Remind yourself that if an answer choice could be false, even in one case, it can be eliminated.

Step 3: Approach Strategically

Pick numbers that make the equation true. Say you start with $j = 4$ and $k = 7$.

(A) $4 + 7$ is odd. True. Can't be eliminated.

(B) $4 + 7$ is even. False. Eliminate.

(C) 4 is odd. False. Eliminate.

(D) 7 is odd. True. Can't be eliminated.

(E) $7 > 4$. True. Can't be eliminated.

Now you'd have to try a different set of numbers, hoping to eliminate some more. **(E)** looks like the easiest one to target, as you just have to think of a j that's greater than or equal to k. You could choose $j = 5$ and $k = 5$. There's no need to test **(C)** or **(B)**, as they've already been eliminated.

(A) $5 + 5$ is odd. False. Eliminate.

(D) 5 is odd. True. Can't be eliminated.

(E) $5 > 5$. False. Eliminate.

Only **(D)** wasn't eliminated, so it must be the correct answer.

Step 4: Confirm Your Answer

Check that your answer makes sense. Is it true that k must be odd? Multiplying any integer by 2 produces an even number, so $2j$ is even. The number 15 is odd, so an odd number must be added to $2j$ to sum to 15. That's k, so indeed, k must be odd.

Next, you'll find in-format "must be/cannot be/could be" questions that can be solved efficiently by picking numbers.

Practice Set: Picking Numbers on Must Be/Cannot Be/Could Be Questions

(Answers and explanations are at the end of the chapter.)

15. If the product of integers a and b is equal to 10, which of the following CANNOT be even?

    I. $ab + b^2$

    II. $(a + b)^2$

    III. $a + b$

    ○   I only

    ○   II only

    ○   III only

    ○   II and III only

    ○   I, II, and III

16. The integer a is less than -1, and the integer d is greater than 1. If $-1 < b < 0$ and $0 < c < 1$, then which of the following must be the greatest negative number?

    ○ $b - a$

    ○ $b - c$

    ○ $b - d$

    ○ $c - a$

    ○ $a - c$

17. In the set S of consecutive integers from 1 to 10, inclusive, D is the subset of all odd numbers, M is the subset of all prime numbers, and Q is the subset of all numbers whose positive square root is also a member of set S. If d is an element of D, m is an element of M, and q is an element of Q, which of the following could be true?

○ $d = \sqrt{mq}$

○ $d = \dfrac{q}{m}$

○ $m = q$

○ $q = \dfrac{m}{d^2}$

○ $q = \sqrt{dm}$

Step 3: Approach Strategically—Backsolving

LEARNING OBJECTIVE

- Backsolve to solve problems with numbers in the answer choices

Backsolving is like picking numbers in reverse. Instead of coming up with a number yourself, you use a number from the answer choices. You'll then work backward through the problem, testing whether an answer choice agrees with the information in the question stem. This is a good approach whenever plugging a choice into the question would allow you to confirm its details in a straightforward way.

You want to backsolve systematically, not randomly. Usually, you should start with either **(B)** or **(D)**. If the choice you pick isn't correct, you'll often be able to figure out whether you need to try a number that's larger or one that's smaller. Since numerical answer choices are always in ascending or descending order on the GMAT, you'll be able to eliminate several choices at once.

Suppose that the choices are arranged in ascending order, so **(A)** is the smallest value and **(E)** is the greatest. Then suppose you start with **(B)**.

- If **(B)** is correct, select it and move on.
- If **(B)** is too great, then **(A)** is correct.
- If **(B)** is too small, then **(C)**, **(D)**, or **(E)** is correct.

Trying **(D)** next will get you to the right choice immediately.

- If **(D)** is correct, select it and move on.
- If **(D)** is too great, then **(C)** is correct.
- If **(D)** is too small, then **(E)** is correct.

Thus, starting with **(B)** or **(D)** will enable you to find the correct choice with one calculation two-fifths of the time and with two calculations the rest of the time, as long as it is apparent whether an incorrect choice is too low or too high. You can apply similar logic when the choices are arranged in descending order.

Sometimes you can use logic to eliminate one or more choices before doing any math. This makes backsolving *really* powerful. If you are left with three consecutive choices, for instance, you can just pick the middle one to backsolve and you will get to the answer immediately just by determining whether that value is too great, too small, or just right.

You can use backsolving for questions where it is not obvious whether a choice is too great or too small, but you may need to test more choices.

Following are a couple of examples of using backsolving with word problems and one example of using backsolving to answer a question that gives you an equation.

Example:

Ron begins reading a book at 4:30 p.m. and reads at a steady pace of 30 pages per hour. Michelle begins reading a copy of the same book at 6:00 p.m. If Michelle started 5 pages behind the page that Ron started on and reads at an average pace of 50 pages per hour, at what time would Ron and Michelle be reading the same page?

- ○ 7:00 p.m.
- ○ 7:30 p.m.
- ○ 7:45 p.m.
- ○ 8:00 p.m.
- ○ 8:30 p.m.

To backsolve, pick an answer choice and see whether Michelle and Ron are on the same page at that time. There's no compelling reason to prefer one choice to another, so just quickly choose (**B**) or (**D**).

If you start with (**B**), then ask, "On what page is Ron at 7:30 p.m.?" He started reading at 4:30 p.m., so he's been reading for 3 hours. His pace is 30 pages per hour. So he's read $30 \times 3 = 90$ pages. Since Michelle started 5 pages behind Ron, she'd need to read 95 pages to be at the same place. She's been reading since 6:00 p.m., so she's read for 1.5 hours. At 50 pages per hour, she's read 75 pages. That's 20 short of what she needs. So (**B**) is not the right answer.

Since Michelle is reading faster than Ron, she'll catch up to him with more time. Therefore, they'll be on the same page sometime after 7:30 p.m. Eliminate (**A**) because it's even earlier than (**B**) and try (**D**) next.

At 8:00 p.m., Ron has read for 3.5 hours. At a pace of 30 pages per hour, he's read 30×3.5, or 105 pages. Since Michelle started 5 pages behind, she'd need to read 110 pages to be at the same place. She's been reading for 2 hours at this point; at 50 pages per hour, she's read 100 pages. That's still 10 short of what she needs to catch up. So (**D**) is also not the right answer, and you need a later time than 8:00 p.m.—choice (**E**) must be correct.

Example:

A crate of apples contains 1 bruised apple for every 30 apples in the crate. Three out of every 4 bruised apples are considered not fit to sell, and every apple that is not fit to sell is bruised. If there are 12 apples not fit to sell in the crate, how many apples are in the crate?

- ○ 270
- ○ 360
- ○ 480
- ○ 600
- ○ 840

If you start backsolving with (**B**), suppose that there are 360 apples in the crate. Then $\frac{360}{30}$ apples, or 12 apples, are bruised. So, $\frac{3}{4}$ of those 12 apples, or 9 apples, are unsalable. This is too few unsalable apples, so (**B**) is too small. Eliminate (**B**) and (**A**) as well.

Testing **(D)**, suppose that there are 600 apples in the crate. Then $\frac{600}{30}$ apples, or 20 apples, are bruised. Of those 20, $\frac{3}{4}$, or 15, are unsalable. That's too many. So **(D)** and **(E)** are both out, and **(C)** must be correct.

Backsolving works for more than just word problems. You can use it when you're solving for a *single* variable in the question stem.

Example:

What is the value of x if $\frac{x+1}{x-3} - \frac{x+2}{x-4} = 0$?

- ○ −2
- ○ −1
- ○ 0
- ○ 1
- ○ 2

Since **(D)** is just +1, it looks easier to work with than **(B)**, so start with that choice:

$$\frac{1+1}{1-3} - \frac{1+2}{1-4} = \frac{2}{-2} - \frac{3}{-3} = -1 - (-1) = 0$$

Therefore, **(D)** is correct, and you don't have to test any more choices.

CONCEPT CHECK

- How does backsolving differ from picking numbers?

  _____

- If the question is such that you can readily determine whether an incorrect choice is too high or too low, what is the most efficient way to backsolve?

  _____

Example answers are in your book's online resources (**kaptest.com/login**).

Applying the Kaplan Method: Backsolving

Now use the Kaplan Method on a Problem Solving question that lends itself to backsolving.

> At a certain zoo, the ratio of sea lions to penguins is 4 to 11. If there are 84 more penguins than sea lions at the zoo, how many sea lions are there?
>
> O 24
>
> O 36
>
> O 48
>
> O 72
>
> O 132

Step 1: Analyze the Question

A zoo has more penguins than sea lions, and you're given both a ratio and a numerical difference between them.

Step 2: State the Task

You need to figure out the number of sea lions. You have a lot to think about during the GMAT, and you don't want to accidentally solve for the number of penguins. Jot down "sea lions" in your scratchwork to keep track of the task.

Step 3: Approach Strategically

The answer choices are numbers, and plugging in the number of sea lions will determine whether the ratio and the difference work, so backsolving is a good approach.

With choice (**B**), the assumption is that there are 36 sea lions. The ratio of sea lions to penguins of 4 to 11 becomes 36 sea lions to some number of penguins. Since 36 is 9 × 4, the number of penguins in this scenario is 9 × 11 = 99. Is that consistent with the rest of the information? There should be 84 more penguins than sea lions, but 99 – 36 is only 63. You can eliminate (**B**).

Now, do you need more or fewer sea lions? Well, you need to increase the difference between them. Since the animals are in a ratio of 4:11, every time you remove 4 sea lions, you'd remove 11 penguins, *shrinking* the difference between them by 7. So you definitely need *more* sea lions—every time you add 4 sea lions, you add 11 penguins, increasing the difference by 7. Eliminate (**A**) as well and test (**D**).

In this case, the ratio of sea lions to penguins of 4 to 11 becomes 72 sea lions to an unknown number of penguins. Since you've doubled the number of sea lions from what you had in choice (**B**), you must double the number of penguins as well, so you've got 198 penguins. Is that consistent with the rest of the information? There should be 84 more penguins than sea lions. But 198 – 72 is more than 100. That's too many more penguins, so eliminate (**D**). You need a smaller difference, which means you need a smaller number of sea lions. (**C**) must be correct.

Step 4: Confirm Your Answer

If you had accidentally answered (**E**), which is the number of penguins, this step would save you from a wrong answer.

Next, you'll find in-format Problem Solving questions that you can try backsolving.

Practice Set: Backsolving

(Answers and explanations are at the end of the chapter.)

18. If $\left(\frac{1}{64}\right)^x = 4{,}096$, $x =$

    ○ $-\frac{1}{3}$

    ○ $-\frac{1}{2}$

    ○ $-\sqrt{2}$

    ○ -2

    ○ -3

19. The length of a rectangle is twice as long as the width, and the rectangle's area is greater than 72 and less than 200. Which of the following could be the length of the rectangle?

    ○   8

    ○   12

    ○   16

    ○   20

    ○   24

20. In a certain beanbag game, players toss beanbags at a board with a hole in it. If the beanbag falls into the hole, the player scores 5 points. A beanbag that lands on the board but misses the hole is worth 2 points. If a toss misses the board entirely, 1 point is deducted from the player's score. Julianna had 20 tosses and missed the board with 3 throws. Her total score was 52. How many times did she toss the beanbag into the hole?

    ○   5

    ○   6

    ○   7

    ○   8

    ○   9

Step 3: Approach Strategically—Estimating and Guessing

LEARNING OBJECTIVES

- Describe how guessing can be an effective strategy for Problem Solving questions
- Describe what it means to use logic to estimate an answer
- Apply effective guessing and estimating strategies to appropriate questions

Making a well-placed guess can sometimes be the best thing you can do on a problem. Because of the severe penalty exacted on those who fail to finish a section, you need to stay on a steady pace. If you fall behind, it's a good idea to guess on a problem that feels very difficult. That way you'll get back lost time instead of falling further behind. And while you shouldn't be afraid to guess, you *should* be afraid to rush! The GMAT builds in twists and writes problems in complicated ways; rushing almost always leads to a misperception of the problem. The test makers base many wrong answers on the most common misperceptions. So rushing through a problem virtually guarantees a wrong answer. It's far better to guess as needed than to rush through an entire section.

Sometimes you just have no idea how to approach a problem. Instead of throwing away 3 or 4 minutes getting frustrated, make a guess. If you don't know how to approach the problem, you aren't likely to choose the right answer in any case, and you can use the time you save to solve other problems that you stand a better chance of answering correctly.

Lastly, there are some problems that are *best* solved using guessing techniques. The two keys to good guessing are (1) elimination of likely wrong answers by using your knowledge of the problem and of the GMAT's tendencies and (2) maintaining your focus on the "big picture"—remembering that your performance on the section as a whole matters much more than your performance on two or three questions. Better to make a guess in 1 minute and be done with a hard problem than spend 6 minutes before finally guessing anyway; the extra time will pay off.

Also, keep in mind that the hardest questions are the ones you'll be most likely to need to guess on—and are also the ones that will hurt your score the *least* when you get them wrong. So don't be afraid to guess!

There are five guessing strategies that you can apply to Problem Solving:

1. Use logic.
2. Estimate the answer.
3. Eliminate numbers appearing in the question stem.
4. Eliminate the oddball.
5. Eliminate uncritical solutions.

Use Logic

Some answers are simply logically impossible. By analyzing and simplifying before attempting to solve, you may learn enough about the problem to eliminate some wrong answer choices. Consider this problem:

> A container holding 12 ounces of a solution that is 1 part alcohol to 2 parts water is added to a container holding 8 ounces of a solution that is 1 part alcohol to 3 parts water. What is the ratio of alcohol to water in the resulting solution?
>
> ○ 2:5
> ○ 3:7
> ○ 3:5
> ○ 4:7
> ○ 7:3

When paraphrased, this problem is saying that you're adding a 1:2 solution to a 1:3 solution. So logically, the correct answer has to be between 1:3 (or $\frac{1}{3}$, or 0.333 . . .) and 1:2 (or $\frac{1}{2}$, or 0.5). **(A)** and **(B)** are both in that range, but all the others are above 1:2. So you can make a guess—with a 50% chance of being right—just by analyzing the problem logically.

In case you were curious, the answer is **(B)**. The 12-ounce solution has 4 ounces of alcohol and 8 ounces of water. The 8-ounce solution has 2 ounces of alcohol and 6 ounces of water. Add the amounts of alcohol and water to get 6 ounces of alcohol and 14 ounces of water for a ratio of 3:7 alcohol to water.

Also, note that Roman numeral questions are good candidates for logic-based guessing. You can often eliminate several choices by evaluating just one statement. Then if you're pressed for time, you can guess from the remaining choices with an improved chance of success.

Estimate the Answer

The GMAT asks some questions that are intended to be solved via estimation. When a question stem includes a word like *approximately*, that's a clear signal that estimation is probably the best approach you can take.

Example:

> The product of all positive even numbers less than or equal to 20 is closest to which of the following?
>
> ○ 10^6
> ○ 10^7
> ○ 10^8
> ○ 10^9
> ○ 10^{10}

If you had a calculator on the Quant section, you could figure out that the product of all those numbers is 3,715,891,200. But with no calculator, what can you do? The keys to the solution are the word "closest" and the big spread of values in the answer choices—each is 10 times the next smaller value. This problem has "estimation" written all over it.

Jot down the numbers in question:

$$2 \times 4 \times 6 \times 8 \times 10 \times 12 \times 14 \times 16 \times 18 \times 20$$

Since each answer is a power of 10, round the larger values to the nearest 10. Note that you round some up but some down, and a couple aren't changing at all, so you're staying close to the actual value.

$$2 \times 4 \times 6 \times 8 \times 10 \times 12 \times 14 \times 16 \times 18 \times 20$$

$$2 \times 4 \times 6 \times 10 \times 10 \times 10 \times 10 \times 20 \times 20 \times 20$$

For the smallest numbers, $2 \times 4 \times 6 = 48$, which is very close to 50.

$$50 \times 10 \times 10 \times 10 \times 10 \times 20 \times 20 \times 20$$

Restate using factors of 10:

$$(5 \times 10) \times 10 \times 10 \times 10 \times 10 \times (2 \times 10) \times (2 \times 10) \times (2 \times 10)$$

That's eight 10s, one 5, and three 2s:

$$2 \times 2 \times 2 \times 5 \times 10^8$$

$$(2 \times 2) \times (2 \times 5) \times 10^8$$

$$4 \times 10 \times 10^8$$

$$4 \times 10^9$$

That's closer to 10^9 than to 10^{10}, so **(D)** is correct. No calculator needed, just the willingness to estimate!

Eliminate Numbers Appearing in the Question Stem

It's part of human psychology to be drawn to the familiar. When you get lost in a problem, you tend to gravitate toward familiar numbers, such as those you've just seen in the question stem. The GMAT doesn't like to reward people who get lost, so such numbers tend to be wrong.

Eliminate the Oddball

This is psychology again. Our eyes are attracted to difference. (Next time you watch a movie or a TV show, notice how often no one else is dressed in the same color as the main character—it's a subtle trick to keep your attention where the director wants it.) Random guessers, then, will be attracted to uniqueness. As the GMAT does not like to reward random guessing, the oddballs should be eliminated.

A word of warning about this technique: the GMAT also uses a little reverse psychology. The test makers know that people tend to be afraid of answers that seem *too* out of line with the others. These outlying values, then, will sometimes be *correct*. What Kaplan means by an "oddball," then, is *not* a number that's notably bigger or smaller but an answer choice that is structurally unique—the only fraction or the only negative number, for example.

Look at these five answer choices, for example:

○ $\sqrt{2}$

○ 2

○ 4

○ 16

○ 2,056

In this case, the answer choice 2,056 is *not* an oddball and should not be eliminated. But $\sqrt{2}$ is and should be.

Eliminate Uncritical Solutions

Because the GMAT is a test of critical thinking, answers that you'd get just by mashing numbers together are usually wrong. Consider this question:

A bag holds 2 red marbles and 3 green marbles. If you removed 2 randomly selected marbles from the bag, without replacement, what is the probability that both would be red?

○ $\frac{1}{10}$

○ $\frac{1}{5}$

○ $\frac{3}{10}$

○ $\frac{2}{5}$

○ $\frac{1}{2}$

It's true that you want 2 of the 5 marbles in the bag. But GMAT questions usually require a little more math than just that, so $\frac{2}{5}$ isn't likely to be correct. (In fact, it's the odds of getting 1 red marble when selecting 1; the probability of getting 2 red when selecting 2 is actually $\frac{1}{10}$.)

Stay Alert for Guessing Opportunities

Believe it or not, there are some GMAT problems for which a guessing strategy is the best approach you could take. Remember that the test makers aren't trying to judge your math skills alone; they are also testing your ability to find efficient solutions to problems. Every so often, they give you a set of choices with only one logically possible answer. Make sure to look at the answer choices before you choose your approach; you might realize that you can estimate.

Example:

If a store owner increases a product's price by 20 percent and then increases this price by another 15 percent, what percent of the original price is the total price increase?

○ 20%

○ 35%

○ 38%

○ 65%

○ 135%

It's true that you could pick $100 for the original price and then solve for the percent increase, but you can solve even faster by thinking logically about the question and the answer choices. The price goes up 20% and then up another 15%. That 15% increase is being applied not to the original price but to the price after the first increase. If it were 15% of the original, then the total increase would be 20% + 15% = 35% (that's the "uncritical solution"). But since the second increase is based on a higher starting price, the total increase will be a little more than 35%. Only choice (**C**) fits the bill, so it must be correct.

If applied strategically, guessing will be a great tool for you on Test Day. It will help keep you on pace, help you to feel confident and in charge of the test, and occasionally reward you with a very quick right answer.

The Four Core Competencies and Problem Solving

Critical Thinking

Consider what a math question is really asking for. For example, it might look as though it's asking you to solve for the values of several variables, but perhaps you really only need their product, not their individual values.

Study the information you are given and think analytically about what will be the most efficient way to derive the answer from that information. Glance at the answer choices to see what form the answer needs to take, such as a percent, a fraction, or a variable expression. Having your "destination" in mind can help you choose a path toward it.

Most problems can be solved in several different ways. For instance, you might have a choice between using algebra or picking numbers for the variables. As you think which approach will be best for a particular question, consider your personal skills and preferences. Strategic approaches are not one-size-fits-all; practice will help you understand what works best for you. Trust your intuition—if you're thinking of a solution that involves lots of difficult math, then look for a different approach.

Paraphrasing

Sometimes the given information is complicated or presented in a less-than-helpful order. Ask yourself, "How might I rephrase this question more simply?" If you are given a word problem, paraphrasing is your first step. Simplify the wording in the question to just the information needed and explicitly state what the question asks for. Translating words into math is a form of paraphrasing. Distill the given information into scratchwork, which should be simple, accurate, and well organized.

Pattern Recognition

Once you have paraphrased the question, look for any relevant patterns that will ease your path to the proper solution. Certain key words and problem setups indicate that particular math concepts are being tested. Your practice with the range of topics covered in this book will help you get familiar with these patterns so you recognize them on Test Day.

Attention to the Right Detail

You may feel as though you don't have time to read the question stem carefully, but not reading carefully is surely a waste of time. It's all too easy to be in a hurry and solve for a value other than what the question asks for. The test makers know this and include choices that are the right answer to the wrong question. For instance, you might work through the calculations to determine the value of the variable y, but the question asks for the value of $2y - 3$. It is almost a certainty that the value of y will be among the incorrect choices.

There are many details in Problem Solving questions that can be vitally important, such as the difference between $\geq$ and $>$. When performing calculations, pay close attention to the individual operations and the order in which you are performing them. Also note—and don't forget as you are solving—any restrictions given in the question, such as $x < 0$.

Details that are not stated can be important as well. For instance, unless a question specifically states that a certain number is an integer, do not assume that the number is an integer. If it's not specified that a number is positive, keep in mind that it could be zero or negative.

Answers and Explanations

Practice Set: The Kaplan Method for Problem Solving

1. (E)

You are asked to identify which of the choices is a possible number of notebooks made, given that notebooks are made in a repeating sequence of 5 colors. On this day, the machine starts with red and ends with black. Thus, it must have produced at least 3 notebooks: red, blue, black. However, 3 is not an answer choice. The next possibility is that the machine ran through the sequence of 5 colors once and then produced the last 3 notebooks. That would be 8 notebooks, but that's not a choice either. Indeed, the choices are all quite a bit greater, so instead of taking the time to count up by 5s, distill the pattern into a rule: the number of notebooks produced is some multiple of 5 plus 3 more. Multiples of 5 end in 0 or 5, so a value that is 3 greater than a multiple of 5 ends in 3 or 8. **(E)**, 78, is the only such value among the choices, making it correct.

2. (D)

The question asks you to determine how many blocks Youssef lives from his office. You're told that it takes him 10 minutes more to walk than to ride his bike, and you're given his rates of movement: he walks 1 block per minute and bikes 1 block per 20 seconds (that is, 3 blocks per minute).

Because the choices are easy-to-work-with numbers, consider working backward from them. Also, look for opportunities to eliminate one or more choices before doing any math. There's a 10-minute difference between Youssef's time walking and his time biking. In 10 minutes, at a rate of 1 block per minute, Youssef would walk 10 blocks. That would put his biking time at zero minutes. That's clearly not possible. Eliminate **(C)**. If he walked even fewer blocks, his biking time would drop into the negative minutes, so eliminate **(A)** and **(B)** as well.

Now test **(D)**: if Youssef lived 15 blocks away, then walking at 1 block a minute would take 15 minutes, and biking at 3 blocks a minute would take 5 minutes. The difference between 15 and 5 is 10 minutes, which is

exactly what the question says. Therefore, **(D)** works and is correct. Confirm that you've solved for the number of blocks and that your logic and arithmetic are correct.

3. (B)

An unknown number of club members split a bill of $867.50, with each member paying at least $42. Some members could have paid more than $42, but none paid less. The question asks for the maximum possible number of members, which can be determined by imagining that as many members as possible paid the minimum amount, or $42 each.

At this point you could count up to $867.50 in easy steps. Ten members paying $42 each would pay $10 \times \$42 = \$420$, so 20 members would pay twice that amount, or $840. One more member paying the minimum would more than cover the bill: $840 + \$42 = \$882$, so 21 members are too many. There must have been 20 members maximum, with one or more members paying more than $42 to make up the difference between $840 and the bill of $867.50. Therefore, **(B)** is correct.

You could also work backward from the answer choices. **(B)** is a good place to start, since 20 is a round number that is easy to work with. As above, 20 members paying $42 each would pay $840, and if one more member paid $42, the book club would have paid more than the bill. So again, the greatest possible number of members paying at least $42 is 20.

Confirm that you read the question stem correctly. For example, if you thought that each member paid exactly $42, you might not have selected **(B)**.

4. (C)

The question tells you that a team won 50% of its first 60 games, or 30 games. It then improved, winning 80% of its remaining games, so that by the end of the season, the team had won 60% of its games overall. The question asks for the total number of games that the team played. Since the team played more than 60 games, you can eliminate **(E)** immediately.

You could solve this by setting up an equation using the weighted averages formula (discussed in the "Ratios, Rates, and Weighted Averages" chapter). If the unknown number of games in the second part of the season is x, then, since 50% is 0.5 and 80% is 0.8, the equation that describes this is $(0.5)(60) + (0.8)(x) = 0.6(60 + x)$. This becomes $30 + 0.8x = 36 + 0.6x$. Subtract $0.6x$ and 30 from both sides of the equation to get $0.2x = 6$ and multiply both sides by 5 to yield $x = 30$. That's the number of remaining games, so the total number of games is $60 + 30 = 90$, or (**C**).

If the translation of words into algebra or the algebra itself is daunting, however, an efficient approach is to backsolve using the given choices. Start with (**B**). If the total number of games is 120, the team played $120 - 60 = 60$ games in the second part of the season. It won 80% of the latter 60 games, for a total of $0.8 \times 60 = 48$ games. Add the initial 30 games won to the 48 games won in the second part of the season to get $30 + 48 = 78$ games won out of a total of 120 games. The winning percentage is 60% overall, which would be $0.6 \times 120 = 72$, so 78 games won is too many. Eliminate (**B**).

Think strategically about which answer choice to try next. The first portion of games has a 50% winning average, while the second portion has an 80% winning average. Since the percentage you calculated for (**B**) was too high and the second portion of games has the higher winning percentage, (**B**) has too much weight on the latter portion of games. You need fewer games in the second portion and, therefore, fewer games total. Eliminate (**A**) as well.

Try (**C**) next because the math will be easier than for (**D**). A total of 90 games means the team played $90 - 60 = 30$ games in the second part of its season. If the team won 80% of those games, it won $0.8 \times 30 = 24$ more games. In total, the team would have won $30 + 24 = 54$ games. Calculate the 60% winning percentage of 90 games: $0.6 \times 90 = 54$. That's the same number of games, so (**C**) is correct.

5. (B)

The question asks how many more new, 6-seat tables than old, 4-seat tables a restaurant has. There are a total of 40 tables, which seat 220 customers.

You can solve this problem by translating the information into equations. Let F be the number of four-seat tables and S the number of 6-seat tables. Because there are 40 tables, $F + S = 40$. The number of people who can be seated at 4-seat tables is $4F$ and the number at 6-seat tables is $6S$. You know the total seating capacity is 220, so $4F + 6S = 220$. Rearrange the first equation to get $F = 40 - S$. Plug that expression for F into the second equation: $4(40 - S) + 6S = 220$. Expand this to get $160 - 4S + 6S = 220$. Subtract 160 from each side and combine the terms with S to get $2S = 220 - 160 = 60$. So, $S = 30$. This means that $F = 40 - 30 = 10$. The question asks for how many *more* new 6-seat tables there are than old 4-seat tables. That is $30 - 10 = 20$, which is (**B**).

The easiest way to make an error in a problem like this one is to solve for the wrong thing. Both the number of new 6-seat tables (30) and the number of old 4-seat tables (10) are present among the choices. A quick check of the question to confirm that the correct answer represents the *difference* between the table types is worthwhile before selecting the choice and moving on.

Practice Set: Picking Numbers with Unknown Values in the Question Stem

6. (E)

This question asks you to determine the value of an expression involving 3 variables given an equation involving those same 3 variables in a different arrangement.

Because this question must have exactly one answer, you can use picking numbers and know that a valid set of values will definitely lead you to the correct answer. The numerator in the given equation can be factored into $4(y - x)$, and it would be convenient to pick numbers such as $y = 2$ and $x = 1$ so that $y - x = 1$ and the entire numerator equals 4. Then for the entire fraction to equal 2, the denominator, $z - x$, must equal 2, making $z = 3$.

Plugging in the chosen values of $x = 1$, $y = 2$, and $z = 3$ into the expression you're asked to evaluate yields $\frac{2(3-1)}{3-2} = 4$, making **(E)** the correct answer. If time permits, check the arithmetic you used to pick numbers for the three variables and your calculation for the value of the second expression.

7. **(D)**

This question asks you to determine the fraction of money remaining after DeShawn donates to Charities A and B. You're told that DeShawn donates $\frac{1}{8}$ of the original amount to Charity A and $\frac{1}{5}$ of the remaining amount to Charity B.

Since there is an unknown original amount and the question is asking for a fraction of this unknown, this is a good opportunity to pick numbers. When given information about fractions of an unknown total, pick a common multiple of the denominators. In this case, pick $40 as the original amount that DeShawn has because it is a multiple of both 5 and 8.

The amount that DeShawn gives to Charity A is $\frac{1}{8} \times \$40 = \$5$. After this donation, he has $\$40 - \$5 = \$35$ remaining. The amount that he gives to Charity B is thus $\frac{1}{5} \times \$35 = \$7$. He now has $\$35 - \$7 = \$28$ remaining. As such, he has $\frac{28}{40} = \frac{7}{10}$ of his original money left. This matches **(D)**. Confirm that you applied the fractions to the correct values (you took an eighth of the *original* amount and a fifth of the *remaining* amount) and that your arithmetic is correct.

8. **(E)**

This question asks for the fraction of stock sold after a store sells 20 percent of its remaining stock each day for 4 days, assuming no additions during these days.

This question asks for a fraction of an unknown total and is thus a good opportunity for picking numbers. Based on the answer choices, 625 is a good pick for the original stock value because it is the denominator of three answer choices and a multiple of 125, the denominator of the two other answer choices. Organize the starting stock, sold stock, and remaining stock for each of the 4 days in a table:

DAY	START	SOLD	REMAINS
1	625	125	500
2	500	100	400
3	400	80	320
4	320	64	256

Since 256 units remain out of 625 starting units, the amount sold is $625 - 256 = 369$, which means the fraction of stock sold is $\frac{369}{625}$, or **(E)**. Confirm that you have found what the question is asking for, which is the fraction of items sold, not items remaining.

Practice Set: Picking Numbers with Percents in the Answer Choices

9. **(C)**

This question asks for the overall percent increase in the bicyclists' speed after a 30% increase followed by a further 10% increase.

A question that asks about a percent increase without specifying the original value is often a good candidate for picking numbers, and that's the case here. Pick 100 because that number works well with percentages. If the bicyclists' original speed is 100 (units can be ignored here) and they increase their speed by 30% , they are now going 30 faster, for a total speed of 130. They then increase their speed by 10%. Since 10% of 130 is 13, their final speed is $130 + 13 = 143$.

The increase in speed is 43, and because the original value is 100, the percent increase is $\frac{43}{100} = 43\%$, or **(C)**. Check to make sure that you answered with the overall percent increase and applied the speed increases separately rather than adding the percent changes.

10. **(C)**

This question asks for the percentage traveled of a round trip. The driver completed the outbound trip followed by 20% of the return trip. Since the driver made it to the customer and started back, you know the driver completed more than half the trip; if you needed to make a strategic guess, you could immediately eliminate **(A)** and **(B)**.

Because the question does not specify any distances and is asking about a percentage, pick 100 as the round-trip distance to make calculations easy. If 100 is the round-trip distance, then the outbound trip must be 50. The driver also completed 20% of the return trip, which is a distance of $(20\%)(50) = (0.2)(50) = 10$.

The driver traveled a distance of $50 + 10 = 60$, and the total round-trip distance is 100. The driver thus traveled $\frac{60}{100} = 60\%$ of the round-trip distance, making **(C)** correct. Confirm that you have answered with the percentage traveled of the round trip.

11. (B)

The question asks by what percentage Sofia's personal productivity per hour increased. You're told that, after hiring a workflow manager, Sofia can produce 20% more boxes while working 20% fewer hours. However, there are two unknowns: the initial number of boxes she produced and the initial number of hours she worked before hiring her manager.

When presented with unknown values, picking numbers is often an efficient approach. In the case of a percent change question, 100 is a great number to pick. Say Sofia's initial production was 100 boxes and she worked 100 hours; then her productivity was 1 box per hour.

If the number of boxes increased by 20%, that is 120 boxes. If her hours were reduced by 20%, they were reduced to 80 hours. Therefore, her new productivity is $\frac{120 \text{ boxes}}{80 \text{ hours}} = 1.5$ boxes per hour. Calculate the percent change in productivity:

$$\text{Percent change} = \frac{\text{Amount of change}}{\text{Original amount}}(100\%)$$
$$= \frac{0.5}{1}(100\%) = 50\%$$

(B) is correct.

Practice Set: Picking Numbers with Variables in the Answer Choices

12. (B)

The question offers a variable, n, that is equivalent to a complex fraction containing the variables j, k, and m. The question asks for the value of $\frac{1}{n-1}$. You'll need to determine a value of n and then insert it into this expression. The variables j, k, and m are restricted from equaling zero to avoid division by zero in the first fraction, and n cannot equal 1 for the same reason in the second fraction.

Because the answer choices are all given in terms of j, k, and m, picking numbers is an efficient strategy. Say each of the three variables is equal to 2. Then you get

$$n = \frac{jkm}{jk + jm + km} = \frac{(2)(2)(2)}{2(2) + 2(2) + 2(2)} = \frac{8}{12} = \frac{2}{3}.$$

Now insert this value into the expression you're trying to find: $\frac{1}{n-1} = \frac{1}{\frac{2}{3}-1} = \frac{1}{-\frac{1}{3}} = -3$. Thus, you need to find the choice that yields a value of -3 when you plug in the numbers you picked:

(A) $\frac{1}{j} + \frac{1}{k} + \frac{1}{m} = \frac{1}{2} + \frac{1}{2} + \frac{1}{2} \neq -3$. Eliminate.

(B) $\frac{jk + jm + km}{jkm - jk - jm - km} = \frac{2(2) + 2(2) + 2(2)}{2(2)(2) - 2(2) - 2(2) - 2(2)}$

$$= \frac{12}{8-12} = \frac{12}{-4} = -3.$$

This value is a match, but test the remaining choices to make sure none of the others also equals -3.

(C) This fraction, $\frac{jk + jm + km}{jkm}$, is just the reciprocal of the one in the question stem, so it's $\frac{1}{n} = \frac{3}{2}$ with the numbers you picked. Eliminate.

(D) This fraction is the reciprocal of that in **(B)**, so its value with your picked numbers is $-\frac{1}{3}$. Eliminate.

(E) $j + k + m = 2 + 2 + 2 \neq -3$. Eliminate.

Since only **(B)** gives the same result as the numbers you picked, **(B)** is correct.

13. (B)

The question asks you to find the number of minutes it will take Jyoti to read r pages of her marketing book. The question specifies that Jyoti can read p pages of her economics book in 15 minutes and that she reads her marketing book at the same rate.

Since there are two unknowns, p and r, pick easily manageable numbers. If you make $p = 15$, then Jyoti reads 15 pages of her economics book in 15 minutes, or 1 page per minute. Since she reads her marketing book at this rate also, the number of pages, r, she reads will equal the number of minutes it takes her to read those pages. Say r is 10, then Jyoti will take 10 minutes to read those pages. This is the value you'll look for in the answer choices.

Plug 15 for p and 10 for r into the answer choices to see which one equals 10.

(A) $\dfrac{r}{15p} = \dfrac{10}{15(15)}$. There's no need to work out the denominator; since it's greater than the numerator, the fraction can't equal 10, so eliminate it.

(B) $\dfrac{15r}{p} = \dfrac{15(10)}{15} = 10$. Keep this, but test the remaining choices.

(C) $\dfrac{15}{rp} = \dfrac{15}{10(15)} = \dfrac{1}{10}$. Not 10. Eliminate.

(D) $\dfrac{15p}{r} = \dfrac{15(15)}{10} = \dfrac{225}{10} = 22.5$. Eliminate.

(E) $\dfrac{p}{15r} = \dfrac{15}{15(10)} = \dfrac{1}{10}$. Eliminate.

(B) is the only choice that yields the right value, so it's correct.

14. (C)

The question asks for the difference in amount that each volunteer will need to contribute to the total goal of a fund-raising drive if the number of volunteers is increased. You're told that there are initially v volunteers, each contributing an equal share to the total goal of d dollars. The question also states that there will be r volunteers added and that, after the addition, each of the volunteers will still contribute equally to the goal, d.

Since you're given only variables for the numbers of volunteers and the amount of money, pick numbers. Pick a value for the dollar amount that is divisible by both the original number of volunteers and the increased number. Say v is 3 and r is 2, then you'll need d to be divisible by both 3 and 5 (because 3 volunteers plus 2 additional equals 5.) Therefore, you can make $d = 15$.

Thus, when there are 3 volunteers, each will pay $5 to reach the goal of $15. When 2 more volunteers are added, each of the 5 volunteers will pay $3. Therefore, using the numbers you've picked, the difference in what each original volunteer pays is $2. Plug the numbers you've chosen into the answer choices to find which equals 2.

(A) $\dfrac{d}{2v + r} = \dfrac{15}{2(3) + 2} = \dfrac{15}{8}$. Eliminate.

(B) $\dfrac{dv}{2v + r^2} = \dfrac{15(3)}{2(3) + 2^2} = \dfrac{45}{10}$. Eliminate.

(C) $\dfrac{dr}{v^2 + vr} = \dfrac{15(2)}{3^2 + 3(2)} = \dfrac{30}{15} = 2$. This is a match, so keep it for now.

(D) $\dfrac{dv}{r^2 + vr} = \dfrac{15(3)}{2^2 + 3(2)} = \dfrac{45}{10}$. Eliminate.

(E) $\dfrac{d(v + r)}{2(vr)^2} = \dfrac{15(3 + 2)}{2(3 \times 2)^2} = \dfrac{75}{72}$. Eliminate.

Only (C) yields the correct value, so it is correct.

Practice Set: Picking Numbers on Must Be/Cannot Be/Could Be Questions

15. (D)

The question states that a and b are integers and says that their product is 10. It asks for the Roman numeral statements that cannot be even. These statements offer various expressions containing the variables a and b. You could use knowledge of number properties or pick numbers to solve.

Because this is a "cannot be" question, evaluate each statement with the aim of yielding an even number so you can eliminate the statement. Both Statement I and Statement II appear in three answer choices, so begin by evaluating one of these. You can quickly list the integers that a and b could be: 1 and 10, 2 and 5, −1 and −10, −2 and −5. Note that in each of these factor pairs, a and b could be either number.

Evaluate Statement I. You know that $ab = 10$. The question is what you're adding to it. If b is 1, then $ab + b^2 = 10 + 1^2 = 11$. That's odd, but that only shows that Statement I can be odd—it doesn't mean the expression *must* be odd. Try $b = 10$. Now $ab + b^2 = 10 + 10^2 = 110$. That's even, so Statement I is not part of the correct answer. Eliminate (**A**) and (**E**).

Both Statements II and III appear twice in the remaining choices. Statement III is a little easier to deal with, so try it next. Because the order of the terms doesn't matter in addition, it doesn't matter which factor-pair value a and b have. No matter which of the four pairs of factors you try, the result is odd: $1 + 10 = 11$; $2 + 5 = 7$; $-1 + (-10) = -11$; $-2 + (-5) = -7$. Statement III is part of the correct answer. Eliminate (**B**).

Now for Statement II. The expression inside the parentheses is the same as Statement III, so it will have one of the values you've already worked out. Squared, the expression is either $(\pm 11)^2 = 121$ or $(\pm 7)^2 = 49$. The value is definitely odd, so Statement II is also part of the correct answer. (**D**) is correct.

16. (B)

This question asks you to determine which of these expressions must produce the greatest negative number (the one closest to zero on the number line). You're given rules about 4 variables: a must be an integer less than -1 (that is, -2 or lower), b must be between -1 and 0, c must be between 0 and 1, and d must be an integer greater than 1 (that is, 2 or greater). Thus, $a < b < c < d$.

Pick numbers that follow the given rules and plug them into the answer choices. Since the correct expression has to always produce the greatest negative number, you can eliminate any that result in a positive number or a negative number that is less than a negative number produced by one of the other choices. If two choices are tied for the greatest negative value with the numbers you pick, pick different numbers and try those choices again. You might try $a = -2$, $b = -0.5$, $c = 0.5$, and $d = 2$.

(**A**) $b - a = -0.5 - (-2) = 1.5$. You may also have recognized that subtracting a smaller number from a larger one always yields a positive result. This expression is always positive, so eliminate (**A**).

(**B**) $b - c = -0.5 - 0.5 = -1$. Keep (**B**) for now.

(**C**) $b - d = -0.5 - 2 = -2.5$. This is less than -1, so eliminate (**C**).

(**D**) $c - a = 0.5 - (-2) = 2.5$. This is positive; eliminate (**D**).

(**E**) $a - c = -2 - 0.5 = -2.5$. You may also have noticed that a is no greater than -2 and c is positive, so $a - c < -2$. This value must be less than (**B**); eliminate.

(**B**) is correct. Ensure that you answered the right question, finding the expression that represents the greatest negative number. A common error would be to choose the negative number with the greatest magnitude (absolute value), which is actually the smallest number.

17. (B)

The question describes S, the set of consecutive integers $\{1, 2, 3, \ldots, 9, 10\}$. The subsets of S are these:

- D, the odd numbers in S, $\{1, 3, 5, 7, 9\}$
- M, the prime numbers in S, $\{2, 3, 5, 7\}$
- Q, the perfect squares in S, $\{1, 4, 9\}$

The question asks which of the equations in the choices *could* be true. Individual elements of the subsets are represented as d, m, and q.

Once you find a choice that could be true, you can select it, since there is only one correct choice. Pick numbers for d, m, and q that are members of the variables' respective subsets to test each choice.

(**A**) This choice states that the square root of mq is an integer d, so mq must be one of the elements of D squared: $1^2 = 1$, $3^2 = 9$, $5^2 = 25$, $7^2 = 49$, $9^2 = 81$. The elements of M are 2, 3, 5, or 7, and the elements of Q are 1, 4, and 9. One times the elements of M is either 2, 3, 5, or 7; none of these is among the possibilities above. Check the products for $q = 4$ and $q = 9$: $4 \times 2 = 8$, $4 \times 3 = 12$, $4 \times 5 = 20$, $4 \times 7 = 28$, $9 \times 2 = 18$, $9 \times 3 = 27$, $9 \times 5 = 45$, and $9 \times 7 = 63$. None of these matches the target numbers either. Eliminate (**A**).

(B) This choice says that when q is divided by m, the result is an integer that is in subset D. If $m = 3$ and $q = 9$, then $d = \dfrac{9}{3} = 3$, and that value is in D. **(B)** is the correct choice because the question asks which choice *could* be true.

Make sure that you found the choice that could be true, not the one that must be false! Also, make sure that you plugged in numbers from the right subset for each variable when testing the choices.

Practice Set: Backsolving

18. (D)

The question stem provides an equation containing a fraction that is raised to an unknown exponent x. The choices represent potential values of x, all of which are negative.

Your task is to use an understanding of exponents rules and critical thinking to determine the value of x. Because each choice is a negative value, you are really raising the number 64 to the positive version of each; e.g.,

$\left(\dfrac{1}{64}\right)^{-\frac{1}{3}} = \dfrac{1}{\left(\dfrac{1}{64}\right)^{\frac{1}{3}}} = 64^{\frac{1}{3}}$. Since raising a positive integer

to a fractional exponent does not result in a larger number, eliminate **(A)** and **(B)**. Also, since raising an integer to $\sqrt{2}$ results in a non-integer, eliminate **(C)**.

Now, since the remaining choices **(D)** and **(E)** are small integers, consider using the backsolving strategy. You'll need to test only one of these two choices to arrive at the correct answer. Test **(D)**: $\left(\dfrac{1}{64}\right)^{-2} = 64^2 = 64(64) = 4{,}096$. This outcome matches that in the question stem, so you have found the correct answer.

Confirm that you carefully applied the rules of exponents in setting up the arithmetic and that you performed your calculations accurately.

19. (C)

The question stem refers to a rectangle and says that the length is twice the width. The rectangle's area, which is length times width, is between 72 and 200, exclusive. You're asked to identify which choice is a possible value of one of the rectangle's longer sides, or its length.

Since the choices are numbers and you must determine a single value, you can use the backsolving strategy. Since you're looking for the longer side, consider testing the larger of **(B)** or **(D)** first—that's **(D)**. If the length measures 20, the width, which is half the length, measures 10. The rectangle's area would then be $(20)(10) = 200$. The area needs to be less than 200, so eliminate **(D)**. **(E)** would produce an even larger area, so eliminate this choice as well.

Now test **(B)**. If the length measures 12, the width measures 6, so the rectangle's area would be $(12)(6) = 72$. The area needs to be greater than 72, so eliminate **(B)** as well as **(A)**. The remaining choice, **(C)**, must be correct.

Confirm that you solved for the longer side of the rectangle. If you accidentally solved for the shorter side, or width, choice **(A)** awaits you. If you have time, you could plug a length of 16 into the question, find the width is equal to 8, and multiply to find the area is a permissible 128.

20. (C)

Julianna scored 52 points on 20 attempts in a game in which points are awarded for tossing a beanbag onto a board or into a hole in the board, but points are deducted for missing the board, which Julianna did 3 times. Find the number of times she tossed the beanbag into the hole, earning 5 points per toss.

You could solve this problem algebraically, but seeing whole numbers in the choices is a clue that backsolving might be easier. Start by simplifying this problem by removing the complicating factor of Julianna's misses. Julianna had 3 misses; without those misses, she would have had $20 - 3 = 17$ attempts and a score of $52 + 3 = 55$. Select one of the choices for the number of beanbags that she tossed into the hole, calculate her score, and compare the result to 55.

If you decide to start with (**B**), then determine that 6 tosses in the hole would have been worth 5 points each for a total of 30 points. There would have been $17 - 6 = 11$ tosses that stayed on the board. These would be worth 2 points each for a score of 22 points. Her total score of $30 + 22 = 52$ points would have been less than 55, so (**B**) is not enough tosses into the hole. Eliminate (**B**) and (**A**) as well and look for a better score.

Try (**D**). Eight successes at 5 points each would be 40 points. There would be $17 - 8 = 9$ tosses at 2 points each, for a total of 18 points. Therefore, 8 tosses into the hole would have resulted in a score before penalties of $40 + 18 = 58$ points. Thus, (**D**) is too great, and (**C**) must be correct.

If you have time, you can confirm by calculating her actual score with 7 tosses into the hole at 5 points each, 10 tosses that hit the board at 2 points each, and 3 misses that deduct a point each:
$5(7) + 2(20 - 7 - 3) - 1(3) = 35 + 20 - 3 = 52$.

CHAPTER 6

QUANTITATIVE REASONING STRATEGY: DATA SUFFICIENCY QUESTIONS

> **LEARNING OBJECTIVES**
>
> - Describe the format and content of Data Sufficiency questions
> - Apply the steps of the Kaplan Method for Data Sufficiency
> - Apply various strategic approaches to answer Data Sufficiency questions
> - Recognize how the four Core Competencies apply to Data Sufficiency questions

Slightly less than half the 31 questions in the Quantitative section are in the Data Sufficiency format; you can expect to see about 14 of these questions. The key to solving these questions is to understand how the Data Sufficiency question type is structured and use that knowledge to work efficiently. Just as with Problem Solving questions, you should aim to spend an average of about 2 minutes per question.

A Data Sufficiency question stem will never give you enough information to solve the problem. Further information is presented *after* the initial question in two "statements." Your goal in a Data Sufficiency question is to determine whether the information in the statements is sufficient to allow you to answer the question. Many Data Sufficiency questions can be answered without finding the solution to the question presented in the stem.

The instructions for Data Sufficiency questions on the GMAT are always the same and look like this:

Directions: In each of the problems, a question is followed by two statements containing certain data. You are to determine whether the data provided by the statements are sufficient to answer the question. Choose the correct answer based upon the statements' data, your knowledge of mathematics, and your familiarity with everyday facts (such as the number of minutes in an hour or cents in a dollar). You must indicate whether:

- ○ Statement (1) ALONE is sufficient, but Statement (2) is not sufficient.
- ○ Statement (2) ALONE is sufficient, but Statement (1) is not sufficient.
- ○ BOTH statements TOGETHER are sufficient, but NEITHER statement ALONE is sufficient.
- ○ EACH statement ALONE is sufficient.
- ○ Statements (1) and (2) TOGETHER are NOT sufficient.

Note: Diagrams accompanying problems agree with information given in the question but may not agree with additional information given in Statements (1) and (2).

All numbers used are real numbers.

The directions may seem confusing at first, but they become clear with use. Here's a simple example:

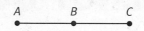

What is the length of segment *AC*?

(1) *B* is the midpoint of *AC*.

(2) *AB* = 5

○   Statement (1) ALONE is sufficient, but Statement (2) is not sufficient.

○   Statement (2) ALONE is sufficient, but Statement (1) is not sufficient.

○   BOTH statements TOGETHER are sufficient, but NEITHER statement ALONE is sufficient.

○   EACH statement ALONE is sufficient.

○   Statements (1) and (2) TOGETHER are NOT sufficient.

The diagram tells you that there is a line segment *AC* with point *B* somewhere between *A* and *C*. A statement will be sufficient if it gives you enough information to figure out the length of *AC*.

Statement (1) tells you that *B* is the midpoint of *AC*. This means that *AB* equals *BC* and that *AC* is twice the length of *AB* and of *BC*. However, Statement (1) does not give an actual value for *AB* or *BC*, so you cannot answer the question using Statement (1) alone.

Statement (2) says that *AB* = 5. However, Statement (2) does not give you any information about *BC*, so the question cannot be answered using Statement (2) alone.

If you use both of the statements together, you know from Statement (1) that *AB* = *BC*, and you know from Statement (2) that *AB* = 5. Therefore, you can find the value of both *AB* and *BC* and you *could* solve for the length of *AC*. Since "Both statements together are sufficient, but neither statement alone is sufficient," the answer to the question is **(C)**.

As in the previous chapter on Problem Solving, and throughout this book, we label the five answer choices with the five letters **(A)**, **(B)**, **(C)**, **(D)**, and **(E)** for ease of reference. Because the answer choices for Data Sufficiency are rather involved, we also have a handy mnemonic, which we'll introduce next in the discussion of the Kaplan Method for Data Sufficiency.

The Kaplan Method for Data Sufficiency

This step-by-step Method is the essential systematic plan of attack for Data Sufficiency, modeled after the approach of students who have mastered this question type. Using this analysis-heavy process will allow you to answer questions efficiently and help you avoid some common Data Sufficiency mistakes.

THE KAPLAN METHOD FOR DATA SUFFICIENCY

STEP 1 Analyze the question stem.
- Determine Value or Yes/No.
- Simplify.
- Identify what is needed to answer the question.

STEP 2 Evaluate the statements using 12TEN.

Step 1: Analyze the Question Stem

Note that this step is not to *read* the question stem. It is to *analyze* the question stem. There are three analytical tasks you should accomplish in this step:

- **Determine Value or Yes/No.** Which type of Data Sufficiency question is this? Depending on whether the question is a Value question or a Yes/No question, the rules for sufficiency are a little different. If you treat the two types the same way, you probably won't get the right answer. Later in this chapter, you'll learn the critical differences between these two types.

- **Simplify.** If the given information is an equation that can be simplified, you should do so up front. Likewise, any word problems should be translated into math or otherwise paraphrased in your scratch-work. When a question asks for the value of a specific variable and gives you a multi-variable equation, isolate the variable being asked for so you can more clearly see what kind of information you need in order to solve.

- **Identify what is needed to answer the question.** What kind of information would get you the answer to the question? The more you think up front about what information would be sufficient, the better you'll be able to evaluate the statements.

Don't rush through this step. The more you glean from the question stem, the easier it will be to find the right answer.

Step 2: Evaluate the Statements Using 12TEN

Since the answer choices depend on first considering each statement alone, don't let the information you learn from one statement carry over into your analysis of the other. Begin by considering each statement separately, in conjunction with the question stem. Remember that each statement is always valid. Don't waste time verifying the statements; just evaluate whether the information lets you answer the question.

On Test Day, you don't want to spend even a second reading the answer choices or thinking about which choice is which. They never change, so you will save yourself much time and confusion by memorizing what the answer choices mean and working with them until you've fully internalized them.

A helpful way to remember how the answer choices are structured is to use the acronym **1-2-TEN**.

1	Only Statement (**1**) is sufficient.
2	Only Statement (**2**) is sufficient.
T	You must put the statements **together** for them to be sufficient.
E	**Each** statement alone is sufficient.
N	**Neither** separately nor together are the statements sufficient.

The **1-2-TEN** mnemonic is extremely helpful for remembering what each of the Data Sufficiency answer choices means. For consistency's sake, when we refer to the five choices to a question, we'll continue to do so by the five letters (**A**), (**B**), (**C**), (**D**), and (**E**), just as we do throughout the rest of the book.

As you evaluate the two statements, use your scratchwork to keep track of which choices you have ruled out as incorrect. Use the following patterns to guide your elimination:

If Statement (1) is sufficient, the answer can only be (**A**) or (**D**). *Eliminate* (**B**), (**C**), *and* (**E**).

If Statement (1) is insufficient, the answer can only be (**B**), (**C**), or (**E**). *Eliminate* (**A**) *and* (**D**).

If Statement (2) is sufficient, the answer can only be (**B**) or (**D**). *Eliminate* (**A**), (**C**), *and* (**E**).

If Statement (2) is insufficient, the answer can only be (**A**), (**C**), or (**E**). *Eliminate* (**B**) *and* (**D**).

A common point of confusion when first learning the mnemonic is about the difference between **T** and **E**. **E** means that *each* statement by itself would allow you to answer the question. So if Statement (1) works by itself and Statement (2) also works by itself, you choose the fourth choice and move on. If neither statement provides enough information on its own, then and only then do you try combining the statements to see if together they provide enough information. If *together* they do, then **T** applies, and you choose the third choice. If there still isn't enough information, you're left with **N** for *neither/none*, and you pick the last choice.

Remember: if either statement by itself is sufficient, then of course the two statements together will also be sufficient. For example, if Statement (1) is sufficient all by itself but Statement (2) is not, when you combine them, Statement (1) does all the work and you still have sufficiency. But you didn't *need* to combine the statements to have sufficiency. (**C**) can be correct *only* when each statement alone is insufficient and combining the statements is necessary to obtain sufficiency.

Apply the Method

Below are a couple of typical Data Sufficiency questions for you to try. As you answer the questions, note the features of this question format. Also consider what you do and don't already know about how to solve. The explanation that follows each question shows how a GMAT expert uses Kaplan's two-step Method for Data Sufficiency, along with certain math concepts, to solve the question efficiently.

A fruit stand sells apples, pears, and oranges. Every apple is the same price, every pear is the same price, and every orange is the same price. If oranges cost $0.50 each, then what is the cost of 5 oranges, 4 apples, and 3 pears?

(1) The cost of 1 apple is $0.30.

(2) The cost of 8 apples and 6 pears is $3.90.

○ Statement (1) ALONE is sufficient, but Statement (2) is not sufficient.

○ Statement (2) ALONE is sufficient, but Statement (1) is not sufficient.

○ BOTH statements TOGETHER are sufficient, but NEITHER statement ALONE is sufficient.

○ EACH statement ALONE is sufficient.

○ Statements (1) and (2) TOGETHER are NOT sufficient.

Step 1: Analyze the Question Stem

This is a Value question that asks for the cost of 5 oranges, 4 apples, and 3 pears. You are given the cost of oranges, so you need enough information to determine the cost of 4 apples and 3 pears.

Step 2: Evaluate the Statements Using 12TEN

Statement (1) provides the cost of apples, but nothing about the cost of pears. This is insufficient, so eliminate **(A)** and **(D)**.

Statement (2) tells you that 8 apples and 6 pears cost $3.90. You cannot determine the individual costs of apples and pears, but what you need is the cost of 4 apples and 3 pears. If you divide the cost of 8 apples and 6 pears in half, that is the cost of 4 apples and 3 pears. Statement (2) is sufficient, and **(B)** is correct. Note that because you've found a statement that works, you do not need to combine the statements—you have the answer.

Now try another one. Spoiler alert: this one has a different answer!

Is the product of x, y, and z equal to 1?

(1) $x + y + z = 3$

(2) x, y, and z are each greater than 0.

○ Statement (1) ALONE is sufficient, but Statement (2) is not sufficient.

○ Statement (2) ALONE is sufficient, but Statement (1) is not sufficient.

○ BOTH statements TOGETHER are sufficient, but NEITHER statement ALONE is sufficient.

○ EACH statement ALONE is sufficient.

○ Statements (1) and (2) TOGETHER are NOT sufficient.

Step 1: Analyze the Question Stem

This is a Yes/No question. If $xyz = 1$, the answer is yes. If $xyz \neq 1$, the answer is no. If a statement always produces a yes or a no answer for all permissible values of x, y, and z, then that statement is sufficient to answer the question.

Step 2: Evaluate the Statements Using 12TEN

Picking numbers for Statement (1), you can see how to get a yes: $x = 1$, $y = 1$, and $z = 1$. Can you pick numbers in such a way that the sum is 3 but the product is not 1? If you consider different kinds of numbers, you can. Zero doesn't alter a sum, but multiplying by zero produces zero. So, if $x = 3$, $y = 0$, and $z = 0$, $x + y + z = 3 + 0 + 0 = 3$, but now $xyz = 3(0)(0) = 0$. In this case, the answer to the question is no. Since you can get both a yes and a no, Statement (1) is insufficient. This means that you can eliminate **(A)** and **(D)** as possible choices.

Now that you've reached a verdict on Statement (1), completely put Statement (1) out of your mind as you evaluate Statement (2). Statement (2) rules out using 0, but not the possibility of using fractions or decimals. So $x = 1$, $y = 1$, and $z = 1$ is also permissible here, but so is something like $x = 100$, $y = 100$, and $z = 100$. So xyz could equal 1, but it could also equal 1,000,000. You can get both a yes and a no here, as well. Statement (2) is also insufficient, so eliminate **(B)**.

Since each statement is insufficient on its own, consider them together. Pick numbers that add to 3 *and* are all positive. Again, $x = 1$, $y = 1$, and $z = 1$ meet the conditions of both statements and answer the question with a yes. Try to think of numbers that are consistent with both statements but *don't* multiply to 1. For example, $x = 2.8$, $y = 0.1$, and $z = 0.1$ fit the bill. They are all positive and sum to 3. However, their product is $2.8(0.1)(0.1) = 0.028$; this answers the question with a no. Since you can get both a yes and a no answer, the statements are insufficient to answer the question unambiguously even when combined. The correct choice is **(E)**.

CONCEPT CHECK

- On a Data Sufficiency question, what analysis should you perform before evaluating the statements?

  _____

- In the Kaplan Method for Data Sufficiency, what do the numbers and letters in the mnemonic 1-2-TEN stand for?

  _____

Example answers are in your book's online resources (**kaptest.com/login**).

Now try the questions in the following practice set. Don't worry if they're challenging at first; you're only getting started working with this unusual question type. For now, do not concentrate on speed—or even on getting the correct answer—but rather on approaching Data Sufficiency questions systematically using the Method. You'll get much more practice with these questions throughout this chapter and the other Quantitative chapters in this book.

Practice Set: The Kaplan Method for Data Sufficiency

Note: Because the Data Sufficiency answer choices are always the same and should be memorized, we have omitted them here. If you need a refresher on the choices or the 12TEN mnemonic, review the preceding section of this chapter.

(Answers and explanations are at the end of the chapter.)

1. How many employees of Company R are surveyors?

    (1) Exactly $\frac{5}{8}$ of the employees of Company R are not surveyors.

    (2) The 18 architects in Company R constitute 25 percent of the company's total employees.

2. If $a^5 \geq -32$ and a is an integer, what is the value of a?

    (1) $6a + 18 \leq 12$

    (2) $a^2 > 2$

3. If $3b - |a| = 27$, what is the value of b?

    (1) $a^2 = 81$

    (2) $a^3 > 0$

4. The nth term of a sequence of distinct positive integers is determined by $a_n = (k^{a_{n-2}})(a_{n-1})$, where $n \geq 3$ and k is a constant. If $a_2 = 4$ and $a_3 = 36$, what is the value of a_5?

   (1) $a_1 = 2$

   (2) $k = 3$

5. A ferry crosses a lake and then returns to its starting point by the same route. The first time it crosses the lake, the ferry travels at 15 kilometers per hour. The ferry's return trip takes 3 hours. How many hours does the ferry take for the first leg of the trip?

   (1) The ferry's average speed for the entire round trip is 12 kilometers per hour.

   (2) The distance the ferry covers to cross the lake once is 30 kilometers.

Step 1: Know the Two Types of Data Sufficiency Questions

LEARNING OBJECTIVE

- Distinguish between Value and Yes/No Data Sufficiency questions

As mentioned in the previous section, there are two types of Data Sufficiency questions, Value questions and Yes/No questions. Your approach to each must be slightly different.

Value Questions

A Value question asks for the exact value of something. If a statement narrows the possibilities down to exactly one number, then it is sufficient. Otherwise, it is not. Of the Data Sufficiency questions you'll see on Test Day, approximately two-thirds will be Value questions.

Take a closer look at how a Value Data Sufficiency question works.

Example:

What is the value of x?

(1) $x^2 - 7x + 6 = 0$

(2) $5x = 30$

Step 1: Analyze the Question Stem

This is a Value question, meaning you need to find the value of x to obtain sufficiency. Sufficiency is obtained when you can identify one, and *only* one, possible value for x.

Step 2: Evaluate the Statements Using 12TEN

Statement (1) can be factored to $(x - 1)(x - 6) = 0$, which means that there are two possible values for x, either 1 or 6. But you don't even need to calculate these two values; once you know there is more than one possible value, you know that Statement (1) must be insufficient. Eliminate **(A)** and **(D)**.

Statement (2) is a linear equation, containing a single variable. Therefore, there can only be one possible result (in this case, $x = 6$), and it is sufficient. Since Statement (1) is insufficient and Statement (2) is sufficient by itself, **(B)** is correct.

CONCEPT CHECK

- To be sufficient to answer a Value question, a statement must

_____

An example answer is in your book's online resources (**kaptest.com/login**).

Following are some Value questions that you can use to hone your skills.

Practice Set: Value Questions

Note: Because the Data Sufficiency answer choices are always the same and should be memorized, we have omitted them here. If you need a refresher on the choices or the 12TEN mnemonic, review the "Kaplan Method for Data Sufficiency" section earlier in this chapter.

(Answers and explanations are at the end of the chapter.)

6. What is the value of $4n - 5m$?

    (1) $\frac{n}{5} = \frac{m}{4}$

    (2) $\frac{n}{4} = \frac{m}{5}$

7. What is the value of $\frac{st}{u}$?

    (1) $s = \frac{3t}{4}$ and $u = 2t$

    (2) $s = u - 10$ and $u = s + t + 2$

8. If z is an integer, what is the units digit of z^3?

    (1) z is a multiple of 5.

    (2) $\sqrt{z}$ is an integer.

9. If d is the product of exactly two distinct prime factors, what is the value of the larger of those prime factors?

    (1) $100 \leq d \leq 120$

    (2) d is an even number.

Yes/No Questions

Yes/No questions are, simply put, questions that call for a yes or a no answer. A key difference between Value questions and Yes/No questions is that a range of values can establish sufficiency for Yes/No questions. For example, if a question asks, "Is $x > 10$?" and a statement says $x < 9$, the answer is, "No, x is never greater than 10."

A common cause of confusion on Yes/No questions is that even when an answer is no, if it is definitely no, that is sufficient to answer the question unambiguously. A statement that allows you to answer the question either "always yes" or "always no" is part of the correct answer; only "sometimes yes, sometimes no" answers are insufficient.

Yes/No questions may not explicitly call for a yes or no answer. Suppose a Data Sufficiency question asks which employee, Jana or Sam, earned more in 2019. You should handle this question the same way as you would a Yes/No question that asked, "Did Jane earn more than Sam last year?" In both cases, you have sufficient information when you determine that only one answer is possible—Jane earned more or Sam earned more—even if you don't know a precise value for either Jane's earnings or Sam's earnings. For example, it's sufficient to know that Jane earned more than $20,000 and that Sam earned less than $16,000.

Applying the Kaplan Method: Yes/No Questions

Try this Yes/No Data Sufficiency question. Think about what makes it a Yes/No question and what would make a statement sufficient. Then see how a GMAT expert uses the Kaplan Method to take the question apart.

> If x is an integer, and $0 < x < 4$, is x prime?
>
> (1) $x > 1$
>
> (2) x is even.

Step 1: Analyze the Question Stem

You need to determine whether x is a prime number or not, so this is a Yes/No question. If you paraphrase the question stem, you learn that x could be 1, 2, or 3. The numbers 2 and 3 are prime, but 1 is not. If a statement tells you that x must be either 2 or 3, you can answer the question with a definite yes; if a statement tells you that x must be 1, you get a definite no.

Step 2: Evaluate the Statements Using 12TEN

Start with Statement (1). Knowing that x is greater than 1 rules out 1, leaving only 2 and 3 as possible values of x. You have the answer: definitely yes. This statement is sufficient. Notice that you don't know which of those two values x equals, but for a Yes/No question, knowing a precise value is often not necessary. Eliminate **(B)**, **(C)**, and **(E)**.

Now set aside Statement (1) and move on to Statement (2). Of the possible values of x (1, 2, and 3), only 2 is even. This statement tells you that x must be 2, and it gives you a definite yes. Statement (2) is also sufficient, so **(D)** is correct.

CONCEPT CHECK

- What is the main difference between a Yes/No and a Value Data Sufficiency question?

  _____

- A statement is sufficient for a Yes/No Data Sufficiency question if it lets you answer the question with either _____ or _____.

Example answers are in your book's online resources (**kaptest.com/login**).

The following practice set contains some questions you can use to practice using the Kaplan Method on Yes/No questions.

Practice Set: Yes/No Questions

Note: Because the Data Sufficiency answer choices are always the same and should be memorized, we have omitted them here. If you need a refresher on the choices or the 12TEN mnemonic, review the "Kaplan Method for Data Sufficiency" section earlier in this chapter.

(Answers and explanations are at the end of the chapter.)

10. Is $\frac{z}{12} - 9$ an integer?

    (1) $\frac{z + 24}{12}$ is an integer.

    (2) z is a multiple of 6.

11. If p and z are positive integers, is pz odd?

    (1) $p + z$ is even.

    (2) z^p is even.

12. Is $0 < \frac{a}{b} < 1$?

    (1) $ab > 1$

    (2) $a - b < 1$

13. If y is an integer and $y > 6$, is $x^3y > 56$?

    (1) $4 < x^2 \leq 9$

    (2) $x^3 + x > x^3$

Step 2: Evaluate the Statements—Picking Numbers

LEARNING OBJECTIVE

- Answer Data Sufficiency questions using the Picking Numbers strategy

An important strategy for Data Sufficiency questions is one you're already familiar with from the previous chapter on Problem Solving: picking numbers. However, you'll use this strategy somewhat differently to answer Data Sufficiency questions.

Picking Numbers in Data Sufficiency

You can pick numbers for many Data Sufficiency questions that contain variables, unknown quantities, or percents of an unknown whole. The main way in which you'll use the Picking Numbers strategy is to test whether statements are sufficient. You'll test whether the statement yields a different answer to the question (e.g., a different value, a yes versus a no) when you plug in different numbers.

Another way you may sometimes use Picking Numbers is in step 1, to get a handle on a question stem that is worded in a particularly complex or abstract way. Sometimes a little thought experimentation with some small, concrete numbers can help you understand an underlying pattern or simply what the question is actually talking about.

Similar to Problem Solving, pick numbers that are *permissible*, that is, that comport with any restrictions established in the question stem and the statement(s) you are evaluating. Also, pick numbers that are *manageable*—the point is to make your life easier, so choose numbers that are easy to work with.

When using this strategy to evaluate statements, always pick at least two different sets of numbers. That's because you are trying to prove that the statements are *insufficient* by producing two different results.

It's usually easier to prove insufficiency than sufficiency. If you plug in a different number and get a different answer to the question, you know the statement is insufficient. If, however, you plug in a different number and get the same answer to the question, it could be that the statement is sufficient, or it could be that you just haven't found a kind of number that yields a different answer.

Fortunately, as you practice this strategy, you'll start to notice the types of numbers that can produce different results, depending on the parameters of the problem. Pay attention to the behavior of positives vs. negatives, fractions vs. integers, odds vs. evens, and so on. Also, don't hesitate to use the numbers 0 and 1 if they are permitted by the question. The unique properties of these numbers mean that they can often produce a different result than any other numbers when plugged into a statement. If you do get the same answer to the question from more than one set of numbers with different characteristics, think critically about whether there is an underlying pattern that means all permissible numbers will produce the same result.

CONCEPT CHECK

- What is your primary goal when picking numbers for Data Sufficiency questions?

  _____

- How might you satisfy yourself that a statement is sufficient when picking numbers to evaluate it?

  _____

Example answers are in your book's online resources (**kaptest.com/login**).

Applying the Kaplan Method: Picking Numbers in Data Sufficiency

Here's a Data Sufficiency question for you to try. The explanation demonstrates how a GMAT expert would use Picking Numbers to solve.

If $a + b = 20$, then what is the value of $c - d$?

(1) $ac - bd + bc - ad = 60$

(2) $d = 4$

Step 1: Analyze the Question Stem

This is a Value question, so to be sufficient, a statement must yield a single value for the expression $c - d$. You are given the value of another expression, $a + b$. To obtain sufficiency, you'll need either values for both c and d or a way to relate the equation $a + b = 20$ to the expression $c - d$.

Step 2: Evaluate the Statements Using 12TEN

As always, think strategically. Since the GMAT doesn't present the statements in any particular order, it's sometimes wise to start by evaluating Statement (2) if it looks easier to evaluate than Statement (1). Here, Statement (2) gives you a value for d but not for c, and it tells you nothing more about $a + b$. Remembering that you started with Statement (2), eliminate **(B)** and **(D)**.

Now tackle Statement (1), remembering to use the information it provides in conjunction with the question stem. Using algebra, the equation $ac - bd + bc - ad = 60$ factors to $(a + b)(c - d) = 60$. You're given $a + b = 20$, so $20(c - d) = 60$, and $c - d = 60 \div 20 = 3$. Statement (1) is sufficient, and **(A)** is correct.

If you don't notice the opportunity to solve algebraically, picking numbers will get you to the answer. Because $a + b = 20$, try $a = 10$ and $b = 10$.

Now, Statement (1) reads:	$10c - 10d + 10c - 10d = 60$
Combine the like terms:	$20c - 20d = 60$
Factor out the 20:	$20(c - d) = 60$
Divide out the 20:	$c - d = 3$

So the expression $c - d$ can equal 3. But you're not finished yet. You have to pick a different set of numbers to see whether you can produce a different answer.

What permissible numbers might be likely to produce a different answer? Since Statement (1) involves subtraction, use a negative number. Try $a = 25$ and $b = -5$.

Now Statement (1) reads:	$25c - (-5)d + (-5)c - 25d = 60$
Move the common terms next to each other:	$25c + (-5)c - (-5)d - 25d = 60$
Simplify the positive and negative signs:	$25c - 5c + 5d - 25d = 60$
Combine like terms:	$20c - 20d = 60$
Factor out the 20:	$20(c - d) = 60$
Divide out the 20:	$c - d = 3$

After picking two sets of numbers that have different properties and receiving the same result, you can say with reasonable confidence that Statement (1) is sufficient.

Following are some questions you can use to practice using the Picking Numbers strategy.

Practice Set: Picking Numbers in Data Sufficiency

Note: Because the Data Sufficiency answer choices are always the same and should be memorized, we have omitted them here. If you need a refresher on the choices or the 12TEN mnemonic, review the "Kaplan Method for Data Sufficiency" section earlier in this chapter.

(Answers and explanations are at the end of the chapter.)

14. Each of *A*, *B*, and *C* represents a single digit in the positive number *ABC*. If the hundreds digit is twice the units digit, is *B* > *A*?

    (1) *C* < 2

    (2) *B* = 9

15. Does the integer *a* have 4 or more distinct prime factors?

    (1) *a* is divisible by 36.

    (2) *a* is divisible by 35.

16. Is $|15 - m| + |m - 15| > 15$?

    (1) *m* > 6

    (2) *m* < 7

Step 2: Evaluate the Statements—Combining Statements

Another key to success on Data Sufficiency questions is knowing how to most effectively combine statements.

Combining Statements

If—and *only* if—each statement on its own is insufficient, you must consider the statements together. One good way to do this is to think of the statements as one long sentence and consider whether that sentence gives you enough information to solve the question. Since this is Data Sufficiency, stop solving as soon as you know that you *could* solve.

The two statements never contradict each other. However, the statements often provide different, complementary information, which may or may not be sufficient to answer the question.

Use the same criteria to evaluate combined statements as you do individual statements. To recap, for a Value question, the combined statements are sufficient if they restrict the quantity being asked about to a single value. Suppose one statement permits more than one value, such as −1, 0, and 1, and the other statement permits values such as 1, 2, and 3. If there is one and only one value in common (1, in this example), then the two statements together are sufficient, and you'll choose (**C**). If there is no value in common or there are more than one value in common, then the combined statements are insufficient, and you'll choose (**E**).

For a Yes/No question, the combined statements are sufficient if they restrict the possible values to a range that answers the question with an "always yes" or "always no." Say a question asks whether Machine X worked faster than Machine Y. If one statement says that the two machines worked the same amount of time and the other statement says that Machine X produced less than Machine Y, then you know X's rate of work was slower than Y's and the answer to the question is no. The combined statements are sufficient to answer the question, and you would choose (**C**).

Combining Statements Drill

The following exercise contains a single Value question stem—"What is the value of *x*?"— and a number of sets of sample statements, which have already been simplified and evaluated for you. Imagine that you had analyzed the statements and gotten the possible values for *x* listed: Which statements, either separately or combined, are sufficient to answer the question?

Choose the appropriate Data Sufficiency answer choice—(A), (B), (C), (D), or (E)—for each pair of statements. Answers follow the exercise.

What is the value of x?

1. (1) $x = -1, 0, 1$

   (2) $x = 0, 1$

2. (1) $x < 3$

   (2) $x > 1$

3. (1) $x = -1, 0$

   (2) $x < 0$

4. (1) $x = -1, 1$

   (2) $x = 1, 2$

5. (1) $x < 4$

   (2) $x < 2$

6. (1) $x = -1, 0$

   (2) $x = -1, 0$

7. (1) $x = -1, 1$

   (2) $x = -1$

8. (1) $x \geq 2$

   (2) $x \leq 2$

9. (1) x is even.

   (2) x is prime.

Combining Statements Drill: Answers

1. (E); x could be 0 or 1.
2. (E); x could be any number between (but not including) 1 and 3. Don't assume that variables are integers.
3. (C); $x = -1$.
4. (C); $x = 1$.
5. (E); x could be any number smaller than 2.
6. (E); x could be 0 or -1. Statements that give redundant information are never sufficient when combined.
7. (B); Statement (2) is sufficient. Note that you would never combine statements in this case.
8. (C); $x = 2$.
9. (C); $x = 2$.

CONCEPT CHECK

- Under what circumstance do you combine statements?

   _____

An example answer is in your book's online resources (**kaptest.com/login**).

Applying the Kaplan Method: Combining Statements

Here's an example of a Data Sufficiency question that involves combining the statements.

If x and y are positive integers, is $\frac{2x}{y}$ an integer?

(1) Some factors of y are also factors of x.

(2) All distinct prime factors of y are also prime factors of x.

Step 1: Analyze the Question Stem

This is a Yes/No question. You can paraphrase the question in the stem as either "Is $2x$ a multiple of y?" or "Does $2x$ divide evenly by y?"

Step 2: Evaluate the Statements Using 12TEN

If you're not comfortable thinking about "factors" and "prime factors" in the abstract, make this question more concrete by picking numbers. Choose permissible, manageable numbers. For Statement (1), that means positive integers with common factors. If you pick $x = 5$ and $y = 5$, that will give you a yes to the original question, since $\frac{2x}{y} = \frac{10}{5} = 2$. But if you pick a different set of numbers, say $x = 2$ and $y = 42$, that will yield the fraction $\frac{4}{42}$. Statement (1) is insufficient; eliminate **(A)** and **(D)**.

Pick numbers for Statement (2), making sure they're permissible. For example, 36 and 6 have the same factors, 2 and 3. Picking the numbers $x = 36$ and $y = 6$ gives you $\frac{2(36)}{6} = \frac{72}{6} = 12$. Choosing $x = 6$ and $y = 36$, on the other hand, gives you $\frac{2(6)}{36} = \frac{12}{36}$. Therefore, Statement (2) is insufficient; eliminate **(B)**.

Now, combining the statements, you will notice something interesting. Statement (2) is more restrictive than Statement (1). So as you combine the statements, ask yourself, "Will any numbers that satisfy Statement (2) also satisfy Statement (1)?" Yes, they will. For instance, $x = 36$ and $y = 6$, which you picked for Statement (2), also work for Statement (1): these numbers will again yield a yes answer. And $x = 6$ and $y = 36$ also work for Statement (1), yielding a no answer. Since combining the statements didn't add any new information and the information presented was insufficient, the answer must be **(E)**.

Practice when and how to combine statements on the questions that follow.

Practice Set: Combining Statements

Note: Because the Data Sufficiency answer choices are always the same and should be memorized, we have omitted them here. If you need a refresher on the choices or the 12TEN mnemonic, review the "Kaplan Method for Data Sufficiency" section earlier in this chapter.

(Answers and explanations are at the end of the chapter.)

17. Is $y^2 < 1$?

   (1) $y > -1$

   (2) $y < 1$

18. A taqueria has exactly two items on its menu, a taco and a burrito. On a particular day, it sold 600 items, exactly half of which were tacos. What was the taqueria's revenue on that day?

   (1) The average price of an item on the menu is $4.50.

   (2) A burrito costs twice as much as a taco.

19. If a and b are positive, what is the value of $a - b$?

   (1) $a^2 + 2ab + b^2 = 36$

   (2) $a^2 - b^2 = 12$

Step 2: Evaluate the Statements—Strategic Guessing

LEARNING OBJECTIVE

- Use strategic guessing when appropriate to manage your pacing on Data Sufficiency questions

Just as on Problem Solving questions, strategic guessing on Data Sufficiency questions is important for your pacing so you don't run out of time before reaching the end of the section.

Strategic Guessing

It's not unusual for Data Sufficiency questions to give you one statement that's significantly more difficult to deal with than the other. You can eliminate some answer choices by looking at the easier statement first, whether that's Statement (1) or (2). Then if you need to guess, your odds of success are better.

Applying the Kaplan Method: Strategic Guessing

Try your hand at this difficult question. Imagine that you are a bit behind pace in the middle of the test and looking to make up time. See if you can narrow down the possibilities quickly.

What was the maximum temperature in City A on Saturday, May 14?

(1) The average (arithmetic mean) of the maximum daily temperatures in City A from Sunday, May 8, to Saturday, May 14, was 72 degrees, which was 2 degrees less than the average (arithmetic mean) of the maximum daily temperatures in City A from Monday, May 9, to Friday, May 13.

(2) The maximum temperature in City A on Saturday, May 14, was 5 degrees greater than the maximum temperature in City A on Sunday, May 8.

Step 1: Analyze the Question Stem

This is a Value question. To obtain sufficiency, you need an exact maximum temperature.

Step 2: Evaluate the Statements Using 12TEN

Statement (1) is long and complicated. Skip it and go to much shorter Statement (2).

Statement (2) tells you that the value you're looking for is 5 degrees more than the temperature on some other day. Without knowing the temperature on that other day, you don't have the information you need. This statement is insufficient. You can eliminate **(B)** and **(D)** and give yourself a one-in-three chance to get the right answer without even evaluating Statement (1).

If you aren't sure how to evaluate Statement (1) or simply don't want to take the time to do so, keep in mind that on the GMAT, complicated or hard-to-evaluate statements are more likely to be sufficient than insufficient. For this reason, you should avoid **(E)** and lean toward **(A)**, unless you have a logical reason to suspect that Statement (1) alone is insufficient. This strategy doesn't guarantee a correct answer, but if you're falling behind on time, it will help you move through the Quantitative section most efficiently. Remember, no one particular question will make or break your GMAT score, but spending too much time on a question and having to rush through several others just to get through the section will hurt your score.

For the record, let's analyze Statement (1). If the average maximum temperature from May 8 to May 14 was 72 degrees, then the sum of the maximum temperatures of those days is $7 \times 72 = 504$ degrees. If the average maximum temperature from May 9 to May 13 was $72 + 2$, or 74 degrees, then the sum of the maximum temperatures of those days was $5 \times 74 = 370$ degrees.

The difference between those two sums is the total of the maximum temperature on May 8, which you can call x, and the maximum temperature on May 14, which you can call y (since these two days were left out of the second time period). So $x + y = 504 - 370 = 134$. Statement (1) by itself is insufficient. But Statement (2) tells you that $y - x = 5$. Taking the statements together, you have the two distinct linear equations $x + y = 134$ and $y - x = 5$. This system of two equations with two variables could be solved for a single value for y, so the statements taken together are sufficient: choice (**C**).

This example demonstrates how guessing can be a good alternative for certain Data Sufficiency questions. By looking at only one statement, you can quickly narrow down the possibilities to two or three choices. Then don't be afraid to guess if necessary to stay on pace. Just be sure you know the rules for eliminating answer choices absolutely cold by Test Day.

The Four Core Competencies and Data Sufficiency

Although Data Sufficiency questions are different from the math questions you saw in school—the answers are English sentences, not math!—they test the same four Core Competencies as the rest of the GMAT.

Critical Thinking

For all Data Sufficiency questions, Critical Thinking is crucial. When you see a Data Sufficiency question, you'll need to be mentally flexible and "switch gears." The focus isn't on solving the problem. Instead, it's all about first figuring out what information you'd need to solve and then whether you've been given that information.

This is similar to many situations in the business world. You'll be facing a high-stakes decision, and if you don't figure out what information you need to make the decision, you could vacillate forever, collecting more and more data but never feeling like you know enough to choose a course of action. Or you might make the mistake of thinking you *do* have enough information to make a sound decision, when in fact you don't.

Critical Thinking on Data Sufficiency starts with step 1 of the Method. Consider what the question is asking for, either a value or a definite yes or no. Study what information the question stem provides and, crucially, does not provide, and think comprehensively about how a statement could give you enough information to answer the question.

Then in step 2, evaluate the statements by performing as few calculations as possible. Be open to picking numbers if doing so will make the problem more concrete and therefore easier. Stop your evaluation of a statement once you know that you *could* answer the question. Data Sufficiency questions are much more like logic puzzles than like math questions.

Paraphrasing

Some question stems in Data Sufficiency may be in the form of a word problem. If so, then apply your paraphrasing skills to translate into math or otherwise simplify so you can clearly identify the missing information. Both the question stem and the statements may require you to simplify or rearrange math. You may want to isolate a variable to see what's needed on the other side of the equation to solve for it, or you might want to make a statement look more like an expression in the question stem so you can more easily determine whether it provides the missing piece.

Pattern Recognition

The Data Sufficiency question is a pattern itself. The statements are new pieces of data and are always true, so don't waste time trying to verify a statement. The fact that the statements are always true has an important corollary that will help you catch errors: the statements will never contradict each other.

Also, the same math patterns show up in Data Sufficiency as in Problem Solving, and key words will often tell you what math concepts are being tested. In some cases, recognizing a pattern—such as a classic quadratic, an isosceles right triangle, or a sequence of evenly spaced integers—can be enough to see that you could—or couldn't—use certain information to answer the question.

Attention to the Right Detail

Attention to the Right Detail is also key to your success on Data Sufficiency. Just as with Problem Solving, be certain that you are considering exactly the right question. Also, don't fail to consider the details that *aren't* mentioned or the restrictions that *don't* exist. Never assume anything in a Data Sufficiency question.

Just as in Problem Solving, many details can be vitally important, such as whether the question asks about *factors* or *multiples*, whether it says $n > x$ or $n < x$, or whether it restricts the range of the value of a variable. Overlooking a detail in the question stem or a statement can make you think you don't have enough information for sufficiency when in fact you do, or vice versa.

Answers and Explanations

Practice Set: The Kaplan Method for Data Sufficiency

1. (C)

This Value question asks how many employees of a particular company are surveyors but provides no other information.

Statement (1) says that $\frac{5}{8}$ of the employees are not surveyors (which means that $\frac{3}{8}$ of the employees *are* surveyors), but there is no way to calculate the number of surveyors without knowing the whole to which those fractions apply. Eliminate (A) and (D).

Statement (2) enables you to find the total number of employees (if 18 of them are 25% of the total, then the total is 4 times as much) but not how many of those employees are surveyors. Statement (2) by itself is insufficient, so eliminate (B).

Combining Statements (1) and (2), you could calculate the total number of employees from Statement (2), and you know what fraction of those employees are surveyors from Statement (1). Therefore, you could determine the number of employees who are surveyors from both statements. (C) is correct.

2. (C)

This Value question asks for the value of a given that a is an integer and that $a^5 \geq -32$. Since $2^5 = 32$, the value of $(-2)^5$ is -32. Thus, the question is saying that $a \geq -2$.

Statement (1) simplifies to $6a \leq -6$ when 18 is subtracted from both sides of the inequality. Divide both sides by 6 to get $a \leq -1$. Since from the question stem you know that $a \geq -2$ and a is an integer, a could be either -1 or -2. Eliminate (A) and (D).

Statement (2), $a^2 > 2$, means that $a > 1$ or $a < -1$. So, a could be any positive integer greater than 1 or it could be -2. Eliminate (B).

Combining Statements (1) and (2), you know from Statement (1) that $a \leq -1$ and from Statement (2) that either $a = -2$ or $a > 1$. The only integer value that works in both statements is -2, so this must be the value of a. (C) is correct.

3. (A)

This Value question asks for the value of b, given that $3b - |a| = 27$. To arrive at the value of b, it is necessary to know the magnitude of the value for a, but not the sign, because the absolute value of a will always be positive.

Statement (1) means that a must be equal to either 9 or -9, but either way, $|a| = 9$. Since Statement (1) is sufficient, eliminate (B), (C), and (E).

Statement (2) indicates that a must be positive, since the cube of a positive number is always positive, but suggests nothing about the magnitude of a; Statement (2) is thus insufficient. Eliminate (D). Because only Statement (1) is sufficient, (A) is correct.

4. (D)

This Value question provides the equation for a sequence of positive integers and the values of the second and third terms, and it asks for the value of the fifth term, a_5. Applying the equation, you can determine that $a_5 = (k^{a_3})(a_4) = (k^{36})(a_4)$ and that $a_4 = (k^{a_2})(a_3) = (k^4)(36)$. Combining these equations gives you $a_5 = (k^{36})((k^4)(36)) = (k^{40})(36)$. Thus, you just need the value of k to calculate a_5. In addition, you can determine the following about k by plugging in the given values:

$$a_3 = (k^{a_1})(a_2)$$
$$36 = (k^{a_1})(4)$$
$$9 = k^{a_1}$$

This means that if you know the value of a_1, you could solve for k.

Statement (1) provides the value of a_1, exactly what you needed to solve for k and ultimately a_5. Since this is a Data Sufficiency question, knowing that you *could* determine the value of a_5 is sufficient; you don't need to do the calculation. Eliminate (B), (C), and (E).

Statement (2) tells you the value of k, which also allows calculation of a_5. This statement is also sufficient. Thus, (D) is correct.

5. (D)

This Value question states that a ferry travels at a rate of 15 kilometers per hour for the first leg of a trip and that it takes 3 hours for the ferry to make the return trip. Both legs are the same distance. For sufficiency, you need to be able to determine how many hours the first leg of the trip takes. This question involves one of the common math formulas you should memorize for Test Day: Distance = Rate × Time.

Make a table to organize the information you know from the question stem so that you can identify what you need to know:

	DISTANCE	RATE (KPH)	TIME (HR)
First leg	d	15	t
Second leg	d	r	3

The question asks for the time (t) of the first leg of the trip. Using the distance formula, you can set up the equation $d = 15t$. Knowing the value of d will be sufficient to calculate t. Notice that knowing the value of r enables you to calculate d.

Statement (1) gives the average speed for the entire trip, allowing you to write a second equation involving d and t. Although you wouldn't do the math on Test Day, here's how it works.

	DISTANCE	RATE (KPH)	TIME (HR)
First Leg	d	15	t
Second Leg	d	r	3
Total journey	$2d$	12	$t + 3$

Since Total distance = Average speed × Total time, $2d = 12 \times (t + 3) = 12t + 36$. From the first leg of the trip, you know that $d = 15t$. So, for the total journey, $2(15t) = 12(t + 3)$ and this could be solved for t. Eliminate **(B)**, **(C)**, and **(E)**.

Statement (2) gives a value for d, which is exactly what you need to solve directly for t. Since both statements are sufficient individually, **(D)** is correct.

Practice Set: Value Questions

6. (A)

This Value question asks for the difference between $4n$ and $5m$. To arrive at this value, it's necessary to know either the values of the terms separately or that $4n$ and $5m$ are equal, since when a quantity is subtracted from an equal quantity, the result will always be 0.

Cross multiplying Statement (1) yields $4n = 5m$, which is sufficient to answer the question with a value of 0. Eliminate **(B)**, **(C)**, and **(E)**.

Statement (2) simplifies to $5n = 4m$, which does not yield the value of either $4n$ or $5m$ and does not establish that $4n = 5m$. Statement (2) is insufficient. Eliminate **(D)**. Since only Statement (1) is sufficient, **(A)** is correct.

7. (C)

This Value question asks for the value of $\frac{st}{u}$ without giving further information. Therefore, either three distinct equations involving these variables or specific values for each of the variables will be sufficient.

Statement (1) provides two distinct equations, which is not enough. Don't take the time to do so on Test Day, but if you did the math, you would find these equations allow you substitute for s and u to put the expression into terms of t:

$$\frac{st}{u} = \frac{\left(\frac{3t}{4}\right)t}{2t} = \frac{\frac{3t^2}{4}}{2t} = \frac{3t^2}{4} \times \frac{1}{2t} = \frac{3t^2}{8t} = \frac{3}{8}t$$

Without a specific value for t, there is no way to determine the value of $\frac{st}{u}$. Statement (1) is insufficient, so eliminate **(A)** and **(D)**.

Statement (2) also provides only two equations, not three, and so is also insufficient. Again, don't take the time to do the math, but if you're interested . . . If you substitute $u - 10$ for s in the second equation, you will find that $t = 8$. You could then substitute 8 for t and $u - 10$ for s in the expression $\frac{st}{u}$, but that results in an expression in terms of u, and without the value of u, you still don't have the answer to the question. Eliminate **(B)**.

Combining the statements provides four distinct equations, which is sufficient to solve for the three variables. (**C**) is correct. Mathematically, from Statement (1) you know that $\frac{st}{u} = \frac{3}{8}t$. If you substitute the value of 8 for the variable t from Statement (2), you find that $\frac{st}{u} = 3$.

8. (E)

This Value question asks for the units digit (the ones digit) of z^3 when z is an integer. Knowing the units digit of z itself will be sufficient, since the units digits of the cubes of integers follow predictable patterns based on the units digit of the original integer. As a thought experiment to better understand the question stem, you could pick a few small integers and cube them to see what happens to the units digit.

Statement (1) means that z has a units digit of either 0 or 5, which means its cube will also have a units digit of 0 or 5, so it's not possible to establish a single value. Eliminate (**A**) and (**D**).

Statement (2) can be rephrased as "z is a perfect square." However, this could mean z is 1, or 9, or 36, or any other perfect square, so it's not sufficient to determine a single value of the units digit of z^3. Eliminate (**B**).

Combining the statements indicates that z is both a multiple of 5 and a perfect square. The smallest value of z that fits is 25, and the next smallest is 100. Since the units digits of these are different, their cubes will also have different units digits, so combining the statements is still not sufficient. (**E**) is correct.

9. (E)

This Value question asks for the value of the larger of two distinct prime factors, given that d is the product of those two prime factors and no other factors except 1 and d. To arrive at an answer, it's necessary to know the either value of d, which would allow for the determination of its prime factors, or just the value of the larger of the two prime factors that produce d.

Statement (1) indicates that d has a value between 100 and 120, inclusive. Because this range includes more than one number that is the product of exactly two distinct prime factors (such as $106 = 2 \times 53$, $115 = 5 \times 23$, and $119 = 7 \times 17$), this statement is not sufficient. Eliminate (**A**) and (**D**).

Statement (2) tells you only that d is even. You know from the question stem that d is the product of two prime factors, so if d is even, the smaller of those two prime factors must be 2 (because all other prime numbers are odd and the product of any two odd numbers is odd, whereas the product of an even times an odd will always be even). However, there's no way to establish an exact value for d or of the larger of the two prime factors. Eliminate (**B**).

Now combine the statements: d has a value from 100 to 120, and it's even. Knowing that one of the prime factors of d is 2, you can determine that the other prime factor must equal $\frac{d}{2}$, so you can divide Statement (1) by 2 to try to solve for this factor: $50 \le \frac{d}{2} \le 60$. There are two prime numbers between 50 and 60: 53 and 59. (You can eliminate non-primes by using divisibility rules; for example, all even numbers in this range are not prime, as are all numbers whose digits sum to a multiple of 3 since they are divisible by 3, and so forth.) Either 53 or 59 might be the larger prime factor of d, so the two statements together are insufficient. Therefore, (**E**) is correct.

Practice Set: Yes/No Questions

10. (A)

This Yes/No question asks whether $\frac{z}{12} - 9$ is an integer. Because 9 is an integer, this question can be simplified to "Is $\frac{z}{12}$ an integer?" This can be further simplified to "Is z a multiple of 12?" A statement will be sufficient if it provides enough information to answer this question unequivocally either yes or no.

Statement (1) presents a fraction that can be split into $\frac{z}{12} + \frac{24}{12}$, which is $\frac{z}{12} + 2$. Since this sum is an integer and 2 is an integer, $\frac{z}{12}$ must also be an integer. This answers the question with a definite yes, so Statement (1) is sufficient. Eliminate (**B**), (**C**), and (**E**).

Statement (2) says that z is a multiple of 6. Picking numbers can help determine whether this is sufficient. If $z = 6$, then $\frac{z}{12}$ is not an integer, but if $z = 12$, then $\frac{z}{12}$ is an integer. Since the question can be answered either yes or no, this statement is not sufficient. (**A**) is correct.

11. (B)

This is a Yes/No question that asks whether the product pz is odd, given that p and z are both positive integers. For pz to be odd, making the answer to the question yes, both p and z must be odd. If either p or z is even, then the answer to the question is no. If a statement establishes either of these cases, then it is sufficient.

Statement (1) says that the sum $(p + z)$ is even. If two integers sum to an even number, the two integers can be either both even or both odd. Since you don't know which is the case, different answers to the question about pz are possible. Statement (1) is insufficient; eliminate (A) and (D).

Statement (2) says that z^p is even. Since raising an odd number to any power results in an odd number, z must be even. Statement (2) provides sufficient information to answer the question (always no), so (B) is correct.

12. (E)

This is a Yes/No question that asks whether $\frac{a}{b}$ is between 0 and 1. Note that for the inequality to be true and the answer to the question to be yes, both a and b must have the same sign and the absolute value of a must be less than that of b. If it's established that either or both of these conditions are not met, then the answer to the question is no.

Statement (1) tells you that ab is greater than 1. That means either that a and b are both positive or that they are both negative. Pick some numbers to test out the possibilities. If $a = -3$ and $b = -2$, then $\frac{a}{b} = \frac{-3}{-2} = \frac{3}{2}$, which is greater than 1, so the answer is no. But, if $a = 2$ and $b = 3$, then $\frac{a}{b} = \frac{2}{3}$, which is between 0 and 1, so the answer is yes. Statement (1) is insufficient. Eliminate (A) and (D).

Statement (2) tells you that $a - b$ is less than 1. You can test this statement using the same pairs of numbers as you did for Statement (1) because both $(-3) - (-2)$ and $2 - 3$ are less than 1. Therefore, Statement (2) is insufficient also. Eliminate (B).

Because each of the statements is insufficient on its own, combine the statements. Since the same cases applied to both statements, combining the statements adds no new information to the analysis, and the combined statements are therefore insufficient. (E) must be correct.

13. (C)

This Yes/No question asks whether there is enough information to determine whether $x^3 y$ is greater than 56. First simplify the question stem. The integer y is at least 7, so $x^3 y > 56$ is effectively the same as $7x^3 > 56$. Note that any value of y greater than 7 would magnify the value of $7x^3$, making it either a greater positive value (if x^3 is positive) or a smaller negative value (if x^3 is negative). This wouldn't change the relationship between $7x^3$ and 56, so you only need to consider the minimum value of $y = 7$. Divide both sides by 7 to get $x^3 > 8$. Take the cube root of both sides to get the final simplification of the question: Is there sufficient information to determine whether $x > 2$?

Statement (1) can be simplified by taking the square root of all parts of the inequality, considering both positive and negative roots. Taking positive square roots results in $2 < x \leq 3$. This gives a yes answer to the question of whether $x > 2$. Taking negative square roots results in $-3 \leq x < -2$, giving a no answer. Since Statement (1) gives both a yes and a no answer, it is insufficient. Eliminate (A) and (D).

Statement (2) can be simplified by subtracting x^3 from both sides to get $x > 0$. In other words, x is positive. This allows for values of x greater than 2 and values of x less than 2. Since Statement (2) gives both yes and no answers to the question of whether $x > 2$, it is insufficient. Eliminate (B).

Since each statement was insufficient individually, consider the two statements together. Statement (2) limits x to positive numbers. That means the only valid range from Statement (1) is $2 < x \leq 3$. Thus, $x > 2$, which is sufficient to answer the question with a definite yes. (C) is correct.

Practice Set: Picking Numbers in Data Sufficiency

14. (B)

This Yes/No question stem says that a three-digit positive number's hundreds digit A is twice the number's units digit C, and it asks whether the tens digit, B, is greater than A. To answer the question about whether the tens digit is greater than the hundreds digit, a statement would need to allow you to establish a consistent numeric relationship between A and B.

If you're not used to thinking about the relationships between digits of numbers, it might help to visualize the possibilities before proceeding. Pick permissible numbers for C, the units digit, to find out the resulting hundreds digit, A. Three-digit numbers in which the hundreds digit is twice the units digit are 2_1, 4_2, 6_3, 8_4, where the blank tens place represents any digit. Note that the range of the units digit is 1 to 4. A units digit of 0 would generate a hundreds digit of $2(0) = 0$, resulting in a two-digit, not a three-digit number. A units digit of 5 would result in a hundreds value of $2(5) = 10$, which is not a digit. The resulting range of the hundreds digit is 2 to 8.

Statement (1) says that C is less than 2. This means that C is equal to 1 and therefore A is equal to $(2)(1) = 2$. The middle digit B, by contrast, can be any digit between 0 and 9 inclusive, so this statement is insufficient. Eliminate (A) and (D).

Statement (2) says that $B = 9$. As determined by the analysis of the question stem, A can be no greater than 8. If you didn't pick numbers up front, do so now, trying to pick a number for C that generates an A-value greater than 9. Since there is no way that A can be greater than B, the answer to the question is always yes. Statement (2) is sufficient, so (B) is correct.

15. (C)

This is a Yes/No question, so you don't need to know the exact value of the number of distinct (different) prime factors of a, just whether there are 4 or more. Every non-prime number can be rewritten as a series of prime numbers multiplied together; those are the number's prime factors.

Statement (1): Pick the simplest number that's divisible by 36, namely 36 itself. That number is 6×6, which means that the prime factors are $2 \times 3 \times 2 \times 3$. Although there are 4 prime factors of 36, there are only 2 distinct prime factors. So if the number is exactly 36, the answer is no. However, the statement only says that a is divisible by 36, so a could be something like $36 \times 5 \times 7 = 1,260$, in which case it *would* have 4 distinct prime factors and the answer would be yes. Statement (1) is insufficient, so eliminate (A) and (D).

Statement (2): Now pick the simplest number that's divisible by 35, which is 35. The prime factors of 35 are 5×7. So if $a = 35$, the answer is no. However, similar to Statement (1), a could be $35 \times 2 \times 3 = 210$, in which case there would be 4 distinct prime factors. So Statement (2) is also insufficient. Eliminate (B) and evaluate the statements together.

If a is divisible by both 36 and 35, it would have to be the product of at least all the prime factors of both numbers. Since 36 has the distinct prime factors 2 and 3, and 35 has the distinct prime factors 5 and 7, any number a that is divisible by both 36 and 35 must have *at least* the 4 distinct prime factors 2, 3, 5, and 7. So considering the statements together, the answer is definitely yes. (C) is correct.

16. (B)

In this Yes/No question, sufficiency means proving that $|15 - m| + |m - 15|$ is either definitely greater than 15 or definitely less than or equal to 15. As the question stem is dealing with a range, picking numbers will help in evaluating the statements.

Statement (1) restricts m to values greater than 6. When picking numbers to evaluate statements, remember to always pick at least two sets of numbers to see if you can get more than one possible answer to the question. Start with a number near the start of the range. First try $m = 7$.

$$|15 - m| + |m - 15| = |15 - 7| + |7 - 15|$$
$$= |8| + |-8|$$
$$= 8 + 8$$
$$= 16$$

Since 16 is greater than 15, $m = 7$ results in a yes answer to the question. A logical next choice could be $m = 15$ since that is the constant within the absolute values.

$$|15 - m| + |m - 15| = |15 - 15| + |15 - 15|$$
$$= |0| + |0|$$
$$= 0 + 0$$
$$= 0$$

Since 0 is less than 15, $m = 15$ results in a no. As $m > 6$ sometimes means yes and sometimes means no, this statement is insufficient. Eliminate (A) and (D).

Statement (2) restricts m to values less than 7. You'll need to pick at least two values once again, so start with $m = 6$.

$$|15 - m| + |m - 15| = |15 - 6| + |6 - 15|$$
$$= |9| + |-9|$$
$$= 9 + 9$$
$$= 18$$

Because 18 is greater than 15, that's a yes. Try $m = 0$.

$$|15 - m| + |m - 15| = |15 - 0| + |0 - 15|$$
$$= |15| + |-15|$$
$$= 15 + 15$$
$$= 30$$

Not only is that a yes, but it also shows that, for this particular situation, as m gets smaller, $|15 - m| + |m - 15|$ gets greater. (If you picked a third, negative number for m, you would see this pattern continue.) This statement will always return an answer of yes to the question. Eliminate (C) and (E). Statement (2) alone is sufficient, so (B) is correct.

Practice Set: Combining Statements

17. (C)

This is a Yes/No question that asks whether y^2 is less than 1. If y is 1 or -1, then y^2 is also 1, and the answer is no. If y is greater than 1 or less than -1, then y^2 is greater than 1, in which case the answer is also no. If, however, y is a fraction between -1 and 1, then y^2 will be a fraction between 0 and 1, in which case the answer would be yes. So, the statements will be sufficient to answer with a definite no if they establish definitively

that $y \geq 1$ or $y \leq -1$, or they will be sufficient to answer with a definite yes if they establish that $-1 < y < 1$.

Statement (1) establishes that y is greater than -1; that means y could be a fraction between -1 and 1, leading to an answer of yes, or y could be 1 or greater, leading to an answer of no. This is insufficient, so eliminate (A) and (D).

Similarly, Statement (2) allows for y to be a fraction between -1 and 1 but also for it to be -1 or lower, also leading to possible answers of yes or no. Eliminate (B).

Together, the statements tell you that y is both greater than -1 and less than 1, which means that $y^2 < 1$ and the answer is yes. The statements together are sufficient, so (C) is correct.

18. (A)

This is a Value question that asks for the revenue of a taqueria that sold 300 burritos and 300 tacos. If b is the price of a burrito and t is the price of a taco, then the revenue is represented by $300b + 300t$, which simplifies to $300(b + t)$. So, the statements will be sufficient to find a value for revenue if they establish the values of b and t, but they will also be sufficient if they establish the value of $b + t$, even if you don't know the individual values.

Statement (1) tells you the average price of the two menu items. Since Average $= \dfrac{\text{Sum of values}}{\text{Number of values}}$, this means that $\dfrac{b + t}{2} = 4.50$, and that simplifies to $b + t = 9$. You could plug that into $300(b + t)$ to find the revenue, so this statement is sufficient. Eliminate (B), (C), and (E).

Statement (2) simply tells you the relationship between the prices. A burrito could be \$4 and a taco \$2, or the prices could be \$10 and \$5. Different possibilities for prices mean different possible values for revenue, so this statement is insufficient. Eliminate (D). Because Statement (1) alone is sufficient, (A) is correct.

19. (C)

For this Value question, to have sufficiency, you must have enough information to find one and only one value for $a - b$. Note that this does not necessarily mean knowing the values of a and b individually. Both variables are positive.

Statement (1) provides a classic quadratic form, $a^2 + 2ab + b^2 = 36$, which can be factored into the binomial form $(a + b)(a + b) = 36$. Thus, $(a + b)^2 = 36$ and, since a and b are positive, $a + b = 6$. While this establishes a value for $a + b$, there's no way to find $a - b$; it could be that $a = 5$ and $b = 1$, or that $a = 2$ and $b = 4$, or any other combination of positive values that sums to 6, and each would yield a different value for $a - b$. Therefore, this statement is insufficient. Eliminate **(A)** and **(D)**.

Statement (2) provides another classic quadratic, which can be translated into the factored form $(a + b)(a - b) = 12$. This again is not enough either to determine exact values for a and b individually or to find the value of $a - b$. Therefore, this statement is insufficient. Eliminate **(B)**.

Combining the statements tells you that $a + b = 6$ and $(a + b)(a - b) = 12$. Plug in $a + b = 6$ to get $6(a - b) = 12$. This is sufficient to get the value of $a - b$. **(C)** is correct.

CHAPTER 7

MATH CONTENT REVIEW: ARITHMETIC AND NUMBER PROPERTIES

LEARNING OBJECTIVES

- Describe which arithmetic and number properties topics are tested on the GMAT
- Apply the Kaplan Methods for Problem Solving and Data Sufficiency to questions testing a variety of arithmetic and number properties concepts

---

Below is an example Problem Solving question with an arithmetic focus. As you try the question, think about what information it gives you, what the question is asking you to do with that information, and what you do and don't already know about how to solve. The explanation that follows demonstrates how a GMAT expert uses the Kaplan Method for Problem Solving and certain arithmetic operations skills to answer this question efficiently.

If x is a number such that $-2 \leq x \leq 2$, which of the following has the largest possible absolute value?

- ○ $3x - 1$
- ○ $x^2 - x$
- ○ $3 - x$
- ○ $x - 3$
- ○ $x^2 + 1$

Step 1: Analyze the Question

This is an abstract question for which the answer choices contain variables, so picking numbers will be an efficient strategy to use. Since you are asked to find the answer choice that yields the largest absolute value, you should pick numbers at the ends of the range of possible values for x. For each value of x you test, you will need to check all the answer choices in case some have the same value.

Step 2: State the Task

Evaluate each choice, using both $x = 2$ or $x = -2$ (the values for x with the greatest possible absolute value), in order to determine which choice will produce the largest absolute value.

Step 3: Approach Strategically

You'll need to plug in those values of x, but first notice choices (**C**) and (**D**): $3 - x$ and $x - 3$ are negatives of each other, which means they have the same absolute value. Therefore, neither can have a greater absolute value than the other, and you can eliminate both of these choices. Notice also that with (**E**), the absolute value will be the same if using 2 or -2, since squaring the x-term will give the same positive value.

Plug in -2 first for x in each of the remaining answer choices. Choice (**A**) gives $3(-2) - 1$, which equals -7. The absolute value of -7 is equal to 7. Choice (**B**) gives $(-2)^2 - (-2) = 4 - (-2) = 6$, which has an absolute value of 6. Choice (**E**) gives $(-2)^2 + 1 = 4 + 1 = 5$, which has an absolute value of 5. You already know that choice (**E**) will yield the same absolute value when $x = 2$, so eliminate (**E**); you already found that (**A**) and (**B**) give a larger possible absolute value.

Now try $x = 2$ with the remaining two answer choices. In choice (**A**), $3(2) - 1 = 6 - 1 = 5$, and the absolute value of 5 is equal to 5. For choice (**B**), $(2)^2 - 2 = 4 - 2 = 2$, and the absolute value of 2 is equal to 2. The largest absolute value you found was for choice (**A**), when $x = -2$. Therefore, (**A**) is correct.

Step 4: Confirm Your Answer

Confirm that your calculations are correct and that you took into account the range of possible values for x.

Arithmetic involves performing operations on numbers, and most of the Quantitative questions you will see on the GMAT involve at least a little arithmetic to solve. The test makers often increase the difficulty of questions by combining various topics, such as absolute value, inequalities, exponents, and fractions, and by asking you to use these skills to solve questions that involve algebra, geometry, or proportions. You will be in a much stronger position on Test Day if you have these operations down cold, freeing up your brain to focus on the more complex critical thinking tasks the high-difficulty questions require.

Number properties are about categories and rules: certain kinds of numbers behave the same ways in all cases. The GMAT test makers love to incorporate number properties in Quantitative questions because they reward your critical thinking ability when you can apply the general rule set, or pattern of behavior, to the specific numbers in the problem. That's why number properties questions constitute approximately 20 percent of GMAT Problem Solving questions and nearly 30 percent of Data Sufficiency questions.

The following sections break down every arithmetic and number properties skill you need to ace the GMAT.

Arithmetic Operations

> **LEARNING OBJECTIVE**
> - Apply the order of operations when solving problems

Always follow the same order when performing arithmetic operations. One mnemonic that can help you remember the order is "Please Excuse My Dear Aunt Sally" (PEMDAS), outlined below, but you may have learned a different one. If an expression has parentheses within parentheses, work from the innermost out.

Example: $30 - 5 \times 4 + (7 - 3)^2 \div 8$

First, perform any operations within **parentheses**.	$30 - 5 \times 4 + 4^2 \div 8$
Next, do the **exponents**.	$30 - 5 \times 4 + 16 \div 8$
Then, do all **multiplication** and **division** in order from left to right.	$30 - \mathbf{20} + \mathbf{2}$
Last, do all **addition** and **subtraction** in order from left to right.	$\mathbf{10} + \mathbf{2}$
Answer:	12

The properties below will not be tested directly on the GMAT (you won't need to define them). Focus rather on understanding how to manipulate numbers using the various properties.

The **commutative property** means that it doesn't matter in what order addition or multiplication is performed. However, division and subtraction are *not* commutative.

Examples: $5 + 8 = 8 + 5$

$2 \times 6 = 6 \times 2$

$3 - 2 \neq 2 - 3$

$6 \div 2 \neq 2 \div 6$

The **associative property** means that addition and multiplication terms can be regrouped without changing the result, but division and subtraction terms *cannot* be regrouped.

Examples: $(a + b) + c = a + (b + c)$ $(a \times b) \times c = a \times (b \times c)$

$(3 + 5) + 8 = 3 + (5 + 8)$ $(4 \times 5) \times 6 = 4 \times (5 \times 6)$

$8 + 8 = 3 + 13$ $20 \times 6 = 4 \times 30$

$16 = 16$ $120 = 120$

The **distributive property** allows you to "distribute" a factor among the terms being added or subtracted; $a(b + c) = ab + ac$.

Example: $4(3 + 7) = 4 \times 3 + 4 \times 7$

$4 \times 10 = 12 + 28$

$40 = 40$

Division can be distributed in a similar way when the sum or difference is in the numerator.

Example: $\dfrac{4 + 6}{2} = \dfrac{4}{2} + \dfrac{6}{2}$

$\dfrac{10}{2} = 2 + 3$

$5 = 5$

However, when the sum or difference is in the denominator, no distribution is possible.

Example: $\dfrac{9}{4+5}$ is *not* equal to $\dfrac{9}{4} + \dfrac{9}{5}$.

The technique of **factoring** uses the distributive property in its reverse form. You can use this property to make mental arithmetic much easier. For instance, you can make multiplication simpler:

Example: $12 \times 19 = 12 \times (20 - 1) = 12 \times 20 - 12 \times 1 = 240 - 12 = 228$

You can also use factoring to make addition or subtraction easier:

Example: $9 + 18 + 27 + 36 = 1(9) + 2(9) + 3(9) + 4(9) = (1 + 2 + 3 + 4)(9) = 10(9) = 90$

You might encounter a question on the GMAT for which unusual symbols are used to represent numbers. If it's specified that the symbols represent digits, they must equal 0, 1, 2, 3, 4, 5, 6, 7, 8, or 9. This use of symbols rather than numbers has no effect on any of the arithmetic operations or properties.

Example: In the equation ♥ × ♪ = ♣, each of the symbols ♥, ♪, and ♣ represents a positive digit. If ♪ is not 0 or 1, and ♥ ÷ ♪ = 2, what is the value of ♣?

The least allowable value for ♪ is 2, which is a very manageable number. So substituting that value, ♥ ÷ ♪ = 2 becomes ♥ ÷ 2 = 2, and ♥ = 4. Substitute these values into ♥ × ♪ = ♣, to get 4 × 2 = ♣ = 8. You can verify that this is the only valid value for ♣ by increasing ♪ to 3, in which case ♥ × ♪ = 6 × 3 = 18. Since 18 is not a single digit, this is not correct.

Arithmetic Operations Drill

Answers follow the drill.

1. $\dfrac{3 + 4(1 + 5)}{9} =$

2. $5 - 3 + 7(3 + 1) - 13(7 - (3 + 2)) =$

3. $\dfrac{6 - 7}{2} \times (3 + 5) + 3\left(\dfrac{18}{3^2}\right) - \dfrac{4^2}{2} - 3 \times (-3) =$

4. $8 + 3 \times \dfrac{-4 + 3 \times 4}{7 + 2 \times 3 + 11} + (-3)(5 - (-1)) =$

5. $77 \times 11 =$

Arithmetic Operations Drill: Answers

1. 3

2. 4

3. 3

4. −9

5. 847

CONCEPT CHECK

- List the order in which arithmetic operations are performed:

  _____

- You can reverse the order of the numbers when _____ or _____, but you cannot reverse their order when _____ or _____.
- You can regroup terms when _____ or _____ without affecting the result, but you cannot regroup terms when _____ or _____.

Example answers are in your book's online resources (**kaptest.com/login**).

Fractions and Decimals

LEARNING OBJECTIVES

- Perform operations on fractions
- Convert between fractions and decimals

A **fraction** describes the number of parts of a whole. For instance, in the fraction $\frac{3}{4}$, the number on top (the **numerator**) describes how many parts there are (3). The number on the bottom (the **denominator**) tells you into how many equal parts the whole is divided (4). The fraction $\frac{3}{4}$ is the same as 3 divided by 4.

When you multiply both the numerator and denominator by the same nonzero number, the value of the fraction is unchanged.

Example: $\quad \frac{1}{2} = \frac{1 \times 2}{2 \times 2} = \frac{2}{4}$

Similarly, dividing both the top and bottom by the same nonzero number leaves the value of the fraction unchanged.

Example: $\quad \frac{5}{10} = \frac{5 \div 5}{10 \div 5} = \frac{1}{2}$

Fractions in the answer choices on the GMAT are given in **lowest terms**. That means that the numerator and the denominator are not divisible by any common integer greater than 1. Restating a fraction in lowest terms is called **reducing** the fraction.

Example: Reduce $\frac{15}{35}$ to its lowest terms.

Both 15 and 35 are divisible by 5, so $\frac{15}{35} = \frac{15 \div 5}{35 \div 5} = \frac{3}{7}$. Alternatively, you can factor the numerator and denominator and reduce by canceling common factors:

$$\frac{15}{35} = \frac{3 \times 5}{7 \times 5} = \frac{3 \times \cancel{5}}{7 \times \cancel{5}} = \frac{3}{7}$$

Fractions whose numerators are greater than their denominators may be converted into **mixed numbers**, and vice versa. Mixed numbers consist of an integer and a fraction.

Example: Convert $\frac{23}{4}$ to a mixed number.

$$\frac{23}{4} = \frac{20}{4} + \frac{3}{4}$$
$$= 5\frac{3}{4}$$

Example: Convert $2\frac{3}{7}$ to a fraction.

$$2\frac{3}{7} = 2 + \frac{3}{7}$$
$$= \frac{14}{7} + \frac{3}{7}$$
$$= \frac{17}{7}$$

Performing Operations on Fractions

For two fractions to be added or subtracted, they must have the same denominator. A **common denominator** is a multiple of each of the denominators of the fractions.

Example: $\frac{3}{5} + \frac{2}{3} - \frac{1}{2}$

The denominators are 5, 3, 2, so a common denominator is $5 \times 3 \times 2 = 30$.

Multiply each fraction by 1 in the form of $\frac{30}{30}$ and cancel:

$$\left(\frac{\cancel{30}^6}{30}\right)\frac{3}{\cancel{5}^1} + \left(\frac{\cancel{30}^{10}}{30}\right)\frac{2}{\cancel{3}^1} - \left(\frac{\cancel{30}^{15}}{30}\right)\frac{1}{\cancel{2}^1}$$

$$\frac{6 \times 3}{30} + \frac{10 \times 2}{30} - \frac{15 \times 1}{30} = \frac{18 + 20 - 15}{30} = \frac{23}{30}$$

The **least (lowest) common denominator (LCD)** is the **least common multiple (LCM)** of the denominators; that means it is the smallest positive number that is a multiple of all the terms. For example, given $\frac{3}{10} + \frac{2}{3} - \frac{1}{2}$, a common denominator is $10 \times 3 \times 2 = 60$. However, the LCD is 30 because it is the smallest number that is evenly divisible by 10, 3, and 2. One way to determine the LCD is to use successively greater multiples of the greatest value. In this case, 10 is not a multiple of 3 and 2, nor is 20. But the next multiple of 10, which is 30, is a multiple of 2 and 3. It is not necessary to use the LCD when combining fractions—any common denominator will work—but the LCD is the smallest and thus often easiest number to use.

To multiply fractions, multiply the numerators together and the denominators together.

Example: $\frac{3}{4} \times \frac{8}{15} = \frac{24}{60} = \frac{2}{5}$

It's often efficient to **cancel** common factors before multiplying, because you can then multiply smaller numbers and you don't have to reduce a large fraction at the end. Here, divide 3 in one numerator and 15 in one denominator by their common factor of 3. Then divide 8 in one numerator and 4 in one denominator by their common factor 4.

$$\frac{{}^1\cancel{3}}{{}_1\cancel{4}} \times \frac{\cancel{8}^2}{\cancel{15}_5} = \frac{1 \times 2}{1 \times 5} = \frac{2}{5}$$

To divide by a fraction, flip the fraction to get its **reciprocal** and multiply by that.

Example: $4 \div \frac{2}{3} = 4 \times \frac{3}{2} = \frac{12}{2} = 6$

A **complex fraction** contains one or more fractions in its numerator or denominator. There are two methods for simplifying complex fractions.

Method I: Use the distributive property. Find the least common multiple of *all* the denominators and multiply all the terms in the top and bottom of the complex fraction by the LCM. This will eliminate all the denominators.

Example:

The LCM of all the denominators, (9, 6, 3, and 2) is 18.

$$\frac{\frac{7}{9} - \frac{1}{6}}{\frac{1}{3} + \frac{1}{2}}$$

$$= \frac{18 \times \left(\frac{7}{9} - \frac{1}{6}\right)}{18 \times \left(\frac{1}{3} + \frac{1}{2}\right)}$$

$$= \frac{\frac{^2\cancel{18}}{1} \times \frac{7}{\cancel{9}_1} - \frac{^3\cancel{18}}{1} \times \frac{1}{\cancel{6}_1}}{\frac{^6\cancel{18}}{1} \times \frac{1}{\cancel{3}_1} + \frac{^9\cancel{18}}{1} \times \frac{1}{\cancel{2}_1}}$$

$$= \frac{2 \times 7 - 3 \times 1}{6 \times 1 + 9 \times 1}$$

$$= \frac{14 - 3}{6 + 9}$$

$$= \frac{11}{15}$$

Method II: Treat the numerator and denominator separately. Combine the terms in each to get a single fraction on the top and a single fraction on the bottom. You are left with the division of two fractions, which you perform by multiplying the top fraction by the reciprocal of the bottom one. This method is preferable when the LCM for all the denominators is large or unwieldy.

Example: $\dfrac{\frac{7}{9} - \frac{1}{6}}{\frac{1}{3} + \frac{1}{2}}$ LCMs are 18 (numerator) and 6 (denominator).

$$\frac{\left(\frac{18}{18}\right)\frac{7}{9} - \left(\frac{18}{18}\right)\frac{1}{6}}{\left(\frac{6}{6}\right)\frac{1}{3} + \left(\frac{6}{6}\right)\frac{1}{2}} = \frac{\frac{14}{18} - \frac{3}{18}}{\frac{2}{6} + \frac{3}{6}} = \frac{\frac{11}{18}}{\frac{5}{6}} = \frac{11}{\cancel{18}^3} \times \frac{\cancel{6}^1}{5} = \frac{11}{15}$$

Comparing Positive Fractions

You might encounter a question that requires you to compare the value of two fractions. If the numerators of fractions are the same, the fraction with the smaller absolute value in the denominator has the greater value.

Example: $\frac{4}{5} > \frac{4}{7}$

If the denominators are the same, the fraction with the larger numerator has the greater value.

Example: $\frac{5}{8} > \frac{3}{8}$

If neither the numerators nor the denominators are the same, express all of the fractions in terms of some common denominator. Then the fraction with the largest numerator will be the largest.

Another way to compare fractions in which all numerators and denominators are either positive or negative is to multiply the numerator of the left fraction by the denominator of the right fraction, and vice versa. Write each product below the fraction whose numerator was used and then compare the products. If the product associated with the numerator of the left fraction is greater, then the left fraction is greater, and vice versa.

Example: Compare $\frac{5}{7}$ and $\frac{9}{11}$.

Compare 5×11 and 9×7.

Because $55 < 63$, $\frac{5}{7} < \frac{9}{11}$.

You can also convert fractions to decimals for straightforward comparison. This technique is especially useful when finding a common denominator seems time-consuming.

Example: Compare $\frac{3}{4}, \frac{5}{8}$, and $\frac{2}{3}$.

$\frac{3}{4} = 0.75$, $\frac{5}{8} = 0.625$, and $\frac{2}{3} = 0.\overline{6666}$

So, $\frac{5}{8} < \frac{2}{3} < \frac{3}{4}$.

Memorizing the common fraction-to-decimal equivalencies is helpful to solving many GMAT problems efficiently. A table of some common fraction-decimal-percent equivalents is provided in the next section on percents.

Another way to compare fractions is to find a "benchmark value" against which the fractions can be compared. This is especially efficient when dealing with large numbers.

Example: Compare $\frac{13}{24}$ and $\frac{33}{68}$.

Both are very close to $\frac{1}{2}$, since $\frac{1}{2} = \frac{12}{24}$ and $\frac{1}{2} = \frac{34}{68}$.

Because $\frac{13}{24} > \frac{1}{2}$ and $\frac{33}{68} < \frac{1}{2}$, $\frac{13}{24} > \frac{33}{68}$.

Decimals

Decimals can be converted to fractions with a power of 10 in the denominator equal to the number of decimal places.

Example: $0.053 = \frac{53}{10^3} = \frac{53}{1,000}$

Numbers are made up of digits in specific places. The GMAT occasionally asks questions using the terms **digit** and **place**, so you should be familiar with the naming convention. Here the place values of the number 315.246 are labeled:

hundreds	tens	units	tenths	hundredths	thousandths
3	1	5	.2	4	6

When a GMAT question specifies that a variable is a **digit**, the only possible values are the integers between 0 and 9, inclusive.

To compare decimals, add zeros after the last digit to the right of the decimal point until all the decimals have the same number of digits. Then ignore the decimal point and compare the values as though they were integers.

Example: Arrange in order from smallest to largest: 0.7, 0.77, 0.07, 0.707, and 0.077.

$$0.7 = 0.700$$
$$0.77 = 0.770$$
$$0.07 = 0.070$$
$$0.707 = 0.707$$
$$0.077 = 0.077$$

Because $70 < 77 < 700 < 707 < 770$, the correct order is $0.07 < 0.077 < 0.7 < 0.707 < 0.77$.

When adding or subtracting decimals, make sure that the decimal points and leading and trailing zeros are properly aligned.

Example:

$$0.5 + 0.05 + 0.005 \ =$$

0.5	(1 decimal place)
0.05	(2 decimal places)
+ 0.005	+ (3 decimal places)
0.555	(3 decimal places)

To multiply two decimals, initially multiply them as you would integers and ignore the decimal places. Then insert the decimal point in the product. The number of decimal places in the product is the sum of the number of decimal places in the factors that are multiplied together.

Example:

0.675	(3 decimal places)
× 0.42	+ (2 decimal places)
1350	
+ 27000	
0.28350	(5 decimal places)

Division—Method I: When dividing a decimal by another decimal, move the decimal point of each number the same number of places until the number you're dividing by is an integer. Then carry out the division as you would with integers, placing the decimal point in the result directly above the decimal point in the number you're dividing into.

Example: $0.675 \div 0.25 =$ Move the decimal point two places to the right
             $67.5 \div 25 =$ to make 0.25 an integer.

$$\begin{array}{r} 2.7 \\ 25\overline{)67.5} \\ -\underline{50} \\ 175 \\ -\underline{175} \\ 0 \end{array}$$

Division—Method II: Turn the division problem into a fraction. This approach can be efficient when the numbers have common factors. Move the decimal point in the numerator and the denominator an equal number of places to make both numbers integers. Then cancel common factors.

Example: $0.675 \div 0.25$

$$\frac{0.675}{0.25} = \frac{675}{250}$$

$$\frac{675}{250} \div \frac{25}{25} = \frac{27}{10} = 2.7$$

Now use the drill to get some practice working with fractions and decimals.

Fractions and Decimals Drill

Answers follow the drill.

1. Reduce $\frac{63}{81}$ to its lowest terms.

2. Convert $\frac{46}{5}$ to a mixed number.

3. $\frac{1}{5} - \frac{1}{3} + \frac{5}{12} =$

4. $\frac{2}{5} \times \frac{-1}{3} \times \frac{3}{7} =$

5. $\frac{1}{8} \div \frac{3}{4} =$

6. $\dfrac{\frac{1}{8} + \frac{1}{12}}{\frac{2}{3} - \frac{1}{5}} =$

7. Which fraction is greater: $\frac{3}{5}$ or $\frac{4}{7}$?

8. What is the decimal value of $\frac{1}{4} + \frac{3}{8}$?

9. $0.005 + 0.555 + 0.05 =$

10. $0.129 \div 0.6 =$

Fractions and Decimals Drill: Answers

1. $\dfrac{7}{9}$

2. $9\dfrac{1}{5}$

3. $\dfrac{17}{60}$

4. $-\dfrac{2}{35}$

5. $\dfrac{1}{6}$

6. $\dfrac{25}{56}$

7. $\dfrac{3}{5}$

8. 0.625

9. 0.61

10. 0.215

CONCEPT CHECK

- How do you add or subtract fractions?

  _____

- How do you divide by a fraction?

  _____

- How do you multiply fractions?

  _____

- What are at least three methods to compare fractions?

  _____

- When multiplying decimals, how do you determine the number of decimal places in the product?

  _____

Example answers are in your book's online resources (**kaptest.com/login**).

Now see how a GMAT expert uses the Kaplan Method to answer a Problem Solving question on fractions.

$$\frac{1}{3} + \left(\frac{2}{3}\right)^2 =$$

○ $\frac{5}{12}$

○ $\frac{17}{27}$

○ $\frac{7}{9}$

○   1

○ $\frac{5}{3}$

Step 1: Analyze the Question

You're given an expression with two fractions, one of which is raised to an exponent, and you're asked which fraction in the choices is equivalent.

Step 2: State the Task

Simplify the expression, following the order of operations (PEMDAS): start with the exponent and then add the fractions by finding a common denominator.

Step 3: Approach Strategically

First, rewrite the exponent as multiplication and solve: $\frac{2}{3} \times \frac{2}{3} = \frac{4}{9}$. Then find a common denominator for the two fractions $\frac{1}{3}$ and $\frac{4}{9}$. Multiply $\frac{1}{3}$ by $\frac{3}{3}$, which yields $\frac{3}{9}$. Now that the denominators are the same, you can add the two fractions, $\frac{3}{9} + \frac{4}{9}$, which gives you the answer, $\frac{7}{9}$, choice (**C**).

Step 4: Confirm Your Answer

Take a moment to verify your math, particularly that you followed the order of operations and accurately converted fractions into forms that have a common denominator. Note that (**D**) would be the result if you had first added the two fractions and then squared the sum.

Next, you'll find some in-format questions involving fractions and decimals.

Practice Set: Fractions and Decimals

(Answers and explanations are at the end of the chapter.)

1. If x and y are positive numbers, is $\frac{x^2}{y} > \frac{x}{y^2}$?

   1. $\frac{x}{y} > 1$
   2. $xy > 1$

2. If a and b are positive numbers, is $8a < 3b$?

   1. $\frac{a}{b} < 0.374$
   2. $b > 2.671a$

3. The equation $\frac{27}{0.75} + \frac{0.025}{\frac{1}{80}} = 19a$ is equivalent to which of the following?

   ○ $\frac{9}{\frac{1}{4}} - a = 40$

   ○ $\frac{54}{a} + \frac{0.25}{\frac{1}{48}} = 38$

   ○ $\frac{27}{0.75} + \frac{2.5}{\frac{1}{8}} = 19a$

   ○ $\frac{\frac{4}{3}}{\frac{1}{27}} + a = 38$

   ○ $\frac{1.9a}{\frac{1}{20}} = 19$

4. The equation $\frac{5a}{2b} + \frac{10}{3} = 5$ is equivalent to each of the following EXCEPT:

○ $3a = 2b$

○ $5a - 2b = \frac{4b}{3}$

○ $\frac{5a}{2b} + 1 = \frac{8}{3}$

○ $3a + 2b - 1 = 2a + 3b$

○ $\frac{a}{2b} = \frac{1}{3}$

Percents

The word *percent* means "per one hundred," so a percent is a fraction of 100 in which the percent represents the part and 100 represents the whole. Therefore, 19 percent (or 19%) means 19 hundredths . . .

or $\dfrac{19}{100}$

or 0.19

or 19 out of every 100 things

or 19 parts out of a whole of 100 parts

GMAT questions sometimes require you to convert among percents, decimals, fractions, and ratios. Even when not required, converting a number from one form to another often makes the arithmetic more efficient.

To make a percent from a decimal or fraction, multiply by 100 percent.

Example: $0.17 = 0.17 \times 100\% = 17\%$

Example: $\dfrac{1}{4} = \dfrac{1}{4} \times 100\% = 25\%$

To convert from a percent to a fraction, divide by 100 percent.

Example: $32\% = \dfrac{32\%}{100\%} = \dfrac{32}{100} = \dfrac{8}{25}$

Example: $\dfrac{1}{2}\% = \dfrac{\frac{1}{2}\%}{100\%} = \dfrac{1}{200}$

To change a percent to a decimal, delete the percent sign and move the decimal point two places to the left. (This is the same as dividing by 100 percent.)

Example: $15\% = 0.15$

Example: $0.8\% = 0.008$

When asked to calculate a percent that is a multiple of 10, it can be easier to break the percent into 10 percent increments.

Example: Find 30% of 260.

Since 10% of 260 is 26, and 30% is three times as much as 10%, 30% of 260 = 3 × 26 = 78.

Being familiar with the following fraction-decimal-percent equivalents can save you a lot of time on questions that require you to perform such conversions.

$$\frac{1}{20} = 0.05 = 5\% \qquad \frac{1}{11} = 0.\overline{09} = 9\frac{1}{11}\% \qquad \frac{1}{10} = 0.1 = 10\% \qquad \frac{1}{9} = 0.1\overline{1} = 11\frac{1}{9}\%$$

$$\frac{1}{8} = 0.125 = 12\frac{1}{2}\% \qquad \frac{1}{6} = 0.1\overline{6} = 16\frac{2}{3}\% \qquad \frac{1}{5} = 0.2 = 20\% \qquad \frac{1}{4} = 0.25 = 25\%$$

$$\frac{1}{3} = 0.3\overline{3} = 33\frac{1}{3}\% \qquad \frac{1}{2} = 0.5 = 50\%$$

Calculating Percents

Here is the three-part **percent formula**:

$$\text{Percent} = \frac{\text{Part}}{\text{Whole}} \times 100\%$$

If you know any two parts, you can solve for the third.

In percent problems, the whole generally is associated with the word *of*, and the part is associated with the word *is*. The percent can be represented as the ratio of the part to the whole, or the *is* to the *of*.

Example: What is 36 percent of 25?

You are given the percent, 36, and the whole, 25. Use the percent formula and rearrange to solve for the part. The first step is to multiply both sides by 25 and divide both sides by 100% to isolate x.

$$\text{Percent} = \frac{\text{Part}}{\text{Whole}} \times 100\%$$

$$36\% = \frac{x}{25} \times 100\%$$

$$x = 36\%\left(\frac{25}{100\%}\right)$$

$$x = 36\left(\frac{25}{100}\right)$$

$$x = 36\left(\frac{1}{4}\right)$$

$$x = 9$$

Note that due to the way the percent formula works, x percent of y is the same as y percent of x. Therefore, you could rephrase the above question as "What is 25 percent of 36?" This is asking for one-fourth of 36, and you may know the answer is 9 without having to do calculations. Such rephrasing can lead to shortcuts on the GMAT.

Example: 13 is $33\frac{1}{3}$ percent of what number?

You are given the part and the percent, and you need to solve for the whole.

$$\text{Percent} = \frac{\text{Part}}{\text{Whole}} \times 100\%$$

$$33\frac{1}{3}\% = \frac{13}{x} \times 100\%$$

$$\left(\frac{33\frac{1}{3}}{100}\right)x = 13$$

$$\frac{1}{3}x = 13$$

$$x = 39$$

Example: 18 is what percent of 3?

You are given the part and the whole, and you need to solve for the percent. Note that the "part" here is greater than the whole to which it's being compared; anticipate the result will be greater than 100%.

$$\text{Percent} = \frac{\text{Part}}{\text{Whole}} \times 100\%$$

$$x\% = \frac{18}{3} \times 100\%$$

$$x\% = 6 \times 100\%$$

$$x\% = 600\%$$

Some problems will ask you to calculate "percent greater than" or "percent less than." In these cases, apply the percentage to the number that follows the word *than*. You may choose to write the percent as a percent, a decimal, or a fraction over 100—whatever makes the math easiest.

Example: If *n* is 15 percent less than 60, what is the value of *n*?

Start with 60, apply 15% to it, and—because the question is asking for a value *less than* 60—subtract the percentage from your starting value.

$$n = 60 - (15\% \times 60)$$

$$n = 60 - (0.15 \times 60)$$

$$n = 0.85 \times 60$$

$$n = 51$$

Example: What is the price of a television that costs 28 percent more than a $50 radio?

Start with $50, apply the 28% to it, and—because the question is asking for a value *more than* $50—add the percentage to your starting value.

$$t = 50 + (28\% \times 50)$$

$$t = 50 + \left(\frac{28}{100} \times 50\right)$$

$$t = 50 + \frac{28}{2}$$

$$t = 50 + 14$$

$$t = 64$$

Calculating Percent Change

Another commonly tested concept on the GMAT is **percent change**. Use the following formula to calculate percent change:

$$\text{Percent change} = \frac{\text{New value} - \text{Original value}}{\text{Original value}} \times 100\%$$

A negative result is a percent decrease, and a positive result is a percent increase.

Example: If a jacket regularly priced at $150 is offered for a discounted price of $120, what is the percent discount?

$$\text{Percent discount} = \frac{\$120 - \$150}{\$150} \times 100\%$$
$$= -\frac{30}{150} \times 100\%$$
$$= -\frac{1}{5} \times 100\% = -20\%$$

The negative sign in front of 20% reflects the fact that the price was reduced.

Some GMAT questions will ask you to find two or more successive percent changes.

Example: The price of an antique is reduced by 20 percent, and then this discounted price is further reduced by 10 percent. If the antique originally cost $200, what is its final price?

First, the price is reduced by 20%. In other words, the price becomes 100% − 20% = 80% of what it originally was. Find this value: 80% of $200 is equal to $\frac{8}{10}$× $200 or $160. Then, *this price* is reduced by 10%. So 10% × $160 = $16, and the final price of the antique is $160 − $16 = $144.

A common error in this kind of problem is to apply both discounts to the original price and calculate a final price of 20% + 10% = 30% less than the starting price, or $140. To answer correctly, apply each percent, one at a time, to the correct base.

Note that, as in this example, two successive decreases cause a total percent decrease of *less* than the sum of the two individual percents. This is because the second percent decrease is taken from a smaller value. Likewise, two percent increases cause a total increase of *more* than the sum of the two percents, since the second percent increase is calculated based on a higher starting point. You may be able to use this fact to eliminate some answer choices.

Now use the drill to get some practice working with percents.

Percents Drill

Answers follow the drill.

1. Find 15 percent of 500.
2. Find 40 percent of 2.
3. Express 65 percent as a decimal and a fraction in lowest terms.
4. Express $\frac{7}{20}$ as a percent.
5. If 21 is 20 percent of n, what is the value of n?
6. If 30 is p percent of 6, how much is p?
7. A house was appraised at $400,000; after one year, its value dropped by 7 percent. What was its new value?
8. The price of an item increases from $25 to $29. What is the percent increase in price?

9. In 1980, a town's population was 20,000. By 1985, the population had increased by 15 percent. Over the next 5 years, the population increased by a further 10 percent. What was the town's population in 1990?

10. In June, the price of a car was $28,000. In July, the dealership increased the price by 10%. In August, the dealership discounted the car by $2,100. What was the total percent change in the price from June to August?

Percents Drill: Answers

1. 75

2. 0.8

3. $0.65 = \dfrac{13}{20}$

4. 35%

5. 105

6. 500

7. $372,000

8. 16%

9. 25,300

10. 2.5%

CONCEPT CHECK

- What is "x percent" expressed as a fraction? _____

- In percent questions, what are the words *is* and *of* typically associated with?

  _____

- When calculating percent change, what values are in the numerator and denominator of the fraction?

  _____

- If a value undergoes two percent decreases in succession, how will the total percent decrease from the starting value relate to the sum of the two percents?

  _____

Example answers are in your book's online resources (**kaptest.com/login**).

Now see how a GMAT expert uses the Kaplan Method to answer a Problem Solving question dealing with percents.

> A pet store always sells pet food at a discount of 10 percent to 30 percent from the manufacturer's suggested retail price. If during a sale, the store discounts an additional 20 percent from the already discounted price, what would be the lowest possible price of a container of pet food that had a manufacturer's suggested retail price of $20?
>
> O $10.00
>
> O $11.20
>
> O $14.40
>
> O $16.00
>
> O $18.00

Step 1: Analyze the Question

The question describes a range of possible discounts that are always applied to pet food as well as a fixed discount that is applied during a sale. It also provides the baseline price of the food. The correct answer will represent the lowest possible price of the food after both discounts are taken.

Step 2: State the Task

Starting at the $20 manufacturer's suggested retail price, apply the maximum possible regular discount (30%) and then the sale discount (20%) to arrive at the sale price of the pet food.

Step 3: Approach Strategically

You can approach the reduction calculation in two ways:

1. You could determine 30% of $20 and then subtract this amount from $20:

$$\$20 \times 0.3 = \$6; \$20 - \$6 = \$14$$

2. You can find the new price directly. Since $100\% - 30\% = 70\%$, the new price is 70% of $20:

$$\$20 \times 0.7 = \$14$$

Regardless of the approach, the price after the first discount is $14.

Now, take the 20% discount off this reduced price. That means there will be 80% of the price left: $14 \times 0.8 = \$11.20$. (**B**) is correct.

Step 4: Confirm Your Answer

Check your arithmetic and re-read the question stem to make sure that you solved for the correct value.

Next, you'll find some in-format questions involving percents.

Practice Set: Percents with Specified Values

(Answers and explanations are at the end of the chapter.)

5.   Four different batches of concrete are combined in a large mixing vat. Batch A, which weighs 1,000 kilograms, contains 30 percent gravel by weight. Batch B, which is twice the weight of batch A, is made up of 40 percent gravel. Batch C weighs 25 percent less than batch B and contains 50 percent gravel. Finally, batch D, which is half the weight of batch A, contains 60 percent gravel. What is the percentage of gravel in the concrete when the four batches are mixed together?

   ○   40%

   ○   43%

   ○   45%

   ○   50%

   ○   55%

6.   In the first quarter of the year, a certain entrepreneur sold 36 percent of the 75 crafts that she put for sale online. In the second quarter of that year, she sold one-fourth of the remaining crafts. What was the percent decrease in the number of crafts the entrepreneur sold from the first quarter to the second?

   ○   12%

   ○   25%

   ○ $55\frac{5}{9}$%

   ○   61%

   ○ $66\frac{2}{3}$%

7. **Survey of Student Preferences**

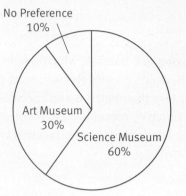

No Preference 10%

Art Museum 30%

Science Museum 60%

The administrators of a certain school survey all 120 students to plan a field trip. Each student can express a preference for only one destination: the science museum, the art museum, or neither. The results of the student survey are shown above. On the day of the field trip, all students who expressed a preference in the survey will attempt to attend their preferred museum. How many students who have a preference do <u>not</u> visit their preferred museum?

(1) Due to transportation constraints, the maximum number of students who can take a field trip to the science museum is 55.

(2) Due to high demand, the art museum can accommodate a maximum of 50 students.

8. A baseball team won 45 percent of the first 80 games it played. How many of the remaining 82 games will the team have to win in order to have won exactly 50 percent of all the games it played?

- ○ 36
- ○ 45
- ○ 50
- ○ 55
- ○ 81

Exponents

> **LEARNING OBJECTIVES**
>
> - Apply exponent rules
> - Convert values to and from scientific notation

In the term $3x^2$, 3 is the **coefficient**, x is the **base**, and 2 is the **exponent**. Exponents are a shorthand way of expressing multiplication. The exponent refers to the number of times the base occurs when it is multiplied by itself. For instance, in 4^3, you multiply 4 three times: $4^3 = 4 \times 4 \times 4 = 64$.

In the expression $3x^2$, only the x is being squared, not the 3. Following the order of operations (PEMDAS), you'd evaluate $3x^2$ by first squaring x and then multiplying by 3. If the expression is $(3x)^2$, however, it's necessary to square both the 3 and the x to yield $9x^2$.

A number multiplied by itself is called the **square** of that number (e.g., 5×5 or 5^2 is 5 squared).

A number multiplied three times is called the **cube** of that number (e.g., $4 \times 4 \times 4$ is 4^3 or 4 cubed).

Exponent Rules

To multiply or divide exponents, they must have the same base. To multiply two powers with the same base, keep the base and *add* the exponents.

Example: $2^2 \times 2^3 = 2^{2+3} = 2^5$

To divide two powers with the same base, keep the base and subtract the exponent in the denominator from the exponent in the numerator.

Example: $\dfrac{4^7}{4^5} = 4^{7-5} = 4^2$

To raise a power to an exponent, multiply the exponents.

Example: $\left(3^2\right)^4 = 3^{2\times4} = 3^8$

To multiply two powers with the same exponent but different bases, multiply the bases and keep the exponent.

Example: $(2^3)(3^3) = (2 \times 3)^3 = 6^3$

When adding or subtracting powers where the bases and exponents are equal, add or subtract the coefficients.

Example: $8(3^7) - 6(3^7) = 2(3^7)$

Example: $12(x^a) + 5(x^a) + 4(x^a) = 21(x^a)$

Any non-zero number raised to the exponent 1 equals itself: $a^1 = a$.

Any number except zero that is raised to the exponent 0 is equal to 1. For example, $3^0 = 1{,}300^0 = 1$, and $a^0 = 1$ where $a \neq 0$. (The value 0^0 is undefined.)

The negative of an exponent indicates a reciprocal. To arrive at an equivalent expression, take the reciprocal of the power and change the sign of the exponent.

$$a^{-n} = \frac{1}{a^n} \text{ or } \left(\frac{1}{a}\right)^n$$

Example: $2^{-3} = \dfrac{1}{2^3} = \dfrac{1}{8}$

Example: $\dfrac{1}{3^{-2}} = 3^2 = 9$

When a negative number is raised to an odd exponent, the result is negative.

Example: $-2^3 = (-2)(-2)(-2) = -8$

When a negative number is raised to an even exponent, the result is positive.

Example: $-2^2 = (-2)(-2) = 4$

Thus, even exponents disguise the sign of their base. From the information that $x^2 = 4$, there is no way to tell whether $x = 2$ or $x = -2$.

When raising a fraction to an integer exponent, you can solve in one of two ways: (1) raise the numerator and the denominator to the exponent separately or (2) multiply the whole fraction by itself the number of times indicated by the exponent.

Example: $\left(\dfrac{2}{3}\right)^2 = \dfrac{2^2}{3^2} = \dfrac{4}{9}$

$\left(\dfrac{2}{3}\right)^2 = \dfrac{2}{3} \times \dfrac{2}{3} = \dfrac{2 \times 2}{3 \times 3} = \dfrac{4}{9}$

Note that the squared value, $\dfrac{4}{9}$, is less than the base, $\dfrac{2}{3}$. Raising a positive fraction less than 1 to a positive exponent greater than 1 results in a smaller value. The higher the exponent, the smaller the result.

Scientific Notation

When a base of 10 is raised to a positive integer exponent, the exponent tells you how many zeros the number would contain if written out.

Example: $10^6 = 1{,}000{,}000$ (6 zeros)

Scientific notation is a means of expressing any value as a number with a magnitude greater than 0 but less than 10, multiplied by 10 raised to a positive integer exponent. A positive exponent on the base of 10 indicates the number of places you'd move the decimal to the right if you wrote the number without using an exponent.

Example: $23{,}140 = 2.314 \times 10{,}000 = 2.314 \times 10^4$

Example: $0.0975 = 9.75 \times 0.01 = 9.75 \times 10^{-2}$

Example: $-850 = -8.5 \times 100 = -8.5 \times 10^2$

Now use the drill to get some practice working with exponents.

Exponents Drill

1. Find the value of 2^4.

2. Express the value of $6^5 \times 6^7$ as a single base raised to an exponent.

3. Express the value of $3^4 \times 5^4$ as a single base raised to an exponent.

4. Express the value of $\dfrac{12^7}{12^3}$ as a single base raised to an exponent.

5. Express the value of $\left(4^4\right)^3$ as a base raised to a single exponent.

6. Find the value of 5^{-2}.

7. Find the value of $\left(\dfrac{3}{5}\right)^2$.

8. Find the value of 10^8.

9. Find the value of 2.75×10^4.

10. Express 429,600 in scientific notation.

Exponents Drill: Answers

1. $2 \times 2 \times 2 \times 2 = 16$

2. $6^{(5+7)} = 6^{12}$

3. $(3 \times 5)^4 = 15^4$

4. $12^{(7-3)} = 12^4$

5. $4^{(4 \times 3)} = 4^{12}$

6. $\dfrac{1}{5^2} = \dfrac{1}{25}$

7. $\dfrac{3}{5} \times \dfrac{3}{5} = \dfrac{9}{25}$

8. $100{,}000{,}000$

9. $2.75 \times 10{,}000 = 27{,}500$

10. 4.296×10^5

CONCEPT CHECK

- What is an exponent telling you to do with its base?

  _____

- How can you re-express a number raised to a negative exponent?

  _____

- What happens to a fraction with a value greater than 0 but less than 1 when it is raised to an exponent greater than 1?

  _____

- How can you re-express 10 raised to a given integer exponent?

  _____

Example answers are in your book's online resources (**kaptest.com/login**).

Now see how a GMAT expert uses the Kaplan Method on a Data Sufficiency question dealing with exponents.

Does $a = b$?

1. $a^2 - b^2 = 0$

2. $1 - \dfrac{a^3}{b^3} = 0$

Step 1: Analyze the Question Stem

This is a Yes/No question. You need to determine whether there is enough information to know whether $a = b$.

Step 2: Evaluate the Statements Using 12TEN

Statement (1) says that $a^2 - b^2 = 0$, which is the same as saying $a^2 = b^2$. Since squared values are always non-negative, if $a^2 = b^2$, then either $a = b$ or $a = -b$. You can test a few cases by picking numbers. If $a = 5$ and $b = 5$, then $a^2 = b^2$, and $a = b$. With these numbers, the answer to the question is yes. But if $a = 5$ and $b = -5$, then a^2 still equals b^2 ($25 = 25$), but a is not equal to b. With these numbers, the answer to the question is no. Because more than one answer to the question is possible, Statement (1) is insufficient. Eliminate **(A)** and **(D)**.

Statement (2) says that $1 - \dfrac{a^3}{b^3} = 0$, which can be simplified as $1 = \dfrac{a^3}{b^3}$ or $a^3 = b^3$. When raised to an odd power, positive numbers yield positive results, and negative numbers yield negative results. For example, $5^3 = 125$ but $-5^3 = -125$. So since $a^3 = b^3$, you can conclude that a and b have the same sign and are equal. The answer to the question is always yes, so Statement (2) is sufficient. **(B)** is correct.

Next, you'll find some in-format questions involving exponents.

Practice Set: Exponents

(Answers and explanations are at the end of the chapter.)

9. At Car Part Corporation, there is a machine that produces brake pads. As the machine works, a wheel assembly turns. After the wheel assembly turns 4.09×10^6 times, the machine needs maintenance. Since being installed, the machine has received maintenance 30 times. Approximately how many total turns had the wheel assembly made when the machine last received maintenance?

    ○ 1.3×10^5

    ○ 1.2×10^7

    ○ 1.2×10^8

    ○ 4.1×10^7

    ○ 7.0×10^8

10. If $\dfrac{2^{5x}}{8^{2x-2}} = 8$, what is the value of x?

    ○ 1

    ○ 2

    ○ 3

    ○ 4

    ○ 5

11. If x is a positive integer, then $9^x + 3^{2x+1} =$

   ○ $3(3^{2x+1})$

   ○ 3^{4x-1}

   ○ 3^{4x+1}

   ○ $4(3^{2x})$

   ○ 12^{2x}

12. What is the value of integer n?

   ○ $n = n^4$

   ○ $1^n \neq n$

Radicals

The **square root** of a number n is a value that, when squared, equals n. This is often represented using the symbol $\sqrt{}$ (called a **radical**). For example, $\sqrt{16} = 4$, since $4^2 = 16$. By convention, a radical represents the positive square root only. So, even though there are two numbers whose square is 16 (both 4 and -4), $\sqrt{16}$ refers to the positive number 4. The negative root would be represented as $-\sqrt{16} = -4$.

Other roots are expressed as $\sqrt[n]{a}$ (read "the nth root of a"). This represents the value that, when raised to the power of n, equals a. For example, $\sqrt[4]{81} = 3$ since $3^4 = 81$. If no n is specified, the radical sign means **square root** (because the root squared equals a). If $n = 3$, that's called a **cube root** (because the root cubed equals a).

Radical Rules

Roots can be expressed as fractional exponents. If a number is raised to an exponent of $\frac{1}{n}$, that is the same as taking the nth root.

Example: $27^{\frac{1}{3}} = \sqrt[3]{27} = 3$

If the numerator of the fraction is not 1, then the formula is $a^{\frac{b}{c}} = \sqrt[c]{a^b}$.

Example: $8^{\frac{2}{3}} = \sqrt[3]{8^2} = \sqrt[3]{64} = 4$

You can add or subtract terms with radicals when the radicals are the same, that is, when they have the same base and the same root. For example, $4\sqrt{2} + 3\sqrt{2} = 7\sqrt{2}$. However, the expressions $\sqrt{2} + \sqrt{3}$ and $\sqrt{15} + \sqrt[3]{15}$ cannot be simplified any further.

To multiply or divide radicals of the same root, multiply or divide the numbers inside the radical signs. If there are numbers outside the radical signs, then multiply or divide those, too.

Example: $\sqrt{3} \times \sqrt{7} = \sqrt{3 \times 7} = \sqrt{21}$

Example: $\sqrt{25} \div \sqrt{5} = \sqrt{25 \div 5} = \sqrt{5}$

Example:

$$\frac{2\sqrt{3} \times 8\sqrt{10}}{4\sqrt{5}} = \frac{(2 \times 8) \times \sqrt{3 \times 10}}{4\sqrt{5}} = \frac{16\sqrt{30}}{4\sqrt{5}} = \frac{16}{4} \times \sqrt{\frac{30}{5}} = 4\sqrt{6}$$

Note that this only works with multiplication. Radicals with addition or subtraction cannot be "split." For example, $\sqrt{16 - 4} \neq \sqrt{16} - \sqrt{4}$.

There are specific procedures for **simplifying radicals**. If the denominator of a fraction contains a radical that cannot be simplified, the fraction must be re-expressed by multiplying the numerator and the denominator by that radical.

Example: $\dfrac{9}{\sqrt{2}} = \dfrac{9 \times \sqrt{2}}{\sqrt{2} \times \sqrt{2}} = \dfrac{9\sqrt{2}}{2}$

If the number inside a radical is a multiple of a perfect square, the expression can be simplified by factoring out the perfect square.

Example: $\sqrt{72} = \sqrt{36 \times 2} = \sqrt{36} \times \sqrt{2} = 6\sqrt{2}$

To rewrite the square root of a decimal without the square root sign, ignore the decimal and consider the value starting with the first nonzero digit. Take the square root of that value. Then insert a decimal so that the original number of decimal places is cut in half.

Example: The number 0.0009 has four decimal places, so its square root should have half as many, or two, decimal places. Ignoring the decimal leaves a value of 9. So, since $\sqrt{9} = 3$, $\sqrt{0.0009} = 0.03$.

Similarly, if a decimal is under a cube root sign, take the cube root of the value without the decimal and reinsert the decimal to cut the number of decimal places by a third.

Example: $\sqrt[3]{0.000125} = 0.05$

Now use the drill to get some practice working with radicals.

Radicals Drill

Simplify the following expressions. Answers follow the drill.

1. $\sqrt[3]{125}$
2. $4^{\frac{3}{2}}$
3. $2\sqrt{10} + 3\sqrt{10} + 4\sqrt{5}$
4. $3\sqrt{2} - 4\sqrt{3} + 2\sqrt{3} - \sqrt{2}$
5. $2\sqrt{12} \times 3\sqrt{3}$
6. $\dfrac{3\sqrt{48}}{6\sqrt{3}}$
7. $\dfrac{10}{\sqrt{2}}$
8. $\sqrt{162}$
9. $\sqrt{a^6}$
10. $\dfrac{\sqrt{0.0144}}{4}$

Radicals Drill: Answers

1. 5
2. 8
3. $5\sqrt{10} + 4\sqrt{5}$
4. $2\sqrt{2} - 2\sqrt{3} = 2(\sqrt{2} - \sqrt{3})$
5. $(2 \times 3) \times (\sqrt{3} \times \sqrt{12}) = 6\sqrt{36} = 6 \times 6 = 36$
6. $\dfrac{3\sqrt{3}\sqrt{16}}{6\sqrt{3}} = \dfrac{12}{6} = 2$

7. $5\sqrt{2}$
8. $9\sqrt{2}$
9. a^3
10. 0.03

CONCEPT CHECK

- A radical is equal to only the _____ square root of the value in the radical.
- When adding or subtracting, when can radicals be combined?

  _____

- How can you simplify a radical?

  _____

- How do you find the square root of a decimal?

  _____

Example answers are in your book's online resources (**kaptest.com/login**).

Now see how a GMAT expert uses the Kaplan Method to answer a Problem Solving question that involves radicals.

$$(\sqrt{3} + \sqrt{7})(\sqrt{3} - \sqrt{7}) =$$

- ○ $-7 - 2\sqrt{3}$
- ○ -4
- ○ 3
- ○ $2\sqrt{7} + 3$
- ○ $7 + 2\sqrt{3}$

Step 1: Analyze the Question

There are two expressions multiplied together. Both expressions involve the addition or subtraction of the same two radicals.

Step 2: State the Task

You need to simplify this quadratic expression, currently in factored form (the topic of quadratics is covered in the "Algebra" chapter).

Step 3: Approach Strategically

Recall that $\sqrt{a} + \sqrt{b}$ does *not* equal $\sqrt{a+b}$. Also, $\sqrt{a} - \sqrt{b}$ does not equal $\sqrt{a-b}$. Thus, the radicals inside the parentheses cannot be combined. Instead, you could multiply out the four pairs of terms (following the mnemonic FOIL). Alternatively, you can save time by recognizing this commonly tested quadratic pattern:

$$(a+b)(a-b) = a^2 - b^2$$

Substitute $\sqrt{3}$ for a, and $\sqrt{7}$ for b:

$$(\sqrt{3} + \sqrt{7})(\sqrt{3} - \sqrt{7}) = (\sqrt{3})^2 - (\sqrt{7})^2 = 3 - 7 = -4$$

That makes **(B)** the correct answer.

Step 4: Confirm Your Answer

Double-check your arithmetic.

Next, you'll find some in-format questions involving radicals.

Practice Set: Radicals

(Answers and explanations are at the end of the chapter.)

13. If a positive number A is equal to 3^x and A, when squared, is equal to the cube root of 27 raised to the fourth power, what is the value of x?

    ○ 81
    ○ 27
    ○ 9
    ○ 2
    ○ 1

14. If $r > 0$, is $\sqrt{r}$ an integer?

    ○ r^2 is an integer.
    ○ $r = m^2$, where m is an integer.

15. $\sqrt{36 - \dfrac{3 \times 23}{4}} =$

    ○ $6 - \dfrac{\sqrt{69}}{2}$
    ○ $\dfrac{3\sqrt{5}}{2}$
    ○ $\dfrac{5\sqrt{3}}{2}$
    ○ $12 - \dfrac{\sqrt{69}}{2}$
    ○ $\dfrac{25\sqrt{3}}{4}$

Interest Rates

> **LEARNING OBJECTIVE**
>
> - Apply the simple and compound interest formulas

On the GMAT, interest rate questions rely on three pieces of information: (1) the principal, or the amount initially invested; (2) the interest rate, or the rate at which the investment grows; and (3) the time period during which the investment accrues interest. Simple and compound interest use different formulas. You can often identify the correct answer to interest rate problems by applying your familiarity with the structure and meaning of these formulas, without doing much or any calculation.

Simple interest is applied only to the principal, not to the interest that has previously accrued. Here's the formula:

(Total of principal and interest) = Principal $\times$ (1 + rt), where r equals the interest rate per time period expressed as a decimal and t equals the number of time periods

Example: If $100 were invested at 12 percent simple annual interest, what would be the total value of the investment after 3 years?

$$\text{Total} = \$100 \times (1 + 0.12 \times 3) = \$100(1.36) = \$136$$

Compound interest is applied to the principal and any previously accrued interest. The previously accrued interest, and thus the base to which the interest rate is applied, increases with each compounding period that elapses. Here's the formula:

(Total of principal and interest) = Principal $\times$ (1 + r)^t, where r equals the interest rate per time period expressed as a decimal and t equals the number of time periods

Example: If $100 were invested at 12 percent interest compounded annually, what would be the total value of the investment after 3 years?

$$\text{Total} = \$100 \times (1 + 0.12)^3 = \$100(1.12)^3$$

Because you don't have the use of a calculator on the GMAT Quantitative section, you will typically see choices for a compound interest rate problem written as expressions similar to $\$100(1.12)^3$. You will not have to calculate values such as 1.12^3.

On Test Day, you might encounter a more difficult question that involves an annual interest rate where the interest is not calculated on an annual basis. In this case, r equals the annual rate divided by the number of times per year it is applied, and t equals the number of years multiplied by the number of times per year interest is applied.

Example: If $100 were invested at 12 percent annual interest, compounded quarterly, what would be the total value of the investment after 3 years?

$$\text{Total} = 100 \times \left(1 + \frac{0.12}{4}\right)^{(3 \times 4)} = 100 \times (1.03)^{12}$$

Now use the drill to get some practice applying the interest rate formulas.

Interest Rates Drill

Answers follow the drill.

1. If $200 were invested at 5 percent simple annual interest, what would be the total value of the investment in 5 years?

2. Joe made a single deposit of x dollars to his bank account and made no withdrawals. If his bank pays interest each year only on his original deposit at an annual rate of 4 percent, and his balance after 3 years is $448, what is the value of x?

3. If $50 were invested at 4 percent compound annual interest, what would be the total value of the investment in 3 years? (Express your answer using an exponent.)

4. Maira made a single deposit of $100 to her bank account and made no withdrawals. If her bank pays 1.5 percent annual interest at 6-month intervals on both her deposit and any accumulated interest, what is the balance in the account 2.5 years later? (Express your answer using an exponent.)

5. Claire deposits $500 to her bank account on January 1, 2021. Her bank pays annual interest of 2 percent, compounded semiannually. Assuming Claire does not make any withdrawals, how much is in her account on January 1, 2024? (Express your answer using an exponent.)

Interest Rate Drill: Answers

1. $200 \times (1 + 0.05 \times 5) = \$200(1.25) = \$250$

2. $\$448 = (x)(1 + 0.04 \times 3) = (x)(1.12); x = \$400$

3. $\$50(1.04)^3$

4. $\$100(1.015)^5$

5. $\$500 \times \left(1 + \dfrac{0.02}{2}\right)^{2\times3} = \$500(1.01)^6$

CONCEPT CHECK

- What is the simple interest formula?

  _____

- What is the compound interest formula?

  _____

- If interest is collected more frequently than once a year but the rate is given in annual terms, how do you adjust the values in the interest formulas?

  _____

Example answers are in your book's online resources (**kaptest.com/login**).

Now see how a GMAT expert uses the Kaplan Method to answer a question that involves interest rates.

> The number of bacteria in a petri dish increased by 50 percent every 2 hours. If there were 108 million bacteria in the dish at 2:00 p.m., at what time were there 32 million bacteria in the dish?
>
> ○   6:00 p.m.
> ○   8:00 p.m.
> ○   6:00 a.m.
> ○   8:00 a.m.
> ○   10:00 a.m.

Step 1: Analyze the Question

This may not look like an interest rate question at first glance, but interest rates are just percent increases applied multiple times. The number of bacteria increases 50% every 2 hours. You could think of this as 50% compounded interest applied once every 2 hours.

Step 2: State the Task

Instead of calculating forward, you have to calculate backward—if there are 108 million in the dish at 2:00 p.m., when were there 32 million?

Step 3: Approach Strategically

Start by setting up the compound interest rate formula, using 32 million as the "original principle" that has had an interest rate applied to it. The interest rate of 50% is converted to 0.5 and plugged in for r. The variable t represents the number of two-hour periods that have elapsed.

Total of principal and interest = Principal $\times (1 + r)^t$

$$108 = 32 \times (1.5)^t$$

$$\frac{108}{32} = (1.5)^t$$

$$\frac{27}{8} = (1.5)^t$$

$$\frac{27}{8} = \left(\frac{3}{2}\right)^t$$

$$\frac{27}{8} = \frac{3^t}{2^t}$$

$$\frac{3^3}{2^3} = \frac{3^t}{2^t}$$

This yields $t = 3$. That's three 2-hour increases for a total of 6 hours. Since there were 108 million at 2:00 p.m., there were 32 million 6 hours earlier at 8:00 a.m. **(D)** is correct.

If you don't feel confident about using the interest rate formula, you could use the backsolving strategy. Try out a time and, starting with 32 million, see whether increasing the number of bacteria by 50% repeatedly is consistent with having 108 million bacteria at 2:00 p.m. Given that the bacteria are "compounding," their number will grow very rapidly, so start with a time shortly before 2:00 p.m. **(D)**, 8:00 a.m., would be a better first choice to try than **(B)**, 8:00 p.m. the previous evening.

Step 4: Confirm Your Answer

Confirm that 32 million increased 50% three times yields a value of 108 million (compounded once yields 48 million, twice yields 72 million, and thrice yields 108 million).

Next, you'll find in-format questions involving interest rates.

Practice Set: Interest Rates

(Answers and explanations are at the end of the chapter.)

16. A certain account pays 1.5 percent compound interest every 3 months. A person invested an initial amount and did not invest any more money in the account after that. If, after exactly 5 years, the amount of money in the account was T dollars, which of the following is an expression for the original number of dollars invested in the account?

   ○ $(1.015)^4 T$

   ○ $(1.015)^{15} T$

   ○ $(1.015)^{20} T$

   ○ $\dfrac{T}{(1.015)^{15}}$

   ○ $\dfrac{T}{(1.015)^{20}}$

17. Binh invested $1,000 in a certificate of deposit (CD) that matured in 4 years. The certificate paid 4 percent annual interest compounded quarterly for the original 4-year term and then 2 percent simple annual interest on the compounded amount after that until the CD was redeemed by the holder. If Binh held his CD for exactly 6 years, how much money did he receive when he redeemed it?

   ○ $1,000 \times (1.01)^{16} \times 1.04$

   ○ $1,000 \times (1.01)^{16} \times (1.02)^2$

   ○ $1,000 \times (1.04)^6$

   ○ $1,000 \times (1.01)^{24}$

   ○ $1,000 \times (1.04)^{16} \times (1.02)^2$

18. The amount of an investment will double in approximately $\frac{70}{p}$ years, where p is the percent interest, compounded annually. If Thelma invests $40,000 in a long-term CD that pays 5 percent interest, compounded annually, what will be the approximate total value of the investment when Thelma is ready to retire 42 years later?

    O $280,000

    O $320,000

    O $360,000

    O $450,000

    O $540,000

Integers and Non-Integers

LEARNING OBJECTIVE

- Apply number property rules for integers and non-integers

Real numbers are all the numbers on the number line. All of the numbers on the GMAT are real. **Integers** are all of the real numbers with no fractional or decimal parts. Integers can be positive (e.g., 3, 105), negative (e.g., -6, -277), or 0. Many number properties questions on the GMAT dealing with integers are Data Sufficiency questions that ask whether a specific term is or is not an integer.

Rational numbers can be expressed as fractions with integers in both the numerator and denominator, such as $\frac{3}{4}$. Whole numbers are rational; for instance, 5 could be written as $\frac{5}{1}$.

Irrational numbers are real numbers that cannot be expressed as fractions, such as $\sqrt{3}$ or π.

When an integer is added to, subtracted from, or multiplied by another integer, the result is an integer.

Examples: $5 + 3 = 8$ $2 - 6 = -4$ $7 \times 5 = 35$

However, when an integer is divided by another integer, the result *may or may not* be an integer.

Examples: $18 \div 6 = 3$, but $\frac{18}{7} = 2\frac{4}{7}$

Now use the drill to get some practice working with integers.

Integers and Non-Integers Drill

Answers follow the drill.

1. Is $3 \times 4 + 11$ an integer?
2. Is $\frac{13}{5}$ an integer?
3. Is $3\sqrt{3}$ an integer?
4. Is $\frac{1}{4} + \frac{1}{8} + \frac{5}{8}$ an integer?
5. Is $\frac{(2\sqrt{3})^4}{48}$ an integer?

Integers and Non-Integers Drill: Answers

1. Yes
2. No
3. No
4. Yes
5. Yes:

$$\frac{(2\sqrt{3})^4}{48} = \frac{2 \times 2 \times 2 \times 2 \times 3 \times 3}{48} = \frac{\cancel{2} \times \cancel{2} \times \cancel{2} \times \cancel{2} \times \cancel{3} \times 3}{\cancel{2} \times \cancel{2} \times \cancel{2} \times \cancel{2} \times \cancel{3}} = 3$$

CONCEPT CHECK

- What is an integer?

_____

- If you add, subtract, or multiply integers, the result will be _____.
- If you divide one integer by another, will the result be an integer?

Example answers are in your book's online resources (**kaptest.com/login**).

Now see how a GMAT expert uses the Kaplan Method to answer a Data Sufficiency question about integers and non-integers.

Is z an integer?

1. $2z$ is an even integer.
2. $4z$ is an even integer.

Step 1: Analyze the Question Stem

This is a Yes/No question about whether z is an integer. Information that answers the question with either "always yes" or "always no" is required for sufficiency.

Step 2: Evaluate the Statements Using 12TEN

Statement (1): Since $2z$ is an even number, z must be an integer because all even numbers can be evenly divided by 2. You can pick numbers to test this. For instance, if $2z = 2$, then $z = 1$. If $2z = -122$, then $z = -61$. Statement (1) is sufficient. Eliminate (**B**), (**C**), and (**E**).

Statement (2) looks similar to Statement (1), but not all even numbers can be evenly divided by 4. You can pick numbers to test the statement. If $4z = 4$, then $z = 1$, which is an integer. But if $4z = 6$, then $z = 1.5$, which is *not* an integer. You can't say that z is always or is never an integer, so Statement (2) is insufficient. (**A**) is correct.

Next, you'll find in-format questions involving integers and non-integers.

Practice Set: Integers and Non-Integers

(Answers and explanations are at the end of the chapter.)

19. If each of d, q, and r is a positive integer such that $dq + r = 3$, what is the value of d?

    (1) The number $\frac{r}{d}$ is less than $0.\overline{66}$.

    (2) The integer $\frac{q}{r}$ is less than 2.

20. If f and g are positive integers, is $\frac{f+g}{f}$ an integer?

    (1) $g = 5f - 4$

    (2) $f = \frac{1}{3}g$

21. If n is a positive integer, is $\frac{\sqrt{n}}{3}$ an integer?

    (1) $\sqrt{\frac{n}{3}}$ is an integer.

    (2) $\sqrt{14n}$ is NOT an integer.

Odds and Evens

LEARNING OBJECTIVE

- Apply the number property rules for odds and evens

The terms **odd** and **even** apply only to integers. Even numbers are divisible by 2, and odd numbers are not divisible by 2. Therefore, even numbers end in the digit 0, 2, 4, 6, or 8. Odd numbers end in the digit 1, 3, 5, 7, or 9. The number 0 is even.

Because whether an integer is odd or even is an either/or proposition, the GMAT tends to test odd and even number properties on Yes/No Data Sufficiency questions.

Here are the number property rules for operations with odds and evens:

$$\text{Odd} \pm \text{Odd} = \text{Even} \qquad \text{Odd} \times \text{Odd} = \text{Odd}$$
$$\text{Even} \pm \text{Even} = \text{Even} \qquad \text{Even} \times \text{Even} = \text{Even}$$
$$\text{Odd} \pm \text{Even} = \text{Odd} \qquad \text{Odd} \times \text{Even} = \text{Even}$$

$$\text{Odd}^{\text{any positive integer}} = \text{Odd}$$

$$\text{Even}^{\text{any positive integer}} = \text{Even}$$

Now use the drill to get some practice working with odds and evens.

Odds and Evens Drill

In the expressions below, h and k are even integers, and o and p are odd integers. Identify which of the expressions are odd and which are even. Answers follow the drill.

1. $o + p$
2. $h - p$
3. $h \times o$
4. $op + k$
5. $k^p - h$

Odds and Evens Drill: Answers

1. Odd + Odd = Even
2. Even − Odd = Odd
3. Even × Odd = Even

4. Odd × Odd = Odd; then Odd + Even = Odd
5. Even^{Odd} = Even; then Even − Even = Even

CONCEPT CHECK

• How can you tell whether an integer is even or odd?

_____

• Which number property rules result in an odd integer?

_____

• Which number property rules result in an even integer?

_____

Example answers are in your book's online resources (**kaptest.com/login**).

Now see how a GMAT expert uses the Kaplan Method to answer a Data Sufficiency question that involves odds and evens.

If x is an integer, is x odd?

(1) $x + 4$ is an odd integer.

(2) $\frac{x}{3}$ is not an even integer.

Step 1: Analyze the Question Stem

This is a Yes/No question. A statement is sufficient if it provides enough information to determine whether x, an integer, is odd. If values permitted by a statement can produce either an even or an odd value for x, the statement is insufficient.

Step 2: Evaluate the Statements Using 12TEN

If $x + 4$ is an odd integer, then x must be odd. That's because 4 is even, and only the sum of an even and an odd number results in an odd number. Statement (1) is sufficient; eliminate (**B**), (**C**), and (**E**).

Statement (2) says that $\frac{x}{3}$ is *not* an even integer. To determine sufficiency, you can pick some numbers for x.

• If $x = 3$, then $\frac{x}{3} = \frac{3}{3} = 1$, which is not an even integer. In this case, the answer to the question is yes, x is odd.

• If $x = 2$, then $\frac{x}{3} = \frac{2}{3}$, which is not an even integer. In this case, the answer to the question is no, x is even.

Because more than one answer to the question is possible, Statement (2) is insufficient. Eliminate (**D**) and choose (**A**).

Next, you'll find in-format questions involving odds and evens.

Practice Set: Odds and Evens

(Answers and explanations are at the end of the chapter.)

22. Set S contains 5 integers, labeled A, B, C, D, and E. If the sum of all of the elements of set S is odd, how many of the elements of set S are even?

    (1) The sum of A and B is odd.

    (2) The product of B, C, and D is odd.

23. If a and b are integers and a is odd, is b even?

    (1) $(a^3 + 1) \times b$ is even.

    (2) $\dfrac{a^2}{b} = b - 4$

24. If m is an odd number and p is a prime number, which of the following must be odd?

    ○ mp

    ○ $m(m + p)$

    ○ $m - p$

    ○ $m^2 + 2p^2 + 1$

    ○ $m^2(m + 2p)$

Positives and Negatives

LEARNING OBJECTIVE

- Apply number property rules for positives and negatives

Numbers that are greater than zero are **positive**. Numbers that are less than zero are **negative**. Because whether an integer is positive or negative is an either/or proposition, the GMAT tends to test positive and negative number properties on Yes/No Data Sufficiency questions.

Numbers with Special Properties

Zero is neither positive nor negative. Adding or subtracting zero from a number does not change the value of the number, and any number multiplied by zero equals zero.

Example: $12 + 0 = 12; 12 \times 0 = 0$

Division by zero is undefined. The fraction $\frac{0}{0}$ is likewise undefined. To avoid this undefined operation, GMAT questions sometimes begin by excluding values that would make the denominator of a fraction in the problem equal to zero.

Example: If $a \neq 0$, is $\frac{x}{a}$ negative?

The numbers 1 and −1 have important properties. Multiplying or dividing a number by 1 does not change the number. Multiplying or dividing a number by −1 changes the sign, but not the absolute value (magnitude) of the number.

Examples: $6 \times (-1) = -6$

$-2 \div (-1) = -(-2) = 2$

Note that when you distribute the − sign across the parentheses, the negative of a negative number is positive. Be certain to distribute the − sign to all terms in parentheses. For instance, $-(2x - y) = -2x + y$.

The **reciprocal** of a non-zero number is 1 divided by the number. The product of a number and its reciprocal is 1.

Example: The reciprocal of 6 is $\frac{1}{6}$, and $6 \times \frac{1}{6} = \frac{6}{6} = 1$.

Example: The reciprocal of $\frac{2}{3}$ is $\frac{1}{\frac{2}{3}} = \frac{3}{2}$, and $\frac{2}{3} \times \frac{3}{2} = 1$.

Note in the second example above that the reciprocal of a fraction can be found by simply switching the numerator and denominator.

The numbers between −1 and +1 other than zero have some important properties, too. The reciprocal of a number between 0 and 1, exclusive, is *greater* than the number itself.

Example: The reciprocal of $\frac{2}{3}$ is $\frac{3}{2}$, which is greater than $\frac{2}{3}$.

The reciprocal of a number between −1 and 0, exclusive, is *less* than the number itself.

Example: The reciprocal of $-\frac{2}{3}$ is $\frac{1}{-\frac{2}{3}} = -\frac{3}{2}$, which is less than $-\frac{2}{3}$.

The square of a number between 0 and 1, exclusive, is less than the number itself.

Example: $\left(\frac{1}{2}\right)^2 = \frac{1}{2} \times \frac{1}{2} = \frac{1}{4}$, which is less than $\frac{1}{2}$.

Multiplying any positive number by a fraction between 0 and 1, exclusive, gives a product smaller than the original number.

Example: $6 \times \frac{1}{4} = \frac{6}{4} = \frac{3}{2}$, which is less than 6.

Multiplying any negative number by a fraction between 0 and 1, exclusive, gives a product greater than the original number.

Example: $-3 \times \frac{1}{6} = -\frac{3}{6} = -\frac{1}{2}$, which is greater than -3.

The special properties of -1, 0, and 1 make them important numbers to consider when you are picking numbers for Data Sufficiency questions, as well as for the "could be/must be" Problem Solving questions. Also, because numbers between -1 and 1 can make things larger or smaller in different ways than do other numbers, they are good numbers to pick when testing whether one expression always has to be less than or greater than another.

Operations with Positives and Negatives

Here are the rules for operations on positive and negative numbers:

- The product or quotient of two numbers with the *same sign*, either positive or negative, is always positive.
- The product or quotient of two numbers with *different signs* is always negative.
- A positive number raised to any power is always positive.
- A negative number raised to an odd power is a negative.
- A negative number raised to an even power is positive.
- The results of addition and subtraction depend upon the signs and the magnitude of the values involved. For instance, $-3 + 10 = 7$, but $3 + (-10) = -7$.
- Subtracting a negative number is the same as adding a positive number.

Now use the drill to get some practice working with positives and negatives.

Positives and Negatives Drill

Answers follow the drill.

1. Is a negative number cubed positive or negative?
2. If $0 < z < 1$, is $z^3 > z^2$?
3. If $-1 < z < 0$, is $z^3 > z^2$?
4. If $-10 < a < b < c < 0 < d$, is $abcd > 0$?
5. What is the product of 12,345 and its reciprocal?

Positives and Negatives Drill: Answers

1. Negative

2. No

3. Yes

4. No

5. 1

CONCEPT CHECK

- Adding zero to a number x results in _____, and multiplying x by zero results in _____.
- Multiplying or dividing a number x by 1 results in _____, and multiplying or dividing x by -1 results in _____.
- When multiplying or dividing numbers with the same sign, the result is always _____.
- When multiplying or dividing two numbers with different signs, the result is always _____.
- Subtracting a negative number is the same as _____ a positive number.

Example answers are in your book's online resources (**kaptest.com/login**).

Now see how a GMAT expert uses the Kaplan Method to answer a Data Sufficiency question involving the properties of positive and negative numbers.

Is $x - 2y + z$ greater than $x + y - z$?

(1) y is positive.

(2) z is negative.

Step 1: Analyze the Question Stem

This is a Yes/No question. For sufficiency, you need information that establishes that the first expression is either always greater than the second expression or is never greater. Simplify the proposed inequality:

$$
\begin{aligned}
x - 2y + z &> x + y - z \\
-2y + z &> y - z \\
z &> 3y - z \\
2z &> 3y
\end{aligned}
$$

Now you can work with the equivalent question stem, "Is $2z > 3y$?"

Step 2: Evaluate the Statements Using 12TEN

Statement (1) says that y is positive. However, you're given no information about z, so this statement is insufficient. Eliminate **(A)** and **(D)**.

Statement (2) says that z is negative. However, you have no information about y, so this statement is insufficient. Eliminate **(B)**.

Consider the statements together. Because y is positive, $3y$ is positive. Because z is negative, $2z$ is negative. Since $2z$ is negative and $3y$ is positive, $2z$ is less than $3y$. It is not true that $2z > 3y$. You can answer the question with a definite no. The two statements taken together are sufficient, and **(C)** is correct.

Next, you'll find in-format questions involving positives and negatives.

Practice Set: Positives and Negatives

(Answers and explanations are at the end of the chapter.)

25. If $x - y = 8$, which of the following must be true?

    I. Both x and y are positive.

    II. If x is positive, y must be positive.

    III. If x is negative, y must be negative.

    ○ I only

    ○ II only

    ○ III only

    ○ I and II

    ○ II and III

26. If $b \neq 0$ and $-1 < \dfrac{a}{b} < 1$, which of the following CANNOT be true?

    ○ $a + b < 0$

    ○ $(a + b)(a - b) > 0$

    ○ $a - b > 0$

    ○ $(a + b)(a - b) < 0$

    ○ $a + b > 0$

27. Is $\dfrac{s - t}{st} < 0$?

    (1) $t < 0 < s$

    (2) $\dfrac{st}{s - t} < -1$

Factors and Multiples

> **LEARNING OBJECTIVE**
> * Apply number property rules for factors and multiples

The GMAT commonly tests the interrelated concepts of factors and multiples. *Factors* and *multiples* are terms that apply only to integers.

The **factors**, or **divisors**, of a number are the positive integers that divide into that number without leaving a remainder (that is, they leave a remainder of 0). When a number is divided by one of its factors, the result is an integer. Some shortcuts for determining divisibility are covered in further detail in the next section on remainders and primes.

Example: The number 36 has nine positive factors: 1, 2, 3, 4, 6, 9, 12, 18, and 36.

* Each of these factors divides into 36 without leaving a remainder.
* Dividing 36 by any of its factors yields an integer (e.g., $36 \div 9 = 4$).

A **factor table** is a tool for systematically finding all of the factors of a given number by listing its **factor pairs**. Always start with 1 and the number you're analyzing, since they are both factors. Then test successively larger numbers in the left column to determine the factors. This table shows the positive factors of 36.

	36 =	
1	×	36
2	×	18
3	×	12
4	×	9
6	×	6

Note that the next factor after 6 in the left column would be 9, but 9 is already listed in the right column. When factors begin to repeat, you know you've found them all.

The **greatest common factor (GCF)** of two or more integers is the largest integer that divides into each of those numbers without leaving a remainder.

Example: The greatest common factor of 16 and 24 is 8, because 8 is the largest number that is a factor of both 16 and 24.

A **multiple** of an integer is the product of that integer and another integer. An integer is a multiple of all its factors, including itself.

Example: The number 36 is a multiple of 1, 2, 3, 4, 6, 9, 12, 18, and 36.

Example: The positive multiples of 3 include 3, 6, 9, 12, 15, . . . , because all these numbers are divisible by 3. This list is generated by multiplying 3 by successive integers: $3 \times 1, 3 \times 2, 3 \times 3, 3 \times 4, 3 \times 5, . . .$

The **least common multiple (LCM)** of two or more numbers is the smallest integer that is divisible by all of those numbers.

Example: The number 24 is the least common multiple of 6 and 8, since 24 is the smallest number that is divisible by both 6 and 8.

Picking numbers is a useful strategy to apply to questions about factors and multiples. When picking numbers, keep in mind the following:

- Every number is both a factor and a multiple of itself.
- 1 is a factor of every integer.
- Zero is a multiple of every integer but not a factor of any integer except itself. GMAT questions often use restrictive language such as "positive multiples of x" to exclude zero.

Now use the drill to get some practice working with factors and multiples.

Factors and Multiples Drill

Answers follow the drill.

1. List all of the factors of 24 as factor pairs.
2. Find the greatest common factor of 12 and 18.
3. Find the greatest common factor of 6, 15, and 21.
4. Find the least common multiple of 4 and 7.
5. Find the least common multiple of 2, 3, and 10.

Factors and Multiples Drill: Answers

1. $24 = (1 \times 24) = (2 \times 12) = (3 \times 8) = (4 \times 6)$ 4. 28

2. 6   5. 30

3. 3

CONCEPT CHECK

- What is the difference between a factor of 10 and a multiple of 10?

  _____

- How do you determine whether x is a factor of y?

  _____

- What is the greatest common factor of two integers?

  _____

- What is the least common multiple of two integers?

  _____

Example answers are in your book's online resources (**kaptest.com/login**).

Now see how a GMAT expert uses the Kaplan Method to answer a Problem Solving question that involves factors and multiples.

> If p, q, and r are positive integers such that q is a factor of r and r is a multiple of p, which of the following must be an integer?
>
> ○ $\dfrac{p + q}{r}$
>
> ○ $\dfrac{r + p}{q}$
>
> ○ $\dfrac{p}{q}$
>
> ○ $\dfrac{pq}{r}$
>
> ○ $\dfrac{r(p + q)}{pq}$

Step 1: Analyze the Question

The question states that p, q, and r are integers greater than 0 and that q is a factor of r, so you know that r is a multiple of q. The question also states that r is a multiple of p. Thus, r is a multiple of both p and q.

Step 2: State the Task

You need to find the answer choice that must be an integer. The choices are fractions, indicating that the concept of divisibility is key to solving. The information in the question is a bit abstract, but if using the rules of factors and multiples is daunting, picking numbers is an excellent strategy to use.

Step 3: Approach Strategically

If $p = 2$ and $q = 3$, then $r = 6$ meets the criteria stated in the question stem. Substitute these values into the answer choices.

(A) $\dfrac{p + q}{r} = \dfrac{2 + 3}{6} = \dfrac{5}{6}$. Not an integer. Eliminate.

(B) $\dfrac{r + p}{q} = \dfrac{6 + 2}{3} = \dfrac{8}{3}$. Not an integer. Eliminate.

(C) $\dfrac{p}{q} = \dfrac{2}{3}$. Not an integer. Eliminate.

(D) $\dfrac{pq}{r} = \dfrac{2(3)}{6} = 1$. An integer. Possibly correct.

(E) $\dfrac{r(p + q)}{pq} = \dfrac{6(2 + 3)}{2(3)} = \dfrac{6(5)}{6} = 5$. An integer, so possibly correct.

Since both **(D)** and **(E)** yielded an integer with the numbers you initially picked, check these answers again by changing at least one of the three numbers. Say r is 12 rather than 6; 12 is a multiple of both 2 and 3 (p and q) so you can leave those values the same.

(D) $\dfrac{pq}{r} = \dfrac{2(3)}{12} = \dfrac{1}{2}$. Not an integer. Eliminate. Choice **(E)** must be correct.

Step 4: Confirm Your Answer

(E) $\dfrac{r(p + q)}{pq} = \dfrac{12(2 + 3)}{2(3)} = \dfrac{12(5)}{6} = 10$. Again, an integer.

Next, you'll find some in-format questions involving factors and multiples.

Practice Set: Factors and Multiples

(Answers and explanations are at the end of the chapter.)

28. If a certain number is divisible by 18 and 24, it must also be divisible by which of the following?

    ○ 30
    ○ 36
    ○ 72
    ○ 216
    ○ 432

29. What is the greatest positive integer x such that 9^{6x} is a factor of 81^{10+x}?

    ○ 2
    ○ 4
    ○ 5
    ○ 6
    ○ 15

30. How many positive integers less than 70 are multiples of either 3 or 4 but not both?

    ○ 17
    ○ 18
    ○ 23
    ○ 30
    ○ 35

31. If a and b are positive integers, is $3a^2b$ divisible by 60?

    (1) a is divisible by 10.

    (2) b is divisible by 18.

32. If integers a and b are distinct factors of 30, which of the following CANNOT be a factor of 30?

    I. $ab + b^2$

    II. $(a + b)^2$

    III. $a + b$

    ○   I only

    ○   II only

    ○   III only

    ○   I and II only

    ○   I, II, and III

Remainders and Primes

> **LEARNING OBJECTIVE**
>
> • Apply number property rules for remainders and primes

As discussed in the previous lesson, factors and multiples concern whether a number is divisible by another number, thus leaving no remainder. You can quickly determine whether a given number is a multiple of 2, 3, 4, 5, 6, 7, 8, 9, or 10.

Divisibility Rules

A number is divisible by **2** if its units digit is even.

Example: 138 is divisible by 2 because 8 is even.

Example: 177 is not divisible by 2 because 7 is not even.

A number is divisible by **3** if the sum of its digits is divisible by 3.

Example: 4,317 is divisible by 3 because $4 + 3 + 1 + 7 = 15$ and 15 is divisible by 3.

Example: 32,863 is not divisible by 3 because $3 + 2 + 8 + 6 + 3 = 22$ and 22 is not divisible by 3.

A number is divisible by **4** if its last two digits compose a two-digit number that is itself divisible by 4. (Here's another test: divide the number by 2; if the result is even—also divisible by 2—the number must be divisible by 4.)

Example: 1,732 is divisible by 4 because 32 is divisible by 4.

Example: 1,246 is not divisible by 4 because 46 is not divisible by 4.

A number is divisible by **5** if its units digit is either a 5 or a 0.

Example: 21,185 is divisible by 5.

Example: 96,780 is divisible by 5.

A number is divisible by **6** if the sum of its digits is divisible by 3 and it is an even number.

Example: 1,146 is divisible by 6 because $1 + 1 + 4 + 6 = 12$, which is divisible by 3, and 1,146 is an even number.

A number is divisible by **7** if the difference between its units digit multiplied by 2 and the number composed of the remaining digits is a multiple of 7.

Example: 147 is divisible by 7 because $14 - 7(2) = 0$, which is divisible by 7.

Example: 682 is not divisible by 7 because $68 - 2(2) = 64$, which is not divisible by 7.

A number is divisible by **8** if its last three digits compose a three-digit number that is itself divisible by 8. (Here's another test: if you divide the number by 2 and divide the result by 2 again, and that result is even, the original number is divisible by 8.)

Example: 76,848 is divisible by 8 because 848 is divisible by 8.

Example: 65,102 is not divisible by 8 because 102 is not divisible by 8.

A number is divisible by **9** if the sum of its digits is divisible by 9.

Example: 16,956 is divisible by 9 because $1 + 6 + 9 + 5 + 6 = 27$, and 27 is divisible by 9.

Example: 4,317 is not divisible by 9 because $4 + 3 + 1 + 7 = 15$, and 15 is not divisible by 9.

A number is divisible by **10** if its units digit is zero.

Example: 67,890 is divisible by 10.

Remainders

A **remainder** is what is left over when an integer is divided by another integer that is not one of its factors. A remainder is always smaller than the number by which you are dividing.

Example: Dividing 9 by 4 yields 2 with a remainder of 1, because two 4s "fit" within 9 ($2 \times 4 = 8$) with 1—the remainder—left over.

Example: Dividing 26 by 6 yields 4 with a remainder of 2, because $6 \times 4 = 24$, leaving 2 remaining.

The GMAT may describe a number like this: "n is a number that, when divided by 7, has a remainder of 2." Usually, the most efficient way to solve a question with such language is to pick a small permissible value for n. In this example, $n = 9$ would be a good choice (because $9 \div 7 = 1$ with a remainder of 2).

Prime Numbers and Prime Factorization

A **prime number** is a positive integer greater than 1 that has only two positive factors, 1 and itself. Note that 1 is not prime; 2 is the smallest prime number and the only even prime. (Every other positive even number has 2 as a factor and, therefore, is not prime.)

Memorizing the prime numbers up to 50 is helpful for the GMAT. They are 2, 3, 5, 7, 11, 13, 17, 19, 23, 29, 31, 37, 41, 43, and 47.

The **prime factorization** of a number is the expression of the number as the product of its prime factors. The easiest way to determine a number's prime factorization is to figure out a pair of factors of the number and then determine their factors, continuing the process until you're left with only prime numbers. No matter which pair of factors you start with, you will end up with the same prime factorization.

Example: Find the prime factorization of 1,050.

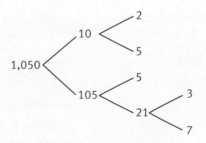

Thus, the prime factorization of 1,050 is $2 \times 3 \times 5^2 \times 7$.

The GMAT asks about not only prime factors but also about *distinct* prime factors. Distinct simply means "different." So $1{,}050 = 2 \times 3 \times 5 \times 5 \times 7$, which is five prime factors but only four distinct ones (2, 3, 5, and 7).

Every factor of a number can be expressed as the product of a subset of that number's prime factors.

Example: The prime factors of 36 are 2, 2, 3, and 3. One factor of 36 is 12, which is equal to $2 \times 2 \times 3$. There are no factors of 36 that have, for example, a prime factor of 5 or three prime factors of 2.

Prime factorization is one of the most valuable tools for the GMAT Quantitative section. Any question about multiples or factors is really, at its heart, a question about prime factors. Quickly jotting down the prime factorizations of the numbers in such questions can provide the key to the solution.

Prime factorization is often the key to dealing with scary-looking exponents as well. If a GMAT question gives you 35^8, rewriting it as $(5 \times 7)^8 = 5^8 \times 7^8$ and understanding that this is really $(5 \times 5 \times 5 \times 5 \times 5 \times 5 \times 5 \times 5) \times (7 \times 7 \times 7 \times 7 \times 7 \times 7 \times 7 \times 7)$ will almost certainly be helpful.

Now use the drill to get some practice working with remainders and primes.

Remainders and Primes Drill

Answers follow the drill.

1. Is 6,438 is divisible by 3?
2. Is 742 is divisible by 4?
3. Is 504 is divisible by 7?
4. Find the remainder when 16 is divided by 7.
5. Find the remainder when 34 is divided by 6.
6. If n is a number that, when divided by 9, has a reminder of 3, what are some small possible values of n?
7. Find the prime factorization of 48.
8. Find the prime factorization of 880.
9. Find the distinct prime factors of 144.
10. Find the fully expanded prime factorization of 42^5.

Remainders and Primes Drill: Answers

1. Yes, because $6 + 4 + 3 + 8 = 21$, which is divisible by 3.
2. No, because 42 is not divisible by 4.
3. Yes, because $50 - (2 \times 4) = 42$, which is divisible by 7.
4. 2
5. 4

6. 3, because $0 \times 9 = 0$ and $0 + 3 = 3$; 12, because $1 \times 9 = 9$ and $9 + 3 = 12$.
7. $2 \times 2 \times 2 \times 2 \times 3 = 2^4 \times 3$
8. $2 \times 2 \times 2 \times 2 \times 5 \times 11 = 2^4 \times 5 \times 11$
9. $144 = 2 \times 2 \times 2 \times 2 \times 3 \times 3$, so the distinct prime factors are 2 and 3.
10. $42^5 = 2^5 \times 3^5 \times 7^5 = (2 \times 2 \times 2 \times 2 \times 2)(3 \times 3 \times 3 \times 3 \times 3)(7 \times 7 \times 7 \times 7 \times 7)$

CONCEPT CHECK

- How do you find the remainder when one number is divided by another number?

  _____

- How do you find the prime factorization of a number?

  _____

- What is the difference between the prime factors and the distinct prime factors of a number?

  _____

- How might you restate a large number raised to an exponent?

  _____

Example answers are in your book's online resources (**kaptest.com/login**).

Now see how a GMAT expert uses the Kaplan Method to answer a Problem Solving question dealing with remainders and primes.

If a and b are prime numbers, which of the following CANNOT be the value of ab?

- ◯ 9
- ◯ 14
- ◯ 21
- ◯ 23
- ◯ 25

Step 1: Analyze the Question

Note that the question doesn't specify that a and b are distinct, so they could be the same or different prime numbers. The correct choice will be the integer that *can't* be the product of a and b, no matter which prime numbers a and b are.

Step 2: State the Task

Since a and b are prime numbers, the question is really asking for the one choice that cannot be the product of just two prime numbers. One approach is to pick numbers that are permissible and systematically apply the numbers to the answer choices.

Step 3: Approach Strategically

Check each choice to see whether it is the product of two prime numbers and eliminate the choices that are.

(A) The product is 9, which can be created by multiplying 3×3. Because 3 is a prime number, 9 is the product of two primes. Eliminate.

(B) The product is 14, which can be created by multiplying 2×7. Because these are both prime, 14 is the product of two primes. Eliminate.

(C) The product is 21, which can be created by multiplying 3×7. Because these are both prime, 21 is the product of two primes. Eliminate.

(D) The number 23 is prime; its only factors are 1 and 23. Because 1 is not a prime number, 23 cannot be the product of two prime numbers. Therefore, **(D)** is correct.

Step 4: Confirm Your Answer

Check whether remaining choice is the product of two primes.

(E) The product is 25, which can be created by multiplying 5×5. Because 5 is a prime number, 25 is the product of two primes. Eliminate.

Next, you'll find some in-format questions involving remainders and primes.

Practice Set: Remainders and Primes

(Answers and explanations are at the end of the chapter.)

33. If n is an integer such that $12 \leq n \leq 24$, is n a prime number?

    (1)   The remainder when n is divided by 4 is 1.

    (2)   The remainder when n is divided by 6 is 1.

34. If $x = 12$, $y = 35$, and $x^2y^2 = 21 \times 28 \times 30 \times z$, what is the value of z?

    ○   10

    ○   12

    ○   15

    ○   21

    ○   30

35. If $a = 5m + 2$ and $b = 5n + 13$, and m and n are positive integers, what is the remainder when $a + b$ is divided by 5?

    ○   0

    ○   1

    ○   2

    ○   3

    ○   4

Answers and Explanations

Practice Set: Fractions and Decimals

1. (B)

This is a Yes/No question. It is given that x and y are positive, so each side of the inequality can be multiplied or divided by x or y without having to flip the inequality sign. The fractions can be eliminated by multiplying both sides by y^2:

$$\frac{x^2}{y}(y^2) > \frac{x}{y^2}(y^2)$$
$$x^2 y > x$$

This can then be simplified further by dividing both sides by x:

$$\frac{x^2 y}{x} > \frac{x}{x}$$
$$xy > 1$$

Simplified this way, the question can be interpreted as asking whether the product of x and y is greater than 1.

Statement (1) indicates that x divided by y is greater than 1. As y is positive, you can multiply both sides of this statement by y to get rid of the fraction:

$$\frac{x}{y}(y) > 1(y)$$
$$x > y$$

However, knowing that x is greater than y does not confirm that the product xy is greater than 1. It's possible that x is 2 and y is 1, resulting in a product of 2. However, it's also possible that x is 2 and y is 0.1, resulting in a product of 0.2. This statement is insufficient, so eliminate **(A)** and **(D)**.

Statement (2) directly confirms that the product of x and y is greater than 1. Thus, this statement alone is sufficient. Eliminate **(C)** and **(E)**. **(B)** is correct.

2. (D)

This Yes/No question asks whether $8a$ is less than $3b$, and it states that both a and b are positive. Sufficiency will require enough information to determine the relative values of a and b.

Statement (1) specifies that $\frac{a}{b}$ is less than 0.374; if you've memorized the commonplace fractions as decimal values, you might recognize that this value is just less than 0.375, which is equal to $\frac{3}{8}$. Since $\frac{a}{b} < 0.374$, it must be less than $\frac{3}{8}$. Substitute $\frac{3}{8}$ for 0.374 to get the expression $\frac{a}{b} < \frac{3}{8}$. Next, cross multiply to get $8a < 3b$. (Note that both variables are positive, so this will not change the direction of the inequality sign.) This answers the question, so the statement is sufficient. Eliminate **(B)**, **(C)**, and **(E)**.

Statement (2) indicates that b is greater than $2.671a$; 2.671 is just greater than $2.6\overline{6}$, which is $2\frac{2}{3} = \frac{8}{3}$. If b is greater than $2.671a$, it must be greater than the lesser value $2.6\overline{6}a$. Thus, the inequality can be safely approximated as $b > \frac{8}{3}a$, which can be rewritten as $3b > 8a$. This statement answers the question, so it is also sufficient. Therefore, **(D)** is correct.

3. (D)

This question asks you to find the answer choice that's equivalent to the equation in the question stem. Begin by simplifying the first term in the equation:

$$\frac{27}{0.75} = \frac{27}{\frac{3}{4}} = 27 \times \frac{4}{3} = 36$$

Now the second term:

$$\frac{0.025}{\frac{1}{80}} = 0.025 \times \frac{80}{1} = 0.25 \times \frac{8}{1} = \frac{1}{4} \times \frac{8}{1} = 2$$

So the equation simplifies to the following:

$$36 + 2 = 38 = 19a$$
$$a = 2$$

Now test the answer choices by plugging in 2 for a to see whether the equation is valid. Remember that to divide by a fraction, you multiply by its reciprocal.

(A) $9 \times 4 - 2 \neq 40$. Eliminate.

(B) $\frac{54}{2} + \frac{1}{4} \times 48 = 27 + 12 \neq 38$. Eliminate.

(C) $27 \times \frac{4}{3} + 2.5 \times 8 = 36 + 20 \neq 38$. Eliminate.

(D) $\frac{4}{3}(27) + 2 = 38$. This expression is equivalent, so **(D)** is correct.

To confirm your answer, check **(E)**: $1.9(2) \times 20 = 3.8 \times 20 = 76 \neq 19$. Eliminate.

4.   (D)

This question asks you to identify the one answer choice that is NOT equivalent to the equation in the question stem. Begin by simplifying the equation in the question stem. Subtract $\frac{10}{3}$ from both sides of the equation to get $\frac{5a}{2b} = \frac{5}{3}$. Next, cross multiply to get $15a = 10b$. Finally, divide both sides by 5 to get $3a = 2b$.

Now simplify each answer choice to see if it matches the expression you derived from the question stem. The one that can't be made to match will be the correct choice.

(A) $3a = 2b$ exactly matches what you found in the stem, so you can eliminate it.

(B): $5a - 2b = \frac{4b}{3} \rightarrow 3(5a - 2b) = 4b \rightarrow 15a - 6b = 4b \rightarrow 15a = 10b \rightarrow 3a = 2b$; this matches, so eliminate it.

(C): $\frac{5a}{2b} + 1 = \frac{8}{3} \rightarrow \frac{5a}{2b} = \frac{8}{3} - 1 \rightarrow \frac{8}{3} - \frac{3}{3} = \frac{5}{3} \rightarrow \frac{5a}{2b} = \frac{5}{3}$ $\rightarrow 15a = 10b \rightarrow 3a = 2b$; eliminate.

(D): $3a + 2b - 1 = 2a + 3b \rightarrow a - b = 1$. This doesn't work, so **(D)** is correct.

(E): $\frac{a}{2b} = \frac{1}{3} \rightarrow 3a = 2b$; eliminate.

Practice Set: Percents

5.   (B)

The question asks for the percentage of gravel in a final concrete mixture composed of four different batches that contain different percentages of gravel. Batch A weighs 1,000 pounds. The weights of the other batches are given in relative terms. Batch B is twice the weight of batch A, or 2,000 kilograms. Batch C weighs 25% less than batch B, so batch C is $(0.75 \times 2000) = 1,500$ kilograms. Batch D is half the weight of batch A, or 500 kilograms.

Calculate the total weight of gravel and the total weight of the complete mixture. Then divide the weight of gravel by that total weight and convert to a percent. Batch A, which weighs 1,000 kilograms (kg), contains 30% gravel, so that is $1,000 \times 0.30 = 300$ kg. Batch B contains $2,000 \times 0.40 = 800$ kg of gravel. The weight of the gravel in batch C is $1,500 \times 0.50 = 750$ kg, and the weight of the gravel in batch D is $500 \times 0.60 = 300$ kg.

The total weight of gravel is $300 + 800 + 750 + 300 = 2,150$ kg, and the weight of the complete mixture is $1,000 + 2,000 + 1,500 + 500 = 5,000$ kg. Therefore, the percentage of gravel is $\frac{2,150}{5,000} \times 100\% = 43\%$. One efficient way to do the division in your head is to multiply top and bottom by 2 to get $\frac{4,300}{10,000}$. Then move the decimal to the left by two spaces to put the fraction over 100: $\frac{43}{100} = 43\%$. **(B)** is correct.

6.   (C)

This question stem contains information about two periods of sales, one as a percent of a total and the other as a fraction of the remaining total. You are asked to calculate the percent decrease in sales from one quarter to the next. To determine this value, you need the number of crafts sold in each quarter.

Translating the first sentence (first quarter), you have $36\% \times 75$ crafts $= 0.36 \times 75$. This arithmetic looks time-consuming. However, 0.75×36 produces the same result, and 0.75 is equal to three-fourths. So there were $\frac{3}{\cancel{4}^{1}} \times \cancel{36}^{9} = 27$ crafts sold.

Next, she sold one-fourth of the remaining crafts. The number of crafts remaining is $75 - 27 = 48$. Therefore, she sold $\frac{1}{\cancel{4}^1} \times \cancel{48}^{12} = 12$.

The percent change formula is this:

$$\text{Percent change} = \frac{\text{New value} - \text{Original value}}{\text{Original value}} \times 100\%$$

Plug in the values for the change:

$$\frac{12 - 27}{27} \times 100\% = \frac{-15}{27} \times 100\% = \frac{-5}{9} \times 100\% =$$

$$\frac{-500\%}{9} = -55\frac{5}{9}\%$$

The negative sign indicates a decrease, so **(C)** is correct.

Make sure you translated each part of the scenario correctly, especially the sentence about the second quarter sales, which describes one-fourth of the *remaining* crafts. Then double-check your work, especially the setup of the percent change calculation.

7. (C)

This is a Value question that asks how many students will *not* be able to visit their preferred museum. This circle graph displays the results of the student survey. Since there are 120 students, you could use the percents in the graph to calculate the number of students who prefer the science museum ($120 \times 0.60 = 72$), the number of students who prefer the art museum ($120 \times 0.30 = 36$), and the number of students who prefer neither museum ($120 \times 0.10 = 12$). With "will attempt to," this question implies that there is some limitation on the number of students who can attend each museum. You can ignore the students who have no preference, as they are irrelevant to this question. The question is asking for the number who expressed a preference for the art museum who did not get to visit that museum plus the number who expressed a preference for the science museum who did not get to visit that museum.

Statement (1) says that no more than 55 students can visit the science museum. Comparing 55 to the number of students who prefer the science museum, 72, means that 17 of those students with this preference won't get their first choice. However, this statement alone provides no information about how many students who want to visit the art museum will be denied the opportunity to attend that museum. Eliminate **(A)** and **(D)**.

Statement (2) says that the limitation for the art museum is 50. Since only 36 students expressed a preference for this museum, none of them would be denied the opportunity. By itself, however, this statement provides no information about the students who want to visit the science museum, so eliminate **(B)**.

Together, the statements allow calculation of the number of students who will not get to attend their preferred museum, whichever it is. The total number of students who did not get to visit their preferred museum is the 17 who couldn't go to the science museum. Thus, **(C)** is correct.

8. (B)

You are given the percentage of games a team has won for the first 80 games and the number of games it has yet to play (82). You are asked to calculate how many more games the team needs to win to end up with a 50% win record. Therefore, you need to calculate the total number of games that will be played, then the number of those that need to be won for a 50% record. Then calculate how many games have already been won and subtract that from the total number of wins needed.

First, add the 80 games that have already been played to the number of remaining games to get the total games: $80 + 82 = 162$. To win 50% of the games, the team would need to win half of these, or 81.

Calculate how many games the team has already won: $45\% \times 80$. You can do this arithmetic a few different ways. Here's one way: since 45% can be expressed as $\frac{45}{100} = \frac{9}{20}$, the calculation can be written as $\frac{9}{\cancel{20}^1} \times \cancel{80}^4 = 9 \times 4 = 36$. Here's another way. First, 50% of 80 is half of 80, or 40. Then, 5% of 80 is half of 10% of 80, which is 8; therefore, 5% of 80 is 4. Finally, 45% of 80 is $40 - 4 = 36$. However, you do the calculation, the team has already won 36 games, and it still needs to win is $81 - 36 = 45$. Choice **(B)** is correct.

Check that your answer is logical: the team would need more than 40 additional wins to make up for the fact that it won less than 50% of its first 80 games. Note that 36 is offered as a choice for those who stop after solving for the number of games already won.

Practice Set: Exponents

9. (C)

This question asks for the *approximate* total number of turns that a machine has gone through after 30 maintenance cycles. The question states that after the machine's wheel assembly turns 4.09×10^6 times, the machine needs maintenance.

Note that the answer choices are given in scientific notation. Since the question only asks for an approximation, estimate $30 \times 4.09 \times 10^6$ as $30 \times 4 \times 10^6$ or 120×10^6. Next, translate 120 into scientific notation: 1.2×10^2.

Now plug in 1.2×10^2 for 120 and simplify:

$$1.2 \times 10^2 \times 10^6 = 1.2 \times 10^8$$

Therefore, (C) is correct.

10. (C)

You need to solve for x in an equation with exponents in the numerator and denominator of a fraction. The bases in the numerator and denominator are not the same, but one of the bases, 8, is equal to the other one, 2, raised to the exponent 3.

Start by multiplying both sides of the equation by the denominator to eliminate the fraction:

$2^{5x} = (8^{2x-2}) \times 8 = (8^{2x-2})(8^1) = 8^{2x-2+1} = 8^{2x-1}$.

Now the equation is $2^{5x} = 8^{2x-1}$. The two bases are different, so make them the same to solve for x. Since $8 = 2^3$, you can substitute 2^3 for 8 in the equation: $2^{5x} = (2^3)^{2x-1}$. Further simplifying yields $2^{5x} = 2^{6x-3}$.

When exponential expressions with the same base have equal values (and the base is not 1, 0, or -1), the exponents must also have equal values. Therefore, $5x = 6x - 3$, so $x = 3$. (C) is correct.

11. (D)

The question asks for the value of $9^x + 3^{2x+1}$ and states that x is a positive integer. Recall that you can only add or subtract numbers with exponents when both the bases and the exponents are the same.

To solve this question algebraically, first convert both powers to a common base. Since $9 = 3^2$, the expression becomes $(3^2)x + 3^{2x+1}$, which further simplifies to $3^{2x} + 3^{2x+1}$. Now consider that 3^{2x+1} can be restated as $(3^{2x})(3^1)$, or $3^{2x} \times 3$. Now the expression reads $3^2x + (3 \times 3^{2x})$, so you have 4 instances of 3^{2x}, which is the same as $4(3^{2x})$. (D) is correct.

You could also solve this question by picking numbers. Try $x = 1$. Then $9^x + 3^{2x+1} = 9^1 + 3^{2+1} = 9 + 27 = 36$. Now substitute 1 for x into each answer choice. Eliminate any choice that does not equal 36 when $x = 1$. You'll find that only (D) equals 36.

12. (C)

This Value question asks for the value of the integer n. A glance at the statements reveals that they test the behavior of exponents.

Statement (1) tells you that $n = n^4$. One possible value for n is 1, since $1 = 1^4$. However, there is one other number, 0, that equals its own fourth power. Statement (1) is insufficient. Eliminate (A) and (D).

Statement (2) tells you only that $1^n \neq n$. No matter what exponent 1 is raised to, the result will remain 1. For example, $1^2 = 1$, as do 1^3 and 1^4. So the only value of n that Statement (2) excludes is $n = 1$. Alone, this statement is insufficient. Eliminate (B) and proceed to combine the statements.

Statement (1) permits only $n = 1$ and $n = 0$. Statement (2) removes $n = 1$ from consideration, leaving $n = 0$ as the only possibility. (C) is correct.

Practice Set: Radicals

13. (D)

The question asks for the value of x and states both that $A = 3^x$ and $A^2 = \left(\sqrt[3]{27}\right)^4$. If $A = 3^x$, then $A^2 = (3^x)^2 = 3^{2x}$. Substitute this value for A^2 into the second equation to get $3^{2x} = \left(\sqrt[3]{27}\right)^4$.

Because $3^3 = 27$, you can substitute 3^3 for that value in the radical and simplify to $3^{2x} = \left(\sqrt[3]{3^3}\right)^4 = 3^4$. Because the bases are the same (and not 1, 0, or -1), you can set the exponents equal and solve: $2x = 4$ and $x = 2$. This matches (D).

You could also use radical sign rules, which tell you that $\sqrt[3]{27}^4 = 27^{\frac{4}{3}}$. Then substitute 3^3 for 27 to make this $(3^3)^{\frac{4}{3}}$. When you raise a power to a power, multiply the exponents: $3 \times \frac{4}{3} = 4$, so the right side of your equation is 3^4. Then, again, set $2x$ equal to 4 and solve.

Backsolving is a great way to confirm your choice. Plug in 2 for x to find that $A = 9$ and therefore $A^2 = 81$. This is indeed equal to 3 (the cube root of 27) to the fourth power.

14. (B)

This Yes/No question states that r is positive, and it asks whether $\sqrt{r}$ is an integer. For $\sqrt{r}$ to be an integer, r must be a perfect square.

Statement (1) says that r^2 is an integer. If $r = 4$, then $r^2 = 4^2 = 16$ is an integer. In this case, $\sqrt{r} = \sqrt{4} = 2$ is an integer, so the answer to the question would be yes. But if $r = 5$, then $r^2 = 5^2 = 25$, which is an integer, but $\sqrt{r} = \sqrt{5}$ is not an integer, and the answer to the question would be no. Because different answers to the question are possible, this statement is insufficient. Eliminate (A) and (D).

Statement (2) says that $r = m^2$, where m is an integer. So, $\sqrt{r} = \sqrt{m^2} = |m|$. Thus, $\sqrt{r}$ must always be an integer. Statement (2) alone is sufficient, so (B) is correct.

15. (C)

The question gives a complicated radical expression with numbers but no variables and asks which choice is equivalent. Use the rules of radicals to simplify the given expression. Subtraction under the radical sign cannot be "split up" under separate radical signs, so the first step is to combine the two terms into one fraction using a common denominator.

$$\sqrt{36 - \frac{3 \times 23}{4}} = \sqrt{\frac{144}{4} - \frac{69}{4}} = \sqrt{\frac{75}{4}}$$

Since all that is left under the radical sign is multiplication and division, you can now split up the factors to facilitate simplification.

$$\sqrt{\frac{75}{4}} = \frac{\sqrt{25 \times 3}}{\sqrt{4}}$$

$$= \frac{\sqrt{25} \times \sqrt{3}}{\sqrt{4}}$$

$$= \frac{5\sqrt{3}}{2}$$

So (C) is correct.

Check your application of the rules for radicals and your arithmetic. Notice that (A) is the answer that awaits those who forget that you cannot split up subtraction and addition under the radical sign.

Practice Set: Interest Rates

16. (E)

The question asks you to identify the expression that represents the original amount of an investment before the application of compound interest. Note that the interest is not annual but is compounded every 3 months. Since there are 12 months per year, the interest compounds 4 times per year. This occurs over a period of 5 years. That's 20 compounding events.

The compound interest formula is $T = P(1 + r)^t$, where P is the initial principle, r is the rate of interest expressed as a decimal, and t is the number of time periods (i.e., the number of compounding events).

The interest rate in this case is 1.5%, so r is 0.015. The number of time periods is 20, so t is 20.

$$T = P(1.015)^{20}$$

The question asks for the initial amount, or P, so rearrange the formula to isolate P:

$$P = \frac{T}{(1.015)^{20}}$$

(E) is correct.

17. (A)

The question asks for the amount of money received when a CD was redeemed, expressed as an arithmetic expression. It states that a $1,000 initial investment paid 4% annual interest for the first 4 years. That interest compounded quarterly, which is to say, it was 1% compounded 4 times a year. After the first 4 years, the investment earned 2% simple annual interest for an additional 2 years.

The formula for compound interest is Principal $\times (1 + r)^t$, where r is the interest rate per time period expressed as a decimal and t is the number of time periods. Since this CD had a 4% annual interest rate compounded 4 times a year over 4 years, $r = \frac{1}{4} \times 0.04 = 0.01$. Because the compounding occurred 4 times per year for 4 years, $t = 4 \times 4 = 16$. Thus, the value of the CD at the end of 4 years was $1,000 \times (1.01)^{16}$.

For the next 2 years, this amount earned simple interest. The formula for simple interest is Principal $\times (1 + rt)$. In this case, the interest rate was 2%, so $r = 0.02$, and it accrued for 2 years, so $t = 2$. So Principal $\times (1 + 0.02(2))$ = Principal $\times 1.04$. Thus, the total value after 6 years was $\$1,000 \times (1.01)^{16} \times 1.04$. **(A)** is correct.

You can confirm your answer, or solve strategically, by applying some logic. The value 1,000 is common to all choices, so ignore it. On their face, **(C)** and **(D)** ignore the second phase of the investment's return. Of the remaining choices, only **(A)** correctly represents the simple interest earned toward the second phase of the investment without an exponent.

18. (B)

The question asks for the approximate value of a $40,000 initial investment after 42 years. The question also gives the doubling rate of $\frac{70}{p}$, where p is the percent interest rate, compounded annually. In this case, that is 5%. Since the question provides a formula to use, avail yourself of it—don't bother reaching for the compound interest formula.

Plug 5 in for p to figure out the number of years it will take the investment to double: $\frac{70}{5} = 14$ years. Now divide 42 years by 14 years to determine the number of times the investment will double: $\frac{42}{14} = 3$ doubling periods.

Thus, the final value of the investment will be $\$40,000 \times 2 \times 2 \times 2 = \$40,000 \times 8 = \$320,000$; **(B)** is correct.

Practice Set: Integers and Non-Integers

19. (D)

This Value question gives an equation with three variables, each defined as a positive integer, and asks for the value of one of the variables. Since each variable is a positive integer, dq is a positive integer. Since $dq + r = 3$, only two possibilities exist. If $dq = 1$, $r = 2$. In this case, both d and q must equal 1. If $dq = 2$, $r = 1$. Here, either $d = 1$ and $q = 2$, or $d = 2$ and $q = 1$. So far, you have enough information to determine that d equals either 1 or 2. A statement that provides enough information to limit d to just one of those two values would be sufficient.

Statement (1) essentially says that $\frac{r}{d}$ is a fraction that is less than $\frac{2}{3}$. For this to be true, r must be less than d, so r would equal 1 and d would equal 2. This statement is sufficient, so eliminate **(B)**, **(C)**, and **(E)**.

Statement (2) says that $\frac{q}{r}$ is an integer that is less than 2. Because both q and r are integers, this means that $\frac{q}{r} = 1$, which can be rewritten as $q = r$. If $q = r = 1$, then $d = 2$. This statement is also sufficient, so **(D)** is correct.

20. (B)

This Yes/No question states that f and g are positive integers and asks whether the fraction $\frac{f+g}{f}$ is an integer. When an integer is divided by an integer, the numerator must be a multiple of the denominator for the result to be an integer.

Statement (1) informs you that $g = 5f - 4$. Substitute that into $\frac{f+g}{f}$ and simplify: $\frac{f + 5f - 4}{f} = \frac{6f - 4}{f} = 6 - \frac{4}{f}$. This is an integer only if 4 is a multiple of f. There is not enough information to determine whether that is true, so eliminate **(A)** and **(D)**.

Statement (2), $f = \frac{1}{3}g$, can be rearranged as $3f = g$. Substitute that into $\frac{f+g}{f}$ to get $\frac{f + 3f}{f} = \frac{4f}{f} = 4$. This is, indeed, an integer, so this statement is sufficient and **(B)** is correct.

21. (A)

This is a Yes/No question about a positive integer n. You need to determine whether $\dfrac{\sqrt{n}}{3}$ is an integer. This fraction is an integer if $\sqrt{n}$ is a multiple of 3. That is the case if n is equal to 9 times any perfect square. That's because $\sqrt{9} = 3$ and the square root of the perfect square would be another integer. The $\sqrt{9}$ would cancel with the 3 in the denominator, leaving the other integer in the numerator. To see this, you can pick numbers:

If $n = 9 \times 1$, then $\dfrac{\sqrt{n}}{3} = \dfrac{\sqrt{9 \times 1}}{3} =$

$\dfrac{\sqrt{9}\,\sqrt{1}}{3} = \dfrac{3 \times 1}{3} = 1.$

If $n = 9 \times 4 = 36$, then $\dfrac{\sqrt{n}}{3} = \dfrac{\sqrt{9 \times 4}}{3} =$

$\dfrac{\sqrt{9}\,\sqrt{4}}{3} = \dfrac{3 \times 2}{3} = 2.$

However, if n is not the product of 9 and a perfect square, the answer to the question is no. For example, if $n = 3$, $\dfrac{\sqrt{n}}{3} = \dfrac{\sqrt{3}}{3}$, which is not an integer.

You can either use logic along with the number property rules or pick numbers to evaluate the statements.

Statement (1) tells you that $\sqrt{\dfrac{n}{3}}$ is an integer. This means that $n = 3x$, where x is some unknown integer that is a perfect square. If none of the factors of x is 3, then there is no way that n can be 9 times a perfect square, so the answer would be no. If, on the other hand, x *does* have a factor of 3, because x is a perfect square, it must have an *even* number of factors of 3. Consequently, n, which is $3x$, would have an *odd* number of factors of 3 and its square root would not even be an integer, let alone an integer that is divisible by 3. Statement (1) is sufficient to answer the question with a no. Eliminate **(B)**, **(C)**, and **(E)**.

As an alternative to the above solution, you could plug in some numbers for n into $\sqrt{\dfrac{n}{3}}$. Use $9 \times 1 = 9$, $9 \times 4 = 36$, and $9 \times 9 = 81$, since those values would make $\dfrac{\sqrt{n}}{3}$ an integer and answer the question with a yes. When substituted for n in $\sqrt{\dfrac{n}{3}}$, none of these values produces an integer, meaning none are valid for Statement (1). Thus, the answer to the question must be no, and this statement is sufficient.

Statement (2) tells you that $\sqrt{14n}$ is not an integer. For any value of n that is not a multiple of 14, that radical is not an integer. However, the question asks whether $\dfrac{\sqrt{n}}{3}$ is an integer. So n could be 9 and $\dfrac{\sqrt{n}}{3}$ would be an integer. On the other hand, there are a myriad of values for which neither $\dfrac{\sqrt{n}}{3}$ nor $\sqrt{14n}$ is an integer. Eliminate **(D)**. Statement (1) alone is sufficient, and the correct choice is **(A)**.

Practice Set: Odds and Evens

22. (C)

This Value question asks how many of the integers in set S are even, given that the sum of all five integers in set S is odd. If the sum of the integers is odd, there has to be an odd number of odd integers in the set. Therefore, set S must contain either 1, 3, or 5 odd integers, which means 4, 2, or 0 even ones.

Statement (1) says that the sum of A and B is odd. When two integers sum to an odd number, one must be even and the other odd. Therefore, there must be 2 or 4 even integers in the set. Since $A + B$ is odd, and the sum of all the integers in the set is odd, the sum of C, D, and E must be even. That could mean that 1 of these 3 is even for a total of 2 even values, or it could mean that all 3 are even, for a total of 4 even values. Thus, Statement (1) is insufficient. Eliminate **(A)** and **(D)**.

Statement (2) says that the product of B, C, and D is odd. An odd product can have only odd factors, so B, C, and D must each be odd. However, this statement says nothing about A or E, which could both be even, in which case 2 of the numbers would be even, or both be odd, which would mean that none of the integers in the set are even. Therefore, this statement is insufficient, and you can eliminate **(B)**.

Now take the statements together. From Statement (1), there must be either 2 or 4 even integers in set S. From Statement (2), you know that there are 0 or 2 even values. Thus, the two statements together show that there must be exactly 2 even integers in set S. **(C)** is correct.

23. (B)

In this Yes/No question, you are told that a is an odd integer and asked whether b, another integer, is even. Therefore, sufficiency means showing that b is either definitely even or definitely odd.

Statement (1) provides an expression that's even. Evaluate it one piece at a time. Since a is odd, a^3 must also be odd (because odd $\times$ odd = odd); therefore, $(a^3 + 1)$ must be even (because odd + odd = even). Since an even times any other integer will always be even, b could be either even or odd and the statement would still hold true. Therefore, Statement (1) is insufficient. Eliminate (A) and (D).

Statement (2) offers an algebraic equation that expresses the relationship between a and b. Solve this to see if there's enough information to determine whether b is even or odd:

$$\frac{a^2}{b} = b - 4$$
$$a^2 = b(b - 4)$$
$$a^2 = b^2 - 4b$$

Use the rules of odds and evens: since a is odd, a^2 must be odd. Thus, you can say that $b^2 - 4b$ must also be odd. Because any even number times any other integer is always even, $4b$ must be even. Therefore, you can say that $b^2 - \text{even} = \text{odd}$.

Since an odd minus an even will always yield an odd, but an even minus an even will always be even, b^2 must be odd. Because two integers multiplied together (in this case, $b \times b$) that produce an odd product must both be odd, b itself must be odd. Thus, Statement (2) is sufficient, and (B) is correct.

24. (E)

In this number properties question, m is an odd number, and p is a prime number. A prime number is a positive integer with exactly two factors: 1 and itself. Examples of prime numbers include 2, 3, 5, and 7. Note that 2 is even, so p may be even or odd. Determine which answer choice must always be odd or, in other words, eliminate any choices that could be even.

For some number properties questions, picking numbers is an efficient strategy. Let m be a small odd number such as 3. Since p is prime, 5 is a good choice for p. Evaluate each choice by plugging in these values and eliminating any choice that produces an even value.

(A) $mp = (3)(5) = 15$. Keep (A).

(B) $m(m + p) = 3(3 + 5) = 3(8) = 24$. Eliminate (B).

(C) $m - p = 3 - 5 = -2$. Eliminate (C).

(D) $m^2 + 2p^2 + 1 = 3^2 + 2(5)^2 + 1 = 9 + 50 + 1 = 60$. Eliminate (D).

(E) $m^2(m + 2p) = 3^2(3 + 2 \times 5) = 9(3 + 10) = 9(13) = 117$. Keep (E).

Both (A) and (E) produced odd values, so they both can be odd. But *must* they be odd? Pick numbers one more time. Pick 2 for p to test an even number for this variable. (A) $mp = (3)(2) = 6$. Eliminate (A). Therefore, (E) must be correct.

You can confirm that (E) is correct: $m^2(m + 2p) = 3^2(3 + 2 \times 2) = 9(3 + 4) = 9(7) = 63$. You can also use number property rules. Because m is odd, m^2 is odd. Then 2 times any integer is even, so $2p$ is even. An odd, m, plus an even is odd, so $m + 2p$ is odd. Thus, this expression is an odd times an odd, and its value must be odd.

Practice Set: Positives and Negatives

25. (C)

This question asks you to identify which of the Roman numeral statements must be true. For "must be true" questions, one example for which the statement is false is sufficient to eliminate the statement from the set of correct answers. Because all the statements specify whether the variables are positive or negative, anticipate that you will use number properties knowledge and/or picking numbers to evaluate the statements.

Start with Statement II, as it shows up most often in the choices. To evaluate whether this statement *must* be true, consider whether a scenario could exist in which $x - y = 8$ and x is positive but y is negative. Subtracting a negative from a positive could yield a positive, and values such as $x = 3$ and $y = -5$ yield a difference of positive 8. Since this scenario could exist, Statement II does not have to be true. Eliminate **(B)**, **(D)**, and **(E)**.

Your analysis of Statement II shows that y can be negative, so Statement I (both x and y are positive) is not always true, and you can eliminate **(A)**. Since there is no a choice for none of the statements, the correct choice is thus **(C)**. You can confirm that Statement III is always true using number properties: if x is negative, then if y were positive, subtracting y would produce an even smaller value; the only way that subtracting y from x will produce a positive value is if y is negative.

26. (B)

The question asks you to identify the statement that cannot be true, given that $\frac{a}{b}$ is a fraction between -1 and 1. The inequality in the question stem means that the absolute value of a is less than the absolute value of b (a is closer to 0); the two values may have the same or different signs.

The choices compare various expressions to 0, so you'll be considering positive and negative number properties as you evaluate the choices. There is no need to evaluate the choices in order. **(A)** and **(E)** are very similar and relatively easy to evaluate. Since both a and b could be negative, their sum could be less than 0, which means **(A)** could be true; since they could be positive, their sum could be greater than 0, which means **(E)** could be true. Eliminate both of these choices.

(C) is a good one to tackle next. This statement is true if $a > b$. The inequality in the question stem allows for a to be positive while b is negative (e.g., $a = 1$ and $b = -2$), so this choice could be true—eliminate it.

(B) and **(D)** contain the same quadratic expression: $(a + b)(a - b)$. Restate this as $a^2 - b^2$. Any non-zero value raised to an even exponent is positive, so the fact that a and/or b could be negative can be ignored. The absolute value of b is greater than that of a, so $b^2 > a^2$. Thus, $a^2 - b^2$ must be negative. **(D)** is always true, while **(B)** is never true. **(B)** is correct.

27. (D)

This Yes/No question asks whether an algebraic expression is negative. The answer will be yes if $s - t$ and st have opposite signs, and the answer will be no if they have the same sign. Thus, a statement is sufficient if it can definitively determine the relationship of the signs of $s - t$ and st.

Statement (1) indicates that s is positive and t is negative. Multiplying terms with opposite signs yields a negative value, so st is negative. The sign of $s - t$ must be positive because a positive minus a negative is identical to a positive plus a positive. Because $(s - t)$ and st have opposite signs, the answer to the question is always yes and Statement (1) is sufficient. Eliminate **(B)**, **(C)**, and **(E)**.

Statement (2) says that the reciprocal of the given expression is less than -1. Since $s - t$ and st must have opposite signs, $\frac{s - t}{st}$ is also negative, making Statement (2) sufficient. Each statement is sufficient on its own, so **(D)** is correct.

Practice Set: Factors and Multiples

28. (C)

The question states that a number is divisible by both 18 and 24, meaning that 18 and 24 divide into the number with no remainder. This is the same as saying that this number is a multiple of both 18 and 24. The question is asking which of the choices divides into the number with no remainder, which is the same as asking which of the choices must be a factor of the number.

An efficient approach is to find the first few multiples of 18 and 24: count by 18s and 24s until you find a number that is on both lists. Counting by 18s: 18, 36, 54, 72 . . . And counting by 24s: 24, 48, 72 . . . The smallest number that's divisible by both 18 and 24 is 72. Thus, you know that the number must be divisible by 72, and (**C**) is correct.

Another approach, most efficient when the choices are large numbers, is prime factorization. Because $18 = 2 \times 3 \times 3$, a number that 18 divides into with no remainder must have at least one factor of 2 and two factors of 3. Because $24 = 2 \times 2 \times 2 \times 3$, a number that 24 divides into with no remainder must have at least three factors of 2 and one factor of 3. Thus, a number that both 18 and 24 can divide into with no remainder must have two factors of 3 (so that 18 works) and three factors of 2 (so that 24 works). That's $2 \times 2 \times 2 \times 3 \times 3 = 72$, (**C**). Be certain that you answered the question that was asked. A common error is to multiply 18 by 24 to get 432 and choose (**E**).

29. (C)
This question states that 9^{6x} can be a factor of 81^{10+x}. Because x is a positive integer, both exponent terms are positive integers. Use the rules of exponents and an understanding of factors and multiples to find the largest possible exponent x that will make 9^{6x} a factor of 81^{10+x}.

To work more easily with the two exponent terms, convert them to the same base. Since 81 is 9^2, 81^{10+x} is $(9^2)^{10+x} = 9^{20+2x}$. Recall that the largest factor of a positive integer is that integer itself (e.g., the greatest factor of 100 is 100). So the largest factor of 9^{20+2x} is a value equivalent to 9^{20+2x}. Therefore, find the x value that makes 9^{6x} equal to 9^{20+2x}. Since the bases are the same, set the exponents equal to each other and solve for x.

$$6x = 20 + 2x$$
$$4x = 20$$
$$x = 5$$

(**C**) is correct.

Plugging 5 back in for x shows that the two exponent terms are equal. You get $9^{6\times5} = 9^{30}$ and $81^{15} = (9^2)^{15} = 9^{30}$.

30. (D)
This question involves multiples of 3 and multiples of 4—or, in other words, numbers that are divisible by 3 or by 4—within the range of 1 to 69. The question asks for the number of multiples of either 3 or 4 but not both. This is equal to the number of values that are multiples of 3 but not 4 plus the number of values that are multiples of 4 but not 3.

Find the number of multiples of 3 that are less than 70 and take out the values that are also multiples of 4. Find the number of multiples of 4 that are less than 70 and take out the values that are also multiples of 3. Add the two values together. When dealing with divisibility, remember that prime factorization can often provide an efficient path to the solution.

The prime factorization of 3 is 3 because it is already a prime number. The prime factorization of 4 is 2×2. Since there are no overlaps in the prime factors needed to make up the two numbers, a number that is a multiple of both 3 and 4 is a multiple of $2 \times 2 \times 3 = 12$.

Dividing 3 into 69 yields 23. Therefore, there are 23 multiples of 3 among the positive integers less than 70. Dividing 12 into 69 yields 5 and a remainder, which means there are 5 positive integers less than 70 that are multiples of both 3 and 4. Subtracting 5 from 23 yields 18, which represents the number of positive integers less than 70 that are multiples of 3 but not 4.

Repeat the process for multiples of 4. Dividing 4 into 69 yields 17 and a remainder. Therefore, there are 17 multiples of 4 among the positive integers less than 70. You have already found that there are 5 positive integers less than 70 that are multiples of both 3 and 4. Subtracting 5 from 17 yields 12—the number of positive integers less than 70 that are multiples of 4 but not 3.

Adding 18 and 12, the two values previously computed, yields 30, making (**D**) correct.

To confirm the answer, you could write out all of the multiples of 3 under 70, then cross out any that are multiples of 4. Next, write out all the multiples of 4 under 70 and cross out any that are multiples of 3. The total number of values that are not crossed out would be 30, confirming (**D**).

31. (A)

This Yes/No question asks whether $3a^2b$ is divisible by 60. In other words, it asks whether $\frac{3a^2b}{60}$ is an integer. The 3 in the numerator cancels out a factor of 3 from the denominator, so it's really asking whether $\frac{a^2b}{20}$ is an integer. For this expression to be an integer, the remaining factors in the denominator have to be canceled out by the numerator. Since $20 = 2 \times 2 \times 5$, the question is really asking whether a^2b contains two 2s and one 5 among its factors.

Statement (1) says that a is divisible by 10. Since $10 = 2 \times 5$, you know that a contains at least one 2 and at least one 5 among its factors. Therefore, the a^2 in the numerator must have at least two 2s and at least two 5s. It doesn't matter what factors b contains, since a^2 alone provides all the factors needed to cancel out the 20. Statement (1) is therefore sufficient. Eliminate **(B)**, **(C)**, and **(E)**.

Since $18 = 2 \times 3 \times 3$, Statement (2) tells you that b has at least one 2 and at least two 3s among its factors. By itself, b does not guarantee two factors of 2, let alone any factor of 5. Therefore, Statement (2) is insufficient. **(A)** is correct.

32. (B)

The question asks for the Roman numeral statements that cannot be a factor of 30. These statements offer various expressions containing the variables a and b, each of which is identified as a distinct factor of 30.

Because this is a "cannot be" question, evaluate each statement with the aim of creating a factor of 30 (so you can eliminate the statement). Both Statement I and Statement II appear in three answer choices, so begin by evaluating one of these. Pick numbers for a and b, starting with a complete list of the factors of 30: 1, 2, 3, 5, 6, 10, 15, and 30; a and b must be two of these.

Evaluate Statement I. Start with small factors of 30 for a and b, since it's more likely that small factors inserted in this expression will yield another factor of 30. If $a = 1$ and $b = 2$, then the expression yields $1(2) + 2^2 = 2 + 4 = 6$. That's a factor of 30, so you can eliminate any expression containing Statement I. Eliminate **(A)**, **(D)**, and **(E)**.

Since you're now down to checking Statement II against Statement III, check Statement III, since it's a simpler expression to evaluate. If $a = 1$ and $b = 2$, then Statement III equals 3, a factor of 30. Eliminate **(C)**. You've already eliminated **(A)**, **(D)**, and **(E)**, so **(B)** is correct.

If you want to confirm that Statement II works, note that it's the square of the sum of two integers, so it must be a perfect square. A quick glance at the list of factors reveals that only 1 is a perfect square, which would require $(a + b)$ to be 1, which is not possible. Therefore, Statement II cannot be a factor of 30.

Practice Set: Remainders and Primes

33. (B)

This Yes/No question states that n is an integer between 12 and 24, inclusive, and asks whether n is a prime number.

Statement (1) tells you that dividing n by 4 leaves a remainder of 1, meaning that n is 1 greater than a multiple of 4. The multiples of 4 within the range are 12, 16, 20, and 24, but 1 more than 24 is outside the range. Thus, the possible values of n are 13, 17, and 21. The first two are, indeed, prime numbers, but 21 is divisible by 3 and 7. Therefore, Statement (1) is insufficient. Eliminate **(A)** and **(D)**.

Statement (2) says that dividing n by 6 leaves a remainder of 1. Thus, according to this statement, n could be $12 + 1 = 13$ or $18 + 1 = 19$. Both of these are prime numbers, so Statement (2) is sufficient. **(B)** is correct.

34. (A)

The question gives the values of x and y and says that x^2y^2 is the product of three integers and a third variable, z. You need to determine the value of z. When the GMAT presents multiplication or division that seems overly complicated, look for a faster approach. This question is a great candidate for prime factorization, since you need to factor a large product to determine the unknown factor z.

Determine the prime factors of the given expression and of each term in the product; then cancel out all the common terms. Those that remain will be the prime factors of z.

$$x^2 = 12^2 = (2 \times 2 \times 3)(2 \times 2 \times 3)$$
$$y^2 = 35^2 = (5 \times 7)(5 \times 7)$$

Thus, you can say that $x^2y^2 = 2 \times 2 \times 2 \times 2 \times 3 \times 3 \times 5 \times 5 \times 7 \times 7$. Now find the prime factors of 21, 28, and 30:

$$21 = 3 \times 7$$
$$28 = 2 \times 2 \times 7$$
$$30 = 2 \times 3 \times 5$$

Therefore, $21 \times 28 \times 30 \times z = 2 \times 2 \times 2 \times 3 \times 3 \times 5 \times 7 \times 7 \times z$. Now compare the two lists of prime factors you've found and cancel out the shared factors to determine what is left over; these will be the factors of z:

$$x^2y^2 = \not{2} \times \not{2} \times \not{2} \times 2 \times \not{3} \times \not{3} \times \not{3} \times 5 \times \not{7} \times 7$$
$$x^2y^2 = \not{2} \times \not{2} \times \not{2} \times \not{3} \times \not{3} \times \not{3} \times \not{7} \times 7 \times z$$
$$z = 2 \times 5 = 10$$

(A) is correct.

35. (A)

This question provides equations for a and b in terms of m and n, respectively, where m and n are positive integers. Use the two equations given to find the remainder when $a + b$ is divided by 5.

Start by determining the value of $a + b$ by adding the two given equations: $a + b = 5m + 2 + 5n + 13 = 5m + 5n + 15$. Notice that all three terms have a common factor of 5, so $a + b = 5(m + n + 3)$. Thus, $(a + b) \div 5 = m + n + 3$. Since m and n are integers, $m + n + 3$ must be an integer. So when $a + b$ is divided by 5, the result is an integer; this means that $a + b$ is a multiple of 5 and there is no remainder when $a + b$ is divided by 5. **(A)** is correct.

To double-check your work, you could pick numbers. Using 2 for m and n will make the arithmetic easy. Now $a = 5(2) + 2 = 12$ and $b = 5(2) + 13 = 23$. Thus, $a + b = 12 + 23 = 25$, which is evenly divisible by 5.

CHAPTER 8

MATH CONTENT REVIEW: ALGEBRA

LEARNING OBJECTIVES

- Identify the algebra techniques that are relevant to a given question that requires algebra to solve
- Apply the Kaplan Methods for Problem Solving and Data Sufficiency to questions testing various algebra skills

Below is an example Problem Solving question with an algebra focus. As you try the question, think about what information it gives you, what the question is asking you to do with that information, and what you do and don't already know about how to solve. The explanation that follows demonstrates how a GMAT expert uses the Kaplan Method for Problem Solving and certain algebra skills to solve this question efficiently.

> If $x + y = 2$ and $x^2 - xy - 10 - 2y^2 = 0$, what does $x - 2y$ equal?
>
> ○ 0
>
> ○ 1
>
> ○ 2
>
> ○ 5
>
> ○ 10

Step 1: Analyze the Question

Use critical thinking to analyze the given information. The GMAT will reward you for recognizing patterns. Here, you are given two variables and two equations, suggesting that information from one equation will help solve for a value in the other. Furthermore, the second equation can be rearranged so a quadratic expression is on one side, suggesting that factoring it will yield results. Simplifying that quadratic is a form of paraphrasing, or restating the information in a way that's more helpful.

Step 2: State the Task

You need to use algebra to simplify and rearrange the two equations and, ultimately, find the value of for $x - 2y$. You're being asked for the value of an expression, not an individual variable, so you may not need to solve for the values of x and y individually.

The answer choices are numbers, not expressions with variables, so there must be a way to write a single equation with $x - 2y$ on one side and a number on the other.

Step 3: Approach Strategically

If you add 10 to both sides of the second equation, you get $x^2 - xy - 2y^2 = 10$. Now you can factor the expression on the left using reverse-FOIL. Since you could get the x^2 term by multiplying x and x, you know both factors will contain x:

$$(x \quad)(x \quad) = 10$$

Next, determine what two factors multiplied together will equal $-2y^2$. You need either $-2y$ and y or $2y$ and $-y$. Since the coefficient of the xy term is negative, choose $-2y$ and y. Then the sum of the outer and inner products will give you $-xy$. Now your equation looks like this:

$$(x + y)(x - 2y) = 10$$

Notice that both factors of $x^2 - xy - 2y^2$ appear in the question stem. You are told that $x + y = 2$, and you are asked to find the value of $x - 2y$.

You can find the value of $x - 2y$ by returning to the equation you've already factored. You know that $(x + y)(x - 2y) = 10$. Since $x + y = 2$, you can replace $(x + y)$ with 2, giving you $2(x - 2y) = 10$, or $x - 2y = 5$. So **(D)** is the correct answer.

Step 4: Confirm Your Answer

Re-read the question stem to check that you have answered the right question. Here, confirm that you have solved for $x - 2y$ and not x or y.

A majority of the questions on the Quantitative section will involve algebra in some way, so strong algebra skills are key to a high score. In this chapter, we'll review the all the concepts and techniques you'll need to deal with algebra as it shows up on the GMAT, starting with translating words into expressions and equations.

Translating Words into Math

> **LEARNING OBJECTIVE**
>
> - Translate word problems into expressions, equations, and inequalities

It's likely that over half of the Quantitative questions you'll see on Test Day will be word problems. Often, the first step in solving these problems is to translate the words into math.

Sometimes the problem will provide letters, or **variables**, to represent unknowns. For example, it might tell you that Greg travels x miles per hour and Harriet travels y miles per hour. In this case, you'd use x and y in your equations.

Other times, you'll need to identify unknowns in the question and choose variables to represent them. When possible, use letters that let you easily remember what they stand for. For example, if Greg and Harriet take trips of unknown length, call the distance Greg travels G and the distance Harriet travels H.

Certain words predictably translate into specific math operations. This table is not exhaustive, but it lists the most common translations you'll need to make. Sometimes a word or phrase can have different meanings depending on how it is used, so context is important as well.

WORD PROBLEMS TRANSLATION TABLE	
ENGLISH	**MATH**
equals, is, was, will be, has, costs, adds up to, the same as, as much as	$=$
less than, smaller than	$<$
less than or equal to, no more than, at most	$\leq$
greater than, more than	$>$
greater than or equal to, at least as much as, at least as many as, no less than, no fewer than	$\geq$
times, of, multiplied by, product of, twice, double, by	$\times$
divided by, per, out of, each, ratio	$\div$
plus, added to, and, sum, combined, more than, greater than	$+$
minus, subtracted from, decreased by, difference between, smaller than, less than, fewer than	$-$
a number, how much, how many, what	x, n, etc.

When the translation seems complicated, don't try to do it all in one step. Instead, translate one short phrase or thought at a time and then put them together. Follow along with this example:

Beatrice's wage is 3 dollars more than twice Alan's wage.

1. Call Beatrice's wage B and Alan's wage A.

2. Break the sentence into pieces and translate each piece.

Beatrice's wage	**is**	**3 dollars more than**	**twice Alan's wage**
↓	↓	↓	↓
B	$=$	$3 +$	$2A$

3. Put the pieces together to make an equation: $B = 3 + 2A$.

Now use the drill to get some practice working with translation.

English-to-Math Translation Drill

Translate the following sentences into algebra. Answers follow the drill.

1. Samantha is 4 years older than Jamal.
2. Mike's score on his geometry test was twice Lidia's score.
3. Arya sold more than three times as many units as Brian sold.
4. w is x less than y.

5. Lucas has 17 fewer dollars than Bianca has.

6. The ratio of $3x$ to $8y$ is 5 to 7.

7. The ratio of salespeople to managers is 9 to 2.

8. The second-grade class has 5 more goldfish than the first-grade class had before the first-graders' recent purchase of 3 goldfish.

9. The sum of Rafael's age and Cindy's age is 17 less than the amount by which Tim's age is greater than Kathy's age.

10. If Mai's salary were increased by $5,000, then the combined salaries of Mai and Anthony would be equal to three times what Mai's salary would be if it were increased by one-half of itself.

English-to-Math Translation Drill: Answers

1. $S = J + 4$

2. $M = 2L$

3. $A > 3B$

4. $w = y - x$

5. $L = B - 17$

6. $\dfrac{3x}{8y} = \dfrac{5}{7}$

7. $\dfrac{S}{M} = \dfrac{9}{2}$

8. $S = (F - 3) + 5$

9. $R + C = (T - K) - 17$

10. $M + 5{,}000 + A = 3\left(M + \dfrac{1}{2}M\right)$

CONCEPT CHECK

- How do you represent unknown values from word problems?

  _____

- What are some words that indicate addition?

  _____

  Subtraction?

  _____

  Multiplication?

  _____

  Division?

  _____

Example answers are in your book's online resources (**kaptest.com/login**).

Now see how a GMAT expert uses the Kaplan Method and words-to-math translation skills to answer a Problem Solving question.

> Charles's and Sarah's current ages are C years and S years, respectively. If 6 years from now, Charles will be at least as old as Sarah was 2 years ago, which of the following must be true?
>
> ○ $C + 6 < S - 2$
> ○ $C + 6 \leq S + 2$
> ○ $C + 6 = S - 2$
> ○ $C + 6 > S - 2$
> ○ $C + 6 \geq S - 2$

Step 1: Analyze the Question

This is a word problem describing the relationship between two people's ages, C and S. The answer choices are equations or inequalities involving C and S. They all begin with $C + 6$, so that part is not in doubt. The differences involve the equal or inequality sign and whether 2 is being added to or subtracted from S.

Step 2: State the Task

Translate the words into math to find the equivalent math "sentence" in the answer choices. There are some time shifts here, with the phrases "6 years from now" and "2 years ago," so you'll need to make sure to include these in your translation.

Step 3: Approach Strategically

Translate one piece at a time:

- Six years from now, Charles's age will be $C + 6$.
- Two years ago, Sarah's age was $S - 2$.

If you were running short on time and needed to make a strategic guess, you could eliminate **(B)** because it does not correctly represent Sarah's age.

Now connect these two algebraic expressions. The phrase "will be *at least* as old as" implies that in 6 years, Charles could be the same age as Sarah 2 years ago, or he could be older. Therefore, use the "greater than or equal to" sign between the two statements:

$$C + 6 \geq S - 2$$

(E) is correct.

Step 4: Confirm Your Answer

Double-check the logic of your translation and that you've used the correct inequality sign.

Next, you'll find some in-format word problems.

Practice Set: Translating Words into Expressions and Equations

(Answers and explanations are at the end of the chapter.)

1. Machine A produces r paper clips per hour. Machine B produces s paper clips per hour. If s is 30 greater than r, which expression represents the number of paper clips the two machines working together produce in t hours?

    ○ $r + s + 30$

    ○ $t(r + s) + 30$

    ○ $t(r + s + 30)$

    ○ $t(2s + 30)$

    ○ $t(2r + 30)$

2. The youngest of 4 children has siblings who are 3, 5, and 8 years older than she is. If the average (arithmetic mean) age of the 4 siblings is 21, what is the age of the youngest sibling?

    ○   17

    ○   18

    ○   19

    ○   21

    ○   22

3. The price of a certain car this year is $42,000, which is 25 percent greater than the cost of the car last year. What was the price of the car last year?

    ○ $27,000

    ○ $28,000

    ○ $31,500

    ○ $33,600

    ○ $34,500

Isolating a Variable

LEARNING OBJECTIVE

* Isolate a variable

Whether the GMAT gives you a mathematical relationship written in algebra, or presents the idea in words and makes you translate into algebra, you then need to use algebra skills to solve the problem. Often, that involves finding the value of a variable or an expression with a variable.

Terms and Expressions

A **term** is a numerical constant or the product of a numerical constant and one or more variables. Examples of terms are 5, $3x$, b, $2ac$, and $4x^2yz$. A number without any variables, such as 5, is called a **constant term**. In the term $3x$, the numerical constant 3 is called a **coefficient**. In a term such as b, 1 is the coefficient.

An **algebraic expression** is a combination of one or more terms, at least one of which contains a variable, and operations (addition, subtraction, multiplication, division, and exponentiation). Examples of expressions are $3xy$, $4ab + 5cd$, and $x^2 - 1$. The general name for expressions with more than one term is **polynomial**. An expression with exactly two terms, such as $4a + 2d$, is a **binomial**.

If you know the value of a variable, you can substitute that value for the variable.

Example: Evaluate $3x^2 - 4x$ when $x = 2$.

Replace every x in the expression with 2 and then carry out the designated operations:

$$3(2^2) - 4(2)$$
$$3(4) - 4(2)$$
$$12 - 8 = 4$$

You can also substitute algebraic terms in place of a variable.

Example: Express $\dfrac{a}{b - a}$ in terms of x and y if $a = 2x$ and $b = 3y$.

Here, replace every a with $2x$ and every b with $3y$:

$$\frac{a}{b - a} = \frac{2x}{3y - 2x}$$

When you work with algebra expressions and equations, follow the same PEMDAS procedures that you use for arithmetic operations. Also, all of the properties of arithmetic operations are applicable to polynomials.

The **commutative property** applies to addition and to multiplication. The order of the terms does not matter, so they can be rearranged.

Examples:

$$2x + 5y = 5y + 2x$$
$$5a \times 3b = 3b \times 5a = 15ab$$

The **associative property** means that when only addition and/or subtraction are involved or only multiplication and/or division are involved, the order of operations does not matter. Be careful when changing the order to ensure that you do not miss any operations or terms. Regrouping can be helpful when **combining like terms**, which is the process of simplifying an expression by subtracting, adding, multiplying, or dividing terms with the same variable component.

Examples:

$$-3x + 5y + 2x + 2y = (2x - 3x) + (5y + 2y) = -x + 7y$$

$$(-2y)\left(\frac{1}{2}x\right)(3y)(-2x) = \left(\frac{1}{2}x\right)(-2x)(-2y)(3y) = 6x^2y^2$$

The **distributive property** is important because it allows you to show expressions with two or more terms in different forms, which can facilitate solving.

Examples:

$$3a(2b - 5c) = (3a \times 2b) - (3a \times 5c) = 6ab - 15ac$$

$$5xy - 10y = (5y)(x) - (5y)(2) = 5y(x - 2)$$

Factoring a polynomial means expressing it as a product of two or more simpler expressions. When there is a single factor common to every term in the polynomial, it can be factored out by using the distributive property. The expressions $3a(2b - 5c)$ and $5y(x - 2)$ above are in factored form, as they are written as the product of two expressions.

Recognizing and applying factors is a technique you can use to simplify complex polynomials. For instance, consider the polynomial $2x^2 - xy - 3y^2 + 6xy$. While there is no common factor for all four terms, there is a common factor of x in the first two terms and a common factor of $3y$ in the second two terms:

1. Group and restate the expression. $x(2x - y) - 3y(y - 2x)$
2. Reverse the minus sign before the second group. $x(2x - y) + 3y(2x - y)$
   These terms now have the common factor $(2x - y)$.
3. Combine the coefficients of $(2x - y)$ and restate. $(x + 3y)(2x - y)$

You can also factor fractions by considering the numerator and denominator separately. The expression $\dfrac{2a}{6b} + \dfrac{2a^2}{3b^2}$ has common factors of $2a$ in the numerator and $3b$ in the denominator, so it is equivalent to $\dfrac{2a}{3b}\left(\dfrac{1}{2} + \dfrac{a}{b}\right)$.

Not all polynomials lend themselves to factoring. For instance, the terms in $7xy + 13xz + 6yz$ have no common factors.

Equations

An **equation** is an algebraic "sentence" that says that two expressions are equal to each other. You can use factoring to simplify equations, too.

To solve for a variable, you can manipulate the equation until you have isolated that variable on one side of the equal sign, leaving any numbers or other variables on the other side. Note that *whenever you perform an operation on one side of the equation, you must perform the same operation on the other side.* Otherwise, the two sides of the equation will no longer be equal.

The steps for isolating a variable are as follows:

1. Eliminate any **fractions** by multiplying both sides by the least common denominator (or by cross multiplying).

2. Put all terms with the variable you're solving for on one **side** by adding or subtracting on both sides.

3. **Combine** like terms.

4. **Factor** out the desired variable.

5. **Divide** to leave the desired variable by itself.

Example: Solve $\frac{x-2}{3} + \frac{x-4}{10} = \frac{x}{2}$.

1. Eliminate fractions by multiplying each term by the least common denominator (LCD). Here the LCD is 30.

$$30\left(\frac{x-2}{3}\right) + 30\left(\frac{x-4}{10}\right) = 30\left(\frac{x}{2}\right)$$
$$10(x-2) + 3(x-4) = 15(x)$$
$$10x - 20 + 3x - 12 = 15x$$

2. Put all terms with the variable on one side by adding or subtracting on both sides. Put all constant terms on the other side of the equation.

$$-20 - 12 = 15x - 10x - 3x$$

3. Combine like terms.

$$-32 = 2x$$

4. Factor out the desired variable.

Does not apply for this equation.

5. Divide to leave the desired variable by itself.

$$x = \frac{-32}{2}$$
$$x = -16$$

To check your work, you can substitute this value for the variable in the original equation. If the equation holds true, you've found the correct answer. In this example, $x = -16$.

$$\frac{-16 - 2}{3} + \frac{-16 - 4}{10} = \frac{-16}{2}$$
$$\frac{-18}{3} + \frac{-20}{10} = \frac{-16}{2}$$
$$-6 + (-2) = -8$$
$$-8 = -8$$

On some problems involving more than one variable, you cannot find a specific value for a variable; you can only solve for one variable in terms of the others. To solve for the desired variable, isolate it on one side of the equation and leave all the other variables on the other side.

Example: In the formula $V = \frac{PN}{R + NT}$, solve for N in terms of P, R, T, and V.

1. Eliminate fractions by cross multiplying.

$$\frac{V}{1} = \frac{PN}{R + NT}$$
$$V(R + NT) = PN$$

2. Remove parentheses by distributing.

$$VR + VNT = PN$$

3. Put all terms containing N on one side and all other terms on the other side.

$$VNT - PN = -VR$$

4. Factor out the common factor N.

$$N(VT - P) = -VR$$

5. Divide by $(VT - P)$ to get N alone.

$$N = \frac{-VR}{VT - P}$$

Note: You can reduce the number of negative terms in the answer by multiplying both the numerator and the denominator of the fraction on the right-hand side by -1.

$$N = \frac{VR}{P - VT}$$

Now use the drill to get some practice isolating a variable.

Isolating a Variable Drill

Answers follow the drill.

Factor the following expressions:

1. $21ab + 7ab^2$

2. $15xy - 9y + 21x$

3. $\dfrac{3q^2 r^2}{10y} - \dfrac{12qr}{15qy}$

4. $42x^4 y^2 + 56x^7 y - 28x^5 y^2$

5. $3 - xy + x - 3y$

Solve the following equations for x:

6. $3x + 4 = 13$

7. $\dfrac{x}{2} - 3 = \dfrac{2x}{3} + 7$

8. $\dfrac{w}{y} = \dfrac{v}{xz}$

9. $3 = \dfrac{2x}{5 + xy}$

10. $2x(a + 2) - 5(a + 2) = 4ax + 8x + a + 2$

Isolating a Variable Drill: Answers

1. $7ab(3 + b)$

2. $3(5xy - 3y + 7x)$

3. $\dfrac{3qr}{5y}\left(\dfrac{qr}{2} - \dfrac{4}{3q}\right)$

4. $14x^4y\left(3y + 4x^3 - 2xy\right)$

5. $x - xy + 3 - 3y = x(1 - y) + 3(1 - y) = (3 + x)(1 - y)$

6. $x = 3$

7. $x = -60$

8. $x = \dfrac{vy}{wz}$

9. $x = \dfrac{-15}{3y - 2}$ or $\dfrac{15}{2 - 3y}$

10. $(2x - 5)(a + 2) = a(4x + 1) + 2(4x + 1)$; $(2x - 5)(a + 2) = (a + 2)(4x + 1)$; $-2x = 6$; $x = -3$

CONCEPT CHECK

- What does isolating a variable mean?

  _____

- What are the five steps to follow in order to isolate a variable?

  _____

- When manipulating an equation to isolate a variable, it's necessary to

  _____

- How do you solve a problem that has more than one variable?

  _____

Example answers are in your book's online resources (**kaptest.com/login**).

Now see how a GMAT expert uses the Kaplan Method to isolate a variable in a Problem Solving question.

If $\dfrac{5}{2 + \frac{3}{n}} = 2$, then $n =$

- ○ $\dfrac{1}{2}$
- ○ 1
- ○ $\dfrac{3}{2}$
- ○ 3
- ○ 6

Step 1: Analyze the Question

In this question, the variable that you need to solve for, n, is buried under two fractions.

Step 2: State the Task

Follow the five-step process to isolate n.

Step 3: Approach Strategically

Begin by multiplying both sides by $2 + \frac{3}{n}$ to get this:

$$5 = 2\left(2 + \frac{3}{n}\right) = 4 + \frac{6}{n}$$

Now multiply everything by n to clear the fraction:

$$5n = n\left(4 + \frac{6}{n}\right)$$
$$5n = 4n + 6$$

Combine like terms:

$$5n - 4n = 4n + 6 - 4n$$
$$n = 6$$

(E) is correct.

Step 4: Confirm Your Answer

You can check your calculations by plugging $n = 6$ into the original equation:

$$\frac{5}{2 + \frac{3}{6}} = \frac{5}{2\frac{1}{2}} = \frac{5}{\frac{5}{2}} = 5 \times \frac{2}{5} = 2$$

Next, you'll find in-format questions involving isolating a variable.

Practice Set: Isolating a Variable

(Answers and explanations are at the end of the chapter.)

4. If $\dfrac{3a - 2ce}{3} = \dfrac{4b - 2de}{2}$, then $\dfrac{e}{3} =$

    ○ $\dfrac{9a - 8b}{6c - 4d}$

    ○ $\dfrac{6a - 3b}{2c - 3d}$

    ○ $\dfrac{3a - 6b}{2c - 3d}$

    ○ $\dfrac{a - 2b}{6c - 9d}$

    ○ $\dfrac{a - 2b}{2c - 3d}$

5. If $2(s - r) = -2\left(\dfrac{r^2 - s^2}{s^2 - r^2}\right)$ and $s^2 - r^2 \neq 0$, then $s - r =$

    ○ -2

    ○ -1

    ○ 0

    ○ 1

    ○ 2

6. A laptop computer uses s fewer watts of electricity than a desktop computer does. In combination, the 2 computers use t watts of electricity. Which of the following expressions represents the desktop computer's electricity usage, in watts?

    ○ $\dfrac{t}{2} - s$

    ○ $\dfrac{t + s}{2}$

    ○ $t(s - 1)$

    ○ $t - \dfrac{s}{2}$

    ○ $t - 2s$

Inequalities

LEARNING OBJECTIVE

- Solve inequalities for a range of values

Four inequality symbols appear on the GMAT:

> greater than	**Example:** $x > 4$ means x is greater than 4.
< less than	**Example:** $x < 0$ means x is less than 0 (x is a negative number).
≥ greater than or equal to	**Example:** $x \geq -2$ means x can be -2 or any number greater than -2.
≤ less than or equal to	**Example:** $x \leq 3.5$ means x can be 3.5 or any number less than 3.5.

One difference between equalities and inequalities is in the result: while the solution to an equality is usually one or possibly two points on the number line, the solution to an inequality is a range of values.

To solve an inequality, use the same approach you'd use to solve an equation, with one possible difference: if the inequality is multiplied or divided by a negative number, the direction of the inequality sign is reversed. To see how this works, consider $1 < 2$. Multiplying both sides by -1 yields the values -1 and -2. Because -1 is to the right of -2 on the number line, $-1 > -2$.

Examples:

$$3a + 4 > 10$$

1. Subtract 4 from both sides.	$3a > 6$
2. Divide both sides by 3.	$a > 2$

$$-2x - 1 \leq 7$$

1. Add 1 to both sides.	$-2x \leq 8$
2. Divide both sides by -2; reverse the direction of the inequality sign.	$x \geq -4$

Note that when you multiply or divide an inequality by a variable, unless the question has given you information about whether the value of the variable is positive or negative, you don't know whether to reverse the inequality sign or not. In Problem Solving, you need to consider both possibilities. In Data Sufficiency, this ambiguity can make a statement insufficient.

Example:

$$3b < 2b^2$$

Divide both sides by b. Write down both possibilities:

if b is pos. OR if b is neg.

$3 < 2b$ OR $3 > 2b$

Divide by 2:

$$\frac{3}{2} < b \text{ OR } \frac{3}{2} > b$$

All negative numbers are less than $\frac{3}{2}$, so b could equal any negative number at all or any positive number greater than $\frac{3}{2}$.

If a question involves a three-part inequality, instead of doing the same thing to *both sides*, do the same thing to *all* parts.

Example:

$$-11 < 2x - 5 < 3$$

1. Add 5 to each part. $\qquad\qquad -6 < 2x < 8$

2. Divide each part by 2. $\qquad\qquad -3 < x < 4$

So x can have any value between -3 and 4, exclusive of those values.

Now use the drill to get some practice working with inequalities.

Inequalities Drill

Solve questions 1 to 5 for y. Answers follow the drill.

1. $y + 5 > 2$
2. $-3 < y - 1$
3. $2y - 9 > -y + 6$
4. $\frac{y}{4} \le 3 - \frac{y}{2}$
5. $5 \ge -y \ge -6$
6. If $\frac{x}{z} > \frac{y}{z}$, is $x > y$?

Inequalities Drill: Answers

1. $y > -3$
2. $y > -2$
3. $y > 5$
4. $\frac{y}{4} + \frac{y}{2} \le 3; y + 2y \le 12; y \le 4$
5. $-5 \le y \le 6$
6. Unknown: if $z > 0$, $x > y$; if $z < 0$, $x < y$.

CONCEPT CHECK

- What are the four inequality signs, and what do they mean?

  _____

- What are two differences between equalities and inequalities?

  _____

- How do you solve a three-part inequality?

  _____

Example answers are in your book's online resources (**kaptest.com/login**).

Now see how a GMAT expert uses the Kaplan Method to answer a Problem Solving question that involves inequalities.

If $x > 4$ and $3x - 2y = 0$, then which of the following must be true?

- ○ $y < -6$
- ○ $y < -4$
- ○ $y < 5$
- ○ $y > 5$
- ○ $y = 6$

Step 1: Analyze the Question

You're given an equation with x and y and an inequality giving you a range of values for x. The answer choices are statements about the value of y. You need to determine which of the statements will always be true of y.

Step 2: State the Task

Because you're interested in the value of y, not x, solve the equation for x in terms of y. Then substitute the resulting expression for x into the inequality. Finally, evaluate the choices and determine which must be true.

Step 3: Approach Strategically

Start by solving the equation for x:

$$3x - 2y = 0$$
$$3x = 2y$$
$$x = \frac{2}{3}y$$

Now substitute $\frac{2}{3}y$ for x in the inequality: $\frac{2}{3}y > 4$. To isolate y, multiple both sides by $\frac{3}{2}$: $y > 6$. Since y is greater than 6, it must also be greater than 5. That's **(D)**.

Step 4: Confirm Your Answer

Check that you solved for y and that you identified the statement that must always be true of y. With the number 6 in it, **(E)** is waiting for the test taker who chooses the familiar-looking number from their calculation. The value of y *could* be 6, but the question asks for what *must* be true.

Next, you'll find some in-format questions involving inequalities.

Practice Set: Inequalities

(Answers and explanations are at the end of the chapter.)

7. Is $a \geq 5$?

    (1) $8a > 32$

    (2) $4a + 6 \leq 25$

8. How many integers n are there such that $-145 < -|-n^2| < -120$?

    ○   0

    ○   2

    ○   4

    ○   11

    ○   12

9. If $\frac{a-b}{c} > 0$, is $c < 0$?

    (1) $a^2 < b^2$

    (2) $b - a < 0$

Absolute Value

LEARNING OBJECTIVE

- Solve equations and inequalities with absolute values

The **absolute value** of a number is the number's distance from zero on the number line. Since absolute value is a distance, it is always non-negative. For instance, both +3 and −3 are 3 units from zero, so their absolute values are both 3. Absolute value is denoted by two vertical lines, so $|3| = 3$ and $|-3| = 3$.

Because absolute value is always non-negative, absolute value conceals the sign of the quantity between the vertical bars. Knowing that $|z| = 3$ does not tell you whether $z = 3$ or $z = -3$. Therefore, you need to take both possibilities into account. You do this by rewriting the equation without the absolute value signs twice, once for the positive value and once for the negative value.

Example:

$$|z + 1| = 3$$

$$z + 1 = 3 \quad \text{OR} \quad z + 1 = -3$$
$$z = 2 \quad \text{OR} \quad z = -4$$

If you plug in either 2 or −4 for z in the original equation, you'll find that it works.

Treat absolute value bars as parentheses: figure out the value inside before performing other operations.

Example: $\quad |-3| + |5| = 3 + 5 = 8$

Handle inequalities with absolute value the same way, except remember to reverse the inequality sign for the negative value.

Example:

$$|2m| > 4$$

$$2m > 4 \quad \text{OR} \quad 2m < -4$$
$$m > 2 \quad \text{OR} \quad m < -2$$

If you plug in a value for m that is greater than 2 or less than −2, you'll find that the original inequality works. For example, if $m = 3$, $|2 \times 3| > 4 \rightarrow 6 > 4$. If $m = -3$, $|2 \times -3| > 4 \rightarrow 6 > 4$.

Now use the drill to get some practice working with absolute value.

Absolute Value Drill

Solve questions 1 to 5 for x. Answers follow the drill.

1. $|x| = \frac{1}{2}$
2. $\left|\frac{x}{2}\right| = 1$
3. $\left|\frac{x - 2}{2}\right| = 1$
4. $|x + 5| < 10$

5. $\left|\dfrac{2x-3}{2}\right| > \dfrac{1}{2}$

6. If $|x - y| = 5$, what is true about the relationship between x and y?

Absolute Value Drill: Answers

1. $x = \dfrac{1}{2}$ OR $x = -\dfrac{1}{2}$

2. $x = 2$ OR $x = -2$

3. $x = 4$ OR $x = 0$

4. $-15 < x < 5$

5. $x > 2$ OR $x < 1$

6. If $|x - y| = 5$, the distance between x and y on the number line is 5 units. It is unknown whether x or y is greater.

CONCEPT CHECK

- Absolute value is always _____.

- In contrast to the absolute value of a number, the quantity *inside* the absolute value bars may be _____, _____, or _____.

- To solve an equation with an absolute value, how many equations must you write?

  _____

- What additional step must you perform when solving an inequality with an absolute value?

  _____

Example answers are in your book's online resources (**kaptest.com/login**).

Now see how a GMAT expert uses the Kaplan Method and an understanding of absolute value to solve a Problem Solving question.

How many possible integer values are there for x, if $|4x - 3| < 6$?

O   One

O   Two

O   Three

O   Four

O   Five

Step 1: Analyze the Question

You're asked for the number of integers that could satisfy a given inequality. The inequality includes the absolute value of an expression.

Step 2: State the Task

Solve the inequality for x and count the number of integers within the range of permissible values for x.

Step 3: Approach Strategically

Because the inequality involves absolute value, write two inequalities and come up with two possible ranges of values for x. Remember to reverse the inequality sign for the negative possibility.

$$|4x - 3| < 6$$

$$
\begin{array}{ccc}
4x - 3 < 6 & \text{OR} & 4x - 3 > -6 \\
4x < 9 & \text{OR} & 4x > -3 \\
x < \dfrac{9}{4} & \text{OR} & x > -\dfrac{3}{4}
\end{array}
$$

The integer values of x lie between $-\dfrac{3}{4}$ and $\dfrac{9}{4}$. To make sure you count them accurately, take a few seconds to sketch a number line and plot the range of x on it:

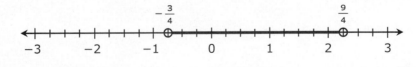

The integer values are 0, 1, and 2. That's three values, so **(C)** is correct.

Step 4: Confirm Your Answer

Double-check that you rewrote the inequality correctly for both the positive and negative values, reversing the sign, and that you answered the question that was asked, which is about the number of integer values of x.

Next, you'll find some in-format questions involving absolute value.

Practice Set: Absolute Value

(Answers and explanations are at the end of the chapter.)

10. Which of the following could be the value of x, if $|12 - 4x| + 2 = 6$?

   ○   −4

   ○   −2

   ○   1

   ○   3

   ○   4

11. If x and y are integers and $z = |x - 2| - |y + 2|$, does $z = 0$?

   (1) $\frac{9}{5} < x < \frac{7}{2}$ and $-3 \leq y < -\frac{21}{11}$

   (2) $2 \leq x < \frac{7}{3}$ and $-\frac{22}{7} < y < -\frac{13}{7}$

12. If $\left|\dfrac{7 - 3j}{2}\right| \leq 4$, then which of the following must be true?

   ○ $j \leq -\frac{1}{3}$

   ○ $j \leq \frac{3}{7}$

   ○ $j \leq 5$

   ○ $j \geq \frac{3}{7}$

   ○ $j \geq 5$

Systems of Linear Equations

LEARNING OBJECTIVES

- Solve systems of linear equations by substitution
- Solve systems of linear equations by combination
- Recognize when fewer equations than variables can be used to solve a system

A system of equations consists of two or more equations that share the same variables. In a system of equations with n distinct variables, you must have at least n distinct linear equations to be able to solve for each variable. This is the **n-equations for n-variables rule**. There are two commonly used ways to solve a system of linear equations: substitution and combination.

Substitution and Combination

To use the **substitution** technique, isolate a variable in one equation. Then plug the value or expression that it equals into its place in the other equation.

Example: Find the values of m and n if $m - 4n = 2$ and $3m + 2n = 20$.

Rearrange the first equation to isolate m: $m = 4n + 2$.

Substitute $4n + 2$ for m in the second equation: $3(4n + 2) + 2n = 20$. This expands to $12n + 6 + 2n = 20$, which simplifies to $14n = 14$, so $n = 1$.

Plug 1 in for n in either equation: $m = 4(1) + 2 = 6$. (Alternatively, $3m + 2(1) = 20$, so $3m = 18$ and $m = 6$.)

To use **combination**, add or subtract whole equations from each other to eliminate a variable. To do this, align the equations vertically and combine like terms.

Example: Find the values of x and y if $3x + 2y = 7$ and $x + 2y = 5$.

The coefficient is the same for the y terms, so subtract to eliminate a term.

$$\begin{aligned}
3x + 2y &= 7 \\
-(x + 2y &= 5) \\
\hline
2x \quad\;\; &= 2 \\
x \quad\;\; &= 1
\end{aligned}$$

Plug in 1 for x in either equation. For example, $1 + 2y = 5$, so $2y = 4$ and $y = 2$.

Sometimes one or both of the equations must be manipulated in order to use combination.

Example: Find the values of x and y if $4x + 3y = 27$ and $3x - 6y = -21$.

Multiply the first equation by 2 to get $8x + 6y = 54$; now the y coefficients have the same absolute value in both equations. Add the second equation to the new equation to eliminate the y term:

$$
\begin{array}{rl}
8x + 6y &= 54 \\
+(3x - 6y &= -21) \\
\hline
11x &= 33 \\
x &= 3
\end{array}
$$

Divide by 11 to get $x = 3$. This value can now be substituted back into either equation to get the value of y. For example, $4(3) + 3y = 27$, so $3y = 27 - 12 = 15$ and $y = 5$.

Sometimes you may need to multiply each of the equations by a different factor so that a pair of terms with the same variable have the same coefficient.

Example: Find the values of x and y if $2x + 3y = 8$ and $3x + 2y = 7$.

Multiply the first equation by 3 and multiply the second equation by 2 so that both x terms have a coefficient of 6. Then subtract one equation from another.

$$
\begin{array}{rl}
6x + 9y &= 24 \\
-(6x + 4y &= 14) \\
\hline
5y &= 10 \\
y &= 2
\end{array}
$$

Substitute 2 for y into either equation to find the value of x. For example $2x + 3(2) = 8$; $x = 1$.

Remember that you need two *distinct* linear equations to solve for the values of two variables. You may encounter a Data Sufficiency question where this rule is important. For instance, given the equations $x + y = 5$ and $3x + 3y = 15$, you *cannot* solve for x and y. Because multiplying the first equation by 3 results in the second equation, the equations are equivalent rather than distinct.

In general, when you can easily isolate one variable and whatever that variable equals is a simple term, substitution is more efficient. Combination works better if the coefficients of one variable are the same in both equations or can easily be made to be the same.

Solving for Expressions with Multiple Variables

Some questions will ask you to solve for a relationship between variables, such as the value of $x + y$ or $x - y$, the average of x and y, or the ratio between the two variables. Data Sufficiency questions, in particular, may require you to recognize whether you have enough information to determine a relationship.

Example: Given that $4x + y = x - 2y + 12$, what is the value of $x + y$?

Get all the x and y terms on one side of the equation by subtracting $x - 2y$ from both sides to get $3x + 3y = 12$. Now divide the equation by 3 to see that $x + y = 4$.

Note that you were able to solve for the value of the expression $x + y$ even though you had only one equation. That's because you didn't need to find the individual values of x and y to answer the question. Although the n-equations for n-variables rule applies when solving for individual variables, it may not apply when solving for a relationship involving more than one variable.

Systems of Linear Equations Drill

Solve the following systems for the values of both variables. Answers follow the drill.

1. $3x - y = 2$ and $x + y = 6$
2. $x = y - 3$ and $5x + 2y = 13$
3. $y = 5 - 2x$ and $6x - 15 = -3y$
4. $6x = 15 + 9y$ and $3y = x - 1$
5. $5x = 2y + 10$ and $5y = 37 - 3x$

Systems of Linear Equations Drill: Answers

1. $x = 2$ and $y = 4$
2. $x = 1$ and $y = 4$
3. No solution because the two equations are equivalent (not distinct)
4. $x = 4$ and $y = 1$
5. $x = 4$ and $y = 5$

CONCEPT CHECK

- To solve for the value of each variable in a system of equations with x different variables, you must have _____.

- Solving one equation for one of the variables and plugging that value into the other equation is called _____.

- Adding or subtracting one equation from the other is called _____.

- If one equation can be manipulated so that it is identical to another equation, then the equations are not _____.

- What might be different about your approach if a question asks for the value of a relationship between variables rather than the value of an individual variable?

_____

Example answers are in your book's online resources (**kaptest.com/login**).

Now see how a GMAT expert uses the Kaplan Method to solve a system of linear equations in a Problem Solving question.

If $x + y = 5y - 13$ and $x - y = 5$, then $x =$

○ 11

○ 12

○ 13

○ 14

○ 15

Step 1: Analyze the Question

The question provides two equations with two variables and asks for the value of one of the variables.

Step 2: State the Task

Use a systems of equations technique to find the value of x. Since the second equation will be easy to rearrange to put y in terms of x, substitution will be an efficient approach.

Step 3: Approach Strategically

Rearrange the first equation to get all terms with variables on one side:

$$x + y = 5y - 13$$
$$x - 4y = -13$$

Simplify the second equation to put y in terms of x. This will let you substitute an expression containing only x into the other equation to solve for x.

$$x - y = 5$$
$$-y = 5 - x$$
$$y = x - 5$$

Substitute $x - 5$ from the second equation for y in the first and solve for x:

$$x - 4(x - 5) = -13$$
$$x - 4x + 20 = -13$$
$$-3x = -33$$
$$x = 11$$

Choice (**A**) is correct.

Step 4: Confirm Your Answer

You can confirm your work by substituting $x = 11$ into either equation to find a value for y. This value for y can then be substituted into the other equation to ensure that $x = 11$.

Next, you'll find in-format questions involving systems of linear equations.

Practice Set: Systems of Linear Equations

(Answers and explanations are at the end of the chapter.)

13. A photographer has visited exactly 42 countries, all of which have been in Africa, Europe, or Asia. If the photographer has been to 6 more countries in Europe than in Asia, and twice as many in Africa as in Europe, how many countries in Asia has the photographer visited?

    ○ 4

    ○ 6

    ○ 12

    ○ 18

    ○ 24

14. Paula has a collection of used books worth $104. Each book is either a mystery or a history. How many books are histories?

    (1) Each mystery is worth $1, and each history is worth $25.

    (2) Paula has exactly 4 mysteries in her collection, which together are worth a total of $4.

15. If $4x + y = 8$ and $y - 3x = 7$, then what is the value of $x + 2y$?

    ○ $\frac{1}{7}$

    ○ 3

    ○ 15

    ○ $\frac{52}{7}$

    ○ $\frac{60}{7}$

16. In 8 years, Leonard will be twice as many years old as Mikala is now. If Leonard were twice as old as he was 2 years ago, and if Mikala were five times as old as she was 2 years ago, the sum of their ages would be 51. What will be the sum of their ages in 3 years?

    ○   12
    ○   14
    ○   19
    ○   22
    ○   25

17. What is the value of b?

    (1) $5b - a = 3b + 5a$

    (2) $4(b - a) = 12 - 4a$

18. What is the value of $a + b$?

    (1) $5a + 2b = 22$

    (2) $3b = 30 - 6a$

19. If the average (arithmetic mean) of x and y is 30 and $3y + z = 180$, what is the value of $\frac{z}{x}$?

    ○ $\frac{1}{6}$
    ○ $\frac{1}{3}$
    ○   1
    ○   3
    ○   6

20. What is the value of g?

    (1) $f + g = 9$

    (2) $3f - 27 = -3g$

21. At a certain diner, Joe ordered 3 doughnuts and a cup of coffee and was charged $2.25. Stella ordered 2 doughnuts and a cup of coffee and was charged $1.70. What is the price of 2 doughnuts?

    ○ $0.55

    ○ $1.00

    ○ $1.10

    ○ $1.30

    ○ $1.80

22. A souvenir shop made $2,400 in revenue selling postcards. If a large postcard costs twice as much as a small postcard, the shop sold 950 large postcards, and it sold no other type of postcard besides these two sizes, then how many small postcards did it sell?

    (1) A large postcard costs $2.

    (2) If the shop had sold 20 percent fewer small postcards, its revenue would have been reduced by $4\frac{1}{6}$ percent.

Quadratic Equations

LEARNING OBJECTIVES

- Solve a quadratic equation by factoring
- Recognize the classic quadratics

The term **quadratic expression** refers to a mathematical expression in the form $ax^2 + bx + c$, where a, b, and c are constants and a does not equal zero. The algebraic rules for solving a linear equation apply to quadratics as well, but there are some specific things to know about handling quadratic equations.

Another way to express a quadratic is as the product of two binomials, such as $(y + 5)(y - 2)$. This can also be "expanded" to the form $ax^2 + bx + c$. A convenient way to do this is to follow the acronym **FOIL**: multiply the **F**irst terms first, then the **O**uter terms, then the **I**nner terms, and finally the **L**ast terms.

Example: $(y + 5)(y - 2)$

$$= (y \times y) + (y \times -2) + (5 \times y) + (5 \times -2)$$

$$= y^2 - 2y + 5y - 10$$

$$= y^2 + 3y - 10$$

Factoring is the reverse of this process. It can be thought of as applying the FOIL method backward, or **"reverse-FOIL."**

Example: $x^2 - 3x + 2$

Using reverse-FOIL, you can factor this into two binomials, each containing an x term. Start by writing down what you know. The product of the first terms is x^2, so the two first terms are each x:

$$x^2 - 3x + 2 = (x \quad)(x \quad)$$

The *product* of the two missing terms will be the *last term* in the polynomial: 2. The *sum* of the two missing terms will be the *coefficient of the second term* of the polynomial: -3. Try the possible integer factors of 2 until you get a pair that adds up to -3. There are two possibilities for the integer factors of 2: either 1 and 2 or -1 and -2. Since $(-1) + (-2) = -3$, you can write -1 and -2 in the empty spaces.

$$x^2 - 3x + 2 = (x - 1)(x - 2)$$

If the coefficient of the constant (the last term) is negative, then the binomials will have different signs (one + and one −). If the coefficient of the constant is positive, then the binomials will both have the same sign as the coefficient in the middle term (two +'s or two −'s), as in the previous example.

Note: Whenever you factor a polynomial, you can check your answer by using FOIL to obtain the original polynomial.

Classic Quadratic Patterns

The process of reverse-FOIL works on all the quadratics you will find on the GMAT. However, there are some patterns called "classic quadratics," which you can factor more quickly by recognizing the pattern.

The **difference of two squares** can be factored according to this pattern: $a^2 - b^2 = (a + b)(a - b)$.

Example: $d^2 - 16 = (d + 4)(d - 4)$

The **square of a binomial** is another quadratic that has a pattern: $(a + b)^2 = a^2 + 2ab + b^2$ and $(a - b)^2 = a^2 - 2ab + b^2$

Example: $x^2 + 6x + 9 = x^2 + 2(x)(3) + 3^2 = (x + 3)^2$

Example: $x^2 - 10x + 25 = x^2 - 2(x)(5) + 5^2 = (x - 5)^2$

All three forms begin and end in a perfect square, which can be helpful in spotting quadratics that follow a pattern:

$$a^2 - b^2$$
$$a^2 + 2ab + b^2$$
$$a^2 - 2ab + b^2$$

Not all the quadratic-like expressions on the GMAT will have a simple x^2 (or something similar) for the first term.

Example: $4x^2 + 52x + 169$

Notice that $4x^2$ is $(2x)^2$, 169 is 13^2, and, for the second term, $(2x \times 13) + (2x \times 13) = 26x + 26x = 52x$, so you can factor this square of a binomial as $(2x + 13)^2$.

Different Presentations of Quadratics

There are some twists that GMAT may add to quadratics. One is to require you to do extensive manipulation to get the equation into the form $ax^2 + bx + c$.

Example: $x - 3 = \dfrac{-4}{x + 2}$ does not look like a quadratic, but when you clear the fraction and rearrange the terms, this becomes the quadratic $x^2 - x - 2$.

Using two variables is another variation. Remember that the first term of a quadratic is the product of the first terms of the binomial equivalent and the third term is the product of the second terms of the binomials.

Example: $x^2 - 3xy - 10y^2$ factors to $(x + 2y)(x - 5y)$.

Factoring a quadratic can be more difficult if the coefficient of the first term is something other than 1.

Example: Factor $6x^2 + x - 12$.

First, list the factors of 6 and -12. For 6, the positive factor pairs are (6×1) and (3×2). For 12, the positive factor pairs are (1×12), (6×2), and (4×3), but one of each pair will be positive and one negative. Some experimentation will reveal that $3 \times 3 = 9$, and $-4 \times 2 = -8$. The sum of these is $9 + (-8) = 1$, which is the coefficient of the middle term. So, $6x^2 + x - 12$ factors to $(3x - 4)(2x + 3)$.

When the coefficient of the first term is not 1, be alert for an opportunity to factor out the coefficient from each term, greatly simplifying your factoring of the remaining quadratic.

Example: $3x^2 + 15x - 42 = 3(x^2 + 5x - 14) = 3(x + 7)(x - 2)$

Occasionally, the GMAT may use radicals in a quadratic equation.

Example: $9x^2 - 5$ is, in fact, a difference of two squares and can be factored as $(3x + \sqrt{5})(3x - \sqrt{5})$.

Solving Quadratic Equations

If the expression $ax^2 + bx + c$ is set equal to zero, there is a special name for it: a **quadratic equation**. On the GMAT, you can find the value or values for x that make the equation work by using the factored form of the equation obtained through reverse-FOIL.

Example: $x^2 - 3x + 2 = 0$

To find the solutions, or **roots**, start by factoring using reverse-FOIL. Factor $x^2 - 3x + 2$ into $(x - 1)(x - 2)$:

$$(x - 1)(x - 2) = 0$$

When the product of two terms is zero, at least one of the terms is zero. If the product of $(x - 1)$ and $(x - 2)$ is equal to zero, that means either the first term equals zero or the second term equals zero. So to find the roots, set each of the two binomials equal to zero. If $x - 1 = 0$, add 1 to both sides to see that $x = 1$. If $x - 2 = 0$, then $x = 2$. You can check that either value works by plugging it back into the equation.

When the second term of each binomial factor is the same, then the quadratic has only one root.

Example: If $(x + 2)(x + 2) = 0$, the sole solution is $x = -2$.

Whether a quadratic has a single value as a solution can be an important piece of information in a Data Sufficiency question.

Now use the drill to get some practice working with quadratics.

Quadratics Drill

Answers follow the drill.

1. Expand $(x + 3)(x - 5)$.
2. Expand $(z - 7)^2$.
3. Factor $a^2 + a - 2$.
4. Factor $4x^2 + 20x + 25$.
5. Factor $a^2 - ab - 20b^2$.
6. Find the root(s) of $x^2 - 11x + 28 = 0$.
7. Find the root(s) of $2x^2 - 12 = x^2 + 6x - 5$.
8. Find the root(s) of $z^2 - 7 = 0$.
9. Find the value(s) of x in terms of y and z for $x^2y^2 - 4xyz + 4z^2 = 0$.
10. Find the root(s) of $y - 7 = \frac{-12}{y}$.

Quadratics Drill: Answers

1. $x^2 - 2x - 15$
2. $z^2 - 14z + 49$
3. $(a + 2)(a - 1)$
4. $(2x + 5)^2$
5. $(a - 5b)(a + 4b)$
6. $(x - 4)(x - 7) = 0$; $x = 4$ or $x = 7$
7. $x^2 - 6x - 7 = 0$; $(x^2 + 1)(x^2 - 7) = 0$; $x = 7$ or $x = -1$
8. $z = \sqrt{7}$ or $z = -\sqrt{7}$
9. $(xy - 2z)(xy - 2z) = 0$; $xy - 2z = 0$; $x = \dfrac{2z}{y}$
10. $y^2 - 7y + 12 = 0$; $y = 3$ or $y = 4$

CONCEPT CHECK

- What are the two forms for a quadratic?

  _____

- What do the letters in the mnemonic FOIL stand for?

  _____

- To solve a quadratic equation, set the right side of the equation equal to _____.

Example answers are in your book's online resources (**kaptest.com/login**).

Now see how a GMAT expert uses the Kaplan Method to answer a Problem Solving question involving quadratics.

If $(a - 3)^2 = 5 - 10a$, then which of the following could be the value of a?

○ −3

○ −2

○ 0

○ 2

○ 3

Step 1: Analyze the Question

The question provides an equation containing a binomial squared, but the equation is not given in a standard quadratic form. You will need to manipulate the equation to set the right side to 0 and then determine the factors.

Step 2: State the Task

Solve for the value of a.

Step 3: Approach Strategically

Simplify the equation by subtracting 5 from both sides and adding $10a$ to both sides to get $(a - 3)^2 - 5 + 10a = 0$.

Next, use the pattern for a binomial squared to expand $(a - 3)^2$ and simplify:

$$(a - 3)(a - 3) - 5 + 10a = 0$$
$$a^2 - 6a + 9 - 5 + 10a = 0$$
$$a^2 + 4a + 4 = 0$$

This is also a pattern of a binomial squared; it factors to $(a + 2)(a + 2) = 0$. There is only one solution, $a = -2$. Choice (**B**) is correct.

Step 4: Confirm Your Answer

You can plug your calculated value for a into the equation in the question stem to confirm that the calculations are correct.

Next, you'll find in-format questions involving quadratic expressions and equations.

Practice Set: Quadratic Equations

(Answers and explanations are at the end of the chapter.)

23. Is $x > 0$?

   (1) $x^2 - 8x + 16 = 0$
   (2) $x^2 - x - 12 = 0$

24. Which of the following expressions could be equal to 0 when $n^2 - 4n = 12$?

   ○ $n^2 - 2n - 15$
   ○ $n^2 - 2n + 1$
   ○ $n^2 + 4n - 12$
   ○ $n^2 - 5n - 6$
   ○ $n^2 + 6n + 5$

25. Which of the following could equal zero for some value of x?

   I. $3x^2 - 12$
   II. $x^4 + x^2 + 1$
   III. $x^2 + 7x + 6$

   ○   I only
   ○   III only
   ○   I and II only
   ○   I and III only
   ○   I, II, and III

26. What is the product of all the possible values of x if $x^2(x + 2) + 7x(x + 2) + 6(x + 2) = 0$?

   ○   −29

   ○   −12

   ○   12

   ○   29

   ○   168

Sequences

A sequence is an ordered list of numbers a_{n-1}, a_n, a_{n+1}, where n denotes the position in the sequence of any individual term; the subscript does not indicate value.

Example:

$$\text{If } n = 2, a_n \text{ is the 2nd number}$$

$$a_{2+1} = a_3, \text{ which is the 3rd number}$$

$$a_{2-1} = a_1, \text{ which is the 1st number}$$

An **arithmetic sequence** is one for which each term after the first is equal to the sum of the preceding term and a constant k, so $a_{n+1} = a_n + k$. A **geometric sequence** is one in which each term after the first is equal to the product of the preceding term and a constant, so $a_{n+1} = ka_n$.

There will be a discernible pattern to a sequence on the GMAT, even if it isn't apparent immediately. Knowing at least one value in the sequence and the relationship that defines the sequence will enable you to derive the value of any number in the sequence.

The relationship that defines the sequence is often presented as an equation using sequence notation.

Example: For all $n \geq 3$, $a_n = a_{n-2} + a_{n-1}$.

This translates to "Starting with the third term in the sequence, the value of the term equals the sum of the preceding two elements."

Now use the drill to get some practice working with sequences.

Sequences Drill

Answers follow the drill.

1. In the sequence S, $s_n = s_{n-1} + 5$. If $s_1 = 3$, what is the value of s_2?

2. For $n \geq 3$, a sequence of numbers is defined as $s_n = s_{n-2} + s_{n-1}$. If $s_3 = 4$ and $s_4 = 6$, what is the value of s_5?

3. A sequence of numbers is defined as follows: $s_n = ks_{n-1}$, where k is a constant. If $s_1 = 1$ and $s_2 = 2$, what is the value of s_3?

4. A sequence of numbers is defined as follows: $s_n = s_{n-2} + s_{n-1} - 2$. If $s_4 = 3$ and $s_5 = 4$, what is the value of s_7?

5. Sequence A is an arithmetic sequence, so $a_n = a_{n-1} + k$. If sequence A consists of consecutive odd integers, what is the value of k?

Sequences Drill: Answers

1. 8
2. 10
3. $2 = k(1)$, so $k = 2$; $s_3 = ks_2 = 2 \times 2 = 4$
4. $s_6 = 3 + 4 - 2 = 5$; $s_7 = 4 + 5 - 2 = 7$
5. 2

CONCEPT CHECK

- In sequence notation, what is the meaning of the subscript in s_n?

  _____

- What is an arithmetic sequence?

  _____

- What is a geometric sequence?

  _____

- In order to find the value of a specific number in a sequence, what two things do you need to know?

  _____

Example answers are in your book's online resources (**kaptest.com/login**).

Now see how a GMAT expert uses the Kaplan Method to solve a Problem Solving question involving sequences.

> In the arithmetic sequence S, where each term is the sum of the previous term and a constant k, the value of s_1 is 3 and the value of s_4 is 15. What is the value of s_6?

- O 18
- O 19
- O 21
- O 23
- O 24

STEP 1: ANALYZE THE QUESTION

The question asks for the value of the sixth term in an arithmetic sequence. To find the value of an element in an arithmetic sequence, you need to know how much is added to each term to get the next term and the value of at least one element. For this question, you are given the values of two elements.

STEP 2: STATE THE TASK

Use the two values provided to determine the constant that's added to each element to generate the arithmetic sequence. Then add that constant twice to s_4 to obtain the value of s_6.

STEP 3: APPROACH STRATEGICALLY

Starting with s_1, k is added to that value to yield s_2. Then k is added to s_2 to yield s_3, and k is added to s_3 to yield s_4. Thus, because s_4 is three elements further along in the sequence than s_1, k is added to s_1 three times to generate s_4, so $s_4 = s_1 + 3k$. Substitute the known values for s_1 and s_4 to get $15 = 3 + 3k$. So, $3k = 12$ and $k = 4$. Because $s_6 = s_4 + 2k$, $s_6 = 15 + 2(4) = 23$. (**D**) is correct.

STEP 4: CONFIRM YOUR ANSWER

Double-check that you used the correct number of intervals between values in the sequence to calculate the amount added to each value and to extend the series to get the value of s_6.

Next, you'll find in-format questions involving sequences.

Practice Set: Sequences

(Answers and explanations are at the end of the chapter.)

27. *l, m, n, o, p*

An arithmetic sequence is a sequence in which each term after the first is equal to the sum of the preceding term and a constant. If the list of letters shown above is an arithmetic sequence, which of the following must also be an arithmetic sequence?

   I. $3l, 3m, 3n, 3o, 3p$
   II. l^2, m^2, n^2, o^2, p^2
   III. $l-5, m-5, n-5, o-5, p-5$

   O   I only
   O   II only
   O   III only
   O   I and III
   O   II and III

28. In a certain sequence of positive integers, the term *tn* is given by the formula $t_n = 3(t_{n-2}) + 2(t_{n-1}) - 1$ for all $n \geq 1$. If $t_6 = 152$ and $t_5 = 51$, what is the value of t_2?

   O   1
   O   2
   O   3
   O   6
   O   17

29. In the infinite sequence S, each term S_n after S_2 is equal to the sum of the two terms S_{n-1} and S_{n-2}. If S_1 is 4, what is the value of S_2?

   (1) $S_3 = 7$

   (2) $S_4 = 10$

Functions and Symbolism

A function describes the operation that is performed on an input to get a single output. The GMAT uses classic function notation, such as $f(x)$, but it also uses some untraditional notation, such as $\diamond$, $\spadesuit$, or $\otimes$. Function or symbolism questions ask you to substitute values or operations in the manner prescribed by the question.

Example: What is the minimum value of the function $f(x) = x^2 - 1$?

This function says that whatever number is between the parentheses gets substituted in place of x in $x^2 - 1$. For instance, $f(2) = 2^2 - 1 = 3$.

One way to solve this would be to test the choices given to see which was the least attainable value for the function, but solving logically is more efficient. Since x^2 cannot be negative, the value of the function will be the least when x^2 is 0. So the least $x^2 - 1$ can be is -1.

Questions offering strange symbols work basically the same way as conventional functions.

Example: If $x \spadesuit y = 3x - y^2$, then what is the value of 8 $\spadesuit$ 2?

The given equation is really just a pattern for substitution. Whatever is to the left of the $\spadesuit$ symbol is x and should be substituted in place of x in $3x - y^2$. Similarly, anything to the right of $\spadesuit$ is y and should be substituted for y.

$$x \spadesuit y = 3x - y^2$$
$$8 \spadesuit 2 = 3(8) - (2)^2$$
$$8 \spadesuit 2 = 24 - 4$$
$$8 \spadesuit 2 = 20$$

For the most part, symbols on the GMAT define operations. Occasionally, as discussed in the "Arithmetic Operations" lesson in the chapter on arithmetic and number properties, the GMAT will use symbols to stand in for numbers.

You may encounter **nested functions** on the GMAT. An example would be $f(g(x))$. Just as with nested parentheses in any arithmetic, always evaluate nested functions from the inside out.

Example: If $s(x) = 3x + 2$ and $t(x) = 7 - 2x$, what is the value of $s(t(2))$?

Start from the inside: $t(2) = 7 - 2(2) = 3$. Now evaluate $s(3)$: $s(3) = 3(3) + 2 = 11$. The value of $s(t(2))$ is 11. A common error is to apply the second function, s, to the original input, 2. However, that input gets transformed into 3 by the first function, t, so $f(s)$ receives 3 as input.

Now use the drill to get some practice working with functions and symbolism.

Functions and Symbolism Drill

Answers follow the drill.

1. If $f(x) = x^2 - x + 2$, then $f(3) =$

2. If $x \, \&\& \, y = \frac{2x}{y}$, then $3 \, \&\& \, 2 =$

3. If $x \clubsuit y = \frac{5x + 3}{y}$ and $3 \clubsuit y = 2$, then $y =$

4. If $f(x) = 3x - 2$ and $g(x) = x^2$, then $f(g(3)) =$

5. If $f(x) = 3x - 2$ and $g(x) = x^2$, then $g(f(3)) =$

Functions and Symbolism Drill: Answers

1. 8

2. 3

3. $\frac{5(3) + 3}{y} = 2$; $y = 9$

4. $g(3) = 9$; $f(9) = 3(9) - 2 = 25$

5. $f(3) = 3(3) - 2 = 7$; $g(7) = 7^2 = 49$

CONCEPT CHECK

- A function describes the operation(s) performed on an _____ to get a unique _____.

- In function notation, the variable within parentheses represents _____.

- On the GMAT, unusual symbols often represent _____.

Example answers are in your book's online resources (**kaptest.com/login**).

Now see how a GMAT expert uses the Kaplan Method to answer a Data Sufficiency question involving a symbolic function.

> The symbol ♣ represents one of the following operations: addition, subtraction, multiplication, or division. What is the value of 6 ♣ 2?
>
> (1) 0 ♣ 3 = 0
>
> (2) 2 ♣ 1 = 2

Step 1: Analyze the Question Stem

This Value question asks whether there is sufficient information to find the value of 6 ♣ 2. You are told that the symbol ♣ can stand for any one of the four operations of addition, subtraction, multiplication, or division.

Step 2: Evaluate the Statements Using 12TEN

Statement (1) tells you that 0 ♣ 3 = 0. The operations that yield this value are:

$$\text{Multiplication: } 0 \times 3 = 0$$
$$\text{Division: } 0 \div 3 = 0$$

So ♣ could stand for multiplication or division. However, $6 \times 2 = 12$ and $6 \div 2 = 3$, so there is more than one possible answer to the question. Statement (1) is insufficient. Eliminate **(A)** and **(D)**.

Statement (2) tells you that 2 ♣ 1 = 2. The operations that yield this value are:

$$\text{Multiplication: } 2 \times 1 = 2$$
$$\text{Division: } 2 \div 1 = 2$$

So again, ♣ could be multiplication or division; as you saw in evaluating the first statement, the value of 6 ♣ 2 changes depending on whether the symbol represents multiplication or division. Statement (2) is insufficient. Eliminate **(B)**.

Taking the statements together, you still know only that ♣ could be multiplication or division. So, the two statements taken together are insufficient. Therefore, **(E)** is correct.

Next, you'll find in-format questions involving functions and symbolism.

Practice Set: Functions and Symbolism

(Answers and explanations are at the end of the chapter.)

30. Let $\boxed{x} = \dfrac{x^2 + 1}{2}$ and $\textcircled{y} = \dfrac{3y}{2}$, for all integers x and y. If $m = 2$, $\boxed{\textcircled{m}}$ is equal to which of the following?

   ○ $\dfrac{13}{8}$

   ○ 3

   ○ $\dfrac{15}{4}$

   ○ 5

   ○ $\dfrac{37}{2}$

31. In the multiplication problem above, each of the symbols ◇, △, and ● represents a positive digit. If ◇ > △, what is the value of ◇ ?

   (1) △ = 1

   (2) ● = 9

32. For all positive numbers x and y, the operation $x \blacklozenge y$ is defined by $x \blacklozenge y = \dfrac{x^2 - x}{2xy}$. If $x \blacklozenge 5 = 2$, then $x =$

    ○ 1
    ○ 5
    ○ 11
    ○ 20
    ○ 21

33. The operation $\sqintop x$ is defined by the equation $\sqintop x = ax - b(x - 1) + c$, where a, b, and c are constants that are positive integers. The value of $\sqintop 0$ is 7. What is the value of b?

    (1) $a = 3$

    (2) $c = 5$

Answers and Explanations

Practice Set: Translating Words into Expressions and Equations

1. (E)

The question states that machine A produces r paper clips per hour and that machine B produces s per hour. Since machine B produces 30 more per hour than machine A, $s = r + 30$. Your task is to determine the algebraic expression for the number of paper clips both machines working together can produce in t hours.

The total output for a period of time is the rate times the amount of time: Paper clips $= \dfrac{\text{Paper clips}}{\text{Hour}} \times$ Hours. The total rate is the sum of the rates of the two machines, $r + (r + 30) = 2r + 30$, and the time is t. Thus, the total number of paper clips is $t(2r + 30)$, which is (E).

You could pick numbers to solve this problem or to confirm your answer. If $r = 10$, then $s = 10 + 30 = 40$. The total production is $10 + 40 = 50$ paper clips each hour. If $t = 2$, then the machines produce $50 \times 2 = 100$ paper clips. When you plug these numbers into the choices, only (E) equals 100.

2. (A)

The question tells you the ages of 4 children relative to the age of the youngest and the average age of all the children, and it asks for the age of the youngest child. This question can be solved using backsolving, but algebra is faster. If you are behind time and need to make a strategic guess, note that if the average age is 21, the youngest child must be under 21, so eliminate (D) and (E) before guessing.

Translate the words into an algebraic equation. Let y be the age of the youngest child. Then the ages of the other children are $y + 3$, $y + 5$, and $y + 8$. The average formula is Average $= \dfrac{\text{Sum of the terms}}{\text{Number of terms}}$. So

$$21 = \frac{y + (y + 3) + (y + 5) + (y + 8)}{4} = \frac{4y + 16}{4}.$$ All the

terms in the fraction are divisible by 4, so this simplifies to $21 = y + 4$, and $y = 21 - 4 = 17$. (A) is correct.

You can confirm your answer by plugging in 17 for y in the equation and verifying that the average age is 21.

3. (D)

The test makers often set up percentage problems to reward those who do two important things. The first is to be careful about what number the percentage is applied to. The second is to remember to look for ways to simplify calculations.

This question tells you that an increase of 25% raises the price of a car to $42,000 and asks for the original price. Call the original price p and converting the words to an equation. To make the arithmetic easier, convert 25% to the fraction $\frac{1}{4}$:

$$p + \frac{1}{4}p = 42{,}000$$

$$\frac{5}{4}p = 42{,}000$$

$$p = 42{,}000 \times \frac{4}{5}$$

$$p = 8{,}400 \times 4$$

$$p = 33{,}600$$

(D) is correct. You can confirm this by adding 25% to the original price. Since 25% is one-quarter, divide 33,600 by 4 to get 8,400. Since $33{,}600 + 8{,}400 = 42{,}000$, this confirms your choice. If the answer you got doesn't check out at this step, it's possible that you applied the 25% increase to $42,000 instead of the unknown original price. Decreasing $42,000 by 25% yields $31,500, (C).

Practice Set: Isolating a Variable

4. (E)

The question asks you to determine the value of $\frac{e}{3}$ based on an equation involving five variables. Since e is on both sides of the equation, there is unlikely to be a shortcut, so use algebra to manipulate the equation so that $\frac{e}{3}$ is on one side and all other terms are on the other side.

Cross multiply the given equation to yield $2(3a - 2ce) = 3(4b - 2de)$. After you distribute the 2 and 3 on the left and right sides, the equation looks like this: $6a - 4ce = 12b - 6de$. Subtract $12b$ and add $4ce$ to both sides: $6a - 12b = 4ce - 6de$. Factor the e out from the right side to arrive at $6a - 12b = e(4c - 6d)$. Divide by $4c + 6d$ to isolate e, making the equation $\dfrac{6a - 12b}{4c - 6d} = e$.

The question asks for $\dfrac{e}{3}$, so multiply the equation by $\dfrac{1}{3}$. Note that because both the coefficients in the numerator are multiples of 3, they cancel out:

$$\frac{e}{3} = \frac{1}{3}\left(\frac{6a - 12b}{4c - 6d}\right) = \frac{2a - 4b}{4c - 6d}.$$

All the remaining coefficients on the right side are multiples of 2. Simplify by dividing out 2 from every term in the numerator and denominator to produce $\dfrac{e}{3} = \dfrac{a - 2b}{2c - 3d}$, making (**E**) the correct answer. Confirm that you have found the term that the question asks for, e, and check your algebra.

5. (D)

This question asks for the value of an expression, $s - r$. When the GMAT asks for an expression, there is often a shortcut besides solving for each variable individually. Note also that you are given only one equation, which means that it is not possible to find the individual variable values.

First, divide both sides of the equation by 2:

$$s - r = -1\left(\frac{r^2 - s^2}{s^2 - r^2}\right)$$

Next, note that the numerator and denominator involve subtraction of the same terms but in opposite order. In this situation, factor out –1 from either the numerator or denominator. For example, doing so for the numerator yields:

$$s - r = (-1)\frac{(-1)(s^2 - r^2)}{s^2 - r^2} = \frac{s^2 - r^2}{s^2 - r^2} = 1$$

The value of $s - r$ is 1, making (**D**) the correct answer. Confirm that you have found the expression that the question asks for.

6. (B)

The question asks for an expression representing the desktop computer's electricity usage given two relationships: (1) the laptop computer's usage and desktop computer's usage relative to each other and (2) the sum of the two usages. Form two equations (one representing

each relationship) and isolate the variable representing the desktop computer's electricity usage.

Using L and D to represent the laptop's electricity usage and the desktop's electricity usage, respectively, the two equations are $L = D - s$ and $D + L = t$. Use substitution and the first equation to rewrite the second equation as $D + (D - s) = t$.

Solve the equation $D + (D - s) = t$ for D, the desktop computer's electricity usage.

$$D + (D - s) = t$$
$$D + D - s = t$$
$$2D - s = t$$
$$2D = t + s$$
$$D = \frac{t + s}{2}$$

Thus, (**B**) is correct. Picking numbers would also be an appropriate strategy for this question. For example, you could decide that the desktop uses 5 watts and that $s = 2$ so that laptop uses $5 - 2 = 3$ watts. Then $t = 5 + 3 = 8$ watts. When you plug in 2 for s and 8 for t, only (**B**) yields 5, the desktop watts you decided on.

Practice Set: Inequalities

7. (B)

In this Yes/No question, sufficiency means demonstrating either that a is equal to or greater than 5 or that a is less than 5.

Simplify Statement (1). If $8a > 32$, then $a > 4$. While it's possible that a is equal to or greater than 5, it's also possible that a is greater than 4 but still less than 5. Eliminate (**A**) and (**D**).

Statement (2) says that $4a + 6 \leq 25$, which simplifies to $4a \leq 19$. Hence, a must be less than 5, because if a were 5, $4a$ would be 20. This means that the answer to the stem question is unequivocally no, making Statement (2) alone sufficient. (**B**) is correct.

8. (C)

The question asks how many integer values of n satisfy the inequality $-145 < -|-n^2| < -120$. Since each part of the inequality has a negative sign, start by multiplying each term by -1 to make it positive. Remember to reverse the direction of the inequality signs because you are multiplying by a negative number: $145 > |-n^2| > 120$. You need to identify the perfect squares between 120 and 145, exclusive, then determine the values of n that, when squared, yield those values.

Since 120 is 1 less than the perfect square 121 (11^2) and 145 is 1 greater than the perfect square 144 (12^2), both 121 and 144 are within the range of permissible values for n^2. Thus, n^2 could equal 11^2 or 12^2.

Squaring any value yields a positive value. The negative sign within the absolute value bars will make n^2 a negative value, but then the absolute value bars will make it positive again. Therefore, if $n^2 = 11^2$, n could equal 11 or -11. If $n^2 = 12^2$, n could equal 12 or -12. That's four possible values for n. Thus, **(C)** is correct.

Ensure that you determined all possible values for n. The result of omitting the negative square roots is **(B)**.

9. (B)

This is a Yes/No question that asks whether c is negative, given that the inequality $\frac{a - b}{c}$ is positive. Since the expression is positive, $a - b$ and c are either both positive or both negative. Thus, a statement that gives information about the sign of the expression $a - b$ would provide sufficient information to determine whether c is positive or negative.

In Statement (1), the fact that a^2 is less than b^2 merely means that $|a| < |b|$. If, for instance, $a = 1$ and $b = 2$, then $a - b$ is negative. But if $a = -1$ and $b = -2$, then $a - b$ is positive. Thus, Statement (1) is insufficient; eliminate **(A)** and **(D)**.

Statement (2) has the terms in the opposite order from the numerator of the given equation. Multiply by -1 and flip the inequality to get $a - b > 0$. Since $a - b$ and c must have the same sign, c must be positive. Statement (2) alone is sufficient, and **(B)** is correct.

Practice Set: Absolute Value

10. (E)

You are given an equation that includes an absolute value containing a term with a variable. The question asks you to find what *could be* the value of x. This implies that x potentially has multiple values, although only one will be in the answer choices. When there is an absolute value in an equation, set up two equations, one for a positive value inside the absolute value bars and one for a negative value inside the bars.

First, simplify by subtracting 2 from both sides of the equation to get $|12 - 4x| = 4$. Now, $12 - 4x$ could equal 4 or -4. Solve for each of the cases separately. For the negative case, subtract 12 from both sides of $12 - 4x = -4$ to get $-4x = -16$. Dividing both sides by (-4) gives you $x = 4$. This is choice **(E)**.

To confirm your answer, you could backsolve by plugging 4 in for x in the original equation: $|12 - 4(4)| + 2 = |12 - 16| + 2 = |-4| + 2 = 4 + 2 = 6$. **(E)** is confirmed as correct.

11. (E)

This is a Yes/No question asking whether $z = 0$. You are given the equation $z = |x - 2| - |y + 2|$. If $z = 0$, then $|y + 2| = |x - 2|$. For sufficiency, the statements will need to provide enough information about the integers x and y to determine whether this equation is valid.

Since you are working with integers, convert the fractions in Statement (1) to mixed numbers: $1\frac{4}{5} < x < 3\frac{1}{2}$ and $-3 \leq y < -1\frac{10}{11}$. The only integers in the range for x are 2 and 3, and the only integers in the range for y are -3 and -2. Try out some combinations of these numbers to see whether they yield different answers to the question. If $x = 2$ and $y = -2$, then $|2 - 2| = |-2 + 2|$ and $z = 0$. The answer to the question would be yes. If, however, $x = 2$ and $y = -3$, then $|2 - 2| \neq |-3 + 2|$. Thus, Statement (1) is insufficient. Eliminate **(A)** and **(D)**.

Statement (2) can be rewritten as $2 \leq x < 2\frac{1}{3}$ and $-3\frac{1}{7} < y < -1\frac{6}{7}$, so you can conclude that x must equal 2 and that y must equal -3 or -2. Thus, by the same logic as for Statement (1), this statement is also insufficient. Eliminate **(B)**.

Combining Statements (1) and (2), you know that x must equal 2 because that is the only value for x that works for both statements. However, in both statements, y could equal -3 or -2. You know from the analysis above that this is insufficient, so **(E)** is correct.

12. (C)

This question involves an inequality with an absolute value. The solution to an inequality will have a range of values, and solving for an absolute value means writing two inequalities, one if the value between the bars is positive and one if it is negative. Note that the question asks for an inequality that *must* be true, not one that *could* be true.

Rewrite the given inequality as two inequalities: $\frac{7 - 3j}{2} \leq 4$ and $\frac{7 - 3j}{2} \geq -4$. Remember to flip the inequality sign for the negative case. Evaluate both inequalities to find the range for j.

For the first inequality:

$$\frac{7 - 3j}{2} \leq 4$$
$$7 - 3j \leq 8$$
$$-3j \leq 1$$
$$j \geq -\frac{1}{3}$$

For the second inequality:

$$\frac{7 - 3j}{2} \geq -4$$
$$7 - 3j \geq -8$$
$$-3j \geq -15$$
$$j \leq 5$$

Therefore, the full range of values for j is $-\frac{1}{3} \leq j \leq 5$.

Examine the choices with that range in mind. Since 5 is the maximum value for the range of j, it is a true statement that $j \leq 5$. **(C)** is the correct choice.

A good way to check your answer to questions involving inequalities is to sketch the solutions to the inequalities on a number line so you can see the range of the solutions.

Practice Set: Systems of Linear Equations

13. (B)

The question provides enough information to set up three equations about the countries a photographer has been to on three continents: Africa (F), Europe (E), and Asia (S). Since there are 42 countries total, $F + E + S = 42$. Also, since the photographer has been to 6 more countries in Europe than in Asia, $E = S + 6$. Twice as many in Africa as in Europe translates to $F = 2E$.

Now, use the resulting system of linear equations to determine the number of countries that were visited in Asia. Since $E = S + 6$, it follows that $F = 2E$ can be written as $F = 2E = 2(S + 6)$. Use substitution to solve for S:

$$F + E + S = 42$$
$$2(S + 6) + (S + 6) + S = 42$$
$$2S + 12 + S + 6 + S = 42$$
$$4S + 18 = 42$$
$$4S = 24$$
$$S = 6$$

Therefore, **(B)** is correct. The photographer has been to 6 countries in Asia.

As always, be sure to answer the right question. **(C)** is the number of countries visited in Europe and **(E)** is the number visited in Africa. If time permits, plug 6 back into the word problem to check your answer and see whether you come up with 42 total countries: Asia = 6; Europe = 6 + 6 = 12; Africa = 2 × 12 = 24. Finally, 6 + 12 + 24 = 42.

14. (C)

This is a Value question. The question stem says that Paula's used book collection, comprising histories and mysteries, is worth \$104 and asks how many are histories. No information is provided about the total number of books or the value of any individual books. Since there are two variables, the numbers of histories and mysteries, you will need two distinct linear equations to get the number of history books.

Statement (1) tells you that the mysteries are $1 apiece and the histories are $25 apiece. If m is the number of mysteries and h is the number of histories, the total worth can be stated as the number of each type of book times the unit worth: $104 = 1m + 25h$. Since you have one equation with two variables, this is insufficient. Eliminate **(A)** and **(D)**.

Statement (2) states that there are exactly 4 mysteries with a total worth of $4. Thus, the total worth of the histories is $104 − $4 = $100. Lacking information about the value per history book, this statement is also insufficient. Eliminate **(B)** and evaluate the statements together.

Statement (1) says that history books are worth $25 each, and from Statement (2), you know that the history books are worth $100. Knowing the value of each history book and the total amount is sufficient to determine the number of history books (4 books, if you're curious), so **(C)** is correct.

15. **(C)**

You're given two linear equations in terms of x and y. When you're asked for an expression, as you are here, see if there's a way to combine the two equations to lead straight to the expression. In this case, you can add them. Rearrange $y − 3x = 7$ to $−3x + y = 7$ so things line up nicely, then combine the equations:

$$\begin{array}{r} 4x + y = 8 \\ +[-3x + y = 7] \\ \hline x + 2y = 15 \end{array}$$

(C) is correct.

16. **(E)**

This question provides information about two people's relative ages at varying points in time. The answer choices represent a sum of *two* unknown ages, so backsolving would not be an efficient strategy. Instead, translate the words into algebra. Let L and M represent Leonard and Mikala's ages now. The question asks for the sum of their ages 3 years from now, which is $(L + 3) + (M + 3) = L + M + 6$.

That Leonard's age in 8 years will be twice Mikala's *current* age can be written as $L + 8 = 2M$. Rearrange this to $L − 2M = −8$.

Leonard's age 2 years ago is $L − 2$, so twice that age is $2(L − 2)$. And 2 years ago, Mikala's age was $M − 2$, so five times that age is $5(M − 2)$. The equation for the second sentence is thus $2(L − 2) + 5(M − 2) = 51$. Distribute the 2 and 5 across the parentheses: $2L − 4 + 5M − 10 = 51$. Simplify to get $2L + 5M = 65$.

There is no way to directly add or subtract these equations to find $L + M$, but if you add the equations, the two terms have the same coefficient, which can then be divided out. Thus, combination is an efficient approach.

$$\begin{array}{r} L − 2M = −8 \\ +(2L + 5M = 65) \\ \hline 3L + 3M = 57 \\ L + M = 19 \end{array}$$

The question asks for the sum of the two ages in 3 years: $L + M + 6 = 19 + 6 = 25$. **(E)** is correct.

Be certain that you correctly untangled the question stem and that you answered the question that was asked. **(C)** is the sum of the ages now. **(D)** is the sum of the ages plus 3 years, but both Leonard and Mikala will each be 3 years older, so 3 needs to be added twice.

17. **(B)**

This Value question asks for the value of b, and the statements contain equations involving a and b. In order to find b, you must have at least the same number of independent equations as variables once extraneous information is removed.

Statement (1) includes both a and b. Combine like terms by adding a to both sides and subtracting $3b$ from both sides, yielding $2b = 6a$. While you can go one step further and divide both sides by 2, at this point there is one equation with two variables, so the statement is insufficient. Eliminate **(A)** and **(D)**.

Statement (2) includes both a and b in the equation. However, note that after distributing the 4, the equation reads: $4b − 4a = 12 − 4a$. Simplify the equation by adding $4a$ to both sides, yielding $4b = 12$. Since the *a* term can be removed, there is one variable and one independent equation, so this statement alone is sufficient. **(B)** is correct.

18. (C)

This Value question asks for the value of the expression $a + b$. One path to sufficiency is to find individual variable values and then find their sum. Alternatively, a statement will be sufficient if would allow you to isolate the expression $a + b$ on one side of an equation.

Statement (1) contains one equation with two variables. No variable can be removed via simplification, nor is it possible to manipulate the equation to leave only $a + b$ on one side. The statement is insufficient, so eliminate **(A)** and **(D)**.

Statement (2) again contains one equation with two variables. Rearranging the equation yields $6a + 3b = 30$, and each term can be divided by 3 to yield $2a + b = 30$. However, there is no way to isolate $a + b$ because the coefficients of the a and b terms are different. This statement is also insufficient, so eliminate **(B)**.

Combine the statements: there are now two distinct equations with two variables, meaning that you could solve for the values of the variables. Choose **(C)**.

19. (D)

This question asks for the value of the expression $\frac{z}{x}$, which can be found either by finding the individual values of z and x then solving or by isolating the expression on one side of an equation. Based on the average information, you can write the equation $\frac{x + y}{2} = 30$. Multiplying by 2 yields the equation: $x + y = 60$. You are also given the second equation $3y + z = 180$.

There are three variables but only two independent equations, so solving for the individual variable values is not feasible. Instead, construct an equivalent expression to the desired $\frac{z}{x}$ using the fact that both variables can be written in terms of y. This allows you to set up an equation with the desired expression isolated on one side. Rearranging the first and second equations yields $x = 60 - y$ and $z = 180 - 3y$, respectively.

Construct the desired $\frac{z}{x}$ in terms of y: $\frac{z}{x} = \frac{180 - 3y}{60 - y}$. Factoring out a 3 from the numerator yields $\frac{z}{x} = \frac{3(60 - y)}{60 - y} = 3$. The correct choice is **(D)**.

Alternatively, you could pick values of x, y, and z that satisfy the two equations. Start with z and choose a value that, when subtracted from 180, leaves a multiple of 3 (so you can divide by 3 and get an integer value for y). If you pick $z = 30$, then according to the second equation, $y = 50$. Since the average of x and y is 30 and y is 20 more than 30, x is 20 less than 30, or 10. Now $\frac{z}{x} = \frac{30}{10} = 3$.

20. (E)

This question asks you to recognize whether there's sufficient information to find a single value of g.

Statement (1) is a linear equation with the variables f and g. To solve for either of two variables, you need two distinct linear equations, so Statement (1) is insufficient. Eliminate **(A)** and **(D)**.

Statement (2) is also a linear equation with the two variables f and g. This is insufficient, so eliminate **(B)**.

Combine the two statements. At first glance, it may seem that the statements together will be sufficient, since you now have two equations for two variables. However, simplifying $3f - 27 = -3g$ by dividing all terms by 3 gives you $f - 9 = -g$, which can be rearranged as $f + g = 9$. This is identical to Statement (1), so the two statements give you only one distinct linear equation. **(E)** is correct.

21. (C)

You're given the totals for two orders, each involving two items, and you're asked for the price of two doughnuts. Let doughnuts be d and a cup of coffee be c, and set up two equations: $3d + c = 2.25$ and $2d + c = 1.70$. Notice that the only difference between the two equations is the number of doughnuts, so use combination and subtract the second equation from the first:

$$\begin{array}{r} 3d + c = 2.25 \\ -(2d + c) = 1.70 \\ \hline d + 0 = 0.55 \end{array}$$

Since $d = 0.55$, the price of 2 doughnuts, or $2d$, is 1.10. **(C)** is correct.

22. (D)

There are four factors that affect the outcome of this problem: (1) the price of a small postcard, (2) the price of a large postcard, (3) the number of small postcards sold, and (4) the number of large postcards sold. That's four variables, so four distinct linear equations would enable you to solve for any of the variables. How many equations do you have already? Well, something-or-other equals $2,400 (that's one), there's a relationship between the prices (that's two), and you get the number of large postcards (that's three). With three equations for four variables, *any new equation* will be sufficient, as long as it is distinct and it doesn't introduce a new variable.

Statement (1) is a new equation and is therefore sufficient. Statement (2) is a more complicated equation, and it would likely be time-consuming to calculate. But it is still a new, distinct equation, and it is therefore sufficient. **(D)** is correct.

Practice Set: Quadratic Equations

23. (A)

For this Yes/No question, sufficiency means determining that x is either definitely positive or definitely not positive (zero or negative). It is not necessary to know the exact value of x.

Statement (1) provides a quadratic equation in which the sign of the constant term (16) is positive. A plus sign here means the value(s) of x are either both positive (in which case the answer to the question is yes) or both negative (in which case the answer is no). Without factoring the quadratic, you know that the roots have a definitive relationship with 0. Since Statement (1) is sufficient, eliminate **(B)**, **(C)**, and **(E)**.

Statement (2) provides a quadratic equation in which the sign of the constant term (-12) is negative. A negative sign in this position of a quadratic guarantees that it has two different roots—one positive and one negative. This statement is therefore insufficient. Eliminate **(D)**. Because only Statement (1) is sufficient, **(A)** is correct.

24. (D)

This question asks which of the answer choices, all of which are quadratic equations that include n, could equal 0. To help figure this out, you're given a quadratic equation involving n. Note that you're not being asked to solve for n.

The given equation $n^2 - 4n = 12$ can be restated as the quadratic equation $n^2 - 4n - 12 = 0$. This equation factors to $(n - 6)(n + 2) = 0$, which means that either of the factors could be 0. The answer choice that has either $n - 6$ or $n + 2$ as a factor therefore could also be equal to 0.

(A) $n^2 - 2n - 15 = (n + 3)(n - 5)$. Eliminate.

(B) $n^2 - 2n + 1 = (n - 1)(n - 1)$. Eliminate.

(C) $n^2 + 4n - 12 = (n - 2)(n + 6)$. Be careful here! The factors of this expression reverse the signs of the factors of the given equation. Eliminate.

(D) $n^2 - 5n - 6 = (n - 6)(n + 1)$. The factor $(n - 6)$ is one of those identified as possibly equaling zero, meaning that this expression could equal zero. **(D)** is correct. There won't be more than one right answer, so after finding the expression that could equal zero, you can stop testing.

25. (D)

This question asks you to determine which of the expressions could equal zero. Since there are multiple exponents in the question, expect to do some factoring.

Statement I shows up the most in the choices, so start there. Factor the expression into $3(x^2 - 4) = 3(x + 2)(x - 2)$. If x is 2 or -2, the expression is 0. Statement I must be part of the correct answer, so eliminate **(B)**.

Evaluate Statement II next. Note that both variable terms, x^4 and x^2, will never be negative, since any real base raised to an even exponent is either zero or positive. Therefore, this expression cannot be less than the constant term, 1. Eliminate **(C)** and **(E)**.

Evaluate Statement III by factoring $x^2 + 7x + 6$ into $(x + 6)(x + 1)$. The expression will be 0 if $x = -6$ or $x = -1$. This statement is part of the correct answer. **(D)** is correct.

26. (B)

Instead of distributing the multiplication, which would lead to a complicated cubic equation, factor out the multiple occurrences of $(x + 2)$, which will leave you with a quadratic equation you can reverse-FOIL and solve.

$$x^2(x + 2) + 7x(x + 2) + 6(x + 2) = 0$$

Factor: $(x + 2)(x^2 + 7x + 6) = 0$

Reverse-FOIL: $(x + 2)(x + 6)(x + 1) = 0$

Solve for x: $x = -2 \text{ or } -6 \text{ or } -1$

Multiply: $-2 \times -6 \times -1 = -12$

(B) is correct.

Practice Set: Sequences

27. (D)

This question provides the definition of an arithmetic sequence and says that l, m, n, o, p is one such sequence. The question asks which of the Roman numeral statements are also arithmetic sequences. It may be helpful to pick numbers to evaluate the statements. Evaluate the statements beginning with Statement III, as it shows up the most often in the answer choices.

Statement III: This statement shifts each element of the original sequence left on the number line by 5 units. That doesn't change the relationship between the elements, so this sequence conforms to the same pattern as the first sequence and is thus still an arithmetic sequence. Picking numbers can make this easier to see. Say the original arithmetic sequence is 6, 9, 12, 15, 18 (adding a constant of 3 each time). Statement III results in the sequence 1, 4, 7, 10, 13. Because each term is still exactly 3 more than its preceding term, this is still an arithmetic sequence. Since Statement III is part of the correct answer, eliminate **(A)** and **(B)**.

Of the remaining statements, Statement I is easier to test. Using the same original sequence you had above, Statement I would have you multiply each term by 3. Doing so results in the sequence 18, 27, 36, 45, 54. This is still an arithmetic sequence as each term is exactly 9 more than its preceding term, so Statement I is part of the correct answer. Eliminate **(C)** and **(E)**. Since you've eliminated four choices, **(D)** must be correct.

To confirm the answer, test Statement II. Using the same sequence picked above, square each term. Just squaring the first three terms ($6^2 = 36$, $9^2 = 81$, $12^2 = 144$) is enough to show that Statement II does not result in an arithmetic sequence. **(D)** is confirmed.

28. (B)

The question stem provides the formula for a sequence, t_n, and the values for the fifth and sixth terms in the sequence, t_5 and t_6. The question asks for the value of the second term in the sequence, t_2. Work backward from the known values until you get to t_2. For t_6, the t_{n-2} term is t_4 and the t_{n-1} term is t_5. Plug the two known values into the formula for the series to get $152 = 3(t_4) + 2(51) - 1$. This simplifies to $3(t_4) = 51$, so $t_4 = 17$. For t_5, the formula is $51 = 3(t_3) + 2(17) - 1$. Thus, $3(t_3) = 51 - 34 + 1 = 18$, and $t_3 = 6$. One more to go! For t_4, $17 = 3(t_2) + 2(6) - 1$. So $3(t_2) = 17 - 12 + 1 = 6$, and $t_2 = 2$, which is **(B)**.

In case you stopped working backward too soon, **(E)** is t_4 and **(D)** is t_3. Checking your scratchwork to make sure you've calculated through to the correct value in the sequence will help you avoid these incorrect choices.

29. (D)

This Value question describes an infinite sequence $S_n = S_{n-1} + S_{n-2}$, gives the value of S_1 as 4, and asks for the value of S_2. Since, $S_3 = S_2 + S_1$, knowing the value of S_3 would suffice. Also, $S_4 = S_3 + S_2$, but that would require the values of both S_4 and S_3 to get S_2.

Statement (1) says that $S_3 = 7$. The analysis above shows that having the value of S_3 enables you to get S_2, so Statement (1) is sufficient. Eliminate **(B)**, **(C)**, and **(E)**.

Statement (2) says that $S_4 = 10$, so $S_3 + S_2 = 10$. You know from the analysis that $S_3 = S_2 + 4$. These are two distinct linear equations containing the terms S_2 and S_3, so you have enough information to determine the values for both S_3 and S_2. Statement (2) is also sufficient. **(D)** is correct.

Practice Set: Functions and Symbolism

30. (D)

This is a symbolism problem containing two definitions and a nested function. Begin with the innermost function and work your way outward to find the value of $\boxed{m}$.

Symbolism problems such as this are equations for which you are asked to plug in a value. To evaluate $\boxed{m}$ for $m = 2$, begin by plugging 2 in for the variable in the circle equation: $\dfrac{3y}{2} = \dfrac{3(2)}{2} = 3$. Now take the result, 3, and plug that into the square equation:

$$\frac{x^2 + 1}{2} = \frac{3^2 + 1}{2}$$
$$= \frac{9 + 1}{2}$$
$$= \frac{10}{2}$$
$$= 5$$

The value of $\boxed{m}$ is 5, so **(D)** is correct.

When working with nested functions, remember to always work from the inside out. Doing so allows you to avoid choices such as **(C)**, which is the result of first applying the square to the value 2, then using the result as input to the circle function.

31. (B)

This Value question represents unknown digits with various symbols. It states that the product of the positive digits $\diamond$ and $\triangle$ is $\bullet$ and that $\diamond > \triangle$, and it asks for the value of the digit $\diamond$. Since all of the symbols are positive digits, each is one of the integers 1, 2, 3, 4, 5, 6, 7, 8, or 9. There is no mention that all the digits are different, so potentially more than one symbol could have the same value.

Statement (1) says that $\triangle = 1$. So the product of $\diamond$ and 1 is $\bullet$. Because the product of any number and 1 is that number, the product of $\diamond$ and 1 is $\diamond$. So $\diamond = \bullet$. You know from the question stem that $\diamond > \triangle$, and because Statement (1) says that $\triangle = 1$, you have $\diamond > 1$. However, you do not know the value of the digit. So $\diamond$ could be any of the eight remaining positive digits 2, 3, 4, 5, 6, 7, 8, and 9. Because there is more than one possible value for $\diamond$, Statement (1) is insufficient. Eliminate **(A)** and **(D)**.

Statement (2) says that $\bullet = 9$. Thus, the product of $\diamond$ and $\triangle$ is 9. There are two ways to write 9 as the product of two digits, 9×1 and 3×3. Because $\diamond \times \triangle = 9$ and you must have $\diamond > \triangle$, it must be the case that $\diamond = 9$ and $\triangle = 1$. Therefore, $\diamond$ has only one possible value, 9. Statement (2) is sufficient, and **(B)** is correct.

32. (E)

This symbolism question states that $x \blacklozenge y$ is defined by the expression $\dfrac{x^2 - x}{2xy}$. The value of $x \blacklozenge 5$ is 2 and the question asks for the value of x.

Because you know that $x \blacklozenge 5 = 2$, replace y with 5 in the defining expression and set it equal to 2: $\dfrac{x^2 - x}{(2x)5} = 2$.

Combine factors in the denominator: $\dfrac{x^2 - x}{10x} = 2$. Next, multiply both sides by $10x$: $x^2 - x = 20x$. Subtract $20x$ from both sides to yield $x^2 - 21x = 0$. Factor out an x from each term on the left: $x(x - 21) = 0$. Thus, either $x = 21$ or $x = 0$. The question stem specifies that x is positive, so you're left with $x = 21$. The correct choice is **(E)**.

Check that you substituted numbers correctly into the definition and verify your calculations, making sure you solve for the value of x and not y. If you plugged in 5 for x and solved for y, the result would be 1, which is **(A)**.

33. (B)

This symbolism question defines the equation $\text{♫} \, x = ax - b(x - 1) + c$, where a, b, and c are positive integers. Given that $\text{♫} \, 0 = 7$, the question asks for the value of b. Substitute 0 for x into the function and set it equal to 7: $a(0) - b(0 - 1) + c = 7$; this simplifies to $b + c = 7$. Therefore, knowing the value of c would enable you to calculate b.

Statement (1) says that $a = 3$. But a is not in the equation $b + c = 7$. Thus, Statement (1) is insufficient. Eliminate **(A)** and **(D)**.

Statement (2) informs you that $c = 5$. You can plug this value into $b + c = 7$ to get the value of b. Therefore, Statement (2) is sufficient to solve for the value of b, and **(B)** is correct.

CHAPTER 9

MATH CONTENT REVIEW: RATIOS, RATES, AND AVERAGES

LEARNING OBJECTIVES

- Describe how ratios, rates, and averages are tested on the GMAT
- Apply the Kaplan Methods for Problem Solving and Data Sufficiency to questions that test ratios, rates, and averages

---

Below is an example Problem Solving question about an average. As you try the question, think about what information it gives you, what the question is asking you to do with that information, and what you do and don't already know about how to solve. The explanation that follows demonstrates how a GMAT expert uses the Kaplan Method for Problem Solving and the average formula to solve this question efficiently.

If the average (arithmetic mean) of x, 25, y, and 30 is $x + y$, which of the following equals the value of x?

- ○ $18\frac{1}{3}y$
- ○ $18\frac{1}{3}+y$
- ○ $18-\frac{3}{y}$
- ○ $y-18\frac{1}{3}$
- ○ $18\frac{1}{3}-y$

Step 1: Analyze the Question

This question tells you that the average of the four terms x, 25, y, and 30 is $x + y$. A quick glance at the answer choices reveals that you are being asked to solve for x in terms of y.

Step 2: State the Task

You'll need to set up the average formula and then isolate x. But don't rush to the conclusion that you have to do a lot of algebra here.

Step 3: Approach Strategically

Think critically about how you can approach this problem to save time. Picking numbers is often a simple way to handle problems in which you need to solve for one variable in terms of another. Once you put the terms in the average formula, you can pick a number for x, solve the problem for y, and then plug that number into the answer choices to get the one that matches your choice for x. The average formula is the sum of terms divided by the number of terms. Here, that would look like this: $\dfrac{x + 25 + y + 30}{4} = x + y$. Multiplying both sides by 4 results in $x + 25 + y + 30 = 4(x + y)$. Distribute the 4 and you have $x + 25 + y + 30 = 4x + 4y$.

Now pick an easy number to substitute for x, such as $x = 1$. That gives you $1 + 25 + y + 30 = 4 + 4y$. Combine like terms, and you have $56 + y = 4 + 4y$. Doing the subtraction necessary to get y and the numbers on different sides of the equation leaves you with $52 = 3y$. Divide each side by 3, and you find that $y = 17\frac{1}{3}$. Since you chose 1 to stand in for x, all you need to do is substitute $17\frac{1}{3}$ in for y and find the choice that equals 1. That's **(E)**.

You could also have solved algebraically. Taking the equation above, $x + 25 + y + 30 = 4x + 4y$, you can continue to simplify by combining like terms until you get $55 = 3x + 3y$. Factoring out a 3 from the right side gives you $55 = 3(x + y)$, and dividing both sides by 3 results in $\frac{55}{3}$. Isolating x and converting $\frac{55}{3}$ to a mixed number results in $x = 18\frac{1}{3} - y$, which corresponds to choice **(E)**.

Step 4: Confirm Your Answer

Using picking numbers can save you valuable time on this problem. You can also solve it with pure algebra, of course, and that approach can be used to confirm your answer if you initially solve by picking numbers.

Once you see past their superficial window dressing, many word problems on the GMAT Quantitative section deal with the commonsense principle of proportionality and require the application of a few easily memorized formulas. On challenging questions, the GMAT test makers will ask you to rearrange the information you're given and then apply these concepts creatively, which takes practice but is absolutely doable. This chapter will give you a solid foundation in these topics.

Ratios

LEARNING OBJECTIVE

- Construct ratios to solve problems

A **ratio** is a comparison of two quantities by division. Ratios may be written with a fraction bar $\left(\frac{x}{y}\right)$, with a colon ($x{:}y$), or in English ("the ratio of x to y"). Ratios are always written in fully reduced form; reduce a ratio the same way you reduce a fraction.

In a ratio of two numbers, the numerator is often associated with the word *of* and the denominator with the word *to*.

$$\text{Ratio} = \frac{\text{Of} \ldots}{\text{To} \ldots}$$

Example: In a box of doughnuts, 12 are sugar and 18 are chocolate. What is the ratio of sugar doughnuts to chocolate doughnuts?

$$\text{Ratio} = \frac{\text{Of sugar}}{\text{To chocolate}} = \frac{12}{18} = \frac{2}{3} \text{ or } 2{:}3$$

Part-to-Part and Part-to-Whole Ratios

A ratio can either represent a **part-to-part** or a **part-to-whole** relationship between quantities or numbers. Additionally, you can convert one type of ratio to another if all the parts together equal the whole and there is no overlap among the parts (i.e., if the whole is equal to the sum of its parts).

Example: The ratio of domestic sales to foreign sales of a certain product is 3:5. What is the ratio of domestic sales to total sales?

The two parts (domestic and foreign sales) together equal the whole (total sales). Because domestic sales are represented by 3 in the ratio and foreign sales are represented by 5, total sales can be represented by $3 + 5 = 8$. Therefore, the ratio of domestic sales to total sales is $\frac{3}{8}$ or 3:8.

Ratios may describe the relationships of more than two terms. As with ratios involving just two terms, you can determine part-to-part and part-to whole relationships.

Example: Given that the ratio of children to parents to teachers in a classroom is 4:3:2 and that there is no one else in the room, what ratios can you determine?

PART-TO-PART RATIOS	PART-TO-WHOLE RATIOS
Ratio of children to parents = 4:3 or $\frac{4}{3}$.	Ratio of children to people = 4:9 or $\frac{4}{9}$.
Ratio of parents to teachers = 3:2 or $\frac{3}{2}$.	Ratio of parents to people = 3:9 = 1:3 or $\frac{1}{3}$.
Ratio of teachers to children = 2:4 = 1:2 or $\frac{1}{2}$.	Ratio of teachers to people = 2:9 or $\frac{2}{9}$.

All the above ratios could also be written in reverse order. For example, the ratio of all the people in the room to children is $\frac{9}{4}$.

You can combine multiple ratios so long as they have an entity in common. So if one ratio is $a{:}b$ and another is $b{:}c$, you can make $a{:}b{:}c$. Before combining ratios, give the common entity the same value in both.

Example: If $a{:}b = 3{:}2$ and $b{:}c$ is 6:1, what is $a{:}b{:}c$?

The entity in common is b, but it has a value of 2 in one ratio and 6 in the other. Multiply $a{:}b$ by 3 to get 9:6. Now b is equal in both ratios, so you can combine them. The ratio $a{:}b{:}c$ is 9:6:1.

You can also combine ratios by multiplying them so that the shared entity cancels out.

Example: If the ratio of apples to bananas is 3:4 and the ratio of bananas to cantaloupes is 6:7, then the ratio of apples to cantaloupes is $\frac{A}{B} \times \frac{B}{C} = \frac{3}{\cancel{4}^2} \times \frac{\cancel{6}^3}{7} = \frac{9}{14}$.

Ratios Versus Actual Numbers

Because ratios are always reduced to their simplest form, they may not reflect the actual values of the parts in the ratio. Recognizing when you can and cannot calculate an actual number of things can be key to solving a Data Sufficiency question.

Example: In a classroom of 30 first-grade students, the ratio of 5-year-olds to all students is 2:5. How many students are 5 years old?

You are given a part-to-whole ratio (5-year-olds to all students) of $\frac{2}{5}$. Multiplying this fraction by the value of the whole gives the value of the corresponding part. There are 30 students, and $\frac{2}{5}$ of them are 5 years old, so the number of 5-year-olds is $\frac{2}{\cancel{5}^1} \times \cancel{30}^6 = 12$.

Note that the actual quantity of a thing will always be a multiple of the number that represents it in a ratio. Keeping this fact in mind can be very helpful in eliminating answer choices in Problem Solving questions before doing any calculations.

Example: A pond contains koi and goldfish and no other fish. The ratio of koi to goldfish in the pond is 2:3. What are possible numbers of koi, goldfish, and total fish?

If the pond contains 2 koi, it has 3 goldfish and 5 fish altogether. If it has twice as many fish, that's 4 koi and 6 goldfish for 10 total fish. But what if the pond held 3 koi? It would have to contain 4.5 goldfish and 7.5 total fish—which isn't possible. (Things that generally exist intact in the real world must be kept intact when working with ratios on the GMAT.)

Given a ratio, you can find actual values by using a common multiplier.

Example: If the ratio of used cars to new cars at a dealership is 2:5, and there are 10 used cars, how many new cars are there?

Since the ratio of used to new cars is 2:5, the number of used cars will be $2x$ and the number of new cars will be $5x$. Since there are 10 used cars, $2x = 10$ and $x = 5$. So, there are $5x = 5(5) = 25$ new cars.

You can often find the actual numbers of entities as long as the question gives you just one actual number of things along with the ratios.

Example: A homecoming party at College Y is initially attended by students and alumni in a ratio of 5 to 1. But after 2 hours, 36 more alumni arrive, changing the ratio of students to alumni to 2 to 1. If the number of students did not change, how many people were at the party when it began?

The only actual number of people referenced is the 36 alumni who show up late. Nonetheless, you can solve for the original (and ending) numbers of students, alumni, and people. Jot down the beginning ratio and the ratio 2 hours later.

BEGINNING RATIO	RATIO 2 HOURS LATER
$\dfrac{S}{A} = \dfrac{5}{1}$	$\dfrac{S}{A + 36} = \dfrac{2}{1}$

Cross multiply each ratio: $S = 5A$ and $S = 2A + 72$. Now you have two expressions that both equal S. Set these expressions equal to each other and solve for A:

$$5A = 2A + 72$$
$$3A = 72$$
$$A = 24$$

The number of alumni at the beginning of the party was 24. The ratio of students to alumni at the start of the party was 5 to 1, so there were $5 + 1 = 6$ times as many people as alumni: $6 \times 24 = 144$ people.

Now use the drill to get some practice working with ratios.

Ratios Drill

Answers follow the drill.

1. If the ratio of red bikes to all other bikes at a bike store is 2:5, what is the ratio of red bikes to total bikes?

2. Given the ratio of 4:3:2 items in a box, what is the minimum total number of items in the box?

3. A game shop hosts weekly events. There are 3 card game events for every 5 board game events. If there are 24 events this week, how many card games did the shop host?

4. A pet store normally sells 5 bags of cat food for every 11 bags of dog food. Additionally, it sells 2 bags of ferret food for every 1 bag of dog food. What is the ratio of cat food to ferret food?

5. A charity donates care packages to needy families that each contain items A, B, and C in the ratio of 5:4:1. Assuming that it stocks these items using the same ratio, what is the minimum number of items it has in stock if it can provide care packages to 75 families?

Ratios Drill: Answers

1. 2:7

2. 9

3. $\dfrac{\text{Card}}{\text{Total}} = \dfrac{3}{3+5} = \dfrac{c}{24}; c = 9$

4. $\dfrac{C}{D} = \dfrac{5}{11}; \dfrac{D}{F} = \dfrac{1}{2} = \dfrac{11}{22}; \dfrac{C}{F} = \dfrac{5}{22}$

5. Minimum of $5 + 4 + 1 = 10$ items/package $\times$ 75 families $= 750$ items

---

CONCEPT CHECK

- What are the two relationships that can be described by a ratio?

  _____

- What are the two approaches you can use to combine two ratios into a common ratio?

  _____

- If the entities in a ratios problem cannot logically be non-integers, what can you deduce about the actual numbers of entities?

  _____

Example answers are in your book's online resources (**kaptest.com/login**).

Now see how a GMAT expert uses the Kaplan Method on a question that involves ratios.

> In a used bookstore, the ratio of hardcover to paperback books is 2:3. If the bookstore acquires 5 of each type of book and the new ratio of hardcover to softcover books is 3:4, what is the total number of books after the acquisition?
>
> ○   12
> ○   20
> ○   25
> ○   35
> ○   70

Step 1: Analyze the Question Stem

You're given the starting and ending ratio of hardcover to paperback books, and you're told that the actual number of each type of book increases by 5.

Step 2: State the Task

Use the given ratios and actual numbers of books to find the actual number of books after 5 books of each type are acquired.

Step 3: Approach Strategically

The final ratio of books is 3:4, so the total number of books has to be a multiple of $3 + 4$, or 7. Only two answer choices meet this criterion. Eliminate (A), (B), and (C).

Now you could backsolve. Try (D). If there are 35 books after the acquisition in a ratio of 3:4, that means the common multiplier is $35 \div 7 = 5$. Thus, after the acquisition, there are $3 \times 5 = 15$ hardcover books and $4 \times 5 = 20$ paperbacks. Since 5 of each type of book were acquired, subtract 5 from each number to get 10 hardcovers and 15 paperbacks. The quantities 10 and 15 are in a ratio of 2:3, which is the starting ratio given in the question stem. (D) is correct.

Step 4: Confirm Your Answer

You can check (E). If there are 70 books after the acquisition in a ratio of 3:4, that means there were $3 \times 10 = 30$ hardcovers and $4 \times 10 = 40$ paperbacks. Subtract 5 from each to get 25 hardcovers and 35 paperbacks, but that's a ratio of 5:7—not the correct starting ratio.

Next, you'll find some in-format questions involving ratios.

Practice Set: Ratios

(Answers and explanations are at the end of the chapter.)

1.   At a certain university, the football program receives 4 times more funding than does the basketball program. Together, the football and basketball programs receive 3 times as much funding as do all other sports programs combined. What is the ratio of funding for the basketball program to funding for all other sports programs, not including the football program?

  ○   1:5

  ○   1:4

  ○   3:5

  ○   3:4

  ○   5:3

2.   If $\frac{a}{b} = \frac{c}{d}$, what is the numerical ratio of b to d?

  (1) $\frac{a}{b} = \frac{3c}{2b}$

  (2) $a = 2$ and $d = 4$.

3.   If the ratio of a to b is 4 to 3 and the ratio of b to c is 1 to 5, what is the ratio of a to c?

  ○ $\frac{4}{15}$

  ○ $\frac{1}{3}$

  ○ $\frac{2}{5}$

  ○ $\frac{4}{5}$

  ○ $\frac{7}{6}$

Proportions

The GMAT will frequently ask you to deal with proportional relationships by working with fractions that represent ratios.

A **proportion** is a comparison of two ratios. A proportion usually consists of an equation in which two ratios, expressed as fractions, are set equal to each other. Occasionally, you may see a proportion written as an inequality. Fractions in proportions represent part-to-part or part-to-whole relationships. When dealing with proportions, it's important to notice what something is a proportion *of*. In the proportion, the numerators of both fractions must represent the same thing, and the denominators of both fractions must represent the same thing.

To solve a proportion, there are two useful approaches. One is **cross multiplication**, in which the numerator from the first ratio is multiplied by the denominator from the second ratio, and then the denominator from the first ratio is multiplied by the numerator of the second ratio. The two products are set equal to each other. Then you solve for the variable in the equation.

Example: Solve for m: $\frac{6}{11} = \frac{m}{33}$.

Using cross multiplication, the equation becomes $6 \times 33 = m \times 11$. Before you spend time multiplying out 6×33, notice that you can instead divide both sides of the equation by 11. This simplifies to $6 \times 3 = m$. Thus, $m = 18$.

The second way, often more efficient, is to use the **common multiplier principle**, in which the known values from each fraction are compared to determine their relationship; then that relationship is applied to the unknown value.

Example: Solve for m: $\frac{6}{11} = \frac{m}{33}$.

Compare the denominators to determine that 33 is 3×11. Since the denominator of the first fraction is multiplied by 3 to yield the denominator of the second fraction, the numerator of the first fraction must also be multiplied by 3 to yield the value of m. (The common multiplier is 3.) Therefore, m must be 3×6. That's 18.

To solve word problems involving proportional relationships, translate the English into math so that the units of the same type are either one above the other or directly across from one another.

Example: The ratio of T-shirts to sweaters in a closet is 4:5. If there are 24 T-shirts in the closet, how many sweaters are there?

Set up a proportion, being careful to line up the units. One way to write the proportion is $\frac{4 \text{ T-shirts}}{5 \text{ sweaters}} = \frac{24 \text{ T-shirts}}{x \text{ sweaters}}$. Note that the label of T-shirts appears in both numerators and the label of sweaters appears in both denominators. The common multiplier can be determined by comparing numerators: since $24 \div 4 = 6$, the common multiplier is 6. Thus, there are $5 \times 6 = 30$ sweaters.

You could also set up the proportion $\frac{4 \text{ T-shirts}}{24 \text{ T-shirts}} = \frac{5 \text{ sweaters}}{x \text{ sweaters}}$, which lines up the clothing types above each other rather than across from each other. You still compare T-shirts to T-shirts to find the common multiplier of 6, which you then apply to the 5 sweaters.

Both arrangements of the proportion could be solved using cross multiplication as well, but using the common multiplier is more efficient.

A question might also ask you to relate the number of items represented by one part of a ratio to the total number of items represented by both parts, or vice versa.

Example: The ratio of pants to shirts in a closet is 6:13. If the total number of pants and shirts is 76, how many shirts are there?

You are given both parts of the ratio, representing pants and shirts. You're also given the actual number of pants and shirts combined. To find the actual number of shirts, set up this proportion comparing the part-to-whole ratio to a ratio of actual values, which the unknown number of shirts represented by s:

$$\frac{\text{Shirts}}{\text{Total}} = \frac{13}{6 + 13} = \frac{s}{76}$$
$$\frac{13}{19} = \frac{s}{76}$$

Because $76 \div 19 = 4$, the common multiplier is 4. Then $13 \times 4 = 52$, and there are 52 shirts.

Now use the drill to get some practice working with proportions.

Proportions Drill

Answers follow the drill.

For questions 1–3, solve for the value of the variable.

1. $\frac{7}{12} = \frac{x}{60}$

2. $\frac{24}{n} = \frac{8}{7}$

3. $\frac{16}{3} = \frac{100}{a}$

4. The ratio of doctors to nurses in a hospital is 3:10. If there are 36 doctors in the hospital, how many nurses are there?

5. The ratio of cars to trucks in a parking lot is 15:2. If there are 225 cars in the lot, how many cars and trucks combined are there?

Proportions Drill: Answers

1. 35

2. 21

3. 18.75

4. 120

5. 255

CONCEPT CHECK

- How do you ensure the values are aligned correctly when setting up a proportion?

  _____

- What is a common multiplier in a proportion?

  _____

- If you are given a ratio and one of the actual values represented in that ratio, what other values can you find?

  _____

Example answers are in your book's online resources (**kaptest.com/login**).

Now see how a GMAT expert uses the Kaplan Method on a Data Sufficiency question that involves proportions.

> A bakery case contains only cookies and pastries. What percentage of the items in the case are chocolate chip cookies?
>
> (1) $\frac{3}{4}$ of the cookies are not chocolate chip.
>
> (2) If the number of pastries were decreased by 25%, the number of pastries would be three times the number of chocolate chip cookies.

Step 1: Analyze the Question Stem

This Value question tells you that there are cookies and pastries in a bakery case, and no other items. The question asks for the percentage of all of the items that are chocolate chip cookies. To have sufficiency, you need information from which you could derive the ratio of chocolate chip cookies to the other cookies and the pastries in the case. The terms "cookies" and "chocolate chip cookies" both start with c and therefore could be confusing; you could decide at this point to refer to the total number of cookies as capital C and the number of chocolate chip cookies as lowercase c to keep them straight.

Step 2: Evaluate the Statements Using 12TEN

Statement (1) says that $\frac{3}{4}$ of the cookies are not chocolate chip, which is the same as saying that $\frac{1}{4}$ of the cookies *are* chocolate chip. However, there is no information given about the fraction of items in the case that are pastries, so this is insufficient. Eliminate **(A)** and **(D)**.

Statement (2) indicates that if the number of pastries (call this P) were reduced by 25%, they would be equal to 3 times the number of chocolate chip cookies. As an equation, this could be written $0.75P = 3c$, or $\frac{3}{4}P = 3c$. This can be simplified to $P = 4c$. There are 4 times as many pastries in the case as chocolate chip cookies. However, there is no information about the relationship between chocolate chip cookies and other cookies, so it's not possible to know what percentage of all the items are chocolate chip cookies. Therefore, Statement (2) is insufficient. Eliminate **(B)**.

Since neither statement was sufficient on its own, try combining them. Statement (1) provides a relationship between chocolate chip cookies and other cookies, and Statement (2) provides a relationship between pastries and chocolate chip cookies. That is sufficient to answer the question, so **(C)** is correct.

For the record, you could set up equations to solve for c. Call the number of total cookies C and the number of total items in the case T. Since from Statement (1), you know that $\frac{1}{4}C = c$, you can say that $C = 4c$. From your work paraphrasing Statement (2), you know that P also equals $4c$. Therefore, $C = P$. Since $C + P = T$ and C and P are equal, $C = \frac{1}{2}T$. Now $c = \frac{1}{4}C = \frac{1}{4}\left(\frac{1}{2}T\right) = \frac{1}{8}T$. Convert to a percent as the question asks: $\frac{1}{8} = 12.5\%$. Thus, 12.5% of all items in the case are chocolate chip cookies.

Next, you'll find some in-format questions involving proportions.

Practice Set: Proportions

(Answers and explanations are at the end of the chapter.)

4. The weight of a certain type of cable is always directly proportional to its length. If 560 meters of this cable weighs 84 kilograms, what is the weight, in kilograms, of 110 meters of the same cable?

    ○   11.5
    ○   16.5
    ○   22
    ○   24.5
    ○   26

5. The ratio of the cost of a wooden plank to the length of a wooden plank is constant. A plank measuring 6 feet long costs $96. Jordan wants to buy planks that measure 10 feet in length, and Kristen wants to buy planks that are 7.5 feet in length. How much more, in dollars, will Jordan pay per plank?

    ○   40
    ○   45
    ○   120
    ○   135
    ○   160

6. There are chips of four different colors in a bucket distributed as follows: $\frac{1}{2}$ are white, $\frac{1}{6}$ are green, $\frac{1}{5}$ are blue, and the remaining 12 chips are red. What is the total number of chips in the bucket?

    ○   38
    ○   78
    ○   90
    ○   102
    ○   120

Rates and Unit Conversions

LEARNING OBJECTIVES

- Solve problems using rate formulas
- Use proportions to perform unit conversions

On the GMAT, the most common rate is a speed, such as miles per hour. But anything with the word *per* is a rate: kilometers per second, miles per gallon, ounces of cheese per party guest, and so forth. A **rate** is any quantity of A per quantity of B.

$$\text{Rate } A \text{ per } B = \frac{\text{Quantity of } A}{\text{Quantity of } B}$$

In general, the amount of work that someone or something does is equal to the rate at which they work multiplied by the amount of time they work. If you know any two values in this three-part formula, you can find the third value.

$$\text{Work} = \text{Rate} \times \text{Time}$$
$$\text{Rate} = \frac{\text{Work}}{\text{Time}}$$
$$\text{Time} = \frac{\text{Work}}{\text{Rate}}$$

One type of work that can be accomplished is to travel a distance, so you'll often see the formulas above written with *Distance* substituted for *Work* and *Speed* substituted for *Time*.

Many rate problems involve conversions from one rate to another. These are best handled by multiplying the various rates so that the units of measure you don't want in your answer cancel out. You may have to invert some of the rates to make the units of measure cancel.

Example: If a car averages 25 miles per gallon and each gallon of gas costs \$2, what is the value of the gas consumed during a trip of 175 miles?

$$\frac{\$2}{1 \text{ gallon}} \times \frac{1 \text{ gallon}}{25 \text{ miles}} \times 175 \text{ miles}$$

Notice that you need to invert *miles per gallon* to *gallons per mile* so the gallons and miles cancel out and you're left with dollars.

$$\frac{\$2}{1 \text{ gallon}} \times \frac{\text{gallon}}{25^1 \text{ miles}} \times 175^7 \text{ miles}$$

$$\$2 \times 7$$

$$\$14$$

Example: If José reads at a constant rate of 2 pages every 5 minutes, how many seconds will it take him to read N pages?

Change the rate you're given in minutes into seconds. There are 60 seconds in a minute, so $\dfrac{2^1 \text{ pages}}{5 \text{ minutes}} \times \dfrac{1 \text{ minute}}{60^{30} \text{ seconds}} = \dfrac{1 \text{ page}}{150 \text{ seconds}}$.

Call the time in seconds T. Set up the proportion relating pages to seconds: $\dfrac{1}{150} = \dfrac{N}{T}$. Cross multiply to get $T = 150N$.

Now use the drill to get some practice working with rates and unit conversion.

Rates and Unit Conversions Drill

Answers follow the drill.

1. What is the distance traveled if an average speed of 40 miles per hour is maintained for 1.5 hours?

2. How many minutes would it take to travel 50 miles at an average speed of 30 miles per hour?

3. How many minutes will it take to pick $20 worth of apples if the price is $2.50 per pound and a worker picks apples at a rate of 4 pounds per minute?

4. A furlong is 220 yards or approximately 200 meters. If there are 1,760 yards in a mile, approximately how many meters are in a mile?

5. Company A can mow L square feet of lawn per hour, and Company B can mow $L + 200$ square feet per hour. How much longer, in minutes, will it take Company A to mow a yard that is M square feet?

Rates and Unit Conversions Drill: Answers

1. 60 miles

2. 100 minutes

3. 2 minutes

4. $\dfrac{\text{Yards}}{\text{Meters}} = \dfrac{220}{200} = \dfrac{11}{10} = \dfrac{1,760}{x}$; $x = 1,600$

5. $60 \dfrac{\text{min}}{\text{hr}} \left(\dfrac{M \text{ sq ft}}{L \dfrac{\text{sq ft}}{\text{hr}}} \right) - 60 \dfrac{\text{min}}{\text{hr}} \left(\dfrac{M \text{ sq ft}}{L + 200 \dfrac{\text{sq ft}}{\text{hr}}} \right)$

$= 60 \left(\dfrac{M}{L} - \dfrac{M}{L + 200} \right)$ minutes

---

CONCEPT CHECK

- What is the general formula for rates?

  _____

- What is the formula for speed?

  _____

- Describe how to set up a rates conversion problem algebraically.

  _____

Example answers are in your book's online resources (**kaptest.com/login**).

Now see how a GMAT expert uses the Kaplan Method to answer a Problem Solving question about rates.

If the city centers of New York and London are 3,471 miles apart, which of the following is closest to the distance between the city centers in inches? (There are 5,280 feet in a mile and 12 inches per foot.)

- ○ 1.75×10^6
- ○ 1.83×10^7
- ○ 2.10×10^8
- ○ 2.10×10^9
- ○ 2.20×10^{10}

Step 1: Analyze the Question

There are some large numbers in this question, but the words "closest to" and the fact that the answer choices are at least a power of 10 apart let you know that you can estimate.

Step 2: State the Task

Use the given equivalencies of feet to miles and inches to feet to convert 3,471 miles into inches, expressed in scientific notation.

Step 3: Approach Strategically

Set up the calculation so the feet and miles cancel out: $3{,}471 \text{ miles} \times \dfrac{5{,}280 \text{ feet}}{1 \text{ mile}} \times \dfrac{12 \text{ inches}}{1 \text{ foot}}$.

That's $3{,}471 \times 5{,}280 \times 12$. Happily, you can estimate: $3{,}500 \times 5{,}000 \times 10 = (3.5 \times 10^3) \times (5 \times 10^3) \times 10^1 = 1.75 \times 10^8$. The only answer that's close (within a power of 10) is (**C**).

Step 4: Confirm Your Answer

Re-read the question stem, making sure that you didn't miss anything about the problem. For example, if you accidentally solved for feet instead of inches, you'd have chosen (**B**).

Next, you'll find in-format questions involving rates and unit conversions.

Practice Set: Rates and Unit Conversions

(Answers and explanations are at the end of the chapter.)

7. Bridget and her friends rent a small bus to go sightseeing. The rate for the bus and driver is $90 per hour, and the total distance of the sightseeing tour is 112 miles. If the total charge for the trip is $420, what is the average speed of the bus in miles per hour?

    O   16.7

    O   21.0

    O   22.5

    O   24.0

    O   25.8

8. Pierre's European car measures fuel economy in terms of liters per kilometer. If the car averages $\frac{1 \text{ liter}}{10 \text{ kilometers}}$ on a trip, what is the car's approximate fuel economy in terms of the standard U.S. measurement of miles per gallon? (Note: 1 gallon is approximately 3.78 liters, and 1 mile is approximately 1.61 kilometers.)

    O   4

    O   16

    O   24

    O   30

    O   40

9. A student can complete x homework questions in h hours. According to his calculations, it will take him 4 days to complete his latest assignment if he works m minutes a day. How many questions are on his latest assignment?

    O $\frac{mx}{60h}$

    O $\frac{15x}{mh}$

    O $\frac{4xh}{m}$

    O $\frac{mx}{15h}$

    O $\frac{4mx}{15h}$

Averages and Weighted Averages

LEARNING OBJECTIVES

- Calculate averages using average formulas and the balance approach
- Find an unknown value given the average
- Apply the weighted average approach to data sets

The average (arithmetic mean) of a group of numbers is defined as the sum of the values divided by the number of values. Here is the **average formula**:

$$\text{Average value} = \frac{\text{Sum of values}}{\text{Number of values}}$$

Example: Henry buys 3 items costing $2.00, $0.75, and $0.25. What is the average price of the items?

$$\text{Average price} = \frac{\text{Sum of prices}}{\text{Number of prices}}$$

$$= \frac{\$2.00 + \$0.75 + \$0.25}{3}$$

$$= \frac{\$3.00}{3}$$

$$= \$1.00$$

If you know any two of the values in this three-part formula, you can solve for the third. For some questions, therefore, you may need to rearrange the formula to Sum of values = Average × Number of values or Number of values = $\frac{\text{Sum of values}}{\text{Average}}$.

Example: Two classes in a school are having a candy sales contest. Each class has a goal of averaging $40 in sales per student. The goal for Class A is $960. How many students are in Class A?

$$\text{Number of values} = \frac{\text{Sum of values}}{\text{Average}} = \frac{\$960}{\$40/\text{student}} = 24 \text{ students}$$

You can save time on calculations if you think of the average as a "balancing point" among the values. That is, the sum of the differences between the average and every number below it must equal the sum of the differences between the average and every number above it.

You've already seen that the average of $2.00, $0.75, and $0.25 is $1.00. The figure shows how that relationship is represented using the **balance approach**. You can think of the values as sitting on a seesaw with the average as the fulcrum.

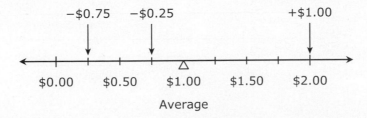

Average

The total of the differences between the average and the values below the average is −$1.00, and the difference between the average and the value above the average is +$1.00. Thus, the values are "in balance" around the average.

Example: The average of 143, 144, 145, and x is 145. What is the value of x?

Find the differences between each given value and the average: $143 − 144 = −2$, $144 − 145 = −1$, and $145 − 145 = 0$. That's a total difference so far of $−2 + (−1) = −3$. Therefore, the remaining value must be 3 above the average to achieve balance. So $x = 145 + 3 = 148$.

Another way to calculate the average is to use the **weighted average formula**:

$$\text{Average} = \frac{\text{Weight}_1\left(\text{Value}_1\right) + \text{Weight}_2\left(\text{Value}_2\right) + \ldots + \text{Weight}_n\left(\text{Value}_n\right)}{\text{Total of weights}}$$

Weighted averages are useful when you don't know the individual value of each element in the group but you do know the values or averages of different portions of the whole.

Example: If two-fifths of the students in a class have an average score of 79 on a test and the remaining three-fifths have an average score of 84, what is the average score for the entire class?

Set up the weighted average formula, weighting the value 79 by 2 (because it is two-fifths of the total) and weighting the value 84 by 3 (because it is three-fifths of the total):

$$\text{Average} = \frac{2(79) + 3(84)}{2 + 3}$$

$$= \frac{158 + 252}{5} = \frac{410}{5} = 82$$

Notice that the average of the whole class comes out closer to 84 than to 79. This will always be the case when the portions of the whole are of different sizes. In fact, this is where the term "weighted average" comes from; the larger the portion of the whole, the more heavily "weighted" that portion is when calculating the overall average. Note that you can use the weighted average formula as long as you have averages for all portions adding up to 100 percent of the whole.

Some questions may present the data in the form of a **frequency table**.

Example: Antony tracked his coffee consumption for 15 days and summarized the data in a table.

NUMBER OF CUPS OF COFFEE CONSUMED	NUMBER OF DAYS
0	3
1	2
2	4
3	4
4	2

Reading the table, you see that Antony had no coffee on 3 days, 1 cup of coffee on 2 days, 2 cups on 4 days, etc. To calculate Antony's average coffee consumption, use the numbers of cups of coffee consumed as the values and weight these values by the numbers of days each occurred.

$$\text{Weighted average} = \frac{3(0) + 2(1) + 4(2) + 4(3) + 2(4)}{3 + 2 + 4 + 4 + 2}$$

This simplifies to $\frac{30}{15} = 2$ cups of coffee per day on average.

Now use the drill to get some practice working with averages.

Averages and Weighted Averages Drill

Answers follow the drill.

1. What is the average of 2, 6, 8, and 12?

2. The average of 1,750, 1,747, 1,744, and x is 1,749. What is the value of x?

3. The average of a group of 3 numbers is 7. What number must be added to bring the new average up to 9?

4. In one year, a business earns 60 percent margins for 8 months and 90 percent margins for 4 months. What is the average margin earned for the year?

5. What is the weighted average of the values below?

Value	Number of Occurrences
2	5
3	3
4	3
5	5
6	4

Averages Drill: Answers

1. 7

2. 1,755

3. 15

4. $\dfrac{(8)(60\%) + (4)(90\%)}{12} = 70\%$

5. $\dfrac{(2)(5) + (3)(3) + (4)(3) + (5)(5) + (6)(4)}{20} = 4$

CONCEPT CHECK

- The average formula is _____.

- Describe the balance approach to calculating an average.

  _____

- What is the weighted average formula?

  _____

Example answers are in your book's online resources (**kaptest.com/login**).

Now see how a GMAT expert uses the Kaplan Method to answer a Data Sufficiency question involving averages.

> If each of the bowlers in a tournament bowled an equal number of games, what is the average (arithmetic mean) score of all the games bowled in the tournament?
>
> (1) Of the bowlers, 70 percent had an average (arithmetic mean) score of 120, and the other 30 percent had an average score of 140.
>
> (2) Each of the 350 bowlers in the tournament bowled 3 games.

Step 1: Analyze the Question Stem

This a Value question that asks for the average score of all games bowled in a tournament. The only information provided is that each person in the tournament bowled the same number of games. To answer the question, you'll need either the number of games and the total of the scores (for the average formula) or some way to calculate a weighted average.

Step 2: Evaluate the Statements Using 12TEN

Statement (2) is straightforward, so starting here makes sense. This tells you the number of games but nothing about the scores. Insufficient. Eliminate **(B)** and **(D)**.

Statement (1) doesn't allow you to figure out the number of games or the sum of the scores. But since the proportions add up to 100% of the total, and you know that all the bowlers bowled the same number of games, you could calculate the overall average using the weighted average approach. Sufficient. **(A)** is correct.

Next, you'll find in-format questions involving averages.

Practice Set: Averages and Weighted Averages

(Answers and explanations are at the end of the chapter.)

10. Bradley's grade in his science class is determined by his scores on 5 tests that each count an equal amount toward his grade. He has received scores of 67, 76, 78, and 94 on the 4 science tests thus far. If the last test consists of 20 equally weighted questions and is graded out of 100 points, how many questions does he need to answer correctly on the last test in order to obtain an average (arithmetic mean) of 80 in his science class?

    ○ 15
    ○ 16
    ○ 17
    ○ 18
    ○ 19

POINTS	# OF ARROWS
0	1
1	1
3	3
5	6
7	8
9	2

11. In a certain archery contest, archers are awarded a different number of points for each arrow, depending upon the accuracy of the shot. If an arrow hits the bull's-eye, 10 points are awarded. The results for one archer are shown in the table above, but the values do not include her bull's-eyes. If the archer's average (arithmetic mean) number of points scored per arrow is 6.0, how many of her attempts were bull's-eyes?

    ○ 0
    ○ 1
    ○ 2
    ○ 3
    ○ 4

12. An exam is given in a certain class. The average (arithmetic mean) of the highest score and the lowest score on the exam is equal to x. If the average score for the entire class is equal to y and there are z students in the class, where $z > 5$, then in terms of x, y, and z, what is the average score for the class, excluding the highest and lowest scores?

- $\frac{zy - 2x}{z}$

- $\frac{zy - 2}{z}$

- $\frac{zx - y}{z - 2}$

- $\frac{zy - 2x}{z - 2}$

- $\frac{zy - x}{z + 2}$

13. The average price of Emily's 5 meals was $20. If none of Emily's meals were free, how many of Emily's meals were priced at $25 or more?

(1) The most expensive of the 5 meals had a price of $50.

(2) The least expensive of the 5 meals had a price of $10.

14. In an increasing sequence of 8 consecutive even integers, the sum of the first 4 integers is 268. What is the sum of all the integers in the sequence?

- 552

- 568

- 574

- 586

- 590

15. In an election, candidate Suarez won 52 percent of the total vote in Counties A and B. He won 61 percent of the vote in County A. If the ratio of people who voted in County A to County B is 3:1, what percent of the vote did candidate Suarez win in County B?

   O   25%

   O   27%

   O   34%

   O   43%

   O   49%

Mixtures

LEARNING OBJECTIVE

- Use the weighted average formula and the balanced average approach to solve for an unknown value in a mixture question

---

Mixture problems can look more complicated than they are because they may describe things such as chemical solutions, which may evoke memories of science labs. Underneath their window dressing, however, mixture problems are just word problems involving weighted averages. Organize the given information and use either the balanced average approach or the weighted average formula to solve.

Suppose you're told that there are several different amounts of solutions containing different concentrations of Substance X. You might be asked to find the percent of Substance X in a mixture of the different solutions, or the question might give you the percent of Substance X in the mixture and ask for the concentration of the substance in one of the component solutions. Either way, you can use the **weighted average formula** to solve:

$$\text{Average} = \frac{\text{Weight}_1(\text{Value}_1) + \text{Weight}_2(\text{Value}_2) + \ldots + \text{Weight}_n(\text{Value}_n)}{\text{Total of weights}}$$

The average on the left is the percent of Substance X in the final mixture. The values are the concentration of Substance X in the components that make up the final mixture, usually given as percents. The components are weighted according to the proportion of each in the final mixture. The weights may be the actual quantities of the components, in which case the "total of weights" is the sum of the quantities. Or they may be fractions or percents of the whole, in which case the "total of weights" is typically 100% or 1 (the whole mixture) and can be ignored in the calculation.

Example: Samuel, Laura, and Remi each bring a bowl of fruit punch to a garden party. Samuel's 20 liters of punch contain 10 percent apple juice by volume, Laura's 10 liters of punch contain 20 percent apple juice by volume, and Remi's 10 liters of punch contain an unknown percentage of apple juice. If they all pour their punch into the same bowl, creating a new mix of 25% apple juice by volume, what is the percentage of apple juice in Remi's punch?

Set up the weighted average formula. Here, the average on the left is the percent of apple juice in the final mixture. The values in parentheses are the concentrations of punch, and the weights are the quantities of each person's punch. The total weight is the total amount of punch. R represents the concentration of apple juice in Remi's punch.

$$25\% = \frac{20(10\%) + 10(20\%) + 10(R)}{20 + 10 + 10}$$

$$25\% = \frac{2 + 2 + 10(R)}{40}$$

$$10 = 4 + 10(R)$$

$$6 = 10(R)$$

$$R = \frac{6}{10}$$

$$R = 0.6 = 60\%$$

Since Samuel and Laura contribute quite a bit of the punch to the mixture and their punches are significantly weaker than the final mixture, it makes sense that Remi's punch is quite a bit stronger than the final mixture.

Just as with other weighted average problems, you can also use the **balance approach** for problems involving mixtures. Here's how the previous example would be solved using the balance approach.

Find the differences between each person's percent value and the combined average of 25%. Since Samuel adds twice as much punch as either Laura or Remi, weight his contribution by a factor of 2.

- Samuel: $10\% - 25\% = -15\% \rightarrow -15\% \times 2 = -30\%$
- Laura: $20\% - 25\% = -5\%$
- Remi: Samuel and Laura together create a value of $-30 + -5 = -35$ below the average. Therefore, to bring the concentrations of apple juice into balance at 25%, Remi's punch must be 35 above the average. Thus, Remi's punch must have a juice concentration of $25\% + 35\% = 60\%$.

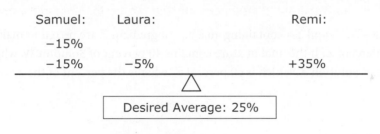

Some mixture problems can be solved without using the concept of weighted average. Instead, you can apply the "percent of" formula. Use the approach that's most intuitive and efficient for you.

Example: A scientist has 10 ounces of a 14 percent alcohol solution. How much water would the scientist have to add to the solution to make the alcohol content equal to 10 percent?

"Percent of" formula: The scientist has 10 ounces of 14% solution, so there are $14\% \times 10 = 1.4$ ounces of alcohol. There's no change to the amount of alcohol; only water is added. Therefore, in the new solution, there will still be 1.4 ounces of alcohol. However, that alcohol will be only 10% of the solution. Set up the equation $10\% \times S = 1.4$. The amount of solution S is 14 ounces. Therefore, the amount of water the scientist needs to add is $14 - 10 = 4$ ounces.

"Balance" approach: The scientist has 10 ounces of 14% solution. Compared to the desired concentration of 10%, that's +4%/ounce × 10 ounces = +40%. The water has a concentration of 0% alcohol, so, compared to the desired concentration of 10%, it contributes $0\% - 10\% = -10\%$ per ounce. To balance out the existing solution, the water needs to contribute −40%. Set up the equation $-10\%/\text{ounce} \times A \text{ ounces} = -40\%$ and solve for A. The scientist needs to add $A = 4$ ounces of water.

Now use the drill to get some practice applying these approaches to mixtures.

Mixtures Drills

Use either the weighted average formula or the balance approach to answer each of the following. Answers showing at least one approach follow the drill.

1. An artist creates a dye by mixing a 20 percent blue solution with a 60 percent blue solution in a ratio of 3 to 2. The dye is what percent blue?

2. A gardener fills a raised bed with soil from two bins. The gardener takes 90 percent of the soil for the bed from a bin containing soil that is 60 percent compost. The gardener takes the remaining soil for the bed from a bin containing soil that is 40 percent compost. What is the percent compost in the raised bed's soil?

3. Jack has two buckets of a salt solution. The first bucket contains 20 ounces of a 35 percent salt solution. The second bucket contains a solution that is 50 percent salt. If Jack combines the contents of each bucket to create a new mixture that is 45 percent salt, how many ounces of solution does the second bucket contain?

4. A chemist prepares a solution containing 60 percent acetone by mixing 5 ounces of Solution A, which is 30 percent acetone, with 15 ounces of Solution B. What is the percent concentration of acetone in Solution B?

5. Three solutions—W, X, and Y—containing an active ingredient Z are mixed to make a solution containing 50 percent Z. If the final mixture contains 40 percent of Solution W, which is 20 percent Z, and 40 percent of Solution X, which is 60 percent Z, what is the percent of the active ingredient in Solution Y?

Mixtures Drills: Answers

1. $\dfrac{3(20\%) + 2(60\%)}{5} = 36\%$

2. $\dfrac{90\%(60) + 10\%(40)}{100\%} = 58\%$

3. 20 oz. $\times$ (-10%/oz.) $= -200\%$; S oz. $\times$ (5%/oz) $= +200\%$; $S = 40$ ounces

4. 5 oz. $\times$ (-30%/oz.) $= -150\%$; 15 oz. $\times$ (A/oz.) $= +150\%$; $A = 10\%$; $60\% + 10\% = 70\%$

5. Weighted average formula:

   $\dfrac{40\%(20) + 40\%(60) + 20\%(x)}{100\%} = 50\%$; $x = 90$

   Balance approach: $4 \times (-30) + 4 \times (10) = -80$; $2 \times d = +80$; $d = +40$; $50 + 40 = 90$

CONCEPT CHECK

- How do problems involving mixtures relate to weighted average problems?

  _____

- How do you plug values into the weighted average formula when solving a mixtures problem involving Substance X?

  _____

- When you use the balance approach to solve a mixtures problem, what is the "balance point"?

  _____

Example answers are in your book's online resources (**kaptest.com/login**).

Now see how a GMAT expert uses the Kaplan Method to solve a question that involves mixtures.

> Two brands of detergent are to be combined. Detergent X contains 20 percent bleach and 80 percent soap, while Detergent Y contains 45 percent bleach and 55 percent soap. If the combined mixture is to be 35 percent bleach, what percent of the final mixture should be Detergent X?
>
> ○ 10%
>
> ○ $32\frac{1}{2}$%
>
> ○ 35%
>
> ○ 40%
>
> ○ 60%

Step 1: Analyze the Question

You are creating a new mixture from two others, Detergent X and Detergent Y. X is 20% bleach, and Y is 45% bleach. The new mixture is to be 35% bleach. You're given no information about the actual volume of any bleach. Because only the final percent of bleach is provided, ignore the information about soap; it is simply the portion of the mixtures that is not bleach.

Step 2: State the Task

You're being asked for the percent of the whole mixture that is Detergent X. Note that you don't need to find an actual quantity of Detergent X, just its relationship to the whole. You can use either the balanced average approach or the weighted average formula. For most students, the balanced average approach will be more efficient.

Step 3: Approach Strategically

At 20% bleach, Detergent X is 15 percentage points below the final concentration of 35%. At 45% bleach, Detergent Y is 10 percentage points above the final concentration. When each of these differences is multiplied by the quantity of the respective detergents, they will equal each other.

Set up an equation that represents the "balance" between what each detergent contributes to the final mixture. Then rearrange the values to find the fraction of the whole that is Detergent X. Here, X is the unknown volume of Detergent X, and Y is the unknown volume of Detergent Y.

$$15X = 10Y$$
$$\frac{X}{Y} = \frac{10}{15} = \frac{2}{3}$$

Since the final mixture consists only of the two detergents, and that whole is made up of 2 parts X and 3 parts Y, the whole can be represented in the ratio by $2 + 3 = 5$. Thus, the ratio of Detergent X to the whole mixture is $\frac{2}{5}$, so Detergent X makes up 40% of the mixture. **(D)** is correct.

Step 4: Confirm Your Answer

Check your answer against the logic of the situation. Since the percent concentration of bleach in Detergent X (20%) is further away from the final percent (35%) than Detergent Y's percent (45%), Detergent X should be less than half the mixture.

Next, you'll find some in-format questions involving mixtures.

Practice Set: Mixtures

(Answers and explanations are at the end of the chapter.)

16. A display case contains a certain number of donuts. Some are chocolate, some are jelly filled, and the rest are plain. One-sixth of the donuts are chocolate. How many chocolate donuts must be added so that one-fourth of the total donuts are chocolate?

    (1) There are 40 plain donuts in the case.

    (2) The ratio of plain donuts to jelly-filled donuts is 2:1.

17. A farmer who grows only two crops, corn and soybeans, has the same combined target output by weight every year. This year, corn makes up 40 percent of the crop and weighs 24 tons. Next year, however, the farmer wants corn to be only 15 percent of the total tonnage. How many more tons of soybeans must the farmer grow next year to maintain the same target output?

    ○ 9

    ○ 15

    ○ 25

    ○ 36

    ○ 51

18. If an amount of a solution containing 10 percent Chemical A is combined with twice as much of a solution that is 30 percent chemical A and four times as much of a solution that is 35 percent Chemical A, what is the concentration of Chemical A in the resulting solution?

    ○ 17.5%

    ○ 20%

    ○ 25%

    ○ 27.5%

    ○ 30%

Rates and Speed—Multi-Part Journeys

> **LEARNING OBJECTIVE**
>
> • Use the average rate formula to solve multi-part journey problems

The GMAT sometimes asks questions about the average rate of speed over a multi-part journey in which the parts are completed at different speeds. Just as you cannot use the averages of two different portions of a group to determine the group's overall average (unless you know the weights of the portions), you also cannot find the average overall speed of a journey from the speeds of two parts unless you know the proportion of time spent or distance traveled in those parts. Instead, you'll need to use the **average rate formula**:

$$\text{Average speed} = \frac{\text{Total distance}}{\text{Total time}}$$

Example: Amol travels 30 miles in 2 hours and then 60 miles in 3 hours. What is his average speed in miles per hour for the entire journey?

> Amol's first rate was 15 miles per hour, and his second rate was 20 miles per hour, so his average rate will fall somewhere between 15 and 20 miles per hour. Amol spent more *time* traveling at 20 miles per hour, so before doing any calculations, you know that his average rate will be closer to 20 than to 15. If you are running short on time, this deduction could allow a strategic guess.

$$\text{Average speed} = \frac{\text{Total miles}}{\text{Total hours}}$$
$$= \frac{(30+60)\text{ miles}}{(2+3)\text{ hours}} = \frac{90\text{ miles}}{5\text{ hours}} = 18\text{ miles/hour}$$

Multi-part journey questions frequently present you with a lot of information. To organize the data, you can create a chart such as this:

	RATE	TIME	DISTANCE
Part 1 of trip			
Part 2 of trip			
Entire trip			

This chart incorporates several relationships. Rate × Time = Distance, so each row of boxes *multiplies across*. The total time and distance are the sum of the time and distance for each part of the trip, so these columns *add down*. However, *rates* do *not* add down; they are calculated by dividing distance by time.

Example: A powerboat crosses a lake at 18 miles per hour and returns at 12 miles per hour. If the time taken turning the boat around is negligible and it returns by the same route, what is the boat's average speed for the round trip, in miles per hour?

Create a chart, using a question mark to indicate the value that the question asks for, and fill in the data given by the problem.

	RATE (MPH)	TIME (HR)	DISTANCE (MILES)
Part 1 of trip	18		
Part 2 of trip	12		
Entire trip	?		

Because the boat travels the same route both times, the distance for both legs must have been the same. You could use the variable D and solve with algebra, but since you are solving for overall rate, any distance will work as long as it's the same for both legs. This means you can pick numbers. You'll be dividing the distance of each leg by the rate for that leg, so picking a number that's a multiple both of 18 and of 12 will make the math work out nicely. Say the lake was 36 miles across.

	RATE (MPH)	TIME (HR)	DISTANCE (MILES)
Part 1 of trip	18		36
Part 2 of trip	12		36
Entire trip	?		

Now you can solve for the times and the total distance:

	RATE (MPH)	TIME (HR)	DISTANCE (MILES)
Part 1 of trip	18	2	36
Part 2 of trip	12	3	36
Entire trip	?	$3 + 2 = 5$	$36 + 36 = 72$

Now you have what you need to solve for average rate: $\frac{\text{Total distance}}{\text{Total time}} = \frac{72}{5} = 14.4$ mph. This answer makes logical sense: since the two rates are 18 and 12 miles per hour and the boat spent more time traveling at the lower speed, the average is closer to 12 than to 18.

Now use the drill to get some practice with multi-part journeys.

Multi-Part Journeys Drill

Answers follow the drill.

1. What is the overall average speed for a trip with one leg of 10 miles completed at a speed of 4 miles per hour and the other leg of 12 miles completed at a speed of 8 miles per hour?

2. The first part of a 2-part train ride took 1 hour at an average speed of 25 miles per hour. If the average speed for the entire ride was 35 miles per hour and the total time was 3 hours, what was the average speed of the second part of the ride?

3. What is the average speed for this 3-part journey?
   leg 1: 120 miles at 40 miles per hour
   leg 2: 40 miles in 2 hours
   leg 3: 2 hours at 25 miles per hour

4. The average speed for a 3-part trip is 32.5 miles per hour. The distances are 120, 50, and 90 miles for the three legs in that order. The average speeds for legs 2 and 3 are 25 and 30 miles per hour, respectively. What was the amount of time needed to complete the first leg?

5. The speed for the first leg of a two-leg journey is r, and the time to complete that leg is t. The speed for the second leg is 50 percent greater, and the time is twice that of the first leg. What is the average speed for the entire journey in terms of r?

Multi-Part Journeys Drill: Answers

1. 5.5 mph

2. 3 hrs × 35 mph = 105 miles total; 105 − 25 = 80 miles for part 2; 80 miles ÷ 2 hrs = 40 mph.

3. Time for leg 1 = 3 hrs; total time = 7 hrs. Distance for leg 3 = 50 miles; total distance = 210 miles. Overall speed = 210 miles ÷ 7 hrs = 30 mph.

4. Total distance = 120 + 50 + 90 = 260 miles. Total time = 260 miles ÷ 32.5 mph = 8 hrs. Time for leg 2 = 50 miles ÷ 25 mph = 2 hrs. Time for leg 3 = 90 miles ÷ 30 mph = 3 hrs. Time for leg 1 = 8 − 2 − 3 = 3 hours.

5. Picking numbers: If $r = 2$ and $t = 1$, distance of leg 1 = 2. Then rate for leg 2 = 3, time for leg 2 = 2, and distance for leg 2 = 2 × 3 = 6. Overall rate = $\frac{2 + 6}{1 + 2} = \frac{8}{3}$. Since $r = 2$, that's $\frac{4}{3}r = 1\frac{1}{3}r$.

CONCEPT CHECK

- What is the formula for overall average rate of speed?

  _____

- What must you know or be able to determine in order to calculate the average speed for an entire multi-part journey?

  _____

- If you set up a chart to solve a multi-part journey question, what will the columns and rows be labeled?

  _____

- Speeds for the legs of a multi-part journey are weighted by the _____ for each leg to get the average for the total trip.

Example answers are in your book's online resources (**kaptest.com/login**).

Now see how a GMAT expert uses the Kaplan Method to answer a Data Sufficiency question involving a multi-part journey.

> What was the average speed of a runner in a race from Point X to Point Z?
>
> (1) The runner's average speed from Point X to Point Y was 10 miles per hour.
>
> (2) The runner's average speed from Point Y to Point Z was 8 miles per hour.

Step 1: Analyze the Question Stem

To answer this Value question, you'll need either the total distance and total time or some information about distance or time that allows you to calculate the runner's overall speed.

Step 2: Evaluate the Statements Using 12TEN

Statement (1) gives you some data about the trip from X to Y but nothing about X to Z. This is insufficient, so eliminate (**A**) and (**D**).

Statement (2) gives you data about the trip from Y to Z but nothing about X to Z. Insufficient. Eliminate (**B**).

Even when combining the two statements, you have no information relating either the times or the distances of either leg. You cannot assume that they were the same distance or time, so the combined statements are insufficient, and (**E**) is correct.

Next, you'll find in-format questions involving multi-part journeys.

Practice Set: Rates and Speed—Multi-Part Journeys

(Answers and explanations are at the end of the chapter.)

19. A motorcyclist started riding at highway marker A, drove 120 miles to highway marker B, and then, without pausing, continued to highway marker C, where she stopped. The average speed of the motorcyclist, over the course of the entire trip, was 45 miles per hour. If the ride from marker A to marker B lasted 3 times as many hours as the rest of the ride, and the distance from marker B to marker C was half of the distance from marker A to marker B, what was the average speed, in miles per hour, of the motorcyclist while driving from marker B to marker C?

- O 40
- O 45
- O 50
- O 55
- O 60

20. Did Jon complete a journey of 40 kilometers in less time than it took Ann to complete the same journey?

(1) Jon traveled at an average speed of 30 kilometers per hour for the first 10 kilometers and then at an average speed of 15 kilometers per hour for the rest of the journey.

(2) Ann traveled at an average speed of 20 kilometers per hour for the entire journey.

21. A hiker walks three sections of a trail that are of equal length. The first section of the trail is flat, and on this section the hiker travels at 3 miles per hour for 1.5 hours. The second section is uphill, and on this section the hiker's pace slows by 25 percent. The third section is downhill, and here his speed doubles. What was the hiker's average speed for the entire three-section hike?

- O 1.5
- O 3
- O 3.25
- O 4.5
- O 9.75

22. A truck driver drove for 2 days. On the second day, she drove 3 hours longer and at an average speed of 15 miles per hour faster than she drove on the first day. If she drove a total of 1,020 miles and spent 21 hours driving during the 2 days, what was her average speed on the first day, in miles per hour?

    ○   25

    ○   30

    ○   35

    ○   40

    ○   45

Combined Rates and Combined Work

> **LEARNING OBJECTIVE**
>
> - Perform calculations involving combined rates
> - Apply the combined work formula

Combined work questions on the GMAT present you with information about different people or machines that perform the same task in different amounts of time because they are working at different rates. If two entities are working together to accomplish a task, then their rates can be added to find their combined rate of work.

Example: Alex can bake 30 cookies per hour, while Nzinga can bake 20 cookies per hour, so together they can bake 30 + 20 = 50 cookies per hour.

Example: Two vehicles are approaching each other. Vehicle A is traveling at 50 miles per hour, and Vehicle B is traveling at 40 miles per hour. Together, they are closing the distance at 40 + 50 = 90 miles per hour.

If two entities are working at cross-purposes, then you subtract one rate from another to find the rate at which the task is being accomplished.

Example: A snowshoer is traveling at 3 miles per hour. A cross-country skier who is 3 miles behind the snowshoer is traveling at 9 miles per hour in the same direction on the same trail. If both continue to travel at their current rate of speed, how much time in hours will elapse before the skier catches up to the snowshoer?

> The snowshoer is traveling away from the skier, so the skier is catching up at a rate of 9 − 3 = 6 mph. There are 3 miles between them to cover. Use the formula Distance = Rate × Time: $3 = 6 \times T$ and $T = 0.5$ hours.

Often, the GMAT will not give you the rates at which people or machines work. Instead, you'll be given the time it takes the entities to perform a task. Individual times cannot be added to find combined times. For example, if Della takes 2 hours to clean a room and Earl takes 3 hours to clean the same room, it does not take them 5 hours working together to clean the room. Logically, if Della can clean the room by herself in 2 hours, she should be able to clean it even faster with help.

To calculate the time needed for all entities working together to finish the job, convert each individual work time into a rate by taking its reciprocal. So if Della can clean a room in 2 hours, her rate of room cleaning is 1 room per 2 hours, or $\frac{1}{2}$ of a room per hour. Then you can add the rates together to find the combined rate. As a final step, convert the combined rate back to time by again taking the reciprocal.

Example: If Della takes 2 hours to clean a room and Earl takes 3 hours to clean the same room, how much time does it take for them to clean the room if they work together?

Della's rate is $\frac{1}{2}$ rooms per hour, and Earl's rate is $\frac{1}{3}$ rooms per hour. Together they can clean $\frac{1}{2} + \frac{1}{3} = \frac{3}{6} + \frac{2}{6} = \frac{5}{6}$ rooms per hour. Take the reciprocal to find it takes them $\frac{6}{5}$ or $1\frac{1}{5}$ hours, or 1 hour 12 minutes, to clean a room when working together.

Here's the general form of the **combined work formula**:

$$\frac{1}{\text{Total time}} = \frac{1}{A} + \frac{1}{B} + \frac{1}{C} + \cdots + \frac{1}{N},$$ where A, B, C, etc. represent the time it takes the individual entities to complete the task by themselves.

If the question presents you with the times of only two people or machines working together, you can save time by using this shortcut version of the combined work formula, where A and B are the times it takes the two people working alone to finish the job:

$$\text{Total time} = \frac{AB}{A + B}$$

Example: Irina can complete a data entry task in 3 hours, and Jess can complete the same data entry task in 2 hours. How many hours does it take Irina and Jess to complete the task if they work together?

$$\text{Total time} = \frac{AB}{A + B} = \frac{3 \times 2}{3 + 2} = \frac{6}{5} \text{ hours, or 1 hour 12 minutes}$$

Sometimes, the GMAT will provide the total work time and ask you to solve for one of the individual work times.

Example: Working together, Jon, David, and Roshan require 2 hours to complete a certain task, if each works at his respective constant rate. If Jon alone can complete the task in 4 hours and David alone can complete the task in 8 hours, how many hours would it take Roshan to complete the task working alone?

$$\frac{1}{T} = \frac{1}{J} + \frac{1}{D} + \frac{1}{R}$$

$$\frac{1}{2} = \frac{1}{4} + \frac{1}{8} + \frac{1}{R}$$

$$\frac{4}{8} = \frac{2}{8} + \frac{1}{8} + \frac{1}{R}$$

$$\frac{1}{8} = \frac{1}{R}$$

$$R = 8 \text{ hours}$$

Now use the drill to get some practice working with combined rates and combined work.

Combined Rates and Combined Work Drills

Answers follow the drill.

1. Two trains are traveling toward each other at a combined rate of 100 miles per hour. If one train is traveling at 60 miles per hour, what is the speed of the other train?

2. Person B, walking at a pace of 40 feet per minute, is currently 400 feet behind Person A. If Person A is walking on the same path and in the same direction at a pace of 30 feet per minute, how long in minutes will Person B walk before catching up to Person A?

3. Machine M can complete a task in 3 hours, and Machine N can complete the same task in 6 hours. How long in hours would it take both machines working together to complete a task?

4. One bulldozer operator can dig a hole of a certain size in 4 days, and another bulldozer operator can dig a hole of the same size in 5 days. In how many days could both operators working together dig 3 holes of this size?

5. Driving a snowplow, Kiran takes 2 hours to clear a parking lot of a certain size, and Milan plows at the same rate. Working individually, Priyanka and Andrew can each plow a parking lot of the same size in 3 hours. How long would it take all four of these people working together to clear 2 parking lots of the given size?

Combined Rates and Combined Work Drills: Answers

1. 40 mph

2. 40 minutes

3. $\frac{3 \times 6}{3 + 6} = 2$ hours

4. $3 \times \frac{4 \times 5}{4 + 5} = \frac{60}{9} = 6\frac{2}{3}$ days

5. Combined rate: $\frac{1}{2} + \frac{1}{2} + \frac{1}{3} + \frac{1}{3} = \frac{10}{6}$ lots per hour. Combined time: $\frac{6}{10}$ hours per lot. Time for 2 lots: $\frac{12}{10} = \frac{6}{5} = 1\frac{1}{5}$ hours, or 1 hour 12 minutes.

CONCEPT CHECK

- Which formula is used when combining three or more individual work times?

  _____

- What is the relationship between work time and work rate?

  _____

- What is the shortcut formula for calculating the time for two entities to complete a task?

  _____

Example answers are in your book's online resources (**kaptest.com/login**).

Now see how a GMAT expert uses the Kaplan Method to answer a Problem Solving question dealing with combined rates and combined work.

> Working alone, Machine X can manufacture 1,000 nails in 12 hours. Working together, Machines X and Y can manufacture 1,000 nails in 5 hours. How many hours does it take Machine Y to manufacture 1,000 nails working alone?
>
> ○ $3\frac{9}{17}$
>
> ○ $5\frac{1}{3}$
>
> ○ 7
>
> ○ $7\frac{1}{5}$
>
> ○ $8\frac{4}{7}$

Step 1: Analyze the Question

You're given the time it takes one machine to perform the task of making 1,000 nails and the time it takes that machine working with another one to complete the same task.

Step 2: State the Task

Use the given information and the combined work formula to find the time it takes Machine Y to make 1,000 nails.

Step 3: Approach Strategically

Since there are two machines and you're given times that are easy numbers to work with, using the formula $T = \dfrac{AB}{A+B}$ will be efficient.

$$5 = \frac{12Y}{12+Y}$$

$$5(12+Y) = 12Y$$

$$60 + 5Y = 12Y$$

$$60 = 7Y$$

$$\frac{60}{7} = Y$$

$$8\frac{4}{7} = Y$$

(E) is correct.

Step 4: Confirm Your Answer

Re-read the question stem, making sure that you solved for rate (not time or number of tasks performed) and for the rate of Machine Y (and not some other rate).

Next, you'll find some in-format questions involving combined rates and combined work.

Practice Set: Combined Rates and Combined Work

(Answers and explanations are at the end of the chapter.)

23. Working at its usual constant rate, Pump A can empty a water storage tank in 3 hours. Pump B, also working at its usual constant rate, can empty half of the same tank in 4 hours. How many hours will it take both pumps working together at their usual respective constant rates to empty half of the tank?

    ○ $\frac{12}{11}$

    ○ $\frac{24}{11}$

    ○ $\frac{24}{7}$

    ○ $\frac{7}{2}$

    ○ $\frac{36}{7}$

24. Machine 1 and Machine 2 working together can produce 12,000 meters of steel cable per hour. Each machine works at a constant rate. Machine 1 by itself can produce 5,000 meters of cable per hour. How many hours would it take Machine 2 working alone to produce 12,000 meters of cable?

    ○ $\frac{7}{12}$

    ○ $\frac{67}{40}$

    ○ $\frac{12}{7}$

    ○ $\frac{11}{5}$

    ○ $\frac{5}{2}$

25. Two trucks travel from Town A to Town B along the same route. The speed limit for the first 30 miles is 60 miles per hour. The speed limit for the next 10 miles is 40 miles per hour, and the limit for the final 60 miles is 55 miles per hour. Truck F has a maximum speed of 70 miles per hour, but Truck S has a speed-limiting governor installed to cap its maximum speed at 50 miles per hour. Truck S departs Town A 12 minutes before Truck F. If each truck travels at the lesser of the speed limit or the maximum speed of the truck, how far from Town B is the point where Truck F catches up with Truck S?

○   5 miles

○   20 miles

○   55 miles

○   95 miles

○   Both trucks arrive at Town B simultaneously.

Answers and Explanations

Practice Set: Ratios

1. (C)

The question gives you enough information to set up two ratios. Select variables to represent the funding unknowns (f for football, b for basketball, and s for other sports programs). The football program gets 4 times as much funding as basketball, so the ratio $f{:}b$ is 4:1. Football and basketball combined get 3 times as much funding as the other sports, so the ratio $(f + b){:}s$ is 3:1. No actual values are given, but that is okay because the question doesn't ask for a value; it asks for the ratio of basketball's funding to funding for other sports (not including football).

Picking numbers is a great strategy to answer ratio questions when no values are given. Numbers need not be realistic; pick easy-to-use values. Let the funding for basketball be $3. Since football receives 4 times as much, its funding is $12. Together, these two programs have $15 in funding, which is 3 times as much as that of all of the other sports combined. Therefore, the other programs receive $5. Finally, since basketball gets $3 and the other sports get $5, the ratio of their funding is 3:5.

Alternatively, you could solve using algebra. Since football gets 4 times more than basketball, $f = 4b$. Together, these two teams' funding is $f + b$, and, substituting $4b$ for f, the total amount is $4b + b = 5b$. That total is 3 times the amount given to the other programs, so $5b = 3s$. Rewriting the equation to solve for $b{:}s$, you obtain the ratio 3:5.

Solving with either method shows that (C) is correct. In a ratio question where the answer represents a part:part ratio, make sure the answer you picked represents the right parts in the right order.

2. (A)

This Value question stem provides a proportion with four variables and asks for the ratio of b to d. Rearranging the proportion to put b over d on one side may help you visualize what is needed: cross multiply to get $ad = bc$, divide both sides by d to get $a = \dfrac{bc}{d}$, and divide both sides by c to get $\dfrac{a}{c} = \dfrac{b}{d}$. Therefore, anything that

gives you the ratio of a to c would enable you to determine the ratio of b to d.

Statement (1) says that $\dfrac{a}{b} = \dfrac{3c}{2b}$. Cross multiply to find that $2ab = 3bc$. Divide both sides by b: $2a = 3c$. This means that $\dfrac{a}{c} = \dfrac{3}{2}$. You've already determined that this is also the ratio of $\dfrac{b}{d}$. This statement is sufficient, so eliminate (B), (C), and (E).

Plug the values in Statement (2) into the equation: $\dfrac{2}{b} = \dfrac{c}{4}$. Cross multiplying results in $bc = 8$. Although the statement provides a value for d, you can't determine the value of b, so this statement is insufficient. (A) is correct.

3. (A)

You are given two ratios, a to b and b to c, and are asked to solve for the ratio of a to c. You can do so by picking numbers or by translating the given information into equations and combining them.

If you use picking numbers, the most straightforward values to choose are $a = 4$ and $b = 3$. If $b = 3$, then c is $5b$, which is 15. That makes the ratio of a to c equal to $\dfrac{4}{15}$. If you use algebra, translate the first equation as $\dfrac{a}{b} = \dfrac{4}{3}$. Translate the second equation as $\dfrac{b}{c} = \dfrac{1}{5}$. You can calculate $\dfrac{a}{c}$ by multiplying $\dfrac{a}{b}$ by $\dfrac{b}{c}$ so that the b's cancel out:

$$\frac{a}{c} = \left(\frac{a}{b}\right)\left(\frac{b}{c}\right) = \left(\frac{4}{3}\right)\left(\frac{1}{5}\right) = \frac{4}{15}$$

However you get there, (A) is correct. Be sure to confirm the order of the words in the question stem ratios to ensure that you have translated the ratios correctly.

Practice Set: Applying Fractions to Proportions

4. (B)

The question gives the weight of a certain length of cable and asks for the weight of a different length of cable, given that the weight is directly proportional to the length. Let w equal the weight of 110 meters of the cable. The cable's weight is proportional to its length, so set up the proportion:

$$\frac{84}{560} = \frac{w}{110}$$

Note the relationship between 560 and 110: 110 is about a fifth of 560 (because $110 \times 5 = 550$, which is nearly 560). Therefore, you can say that the unknown weight of

110 meters of cable must be about a fifth of 84. A fifth of 100 is 20, so the correct answer must be a bit less than 20. Among the choices, only (**A**) and (**B**) are less than 20, and (**A**), at only slightly more than half of 20, is too small. (**B**), 16.5, is correct.

If you didn't spot this opportunity to estimate, you could do the math like this:

$$\frac{84}{560} = \frac{w}{110}$$
$$(84)(110) = 560w$$
$$(84)(11) = 56w$$
$$(21)(11) = 14w$$
$$(3)(11) = 2w$$
$$33 = 2w$$
$$w = 16.5$$

To confirm, rewrite the original proportion you set up to solve and plug in your answer for w. Do the two fractions look roughly proportional?

5. (A)

You're given a ratio of the length of a plank to cost of that plank and the lengths of two planks. The question asks for the difference between the costs of the planks. Express the cost of the planks as a ratio: $\frac{\$}{\text{foot}} = \frac{96}{6} = \frac{16}{1}$. In other words, planks cost $16 per foot. The plank that Jordan wants to buy is $10 - 7.5 = 2.5$ feet longer than the plank that Kristen wants to buy. Let x be the cost of the 2.5-foot difference, so $\frac{16}{1} = \frac{x}{2.5}$. Cross multiply to get $x = 16 \times 2.5 = 40$. This matches (**A**). Check that you correctly converted the wording in the stem into the proper ratios.

6. (C)

This question presents colored chips as parts that make up a whole and asks for the total number of chips. Most of the parts are identified as fractions of the whole, while one part is identified as a specific quantity.

There is more than one way to approach this question. One strategy is to determine what fraction of the total the 12 red chips are and then use that information to calculate the total number. Rewrite the three given

fractions with their common denominator of 30 and add those rewritten fractions:

$$\left(\frac{15}{15}\right)\left(\frac{1}{2}\right) + \left(\frac{5}{5}\right)\left(\frac{1}{6}\right) + \left(\frac{6}{6}\right)\left(\frac{1}{5}\right) = \frac{15}{30} + \frac{5}{30} + \frac{6}{30} = \frac{26}{30}$$

So the rest of the chips, $\frac{30}{30} - \frac{26}{30} = \frac{4}{30} = \frac{2}{15}$, are the 12 red ones. Solve for the total number of chips, x, by setting up the proportion of part-to-whole ratios, $\frac{\text{Red chips}}{\text{All chips}} = \frac{12}{x} = \frac{2}{15}$. Cross multiply: $2x = 180$. Thus, $x = 90$, and (**C**) is correct.

Alternatively, you could backsolve. Since $\frac{1}{2}, \frac{1}{6}$, and $\frac{1}{5}$ of the chips are integers, the total number of chips must be divisible by 2, 5, and 6. Thus, the total is divisible by the least common multiple of 2, 5, and 6, which is 30. Use this deduction to eliminate (**A**), (**B**), and (**D**). Select one of the two remaining choices to backsolve. For (**C**), 90, there would be $\frac{1}{2} \times 90 = 45$ white chips, $\frac{1}{6} \times 90 = 15$ green chips, and $\frac{1}{5} \times 90 = 18$ blue chips. Thus, $90 - 45 - 15 - 18 = 12$ chips would be red—and that is the number of red chips given in the question. (**C**) is correct. Confirm that you solved for the total number of chips; (**B**) represents the number of chips represented by the fractions.

Practice Set: Rates and Speed—Converting Rates

7. (D)

You are provided with three pieces of information about a trip: the per-hour rate to rent a bus and driver, the distance traveled, and the total charge. Use this information to determine the average speed of the bus.

Since the question asks for speed, use the formula $\text{Speed} = \frac{\text{Distance}}{\text{Time}}$. The distance is given, so calculate time using the cost and hourly rate: $\frac{\$420/\text{hour}}{\$90} = \frac{14}{3}$ hours. So, $\text{Speed} = \frac{112 \text{ miles}}{\frac{14}{3} \text{ hrs}}$. Then invert the denominator and multiply: $112 \times \frac{3}{14} = 8 \times 3 = 24$. So the average speed is 24 miles per hour. Check your calculations and units before selecting (**D**).

8. (C)

You're given a rate and asked for the equivalent rate with two different units. Note that the question asks for an approximate value and the values in the answer choices are fairly far apart, so plan to make some estimates rather than perform precise calculations.

Since the ultimate result will be in terms of $\dfrac{\text{Distance}}{\text{Volume}}$, start by inverting $\dfrac{1 \text{ liter}}{10 \text{ kilometers}}$ to get $\dfrac{10 \text{ kilometers}}{1 \text{ liter}}$. Convert the terms one by one to avoid confusion. Start with distance. Since 1 mile = 1.61 kilometers:

$$10 \text{ kilometers} \times \frac{1 \text{ mile}}{1.61 \text{ kilometers}} \approx 10 \times \frac{1}{\frac{8}{5}}$$

$$= 10 \times \frac{5}{8} = \text{just over 6 miles}$$

Given that 1 gallon = 3.78 liters:

$$1 \text{ liter} \times \frac{1 \text{ gallon}}{3.78 \text{ liters}} \approx 1 \times \frac{1 \text{ gallon}}{4} = 0.25 \text{ gallons}$$

Finally, $\dfrac{6 \text{ miles}}{0.25 \text{ gallons}} = \dfrac{24 \text{ miles}}{1 \text{ gallon}}$. **(C)** is correct.

Re-read the question stem, making sure that you didn't miss any important details in the problem. Be certain that you paid close attention to the units throughout your calculations, setting up the equations so that you ended up with miles per gallon.

9. (D)

This question asks you to identify the algebraic expression that represents the number of questions on the student's assignment, given his rate of work and the amount of time he works. The stem gives you two rates expressed in variables (x questions per h hours, m minutes per 1 day) and a time as a number (4 days).

With so many variables involved, this question can seem abstract, and setting up the algebra may be daunting. Picking numbers is a good strategy here.

Since there are 60 minutes in 1 hour, let $m = 60$. So he works for 60 minutes (1 hour) each day. Then pick small numbers for x and h that are factors/multiples of each other and of 60, since rate calculations involve division. You might let $x = 6$ and $h = 2$. Based on the numbers picked, the student completes 6 questions every 2 hours, or 3 questions an hour. The student is going to work

1 hour a day for 4 days, or 4 hours total. That means there must be $\dfrac{3 \text{ questions}}{1 \text{ hour}} \times 4 \text{ hours} = 12 \text{ questions}$ on the latest assignment.

Plug the numbers you picked into the answer choices to see which yields the same answer of 12:

(A) $\dfrac{mx}{60h} = \dfrac{60(6)}{60(2)} = \dfrac{6}{2} \neq 12$. Eliminate.

(B) $\dfrac{15x}{mh} = \dfrac{15(6)}{60(2)} = \dfrac{1(3)}{4(1)} \neq 12$. Eliminate.

(C) $\dfrac{4xh}{m} = \dfrac{4(6)(2)}{60} = \dfrac{4 \times 2}{10} = \dfrac{8}{10} \neq 12$. Eliminate.

(D) $\dfrac{mx}{15h} = \dfrac{(60)(6)}{15(2)} = \dfrac{(4)(3)}{1(1)} = 12$. Keep this one.

(E) $\dfrac{4mx}{15h} = \dfrac{4(60)(6)}{15(2)} = \dfrac{4(4)(3)}{1(1)} \neq 12$. Eliminate.

Only **(D)** yields a result of 12 and is correct.

Alternatively, this question can be solved via by using unit conversion. The student will work m minutes per day. Because *per* indicates a rate, and rates can be represented as fractions, you have the fraction $\dfrac{m \text{ minutes}}{1 \text{ day}}$. Because the student completes x questions in h hours, that rate can be represented as $\dfrac{x \text{ questions}}{h \text{ hours}}$. Multiply the rates, orienting the fractions so that all units except questions cancel out.

$$4 \text{ days} \times \frac{m \text{ minutes}}{1 \text{ day}} \times \frac{1 \text{ hour}}{60 \text{ minutes}} \times \frac{x \text{ questions}}{h \text{ hours}}$$

$$= \frac{4mx}{60h} = \frac{mx}{15h} \text{ questions}$$

Practice Set: Averages

10. (C)

Bradley wants an average score of 80 out of 100. His final test has 20 questions on it worth 100 points, so he will earn $\dfrac{100}{20} = 5$ points per question. The question asks for the number of correct answers Bradley needs on this fifth test to get an overall average of 80, given his scores on the first four tests.

The numbers here are relatively large, so calculating an average using the average formula, while doable, is somewhat cumbersome. Using the "balanced average" strategy will let you work with smaller numbers.

The goal average is 80. Bradley currently has three scores less than 80: 67, 76, and 78. These are, respectively, 13, 4, and 2 points less than 80. Therefore, he has a sum of $13 + 4 + 2 = 19$ points below the average (to the left of the average, if you're sketching this). He has one score greater than 80: 94, which is 14 points greater than 80 (to the right of 80). To balance the 19 points on the left with the 14 points on the right, Bradley needs 5 points more on the right. The score that adds 5 points to the right is $80 + 5 = 85$.

Translate 85 points into questions correct on the test: $\dfrac{85 \text{ pts}}{5 \text{ pts/question}} = 17$ questions. **(C)** is correct.

To confirm your answer, you could plug 85 back into the question. That score results in an average of $\dfrac{85 + 67 + 76 + 78 + 94}{5} = \dfrac{400}{5} = 80$.

11. (D)

This is a weighted average question that asks for the number of 10-point arrows an archer shot if her average was 6.0 points per arrow. The frequency of each point value except 10 is given in a table.

You can backsolve or do straight-ahead math. Either way, you first find the total number of arrows and points scored that are shown in the table. Add the number of arrows: $1 + 1 + 3 + 6 + 8 + 2 = 21$ arrows. Then find the total points shown: $(0)(1) + (1)(1) + (3)(3) + (5)(6) + (7)(8) + (9)(2) = 114$.

If you use backsolving, first note that the bull's-eyes score more than any of the other arrows, so a larger number of bull's-eyes will pull the average up. You might start with **(B)**, 1 arrow that scored 10 points. In this case, the archer would have shot $21 + 1 = 22$ arrows and scored $114 + 10 = 124$ points. When you begin to divide 124 by 22, you get 5 and a remainder. You are looking for an average of 6, so this is not enough 10-point arrows. Eliminate **(A)** and **(B)** and move on to **(D)**: $21 + 3 = 24$ arrows and $114 + (3)(10) = 144$ points. When you divide 144 by 24, you get 6—which is the desired average. **(D)** is correct.

If you choose to do regular math, a weighted average is the sum of each value times its frequency divided by the total number of values. Let x be the unknown number of bull's-eyes. Then, $6 = \dfrac{114 + 10x}{21 + x}$. Multiply both sides by $21 + x$ to get $126 + 6x = 114 + 10x$. This simplifies to $12 = 4x$, so $x = 3$. Again, **(D)** is correct.

If you didn't backsolve, you could confirm your choice by plugging in 3 for x to get $\dfrac{114 + 10(3)}{21 + 3} = \dfrac{144}{24} = 6$. If you backsolved, confirm that you correctly added the number of arrows and the corresponding number of points before finding the average.

12. (D)

The question asks you to find an algebraic expression that represents the average exam score of a class, excluding the highest and lowest scores. The mean of the highest score and the lowest score on the exam is x. The mean for all the scores is y, and there are z students in the class.

Rather than get involved in complicated algebra or pick numbers, first apply some logic.

$\text{Average} = \dfrac{\text{Total of scores}}{\text{Number of scores}}$. So, given that the average of the high and low scores is x, their total is $2x$. Therefore, the expression for the average without them will subtract $2x$ from the total of the scores. Only **(A)** and **(D)** have a $-2x$ term in the numerator. Then, with those 2 scores are removed, there are $z - 2$ scores left. That should be the denominator. **(D)** is correct. Many GMAT word problems have answer choices that can be eliminated without doing much math.

Re-read the question stem, making sure that you didn't miss anything about the problem.

13. (C)

This is a Value question that asks how many meals, out of 5 meals with a $20 average price, cost $25 or more. Given that average, the sum of the prices of all 5 meals is $5 \times \$20 = \$100$.

Statement (1) says that the most expensive meal had a price of $50. The other 4 meals together must have cost $100 - \$50 = \$50$. It could be that 1 of these meals was

$25 or more and each of the other 3 was less than $25, or it could be that each of the 4 meals was less than $25. So, counting the $50 meal, there could have been either 1 or 2 meals that cost $25 or more. Statement (1) is insufficient, so eliminate **(A)** and **(D)**.

Statement (2) says that the least expensive of the 5 meals had a price of $10, so the prices of the 4 most expensive meals sum to $90. It could be that 3 of these 4 meals are $25 each and the fourth is $15, or that 2 are $25 each and 2 are $20 each, or that 1 meal is $45 and the other 3 are $15 each. Since there could be 1, 2, or 3 meals that cost at least $25, this statement is insufficient. Eliminate **(B)**.

Now consider the statements together. Since the most expensive meal cost $50 and the least expensive meal cost $10, the remaining 3 meals together cost $100 − $50 − $10 = $40. How might this $40 be distributed among the remaining 3 meals? Since Emily's least expensive meal was $10, each of these 3 remaining meals must cost more than $10, so 2 of the 3 together must cost over $20; therefore, the third cannot be as much as $25. The $50 meal would have to be the only one with a price of at least $25. The two statements combined are sufficient to determine an exact number of meals that cost at least $25, and the correct choice is **(C)**.

14. (B)

You are asked to determine the sum of all the integers in the sequence, and you are given the sum of the first 4 of 8 integers. Since you are given the sum of the first half of the sequence, you can use the average formula to solve this strategically. Since the sum of 4 terms is 268, the average is $268 \div 4 = 67$, which means the first 4 even integers must be 64, 66, 68, and 70, and the next 4 must be 72, 74, 76, and 78. The sum of all 8 is 568, so **(B)** is correct.

15. (A)

The question asks what percent of voters in County B voted for a candidate. It provides the percentages of votes a candidate won in two counties and gives the ratio of the number of voters in the two counties. You can make quick work of this problem using the balance approach. Suarez ends up at 52%, and County A is 9 points above this at 61%. Moreover, there are 3 people

in County A for every 1 person in County B, so multiply A's 9-point surplus by 3 to get a 27-point surplus. To bring the vote percentage into balance at 52%, County B has to be 27 points below 52%, or 25%. **(A)** is correct.

Or you can use a formula that handles this question:

$$(\text{Proportion A})(\text{Weight of A}) + (\text{Proportion B})(\text{Weight of B}) = (\text{Total proportion})(\text{Total weight})$$

Let b represent the proportion of the vote Smith won in County B and weight the proportion of voters in County A by a factor of 3:

$$(0.61)(3) + (b)(1) = (0.52)(3 + 1)$$
$$1.83 + b = (0.52)(4)$$
$$1.83 + b = 2.08$$
$$b = 2.08 - 1.83$$
$$b = 0.25$$

Not comfortable with the balance approach or the formula? Picking numbers also works. Since the ratio of voters is 3:1, pick a total number of voters that's a multiple of 4. The number 400 works. Now there were 300 voters in County A, and 61% of them voted for Suarez—that's 183 votes for Suarez. Overall, he got 52% of 400 votes, or 208 votes. Therefore, he must have received 208 − 183, or 25 out of the 100 votes available in County B. That's 25%.

Practice Set: Mixtures

16. (C)

This Value question asks how many chocolate donuts must be added to a display case to increase the number of those donuts from one-sixth to one-fourth of the total number of donuts. If you had enough information to determine how many donuts are in the case, then using the two fractions in the question stem, you could determine the number of chocolate donuts.

Statement (1): While this tells you the number of plain donuts in the case, you don't know how many donuts there are in total. Thus, Statement (1) is insufficient. Eliminate **(A)** and **(D)**.

Now evaluate Statement (2), which provides a ratio between plain donuts and jelly-filled donuts. This tells you how the $\frac{5}{6}$ of donuts that aren't chocolate are divvied up between plain and jelly, but since there is no actual number of any of the donut types, this statement does not allow calculation of the total number of donuts. Statement (2) is not sufficient. Eliminate **(B)**.

Now combining the statements, you know the number of plain donuts and the ratio of plain to jelly-filled donuts. These facts would enable you to calculate the total of plain and jelly-filled donuts (40 and 20, respectively, for a total of 60). The fact that $\frac{1}{6}$ of the donuts are chocolate means that $\frac{5}{6}$ are plain or jelly. Thus, you could apply this ratio to find the total number of donuts $\left(\frac{5}{6}(\text{Total}) = 60;\right.$ $\left.\text{Total} = 72\right)$. The statements together are sufficient, and **(C)** is correct.

If this were a Problem Solving question, here's the final calculation you'd perform to find the number of additional chocolate donuts, where c is the number of added chocolate donuts:

$$12 + c = \frac{1}{4}(72 + c)$$
$$12 + c = 18 + \frac{1}{4}c$$
$$\frac{3}{4}c = 6$$
$$c = 8$$

17. (B)

The question says that a farmer who grows only corn and soybeans has the same total target output for crops each year. This year, 24 tons of corn makes up 40% of the output; next year, she wants to grow the same total output but have only 15% be corn. Since the total output remains the same, she is going to grow less corn and more soybeans.

Translate the information into equations to determine how many more tons of soybeans the farmer must grow. First, use the fact that 24 tons of corn makes up 40% of the target output, t. That equation is $\frac{4}{10}t = 24$. Multiply both sides by $\frac{4}{10}$ to get $t = 60$.

Next year, corn will only be 15% of the total output, so that will be $0.15 \times 60 = 9$. This is $24 - 9 = 15$ fewer tons than for the current year. Therefore, the farmer will need to grow 15 more tons of soybeans. **(B)** is correct.

Make sure you've answered the right question. **(A)** represents the amount of corn the farmer will grow next year, **(D)** represents the total amount of soybeans grown this year, and **(E)** represents the total amount of soybeans to be grown next year.

18. (E)

The question provides the relative amounts of solutions containing different stated concentrations of a chemical. These different solutions are combined in the ratio 1:2:4. The question asks for the concentration of Chemical A in the total solution.

One unit of the 10% solution contains $1 \times 0.1 = 0.1$ units of Chemical A; 2 units of the 30% solution contain $2 \times 0.3 = 0.6$ units; 4 units of the 35% solution contain $4 \times 0.35 = 1.4$ units. So the total amount of Chemical A is $0.1 + 0.6 + 1.4 = 2.1$ units. The total volume of the combined solution is $1 + 2 + 4 = 7$ units. Thus, the resulting concentration is $\frac{2.1}{7} = \frac{3}{10} = 30\%$. **(E)** is correct.

You can check your result of 30% using the balance approach. One unit of the 10% solution is $1(30 - 10) = 20$ below the overall 30%. The 30% solution is the same as the overall concentration, and 4 units of the 35% solution are $4(35 - 30) = 20$ above the overall 30%. Thus, the concentrations are "in balance" when the average of 30% is used.

Practice Set: Rates and Speed—Multi-Part Journeys

19. (E)

A motorcyclist rides from highway marker to highway marker for different distances and durations and at different speeds. The question asks for the average speed, in miles per hour (mph), of the motorcyclist while driving from marker B to marker C.

With so much information to keep track of, one way to approach this problem is first to organize the information in a table:

	RATE (MPH)	TIME (HR)	DISTANCE (MILES)
Marker A to marker B			120
Marker B to marker C	?		
Overall	45		

Use t for the amount of time, in hours, that it took to ride from B to C. The ride from A to B took 3 times as long as the ride from B to C, or $3t$. Thus, the total time for the journey was $4t$. The distance from B to C is half the distance from A to B: $\frac{1}{2} \times 120 = 60$. Finally, fill in the total distance of $120 + 60 = 180$.

	RATE (MPH)	TIME (HR)	DISTANCE (MILES)
Marker A to marker B		$3t$	120
Marker B to marker C	?	t	60
Overall	45	$4t$	180

It took $4t$ hours to go 180 miles at 45 miles per hour. Since Distance = Rate × Time, $180 = 45 \times 4t$. Thus $180 = 180t$ and t is 1. You can now finish the table:

	RATE (MPH)	TIME (HR)	DISTANCE (MILES)
Marker A to marker B	40	3	120
Marker B to marker C	60	1	60
Overall	45	4	180

The average speed from marker B to marker C is found by dividing the distance for that leg of the journey, 60 miles, by the time for that leg, 1 hour, to get 60 miles per hour. **(E)** is correct.

When using a table to organize information, ensure that the different pieces of information are in the correct parts of the table. Also remember that, unlike time and distance, for which the values in the columns sum to get the total, the only way to calculate rate is to divide the distance for that row by the corresponding time.

20. (C)

This is a Yes/No question that asks you to compare the time it took two people to complete the same journey of 40 kilometers. Since Distance = Rate × Time, you'll need each person's rate.

Statement (1) gives you Jon's speeds for each leg of his journey and allows you, in combination with the total distance from the question stem, to calculate his time for each leg and thus his total time. But there is no information about Ann. Statement (1) is insufficient. Eliminate **(A)** and **(D)**.

Statement (2) gives you Ann's speed, which is enough information to determine her time. But there is no information about Jon. Statement (2) is insufficient. Eliminate **(B)**.

Combining the two statements, you have enough information to determine both times, and you'd then be able to compare them. **(C)** is correct.

21. (B)

The question asks for the average speed for an entire hike, which consists of three parts of equal distance traveled at different speeds. The speed for the first section is 3 miles per hour (mph), and the time is 1.5 hours. Since Distance = Rate × Time, the distance for this section is 3 mph × 1.5 hour = 4.5 miles. The speeds for the second and third parts of the journey are given in terms of the speed for the previous part. To find the average rate of speed for the entire journey, you'll need the total distance hiked and the total time the hike took.

The time needed for the second section will be distance divided by speed. The hiker's speed on the second section is 25% less than the speed on the first section, or 100% − 25% = 75% of the starting speed; calculate 0.75 × 3 mph = 2.25 mph. Thus, the time needed for the second section of the hike is 4.5 miles ÷ 2.25 mph = 2 hours.

For the third section, apply the same process: the hiker's rate is twice his rate on the second section, so that's 2×2.25 mph $= 4.5$ mph. Again, the distance is 4.5 miles, so the time needed is 4.5 miles $\div$ 4.5 mph $= 1$ hour. Therefore, the time for the entire hike is 1.5 hours $+$ 2 hours $+$ 1 hour $= 4.5$ hours.

Finally, calculate the average rate for the journey:
$\dfrac{3 \times 4.5 \text{ miles}}{4.5 \text{ hours}} = 3$ mph. **(B)** is correct.

If you set up a table to organize the information, it would look like this:

	RATE (MPH)	TIME (HR)	DISTANCE (MILES)
Part 1 of hike	3	1.5	$3 \times 1.5 = 4.5$
Part 2 of hike	$0.75 \times 3 = 2.25$	$4.5 \div 2.25 = 2$	4.5
Part 3 of hike	$2 \times 2.25 = 4.5$	$4.5 \div 4.5 = 1$	4.5
Entire hike	$(3 \times 4.5) \div 4.5 = 3$	$1.5 + 2 + 1 = 4.5$	3×4.5

Be sure that you've properly applied the percent adjustments to the appropriate speeds for each section of the hike and that you used the correct formula, Average rate $=$ Total distance $\div$ Total time, to find the final value.

22. (D)

This is a multi-stage journey question that asks for an average speed for the first day of a two-day journey. Transfer the data from the question stem into a chart.

You know the total time will be 21 hours, so you can't just pick a number. Use t for time on the first day. That makes time on the second day $t + 3$. Set r as the speed on the first day; this is what you've solving for. Then $r + 15$ is speed on the second day. The total distance is given as 1,020 miles.

	RATE (MPH)	TIME (HR)	DISTANCE (MILES)
Day 1	r	t	
Day 2	$r + 15$	$t + 3$	
Entire trip		21	1,020

Solve for t: $t + (t + 3) = 21$. Combine terms to get $2t + 3 = 21$. Subtract 3 from both sides to see that $2t = 18$ and then that $t = 9$. That allows you to find distance for each day by multiplying (Rate $\times$ Time $=$ Distance). Enter these values into that chart:

	RATE (MPH)	TIME (HR)	DISTANCE (MILES)
Day 1	r	9	$9r$
Day 2	$r + 15$	12	$12(r + 15)$
Entire trip		21	1,020

Now, working with the information in the distance column, you can write an equation to solve for r:

$$9r + 12(r + 15) = 1,020$$
$$9r + 12r + 180 = 1,020$$
$$21r = 840$$
$$r = 40$$

(D) is correct. Review the question stem, making sure that you didn't miss anything about the problem. For example, if you inverted some information about the 2 days, you could end up with **(A)**.

Practice Set: Combined Rates and Combined Work

23. (A)

The question asks how long it takes two pumps working together to empty half a tank. Pump A takes 3 hours to empty the tank, and Pump B takes 4 hours to empty half the same tank—that is, it would take Pump B 8 hours to empty the whole tank.

While you could calculate this problem using the combined work formula, some critical thinking can go far here. Since Pump A by itself can empty the tank in 3 hours, it stands to reason that Pump A and Pump B working together must be able to empty the tank in fewer than 3 hours. Notice that (C), (D), and (E) are all greater than 3, so eliminate them. Furthermore, you're trying to find how long it would take the two pumps to empty only half of the tank, so logically, that must be less than half of 3 hours, or 1.5 hours. Since (B) is greater than 1.5, you can eliminate it as well. Thus, the correct answer is the only remaining choice, (A).

You can also use the combined work formula, $T = \dfrac{AB}{A+B}$, to solve, or use it to check your work if you used the critical thinking approach.

$$T = \frac{3 \times 8}{3 + 8}$$

$$T = \frac{24}{11}$$

So it takes Pump A and Pump B working together $\dfrac{24}{11}$ hours to empty the whole tank. Since you need to find how long it would take to empty just half the tank, that's $\dfrac{24}{11} \div 2 = \dfrac{12}{11}$ hours. Note that (B) is the time to empty the whole tank.

24. (C)

In this combined work problem, you're given the time it takes two machines together to complete a job and the portion of the job one of the two machines can do in the same amount of time. Your task is to determine how long it would take the second machine, working alone, to complete the entire job.

Since Machine 1 by itself can produce 5,000 meters of cable in 1 hour, Machine 2 by itself can complete $12,000 - 5,000 = 7,000$ meters in an hour. To produce 12,000 meters of cable, Machine 2 would require $\dfrac{12,000 \text{ meters}}{7,000 \text{ meters/hour}} = \dfrac{12}{7}$ hour. (C) is correct.

You can solve, or confirm your answer, with an alternative approach. Machine 1 can do $\dfrac{5}{12}$ of the job (making 12,000 meters of cable) in 1 hour, so you can deduce that Machine 2 must be able to complete $\dfrac{12}{12} - \dfrac{5}{12} = \dfrac{7}{12}$ of the job in 1 hour. Set up a proportion of

jobs to hours and solve for the hours for 1 job for Machine 2:

$$\frac{\text{Jobs}}{\text{Hours}} = \frac{\frac{7}{12}}{1} = \frac{1}{x}$$

Cross multiply: $\dfrac{7}{12}x = 1$, and $x = \dfrac{12}{7}$.

25. (A)

Because two trucks are traveling the same route and the slower truck sets out on the journey before the faster truck, this is an overtaking problem. The relative speed of the two trucks is the *difference* between their speeds; this is the rate at which the faster truck catches up to the slower truck. There are limiting factors included in the question, including the speed limits on the roads and the maximum speeds of the trucks.

- For the first 30 miles, Truck F travels at 60 mph and Truck S at 50 mph, so F is traveling 10 mph faster than S.

- Both trucks travel the next 10 miles at 40 mph.

- For the final 60 miles, Truck F travels at 55 mph and Truck S at 50 mph, so F is traveling 5 mph faster than S.

Determine the distance from Town B to the point where Truck F overtakes Truck S.

Since there are different speeds involved in the three segments of the journey, analyze this piece by piece. The first leg is 30 miles. Using the formula Distance = Rate × Time rearranged as Time = $\dfrac{\text{Distance}}{\text{Rate}}$, Truck S traverses this leg in $\dfrac{30}{50} = 0.6$ hours. Truck F starts 12 minutes later, or $\dfrac{12}{60} = \dfrac{1}{5} = 0.2$ hours later. It completes this leg in $\dfrac{30}{60} = 0.5$ hours, which is 0.1 hours less than the time for S. However, since Truck F started 0.2 hours after Truck S, Truck F arrives at the end of the 30-mile leg 0.1 hour after Truck S.

The trucks will complete the 10-mile segment in the same amount of time since they both are limited to 40 mph, so Truck F will begin the final 60-mile leg 0.1 hour after Truck S does.

For the last 60 miles, Truck F overtakes Truck S at a rate of 5 mph. Truck S starts this leg 0.1 hour before Truck F. Traveling at 50 mph, that is a 50 × 0.1 = 5-mile head start. So given that F is traveling 5 mph faster, it would catch up with S in exactly an hour. The point at which this occurs would be 1 hour × 55 mph = 55 miles from the start of the leg. Because the entire segment is 60 miles long, this point is 60 − 55 = 5 miles from town B. **(A)** is correct.

The challenging part of this question is all the details regarding distances and speeds. Re-read the question stem, making sure that you used the correct values, and check your calculations. **(C)** is the distance the trucks traveled on the last leg before F catches up to S. **(D)** is the correct distance from Town A rather than from Town B.

CHAPTER 10

MATH CONTENT REVIEW: SETS AND STATISTICS

> **LEARNING OBJECTIVES**
>
> - Identify the properties of sets and statistics that are relevant to a given question
> - Apply the Kaplan Methods for Problem Solving and Data Sufficiency to a variety of questions that involve sets and statistics

Below is an example Data Sufficiency question dealing with probability. As you try the question, think about what information it gives you, what the question is asking you to do with that information, and what you do and don't already know about how to solve. The explanation that follows demonstrates how a GMAT expert uses the Kaplan Method for Data Sufficiency and an understanding of probability to solve this question efficiently.

> Lian has 3 bags of marbles, each bag containing at least 1 blue marble, at least 1 red marble, and no marbles of another color. If Lian selects 1 marble at random from each bag, what is the probability that all 3 marbles that she selects will be red?
>
> (1) There is a total of 5 red marbles and 5 blue marbles in the 3 bags.
> (2) The ratios of red to blue marbles in the 3 bags are 2:1, 1:1, and 1:2.

Step 1: Analyze the Question Stem

This is a Value question asking for the probability that when 1 marble is chosen at random from each of 3 bags, each marble chosen is red. To find the probability of independent events, you multiply together the probabilities of each event (i.e., drawing a red marble from one bag). From the question stem, you know that each bag contains only blue and red marbles and it holds at least 1 blue marble and at least 1 red marble. Since you're asked for a probability and probability is a ratio, you don't necessarily need to know the number of red marbles and total marbles in each bag; critical thinking tells you that a statement is sufficient if it gives you the relationship between red and total marbles in every bag.

Step 2: Evaluate the Statements Using 12TEN

Statement (1) tells you that a total of 5 red marbles and 5 blue marbles are distributed among the 3 bags. Because there are different ways to distribute the marbles among the bags, there are different possible ratios of red to total marbles in each bag and thus different probabilities. Picking some permissible numbers can help make this clear.

If Bag 1 contains 3 blue marbles and 3 red marbles, while Bags 2 and 3 each contain 1 blue marble and 1 red marble, then the probability that all 3 marbles chosen are red can be calculated as follows:

$$\frac{\text{Bag 1 red}}{\text{Bag 1 total}} \times \frac{\text{Bag 2 red}}{\text{Bag 2 total}} \times \frac{\text{Bag 3 red}}{\text{Bag 3 total}} = \frac{1}{2} \times \frac{1}{2} \times \frac{1}{2} = \frac{1}{8}$$

Pay attention to the detail that these probabilities relate red marbles to total marbles, not red marbles to blue marbles.

If, however, Bag 1 contains 3 blue marbles and 1 red marble, Bag 2 contains 1 blue marble and 3 red marbles, and Bag 3 contains 1 blue marble and 1 red marble, then the probability that all 3 marbles chosen are red is $\frac{1}{4} \times \frac{3}{4} \times \frac{1}{2} = \frac{3}{32}$.

Because different answers to the question are possible when you pick different numbers, Statement (1) is insufficient. Eliminate choices (**A**) and (**D**).

Now look at Statement (2). You are told the ratio of red to blue marbles in each bag. So you can say that the probability of picking a red marble from one bag is $\frac{2}{3}$, the probability of picking a red marble from another bag is $\frac{1}{2}$, and the probability of picking a marble from the remaining bag is $\frac{1}{3}$. The probability of picking a red marble from each of the 3 bags is $\frac{2}{3} \times \frac{1}{2} \times \frac{1}{3}$. Since you could calculate this probability, Statement (2) is sufficient, and (**B**) is correct.

Now let's look at each of the concepts related to sets and statistics that show up on the GMAT Quantitative section, starting with median, mode, range, and standard deviation.

Mean, Median, Mode, Range, and Standard Deviation

LEARNING OBJECTIVES

- Calculate mean, median, mode, and range
- Describe standard deviation and compare standard deviations of sets

The GMAT tests mean, median, and mode. These are measures of central tendency, or indicators of the middle or typical value of a group of numbers. The exam also tests range and standard deviation. These are measures of dispersion, or indicators of how spread out a group of numbers is.

Mean, Median, and Mode

Another term for *average*, described in the chapter on "Ratios, Rates, and Weighted Averages," is **mean**. In math, there are several types of mean, but on the GMAT, the only mean you will see is the arithmetic mean, which is calculated using the familiar average formula:

$$\frac{\text{Sum of terms}}{\text{Number of terms}} = \text{Mean (Average)}$$

Example: What is the mean of {1, 3, 5, 6, 100}?

$$\frac{1 + 3 + 5 + 6 + 100}{5} = 23$$

When a group of numbers is arranged in order, if there is an odd number of values, the **median** is the middle value. If there is an even number of values, the median is the average of the two middle values.

Example: What is the median of {1, 3, 5, 6, 100}?

The median is 5.

Example: What is the median of {1, 2, 5, 6, 100, 101}?

$$\frac{5 + 6}{2} = 5.5$$

The **mode** is the number that appears most frequently in a group of numbers, when at least one value appears more than once.

Example: What is the mode of {1, 3, 5, 6, 6, 100}?

All values occur once except for 6, which appears twice. The mode is 6.

There can be more than one mode if more than one value appears equally often.

Example: What is the mode of {1, 1, 3, 3, 3, 5, 6, 6, 6, 100}?

The greatest frequency that a number occurs in the set is three times, and both 3 and 6 occur three times. Therefore, 3 and 6 are the modes.

If no value appears more than once, there is no mode. For example, the set {1, 3, 5, 6, 100} has no mode.

Note that the mean, median, and mode of a set may vary greatly. For example, the mean of {1, 3, 5, 6, 100} is 23 while the median is only 5. In general, outlier values—values that are very different from the others, such as 100 in this example—have a greater effect on mean than on median.

Now use the drill to practice finding the mean, median, and mode.

Mean, Median, and Mode Drill

Answers follow the drill.

1. What is the median of {5, −1, 1, 500, 50}?
2. What is the median of {−100, 100, −6, 2, 0, −81}?
3. What is/are the mode(s) of {7, −3, 4, 7, −1, −12, 5}?
4. What is/are the mode(s) of {23, 17, 3, 17, 11, 23, 19}?
5. Set A = {0, 0, 3, 4, 7, 70}. Which is greatest: the mean, median, or mode of set A? Which is least?

Mean, Median, and Mode Drill: Answers

1. Arranged in order: $\{-1, 1, 5, 50, 500\}$. The median is 5.

2. Arranged in order: $\{-100, -81, -6, 0, 2, 100\}$. The median is $\frac{-6 + 0}{2} = -3$.

3. The mode is 7.

4. The modes are 17 and 23.

5. The mean is $\frac{0 + 0 + 3 + 4 + 7 + 70}{6} = 14$. The median is $\frac{3 + 4}{2} = 3.5$. The mode is 0. The greatest value is the mean, and the least is the mode.

Range and Standard Deviation

Range is the positive difference between the largest and smallest value in a set. You can think of range as the distance between the values on a number line.

Example: What is the range of the set $\{1, 3, 5, 6, 100\}$?

$$100 - 1 = 99$$

Example: What is the range of the set $\{-10, 3, 5, 6, 100\}$?

$$100 - (-10) = 110$$

Standard deviation measures how close or far the values in a set are from the average of the set. It is highly unlikely that you'll need to calculate standard deviation on Test Day. However, you should understand how it is calculated so that you can do the following:

- Determine whether you have sufficient information to calculate standard deviation (to answer a Data Sufficiency question)
- Determine whether standard deviation is greater than, less than, or the same for different sets.

Standard deviation is calculated by following these steps:

1. Find the average of the set.

2. Subtract the average of the set from each term in that set.

3. Square each result.

4. Take the average of those squares.

5. Calculate the positive square root of that average.

Example: In a set of four terms, three of the terms are 2 less than the average, and the other term is 6 greater than the average. Could you calculate the standard deviation of the set?

Yes, you could calculate the standard deviation, even though you don't know the average. Because you're given the difference of each value from the average, you'd start with step 3 by squaring each of the three differences of 2 and the single difference of 6.

When the degree of dispersion of a set does not change, the standard deviation doesn't change. Therefore, adding the same number to, or subtracting the same number from, every term in a set does not change the set's standard deviation.

Example: What is the difference between the standard deviation of {1, 2, 3} and the standard deviation of {101, 102, 103}?

The values in the second set are the values in the first set plus 100. The standard deviations of the two sets are the same, because the numbers are equally spread out around their respective means. Therefore, the difference in the standard deviations is zero.

Multiplying every value in a set by a number with an absolute value greater than 1 causes the standard deviation to increase.

Example: Which set has the greater standard deviation: {1, 2, 3} or {−2, −4, −6}?

The values in the second set are the values in the first one multiplied by −2. The values are more spread out in the second set, so it has the greater standard deviation.

Dividing every value in a set by a number with an absolute value greater than 1 causes the standard deviation to decrease.

Example: Which set has the greater standard deviation: {25, 10, 5} or {5, 2, 1}?

The values in the second set are the values in the first one divided by 5. The values are more spread out in the first set, so it has the greater standard deviation.

In addition, the GMAT may test your understanding of standard deviation when the distribution of a group of values is symmetric around the mean. This is the so-called **normal distribution** or "bell curve." In such a distribution:

- About 68 percent of values fall within 1 standard deviation of the mean.
- About 95 percent of values fall within 2 standard deviations of the mean.
- Nearly 100 percent of values fall within 3 standard deviations of the mean.

Example: Given a normal distribution, what percent of values fall within 1 standard deviation above the mean?

To find the percent of values that fall within 1 standard deviation either *above* or *below* the mean, divide 68 percent in half: about 34 percent of values in a normal distribution fall within 1 SD above the mean. Another 34 percent fall within 1 SD below the mean.

Example: What percent of values fall between 1 and 2 standard deviations below the mean?

To find the percent of values that fall between 1 and 2 standard deviations either *above* or *below* the mean, first subtract 68 percent from 95 percent and then divide that value by 2. So first, $95 - 68 = 27$ and then $27 \div 2 \approx 14$; approximately 14 percent of values fall between 1 and 2 SD below the mean. Another 14 percent fall between 1 and 2 SD above the mean.

Now use the drill to get some practice working with range and standard deviation.

Range and Standard Deviation Drill

Answers follow the drill.

1. What is the range of {1, 3, 10, 12}?

2. What is the range of {90, −3, 64, −52, −65}?

For questions 3–5, determine which set has the greater standard deviation or whether the standard deviations are equal.

3. Set $G = \{2, 4, 6\}$. Set $H = \{1, 3, 5\}$.

4. Set $S = \{1, 10, 100\}$. Set $T = \{0.1, 1, 10\}$.

5. Set $U = \{6, 2, 1\}$. Set $V = \left\{1, \frac{1}{2}, 3\right\}$.

Range and Standard Deviation Drill: Answers

1. $12 - 1 = 11$

2. $90 - (-65) = 155$

3. The values in set H are the values in set G plus 2. The standard deviations are equal.

4. The values in the set T are the values in set S divided by 10. Therefore, set S has the greater standard deviation.

5. The values in set U are the values in set V multiplied by 2, so set U has the greater standard deviation.

CONCEPT CHECK

- What is the formula for arithmetic mean?

  _____

- When do you find the median by putting values in order and choosing the middle value?

  _____

- When do you find the median by putting values in order and averaging the two middle values?

  _____

- What is the mode of a set? Can there be more than one mode? No modes?

  _____

- How do you calculate the value of the range of a set?

  _____

- What is the effect of adding x to each value in a set on that set's standard deviation? Subtracting x from each value?

  _____

- If $y > 1$ or $y < -1$, what is the effect on the standard deviation of a set of multiplying each value in the set by y? Dividing each value by y?

  _____

Example answers are in your book's online resources (**kaptest.com/login**).

Now see how a GMAT expert uses the Kaplan Method and an understanding of median, range, and standard deviation to solve a Data Sufficiency question.

> Set $L = \{12, 8, 10, 14,$ and $6\}$. If two numbers are removed from set L, what is the standard deviation of the new set?
>
> (1) The range of the new set is 8.
> (2) The median of the new set is 8.

Step 1: Analyze the Question Stem

This is a Value question. You know that two numbers are removed from a set, but you don't know which two numbers. A statement will be sufficient if it provides enough information to calculate the standard deviation of the new set.

Step 2: Evaluate the Statements Using 12TEN

Statement (1): You are told that the range of the new list is 8. The only way to have a range of 8 is for both 6 and 14 to appear in the new list, because any other pair of numbers in the original list will be less than 8 apart. So the new list must contain 6 and 14.

The new list will also contain one of the numbers 8, 10, and 12. If, for example, the third number in the list is 10, then the list will be 6, 10, and 14. If the third number in the list is 12, then the numbers in the list will be 6, 12, and 14. The standard deviation of the list 6, 10, and 14 is different from the standard deviation of the list 6, 12, and 14 because the numbers in the two lists are spread out differently around the respective means.

More than one standard deviation is possible, and therefore more than one answer to the question is possible. Statement (1) is insufficient. Eliminate (**A**) and (**D**).

Statement (2) says that the median of the new set is 8. Because there will be an odd number (three) of members of the new set, 8 has to appear in the set in order for 8 to be the median. Additionally, since 8 must be in the middle of the new set and there is only one possible value less than 8, you know that 6 must also be in the set. The new set could be {6, 8, 10}, which has a median of 8. However, the new set could also be {6, 8, 14}, which also has a median of 8.

The numbers in the set {6, 8, 10} are less spread out than the numbers in the set {6, 8, 14}, so the sets' standard deviations are different. Therefore, more than one answer to the question is possible. Statement (2) is insufficient, so eliminate (**B**).

Having determined that Statement (1) and Statement (2) are each insufficient on their own, look at the statements together. You know from Statement (1) that 6 and 14 must be in the set, and you know from Statement (2) that 6 and 8 must be in the set. The statements taken together tell you that the set must consist of 6, 8, and 14. Because there is only one possible set, there can only be one standard deviation. The statements taken together are sufficient. (**C**) is correct.

Next, you'll find in-format questions involving measures of central tendency and measures of dispersion.

Practice Set: Mean, Median, Mode, Range, and Standard Deviation

(Answers and explanations are at the end of the chapter.)

1. Data set S contains the elements $\{-5, x, 2, 0, -1, 1, 9\}$. What is the value of x?

    (1) The average (arithmetic mean) of data set S is 2.
    (2) The median of data set S is 1.

2. If the range of the eight numbers 17, 8, 14, 28, 9, 4, 11, and n is 25, what is the difference between the greatest possible value of n and the least possible value of n?

    ○ 1
    ○ 3
    ○ 21
    ○ 26
    ○ 29

3. In the set of numbers $\{a, b, c\}$, a is the average (arithmetic mean) of the list and $b + c = 0$. What is the standard deviation of a, b, and c?

    (1) $b - a = 2$
    (2) $c - a = -2$

4. Given the set of even numbers $\{2, 18, 32, x, y\}$, what is the median of the set?

    (1) $y(y - 1) = 30$
    (2) $(x - y)^3 \leq 0$

Sets of Equally Spaced Integers

> **LEARNING OBJECTIVE**
>
> - Calculate the mean, median, sum, and number of terms of a set of equally spaced integers

The average, or mean, of a set of equally spaced integers equals its median.

Example: What is the mean of 1, 2, 3, 4, and 5? What is the median of this series of numbers?

$$\frac{1+2+3+4+5}{5} = \frac{15}{5} = 3$$

For this set, 3 is both the mean and the median.

There is another way to calculate the mean of the above set. The average of a series of equally spaced integers is the same as the average of its first and last terms.

Example: What is the mean of 1, 2, 3, 4, and 5?

$$\frac{1+5}{2} = \frac{6}{2} = 3$$

Example: What is the sum of all the integers between 1 and 66 inclusive?

Since consecutive integers are equally spaced, you can find the average by averaging the first and last terms: $\frac{1+66}{2} = \frac{67}{2}$. As described in the chapter on "Averages and Weighted Averages," if you know the average of a group of numbers and how many numbers are in the group, you can find the sum of the numbers by rearranging the average formula: Sum of values = Average value × Number of values. So, the sum of the values is $\frac{67}{2} \times 66 = \frac{67}{2} \times \cancel{66}^{33} = 2{,}211$. You still have to calculate 67 × 33, but that is much easier than adding all 66 numbers!

To find the number of terms in a set of equally spaced integers, divide the difference between the greatest and least values by the interval between the integers and then add 1.

Example: How many integers are in the sequence of consecutive integers from 47 to 108, inclusive?

$$\frac{108-47}{1} + 1 = 61 + 1 = 62$$

Example: How many terms are in the sequence of multiples of 5 between 25 and 75?

$$\frac{75-25}{5} + 1 = \frac{50}{5} + 1 = 10 + 1 = 11$$

Now use the drill to get some practice working with sets of equally spaced integers.

Sets of Equally Spaced Integers Drill

Answers follow the drill.

1. What are the mean and the median of the sequence of consecutive integers from 450 to 498?

2. How many numbers are in the sequence of consecutive integers between 248 and 364, inclusive?

3. How many numbers are in a sequence of the multiples of 3 from 27 to 78?

4. What is the sum of the sequence of consecutive integers from 10 to 30?

5. What is the sum of all odd numbers from 3 to 33?

Sets of Equally Spaced Integers Drill: Answers

1. 474

2. 117

3. 18

4. average = 20; number of values = 21; $20 \times 21 = 420$

5. average = 18; number of values = 16; $18 \times 16 = 288$

CONCEPT CHECK

* In a sequence of equally spaced integers, the average, or mean, equals the _____.

* How do you find the number of terms in a sequence of equally spaced integers?

  _____

* How do you find the sum of a sequence of equally spaced integers?

  _____

Example answers are in your book's online resources (**kaptest.com/login**).

Now see how a GMAT expert uses the Kaplan Method to solve a Problem Solving question involving a sequence of evenly spaced entities.

> In a new housing development, trees are to be planted in a straight line along a 166-foot stretch of sidewalk. Each tree will be planted in a square plot with sides measuring 1 foot. If there must be 14 feet between each plot, what is the maximum number of trees that can be planted?
>
> ○   8
> ○   9
> ○   10
> ○   11
> ○   12

Step 1: Analyze the Question

This word problem describes a series of evenly spaced trees. A quick sketch of the situation will help you picture it clearly.

Therefore, one tree and one space together take up 1 foot + 14 feet = 15 feet.

Step 2: State the Task

To find the maximum number of trees that can be planted, use the same math as you would to calculate the number of equally spaced integers in a sequence.

Step 3: Approach Strategically

First, divide the total length of the sidewalk by the length taken up by one tree-plus-space unit.

$$166 \div 15 = 11, \text{ with a remainder of 1 foot}$$

You can plant 1 last tree in the remaining foot, bringing the total number of trees to 12. This means along the sidewalk, you can plant 12 trees with 11 spaces between them, as long as you start and end with a tree. **(E)** is correct.

Step 4: Confirm Your Answer

Check to be sure your answer makes sense in the context of the question. Did you take into account the remainder of the division? Will an entire tree fit in the remaining space? You can use these questions to confirm your work.

Next, you'll find in-format questions involving sets of equally spaced integers.

Practice Set: Sequences of Integers

(Answers and explanations are at the end of the chapter.)

5. The sum of a sequence of consecutive integers is 1,125 and the median is 45. What is the value of the greatest integer in the sequence?

    ○ 33
    ○ 45
    ○ 56
    ○ 57
    ○ 58

6. What is the sum of the multiples of 4 between 13 and 125 inclusive?

    ○ 1,890
    ○ 1,960
    ○ 2,200
    ○ 3,780
    ○ 4,400

7. If z is the sum of three consecutive odd positive integers, is z evenly divisible by 9?

    (1) When the smallest of the three numbers is divided by 3, the remainder is 1.
    (2) The smallest of the three numbers is divisible by 7.

8. The sum of a sequence of six consecutive positive integers is Z. The sum of terms in a different sequence of five consecutive integers is $Z - 5$. If the greatest term of the five-number sequence is 40, what is the difference between the median term of the five-number sequence and the least term of the six-number sequence?

    ○ 5
    ○ 7
    ○ 8
    ○ 9
    ○ 10

Combinations and Permutations

LEARNING OBJECTIVE

- Solve combinations and permutations problems

The GMAT may ask you to count the number of possible ways to select a subgroup from a larger group.

If the selection is *unordered*, then it's a **combinations** question. For example, you might be asked to count the number of groups of three employees who could be shortlisted for a marketing award; shortlisting Wilma, Xavier, and Zac is the same as shortlisting Zac, Xavier, and Wilma.

If the selection is *ordered*, it's a **permutations** question. For instance, you could be asked how many ways two people could be elected to class government positions, and President Mario and Vice President Nadine is a different outcome than President Nadine and Vice President Mario.

Once you know which type of selection a question calls for, you can apply the appropriate formula.

The formulas for determining the numbers of both unordered and ordered selections make use of factorials. The notation for factorials is $n!$, where n is a positive integer. This means $n(n-1)(n-2)\dots$ until you get all the way down to 1.

Example: $5! = 5 \times 4 \times 3 \times 2 \times 1$

You can save time when factorials show up in fractions by using cancellation.

Example: Calculate $\dfrac{6!}{4!}$.

You could write out $\dfrac{6 \times 5 \times 4 \times 3 \times 2 \times 1}{4 \times 3 \times 2 \times 1}$ and cancel. But notice that the last four terms in the numerator are the same as 4!. So, instead of writing down all these numbers, you go straight to $\dfrac{6!}{4!} = 6 \times 5 = 30$.

Combinations

The **combinations formula** is used when solving for the number of k unordered selections one can make from a group of n items, where $k \leq n$. This is usually referred to as $_nC_k$, which is often said as "n choose k."

$$_nC_k = \frac{n!}{k!(n-k)!}$$

Note that because of how the denominator is structured, $_nC_k$ and $_nC_{(n-k)}$ are equal. Selecting the k that you want from a group of n is the same as selecting the $n-k$ that you *don't* want from the group of n.

Example: A company is selecting 4 members of its board of directors to sit on an ethics subcommittee. If the board has 9 members who can serve on the subcommittee, how many different selections of members could the company make?

Since the order in which you select the members doesn't change the composition of the committee, this is a combinations question. You are choosing 4 members from 9 options, so $n = 9$ and $k = 4$.

$$_9C_4 = \frac{9!}{4!(9-4)!}$$

$$\frac{9!}{4!5!} = \frac{9 \times 8 \times 7 \times 6}{4 \times 3 \times 2 \times 1}$$

Because you do not have a calculator for the Quantitative section of the GMAT, take advantage of opportunities to simplify before multiplying by canceling common factors in the numerator and denominator.

$$\frac{9 \times \cancel{8}^2 \times 7 \times \cancel{6}^1}{\cancel{4}^1 \times \cancel{3}^1 \times \cancel{2}^1 \times 1} = 9 \times 2 \times 7 = 126 \text{ different selections}$$

Some questions will require multiple iterations of the formula.

Example: County X holds an annual math competition, and each county high school sends a team of 4 students. If School A has 6 juniors and 7 seniors who can be on the school's team, and a team must consist of 2 juniors and 2 seniors, how many different teams might School A send to the competition?

The order of selection doesn't matter here, so you can use the combinations formula. However, if you lump all the students together and calculate $_{13}C_4$, you'd count some all-juniors teams and all-seniors teams. The question explicitly says you can only select 2 juniors and 2 seniors, so you are choosing 2 juniors from 6 and 2 seniors from 7—and then combining the 2 of each class to make the team of 4. When you need to make one selection *and* another selection to achieve the end result, *multiply* the two numbers of combinations.

$$_6C_2 \text{ and } _7C_2$$

$$\frac{6!}{2!4!} \times \frac{7!}{2!5!} = \frac{\cancel{6}^3 \times 5}{\cancel{2}^1 \times 1} \times \frac{7 \times \cancel{6}^3}{\cancel{2}^1 \times 1} = 3 \times 5 \times 7 \times 3 = 315$$

There are 315 possible teams consisting of 2 juniors and 2 seniors.

Permutations

If the order of selection matters, you can use the **permutation formulas**:

Number of permutations (arrangements) of n items $= n!$

Number of permutations of k items selected from $n = {}_nP_k = \frac{n!}{(n-k)!}$

Example: How many ways are there to arrange the letters in the word ASCENT?

ASCENT is different from TNECSA, so order matters here. There are 6 different letters in the word, so you must calculate the permutations of 6 different items:

$$6! = 6 \times 5 \times 4 \times 3 \times 2 \times 1 = 720$$

Another way to solve is to draw blanks for the arranged items and then write in the number of possibilities for each blank. Finally, multiply the numbers together. Many high-difficulty GMAT permutation questions resist formulaic treatment but are easier to complete with the "draw blanks" approach, sometimes called the "slots" approach.

Here's how you would use this technique to solve the ASCENT problem:

ASCENT has 6 letters, so you need 6 blanks:

$$\underline{} \times \underline{} \times \underline{} \times \underline{} \times \underline{} \times \underline{}$$

There are 6 letters you might place in the first blank (A, S, C, E, N, or T):

$$\underline{6} \times \underline{} \times \underline{} \times \underline{} \times \underline{} \times \underline{}$$

No matter which letter you place there, there are 5 possibilities for the next blank:

$$\underline{6} \times \underline{5} \times \underline{} \times \underline{} \times \underline{} \times \underline{}$$

There will be 4 for the next, 3 thereafter, 2 after that, and just 1 letter left for the last:

$$\underline{6} \times \underline{5} \times \underline{4} \times \underline{3} \times \underline{2} \times \underline{1} = 720$$

Notice that you wind up reproducing the arrangements formula, $n!$, so knowing the formulas can save you time on Test Day.

Example: There are 6 people at a family reunion, 3 children and 3 adults. They will be lined up single file for a photo, alternating children and adults. How many arrangements of people are possible for this photo?

You know you'll have 6 "blanks," but you don't know whether to begin with a child or with an adult. It could be either one. When you can achieve the end result by making one arrangement *or* another arrangement, *add* the two numbers of permutations.

$$cacaca \text{ or } acacac$$

$$\underline{} \times \underline{} \times \underline{} \times \underline{} \times \underline{} \times \underline{} + \underline{} \times \underline{} \times \underline{} \times \underline{} \times \underline{} \times \underline{}$$

Any of the 3 children could go in the first spot, and any of the 3 adults in the second:

$$\underline{3} \times \underline{3} \times \underline{} \times \underline{} \times \underline{} + \underline{} \times \underline{} \times \underline{} \times \underline{} \times \underline{} \times \underline{}$$

The next spot can be filled with either of the remaining 2 children; the one after by either of the 2 remaining adults. Then the last child and the last adult take their places:

$$\underline{3} \times \underline{3} \times \underline{2} \times \underline{2} \times \underline{1} \times \underline{1} + \underline{} \times \underline{} \times \underline{} \times \underline{} \times \underline{} \times \underline{}$$

That's the child-first possibility. The same numbers of children and adults apply to the adult-first possibility, so you get this:

$$\underline{3} \times \underline{3} \times \underline{2} \times \underline{2} \times \underline{1} \times \underline{1} + \underline{3} \times \underline{3} \times \underline{2} \times \underline{2} \times \underline{1} \times \underline{1}$$

$$9 \times 4 \times 1 + 9 \times 4 \times 1$$

There are $36 + 36 = 72$ possible arrangements of alternating 3 children and 3 adults.

Some questions involve groups of elements in which some elements are identical. These questions require both ordered and unordered selection.

Example: How many ways are there to arrange the letters in the word ASSETS?

Think about putting a "tag" on the S's … $AS_1S_2ETS_3$. If you calculated 6! as you did for ASCENT, you'd be counting $AS_1S_2ETS_3$ and $AS_3S_1ETS_2$ as different words, even though with the tags gone, you can see that they aren't (ASSETS is the same as ASSETS). This mean you'll need to eliminate all the redundant arrangements from the 6! total.

Since there are 3 S's in the word ASSETS, there are 3! ways to rearrange those S's without changing the result. You need to count every group of 3! within the 6! total as only 1 arrangement.

Thus, instead of 6! arrangements, as there were for ASCENT, the word ASSETS has $\frac{6!}{3!}$.

$$\frac{6!}{3!} = 6 \times 5 \times 4 = 120$$

If two letters repeat, you need to divide out the redundant arrangements of both letters. For instance, the number of arrangements of the letters in the word REASSESS (2 E's and 4 S's) is $\frac{8!}{4!2!}$.

Example: A restaurant is hanging 7 large tiles on its wall in a single row. How many arrangements of tiles are possible if there are 3 identical white tiles and 4 identical blue tiles?

This problem essentially asks for the arrangements of WWWBBBB. Since all the white tiles are indistinguishable from one another, as are the blue tiles, you need to divide out the number of redundant arrangements from the 7! total arrangements:

$$\frac{7!}{3!4!} = \frac{7 \times \cancel{6}^1 \times 5}{\cancel{3 \times 2 \times 1}^1} = 7 \times 5 = 35$$

Now use the drill to get some practice working with combinations and permutations.

Combinations and Permutations Drill

Answers follow the drill.

1. Joe wants to give a friend 3 books out of the 8 books he's recently read. How many different groups of books might he give his friend?

2. Sofia wants to arrange 3 of her 8 books on a shelf. How many ways can she arrange the books?

3. How many ways are there to form a team consisting of 2 marketing managers and 3 sales managers if there are 6 marketing managers and 5 sales managers to choose from?

4. Bogdan has 2 identical boxes of Cereal A and 5 identical boxes of Cereal B. How many different ways can he arrange the 7 boxes of cereal on a shelf?

5. A team consisting of 2 juniors and 3 seniors wants to take a group photo in which no juniors are standing next to each other and no seniors are standing next to each other. How many arrangements of students are possible?

Combinations and Permutations Drill: Answers

1. $_8C_3 = 56$
2. $_8P_3 = 8 \times 7 \times 6 = 336$
3. $_6C_2 \times _5C_3 = 15 \times 10 = 150$
4. $\dfrac{7!}{5!2!} = 21$
5. SJSJS: $3 \times 2 \times 2 \times 1 \times 1 = 12$

CONCEPT CHECK

- How do you know a question is asking you to calculate combinations? Permutations?

  _____

- What is the combinations formula?

  _____

- What are the permutations formulas, and when do you use each?

  _____

Example answers are in your book's online resources (**kaptest.com/login**).

Now see how a GMAT expert would solve a question dealing with combinations and permutations.

> Six children—Arya, Betsy, Chen, Daniel, Emily, and Franco—are to be seated in a single row of 6 chairs. If Betsy cannot sit next to Emily, how many different arrangements of the 6 children are possible?

- ○ 240
- ○ 480
- ○ 540
- ○ 720
- ○ 840

Step 1: Analyze the Question

You have to arrange 6 children in 6 chairs (so order matters), but 2 of the children can't sit together.

Step 2: State the Task

You need to calculate the number of different arrangements of children given the conditions. To do so, first calculate the total number of possible arrangements of the children. Then subtract the number of arrangements in which Betsy is next to Emily.

Step 3: Approach Strategically

The possible number of arrangements of 6 elements is $6! = 6 \times 5 \times 4 \times 3 \times 2 \times 1 = 720$.

Now calculate the number of unacceptable arrangements. If you number the seats from left to right, there are 5 ways they could sit together if Betsy is on the left and Emily is on the right:

Seats 1 & 2

Seats 2 & 3

Seats 3 & 4

Seats 4 & 5

Seats 5 & 6

There are 5 more ways if Emily is on the left and Betsy is on the right, for a total of 10. For any one of those 10 arrangements of Betsy and Emily, the 4 remaining children could be seated in 4! ways: $4! = 4 \times 3 \times 2 \times 1 = 24$. So you need to subtract $10 \times 24 = 240$ arrangements that include Betsy and Emily sitting together from your original total of 720: $720 - 240 = 480$. **(B)** is correct.

Step 4: Confirm Your Answer

Verify that you understood the scenario in the question stem and that your calculations are correct.

Next, you'll find in-format questions involving combinations and permutations.

Practice Set: Combinations and Permutations

(Answers and explanations are at the end of the chapter.)

9. A company plans to award prizes to its top 3 salespeople, with the largest prize going to the top salesperson, the next-largest prize to the next salesperson, and a smaller prize to the third-ranking salesperson. If the company has 12 salespeople on staff, how many different arrangements of winners are possible?

    O   1,728
    O   1,440
    O   1,320
    O   220
    O   6

10. How many organizational structures can be formed that consist of Division A; at least one of Divisions B and C; at least two of Divisions D, E, and F; and at least two of Divisions G, H, J, and K?

    O   60
    O   90
    O   99
    O   120
    O   132

11. Of the 5 distinguishable wires that lead into an apartment complex; 2 are for cable television service and 3 are for internet service. Using these wires, how many distinct combinations of 3 wires are there such that at least 1 of the wires is for cable television?

    O   6
    O   7
    O   8
    O   9
    O   10

12. When cleaning her house, Carlotta discovered an old box of candles and figurines, each of which is unique. She wants to display the items on a shelf. How many different ways can she place the items in a row on the shelf if she alternates between candles and figurines?

    (1) If only the figurines were lined up, 40,320 different arrangements would be possible.
    (2) Carlotta has one more candle than figurine.

13. There are 6 identical chips, each of which has 1 red side and 1 blue side. How many more ways are there to arrange the chips in a straight line with 3 red sides and 3 blue sides showing than there are to similarly arrange the chips with 4 red sides and 2 blue sides showing?

    O   3
    O   5
    O   6
    O   15
    O   20

Probability

> **LEARNING OBJECTIVES**
>
> - Calculate probabilities based on data sets
> - Distinguish between independent and dependent events

Probability is the likelihood that a desired outcome will occur. It is often written as a fraction, but can also be expressed as a decimal or percent. Here is the formula for the probability of events with equally likely outcomes:

$$\text{Probability} = \frac{\text{Number of desired outcomes}}{\text{Number of total possible outcomes}}$$

Example: If there are 12 shirts in a drawer and 9 of them are white, the probability of picking a white shirt from the drawer at random is $\frac{9}{12} = \frac{3}{4} = 0.75 = 75\%$.

Events are **independent** if the outcome of one occurrence does not affect the outcome of another. For example, the flipping of a coin does not affect the outcome of the next flip. To find the probability of multiple independent events, multiply the chance that each event occurs. Thus, the chance of getting two heads in a row in two coin flips is $\frac{1}{2} \times \frac{1}{2} = \frac{1}{4}$.

Events are **dependent** if the occurrence of one impacts the probability of the next. For instance, if you randomly draw a black card from a deck of black and red cards and don't replace the card, that reduces both the number of black cards and the total number of cards in the deck. If the deck consists of 2 red and 2 black cards, the chance of drawing two black cards in a row without replacement is $\frac{2}{4} \times \frac{1}{3} = \frac{1}{6}$.

Note that for both independent and dependent events, when you need results from more than one event to generate an overall result (e.g., two heads, two black cards), you *multiply* the probabilities of each event. In other words, when you need an outcome from one event *and* another event, you multiply.

You can also find the probability of more than one **mutually exclusive events**—those that cannot happen simultaneously—by adding their individual probabilities of occurrence.

Example: Of the 12 shirts in a drawer, 4 are white, 5 are blue, and 3 are green. If you choose 1 shirt at random, what is the probability that the shirt is either white or green?

> If you choose only 1 shirt, that shirt cannot be more than one color. Thus, drawing a white shirt excludes the possibility of picking a green shirt, and vice versa. The probability of picking a white shirt at random is $\frac{4}{12}$. The probability of picking a green shirt at random is $\frac{3}{12}$. The probability that the chosen shirt is either white or green is, therefore, $\frac{4}{12} + \frac{3}{12} = \frac{7}{12}$.

Note that when you can achieve an overall result (e.g., a white or green shirt) in one way *or* another way, you *add* the probabilities of the events.

When dealing with the probability of **non-mutually exclusive events**—those that can happen simultaneously—the formula to find the probability that one or both of the events happens is $P(A \text{ or } B) = P(A) + P(B) - P(A \text{ and } B)$. Similar to the overlapping sets formula you'll review in the next lesson, it's necessary to subtract the probability that both events happen from the sum of the probabilities that at least one occurs to avoid double-counting that probability.

Example: If you roll two six-sided dice with the numbers 1 through 6 on their faces, what is the probability of rolling an even number on the first die or a value less than 4 on the second die?

Note the "or" in this question. The word *or* is an indicator that you'll *add* probabilities at some point in your calculations There are 6 total outcomes when you roll a die. There are 3 outcomes that are even (2, 4, 6), so $P(A) = \frac{3}{6} = \frac{1}{2}$. There are 3 outcomes that are less than 4 (1, 2, 3), so $P(B) = \frac{3}{6} = \frac{1}{2}$. Since the two events are independent, the probability that both occur is $P(A \text{ and } B) = \frac{1}{2} \times \frac{1}{2} = \frac{1}{4}$. Now plug these probabilities into the formula to find the chance that *either* event occurs:

$$P(A \text{ or } B) = P(A) + P(B) - P(A \text{ and } B)$$

$$P(A \text{ or } B) = \frac{1}{2} + \frac{1}{2} - \frac{1}{4}$$

$$P(A \text{ or } B) = \frac{3}{4}$$

Broadly speaking, there are five approaches you can take to probability questions.

Approach 1: Multiply the probabilities of individual events. This works best when you know the probability for each event and you need to find the probability that all the events occur (e.g., the probability that the first flip of a coin lands heads up *and* the second flip lands tails up). Make sure to pay attention to what effect, if any, the outcome of the first event has on the second, the second on the third, and so on.

Example: If 3 people are chosen at random from a class with 6 children and 4 adults, what is the probability that all 3 people chosen will be children?

The probability that the first person chosen will be a child is $\frac{6}{10}$. After that person is chosen, there are 9 people remaining, 5 of whom are children. So the probability of choosing a child for the second person is $\frac{5}{9}$. Finally, for the third pick, there are 8 total people remaining, 4 of whom are children. The probability of choosing a child for the third person is therefore $\frac{4}{8}$.

The probability that all 3 people chosen will be children is $\frac{6^2}{10^2} \times \frac{5^1}{9^3} \times \frac{4^1}{8^2} = \frac{2}{12} = \frac{1}{6}$.

Approach 2: Subtract the probability of the undesired outcomes from 1. This approach works best when calculating the probability of a large number of desired outcomes would be time-consuming but calculating the probability of one or two undesired outcomes would be faster. In probability, the total of all possible outcomes is always 1, so subtracting the probability of undesired outcomes from 1 yields the probability of the desired outcomes.

Example: If a fair coin is flipped 3 times, what is the probability of getting at least 1 tail?

A fair coin will land heads up 50 percent of the time. What's desired is 1 tail, 2 tails, or 3 tails in 3 flips. That's a lot to keep track of. But there's only one outcome that doesn't meet the criterion: 3 heads in a row. Calculate the probability of getting 3 heads in a row and then subtract that from 1.

Total − Undesired

$$1 - HHH = 1 - \frac{1}{2} \times \frac{1}{2} \times \frac{1}{2} = 1 - \frac{1}{8} = \frac{7}{8}$$

Approach 3: Solve for the probability of one possible desired outcome; then multiply by all the different ways to get that outcome. This method works best when you need to know the probability that an event will occur a certain number of times, but the order of those occurrences doesn't matter.

Example: If a fair coin is flipped 5 times, what is the probability of getting exactly 3 heads?

It's clear what you desire—3 heads and 2 tails—but you don't have to get them in any particular order. HTHTH would be fine, as would HHHTT, TTHHH, and so forth. So Approach 1 wouldn't work well for this problem. But you can use Approach 1 to figure out the probability of one of these outcomes:

$$\frac{1}{2} \times \frac{1}{2} \times \frac{1}{2} \times \frac{1}{2} \times \frac{1}{2} = \frac{1}{32}$$

Now multiply this result by the number of ways you could get this outcome—in other words, by the number of ways you could rearrange the letters in HHHTT.

Use the combinations formula to solve for the number of arrangements of HHHTT. You can think of this as finding the number of combinations of 3 heads out of 5 coins; or the number of combinations of 2 tails out of 5 points; or of finding the total number of arrangements, 5!, and dividing out the indistinguishable outcomes. All result in the same math:

$$\frac{5!}{3!2!} = \frac{5 \times 4 \times 3 \times 2 \times 1}{3 \times 2 \times 1 \times 2 \times 1} = 5 \times 2 = 10$$

There are 10 different ways to get 3 heads and 2 tails. Each one of those outcomes has a probability of $\frac{1}{32}$, so the probability of getting exactly 3 heads in 5 coin flips is $\frac{1}{32} \times 10 = \frac{5}{16}$.

Approach 4: Find the numerator and denominator of the probability formula separately. You can calculate the total number of possible outcomes and the total number of desired outcomes, then put them together in one big fraction (instead of multiplying lots of little fractions together). Like Approach 3, this one works best when what you want is very specific but the order in which it happens is not.

Example: A bag holds 4 red marbles, 5 blue marbles, and 2 green marbles. If 5 marbles are selected one after another without replacement, what is the probability of drawing 2 red marbles, 2 blue marbles, and 1 green marble?

Start by thinking about all the possible outcomes. You are reaching into a bag of 11 marbles and pulling out 5. (The fact that they are pulled out one by one doesn't change anything; in the end, you still have 5 marbles.) Quite literally, this is "11 choose 5," $_{11}C_5$.

Number of possible selections $= {}_{11}C_5 =$

$$\frac{11!}{5!6!} = \frac{11 \times 10 \times 9 \times 8 \times 7 \times 6 \times 5 \times 4 \times 3 \times 2 \times 1}{5 \times 4 \times 3 \times 2 \times 1 \times 6 \times 5 \times 4 \times 3 \times 2 \times 1} = 11 \times 2 \times 3 \times 7$$

Save yourself some work: don't multiply out factors that may later cancel. You can leave the expression as $11 \times 2 \times 3 \times 7$ for now.

Now, what is desired? You want 2 of the 4 red marbles, literally "4, choose 2," or $_4C_2$. You also want 2 of the 5 blue marbles ($_5C_2$) and 1 of the 2 green marbles ($_2C_1$).

Number of desired selections $= {}_4C_2$ and $_5C_2$ and $_2C_1$.

$$\frac{4!}{2!2!} \times \frac{5!}{2!3!} \times \frac{2!}{1!1!}$$

$$\frac{4 \times 3 \times 2 \times 1}{2 \times 1 \times 2 \times 1} \times \frac{5 \times 4 \times 3 \times 2 \times 1}{2 \times 1 \times 3 \times 2 \times 1} \times \frac{2 \times 1}{1 \times 1}$$

$$6 \times 10 \times 2$$

Now put the fraction together:

$$\frac{\text{Number of desired outcomes}}{\text{Number of total possible outcomes}} = \frac{6 \times 10 \times 2}{11 \times 2 \times 3 \times 7} = \frac{10 \times 2}{11 \times 7} = \frac{20}{77}$$

Approach 5: Just total up the outcomes. This approach works best when the numbers involved are so small that there's really no need to waste time thinking of or doing the arithmetic calculation.

Example: If a fair coin is flipped 2 times, what is the probability of getting exactly 1 head?

Two coin flips aren't very many. List out the possible results:

HH, HT, TH, TT

Of these 4 possibilities, 2 have exactly 1 head—HT and TH. So the probability of getting exactly 1 head in 2 flips is $\frac{2}{4}$, or $\frac{1}{2}$.

Take your time thinking probability questions through—spending the time to select the most efficient approach will be time well spent!

Now use the drill to get some practice working with probability.

Probability Drill

Express your answers as fractions. Answers follow the drill.

1. Of the 11 students in a classroom, 5 are history majors, 3 are business majors, and 3 are chemistry majors. If 1 student is chosen at random, what is the probability that the student is either a history or business major?

2. Audre has 3 red shirts, 6 blue shirts, and 2 yellow shirts in a drawer. She chooses a shirt to wear at random each morning from the drawer, and she places shirts she has worn in the laundry hamper. What is the probability that she will choose a red shirt today and a red shirt again tomorrow?

3. If Roy rolls 3 six-sided dice (each with numbers 1–6 on their faces), what is the chance that Roy will roll exactly 2 even numbers?

4. A box contains 5 books: 1 is fiction, 2 are biographies, and 2 are textbooks. If 3 books are selected at random and are placed back in the box each time, what is the probability that none of them are textbooks?

5. If 3 games are chosen at random, without replacement, from a shelf with 4 strategy games and 3 story-telling games, what is the probability that all 3 chosen games will be strategy games?

Probability Drill: Answers

1. $\frac{8}{11}$
2. $\frac{3}{11} \times \frac{2}{10} = \frac{3}{55}$
3. $\frac{1}{2} \times \frac{1}{2} \times \frac{1}{2} = \frac{1}{8}$; $3 \times \frac{1}{8} = \frac{3}{8}$
4. $\frac{3}{5} \times \frac{3}{5} \times \frac{3}{5} = \frac{27}{125}$
5. $_7C_3 = \frac{7!}{3!4!} = 35$; $_4C_3 = \frac{4!}{3!1!} = 4$; $\frac{4}{35}$

CONCEPT CHECK

- What is the formula for the probability of events with equally likely outcomes?

  _____

- The sum of the probabilities of a complete set of mutually exclusive events is _____.

- How do you find the probability that one *and* another of two independent events will occur?

  _____

- How do you find the probability that one *or* another of two mutually exclusive events will occur?

  _____

Example answers are in your book's online resources (**kaptest.com/login**).

Now see how a GMAT expert uses the Kaplan Method to answer a Problem Solving question on probability.

> Halona tossed a fair coin 3 times. What is the probability that the coin landed heads up exactly twice?

- ◯ 0.125
- ◯ 0.250
- ◯ 0.375
- ◯ 0.750
- ◯ 0.875

Step 1: Analyze the Question

Each coin toss has a $\frac{1}{2}$ chance of being heads and a $\frac{1}{2}$ chance of being tails, and each toss has no effect on the probability of any other toss. The coin is tossed 3 times, and the correct answer is the probability, expressed as a decimal, that two flips result in heads and one result results in tails in any order.

Step 2: State the Task

To calculate the probability of exactly 2 heads in 3 flips, you could use several approaches. Because there are only 3 flips and only 2 possible results for each flip, just listing and counting possibilities will probably be fastest.

Step 3: Approach Strategically

Write out all the ways flipping a coin 3 times could turn out and count how many results include exactly 2 heads. Be systematic, so you don't miss anything. The possible results are HHH, HHT, HTH, HTT, THH, THT, TTH, TTT. That's 8 possible outcomes, 3 of which have exactly 2 heads, so that's $\frac{3}{8} = 0.375$. **(C)** is correct.

If you prefer a math-based approach, you could calculate the probability of one desired outcome and then multiply by the number of desired outcomes. Consider the result HHT. Each outcome, H or T, has a probability of $\frac{1}{2}$, and you need the first flip, the second flip, *and* the third flip to get HHT. Therefore, you multiply the probabilities: $\frac{1}{2} \times \frac{1}{2} \times \frac{1}{2} = \frac{1}{8}$, or 0.125. The number of ways of getting 2 Hs and 1 T is calculated in the same manner as rearranged-letter problems, taking into account 3 letters but dividing out the 2 indistinguishable Hs: $\frac{3!}{2!} = 3$. So again, the probability of getting exactly 2 heads in 3 flips is $0.125 \times 3 = 0.375$.

Step 4: Confirm Your Answer

Re-read the question stem, confirming that you answered the question that was asked, and check your work.

Next, you'll find in-format questions involving probability.

Practice Set: Probability

(Answers and explanations are at the end of the chapter.)

14. A garden shed contains a total of 8 bags of yard care supplies. There are 3 bags of fertilizer and 2 bags of grass seed, and the remaining bags are of mulch. If 3 bags are selected from the shed at random, one at a time without replacement, what is the probability that none of the bags are of mulch?

    ○ $\frac{1}{56}$

    ○ $\frac{15}{128}$

    ○ $\frac{5}{28}$

    ○ $\frac{125}{336}$

    ○ $\frac{3}{8}$

15. A bag contains 4 red marbles and 5 marbles of other colors. A second bag contains 3 red marbles and 6 marbles of other colors. If 1 marble is selected at random from each bag, what is the probability that exactly 1 of the marbles will be red?

    ○ $\frac{4}{27}$

    ○ $\frac{7}{18}$

    ○ $\frac{13}{27}$

    ○ $\frac{17}{27}$

    ○ $\frac{55}{81}$

16. A certain event has only outcomes *A* or *B*, and they are equally likely and mutually exclusive. Out of 5 random occurrences of the event, what is the probability that fewer than half result in an outcome of *A*?

    ○ $\frac{3}{16}$

    ○ $\frac{5}{16}$

    ○ $\frac{1}{3}$

    ○ $\frac{2}{5}$

    ○ $\frac{1}{2}$

17. A student is entered in a college housing lottery for two consecutive years. What is the probability that the student receives housing through the lottery for at least one of these years?

    (1) Of the students in the lottery, 80 percent do not receive housing through the lottery in any given year.

    (2) Each year, 1 of 5 students receives housing through the lottery.

Overlapping Sets

LEARNING OBJECTIVE

- Solve an overlapping sets problem by using a Venn diagram, a formula, or a chart

Overlapping set problems on the GMAT involve a larger group that is subdivided into two or more potentially overlapping subgroups. For example, say there are 12 dog owners and 14 cat owners in a group of 20 people. Since 12 plus 14 is more than 20, the only way this situation makes sense is if some people own both a dog and a cat. Therefore, people who own both a cat and a dog represent the overlap between each set of pet owners. It is also possible that some people own neither kind of pet.

There are three ways to solve these problems.

Approach 1: Organize the given information using a **Venn diagram**. This approach uses partially overlapping circles to represent the data visually.

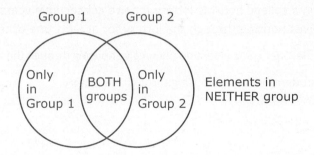

Example: All the students in a class study either forensics or statistics or both. There are 16 forensics students, 3 of whom also study statistics. How many statistics students are in the class if the class has 25 students altogether?

> Since all the students study at least one of these two subjects, there's no need to account for any students who fall outside the two circles.
>
> Since the question states that 3 of the forensics students also study statistics, write a 3 in the "Both" region.
>
> Next, label one circle "F" for forensics and indicate there are 16 total forensics students. Subtract the 3 forensics students already accounted for and write 13 in the "forensics only" part of that circle.
>
> Now, since the "Forensics only" and "Both" groups total 16 and there are 25 students in the class, $25 - 16 = 9$ students study only statistics, the only region in the diagram that remains to be filled. Thus, $9 + 3 = 12$ is the total number of statistics students.

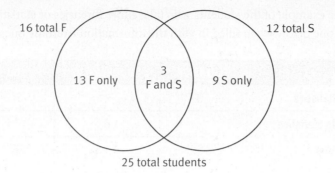

Approach 2: Use the **overlapping sets formula**. When there are two sets, the formula is this:

$$\text{Total} = \text{Group 1} + \text{Group 2} - \text{Both} + \text{Neither}$$

Just as you split out the "Both" group in the Venn diagram so you count those students only once, even though they are members of both groups, you subtract the "Both" group in the formula, since you've already counted those students in Group 1 and Group 2.

For the above example, the formula would read Total = Forensics + Statistics − Both + Neither. When you plug in the numbers, that's $25 = 16 + S - 3 + 0$, and you would solve for $S = 12$. Here's another example.

Example: An office manager orders 27 pizzas for a party. Of these, 15 have pepperoni and 10 have mushrooms. If 4 pizzas have no toppings at all, and no other toppings are ordered, how many pizzas have both kinds of toppings?

$$\text{Pepperoni} + \text{Mushrooms} - \text{Both} + \text{Neither} = \text{Total}$$
$$15 + 10 - \text{Both} + 4 = 27$$
$$29 - \text{Both} = 27$$
$$\text{Both} = 2$$

Approach 3: Organize the given information using a chart you quickly set up, like a little spreadsheet. This can work well when there are two overlapping sets but is not effective for three sets.

	IN GROUP 1	NOT IN GROUP 1	TOTAL
In Group 2			
Not in Group 2			
Total			

To continue with the example of the students who take either forensics or statistics or both, that chart would look like the one below when filled in with the information from the question stem.

	FORENSICS	NO FORENSICS	TOTAL
Statistics	3		?
No Statistics		0	
Total	16		25

The column heads describe one characteristic of the students (they take forensics or they don't), and the row labels describe the other (they take statistics or they don't). You can see that the 16 students who take forensics are in the Total cell of the Forensics column. The 3 students who take both classes are in the cell in the Forensics column and the Statistics row. The 25 total students are at the lower right. The question mark represents what the question is asking for.

Next, fill in the missing information by adding and subtracting until you find the needed value. One path to a solution is to first subtract 3 from 16 and write 13 in the Forensics/No Statistics cell, then add 0 to find a total of 13 in the No Statistics row, and finally subtract 13 from 25 to find a total of 12 for the Statistics row.

	FORENSICS	NO FORENSICS	TOTAL
Statistics	3		**12**
No Statistics	**13**	0	**13**
Total	16		25

Here's another example.

Example: A company has 200 employees, 90 of whom belong to a union. If there are 95 part-time non-union employees and 80 full-time union employees, then how many full-time employees work for the company?

Build the chart and add the data you've been given. Use a question mark to keep track of the value the question is asking for.

	IN UNION	NOT IN UNION	TOTAL
Full-time	80		?
Part-time		95	
Total	90		200

Whenever two boxes in the same column or row have been filled, you will be able to calculate the remaining box. So, you can now calculate the total number of nonunion employees ($200 - 90 = 110$) and the number of part-time union employees ($90 - 80 = 10$):

	IN UNION	NOT IN UNION	TOTAL
Full-time	80		?
Part-time	10	95	
Total	90	110	200

And now either calculate full-time nonunion employees ($110 - 95 = 15$) or the total number of part-time employees ($10 + 95 = 105$):

	IN UNION	NOT IN UNION	TOTAL
Full-time	80	15	?
Part-time	10	95	105
Total	90	110	200

Either way, you can then calculate the total number of full-time employees ($80 + 15 = 95$ or $200 - 105 = 95$):

	IN UNION	NOT IN UNION	TOTAL
Full-time	80	15	95
Part-time	10	95	105
Total	90	110	200

The chart approach is especially effective for solving overlapping sets problem when the question provides information from different perspectives while describing the same group (such as people who like books vs. people who don't like books.)

While you can solve an overlapping sets question using any of the above methods, some approaches are better suited to a particular setup than others. Practice all of them so you get a sense of which approach is best suited to different presentations of information and which approach or approaches you simply prefer.

Three Overlapping Sets

Questions that involve three overlapping sets occasionally make an appearance on the GMAT. You can use either a Venn diagram or a formula to solve these problems. The key thing to remember is that some entities will be included in two sets and will need to be subtracted out to avoid double counting—and some entities will be included in all three sets and therefore will need to be subtracted out *twice* to avoid triple counting.

Here is the formula that accounts for the subtraction that must occur:

$$\text{Total} = \text{Group 1} + \text{Group 2} + \text{Group 3} - \text{Both}_{1,2} - \text{Both}_{2,3} - \text{Both}_{1,3} - 2(\text{Triple}_{1,2,3}) + \text{None}$$

Example: In a class, every student received at least one letter grade, and no students got a grade other than A, B, or C. There are 22 students who received As on their report card, 12 who received Bs, and 21 who received Cs. If there are 36 total students in the class, and if 5 received only As and Bs, 3 received only Bs and Cs, and 3 received only As and Cs, how many got As, Bs, and Cs on their report card?

You need to solve for the number of students who are in all three groups. Plug the given numbers into the formula. Because every student got at least one of the three grades, you can ignore the "None" group.

$36 = 22 + 12 + 21 - 5 - 3 - 3 - 2(\text{Triple}_{1,2,3})$

$36 = 55 - 11 - 2T$

$36 = 44 - 2T$

$2T = 8$

$T = 4$

Four students received at least one of each grade. Here's how the given information and the answer to the question look when sketched in a Venn diagram.

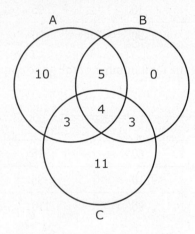

Now use the drill to get some practice working with overlapping sets.

Overlapping Sets Drills

Answers follow the drill.

1. In a class of 80 students, 30 students play sports, 60 are in the drama club, and 5 are involved in neither sports nor drama. How many students participate in both sports and drama club?

2. In a group of 24 dogs, if 15 of the dogs know to sit on command, 10 of the dogs know to heel on command, and 2 dogs know both commands, how many dogs have not yet learned either command?

3. Company X hired 120 employees, all of whom have experience in at least one of programming or sales. If 80 of the new employees have experience in sales and 40 have experience in both sales and programming, how many have programming experience?

4. The local Nordic club has 500 members. There are 40 members who do not currently ski due to injuries. All the other members engage in either classic skiing or skate skiing or both. If 400 members skate ski and 300 members engage in both types of skiing, how many members engage in classic skiing only?

5. A company assigns 100 executives to oversee operations in Africa, Asia, and South America. There are 50 executives assigned to Africa; 10 of those also have responsibilities in Asia and another 10 also have responsibilities in South America. There are 60 executives assigned only to Asia and 40 assigned only to South America, and 5 executives have responsibilities on all three continents. How many executives are assigned to both Asia and South America?

Overlapping Sets Drills: Answers

1. 15
2. 1
3. 80
4. 60
5. $100 = 50 + 60 + 40 - 10 - 10 - \text{Both}_{\text{Asia+SA}} - 2(5)$; $\text{Both}_{\text{Asia+SA}} = 20$

CONCEPT CHECK

- What is the formula for solving problems with two overlapping sets?

- What is the formula for solving problems with three overlapping sets?

- In the overlapping sets formula, why is the "Both" term subtracted?

- Describe some of the advantages of the chart approach.

Example answers are in your book's online resources (**kaptest.com/login**).

Now see how a GMAT expert uses the Kaplan Method to answer a Problem Solving question that involves overlapping sets.

> A polling company surveyed voters in a certain country, giving respondents a choice of registering either favorable or unfavorable impressions of two political parties. It found that 35 percent of that country's voters had an unfavorable impression of both of the country's major political parties and that 20 percent had a favorable impression only of Party A. If 1 voter had a favorable impression of both parties for every 2 voters who had a favorable impression only of Party B, what percentage of the country's voters had a favorable impression of both parties?

- ○ 15
- ○ 20
- ○ 30
- ○ 35
- ○ 45

Step 1: Analyze the Question

Among the voters polled, there are two major categories: those who like Party A and those who like Party B. Some voters don't like either party, and some voters like both parties—the question is about these voters. You aren't given any actual numbers of voters, only percents of the total and a ratio between two parts. Because there's a lot of information to keep track of, a chart will be helpful.

	FAVORABLE B	NOT FAVORABLE B	TOTAL
Favorable A	?		
Not favorable A			
Total			

Step 2: State the Task

Calculate the percentage of registered voters who like both parties—in other words, the value in the upper left-hand box.

Step 3: Approach Strategically

Start by putting the information into the chart. Because you're given no total number of voters but you are asked to work with percents, picking 100 for the total will make the calculations simpler.

	FAVORABLE B	NOT FAVORABLE B	TOTAL
Favorable A	?	20	
Not favorable A		35	
Total			100

The other piece of data is "1 registered voter has a favorable impression of both parties for every 2 registered voters who have a favorable impression only of Party B." In other words, the ratio of "favorable A and favorable B" to "favorable B and not favorable A" is 1:2. You can represent that relationship with x and $2x$.

	FAVORABLE B	NOT FAVORABLE B	TOTAL
Favorable A	x	20	
Not favorable A	$2x$	35	
Total			100

Use addition and subtraction to fill in the rest of the chart:

	FAVORABLE B	NOT FAVORABLE B	TOTAL
Favorable A	x	20	$20 + x$
Not favorable A	$2x$	35	$35 + 2x$
Total	$3x$	55	100

Whether you use the Total column or the Total row, you solve the same equation to find x:

$$3x + 55 = 100$$
$$3x = 45$$
$$x = 15$$

(A) is correct.

Step 4: Confirm Your Answer

Confirm that you solved for the right value; values of other cells in the table show up in the incorrect choices.

Next, you'll find in-format questions involving overlapping sets.

Practice Set: Overlapping Sets

(Answers and explanations are at the end of the chapter.)

18. Of the 65 books released last year by a particular publishing house, 25 were no more than 200 pages. The publisher released 35 fiction books, of which 20 were more than 200 pages, and it also published nonfiction books. How many nonfiction books of no more than 200 pages did the publishing house release last year?

    ○ 5

    ○ 10

    ○ 20

    ○ 30

    ○ 35

19. Three hundred students at College Q study a foreign language. Of these students, 110 study French and 170 study Spanish. If at least 90 students who study a foreign language at College Q study neither French nor Spanish, then the number of students who study Spanish but not French could be any number from

    ○ 10 to 40

    ○ 40 to 100

    ○ 60 to 100

    ○ 60 to 110

    ○ 70 to 110

20. The *Financial News Daily* has 25 reporters covering Asia, 20 covering Europe, and 20 covering North America. If 4 reporters cover Asia and Europe but not North America, 6 reporters cover Asia and North America but not Europe, and 7 reporters cover Europe and North America but not Asia, how many reporters cover all three continents (Asia, Europe, and North America)?

    (1) The *Financial News Daily* has 38 reporters in total covering at least 1 of the following continents: Asia, Europe, and North America.

    (2) There are more *Financial News Daily* reporters covering Asia and North America but not Europe than there are *Financial News Daily* reporters covering all three of the continents.

Answers and explanations follow on the next page. ▶ ▶ ▶

Answers and Explanations

Practice Set: Mean, Median, Mode, Range, and Standard Deviation

1. (A)

This Value question asks for the value of x and provides the set $\{-5, x, 2, 0, -1, 1, 9\}$. Sufficiency means having enough information to find one exact value of x.

Statement (1): the average of a set of numbers is $\dfrac{\text{Sum of values}}{\text{Number of values}}$, so you can write the following equation:

$$\frac{-5 + x + 2 + 0 + (-1) + 1 + 9}{7} = 2$$

This is sufficient to solve for x, so eliminate **(B)**, **(C)**, and **(E)**.

Statement (2): In order to determine the median of a list of numbers, the numbers must be placed in numerical order. Begin by ordering the known values: $\{-5, -1, 0, 1, 2, 9\}$. Since there are seven values including x, the fourth term will be the median. If the 1 currently identified in the set is the median, then x must be greater than 1. Alternatively, x itself could be 1, and 1 would still be the median. Thus, x could be any value equal to or greater than 1. This statement is insufficient, so **(A)** is correct.

2. (D)

The question presents a set of eight specific numbers and one variable, n, and indicates that the range of this set is 25. It asks for the difference between the largest and smallest possible values of n. Since the range of the largest and smallest specified values is $28 - 4 = 24$, n must be either 1 greater than 28 or 1 less than 4 to create a range of 25.

Therefore, n is either 29 or 3. The difference of these two values is $29 - 3 = 26$, so **(D)** is correct.

3. (D)

This Value questions asks for the standard deviation of a, b and c. It indicates that a is the average of the three values. Furthermore, the sum of b and c is 0. This means either b and c both equal 0, or they have opposite values (for example, 5 and –5 or 1 and –1).

Since b and c are balanced around 0 (their absolute values are equal), a must be halfway between b and c and thus equal to 0. Standard deviation is calculated by finding each number's distance from the mean as a first step. So to be able to determine the standard deviation of a, b, and c, a statement would need to provide the specific value of b or c, the difference between them, or the difference between either value and a.

Statement (1) tells you that $b - a = 2$. Since you know that $a = 0$, you can find that $b = 2$. Thus, you know that c must be –2. These values are sufficient to find the standard deviation. Eliminate **(B)**, **(C)**, and **(E)**.

Statement (2) tells you that $c - a = -2$. Since you know that $a = 0$, you can find that $c = -2$. Thus, you know that a must be 2. Again, this is enough to find the standard deviation, so **(D)** is correct.

4. (C)

This Value question asks for the median of the set $\{2, 18, 32, x, y\}$; it also specifies that the values in the set are all even. It will be necessary to find the positions of x and y in the set relative to the middle value. This might mean finding their exact values or finding some upper or lower limit to their values, so you know where in the set they fall.

Statement (1) is a quadratic equation with one variable, so you can find the value (or values) of y. However, there's no information about where x falls in the set, so you can't determine the median with it alone. Eliminate **(A)** and **(D)**.

Statement (2) provides information about the relationship between the two variables, allowing two potential scenarios:

1. If $(x - y)^3 = 0$, $x - y = 0$, so $x = y$

2. If $(x - y)^3 < 0$, $x - y < 0$, so $x < y$

However, this does not provide information about the relationship between either variable and the other numbers in the set, which makes it insufficient. Eliminate **(B)**.

Now combine the statements. You were able to eliminate Statement (1) without taking the time to solve for y, but it's now worthwhile to do so:

$$y(y - 1) = 30$$
$$y^2 - y = 30$$
$$y^2 - y - 30 = 0$$
$$(y - 6)(y + 5) = 0$$
$$y = 6 \text{ or } y = -5$$

The question stem indicates that the set contains only even numbers, so you know that $y = 6$.

There are two numbers greater than y in the set, 18 and 32, and at least one number, 2, less than y. In other words, y is definitely between 2 and 18. Based on Statement (2), x is less than or equal to y, which would mean that x is less than or equal to 6. If it's less than 6, y is the median, and that's 6. If $x = 6$, then either x or y could be taken as the median, which is still 6. Therefore, combining the statements is sufficient, and **(C)** is correct.

Practice Set: Sequences of Integers

5. (D)

The question asks for the largest integer in a sequence of consecutive integers. The sequence has a sum of 1,125 and a median of 45. In a sequence of consecutive integers, the median equals the average (arithmetic mean).

Use the formula for averages to determine how many integers are in the sequence. Then use that information and the given median to find the value of the greatest number in the sequence.

Rearrange the averages formula to get Number of values $= \dfrac{\text{Sum of values}}{\text{Average}}$. So that is $\dfrac{1{,}125}{45} = 25$. In a list of 25 consecutive integers, 12 integers will be less than the middle value and 12 will be greater than the middle value. So the greatest value in the sequence is $45 + 12 = 57$. **(D)** is correct.

6. (B)

The question asks for the sum of the multiples of 4 between 13 and 125. Begin by finding the smallest and largest multiple of 4 from the list. In this range, the smallest multiple of 4 is 16, and the largest is 124. Thus, the set of values in this question is really the multiples of 4 from 16 to 124 inclusive.

To find the sum, you need to calculate the average of the terms in the set and then multiply that by the number of terms in the set.

$$\text{Average} = \frac{\text{Sum of terms}}{\text{Number of terms}}$$
$$\text{Sum of terms} = \text{Average} \times \text{Number of terms}$$

The average of a set of consecutive numbers equals the average of the smallest and largest terms. The average of these two numbers is $\dfrac{16 + 124}{2} = \dfrac{140}{2} = 70$. So the average of all terms in this set is 70.

Now find the number of multiples of 4 between 16 and 124 inclusive. You could simply list all of the terms in the sequence, but that would be time-consuming. A great shortcut to determine this value is to find the difference between the smallest and largest terms and add 1. Because the numbers in this set are multiples of 4, you must divide the difference by 4 before adding 1. Therefore, the number of terms in this set is $\dfrac{124 - 16}{4} + 1 = \dfrac{108}{4} + 1 = 27 + 1 = 28$.

Thus, the average of the terms in the set is 70, and the number of terms in the set is 28. Therefore, the sum of the terms in the set is $28 \times 70 = 1{,}960$. Note that you can shortcut some of the multiplication here by noticing that $8 \times 70 = 560$, so the answer will have to end in a 60, and only **(B)** does so. **(B)** is correct.

7. (A)

This Yes/No question states that z is the sum of three consecutive odd positive integers. Call the smallest integer x and write the other two as $(x + 2)$ and $(x + 4)$, respectively. Therefore, the sum of the three integers is $x + (x + 2) + (x + 4)$ or, combining like terms, $3x + 6$. Finally, factor to find that the sum is $3(x + 2)$. So the question is really asking, "Is $3(x + 2)$ evenly divisible by 9?"

Statement (1): When x is divided by 3, the remainder is 1. So x is 3 times some integer plus 1. Call that integer y and substitute $3y + 1$ for x in the expression above to get $3(3y + 1 + 2) = 3(3y + 3)$. When the factor is distributed, this is $9y + 9$. Since y is an integer, this expression must be divisible by 9. So the answer is always yes, and Statement (1) is sufficient. Eliminate (B), (C), and (E).

Statement (2): You can check this statement for sufficiency by picking numbers. If $x = 7$, then the sum is $3(7 + 2) = 27$, which is divisible by 9. However, if $x = 21$, the next odd number divisible by 7, then the sum is $3(21 + 2) = 69$, which is not divisible by 9. Therefore, Statement (2) is insufficient, so (A) is correct.

8. (C)

There are two sequences of integers. The sum of the sequence with six consecutive integers is Z. The sum of the sequence with five consecutive integers is $Z - 5$. The greatest integer in this latter sequence is 40. The question asks for the difference between the median value of the five-term sequence and the smallest value of the six-term sequence.

If the greatest term in the five-number sequence is 40, that sequence must be 36, 37, 38, 39, 40. The sum of a sequence of integers is the average (arithmetic mean) times the number of terms. Since this sequence has an odd number of equally spaced terms, the middle or median value, 38, is also the mean. Thus, the sum of terms in this sequence is the mean times the number of terms: $38 \times 5 = 190$. This sum is equivalent to $Z - 5$, so $Z = 195$.

To find the smallest value in the six-term sequence, start by finding the average: $\text{Average} = \dfrac{\text{Sum of terms}}{\text{Number of terms}}$ yields $195 \div 6 = 32.5$. This sequence has an even number of terms, so the mean is the average of the two middle terms when all of the terms are arranged in numeric order. Therefore, the third and fourth terms in the sequence must be 32 and 33, so the entire sequence is 30, 31, 32, 33, 34, 35. Thus, the difference between the third term of the five-number sequence (38) and the smallest term of the six-number sequence (30) is 8, which is (C).

Practice Set: Combinations and Permutations

9. (C)

This question asks you to calculate the number of ways you can distribute first, second, and third place prizes among 12 people. Since order matters, this is a permutations question. Count the number of possibilities for each prize and multiply.

Any of 12 people might win first place, leaving 11 possible choices for second. This leaves 10 possible winners for third. Hence, these prizes could be awarded $12 \times 11 \times 10 = 1{,}320$ possible ways. (C) is correct. (D) is the result of erroneously applying the combinations formula to this problem.

10. (E)

The question asks how many organizational structures can be created among 10 divisions and provides the parameters for including the divisions. Since nothing indicates that order matters (an organization having Divisions A and B is exactly like that organization having Divisions B and A), this is a combinations question.

Since Division A must be part of the organization, there is only 1 way to choose that unit.

If at least one of B and C must be in the organization, only B, only C, or both could be in it, making for 3 possible ways to choose from these divisions.

At least two of D, E, and F must be part of the organization. If only two join, there are 3 possible outcomes: D and E, D and F, or E and F. Or all three could be included, which is 1 more outcome. So there are 4 possible ways to choose this group of units.

Finally, at least two of G, H, J, and K must be included. If two are included, there are
$$_4C_2 = \frac{4!}{(2!)(4-2)!} = \frac{4 \times 3 \times \cancel{(2!)}}{2 \times 1 \times \cancel{(2!)}} = 6 \text{ possible outcomes.}$$
If only three of these divisions are used, there are four ways to leave one division out, so that's 4 possible outcomes. If all four are included, that's 1 more outcome. Thus, there are $6 + 4 + 1 = 11$ possible ways to choose divisions from this group.

To find the number of organizational structures that can be formed from these various groups, multiply the numbers of ways of selecting each group: $1 \times 3 \times 4 \times 11 = 132$. **(E)** is correct.

Make sure you counted all of the possibilities for including the divisions when determining the number of possible organizational structures.

11. (D)

The question asks how many distinct combinations of three wires can be made with at least one of them being a cable television wire. There are 2 cable television and 3 internet wires to choose from. Because these are distinct combinations, the order of the wires will not matter; you can apply the combinations formula.

Notice the phrase "at least" in the question stem. When combination and permutation problems use that phrase, solving for the total and then subtracting the undesired outcomes is usually a more efficient approach. The total is the number of ways one could select any 3 wires from 5. The undesired outcome is selecting only internet wires. Use the combinations formula, $\frac{n!}{k!(n-k)!}$, to find the total number of ways to choose 3 wires out of 5:

$$\frac{5!}{3!(5-3)!} = \frac{5!}{3!2!} = \frac{5(4)(3!)}{3!2!} = \frac{5(4)}{2} = 5(2) = 10$$

You now know that there are 10 subsets of 3 wires. Now turn your attention to what is undesired—selecting only internet wires. Because there are only 3 internet wires, there is only 1 possible way to choose 3 of the 5 wires such that all are internet wires. Thus, there are $10 - 1 = 9$ ways to choose 3 wires such that at least 1 of the wires would be for cable. **(D)** is correct.

Pay careful attention to exactly what the question stem is asking. Notice that **(E)** is simply the total number of possible outcomes.

12. (C)

This Value question describes lining up different candles and figurines in such a way that no two of the same type of object are adjacent to each other and asks how many different arrangements can be made. In order to determine that value, you would need to know the exact number of each object.

Statement (1) tells you that 40,320 arrangements can be made using only the distinct figurines. If the number of figurines is f, then the number of arrangements is $f! = 40{,}320$. You could solve this for the number of figurines, but there's no need to do so on Test Day (for the record, $8! = 40{,}320$). However, you still don't know the number of candles, so there is no way to determine the total number of possible arrangements. Thus, Statement (1) is insufficient. Eliminate **(A)** and **(D)**.

Statement (2) informs you that there's one more candle than figurine, but does not tell you exactly how many there are. This is insufficient, so eliminate **(B)** and proceed to evaluate the statements together.

Statement (1) enables you to calculate the number of figurines and Statement (2) tells you that there's one more candle. So you know the numbers of each object, which is sufficient to determine the number of arrangements. **(C)** is correct.

13. (B)

The question states that there are 6 identical chips, each with a red side and a blue side, and asks for the difference between the number of ways that 3 red-sided and 3 blue-sided chips can be arranged and the number of ways 4 red-sided and 2 blue-sided chips can be arranged. Since the chips are identical, there is no way to distinguish among any chips with the same color showing.

If the chips were all different from each other, there would be 6! ways to arrange them. However, that number must be reduced by factors that represent the number of ways that the red sides can be arranged and the blue sides can be arranged, since all of these configurations are identical.

For 3 of each color, divide 6! by 3! twice to represent the indistinguishable arrangements of 3 blue and 3 red chips. Thus, the number of ways to arrange the chips is $\frac{6!}{3!(3!)} = \frac{6 \times 5 \times 4}{3 \times 2 \times 1} = 5 \times 4 = 20$. Similarly, the number of ways to arrange 4 reds and 2 blues is $\frac{6!}{4!(2!)} = \frac{6 \times 5}{2 \times 1} = 3 \times 5 = 15$. Since $20 - 15 = 5$, **(B)** is correct.

Check that you answered the question that is actually asked. (**C**) is merely the number of chips, and (**D**) and (**E**) represent the number of arrangements for each of the two configurations.

Practice Set: Probability

14. (C)

The question asks for the probability of randomly choosing (without replacement) 3 bags of mulch from 8 total bags of yard care supplies. You are given that $3 + 2 = 5$ of the bags are not mulch. Probability is $\dfrac{\text{Number of desired outcomes}}{\text{Number of total possible outcomes}}$. There are 8 total bags and 5 of them do not have mulch, so the first time you pick a bag out of the shed, there is a $\frac{5}{8}$ chance of getting a non-mulch bag. This bag is not replaced, so now there are 7 total bags and 4 are non-mulch: that's a $\frac{4}{7}$ probability. There is a $\frac{3}{6} = \frac{1}{2}$ chance of picking a non-mulch bag for the third selection.

To achieve the desired result, you need to get 1 non-mulch bag *and* a second one *and* a third one. This means you multiply the individual events' probabilities: $\frac{5}{8} \times \frac{4}{7} \times \frac{1}{2}$. Simplify this to get $\frac{5}{8\,2} \times \frac{\cancel{4}\,1}{7} \times \frac{1}{2} = \frac{5}{28}$. (**C**) is correct.

15. (C)

The question says that there are 2 different bags containing 9 marbles each. One bag contains 4 red marbles, and the other bag has 3 red marbles. The question asks for the probability that exactly 1 of the 2 marbles that is selected randomly from each of the bags is red.

There are two ways to select exactly 1 red marble. One way is to select a red marble from the first bag and a non-red marble from the second bag. The other way is to select a non-red marble from the first bag and a red marble from the second bag. Since the desired result can be attained in one manner or another, add these two probabilities to get the total probability of selecting exactly 1 red marble.

The probability that the red marble is chosen from the first bag is $\frac{4}{9}$, and the probability that a non-red marble is chosen from the second bag is $\frac{9-3}{9} = \frac{6}{9}$. Since both of these outcomes must occur, multiply their probabilities to get $\frac{4}{9} \times \frac{6}{9} = \frac{24}{81}$. There is no need to simplify at this point because you will be adding this to another fraction.

The probability that a non-red marble is chosen from the first bag is $\frac{9-4}{9} = \frac{5}{9}$, and the probability that a red marble is chosen from the second bag is $\frac{3}{9}$. Since both of these outcomes must occur, multiply their probabilities to get $\frac{5}{9} \times \frac{3}{9} = \frac{15}{81}$.

Now, add the probabilities of the two desired outcomes; the probability that exactly 1 of the chosen marbles is red is $\frac{24}{81} + \frac{15}{81} = \frac{39}{81} = \frac{13}{27}$. (**C**) is correct. Confirm that these two scenarios are the only two ways in which the desired outcome can occur. (**A**) is the probability that both marbles will be red, and (**D**) is the probability that one *or* both will be red.

16. (E)

The question asks out of 5 random occurrences of an event, what is the probability that fewer than half result in an outcome of *A*? It states that the event has two equally likely outcomes and that they are mutually exclusive. In other words, every time the event happens, there's a 50% chance of outcome *A* and a 50% chance of outcome *B*.

The probability that less than half of 5 trials have an outcome of *A* is the total of the probability of 0, 1, or 2 outcome *A*s. Use the probability formula, Probability $= \dfrac{\text{Number of desired outcomes}}{\text{Number of total possible outcomes}}$, to determine this probability.

Since each occurrence has 2 possible outcomes, and there are 5 occurrences, the total number of possible outcomes is $2^5 = 32$. There is only 1 way to have no *A*s, that is, 5 *B*s. There are 5 ways to have 1 *A*, since that singular *A* could occur on any 1 of the 5 trials.

There are 2 ways to find the number of ways to get 2 *A*s. You could actually count the ways: AABBB, ABABB, ABBAB, ABBBA, BAABB, BABAB, BABBA, BBAAB, BBABA, and BBBAA, for a total of 10 different ways. Alternatively, you could use the combinations formula to find the number of combinations of 2 *A*s out of 5 events:

$$_5C_2 = \frac{5!}{2!(3!)} = \frac{5 \times 4 \times \cancel{3} \times \cancel{2} \times \cancel{1}}{2 \times 1(\cancel{3} \times \cancel{2} \times \cancel{1})} = \frac{20}{2} = 10$$

The total number of ways to obtain the desired outcome is thus $1 + 5 + 10 = 16$, so the probability is $\frac{16}{32} = \frac{1}{2}$. (**E**) is correct.

Be certain that you answered the question that was asked and that you counted only the ways to get 2 or fewer outcomes of *A* since (**E**) is the greatest probability among the choices.

17. (D)

This Value question asks for the probability that a student receives housing in at least one of two consecutive years. In order to calculate that probability, you would need to know the probability of getting housing in each year.

Statement (1): This gives you the probability of *not* getting into housing. An 80% chance of not getting housing each year means a 20% chance of getting housing each year. The exact answer isn't something that you need to worry about, since this isn't Problem Solving. You know an answer can be calculated, so Statement (1) is sufficient. Eliminate choices (**B**), (**C**), and (**E**).

Statement (2): This isn't given in percentage form, but any proportion will serve. This, too, gives you the likelihood of getting housing in any given year. Each statement is sufficient. (**D**) is correct.

Practice Set: Overlapping Sets

18. (B)

This question provides you with information about a group of 65 books; every book is classified as either fiction or nonfiction and as either greater than 200 pages or less than or equal to 200 pages (call these "long books and short books"). The question asks for the total

number of nonfiction books "of no more than 200 pages"—in other words, short nonfiction books.

Organize the given information into a table:

	FICTION	NONFICTION	TOTAL
Short		?	25
Long	20		
Total	35		65

With everything organized, fill in the blanks. Once you have two entries in a row or column, you can fill in the third entry for that row or column. If the two known values are subtotals, add them to get the total; if one of the known values is a total, subtract the known subtotal from the total to get the other subtotal. The complete table would look like the one below. However, you would not need to fill in the cells for long nonfiction or total nonfiction to get the number of short fiction books.

	FICTION	NONFICTION	TOTAL
Short	15	10	25
Long	20	20	40
Total	35	30	65

Arrive at the correct answer either by subtracting 15 short fiction books from 25 total short books in the first row or by subtracting 20 long nonfiction books from 30 total nonfiction books in the second column. The number of short nonfiction books is 10. (**B**) is correct.

When using a table, check to make sure that you answer with the right piece of information; three of the incorrect choices are numbers that fill in other cells in the table. Also, double-check that you answered the right question; for example, if you read the question as "How many nonfiction books of more than 200 pages" instead of "*no* more than 200 pages," you may have chosen (**C**).

19. (C)

The question asks for the range of the number of students who may study Spanish but not French. The students are split into two potentially overlapping sets—those who study Spanish and those who study French—so this is an overlapping sets problem.

To organize the data, draw a table and enter the data from the question stem:

	FRENCH	NOT FRENCH	TOTAL
Spanish		?	170
Not Spanish		at least 90	
Total	110		300

From this, you can figure out how many do *not* study each language:

	FRENCH	NOT FRENCH	TOTAL
Spanish		?	170
Not Spanish		at least 90	130
Total	110	190	300

Since the total of the "not Spanish" row is 130, there could be no more than 130 in the "not Spanish and not French" category. (More than 130 would require a negative number of students in the "French and not Spanish" category.)

	FRENCH	NOT FRENCH	TOTAL
Spanish		?	170
Not Spanish		90 to 130	130
Total	110	190	300

The "Spanish and not French" category must add with "90 to 130" to yield 190. There could be as many as 100 (since $100 + 90 = 190$) or as few as 60 (since $60 + 130 = 190$). **(C)** is correct.

Re-read the question stem, making sure that you didn't accidentally misread anything. For example, **(E)** is the value of the "Spanish and French" category.

20. (A)

This is a Value question. It is asking for the number of reporters who cover all three continents. Since the reporters may cover one, two, or three continents, this is

an overlapping sets question. With *three* sets, a chart-based approach would be too unwieldy. A better way to visualize three overlapping sets is with a Venn diagram. Take care to put the totals for each continent just outside the circles so that you don't lose the distinction between the number covering a continent and the number covering *only* that continent.

So that you know what you need, put an x in the "all three continents" space on the diagram.

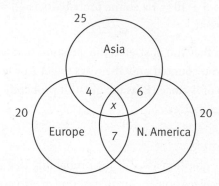

A total of 25 reporters cover Asia, 6 of whom also cover only North America, 4 of whom also cover only Europe, and x of whom also cover both Europe and North America. Therefore, $25 - (6 + 4 + x)$, or $15 - x$, cover only Asia.

Similarly, $20 - (4 + 7 + x)$, or $9 - x$, cover only Europe, and $20 - (7 + 6 + x)$, or $7 - x$, cover only North America.

Put those expressions into your diagram:

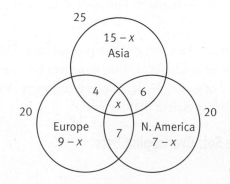

Many kinds of information, therefore, would allow you to figure out the number of reporters who cover all three continents. Any data that lets you make an equation with x would be sufficient.

Statement (1) says that the grand total of all the reporters is 38. In other words, if you added up all the various subcategories, you'd get 38. That's sufficient, as the only unknown in that equation would be x. Eliminate **(B)**, **(C)**, and **(E)**.

Although you wouldn't want to set the whole thing up (you'd stop as soon as you knew that you *could* set up the equation), here's what it would be:

$$(15 - x) + (9 - x) + (7 - x) + 4 + 7 + 6 + x = 38$$

Statement (2) is only saying that $x < 6$. That narrows down the range of possible values of x but does not lead to a unique solution. Statement (2) is insufficient. **(A)** is correct.

CHAPTER 11

MATH CONTENT REVIEW: GEOMETRY

LEARNING OBJECTIVES

- Identify the geometry rules that are relevant to a given geometry question
- Apply the Kaplan Methods for Problem Solving and Data Sufficiency to questions dealing with geometry

Below is an example Problem Solving question with an geometry focus. As you try the question, think about what information it gives you, what the question is asking you to do with that information, and what you do and don't already know about how to solve. The explanation that follows demonstrates how a GMAT expert uses the Kaplan Method for Problem Solving and certain geometry rules to solve this question efficiently.

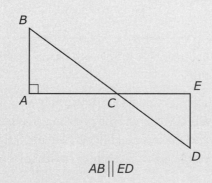

$AB \parallel ED$

<u>Note:</u> Figure not drawn to scale.

In the figure above, $ED = 1$, $CD = 2$, $AE = 6\sqrt{3}$. What is the perimeter of $\triangle ABC$?

- ○ $3\sqrt{3}$
- ○ $10 + 5\sqrt{3}$
- ○ $10\sqrt{3}$
- ○ $15 + 5\sqrt{3}$
- ○ $25\sqrt{3}$

Step 1: Analyze the Question

Apply some critical thinking and a knowledge of geometry rules to make some deductions. The image shows two triangles that meet at a certain point, and you're told that two of the line segments that form their sides are parallel. Additionally, you're given that angle *BAC* is a right angle, which makes triangle *ABC* a right triangle. Pay attention to the detail that *AB* and *ED* are parallel: this means that angles *ABC* and *CDE* are equal, because they are alternate interior angles formed by two parallel lines cut by a transversal. Angles *BCA* and *DCE* are also equal, since these are vertical angles. And since the measure of all interior angles of a triangle must add up to 180, angles *BAC* and *CED* must also be equal. Therefore, these are two similar right triangles. The question stem also gives you the measures of three line segments in the figure.

Step 2: State the Task

You're asked to find the perimeter of triangle *ABC*. The perimeter of a polygon is the sum of its side lengths, so use information about the side lengths of triangle *CDE* to figure out the side lengths of *ABC*.

Step 3: Approach Strategically

Since *CDE* is a right triangle with one leg equal to 1 and a hypotenuse equal to 2, you can apply a special right triangle pattern. The ratio of these sides means that this is a 30°-60°-90° triangle and the side lengths are in the ratio $1:\sqrt{3}:2$. Therefore, side *CE* must have a length of $\sqrt{3}$. Since you are given that *AE* equals $6\sqrt{3}$, leg *AC* must equal $6\sqrt{3} - \sqrt{3} = 5\sqrt{3}$.

Since the two triangles are similar, the three sides *AB*:*AC*:*BC* must also follow the ratio of $1:\sqrt{3}:2$. Because *AC* equals $5\sqrt{3}$, *AB* must equal 5, and *BC* must equal 10. Therefore, the perimeter of triangle *ABC* is $5\sqrt{3} + 5 + 10$, or $15 + 5\sqrt{3}$. Choice (**D**) is correct.

Step 4: Confirm Your Answer

Make sure you used the correct side length ratio, that for a 30°-60°-90° triangle, and that you correctly combined like terms when summing the side lengths.

Geometry is not heavily tested on the Quantitative section; you may see only a few geometry questions. However, because geometry is highly rule driven, if you know the rules and can recognize when to apply which rule, even geometry questions that most test takers find difficult will be straightforward for you. In this chapter, we'll review all the formulas you'll need to deal with geometry as it shows up on the GMAT, starting with the rules governing lines and angles.

Lines and Angles

A **line** is a one-dimensional abstraction—infinitely long with no width. Two points determine a straight line; given any two points, there is exactly one straight line that passes through them.

A line **segment** is a section of a straight line of finite length with two endpoints. A line segment is named for its endpoints, as in segment AB below. The **midpoint** is the point that divides a line segment into two equal parts. A **ray** is a part of a line that has a fixed starting point but no endpoint.

Example:

In the figure above, A and B are the endpoints of the line segment AB, and M is the midpoint. What is the length of AB?

Since AM is 6, MB is also 6, so AB is $6 + 6$, or 12.

Two straight lines are **parallel** if they lie in the same plane and never intersect each other. If line ℓ_1 is parallel to line ℓ_2, you write $\ell_1 \parallel \ell_2$.

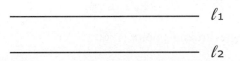

Two straight lines are **perpendicular** if they intersect at a 90° angle. If line ℓ_1 is perpendicular to line ℓ_2, you write $\ell_1 \perp \ell_2$. If $\ell_1 \perp \ell_2$ and $\ell_2 \perp \ell_3$, then $\ell_1 \parallel \ell_3$.

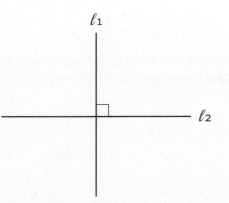

An **angle** is formed by two lines or line segments intersecting at a point. The point of intersection is called the **vertex** of the angle. On the GMAT, angles are measured in degrees (°). Angle x, $\angle ABC$, and $\angle B$ all denote the same angle in this diagram:

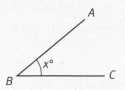

An **acute angle** is an angle whose degree measure is less than 90°. A **right angle** is an angle whose degree measure is exactly 90°. An **obtuse angle** is an angle whose degree measure is greater than 90° and less than 180°. A **straight angle** is an angle whose degree measure is exactly 180°.

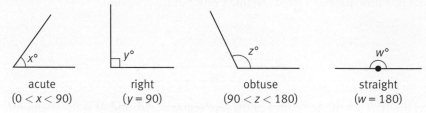

acute	right	obtuse	straight
$(0 < x < 90)$	$(y = 90)$	$(90 < z < 180)$	$(w = 180)$

The **sum of the measures of the angles** on one side of a straight line is 180°.

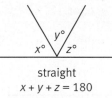

straight
$x + y + z = 180$

The sum of the measures of the angles around a point is 360°.

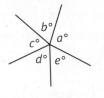

$a + b + c + d + e = 360$

Two angles are **supplementary** if together they make up a straight angle (i.e., if the sum of their measures is 180°). Two angles are **complementary** if together they make up a right angle (i.e., if the sum of their measures is 90°).

$c + d = 180$
supplementary

$a + b = 90$
complementary

A line or line segment **bisects** an angle if it splits the angle into two smaller, equal angles. Line segment BD below bisects $\angle ABC$, and $\angle ABD$ has the same measure as $\angle DBC$. The two smaller angles are each half the size of $\angle ABC$.

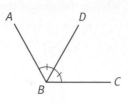

Vertical angles are a pair of opposite angles formed by two intersecting lines or line segments. At the point of intersection, two pairs of vertical angles are formed. Angles a and c below are vertical angles, as are b and d.

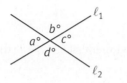

The two angles in a pair of vertical angles have the same degree measure. In the previous diagram, $a = c$ and $b = d$. In addition, since ℓ_1 and line ℓ_2 are straight lines, $a + b = c + d = a + d = b + c = 180°$. In other words, each angle is supplementary to each of its two adjacent angles.

If two parallel lines intersect a third line (called a **transversal**), the third line will intersect each of the parallel lines at the same angle. In the figure below, $a = e$ because the transversal intersects lines ℓ_1 and ℓ_2 at the same angle. Since a and e are equal, and $c = a$ and $e = g$ (vertical angles), you know that $a = c = e = g$. Similarly, $b = d = f = h$.

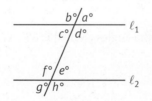

In other words, when two parallel lines intersect a third line, all acute angles formed are equal, all obtuse angles formed are equal, and any acute angle is supplementary to any obtuse angle.

Now use the drill to get some practice working with lines and angles.

Lines and Angles Drill

Answers follow the drill.

1. If line *AB* is perpendicular to line *YZ*, what is the sum of the measures of any three of the angles created by the intersection of the lines?

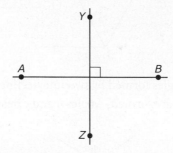

2. Angle *TOM* is 44°. It is bisected by segment *BO*. What is the measure of angle *BOT*?

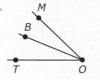

3. *BCD* is a straight line, and ∠*BCZ* is 30°. What is the measure of ∠*ZCD*?

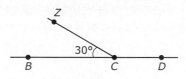

4. Lines *PO* and *BC* intersect. One of the angles created is 88°. What are the measures of the other three angles?

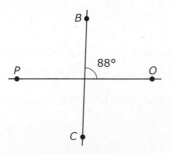

5. Parallel lines ℓ_1 and ℓ_2 are intersected by a transversal *AB*. If the measure of one of the angles formed is 125°, what are the measures of the other seven angles formed?

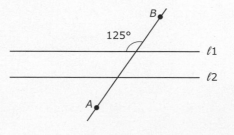

Lines and Angles Drill: Answers

1. 270°

2. 22°

3. 150°

4. 88°, 92°, and 92°

5. Three of the angles are 125°; four of the angles are 55°.

Now see how a GMAT expert uses the Kaplan Method to answer a Problem Solving question involving lines and angles.

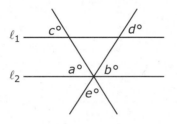

If ℓ_1 is parallel to ℓ_2 in the figure above, which of the following expressions must equal 180?

I. $a + b$

II. $c + e$

III. $c + d + e$

○ I only

○ II only

○ III only

○ II and III only

○ I, II, and III

Step 1: Analyze the Question

Before evaluating the statements, take some time to understand the information you've been given in the question stem and figure. The question stem tells you that ℓ_1 and ℓ_2 are parallel. Since ℓ_1 and ℓ_2 are parallel, you know that the corresponding angles created by the transversals (intersecting lines) are of equal measure. Specifically, that means $a = c$ and $b = d$.

Looking at the figure, you see that angles a and b, plus that third angle between them, compose a straight line, which is 180°. Since angle e is the "vertical angle" of that third angle, their measures are the same. So you can deduce that $a + b + e = 180$.

Step 2: State the Task

Your task is to determine which of the three Roman numeral statements are equal to 180. You just deduced that $a + b + e = 180$, so if a statement is equal to $a + b + e$, then it is also equal to 180.

Step 3: Approach Strategically

Statement III looks similar to what you're after and appears in several answer choices. Does $c + d + e = a + b + e$? Since $a = c$ and $b = d$, the two expressions are equal and, therefore, equal to 180. The correct answer must contain Statement III, so eliminate **(A)** and **(B)**.

Statement II appears twice in the remaining statements, so evaluate it next. Does $c + e = a + b + e$? You deduced earlier that $c + d + e = a + b + e$. The only way, then, that $c + e$ could equal $a + b + e$ is if d were equal to 0. You have no idea what its value is, but it's definitely not 0. So Statement II is not part of the correct answer. Eliminate **(D)** and **(E)**, leaving only the correct choice, **(C)**.

Step 4: Confirm Your Answer

Confirm that you read the figure correctly and double-check the logic of your deductions.

Next, you'll find some in-format questions involving lines and angles.

Practice Set: Lines and Angles

(Answers and explanations are at the end of the chapter.)

1.

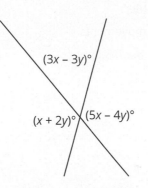

Note: Not drawn to scale.

In the figure above, what is the value of y?

○   36

○   54

○   90

○   126

○   180

2.

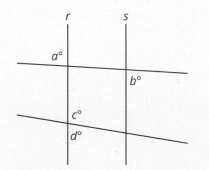

In the figure above, if lines r and s are parallel, what is the value of $a + b$?

(1) $c - a = 25$

(2) $a - d = 15$

3. A certain line segment rotates consistently in one direction in 45° increments around one of its endpoints E. The segment loses half of its length every 45° that it rotates, and it stops rotating when it reaches less than 5 percent of its starting length. Did the segment stop rotating?

    (1) The segment rotated at least 180°.

    (2) The segment made at most 5 movements.

Triangles

A **triangle** is a closed figure with three interior angles and three straight sides. The sum of the **interior angles** of any triangle is 180°.

Each interior angle is supplementary to an adjacent **exterior angle**. The degree measure of an exterior angle is equal to the sum of the measures of the two nonadjacent (remote) interior angles.

Example: In the figure below, a, b, and c are interior angles. Therefore, $a + b + c = 180$. In addition, d is supplementary to c; therefore, $d + c = 180$. So $d + c = a + b + c$, and $d = a + b$. Thus, the exterior angle d is equal to the sum of the two remote interior angles a and b.

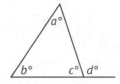

The **altitude** (or height) of a triangle is the perpendicular distance from a vertex to the side opposite the vertex. The altitude can fall inside the triangle, outside the triangle, or, in right triangles, on one of the sides.

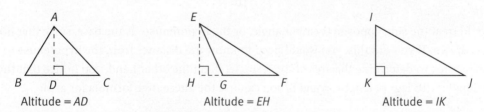

Altitude = AD   Altitude = EH   Altitude = IK

The length of any side of a triangle is less than the sum of the lengths of the other two sides, and it is greater than the positive difference of the lengths of the other two sides. These relationships are known as the **triangle inequality theorem**.

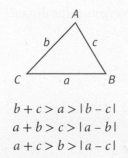

$$b + c > a > |b - c|$$
$$a + b > c > |a - b|$$
$$a + c > b > |a - c|$$

If the lengths of two sides of a triangle are unequal, the greater angle lies opposite the longer side and vice versa. In the figure above, if $\angle A > \angle B > \angle C$, then $a > b > c$.

The formula for the **area** of a triangle is $\frac{1}{2} \times$ Base $\times$ Height.

Example: What is the area of the triangle below?

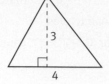

The base has length 4 and the altitude length 3, so you can write:

$$A = \frac{1}{2}bh$$
$$= \frac{1}{2} \times 4 \times 3 = 6$$

Remember that the height (or altitude) must be perpendicular to the base. In a **right triangle**, two sides of a triangle are perpendicular to each other, so they can serve as the base and height. In a right triangle, the two perpendicular sides are called the **legs**. Thus, the area is one-half the product of the legs:

$$A = \frac{1}{2}bh$$
$$= \frac{1}{2} \times l_1 \times l_2$$

Example: What is the area of the triangle below?

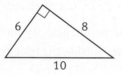

You could treat the side opposite the right angle, or the **hypotenuse**, as the base, since that how the figure is drawn. If you did this, you would need to know the distance from the hypotenuse to the opposite vertex to determine the area of the triangle. If, on the other hand, you notice that this is a right triangle with legs of lengths 6 and 8, you can use the alternative formula for area:

$$A = \frac{1}{2} \times l_1 \times l_2$$
$$= \frac{1}{2} \times 6 \times 8$$
$$= 24$$

The **perimeter** of a triangle, or indeed any polygon, is the distance around it. In other words, the perimeter is equal to the sum of the lengths of the sides.

Example: What is the perimeter of the triangle below?

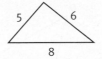

The sides are of length 5, 6, and 8. Therefore, the perimeter is 5 + 6 + 8, or 19.

An **isosceles** triangle has two sides of equal length. The two equal sides are called **legs**, and the third side is called the **base**. Since the two legs have the same length, the two angles opposite the legs must have the same measure.

Example: In the figure below, $PQ = PR$ and $\angle Q = \angle R$.

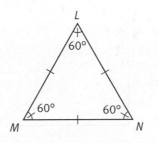

An **equilateral** triangle has three sides of equal length and three 60° angles.

Example: In the figure below, $LM = LN = MN$ and $\angle L = \angle M = \angle N = 60°$.

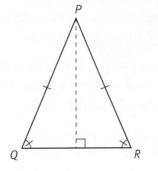

Triangles are **similar** if corresponding angles have the same measure. For instance, any two triangles whose angles measure 30°, 60°, and 90° are similar. In similar triangles, corresponding side lengths are proportional to one another. In other words, similar triangles are the same shape but not necessarily the same size. Triangles are **congruent** if corresponding angles have the same measure and corresponding sides have the same length.

Example: What is the perimeter of $\triangle DEF$ below?

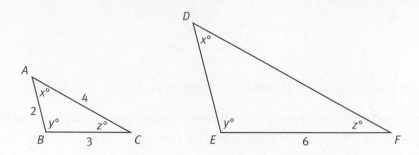

Each triangle has an $x°$ angle, a $y°$ angle, and a $z°$ angle; therefore, the triangles are similar, and corresponding sides are proportional to one another. BC and EF are corresponding sides, because each is opposite the $x°$ angle. Since EF is twice the length of BC, each side of $\triangle DEF$ must be twice the length of the corresponding side of $\triangle ABC$. Therefore, $DE = 2(AB) = 4$, and $DF = 2(AC) = 8$. The perimeter of $\triangle DEF$ is $4 + 6 + 8 = 18$.

The ratio of the areas of two similar triangles is the square of the ratio of the corresponding lengths. For instance, in the example above, since each side of $\triangle DEF$ is 2 times the length of the corresponding side of $\triangle ABC$, $\triangle DEF$ must have 2^2 or 4 times the area of $\triangle ABC$.

$$\frac{\text{Area } \triangle DEF}{\text{Area } \triangle ABC} = \left(\frac{EF}{BC}\right)^2 = \left(\frac{6}{3}\right)^2 = \left(\frac{2}{1}\right)^2 = 4$$

A right triangle has one interior angle of 90°, which is also the largest angle of the triangle. The hypotenuse, opposite the right angle, is the longest side.

The **Pythagorean theorem** applies to all right triangles and states that the square of the hypotenuse is equal to the sum of the squares of the legs.

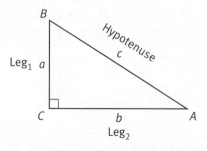

$$(\text{Leg}_1)^2 + (\text{Leg}_2)^2 = (\text{Hypotenuse})^2$$

or

$$a^2 + b^2 = c^2$$

Example: What is the length of the hypotenuse of a right triangle with legs of length 5 and 10?

$$5^2 + 10^2 = \text{Hypotenuse}^2$$
$$25 + 100 = \text{Hypotenuse}^2$$
$$\sqrt{125} = \text{Hypotenuse}$$
$$5\sqrt{5} = \text{Hypotenuse}$$

Some sets of integers happen to satisfy the Pythagorean theorem. These sets of integers are commonly referred to as **Pythagorean triples**. One very common triple is the 3-4-5 triangle. Since $3^2 + 4^2 = 5^2$, if you have a right triangle with legs of 3 and 4, the hypotenuse *must* be 5. This is the most common kind of right triangle on the GMAT. You should be familiar with the numbers so that whenever you see a right triangle with legs of 3 and 4, you will immediately know the hypotenuse must be 5. In addition, any multiple of these lengths makes a Pythagorean triple; for instance, $6^2 + 8^2 = 10^2$, so 6, 8, and 10 (that is, 2 times a 3:4:5 triple) also make a right triangle. Other triples that you may see on the GMAT include 5-12-13 and 8-15-17 (and their multiples).

Additionally, there are two special kinds of right triangles that always have side lengths in the same ratios:

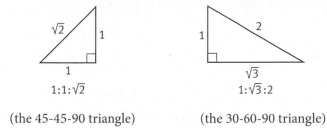

(the 45-45-90 triangle)   (the 30-60-90 triangle)

These two special right triangles appear frequently, so you are very likely to see them. Often, the GMAT will present them in predictable ways. For example, the diagonal of a square creates two **45°-45°-90° triangles** (also known as **isosceles right triangles**). And bisecting an equilateral triangle creates two **30°-60°-90° triangles**, allowing you to determine the height and area of the equilateral triangle:

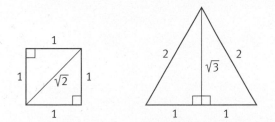

Easily recognizable right triangle patterns—the triples and special right triangles—allow you to save time by avoiding the Pythagorean theorem on a large portion of GMAT geometry questions.

Now use the drill to get some practice working with triangles.

Triangles Drill

Answers follow the drill.

1. Find the area of a triangle with a base of 14 and a height of 9.

2. Triangle *ABC* is similar to triangle *PQR*; side *AB* is 6 and corresponding side *PQ* is 18. If side *BC* is 7, how long is corresponding side *QR*?

3. Find the hypotenuse of a right triangle with leg lengths of 2 and 3.

4. A right triangle has leg lengths of 3 and 4; what is the length of its hypotenuse?

5. The shorter leg of a right triangle is 5 and the hypotenuse is 13; what is the length of the longer leg?

6. A right triangle has a hypotenuse of 10 and one leg length of 8; what is the length of the other leg?

7. A 45°-45°-90° right triangle has leg lengths of 12. What is the length of its hypotenuse?

8. A square has side lengths of 15; what is the length of its diagonal?

9. The shorter leg of a 30°-60°-90° triangle has a length of 100. What are the lengths of the longer leg and the hypotenuse, respectively?

10. An equilateral triangle has side lengths of 10. What is its height?

Triangles Drill: Answers

1. $\frac{1}{2} \times 14 \times 9 = 63$
2. 21
3. $\sqrt{2^2 + 3^2} = \sqrt{4 + 9} = \sqrt{13}$
4. 5; this is a 3-4-5 Pythagorean triple
5. 12; this is a 5-12-13 Pythagorean triple

6. 6; this is a multiple of a 3-4-5 triple
7. $12\sqrt{2}$
8. $15\sqrt{2}$
9. $100\sqrt{3}$ and 200
10. $5\sqrt{3}$

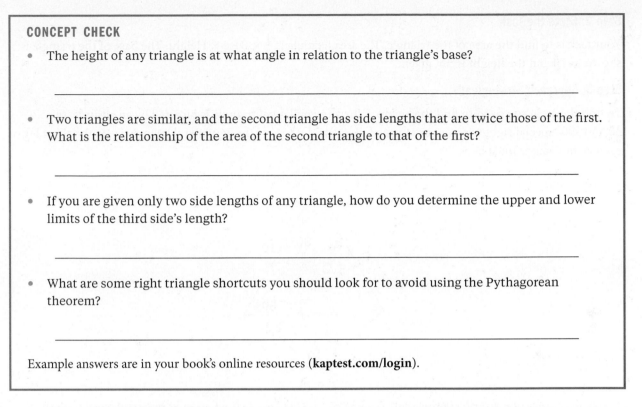

CONCEPT CHECK

- The height of any triangle is at what angle in relation to the triangle's base?

  _____

- Two triangles are similar, and the second triangle has side lengths that are twice those of the first. What is the relationship of the area of the second triangle to that of the first?

  _____

- If you are given only two side lengths of any triangle, how do you determine the upper and lower limits of the third side's length?

  _____

- What are some right triangle shortcuts you should look for to avoid using the Pythagorean theorem?

  _____

Example answers are in your book's online resources (**kaptest.com/login**).

Now see how a GMAT expert uses the Kaplan Method on a Problem Solving question dealing with triangles.

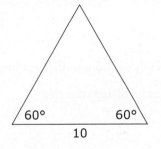

What is the area of the triangle shown above?

- ○ $10\sqrt{3}$
- ○ $25\sqrt{3}$
- ○ 67
- ○ $50\sqrt{3}$
- ○ 100

Step 1: Analyze the Question

This question tests your knowledge of triangle properties. Two of the angles in the given triangle are 60° each, so the third angle must also be 60°, since the angles of every triangle sum to 180°. Thus, the triangle is equilateral.

Step 2: State the Task

Your task is to find the area of the triangle. The area formula is $\frac{1}{2} \times$ Base $\times$ Height. The base of the triangle is shown as 10, but the height is not given.

Step 3: Approach Strategically

To find the area, you need to find the height. When an equilateral triangle is bisected by an altitude, two 30°-60°-90° special right triangles are formed. Because the base of the equilateral triangle is 10, the short leg of each right triangle must be 5.

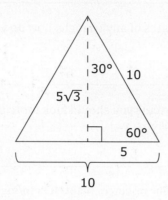

The ratio of sides of a 30°-60°-90° triangle is $x : x\sqrt{3} : 2x$. Since $x = 5$, the height of the equilateral triangle is $5\sqrt{3}$. Thus, the area is $\frac{1}{2} \times 10 \times 5\sqrt{3} = 25\sqrt{3}$. **(B)** is the correct answer.

Step 4: Confirm Your Answer

Double-check that you've used the correct dimensions in the area formula.

Next, you'll find some in-format questions involving triangles.

Practice Set: Triangles

(Answers and explanations are at the end of the chapter.)

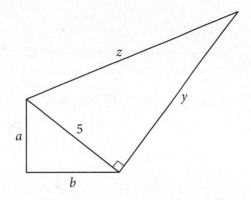

4. Based on the figure shown, which of the following could be true?

    I. $a = b$

    II. $y = z$

    III. $a^2 + b^2 = z^2 - y^2$

    O   None

    O   I only

    O   II only

    O   I and III only

    O   I, II, and III

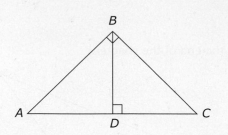

5.   In the figure above, if ∠ABC is a right angle and $\overline{BD}$ bisects $\overline{AC}$, then what is the ratio of BC to AC?

   ○ $\dfrac{\sqrt{2}}{4}$

   ○ $\dfrac{\sqrt{2}}{3}$

   ○ $\dfrac{1}{2}$

   ○ $\dfrac{\sqrt{2}}{2}$

   ○ $\sqrt{2}$

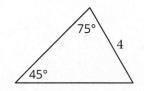

6.   What is the area of the triangle in the figure above?

   ○ $2 + 2\sqrt{3}$

   ○ $4\sqrt{3}$

   ○ $6 + 2\sqrt{3}$

   ○ $6\sqrt{3}$

   ○   12

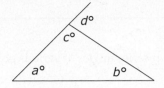

7. In the figure above, what is the value of *b*?

    1. $a + c + d = 225$
    2. $d - a = 55$

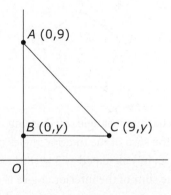

8. In the rectangular coordinate system above, triangle *ABC* has an area of 27 square units. Vertex *A* is at point (0,9), vertex *B* is at point (0,*y*), and vertex *C* is at point (9,*y*). What is the value of *y*?

    ○ 1
    ○ 2
    ○ 3
    ○ 4
    ○ 6

Polygons

LEARNING OBJECTIVE

- Calculate the area, perimeter, and interior angles of various polygons

A **polygon** is a closed figure whose sides are straight line segments. The **perimeter** of a polygon is the distance around the polygon, or the sum of the lengths of the sides. A **vertex** of a polygon is the point where two adjacent sides meet. A **diagonal** of a polygon is a line segment connecting two nonadjacent vertices.

The number of sides determines the specific name of the polygon. A **triangle** has three sides, a **quadrilateral** has four sides, a **pentagon** has five sides, and a **hexagon** has six sides.

The sum of the **interior angles** of a triangle is 180°. The sum of the interior angles of a quadrilateral is 360°. Larger polygons can be divided into smaller components to aid in the calculation of their interior angles. As a general rule, any polygon with n sides can be split into $n - 2$ triangles, so the sum of all the angles inside a polygon with n sides is $(n - 2)180°$.

Example:

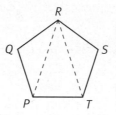

This pentagon has been divided into three triangles by drawing diagonals from a given vertex to all other nonadjacent vertices. Since the sum of the interior angles of each triangle is 180°, the sum of the interior angles of a pentagon can be calculated as $3 \times 180° = 540°$. A pentagon has 5 sides, so in terms of the formula, $n = 5$ and the sum of the interior angles is $(5 - 2)180°$.

A **regular** polygon has sides of equal length and interior angles of equal measure. In a regular polygon with n sides and thus n angles, each angle can be calculated as $\dfrac{(n - 2)\,180°}{n}$. So, each angle in a regular pentagon (5 equal sides) would measure $\dfrac{(5 - 2)180°}{5} = \dfrac{540°}{5} = 108°$.

A **parallelogram** is a quadrilateral with equal and parallel opposite sides. The height of a parallelogram is the length of a perpendicular line segment drawn from the base up to the side opposite that base.

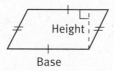

The angles opposite each other are equal. The diagonals of a parallelogram do not necessarily have equal length, but they do bisect each other. The **area of a parallelogram** is equal to Base × Height.

A **rectangle** is a parallelogram with four equal angles, each a right angle.

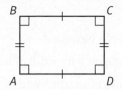

The diagonals of a rectangle have equal length and bisect each other. The **area of a rectangle** equals the product of the lengths of two adjacent sides, or Length × Width.

A **square** is a rectangle with four equal sides. The **area of a square** is thus one of its sides squared, or s^2.

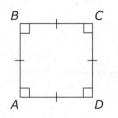

A **trapezoid** is a quadrilateral with one pair of parallel sides. Those parallel sides are the bases. The height of a trapezoid is a perpendicular line connecting the two bases.

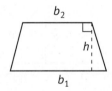

The **area of a trapezoid** is equal to one-half the sum of the bases multiplied by the height: $\frac{1}{2}(b_1 + b_2)(h)$.

Now use the drill to get some practice working with polygons.

Polygons Drill

Answers follow the drill.

1. What is the sum of the interior angles of a hexagon?
2. What is the perimeter of a regular pentagon with sides of length 6?
3. What is the area of a rectangle with sides of length 5 and 9?
4. What is the area of the following parallelogram?

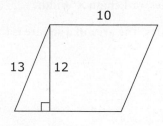

5. What is the area of the following trapezoid?

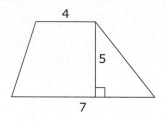

Polygons Drill: Answers

1. 720°
2. 30
3. 45

4. 120
5. 27.5

CONCEPT CHECK

- What are the characteristics that define a regular polygon?

  _____

- The perimeter of a polygon is equal to the _____.
- A rectangle is a quadrilateral in which all angles are _____.
- In a parallelogram, _____ angles are equal, as are the lengths of _____ sides.
- To find the height of a parallelogram or a trapezoid, draw a _____ line connecting the base to the _____.

Example answers are in your book's online resources (**kaptest.com/login**).

Now see how a GMAT expert uses the Kaplan Method and an understanding of polygons to answer a Problem Solving question.

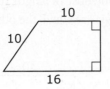

What is the perimeter of the figure above?

- ○ 43
- ○ 44
- ○ 46
- ○ 47
- ○ 48

Step 1: Analyze the Question

The question asks for the perimeter of the figure, a quadrilateral. The lengths of three of the sides are given.

Step 2: State the Task

To solve for the perimeter, you need to determine the length of the unlabeled side.

Step 3: Approach Strategically

Break the polygon down into smaller, more manageable figures. In this case, you can break the shape into a rectangle and a right triangle. Draw a perpendicular height from the left endpoint of the top side down to the bottom side.

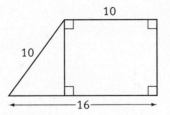

Because the lengths of the opposite sides of a rectangle are equal, the horizontal sides of the rectangle both have a length of 10. This means that the horizontal leg of the right triangle has a length of $16 - 10 = 6$.

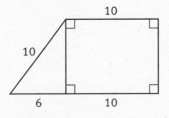

To solve for the vertical leg of the right triangle, you can use the Pythagorean theorem or you can recognize that the two known sides fit the ratio of a special 3:4:5 right triangle. Each side is a part of the ratio multiplied by 2. The leg of length 6 is 3×2, and the hypotenuse of length 10 is 5×2. So the length of the vertical leg is $4 \times 2 = 8$. Because opposite sides of a rectangle are equal, the other vertical side of the rectangle also has a length of 8.

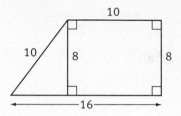

The perimeter is the sum of the length of the sides: $16 + 10 + 10 + 8 = 44$. That's choice **(B)**.

If you were short on time and needed to make a strategic guess, just drawing the height could help eliminate a few choices quickly. The height is equal to the missing side. It is also the vertical leg of a right triangle, which means it must be shorter than the hypotenuse. So, the height, and thus the missing side, must be less than 10. That means the perimeter of the whole figure must be less than $16 + 10 + 10 + 10 = 46$, eliminating **(C)**, **(D)**, and **(E)** and leaving you with a 50/50 chance of guessing the correct answer.

Step 4: Confirm Your Answer

Read back over the problem, confirming that your solution accurately reflects the information in the question.

Next, you'll find some in-format questions involving polygons.

Practice Set: Polygons

(Answers and explanations are at the end of the chapter.)

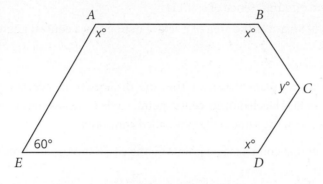

Note: Not drawn to scale.

9.   In the figure shown above, *AB* and *DE* are parallel. What is the value of *y*?

     O   110

     O   120

     O   135

     O   150

     O   160

10. A contractor uses half of the available concrete to pour an 8-foot by 12-foot rectangular base for
     a monument. If she uses the rest of the concrete to create a uniform-width walkway all the way
     around the base of the monument, using the same amount of concrete per square foot as for the
     base, what is the maximum possible width of the walkway?

     O   1 foot

     O   2 feet

     O   3 feet

     O   4 feet

     O   6 feet

11. Is the length of a side of square *S* greater than the length of a side of equilateral triangle *T*?

     (1) The sum of the lengths of a side of *S* and a side of *T* is 22.

     (2) The ratio of the perimeter of square *S* to the perimeter of triangle *T* is 5 to 6.

Circles

LEARNING OBJECTIVES

- Calculate the area and circumference of a circle
- Calculate the length of an arc or the area of a sector defined by a central angle

A **circle** is the set of all points in a plane that are at the same distance from a certain point. This point is called the **center** of the circle. A circle is labeled by its center point: circle O means the circle with center point O. Two circles of different sizes with the same center are called **concentric**.

A **diameter** is a line segment that connects two points on the circle and passes through the center of the circle. In circle O, AB is a diameter.

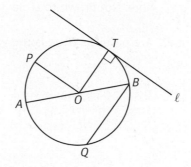

A **radius** is a line segment from the center of the circle to any point on the circle. The radius of a circle is one-half the length of the diameter. In circle O, $\overline{OA}$, $\overline{OB}$, $\overline{OP}$, and $\overline{OT}$ are radii.

A **chord** is a line segment joining two points on the circle. In circle O, $\overline{AB}$ and $\overline{QB}$ are chords. A diameter of a circle is the longest possible chord of the circle.

An **inscribed angle** is one that has its vertex on the circumference of a circle. Here, angle ABC is inscribed.

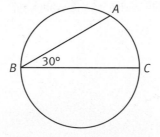

An inscribed angle also has a relationship with minor arc length. For an inscribed angle measuring n degrees:

$$\text{Arc length} = \left(\tfrac{n}{180}\right) \times \text{Circumference}$$

In other words, an angle that's inscribed defines an arc twice as long as one defined by a central angle of equal angle measure.

A **central angle** is an angle formed by two radii. In circle O, $\angle AOP$, $\angle POT$, $\angle POB$, among others, are central angles.

A line that touches only one point on the circumference of the circle is **tangent** to that circle. A line drawn tangent to a circle is perpendicular to the radius at the point of tangency. Line ℓ is tangent to circle O at point T.

Circumference and Area

The distance around a circle is called the **circumference**. The number π (pi) is the ratio of a circle's circumference to its diameter. The value of π is $3.14159265\ldots$, usually approximated as 3.14. For the GMAT, it is usually sufficient to remember that π is a little more than 3.

Since π equals the ratio of the circumference to the diameter (that is, $\pi = \frac{C}{d}$), a **formula for the circumference** is $C = \pi d$ or $C = 2\pi r$.

An **arc** is a portion of the circumference of a circle. In the figure below, AB is an arc of the circle that spans central angle AOB. The shorter distance between A and B along the circle is called the **minor arc**; the longer distance AXB is the **major arc**. An arc that is exactly half the circumference of the circle is called a **semicircle** (in other words, half a circle).

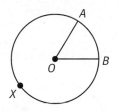

The ratio of an arc's length to the circle's circumference equals the ratio of the degree measure of the arc's central angle to the degree measure of the circle. The degree measure of a circle is always 360°. Thus, for an arc with a central angle measuring n degrees:

$$\text{Arc length} = \left(\frac{n}{360}\right) \times \text{Circumference}$$

$$= \frac{n}{360} \times 2\pi r$$

Example:

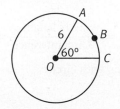

What is the length of arc ABC of the circle with center O above?

Since circumference $= 2\pi r$ and the radius is 6, the circumference is $2 \times \pi \times 6 = 12\pi$. Because $\angle AOC$ measures 60°, the arc is $\frac{60}{360}$, or one-sixth, of the circumference. Therefore, the length of the arc is $\frac{1}{6} \times 12\pi$, or 2π.

The **area of a circle** is given by this formula:

$$\text{Area} = \pi r^2$$

A **sector** is a portion of the circle bounded by two radii and an arc. In the circle below with center O, $OABC$ is a sector. To determine the area of a sector of a circle, use a similar method to the one you used to find the length of an arc: first determine what fraction of 360° the degree measure of the central angle of the sector is and then multiply that fraction by the area of the circle.

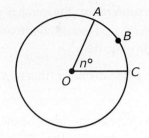

$$\text{Area of sector} = \left(\frac{n}{360}\right) \times \text{Area of circle}$$

$$= \frac{n}{360} \times \pi r^2$$

Example: What is the area of sector $OABC$ in the circle with center O below?

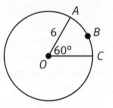

Since $\angle AOC$ measures 60°, a 60° "slice" is $\frac{60}{360}$, or one-sixth, of the circle. So the sector has an area of $\frac{1}{6} \times \pi r^2 = \frac{1}{6} \times \pi(6)^2 = \frac{1}{6} \times 36\pi = 6\pi$.

Because of the proportional relationships of central angle to 360°, arc length to circumference, and sector area to area of the circle, given any one of the three ratios in the following proportion, you can solve for all of the remaining values in the proportion:

$$\frac{\text{Central angle}}{360} = \frac{\text{Arc length}}{\text{Circumference}} = \frac{\text{Area of sector}}{\text{Area of circle}}$$

Now use the drill to get some practice working with circles.

Circles Drill

Answers follow the drill.

1. What is the circumference of a circle with a radius of 7?
2. The area of a circle is 81π. What is the diameter of the circle?
3. Circle *A* has an area of 25π. Circle *B* has twice the radius of circle *A*. What is the area of circle *B*?
4. A circle has a diameter of 10. What is the area of a sector with a central angle of 72°?
5. Minor arc *AB* has a length of 3π on a circle with a radius of 6. What is the central angle of minor arc *AB*?

Circles Drill: Answers

1. 14π

2. 18

3. 100π

4. $r = 5$; area $= 25\pi$; $\dfrac{72}{360} = \dfrac{1}{5}$; $\dfrac{1}{5} \times 25\pi = 5\pi$

5. $C = 12\pi$; $\dfrac{3\pi}{12\pi} = \dfrac{1}{4}$; $\dfrac{1}{4} \times 360° = 90°$

CONCEPT CHECK

- How does a circle's circumference relate to its diameter?

  _____

- How does a circle's area relate to its radius?

  _____

- How does the central angle of a sector relate to the area of the sector and the length of its arc?

  _____

Example answers are in your book's online resources (**kaptest.com/login**).

Now see how a GMAT expert uses the Kaplan Method to answer a Problem Solving question involving circles.

If the diameter of a circle increases by 50 percent, by what percent will the area of the circle increase?

- ○ 25%
- ○ 50%
- ○ 100%
- ○ 125%
- ○ 225%

Step 1: Analyze the Question

Beyond saying that the diameter increases by 50%, the question stem gives no other information about the circle, either before or after it grows. This could be a great candidate for picking numbers.

Step 2: State the Task

You want the percent increase of area from the small circle to the large one. Pick a number for the starting diameter that will work well in the area formula. Then use the percent change formula to work out the effect of the increase arithmetically.

Step 3: Approach Strategically

To make your calculations manageable, consider that the area of a circle is given in terms of its radius and the radius is $\frac{1}{2}$ of the diameter. So you want the diameter to be a multiple of 2. Further, you want 1.5 times the diameter to also be an even number. So suppose that the original diameter is 4. Then the original radius is $\frac{1}{2}(4) = 2$. Therefore, the area of the original circle is $\pi r^2 = \pi(2)^2 = 4\pi$.

Now increase the diameter of 4 by 50%, or $\frac{1}{2}$. The new diameter is $4 + \frac{1}{2}(4) = 4 + 2 = 6$. Therefore, the new radius is $\frac{1}{2}(6) = 3$. The area of the new circle is $\pi r^2 = \pi(3)^2 = 9\pi$.

To calculate the percent increase in the circle's area, use the percent change formula:

$$\text{Percent increase} = \frac{\text{New value} - \text{Original value}}{\text{Original value}} \times 100\%$$

$$= \frac{9\pi - 4\pi}{4\pi} \times 100\%$$

$$= \frac{5\pi}{4\pi} \times 100\%$$

$$= \frac{5}{4} \times 100\%$$

$$= 1.25 \times 100\%$$

$$= 125\%$$

The correct choice is **(D)**.

Step 4: Confirm Your Answer

Be sure you've solved for the percent increase of the area of the second circle in comparison to the area of the first, rather than another value. If you solved for how much the larger area is as a percent of the smaller, you probably chose **(E)**.

Now try some test-like questions that require the use of circle rules.

Practice Set: Circles

(Answers and explanations are at the end of the chapter.)

12. The length of an arc on circle C formed by a central angle measuring 60° is 12. What is the diameter of the circle?

    ○ $\frac{18}{\pi}$

    ○ $\frac{36}{\pi}$

    ○ 6π

    ○ $\frac{72}{\pi}$

    ○ 12π

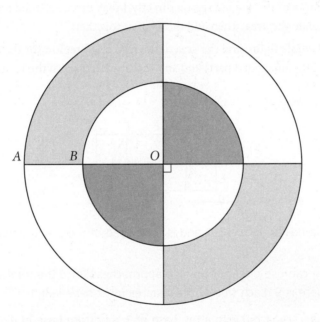

13. The figure above represents a circular garden, with center O. AB is 4 feet, and BO is 3 feet. The gardener plans to plant sunflowers in the two light gray sections and tulips in the two dark gray sections. How much more area, in square feet, will be covered by sunflowers than tulips?

    ○ $\frac{9}{2}\pi$

    ○ 8π

    ○ $\frac{31}{2}\pi$

    ○ 20π

    ○ 31π

14. If two circles overlap each other, what is the area of that overlap?

    (1) The edge of each circle intersects the center of the other circle.

    (2) The sum of the circumferences of the two circles is 12π.

Multiple Figures

> **LEARNING OBJECTIVES**
>
> - Calculate the area, perimeter, and interior and exterior angles of various figures
> - Break down complex figures into simpler components

Questions on the GMAT that deal with multiple figures test your understanding of various geometrical concepts and relationships. One common kind of multiple-figures question involves irregularly shaped regions formed by two or more overlapping figures, often with one region shaded. When you are asked to find the area of the shaded or unshaded portion, either one or both of the following methods may work:

1. If you can't find the area of the shaded region directly, break up the shaded area into smaller pieces for which you can calculate the area. Then add those areas together.

2. Find the area of the whole figure and the area of the unshaded region (or the shaded region if you are asked for the area of the unshaded part) and subtract the latter from the former.

Example:

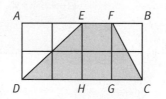

Rectangle *ABCD* above has an area of 72 and is composed of 8 equal squares. Find the area of the shaded region.

For this problem, you can use either of the two approaches. Since the total area of 8 squares is 72, the area of each square is 9. Each side of the squares must have length $\sqrt{9} = 3$.

1. The shaded area is a trapezoid with a top base of 3, a bottom base of $4 \times 3 = 12$, and a height of $2 \times 3 = 6$. Use the formula for the area of a trapezoid, $\frac{1}{2}(b_1 + b_2)(h)$, to get $\frac{1}{2}(3 + 12)(6) = \frac{1}{2}(15)(6) = 15 \times 3 = 45$.

2. The area of the whole rectangle *ABCD* is 72. The area of unshaded triangle *AED* is $\frac{1}{2} \times 6 \times 6$, or 18. The area of unshaded triangle *FBC* is $\frac{1}{2} \times 6 \times 3$, or 9. Therefore, the total unshaded area is $18 + 9 = 27$. The area of the shaded region is the area of the rectangle minus the unshaded area, or $72 - 27 = 45$.

A polygon is **inscribed** in a circle if all the vertices of the polygon lie on the circle. A polygon is **circumscribed** about a circle if all the sides of the polygon are tangent to the circle.

Square *ABCD* is inscribed in circle *O*. (Alternatively, circle *O* is circumscribed about square *ABCD*.)

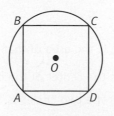

Square *PQRS* is circumscribed about circle *O*. (Alternatively, circle *O* is inscribed in square *PQRS*.)

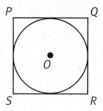

A triangle inscribed in a circle such that one side of the triangle is a diameter of the circle is always a right triangle, so the angle on the circle is 90°. The diameter of the circle is the hypotenuse.

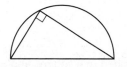

Other questions may ask you to find lengths or the measure of angles. If you do not initially see how to calculate the requested value, begin by looking for measurements that are shared across figures so that you can take information about one figure and apply it to another. A good approach is to draw a sketch and begin filling in the dimensions and/or angles that you can derive until you see relationships that will let you find the requested value.

Example: In the figure below, *H* is the midpoint of the diameter of the semicircle. Triangles *DHF* and *GHF* are inscribed in the semicircle. The measure of ∠*DHG* is 120°. What is the measure of ∠*FHG*?

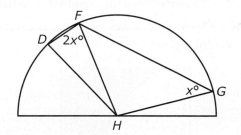

Start by using the given information and properties to fill in additional values. Radii *HD*, *HF*, and *HG* have the same length and form isosceles triangles *DHF* and *GHF*. Isosceles triangles have congruent base angles, so ∠*HFG* = *x* and ∠*HDF* = 2*x*. The sum of the four angles of quadrilateral *HDFG* must be 360. So $2x + 2x + x + x + 120 = 360$. This simplifies to $6x = 240$, so $x = 40$. Triangle *FHG* has two 40° angles and the central angle *FHG*. So the measure of ∠*FHG* is $180° - 40° - 40° = 100°$.

Now use the drill to get some practice working with multiple figures.

Multiple Figures Drill

Answers follow the drill.

1. In the figure shown, what is the value of x?

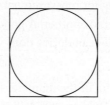

2. In the figure shown, the circle is inscribed in a square, and each side of the square has a length of 4. What is the circumference of the circle?

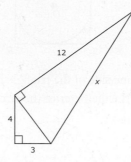

3. A rectangle is circumscribed about a semicircle with a radius of 3. What is the area of the rectangle?

4. In the figure shown, the arc of the quarter circle has length 6π. The rectangle has a perimeter of 60. What is the perimeter of the shaded region?

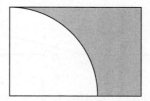

5. The hypotenuse of right triangle ABC is the diameter of the circle. If the diameter of the circle is 18, what is the area of the shaded region?

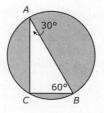

Multiple Figures Drill: Answers

1. 13

2. 4π

3. $3 \times 6 = 18$

4. $C = 4 \times 6\pi = 24\pi$; $r = 12$; $6 + 12 + 18 + 6\pi$
   $= 36 + 6\pi$

5. $81\pi - \left(\frac{1}{2} \times 9 \times 9\sqrt{3}\right) = 81\left(\pi - \frac{\sqrt{3}}{2}\right)$

CONCEPT CHECK

- What are two approaches to questions that ask for the area of a shaded region?

  _____

- What must be true when a polygon is inscribed in a circle?

  _____

- What must be true when a polygon is circumscribed around a circle?

  _____

- Some questions may ask you to find lengths or the measure of angles. If you do not initially see how to calculate the requested value in the question, how should you proceed?

  _____

Example answers are in your book's online resources (**kaptest.com/login**).

Now see how a GMAT expert uses the Kaplan Method to answer a Problem Solving question with multiple figures.

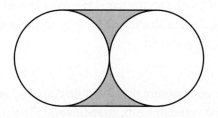

Each circle in the figure above has a diameter of 10, and the line segments are tangent to the circles. What is the area of the shaded region?

○ 50 − 10π

○ 100 − 25π

○ 100 − 10π

○ 150 − 25π

○ 200 − 50π

Step 1: Analyze the Question

Because the line segments are tangent to the circles, they touch the circles at the top and bottom extremes of the circles and are parallel. Moreover, because they go from the uppermost point on one circle to the upper-most point on the other circle, they are the length of two radii, or one diameter. Draw a sketch and connect the points of tangency between the lines and the circles.

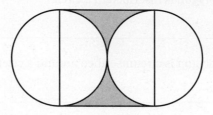

The new lines are diameters of the circles. Because they meet the lines at the points of tangency, the angles with those lines are right angles. Thus, the diameters and the original lines create a square.

Step 2: State the Task

Find the area of the shaded region, which is the area between the lines that is not within the circles.

Step 3: Approach Strategically

There is no simple way to calculate the shaded area directly. However, you can find that area by subtracting the unshaded area within the circles from the area of the square that you created.

Because the diameter of each circle is 10. the square has side length 10 and area $10^2 = 100$. The unshaded portion, 2 semicircles, makes up one circle with a diameter of 10 and radius of 5. So that area is $\pi(5)^2 = 25\pi$. So, the unshaded area is $100 - 25\pi$. **(B)** is correct.

Step 4: Confirm Your Answer

Re-read the question and the figure, making sure that you didn't misread anything or solve for the wrong measure. Be certain, for example, that you didn't mix up radius and diameter.

Next, you'll find in-format questions involving multiple figures.

Practice Set: Multiple Figures

(Answers and explanations are at the end of the chapter.)

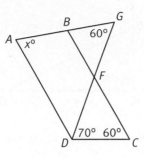

15. In the figure above, what is the value of *x*?

    (1) *AD* ∥ *BC*

    (2) ∠*ADF* = 50°

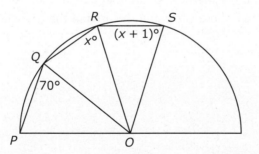

16. In the figure above, point *O* is the center of the semicircle, and *PQ* is parallel to *OS*. What is the measure of ∠*ROS*?

    ○   34°

    ○   36°

    ○   54.5°

    ○   72°

    ○   73°

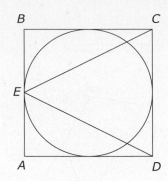

17. In the figure above, a circle is inscribed in square *ABCD*. What is the area of Δ*CDE*?

   (1) The circle has a radius of length 3.

   (2) Δ*CDE* is isosceles.

18. An isosceles triangle is inscribed in a circle such that one of the triangle's sides coincides with the circle's longest chord. If the measure of another side of the triangle is 5, what is the positive difference between the area of the circle and the area of the triangle?

   ○ $\frac{25}{2}(1 - \pi)$

   ○ $25(\pi - 1)$

   ○ $\frac{25}{2}(\pi + 1)$

   ○ $\frac{25}{2}(\pi - 1)$

   ○ $\frac{25}{4}(\pi - 1)$

Solids

LEARNING OBJECTIVE

- Calculate the volume and surface area of common solids

A **solid** is a three-dimensional figure (a figure having length, width, and height). If a diagram represents a three-dimensional figure, that fact will be specified in the accompanying text.

Rectangular solids (including cubes) and cylinders are the most common solids on the GMAT. These are both **prismatic solids**, meaning that their cross sections parallel to the base have constant dimensions. Other solids, such as spheres, may appear, but questions typically will require you only to understand that solid's properties and not to apply any special formula.

The **vertices** of a solid are the points at its corners. For example, a cube has eight vertices. The **edges** of a solid are the line segments that connect the vertices and form the sides of each face of the solid. A cube has 12 edges. The **faces** of a solid are the polygons that are the external boundaries of the solid. A cube has six faces, all squares.

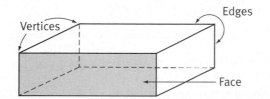

The **volume** of a solid is the amount of space enclosed by that solid. The volume of any prismatic solid is equal to the area of its base times its height. The **surface area** of a solid is equal to the sum of the areas of the solid's exterior surfaces.

A **rectangular solid** has six rectangular faces (all edges meet at right angles). Examples include cereal boxes and bricks.

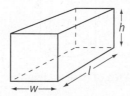

Volume = Area of base × Height = Length × Width × Height $V = l \times w \times h$

Surface area = Sum of areas of faces $SA = 2lw + 2lh + 2wh$

Example: The edges of a rectangular solid measure 3, 5, and 7. What are the volume and surface area of this solid?

$$V = l \times w \times h = 3 \times 5 \times 7 = 105$$

$$SA = 2lw + 2lh + 2wh = 2(3 \times 5) + 2(3 \times 7) + 2(5 \times 7)$$

$$= 30 + 42 + 70 = 142$$

Some geometry questions could ask you to calculate the length of a rectangular solid's longest diagonal.

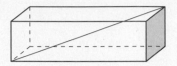

There's a simple formula to calculate the diagonal. It looks a lot like the Pythagorean theorem (in fact, it's derived from that theorem): $\text{Diagonal}^2 = \text{Length}^2 + \text{Width}^2 + \text{Height}^2$.

A **cube** is a rectangular solid whose edges are all equal ($l = w = h$), such as a sugar cube. All faces of a cube are squares.

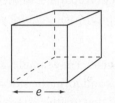

Volume = Area of base × Height = Edge^3 $\qquad V = l \times w \times h = e^3$

Surface area = Sum of areas of faces = 6 × Edge^2 $\qquad SA = 6e^2$

Example: What are the volume and surface area of a cube with edges of length 3?

$$V = e^3 = 3^3 = 27 \qquad SA = 6e^2 = 6(3^2) = 6(9) = 54$$

A **cylinder** is a prismatic solid whose horizontal cross section is a circle. An example is a soup can. You need two pieces of information to find the volume and surface area of a cylinder: the radius of the base and the height.

Volume = Area of base × Height $\qquad \pi r^2 \times h$

You can think of the surface area of a cylinder as having two parts: one part is the top and bottom (the circles), and the other part is the **lateral surface**. For the lateral surface area, think of removing a can's label. When unrolled, it's actually in the shape of a rectangle. One side is the height of the can, and the other side is the distance around the circle, or circumference.

The area of the top and bottom is $\pi r^2 + \pi r^2 = 2\pi r^2$.

The lateral surface area (LSA) = Circumference of base × Height = $2\pi r \times h$.

So, the total surface area (SA) of a cylinder is $2\pi r^2 + 2\pi r h$.

Example: What are the volume and surface area of a cylinder with radius 5 and height 10?

$$V = \pi r^2 \times h = 5^2\pi \times 10 = 25\pi \times 10 = 250\pi$$

$$SA = 2\pi r^2 + 2\pi rh = 2\pi(5^2) + 2\pi(5 \times 10) = 2\pi(25) + 2\pi(50) = 150\pi$$

You might see a question on the GMAT that requires you to understand what a sphere is, though any formulas you need to solve will be provided. A **sphere** is made up of all the points in space a certain distance from a center point; it's like a three-dimensional circle. The distance from the center to a point on the sphere is the radius of the sphere. A basketball is a good example of a sphere.

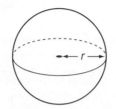

Now use the drill to get some practice working with solids.

Solids Drill

Answers follow the drill.

1. What is the volume of a rectangular solid with length 10 inches, width 5 inches, and height 6 inches?

2. What is the surface area of a rectangular solid with length 10 inches, width 5 inches, and height 6 inches?

3. What is the volume of a cylinder with radius 3 centimeters and height 5 centimeters?

4. What is the surface area of a cylinder with radius 10 inches and height 12 inches?

5. What is the volume of a cube with edges 2 meters in length?

6. What is the surface area of a cube with a volume of 125 cubic inches?

7. What is the length of the longest diagonal of a rectangular solid with dimensions of 3, 4, and 12 units?

8. A rectangular solid has a volume of 168 cubic inches. If the length is 7 inches and the height is 4 inches, what is the width?

9. If 1,000 cubic centimeters of liquid are poured into a cylinder with a radius of 5 without filling the cylinder, the top of the liquid will be how many centimeters above the base of the cylinder?

10. A rectangular solid with a length of 9 inches and a width of 4 inches has the same volume as a cube with 6-inch edges. How much greater is the surface area of the rectangular solid than that of the cube?

Solids Drill: Answers

1. 300 cubic inches

2. 280 square inches

3. 45π cubic centimeters

4. 440π square inches

5. 8 cubic meters

6. 150 square inches

7. 13 units

8. 6 inches

9. $h = \dfrac{V}{\pi r^2} = \dfrac{1{,}000}{25\pi} = \dfrac{40}{\pi}$ centimeters

10. Volume of cube = 216; height of rectangular solid = $\dfrac{216}{9 \times 4}$ = 6. SA of cube = 216; SA of rectangular solid = $2(9 \times 4 + 4 \times 6 + 9 \times 6)$ = 228. Difference is 228 square inches − 216 square inches = 12 square inches.

CONCEPT CHECK

- If the cross sections of a solid that are parallel to the base have constant dimensions, the solid is

  _____

- What is the general formula for the volume of a prismatic solid?

  _____

- How do you calculate the surface area of a solid with flat faces?

  _____

- What is the formula for the surface area of a cylinder?

  _____

- What is the formula for the longest interior diagonal of a rectangular solid?

  _____

Example answers are in your book's online resources (**kaptest.com/login**).

Now see how a GMAT expert uses the Kaplan Method and an understanding of solids to answer a Data Sufficiency question.

> A rectangular fish tank has uniform depth. How long does it take to fill the tank with water?
>
> (1) The tank is 4 feet wide and 10 feet long.
>
> (2) The tank is filled with water at a rate of 1.5 cubic feet per minute.

Step 1: Analyze the Question Stem

This Value question requires you to determine whether there is sufficient information to find how long it takes to fill a rectangular tank with water. Not only do you need the volume of the tank, which requires knowing length, width, and height, but you also need the rate at which the tank is being filled.

Step 2: Evaluate the Statements Using 12TEN

Statement (1) tells you that the tank is 4 feet wide and 10 feet long. Because you are not given any information about the depth, you cannot determine the volume of the tank. Furthermore, you are not given any information about the rate at which the tank is filled with water. This statement is insufficient. Eliminate (**A**) and (**D**).

Statement (2) tells you that the tank is being filled at a rate of 1.5 cubic feet per minute. You have no information with which to determine the volume of the tank. Eliminate (**B**).

Now combine the statements. You know the length of the tank, the width of the tank, and the rate at which it is being filled. Because you do not know the depth of the tank, you still cannot determine its volume. The two statements taken together are insufficient, and (**E**) is correct.

Next, you'll find some in-format questions involving solids.

Practice Set: Solids

(Answers and explanations are at the end of the chapter.)

19. A cylindrical tank with a height of 8 feet is completely full of gasoline. This gasoline is pumped into an empty cylindrical tank with a diameter of 24 feet and a height of 18 feet. If the gasoline reaches a height of 2 feet in this tank, what is the diameter, in feet, of the original tank?

    ○ 3

    ○ 6

    ○ 8

    ○ 10

    ○ 12

20. A rectangular solid has the dimensions 4, 5, and x. If the number of units in the solid's volume and the number of units in that solid's surface area are the same, what is the sum of the areas of the two largest faces of the solid?

    ○ 20

    ○ 40

    ○ 100

    ○ 200

    ○ 400

21. A cube with an edge length of 6 contains the largest possible sphere that completely fits inside of it. If the volume V of a sphere with radius r is given by the formula $V = \frac{4}{3}\pi r^3$, what is the volume inside the cube that is not occupied by the sphere?

    ○ $36(\pi^3 - 6)$

    ○ 36π

    ○ $36(6 - \pi)$

    ○ $36(\pi - 1)$

    ○ $36(4 - \pi)$

Linear Equations and the Coordinate System

LEARNING OBJECTIVES

- Describe the slopes of parallel and perpendicular lines and calculate the slope of a line given two points
- Write the equation of a line in slope-intercept form
- Calculate the distance between two points on a coordinate plane

When you see a **coordinate system** on the GMAT, it will consist of a horizontal x-axis and a vertical y-axis that intersect at right angles. This space is also called a **coordinate plane**. The quadrants of the coordinate system are by convention referred to by Roman numerals.

The point of intersection is called the **origin** and has the coordinates (0,0), where the first number in the coordinate pair represents the position of a point with respect to the x-axis and the second number represents the position of a point with respect to the y-axis. For example, the point (3,5) lies 3 units to the right of the origin and 5 units above it. The point (−2,−1) lies two units to the left of the origin and 1 unit below it.

The **slope** of a line on a coordinate plane tells you about the steepness of the line and whether it rises or falls as you move to the right along it. If a line gets higher as you move to the right, it has a positive slope. If it goes down as you move to the right, it has a negative slope. If the line is horizontal (parallel to the x-axis), it has a slope of zero. If it's vertical (parallel to the y-axis), it has an undefined slope.

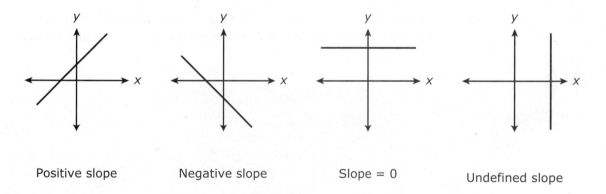

Positive slope   Negative slope   Slope = 0   Undefined slope

To find the slope of a line, use the following formula:

$$\text{Slope} = \frac{\text{Rise}}{\text{Run}} = \frac{\text{Change in } y}{\text{Change in } x} = \frac{y_2 - y_1}{x_2 - x_1}$$

Rise means the difference between the y-coordinate values of two points on the line, and **run** means the difference between the x-coordinate values of the same two points.

Example: What is the slope of the line that contains the points (1,2) and (4,−4)?

$$\text{Slope} = \frac{-4 - 2}{4 - 1} = \frac{-6}{3} = -2$$

To determine the slope of a line from an equation, put the equation into **slope-intercept form**: $y = mx + b$, where the slope is m.

Example: What is the slope of the line given by the equation $3x + 2y = 4$?

$$3x + 2y = 4$$
$$2y = -3x + 4$$
$$y = -\frac{3}{2}x + 2, \text{ so } m \text{ is } -\frac{3}{2}$$

Perpendicular lines have slopes that are negative reciprocals of one another. For the line in this example, with a slope of $-\frac{3}{2}$, a perpendicular line would have a slope of $\frac{2}{3}$. **Parallel lines** have the same slope. For example, the line in this example is parallel to another line with the equation $y = -\frac{3}{2}x - 100$.

Some GMAT questions may present lines in the form $x = cy + d$. Because this equation is set equal to x rather than y, c is *not* the slope. You need to put the line in $y = mx + b$ form to find the slope:

$$x = cy + d$$
$$cy = x - d$$
$$y = \frac{x - d}{c}$$
$$y = \frac{x}{c} - \frac{d}{c}$$
$$y = \frac{1}{c}x - \frac{d}{c}$$

Thus, the slope is $\frac{1}{c}$.

The word *intercept* in "slope-intercept form" is there because b is the value of the **y-intercept**—the point at which the line crosses the y-axis. Another way to think of the y-intercept is as the point on the line at which $x = 0$, that is, $(0,b)$.

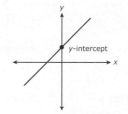

When you know the slope of a line and the x- and y-coordinates of a point on that line, you can find the y-intercept by plugging in the known values to the slope-intercept form and solving for b.

Example: What is the y-intercept of a line that includes the point $(-5,3)$ and has a slope of 2?

$$y = mx + b$$
$$3 = 2(-5) + b$$
$$3 = -10 + b$$
$$13 = b$$

Additionally, you can use this information to define the line in slope-intercept form: $y = 2x + 10$.

To determine the distance between any two points on a coordinate plane, you can use the Pythagorean theorem.

Example: What is the length of AB?

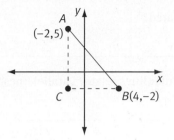

Sketch lines from points A and B parallel to the axes. They will form a right triangle, and their intersection will have the same x-coordinate as one point and the same y-coordinate as the other. Because the new lines aren't diagonal, their length can be found by reading the coordinates. In this example, the length of AC is 7 because the line drops down 5 from A to the x-axis and then another 2 to C. Similarly, the length of BC is 6.

Now use the Pythagorean theorem to calculate AB:

$$AB^2 = BC^2 + AC^2$$
$$AB^2 = 6^2 + 7^2$$
$$AB^2 = 36 + 49$$
$$AB^2 = 85$$
$$AB = \sqrt{85}$$

Now use the drill to get some practice working with linear equations and the coordinate system.

Linear Equations and the Coordinate System Drill

Answers follow the drill.

1. Find the slope of the line $7x + 2y = 16$.
2. Find the y-intercept of a line that has a slope of -5 and includes the point $(20,-60)$.
3. Find the y-intercept of the line that includes the points $(2,7)$ and $(6,15)$.
4. Write the line that includes the points $(0,8)$ and $(-24,20)$ in slope-intercept form.
5. Find the length of the line segment with endpoints $(1,5)$ and $(5,1)$.

Linear Equations and the Coordinate System Drill: Answers

1. $-\dfrac{7}{2}$

2. 40

3. $m = \dfrac{15 - 7}{6 - 2} = 2; 7 = 2(2) + b; b = 3$

4. $m = \dfrac{20 - 8}{-24 - 0} = -\dfrac{1}{2}; y = -\dfrac{1}{2}x + 8$

5. $4^2 + 4^2 = C^2; C = \sqrt{32} = 4\sqrt{2}$

CONCEPT CHECK

- How is the slope of a line calculated?

  _____

- How do the slopes of perpendicular lines relate? Parallel lines?

  _____

- What is the slope-intercept form of a line?

  _____

- What information do you need to find the *y*-intercept of a line?

  _____

- How can you find the length of a line segment, given its endpoints on the coordinate plane?

  _____

Example answers are in your book's online resources (**kaptest.com/login**).

Now see how a GMAT expert uses the Kaplan Method to answer a Data Sufficiency question about coordinate geometry:

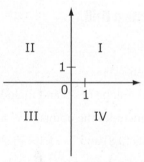

If $st > 0$, in which quadrant of the coordinate system above does the point (s,t) lie?

(1) $(s,-t)$ lies in quadrant II.

(2) s is negative.

Step 1: Analyze the Question Stem

In this Value question, you are asked to determine which quadrant point (s,t) is in. You are told in the question stem that $st > 0$, which means that s and t are either both positive (in quadrant I) or both negative (in quadrant III).

Step 2: Evaluate the Statements Using 12TEN

Statement (1): You know that $(s,-t)$ lies in quadrant II, which tells you that s is negative and $-t$ is positive, so t must be negative. Because s and t are both negative, (s,t) is in quadrant III, and the statement is sufficient. Eliminate **(B)**, **(C)**, and **(E)**.

Statement (2): You are told that s is negative, which is also sufficient, because you already deduced from the question stem that s and t have the same sign. The correct choice is **(D)**.

Next, you'll find some in-format questions involving linear equations and the coordinate system.

Practice Set: Coordinate Geometry

(Answers and explanations are at the end of the chapter.)

22. Line ℓ_1 is given by the equation $y = mx + 3$, and line ℓ_2 is given by the equation $y = nx - 7$, where m and n are constants. Is ℓ_1 parallel to ℓ_2?

    (1) $m^2 - n^2 = 0$

    (2) mn is positive.

23. In the xy-coordinate system, if (m,n) and $(m + 2, n + k)$ are two points on the line with the equation $x = 2y + 5$, then $k =$

    ○ $\frac{1}{2}$

    ○ 1

    ○ 2

    ○ $\frac{5}{2}$

    ○ 4

Answers and explanations follow on the next page. ▶ ▶ ▶

Answers and Explanations

Practice Set: Lines and Angles

1. (A)

The figure shows two intersecting lines with the measure of three of the angles given in terms of variables x and y. The question asks for the value of y.

Use the properties of lines and angles to create equations. Vertical angles are equal, so $x + 2y = 5x - 4y$. Angles along a straight line add up to 180°, so $x + 2y + 3x - 3y = 180$. By the same logic, $5x - 4y + 3x - 3y = 180$. Determine the value of y by using any two of the relationships. For example, start by simplifying the first equation: $x + 2y = 5x - 4y$, so $6y = 4x$.

The second equation, $x + 2y + 3x - 3y = 180$, simplifies to $4x - y = 180$. Note that the $4x$ term appears in both simplified equations, $6y = 4x$ and $4x - y = 180$. Replace the $4x$ in the second equation with the $6y$ from the first equation to get $6y - y = 180$, so $5y = 180$ and $y = 36$.

(A) is correct. (Note that you could have chosen a third relationship to use, but only two distinct linear equations are needed to solve for two variables. Other options would give you the same solution.)

Make sure that you copied the expressions correctly from the figure and solved for the value of y, not x, which is (B), 54.

2. (C)

This is a Value question. You're given a figure and told that lines r and s are parallel, which makes the other lines in the figure transversals. When a transversal intersects a pair of parallel lines, all acute angles formed by that transversal are equal, and all obtuse angles formed are equal. Therefore, since angle a and angle b are both acute angles on the same transversal, they're equal to each other. So in order to determine the value of $a + b$, all you need to know is the value of either angle. Angles c and d are on a different transversal from angles a and b, so those pairs of angles cannot be compared. However, angles c and d form a straight line, so $c + d = 180$.

Statement (1) indicates that $c - a = 25$. This doesn't give you enough information to pin down the value of any of the angles. Eliminate (A) and (D).

Statement (2) says that $a - d = 15$. Similar to Statement (1), this tells you that angle a is greater than angle d but gives no clue as to their values. Eliminate (B) and evaluate the statements together.

Taken together, there are three variables (a, c, and d) and three distinct linear equations: $c + d = 180$, $c - a = 25$, and $a - d = 15$. This would enable you to solve for each of those variables, including a. From that, you would also know the value of b, since $a = b$, and you could find the sum $a + b$. So, together, the statements are sufficient. (C) is correct.

3. (E)

This Yes/No question asks if a certain line segment stops rotating and gives a detailed description of the line's behavior. Simplify the question stem by determining the number of degrees that the segment has to rotate to be less than 5% of its starting length. That will be when it stops rotating. Pick 100 to represent the segment's initial length, so when the segment is 5% of its starting length, its length is 5:

- After the first 45° rotation, the segment measures half of 100, or 50.
- After 90°, it measures 25.
- After 135°, it measures 12.5.
- After 180°, it measures 6.25.
- After 225°, it measures half of 6.25. This is less than 5.

The segment will therefore reach less than 5% of its starting length after moving five 45° increments, or 225°. Thus, the question becomes, "Did the segment make 5 movements?" or "Did it rotate 225°?"

Statement (1) says that the segment rotated *at least* 180°. If the segment rotated exactly 180°, the answer is no. However, the segment could have rotated 225°, and then the answer would be yes. Statement (1) is insufficient, so eliminate (A) and (D).

Statement (2) says that the segment made *no more than* 5 movements. If the segment made 5 movements, the answer is yes, but if the segment made fewer movements, the answer is no. Statement (2) is insufficient, so eliminate **(B)** and combine the statements.

Combining Statements (1) and (2) produces this statement: the segment rotated at least 180° *and* made at most 5 movements. This leaves open the possibility that it moved 4 times (for 180°) or 5 times (for 225°). The answer to the question could still be yes or no, so **(E)** is correct.

Practice Set: Triangles

4. **(D)**

This question asks which Roman numeral statement(s) *could* be true. The figure consists of two triangles that share a side of length 5. One triangle's other two sides measure a and b, while the other triangle's remaining sides measure y and z. Additionally, the latter triangle contains a right angle. Since z is opposite that right angle, z is that triangle's hypotenuse, and y and 5 are that triangle's legs.

Roman numeral I appears most frequently in the choices. It says that sides a and b have the same length. Since you are not given any information for that triangle other than its remaining side's length of 5, the lengths of a and b could be either equal or unequal to each other. Since this statement *could* be true, eliminate those choices that do not contain Roman numeral I, which are **(A)** and **(C)**.

Next, consider Roman numeral II. Since z is the triangle's hypotenuse, it must be that triangle's longest side, so $z > y$. Roman numeral II, therefore, must be false. Eliminate **(E)**.

Finally, examine Roman numeral III: $a^2 + b^2 = z^2 - y^2$. Recall the Pythagorean theorem: the sum of the squared leg lengths equals the squared hypotenuse length. So $y^2 + 5^2 = z^2$. Now subtract y^2 from both sides to obtain $z^2 - y^2 = 5^2$. For the triangle with side lengths a and b, no angles are given. So, it could be a right triangle, too. If it were, you could treat the sides of lengths a and b as the triangle's legs and the side of length 5 as that triangle's hypotenuse to get $a^2 + b^2 = 5^2$. Since $z^2 - y^2$ must equal 5^2 and $a^2 + b^2$ could equal 5^2 as well, it could be true that $a^2 + b^2 = z^2 - y^2$. Since Roman numeral III also could be true, **(D)** is correct.

5. **(D)**

This question asks for the ratio of the lengths of two sides of a right triangle. The figure shows that right triangle, and you're told that BD bisects the hypotenuse of the triangle. This means that it also bisects $\angle ABC$; that is, $\angle ABD$ and $\angle CBD$ both measure 45°.

Line segment BD divides right triangle ABC into two right triangles. Each of the two smaller triangles consists of a 90° angle at vertex D, a 45° angle at vertex B, and a $180° - (90° + 45°) = 45°$ angle at the third vertex. Thus, the angles at vertices A and C are 45°, and the large triangle is a 45°-45°-90° triangle. This means that the corresponding side ratios are $x:x:x\sqrt{2}$. Leg BC is represented in this ratio by x and hypotenuse AC by $x\sqrt{2}$, making the ratio of BC to AC equal to $\dfrac{x}{x\sqrt{2}}$.

Cancel the x terms and rationalize the denominator: $\dfrac{\cancel{x}(\sqrt{2})}{\cancel{x}\sqrt{2}(\sqrt{2})} = \dfrac{\sqrt{2}}{2}$. **(D)** is correct.

Make sure you answer with the ratio of the right sides in the right order. **(E)** is the reciprocal of the correct choice, reduced to its simplest form.

6.   (C)

The question asks for the area of the triangle, which is $\frac{1}{2} \times$ base $\times$ height. An angle measurement is missing from the diagram. Since the interior angles in a triangle add to 180°, the missing angle must be 180° – (45° + 75°), or 60°. Note that two of the angle measurements, 60° and 45°, are part of two of the GMAT's most commonly used shapes, the 45°-45°-90° special right triangle and the 30°-60°-90° special right triangle. If a special right triangle appears in a GMAT problem, it is probably key to the solution.

Divide the triangle into two smaller right triangles by drawing an altitude from the 75° angle to the horizontal base. This will create a 45°-45°-90° triangle on the left side of the altitude and a 30°-60°-90° triangle on the right side of the altitude.

The 30°-60°-90° triangle on the right side of the altitude has a hypotenuse of 4. The ratio of sides of a 30°-60°-90° triangle is $x : x\sqrt{3} : 2x$, where x is the shorter leg, $x\sqrt{3}$ is the longer leg, and $2x$ is the hypotenuse. Therefore, you can deduce that the shorter leg is 2 and the longer leg (the altitude) is $2\sqrt{3}$.

You now also know the length of the legs of the 45°-45°-90° triangle: $2\sqrt{3}$. Therefore, the horizontal base of the large triangle is $2\sqrt{3} + 2$ and the height is $2\sqrt{3}$.

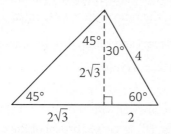

Now plug the known dimensions into the triangle area formula: Area $= \frac{1}{2} \times (2\sqrt{3} + 2) \times 2\sqrt{3} = \frac{1}{2} \times (4 \times 3 + 4\sqrt{3}) = 6 + 2\sqrt{3}$. Therefore, **(C)** is correct.

7.   (B)

The question asks for the measure of angle b in the figure. No numerical values are given on the figure. In this problem, there are a triangle and a straight line, both of which have angles that add to 180°. Hence, you can create two equations:

$$a + b + c = 180 \text{ and } d + c = 180$$

Since both $(a + b + c)$ and $(d + c)$ equal 180, you can set them equal to each other. To solve for b, isolate it on one side:

$$a + b + c = d + c$$
$$a + b = d$$
$$b = d - a$$

So, to solve for b, you need the value of $d - a$.

Statement (1) says that $a + c + d = 225$. Since $c + d = 180$, you could solve for a, but there is no way to derive the value of $d - a$ from this, so Statement (1) is insufficient. Eliminate **(A)** and **(D)**.

Statement (2) gives you the value of $d - a$, so it is sufficient. **(B)** is correct.

8.   (C)

The question asks for the y-coordinate of points B and C on the graph. You're given the x- and y-coordinates of one of the three vertices of triangle ABC, the x-coordinates of vertices B and C, and the area of the triangle. Since the y-coordinates of the two vertices are the same, side BC of the triangle is parallel to the x-axis. Side AB lies on the y-axis, so this is a right triangle.

Use the formula for the area of a triangle to determine the missing coordinate:

The area of triangle $ABC = \left(\frac{1}{2}\right)$(Base)(Height) $= 27$.

The y-coordinates of the base (BC) do not change, so the length is the difference between the x-coordinate values: $9 - 0 = 9$. Plug that into the area formula to solve for the height: $\left(\frac{1}{2}\right)(9)$(Height) $= 27$, which means $9 \times$ Height $= 54$, so Height $= 54 \div 9 = 6$. Because the height (AB) is a vertical line, the x-coordinates do not change and its length is the difference between its y-coordinate values: $9 - y = 6$. Thus, $y = 3$. The correct choice is **(C)**.

Use the height you've calculated from the *y*-coordinate you've found to check whether the area matches that in the question stem. Note also that 6 in (**E**) is the height of the triangle, not the value of *y*.

Practice Set: Polygons

9. (B)

This question asks you to find the value of *y*, an interior angle of an irregular pentagon that has two parallel sides, three angles that are equal (labeled *x*°) and one angle of 60°. To efficiently answer this question, use the properties of parallel lines and the formula for the sum of the interior angles of a polygon.

Because *AB* and *DE* are parallel, *AE* is a transversal, and angle *x* and the 60° angle are supplementary. So $x + 60 = 180$, and $x = 120$. Use the formula for the sum of interior angles of a polygon: Sum of interior angles = 180(Number of sides − 2)°. The polygon has 5 sides, so the sum of the interior angles is $180(5 − 2)° = 180(3)° = 540°$. Therefore, $60 + 3x + y = 540$. Substitute 120 for *x* and solve for *y*: $60 + 3(120) + y = 540$; $420 + y = 540$, and $y = 120$. (**B**) is correct. Quickly confirm by summing the angles: $60 + 360 + 120 = 540$.

10. (B)

The question asks for the maximum width of a walkway that surrounds an 8- by 12-foot rectangular base of a monument. The base and the walkway are made with equal volumes of concrete and equal amounts of concrete per square foot. Use the geometry formula for area of a rectangle to determine the maximum width of the walkway.

Draw a sketch to illustrate the scenario:

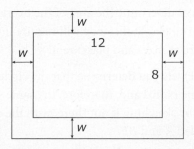

Since the amounts of concrete used for the base and the walkway are the same, the contractor will have enough concrete to make a walkway that has an area of $8 \times 12 = 96$ square feet. The area of the walkway is the area of the larger rectangle formed by the perimeter of the walkway minus the area of the rectangular base. An efficient approach to this question is to use the choices to calculate the area of the walkway. Since you're looking for the maximum width, test (**D**) first. If the walkway is 4 feet wide, the larger rectangle would be 16 by 20 feet since 4 feet are added to each side. The area of the larger rectangle would be $16 \times 20 = 320$ square feet. But $320 − 96 = 224$ square feet, which is too large. Eliminate (**D**) and (**E**).

Test (**B**) next. If the walkway is 2 feet wide, the larger rectangle would be 12 by 16 feet. The area of the larger rectangle would be $12 \times 16 = 192$ square feet. $192 − 96 = 96$ square feet. The two areas are equal, so (**B**) is correct.

11. (B)

This Yes/No question asks you to determine whether there is enough information to establish the relationship between the length of one side of a square and the length of one side of an equilateral triangle. Sufficient information may not yield the actual lengths of the sides but will define the relationship between the sides of the two figures.

Statement (1) says the length of a side of the square and the side of a triangle add to 22. Quickly pick numbers to test: if the side of the square were 1 and the side of the triangle were 21, the answer to the question would be no. But the situation could also be reversed: the side of the square could be 21 and that of the triangle 1, and the answer to the question would be yes. Because different answers to the question are possible, Statement (1) is insufficient. Eliminate (**A**) and (**D**).

Statement (2) says that the ratio of the perimeter of the square to the perimeter of the triangle is 5 to 6. Call the side of the square s; then the perimeter of the square is the sum of the sides, or $4s$. Call the side of the triangle t; then the perimeter of the equilateral triangle is the sum of the sides, or $3t$. Set up the proportion $\frac{4s}{3t} = \frac{5}{6}$. Since this equation establishes a definite relationship between s and t, solving the equation would answer the question with a definite yes or no. Note that you don't have to solve for the ratio in order to know that Statement (2) is sufficient. **(B)** is correct.

For the record, you could cross multiply $\frac{4s}{3t} = \frac{5}{6}$ to get $24s = 15t$, then rearrange this to get $\frac{s}{t} = \frac{15}{24}$. The length of a side of the square s is less than the length of a side of the triangle t, and the answer to the question is no.

Practice Set: Circles

12. (D)

The question asks for the diameter of the circle. It tells you that the length of an arc formed by a 60° central angle is 12.

To get the diameter, first set up a proportion to figure out the full circumference of the 360° circle:

$$\frac{\text{Length of arc}}{\text{Circumference}} = \frac{\text{Central angle}}{360°}$$

$$\frac{12}{\text{Circumference}} = \frac{60°}{360°}$$

$$\frac{12}{\text{Circumference}} = \frac{1}{6}$$

$$\text{Circumference} = 72$$

Because Circumference $= \pi \times$ Diameter,

$$\text{Diameter} = \frac{\text{Circumference}}{\pi} = \frac{72}{\pi}.$$ **(D)** is correct.

Be certain that you answered the question that was asked; **(B)** is the radius, not the diameter.

13. (C)

The question asks for the difference in areas dedicated to the two types of flowers. The garden consists of one circle inside a larger circle. The only numbers given are the radius of the inner circle (3) and the distance from that circle's edge to the edge of the larger circle (4). Thus the radius of the larger circle is $3 + 4 = 7$.

Each of the two tulip regions is a quarter of the inner circle, for a total area of $\frac{1}{2}$ of the inner circle. Each of the two sunflower regions is a quarter of the ring between the outer and inner circles, for a total area of $\frac{1}{2}$ of the ring area. To find the answer to the question, subtract half of the inner circle area from half of the ring area.

The area of the inner circle is $\pi r^2 = \pi(3)^2 = 9\pi$. The area covered by tulips is thus $\frac{1}{2} \times 9\pi = \frac{9}{2}\pi$. The area of the outer circle is $\pi r^2 = \pi(7)^2 = 49\pi$. The total area of the ring is the difference between the areas of the outer and inner circles, or $49\pi - 9\pi = 40\pi$. The area covered by sunflowers is thus half of this, or 20π.

Armed with these figures you can determine that the difference in areas is $20\pi - \frac{9}{2}\pi$. Since $\frac{9}{2}$ is a little less than 5, you can estimate that the answer will be less than 20π but greater than 15π, leading you to **(C)**. If you prefer, you can do the full calculation:

$$20\pi - \frac{9}{2} = \frac{40}{2}\pi - \frac{9}{2}\pi$$
$$= \frac{31}{2}\pi$$

(C) is correct. This is an involved question, so double check that you used the correct formulas for area and took half of the various areas to get the planted areas.

14. (C)

This Value question asks whether there is enough information to determine the area of the overlap between two circles. Sufficiency will require information about the circles' sizes and placement.

Statement (1) lets you determine that the circles must have the same radius and, therefore, the same size. You can see this by sketching it out (here, with the circles' centers labeled A and B):

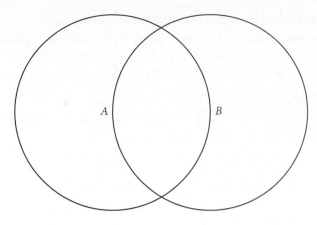

Without knowing the measure of the radii, however, there is no way to determine the area of the overlap. Statement (1) is therefore insufficient. Eliminate (**A**) and (**D**).

Statement (2) provides the sum of the circles' circumferences, but it doesn't give any information about the circles' relative sizes or their placement in relation to each other. Therefore, finding the area of overlap is impossible. Since Statement (2) is insufficient, eliminate (**B**) and combine the two statements.

From Statement (1), you know the circles are the same size. From Statement (2), you know the sum of their circumferences (12π). Thus, you could divide 12π by 2 to get each circumference (6π) and from there figure out the radius of each circle. To determine whether this is sufficient to answer the question, sketch several radii to create two congruent, equilateral triangles. Note that every straight line in the following diagram is a radius of one or both of the circles (and thus has the same length). Because the triangles have sides of equal length, every interior angle of the triangles is 60°.

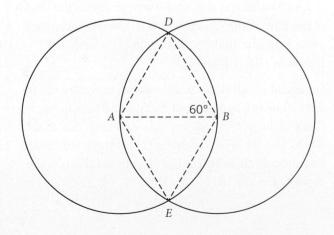

You could then draw a perpendicular line from any vertex to the opposite side, creating two 30-60-90 triangles, and then use the rules of 30-60-90 triangles to calculate the area of each triangle. As for the rest of the overlapped area, note that it consists of four wedges. If you calculated the area of circle A's sector DBE (formed by angle DAE, which is $60 + 60 = 120°$ and therefore $\frac{1}{3}$ of the total circle area) and then subtracted the area of the two triangles, you would have the area of two of the wedges. The other two wedges have the same area. If all of this was added to the area of the two triangles, you would have the total area of the overlapped portion. Since this is a Data Sufficiency question, you wouldn't want to spend time actually doing all of these calculations. But knowing that you could is enough to conclude the two statements together are sufficient to answer the question. (**C**) is correct.

Practice Set: Multiple Figures

15. (D)

This Value question asks for the measure of angle x in a complex figure. You can make the following observations from the figure:

In triangle DFC, the measure of angle DFC is $180° - 70° - 60° = 50°$.

Angle BFG is vertical to angle DFC, so the measure of angle BFG is also 50°.

In triangle FBG, the measure of angle GBF is $180° - 50° - 60° = 70°$.

Angle ABF completes a straight line with angle GBF, so the measure of angle ABF is $180° - 70° = 110°$.

Angles GFC and BFD each complete a straight line with angle DFC, so the measure of each of these angles is $180° - 50° = 130°$.

There are many things that would give you the value of x. You have two of the angles in quadrilateral $ABFD$, so getting the measure of angle ADF would give you the third and allow you to solve for x (all quadrilaterals have interior angles that sum to 360°). It's a complex figure, so there may be other ways to solve for x as well. You'll need to think carefully about any information you're given.

Statement (1) states that *AD* is parallel to *BC*. Therefore, angle *GBF* and the angle marked *x*° must be equal. Because the measure of angle *GBF* is 70°, the measure of the angle marked *x*° must be 70°. Thus, *x* = 70. Statement (1) is sufficient. You can eliminate **(B)**, **(C)**, and **(E)**.

Statement (2) tells you that ∠*ADF* = 50°. This means that the measures of the angles in triangle *AGD* are *x*°, 60°, and 50°, so you could solve for *x*. Statement (2) is sufficient; **(D)** is correct.

16. (A)

This question asks for the measure of ∠*ROS*. The given figure consists of three triangles inscribed in a semicircle. You are told that *PQ* is parallel to *OS*. The measure of ∠*PQO* is 70°, and the measure of two other angles is given in terms of *x*.

Use any concrete information given to determine the starting point to unravel this complex figure:

1. Two of the three sides of each of the three inscribed triangles are radii of the semicircle. That means the three inscribed triangles are isosceles.

2. Since *PQ* is parallel to *OS*, *QO* is a transversal. When a transversal intersects with a pair of parallel lines, alternate interior angles are equal. In this case, since ∠*PQO* = 70°, ∠*QOS* must also be 70°.

Add this information to your sketch of △*QOR* and △*ROS*:

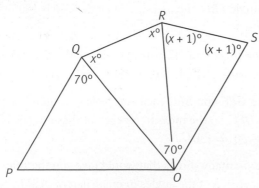

You can't bisect ∠*QOS* to find the answer because GMAT figures are not necessarily drawn to scale. Instead you'll need to solve for *x*. To do so, recall that a triangle's interior angles sum to 180°. If you add up all six interior angles from △*QOR* and △*ROS*, you'll have a sum of 360°. You can now set up an equation to solve for the value of *x*.

$$x + x + (x + 1) + (x + 1) + 70 = 360$$
$$4x + 72 = 360$$
$$4x = 288$$
$$x = 72$$

Since *x* = 72, each of the two base angles in △*ROS* is 72 + 1 = 73°. Therefore, the measure of ∠*ROS* is 180 − 2(73) = 180 − 146 = 34°. The correct answer is **(A)**.

If you were pressed for time, a bit of Critical Thinking would reveal that isosceles triangles with base angles of approximately 70° cannot possibly allow a remaining angle as large as **(C)**, **(D)**, or **(E)** would indicate.

17. (A)

This Value question asks for the area of triangle *CDE*. The area of a triangle is equal to $\frac{1}{2} \times$ Base × Height. You can use *CD* as a base, and the height would be the length of a perpendicular drawn from point *E* to *CD*. Since that perpendicular line would be equal in length to *BC*, you only need to learn the length of the sides of square *ABCD* to know the length of both the base (*CD*) and the height (equal to *BC*) of triangle *CDE*.

Statement (1) says that the radius of the inscribed circle is 3, so its diameter is 6. That diameter equals the length of the sides of the square, which is what you need to answer the question. So, Statement (1) is sufficient. Eliminate **(B)**, **(C)**, and **(E)**.

Statement (2) gives no measurements to work with. It does allow you to figure out that point *E* bisects *AB*, but that still doesn't provide any measurements that enable you to find the area. Statement (2) is insufficient. Since Statement (1) is sufficient but Statement (2) is not, the correct choice is **(A)**.

18. (D)

The question asks for the difference in area between the area of a circle and a triangle. That triangle is inscribed in the circle, which means that each vertex of the triangle is on the circumference of the circle. Furthermore, "one of the triangle's sides coincides with the circle's longest chord" means that one side of the triangle is the diameter of the circle. When a side of a triangle inscribed in a circle is a diameter of the circle, the vertex across from the diameter is a right angle, so the triangle is a right triangle with the diameter as its hypotenuse. You're also told that the measure of another side of this triangle is 5. Since the triangle is said to be isosceles, the third side must also have a length of 5, and the angles opposite those sides must also be of equal measure. Since one angle already measures 90°, each of the other two measures 45°. Thus, the inscribed figure is a 45-45-90 triangle.

Sketching on your notepad to visualize the figures would be helpful. Your sketch might look something like this:

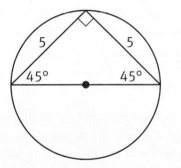

You could start by finding the area of the triangle. Since it is a right triangle, one leg is the triangle's base, and the other leg is the height. Substitute those lengths into the formula for the area of a triangle: $\frac{1}{2} bh = \frac{1}{2}(5)(5) = \frac{25}{2}$.

The formula for area of a circle is πr^2, so to find the area of the circle, you need to know the radius. In this figure, the radius of the circle is half the length of the triangle's hypotenuse. Because the triangle is a 45-45-90 triangle, the measures of the sides are in the ratio $1:1:\sqrt{2}$. Thus, since each of the two legs measures 5, the hypotenuse measures $5\sqrt{2}$. This is also the circle's diameter, so the radius is half of $5\sqrt{2}$, or $\frac{5\sqrt{2}}{2}$. Thus, the circle's area is:

$$\pi r^2 = \pi \left(\frac{5\sqrt{2}}{2}\right)^2 = \pi \left[\frac{(5)^2 (\sqrt{2})^2}{(2)^2}\right] = \pi \left(\frac{25 \times 2}{2^2}\right) = \frac{25\pi}{2}$$

Finally, the area of the circle minus the area of the triangle is $\frac{25\pi}{2} - \frac{25}{2} = \frac{25}{2}(\pi - 1)$, which matches **(D)**.

Ensure that you answered the question, which asks for the positive difference in areas between the circle and the triangle. **(A)** is the area of the triangle minus the area of the circle, and **(C)** is the sum of the two areas.

Practice Set: Solids

19. (E)

Gasoline is pumped from one cylindrical tank into another. The question asks for the diameter of the first tank. That tank starts completely full of gasoline and its height is 8 feet. The diameter of the second tank is 24 feet and its height is 18 feet, but what is relevant is the height that the gasoline reaches in that second tank, which is 2 feet. The key to such a transference problem is noting that the volume of the gasoline in the original tank must equal the volume of the gasoline in the new tank.

The volume of a circular cylinder is $\pi r^2 h$. The second cylinder has a diameter of 24 feet, so its radius must be 12 feet. The gasoline fills it to a height of 2 feet. Thus, the volume of the gasoline in that tank is $\pi(12)^2(2) = 288\pi$ ft^3.

Now, plug this value back into the volume formula for the first cylinder to find its diameter: $288\pi = \pi r^2(8)$, so $r^2 = 36$ and $r = 6$ ft. Finally, double the radius to find the diameter, which is 12 ft. The answer is **(E)**.

20. (D)

The question stem tells you that the number of units in a rectangular solid's volume and the number of units in that solid's surface area are the same. Recall that the volume of a rectangular solid is Length × Width × Height and that the surface area is the sum of the areas of all six faces. You are also given specific values (4 and 5) for two of the three dimensions of the solid. The question asks for the sum of the areas of the two largest faces of the solid.

The solid's volume and surface area are equal values, so $lwh = 2lw + 2lh + 2wh$. Since you are not told which dimensions 4 and 5 represent, simply substitute those values into this equation in a consistent way, assigning x to the third dimension. If, say, $l = 4$ and $w = 5$, then $4(5)x = 2(4)(5) + 2(4)x + 2(5)x$. Now, solve for x:

$$20x = 2(4)(5) + 2(4)x + 2(5)x$$
$$20x = 40 + 8x + 10x$$
$$2x = 40$$
$$x = 20$$

Because 20 is greater than 4 or 5, 20 is the largest edge dimension of the solid. Use that value and the second-largest dimension's measure to find the area of each of the largest faces of the solid: $20(5) = 100$. Finally, since opposite faces of a rectangular solid have the same area, double 100 to determine the sum of the areas of those two largest faces: $2(100) = 200$. **(D)** is correct.

Ensure that you answered the question asked. For example, if you stopped working after solving for x, you might have selected **(A)**. If you forgot to double the area in the last step, **(C)** was waiting for you.

21. (C)

The question asks for the volume of empty space inside a cube that has the largest possible sphere inside it. An edge of the cube has a length of 6 units, so that is also the diameter of the sphere. The empty space is the volume of the cube less the volume of the sphere.

You're given concrete information about the cube, so start by finding its volume: $V_{cube} = e^3 = 6^3 = 216$

Now use the given formula to find the volume of the sphere. Since the length of the sphere's diameter is 6, the sphere's radius is half that, or 3. Plug this in for r in the formula:

$$V = \frac{4}{3}\pi r^3 = \frac{4}{3}(3^3)\pi = 4(3^2)\pi = 4(9)\pi = 36\pi$$

Now, determine the volume of the empty space in the cube: $V_{cube} - V_{sphere} = 216 - 36\pi$. This doesn't look like any of the answer choices, which all begin with a factor of 36. Factor 36 out of this expression to get $36(6 - \pi)$.

This matches **(C)**, which is the correct choice.

Practice Set: Coordinate Geometry

22. (C)

This is a Yes/No question asking whether two lines, each of which is represented by a unique equation, are parallel. Since two lines are parallel if they have the same slope, the statements are sufficient if they provide enough information to determine whether m and n, the slopes of lines ℓ_1 and ℓ_2, respectively, are equal.

Statement (1) says that $m^2 - n^2 = 0$. This is one of the "classic" quadratics; it factors to $(m + n)(m - n) = 0$. This means that $m = n$ or $-n$. In other words, m and n have the same magnitude, but they could have either the same sign or opposite signs. So, if they had the same sign, the slopes would be equal and the answer to the question would be yes, but if they had opposite signs, the slopes would not be equal and the answer would be no. Thus, this statement is insufficient; eliminate **(A)** and **(D)**.

Statement (2) says that the product of m and n is positive. This means that m and n have the same sign; they're either both positive or both negative. Without more information, though, there's no way to know whether they're equal, so this statement is insufficient. Eliminate **(B)**.

Now, combine the statements. According to (1), $m = n$ or $-n$, but according to (2), m and n must have the same sign. That leaves $m = n$ as the only possibility. Even though there's not enough information to determine what the slopes are, they must be equal to each other. Choose **(C)**.

23. (B)

The question asks for the value of k, given that (m,n) and $(m + 2, n + k)$ are two points on the line with the equation $x = 2y + 5$. For any question involving the equation of a line, a good place to start is the slope-intercept form of the line, $y = mx + b$. Remember that if you have two points on a line, you can derive the entire equation, and if you have an equation of the line, you can calculate any points on that line.

The equation of the line in the question stem is defined as $x = 2y + 5$. Isolate y to put this into slope-intercept form:

$$x = 2y + 5$$
$$x - 5 = 2y$$
$$\frac{x - 5}{2} = y$$
$$y = \frac{1}{2}x - \frac{5}{2}$$

So the slope of this line is $\frac{1}{2}$. Therefore, you know that, because there is an increase of 2 units in the x direction when moving from m to $m + 2$, there must be a change of half that, or 1 unit in the y direction when moving from n to $n + k$. So $k = 1$.

You could also pick numbers. Choose the y-coordinate of the point (m,n) to be 0 to allow for easier calculations. Using the given equation, calculate the x-coordinate: $x = 2y + 5 = 2(0) + 5 = 5$. So (m,n) is the point $(5,0)$.

Now plug $(5,0)$ for m and n into the next point: $(m + 2, n + k)$. That yields $(7,k)$. Plug an x-coordinate of 7 into the equation to solve for k, the y-coordinate: $7 = 2k + 5$. Thus, $2 = 2k$ and $k = 1$. Either way, (**B**) is correct.

Re-read the question, making sure that you didn't miss anything. For example, if you thought that the original equation was $y = 2x + 5$, then you would have answered (**E**).

CHAPTER 12

QUANTITATIVE REASONING: PUTTING IT ALL TOGETHER—ADVANCED PRACTICE

In this chapter, you'll find two 20-question practice sets consisting entirely of questions most test takers find challenging. The first practice set contains Problem Solving questions; the second contains Data Sufficiency questions. Following each practice set, you'll find complete explanations for every question.

How to Use These Practice Sets

Use these question sets to hone your Critical Thinking skills if you are aiming for a very high GMAT score. If you are not yet comfortable with the practice questions in the preceding chapters of this book, then continue to review the arithmetic, algebra, geometry, and other topics presented there until you are able to find the correct answers to most of those practice questions. Then you'll be ready to tackle the tougher questions here.

If you are ready to do so, set a timer, giving yourself 2 minutes for each question. If you decided to do five Problem Solving questions and five Data Sufficiency questions in one sitting, for example, you would put 20 minutes on the timer.

As always, be sure to *review the explanation* to every problem you do in this chapter. Noting a different way to work through a problem, even if you got that problem right, is a powerful way to enhance your Critical Thinking skills—and it's ultimately those skills that you will be relying on in order to achieve a very high score on Test Day.

Ready to take your Quantitative score to the next level? Then turn the page and begin work!

Advanced Problem Solving Practice Set

(Answers and explanations are at the end of the chapter.)

1. A weekend farm stand sells only peaches. On Saturday, the farm stand has T peaches to sell, at a profit of m cents each. Any peaches remaining for sale on Sunday will be marked down and sold at a profit of $(m - n)$ cents each. If all peaches available for sale on Saturday morning are sold by Sunday evening, how many peaches, in terms of T, m, and n, does the stand need to sell on Saturday in order to make the same profit on each day?

    ○ $\dfrac{Tm}{m - n}$

    ○ $\dfrac{Tm}{n - m}$

    ○ $\dfrac{m(m - n)}{T}$

    ○ $\dfrac{T}{m - n}$

    ○ $\dfrac{T(m - n)}{2m - n}$

2. Set X consists of at least 2 members and is a set of consecutive odd integers with an average (arithmetic mean) of 37. Set Y consists of at least 10 members and is also a set of consecutive odd integers with an average (arithmetic mean) of 37. Set Z consists of all of the members of both set X and set Y. Which of the following statements must be true?

    I.   The standard deviation of set Z is not equal to the standard deviation of set X.

    II. The standard deviation of set Z is equal to the standard deviation of set Y.

    III. The average (arithmetic mean) of set Z is 37.

    ○ I only

    ○ II only

    ○ III only

    ○ I and III

    ○ II and III

3. The number 10,010 has how many positive integer factors?

   O 31

   O 32

   O 33

   O 34

   O 35

4. A department of motor vehicles asks visitors to draw numbered tickets from a dispenser so that they can be served in order by number. Six friends have graduated from truck-driving school and go to the department to get commercial driving licenses. They draw tickets and find that their numbers are a set of evenly spaced integers with a range of 10. Which of the following could NOT be the sum of their numbers?

   O 1,254

   O 1,428

   O 3,972

   O 4,316

   O 8,010

5. For all values of x, y, and z, $x \lozenge y \lozenge z = x^2(y - 1)(z + 2)$. If $a < 0$, which of the following shows R, S, and T arranged in order from least to greatest?

    $R: 1 \lozenge a \lozenge 3$

    $S: 3 \lozenge a \lozenge 1$

    $T: a \lozenge 3 \lozenge 1$

    ○ R, S, T

    ○ T, S, R

    ○ R, T, S

    ○ T, R, S

    ○ S, R, T

6. If a and b are integers, and $2a + b = 17$, then $8a + b$ cannot equal which of the following?

    ○   −1

    ○   33

    ○   35

    ○   65

    ○   71

7. Two workers have different pay scales. Worker A receives $50 for any day worked plus $15 per hour. Worker B receives $27 per hour. Both workers may work for a fraction of an hour and be paid in proportion to their respective hourly rates. If Worker A arrives at 9:21 a.m. and receives the $50 upon arrival and Worker B arrives at 10:09 a.m., assuming both work continuously, at what time would their earnings be identical?

    ○   11:09 a.m.

    ○   12:01 p.m.

    ○   2:31 p.m.

    ○   3:19 p.m.

    ○   3:36 p.m.

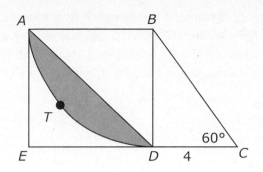

8. In the figure above, *ABDE* is a square, and arc *ATD* is part of a circle with center *B*. The measure of angle *BCD* is 60°, and line segment *CD* has a length of 4. What is the area of the shaded region?

    ○   16π − 32

    ○   12π − 24

    ○   12π − 48

    ○   48π − 24

    ○   48π − 48

9. When the cube of a non-zero number *y* is subtracted from 35, the result is equal to the result of dividing 216 by the cube of that number *y*. What is the sum of all the possible values of *y*?

    ○ $\frac{5}{2}$

    ○   5

    ○   6

    ○   10

    ○   12

10. One letter is selected at random from the five letters V, W, X, Y, and Z, and event *A* is the event that the letter V is selected. A fair six-sided die with sides numbered 1, 2, 3, 4, 5, and 6 is rolled, and event *B* is the event that a 5 or a 6 shows. A fair coin is tossed, and event *C* is the event that a head shows. What is the probability that event *A* occurs and at least one of the events *B* and *C* occurs?

   ○ $\frac{1}{30}$

   ○ $\frac{1}{15}$

   ○ $\frac{1}{10}$

   ○ $\frac{2}{15}$

   ○ $\frac{1}{5}$

11. A car traveled from Town A to Town B. The car traveled the first $\frac{3}{8}$ of the distance from Town A to Town B at an average speed of *x* miles per hour, where $x > 0$. The car traveled the remaining distance at an average speed of *y* miles per hour, where $y > 0$. The car traveled the entire distance from Town A to Town B at an average speed of *z* miles per hour. Which of the following equations gives *y* in terms of *x* and *z*?

   ○ $y = \frac{3x + 5z}{8}$

   ○ $y = \frac{5xz}{8x + 3z}$

   ○ $y = \frac{8x - 3z}{5xz}$

   ○ $y = \frac{3xz}{8x - 5z}$

   ○ $y = \frac{5xz}{8x - 3z}$

12. An ornithologist has studied a particular population of starlings and discovered that their population has increased by 400 percent every 10 years starting in 1890. If the initial population in 1890 was 256 birds, how large was the population of starlings in 1970?

   - ○ 102,400
   - ○ 10,000,000
   - ○ 16,777,216
   - ○ 20,000,000
   - ○ 100,000,000

13. If $(x^2 + 8)yz < 0$, $wz > 0$, and $xyz < 0$, then which of the following must be true?

   - I. $x < 0$
   - II. $wy < 0$
   - III. $yz < 0$

   - ○ II only
   - ○ III only
   - ○ I and III only
   - ○ II and III only
   - ○ I, II, and III

14. If $\dfrac{61^2 - 1}{h}$ is an integer, then h could be divisible by each of the following EXCEPT

   - ○ 8
   - ○ 12
   - ○ 15
   - ○ 18
   - ○ 31

15. If a, b, and c are integers such that $0 < a < b < c$, and a is even, b is prime, and c is odd, which of the following is a possible value for abc?

    ○   5
    ○   12
    ○   16
    ○   34
    ○   54

16. A fair die with sides numbered 1, 2, 3, 4, 5, and 6 is to be rolled 4 times. What is the probability that, on at least one roll, the number showing will be less than 3?

    ○ $\frac{65}{81}$
    ○ $\frac{67}{81}$
    ○ $\frac{8}{9}$
    ○ $\frac{26}{27}$
    ○ $\frac{80}{81}$

17. There are 816 students enrolled at a certain high school. Each of these students is taking at least one of the subjects economics, geography, and biology. The sum of the number of students taking exactly one of these subjects and the number of students taking all three of these subjects is 5 times the number of students taking exactly two of these subjects. The ratio of the number of students taking only the two subjects economics and geography to the number of students taking only the two subjects economics and biology to the number of students taking only the two subjects geography and biology is 3:6:8. How many of the students enrolled at this high school are taking only the two subjects geography and biology?

- ○ 35
- ○ 42
- ○ 64
- ○ 136
- ○ 240

18. Working alone at a constant rate, Machine P produces a widgets in 3 hours. Working alone at a constant rate, Machine Q produces b widgets in 4 hours. If Machines P and Q work together for c hours, then in terms of a, b, and c, how many widgets will Machines P and Q produce?

- ○ $\dfrac{3ac + 4bc}{12}$
- ○ $\dfrac{4ac + 3bc}{12}$
- ○ $\dfrac{4ac + 3bc}{6}$
- ○ $4ac + 3bc$
- ○ $\dfrac{ac + 2bc}{4}$

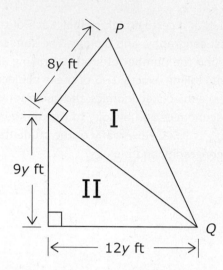

19. In the figure above, the perimeter of triangle I is 16 feet greater than the perimeter of triangle II. What is the length of *PQ*, in feet?

○ 27

○ 51

○ 68

○ 75

○ 85

20. If $x > 0$, $y > 0$, and $\dfrac{7x^2 + 72xy + 4y^2}{4x^2 + 12xy + 5y^2} = 4$, what is the value of $\dfrac{x + y}{y}$?

○ $\dfrac{3}{4}$

○ $\dfrac{4}{3}$

○ $\dfrac{10}{7}$

○ $\dfrac{7}{4}$

○ $\dfrac{7}{3}$

Advanced Data Sufficiency Practice Set

Note: Because the Data Sufficiency answer choices are always the same and should be memorized, we have omitted them here. If you need a refresher on the choices or the 12TEN mnemonic, review Chapter 6 on Data Sufficiency strategy.

(Answers and explanations are at the end of the chapter.)

1. If x and y are positive even integers, is $(40x)x$ divisible by y?

    (1) $x = \frac{1}{128}y$

    (2) y is a multiple of 160.

2. If $a \neq 0$, $\frac{x}{y} = -\frac{1}{a}$, and $\frac{y}{z} = \frac{b}{3}$, is $\frac{x}{z} > \frac{1}{2}$?

    (1) $a^2 - 2a - 3 = 0$

    (2) $b^2 - 4b + 4 = 1$

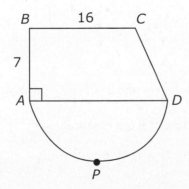

3. In the figure above, what is the area of semicircle *DPA*?

    (1) The area of quadrilateral *ABCD* is 140.

    (2) The length of the line segment whose endpoints are *B* and *D* is 25.

4. Is x divisible by 39?

    (1) x divided by 65 results in a remainder of 7.

    (2) x divided by 36 results in a remainder of 15.

5. If a and b are positive integers with different units digits, and b is the square of an integer, is a also the square of an integer?

    (1) The units digit of $a + b$ is 8.

    (2) $b = 121$

6. What is the value of $8x + y$?

    (1) $3x - 2y + z = 10$

    (2) $2(x + 3y) - (y + 2z) = -25$

7. If b and c are two-digit positive integers and $b - c = 22d$, is d an integer?

    (1) The tens digit and the units digit of b are identical.

    (2) $\frac{b + c}{22} = x$, and x is an integer.

8. The integers x and y are positive, $x > y + 8$, and $y > 8$. What is the remainder when $x^2 - y^2$ is divided by 8?

    (1) The remainder when $x + y$ is divided by 8 is 7.

    (2) The remainder when $x - y$ is divided by 8 is 5.

9. If $x > y > 0$, does $3^{x+1} + 3(2^y) = 12v$?

    (1) $\dfrac{3^{2x} - 2^{2y}}{3^x - 2^y} = 4v$

    (2) $2(3^{x+2}) + 9(2^{y+1}) = 72v$

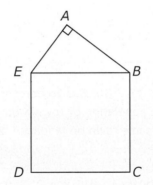

10. In the figure above, the measure of angle *EAB* in triangle *ABE* is 90°, and *BCDE* is a square. What is the length of *AB*?

    (1) The length of *AE* is 12, and the ratio of the area of triangle *ABE* to the area of square *BCDE* is $\dfrac{6}{25}$.

    (2) The perimeter of square *BCDE* is 80 and the ratio of the length of *AE* to the length of *AB* is 3 to 4.

11. In the sequence T, the first term is the non-zero number a, and each term after the first term is equal to the non-zero number r multiplied by the previous term. What is the value of the fourth term of the sequence?

    (1) The sum of the first two terms of the sequence is 16.

    (2) The 18th term of the sequence is 81 times the 14th term of the sequence.

12. A person is to be selected at random from the group T of people. What is the probability that the person selected is a member of club E?

    (1) The probability that a person selected at random from group T is not a member of club D and is not a member of club E is $\frac{1}{4}$.

    (2) The probability that a person selected at random from group T is a member of club D and not a member of club E is $\frac{5}{12}$.

13. The population of Town X on January 1, 2010, was 56 percent greater than the population of the same town on January 1, 2005. The population of Town X on January 1, 2015, was 75 percent greater than the population of the same town on January 1, 2010. What was the population of Town X on January 1, 2005?

    (1) The population of Town X on January 1, 2015, was 21,840.

    (2) The increase in the population of Town X from January 1, 2010, to January 1, 2015, was 4,880 greater than the increase in the population of Town X from January 1, 2005, to January 1, 2010.

14. What is the value of $x - 3z$?

    (1) $x + 4y = 3$

    (2) $x^2 + 4xy - 3xz - 12yz = 24$

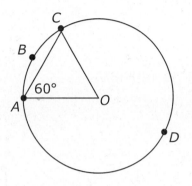

15. In the figure above, the center of the circle is O, and the measure of angle CAO is 60°. What is the perimeter of triangle OAC?

    (1) The length of arc CDA is 16π greater than the length of arc ABC.

    (2) The area of triangle OAC is $36\sqrt{3}$.

16. If x and y are integers and $3x > 8y$, is $y > -18$?

    (1) $-9 < x < 20$

    (2) $y = \dfrac{(x - 42)}{5}$

17. Over the course of 5 days, Monday through Friday, Danny collects a total of 76 baseball cards. Each day, he collects a different number of cards. If Danny collects the largest number of cards on Friday and the second largest number of cards on Thursday, did Danny collect more than 8 cards on Thursday?

    (1) On Friday, Danny collected 49 cards.

    (2) On one of the first 3 days, Danny collected 6 cards.

18. If $y = x^2$, is the equation $(2^{5y})(4^{120}) = 16^{20x}$ true?

    (1) $(4 - x)(12 - x) = 0$
    (2) $(x - 4)(x - 8)(x - 24) = 0$

19. The ratio of the number of students in an auditorium who are seniors to the number of students in the auditorium who are not seniors is 7:5. How many students are there in the auditorium?

    (1) The ratio of the number of students who are seniors who are taking history to the number of students who are not seniors who are taking history is 21:5.

    (2) Of the students in the auditorium who are seniors, $\frac{3}{5}$ are taking history; of the students in the auditorium who are not seniors, $\frac{1}{5}$ are taking history; and the number of seniors in the auditorium who are taking history is 208 greater than the number of students in the auditorium who are not seniors and taking history.

20. If $y > 0$, is $\frac{x}{y} < 3$?

    (1) $x(x + y) - 4y(x + y) < 0$
    (2) $5(y + 8) < 20y - 3x + 40$

Answers and explanations follow on the next page. ▶ ▶ ▶

Answers and Explanations

Advanced Problem Solving Practice Set

1. (E)

The question asks how many peaches must be sold on Saturday to make the profits for Saturday's sales equal to the profits from Sunday's sales. There are a total of T peaches, all of which are to be sold during the course of the weekend. On Saturday, the profit for each peach is m cents. On Sunday, the profit for each peach is $(m - n)$ cents.

Start by setting up expressions for Saturday's profit and Sunday's profit, and then set those expressions equal. Call the number of peaches to be sold on Saturday x. The total profit for Saturday will be (m cents per peach) times (x peaches), which is mx cents. On Sunday, there will be $(T - x)$ peaches left, each of which will bring a profit of $(m - n)$ cents. The total profit for Sunday will be $(m - n)(T - x)$ cents. Saturday's profit must equal Sunday's profit: $mx = (m - n)(T - x)$. The question asks for the number of peaches to be sold on Saturday, so solve for x:

$$mx = (m - n)(T - x)$$
$$mx = mT - mx - nT + nx$$
$$2mx - nx = mT - nT$$
$$(2m - n)x = mT - nT$$
$$x = \frac{mT - nT}{2m - n}$$

None of the answer choices are written as $\frac{mT - nT}{2m - n}$.
However, $\frac{mT - nT}{2m - n} = \frac{T(m - n)}{2m - n}$. **(E)** is correct.

Alternatively, you could have solved by picking numbers. If the farm sold 1 peach on Saturday for 10 cents profit and 2 on Sunday for 5 cents profit each, then $m = 10$, $T = 1 + 2 = 3$, and $n = 10 - 5 = 5$. Evaluate the choices to see which equals 1. **(A)** is 6, **(B)** is −6, **(C)** is $16\frac{2}{3}$, **(D)** is $\frac{3}{5}$, and **(E)** is 1.

2. (C)

This Roman numeral question asks which statement(s) about sets X, Y, and Z *must* be true. Set X has at least 2 members and consists of consecutive odd integers that have a mean of 37. For any set of evenly spaced numbers,

the mean equals the median, so the median of set X is also 37. For a set of consecutive odd integers to have an average that is an odd integer, there must be an odd number of members. So set X must contain at least 3 members.

Set Y has the same mean and median as set X, but a greater minimum number of members (10). There must be an odd number of members, so set Y must contain at least 11 members. Note that neither set X nor set Y has a maximum number of terms.

Set Z contains all the members of both set X and set Y. Because sets contain only unique values, set Z equals either set X or set Y, whichever has the greater number of members. (For instance, if set X is {35, 37, 39} and set Y is {33, 35, 37, 39, 41}, then set Z equals set Y.) When sets X and Y have the same number of members, set Z equals both sets X and Y.

Of the Roman numeral statements, III is the most frequently mentioned in the answer choices and, conveniently, also the easiest to consider. Set Z will always equal set X and/or Y, and both set X and set Y have a mean of 37. Therefore, set Z will also always have a mean of 37. Statement III is part of the correct answer. Eliminate **(A)** and **(B)**.

The other two options involve the standard deviation of set Z. Recall that standard deviation refers to how spread out a set of numbers is. Like many GMAT questions involving standard deviation, this one does not require calculation of the actual value. When two sets have equally spaced numbers and the spacing in both sets is the same, the set with the greater number of numbers has the greater standard deviation. While the standard deviation of set Z will always be equal to either (or both) the standard deviation of set X or Y, it is not necessarily different than the standard deviation of set X, nor is it necessarily equal to the standard deviation of set Y. This eliminates **(D)** and **(E)**, making **(C)** the correct answer.

Quickly confirm by recognizing that when set X has more members than set Y, both Statements I and II are not true. Statement III is the only one that is true under all circumstances.

3. (B)

The question asks for the total number of positive factors of 10,010. The answer choices indicate that there must be more than 30 factors. Because factors come in pairs, you can eliminate **(A)**, **(C)**, and **(E)** immediately because they are odd numbers.

Start by finding the prime factorization of 10,010, and then use those prime factors to find the total number of factors:

- The number 10,010 ends in zero, so it's divisible by 10, or 2×5.

- Now use divisibility rules to investigate the factor 1,001. This is not an even number, so it isn't divisible by 2. Its digits do not sum to 3, so it isn't divisible by 3. It doesn't end in 5 or 0, so 5 is also not a factor. What about 7? This divisibility rule is applicable only rarely on the GMAT. If you happen to know it, use it. Otherwise do the long division to see that $1,001 \div 7 = 143$.

- For 143, you've already checked the prime factors up to 11. There is a divisibility rule for 11, but finding that $143 \div 11 = 13$ is relatively straightforward.

The full prime factorization of 10,010, then, is $2 \times 5 \times 7 \times 11 \times 13$. Once you have its prime factorization, the fastest way to determine how many factors a number has is to add 1 to each exponent in the prime factorization and multiply the resulting values. You can write the prime factorization of 10,010 as $2^1 \times 5^1 \times 7^1 \times 11^1 \times 13^1$. Now add 1 to each exponent and multiply: $(1 + 1)(1 + 1)(1 + 1)(1 + 1)(1 + 1) = (2)(2)(2)(2)(2) = 32$. The correct choice is **(B)**.

If you didn't know the trick above, you can use combinations to total up the number of factors. There are 5 factors of 10,010 that consist of just one of the prime factors. Use the formula for combinations of 2 of the 5 factors, $\frac{5!}{2!3!} = \frac{5 \times 4}{2 \times 1} = 10$, to see that there are 10 factors that consist of 2 of the prime factors. The math for combinations of 3 factors is the same, so there are 10 of those as well. There are 5 ways to leave out one prime factor, so that is the number of four-factor combinations. Finally, there is $10,010 \times 1$, which consists of 2 factors. The total is $5 + 10 + 10 + 5 + 2 = 32$ factors.

Do a quick check to make sure you included all the prime factors you discovered and that you counted the factors 10,010 and 1.

4. (D)

The question asks which choice could NOT be the sum of six evenly spaced integers with a range of 10. You could pick two numbers with a range of 10, such as 1 and 11 to see how six evenly spaced integers could fit in the range to find that the integers must be 2 apart.

Alternatively, the formula for the number of members in a set of evenly spaced integers is this:

$$\text{\# of numbers} = \frac{\text{Range}}{\text{Interval}} + 1$$

In this case:

$$6 = \frac{10}{\text{Interval}} + 1$$
$$6(\text{Interval}) = 10 + 1(\text{Interval})$$
$$5(\text{Interval}) = 10$$
$$\text{Interval} = 2$$

Anytime the GMAT uses a small set of evenly spaced integers, remember that a single variable is sufficient to represent the series. Thus, x can represent the first integer, and the six integers can be written x, $x + 2$, $x + 4$, $x + 6$, $x + 8$, $x + 10$. The sum of these would be $6x + 30$, or $6(x + 5)$. While you do not know the value of this expression (since you do not know the value of x), you do know it is a multiple of 6. The correct choice is the one that is *not* a multiple of 6.

Use the rule for divisibility by 6, which combines the rules for divisibility by 2 and 3. All the answer choices are even, so just use the rule for divisibility by 3.

(A): $1 + 2 + 5 + 4 = 12$. Eliminate.

(B): $1 + 4 + 2 + 8 = 15$. Eliminate.

(C): $3 + 9 + 7 + 2 = 21$. Eliminate.

(D): $4 + 3 + 1 + 6 = 14$, which is *not* divisible by 3. This is the correct choice.

If you divide 4,316 by 6, you get 719 with a remainder of 2. Therefore, 4,316 is not divisible by 6, and **(D)** is correct.

5.   (E)

The question requires you to use the symbolic equation given and evaluate R, S, and T, placing them in order from smallest to largest. Using this symbolism as a function, substitute 1, 3, and a for x, y, and z in the various orders shown. Keep in mind that a is negative.

Calculate the values of R, S, and T and rank them in order from smallest to largest. Again, $x \lozenge y \lozenge z = x^2 (y - 1)(z + 2)$.

$$
\begin{aligned}
R: 1 \lozenge a \lozenge 3 &= 1^2 (a - 1)(3 + 2) \\
&= 1(a - 1)(5) \\
&= 5(a - 1) = 5a - 5 \\
S: 3 \lozenge a \lozenge 1 &= 3^2 (a - 1)(1 + 2) \\
&= 9(a - 1)(3) \\
&= 27(a - 1) = 27a - 27 \\
T: a \lozenge 3 \lozenge 1 &= a^2 (3 - 1)(1 + 2) \\
&= a^2 (2)(3) = 6a^2
\end{aligned}
$$

T must be a positive value because the a is squared and multiplied by a positive number. Because a is negative, the expressions that result for R and S subtract a positive value from a negative value, making them both negative numbers. Therefore, T must be the greatest of the choices. Eliminate (B), (C), and (D).

Next compare R and S. Both involve multiplying the negative value a by a constant and then subtracting a positive integer. You may find it easier to compare R as $5(a - 1)$ and S as $27(a - 1)$: since $(a - 1)$ is negative, R must be greater than S. (E) is the correct choice.

You could pick numbers for a to confirm your answer. For example, if $a = -1$, then $R = 5a - 5 = 5(-1) - 5 = -10$, $S = 27a - 27 = 27(-1) - 27 = -54$, and $T = 6(-1^2) = 6$. For any permissible value of a, S is always less than R and T is always positive, again making (E) correct.

6.   (B)

The question asks what $8a + b$ *cannot* equal, given that $2a + b = 17$. The correct choice will violate that equality.

Since you have only one equation, you can't solve for either variable, but you can still substitute and have just one variable in the expression you're evaluating. Substituting for either variable would work, but it is easier to substitute for b, since all you have to do is put $2a$ on the

other side of the equation. If $b = -2a + 17$, then the expression $8a + b = 8a + (-2a + 17) = 6a + 17$. Since $6a$ is a multiple of 6, subtract 17 from each choice to see if the result is a multiple of 6. Eliminate the choice if the result of the subtraction is a multiple of 6. (Alternatively, since 17 is one less than 18, which is a multiple of 6, you could add 1 to each choice and check that result for divisibility by 6.)

(A): $-1 - 17 = -18$, a multiple of 6. Eliminate.

(B): $33 - 17 = 16$, which is not a multiple of 6. **(B)** is correct.

You can check this using substitution. If $6a + 17 = 33$, then $6a = 16$ and $a = \dfrac{8}{3}$, which is not an integer. **(B)** is correct.

7.   (D)

The question asks at what time of day two workers with different pay scales and different starting times would have the same earnings. Worker A starts at 9:21 a.m. and earns \$50 plus \$15 per hour. Worker B starts at 10:09 a.m. and earns \$27 per hour.

Even though this is about wages and money, it's a combined rates question, just like one that asks when a faster train overtakes a slower train. While it's possible to backsolve, it would be necessary to plug each time into two different formulas, making this approach both time-consuming and potentially error-prone. Instead, you can use four steps to get the answer efficiently.

Worker A works for 48 minutes before B begins, so you want to know how much money A has already made. In combined work problems, calculations are easiest if you state time as a fraction, and 48 minutes is $\dfrac{4}{5}$ of an hour. Thus, $15 \times \dfrac{4}{5} = \$12$ earned. Also, A gets \$50 right off the bat, so A is \$12 + \$50 = \$62 up when B begins working.

The second step is to combine rates. In this case, think about B catching up to A. Worker A makes \$15 an hour and Worker B makes \$27 an hour, so for each hour they both work, B gains on A by \$12.

The third step is to divide the distance/work/earnings by the combined rate to get the time, so divide \$62 by \$12 per hour, and get $5\dfrac{2}{12}$ or $5\dfrac{1}{6}$ hours. A sixth of an hour is 10 minutes, so for Worker B to overcome the initial difference they must both work for 5 hours and 10 minutes, beginning at the time that B started.

The last step is to add the time worked to the starting time. In this case, add 5 hours 10 minutes to the first time when both started working, 10:09 a.m., and get 3:19 p.m. **(D)** is the correct answer.

When taking the four steps described above leads to an answer that exactly matches one of the choices, you can feel fairly confident that you have solved correctly. However, to confirm, you could find that Worker A worked for 5 hours 58 minutes and so, at $15 an hour, made $89.50 + $50, or $139.50. Worker B worked for 5 hours 10 minutes at $27 an hour, which also yields $139.50. Again, **(D)** is correct.

8. (B)

The question asks for the area of a shaded region between an arc of a circle and a chord. In this case, the shaded region is the result of removing triangle ABD, whose area is half the area of square $ABDE$, from the sector of a circle. The question provides two important measurements for triangle BCD: angle BCD measures 60° and side CD has a length of 4. Subtract half the area of the square from the area of the circle sector to calculate the area of the shaded region.

The area of a sector of a circle has the same proportional relationship to the area of the full circle as its central angle does to 360°. This sector has a central angle which is interior angle ABD of the square. So, the measure of angle ABD is 90°. Because 90° is one-fourth of 360°, the sector defined by arc ATD has an area one-fourth of that of the full circle. To calculate the area of both the half square and quarter circle, determine the length of BD, which is both a radius of the circle and a side of the square. Triangle BCD is a 30-60-90 triangle, and its sides, therefore, have the proportion $x : \sqrt{3}x : 2x$. Side CD is opposite the 30° angle and is therefore represented by the x in this proportional relationship. Side BD thus has a length of $4\sqrt{3}$. The area of the square is $(4\sqrt{3})^2$ $= 16 \times 3 = 48$, so the area of triangle ABD is 24. The area of the circle is $\pi(4\sqrt{3})^2 = 48\pi$, and the quarter circle has an area of $\frac{1}{4}(48\pi) = 12\pi$. Therefore, the area of

the shaded region is $12\pi - 24$, and the correct answer is **(B)**.

9. (B)

The question asks for the sum of all possible values of y given the information in the question. Start by translating the English into math. The cube of the number y is y^3. The result of subtracting the cube of the number y from 35 is $35 - y^3$. When 216 is divided by y^3, the result is $\frac{216}{y^3}$. So $35 - y^3 = \frac{216}{y^3}$.

Multiply both sides of the equation by y^3 to get $35y^3 - y^6 = 216$, which is $35y^3 - y^6 - 216 = 0$. Multiply all terms by –1 and rearrange: $y^6 - 35y^3 + 216 = 0$.

Notice that $y^6 - 35y^3 + 216 = 0$ is a quadratic equation with y^3 as the unknown. The equation $(y^3)^2 - 35y^3 + 216 = 0$ factors to $(y^3 - 8)(y^3 - 27) = 0$. So $y^3 = 8$ or 27. If $y^3 = 8$, then $y = 2$; if $y^3 = 27$, then $y = 3$. The sum of all the possible values of y is $2 + 3 = 5$.

(B) is correct.

You can check that you have the correct values of y by plugging them into the equation $35 - y^3 = \frac{216}{y^3}$. If $y = 2$, you get $35 - 8 = \frac{216}{8}$, or $27 = 27$. If $y = 3$, you get $35 - 27 = \frac{216}{27}$, or $8 = 8$.

10. (D)

This probability question asks for the probability that event A occurs *and* that either one *or* both of the events B and C occur. These are three separate and independent events that are defined in the stem.

The probability of an event is $\frac{\text{Number of desired outcomes}}{\text{Number of possible outcomes}}$. For event A, one letter is selected at random from five letters, so the probability that event A occurs is $\frac{1}{5}$. For event B, a 5 or 6 must occur from the 6 possible outcomes, so the probability that event B occurs is $\frac{2}{6} = \frac{1}{3}$. For event C, a head comes up 1 out of 2 possible outcomes, heads and tails, so the probability that event C occurs is $\frac{1}{2}$.

These can be written as $P(A) = \frac{1}{5}$, $P(B) = \frac{1}{3}$, and $P(C) = \frac{1}{2}$.

The probability that event A occurs *and* at least one of the events B and C occurs is $P(A) \times P(B \text{ or } C)$. To find $P(B \text{ or } C)$, apply the generalized formula for two events, $P(B \text{ or } C) = P(B) + P(C) - P(B \text{ and } C)$. The events B and C are independent, so $P(B \text{ and } C) = P(B)P(C)$.

Replacing $P(B \text{ and } C)$ with $P(B)P(C)$, you have $P(B \text{ or } C) = P(B) + P(C) - P(B)P(C)$. Then substitute in $P(B) = \frac{1}{3}$ and $P(C) = \frac{1}{2}$:

$$P(B \text{ or } C) = \frac{1}{3} + - \times \frac{1}{2}\frac{1}{3}\frac{1}{2}$$
$$= \frac{2}{6} + - \frac{3}{6}\frac{1}{6}$$
$$= \frac{4}{6}$$
$$= \frac{2}{3}$$

Now find the probability that event A occurs *and* at least one of the events B and C occurs:

$$P(A) \times P(B \text{ or } C) = \frac{1}{5} \times \frac{2}{3} = \frac{2}{15}$$

(D) is correct.

You can check that you have calculated $P(B \text{ or } C)$ correctly by calculating the probability that neither B nor C occurs and subtracting from 1. $P(\sim B) = \frac{2}{3}$ and $P(\sim C) = \frac{1}{2}$, so

$$P(B \text{ or } C) = 1 - \frac{2}{3} \times \frac{1}{2} = 1 - \frac{1}{3} = \frac{2}{3}.$$

11. (E)

The question asks for y, the speed of the car on the second leg of the journey, in terms of x, the speed of the car on the first leg, and z, the average speed for the entire journey. The car traveled $\frac{3}{8}$ of the distance at x mph and the final $\frac{5}{8}$ of the distance at y mph. Its average speed over the entire distance traveled is z mph. Since there are variables in both the question and the choices, picking numbers can be an efficient strategy. However, the key concept this questions is testing, average speed, means that you must pick your numbers carefully.

Recall that Average speed $= \dfrac{\text{Total distance}}{\text{Total time}}$. 80 is a good number to pick for the total distance since that yields a first part of 30 miles and a second part of

50 miles. Since the total time will be the sum of the times on each part, use Time $= \dfrac{\text{Distance}}{\text{Speed}}$ to choose speeds that divide evenly into the distances you picked. 10 mph for the first part and 25 mph for the second part are good choices. So the time spent on the first leg is $30 \div 10 = 3$ hours, and the time spent on the second leg is $50 \div 25 = 2$ hours. Next, calculate the average speed: $\frac{80}{3+2} = \frac{80}{5} = 16$ mph. The values you will use to test the choices are $x = 10$ and $z = 16$, and you will eliminate choices that do not yield $y = 25$. You don't need to complete the calculations: as soon as you know a choice will not equal 25, eliminate it and move on.

Testing **(A)**:
$$\frac{3x + 5z}{8} = \frac{3(10) + 5(16)}{8} = \frac{110}{8} \neq 25 \text{ Eliminate.}$$

Testing **(B)**:
$$\frac{5xz}{8x + 3z} = \frac{5(10)(16)}{8(10) + 3(16)} = \frac{800}{80 + 48} = \frac{800}{128} \neq 25$$
Eliminate. Also note that $5xz$ appears in two other choices. Use 800, the value you calculated here, to speed your evaluation of later choices.

Testing **(C)**: If you use your work on **(B)**, you can eliminate **(C)** immediately because the numerator is less than 128, the denominator from **(B)**, and the denominator is 800. **(C)** will be a fraction less than 1. For the record: $\frac{8x - 3z}{5xz} = \frac{8(10) - 3(16)}{5(10)(16)} = \frac{32}{800}$

Testing **(D)**:
$$\frac{3xz}{8x - 5z} = \frac{3(10)(16)}{8(10) - 5(16)} = \frac{480}{0} \neq 25 \text{ Eliminate.}$$

(E) must be correct. To confirm:
$$\frac{5xz}{8x - 3z} = \frac{5(10)(16)}{8(10) - 3(16)} = \frac{800}{32} = \frac{100}{4} = 25.$$

12. (E)

The question asks for the population of starlings in 1970. You know that the initial population of starlings in 1890 was 256 and that the population increases by 400% every 10 years. Because you need an exponential function to answer this question, use the compound interest formula.

Although this question does not deal with money, notice that the given facts fit the compound interest formula perfectly. The formula, as applied to money, is Total of

Principal and Interest = Principal $\times (1 + r)^t$, where r is the interest rate per time period and t is the number of time periods. In this question, the total of "principal and interest" is the final population of starlings in 1970, the "principal" is the initial population (256), the "interest rate" is the population growth rate expressed as a decimal (4.00), and t is the number of 10-year periods from 1890 to 1970 (8). Thus, you have the following:

1970 population $= 256 \times (1 + 4)^8 = 256 \times 5^8$

At this point, you could do the arithmetic, but without a calculator, this approach would be time-consuming and potentially prone to errors. When tedious arithmetic arises on the GMAT, there is often a more strategic way to get to the answer. If you notice that 256 is a power of 2, you can use the exponent rules to make your task much simpler:

$256 \times 5^8 = 2^8 \times 5^8 = (2 \times 5)^8 = 10^8 = 100,000,000$

The correct answer is **(E)**.

13. **(D)**

The question asks you to determine the possible positive and negative number properties of four variables, w, x, y, and z. Three inequalities provide relationships among the variables. Review the inequalities and jot down what each tells you about the variables. Since $wz > 0$ and $xyz < 0$, each of the variables w, x, y, and z is non-zero. In the first inequality, $(x^2 + 8)yz < 0$, since x^2 is positive and 8 is positive, $x^2 + 8$ is positive, so it must be that yz is negative. Thus, y and z have opposite signs. Since $wz > 0$, both w and z must have the same sign. Finally, in order for xyz to be negative, either one or all of the three variables x, y, and z must be negative. But since you know only one of y and z is negative, all three variables cannot be negative, so x must be positive.

Now use this information to evaluate the Roman numeral statements. Usually, the most efficient way to solve this type of question is to start with the Roman numeral statement that appears most often in the answer choices; in this case, that is Statement III, $yz < 0$. You already determined that y and z have opposite signs, so this statement must be true. You can eliminate **(A)**.

Evaluate Statement II next. You determined that w and z have the same sign. Therefore, if y times z is negative, then y times w must also be negative, and Statement II must be true. You can now eliminate **(B)** and **(C)**.

Finally, if xyz is negative and yz is also negative, then x must be positive. Eliminate **(E)**. **(D)** is correct.

14. **(D)**

This question asks you to determine which choice does *not* divide evenly into $61^2 - 1$. Calculating the actual value of the numerator would be too time-consuming, but it's presented in the form of the difference of two perfect squares (61^2 and 1^2). This is one of the classic quadratics: $61^2 - 1^2 = (61 + 1)(61 - 1)$, or $(62)(60)$.

Rather than find the product of 60 and 62 and then divide that by each of the answer choices, reduce the numerator and denominator by shared factors.

Testing **(A)**: $\dfrac{(62)(60)}{8} = \dfrac{(\cancel{2})(31)(\cancel{4})(15)}{(\cancel{2})(\cancel{4})}$ Eliminate.

(B), **(C)**, and **(E)** are a little more straightforward; since 12 itself is a factor of 60, 15 is also a factor of 60, and 31 is a factor of 62. The only choice that is not a factor of either number is 18. The correct answer is **(D)**.

You can quickly check that 18 is not a factor of the product of 60 and 62 by breaking down 18, 60, and 62 into their prime factors:

$\dfrac{60 \times 62}{18} = \dfrac{\cancel{2} \times 2 \times \cancel{3} \times 5 \times 2 \times 31}{\cancel{2} \times \cancel{3} \times 3}$. Notice that the 2 in the denominator cancels out one of the 2s in the numerator, but only one of the 3s in the denominator cancels out. So the denominator will have a 3 remaining that cannot be canceled out. Therefore, the product of 60 and 62 is *not* divisible by 18, and **(D)** is correct.

15. **(E)**

This question asks which of the choices is a *possible* value for *abc*. (Note that this doesn't mean that the correct choice is the *only* possible value for *abc*).

You know that a, b, and c are positive integers. Because a is an even number, it must be at least 2. Since b is both a prime number and greater than a, it must be odd and at least 3. Because c is an odd number that is greater than b, it must be at least 5. Therefore, the least possible value for *abc* is $2 \times 3 \times 5 = 30$. Eliminate **(A)**, **(B)**, and **(C)**.

Now consider (D). There is no way to increment a, b, or c to their next permissible value and have the product increase from 30 to 34. For example, consider other possible values with each variable increased to its next permissible value:

If $a = 4$, then $abc = 4 \times 5 \times 7 = 140$.
If $b = 5$, then $abc = 2 \times 5 \times 7 = 70$.
If $c = 7$, then $abc = 2 \times 3 \times 7 = 42$.

When you increase any one of a, b, or c to their next permissible value, the result is greater than 34, so eliminate (D) and choose (E). Indeed, $2 \times 3 \times 9 = 54$, and 9 is a valid value for c.

16. (A)

The question asks for the probability that a 1 or a 2 will appear at least once when a die is rolled 4 times. The probability that *at least* 1 roll is a 1 or 2 includes the probabilities that 1, 2, 3, or 4 rolls result in a 1 or 2. Instead of calculating all those probabilities separately and adding them together, find the probability that *no* rolls result in a 1 or 2, and then subtract that probability from 1.

Start by finding the probability that each of the 4 rolls results in at least a 3. The probability formula is as follows:

$$\text{Probability} = \frac{\text{Number of desired outcomes}}{\text{Number of possible outcomes}}$$

When rolling the die once, there are 4 desired outcomes (3, 4, 5, and 6) and there are 6 possible outcomes (1, 2, 3, 4, 5, and 6). The probability that when the die is rolled once a number greater than or equal to 3 results is $\frac{4}{6} = \frac{2}{3}$. Since the results of the 4 rolls of the dice are independent of each other, the probability that all 4 rolls result in a number greater than or equal to 3 is $\frac{2}{3} \times \frac{2}{3} \times \frac{2}{3} \times \frac{2}{3} = \frac{2 \times 2 \times 2 \times 2}{3 \times 3 \times 3 \times 3} = \frac{16}{81}$. It follows that the probability that at least 1 roll results in a number less than 3 is $1 - \frac{16}{81} = \frac{81}{81} - \frac{16}{81} = \frac{81 - 16}{81} = \frac{65}{81}$.

(A) is correct.

17. (C)

This question asks for the number of students taking one particular two-subject combination: geography and biology. You are given the total number of students (816), the relationship between students taking two subjects and the total number of students taking one or three of the subjects, and ratios of the various two-subject combinations. Since the group that you're interested in, the geography and biology group, is a part of the given ratio, begin there.

Since the geography and biology group are represented by 8 in the ratio, the actual number of these students must be a multiple of 8. Although you don't know the exact number, you can't have a fraction of a student, so the correct answer will be some multiple of 8. Eliminate (A) and (B) because they are not multiples of 8.

Now backsolve, starting by testing (D). If there are 136 geography and biology students, $\frac{136}{8} = 17$ so multiply the other terms in the ratio by 17 to find the number of the other two-subject students: $3 \times 17 = 51$ and $6 \times 17 = 102$. So the total of two-subject students is $51 + 102 + 136 = 289$.

The second sentence of the question says the sum of the number of one- or three-subject students equals 5 times the number of two-subject students. You could set up an equation, but you have over 200 two-subject students: $5 \times 200 = 1,000$ and the total number of students is 816. (D) is too large, so (C) must be correct.

To confirm your answer, quickly test (C). If there are 64 geography and biology students, $\frac{64}{8} = 8$, so multiply the other terms in the ratio by 8 to find the number of the other two-subject students: $3 \times 8 = 24$ and $6 \times 8 = 48$. So the total of two-subject students is $24 + 48 + 64 = 136$. The sum of the number of one- or three-subject students equals 5 times the number of two-subject students, so the total of one- or three-subject students is $5 \times 136 = 680$, and $680 + 136 = 816$, which is the total number of students in the school.

18. (B)

The question asks for the expression that represents the number of widgets two machines working at different rates can produce. You are given variables for the number of widgets produced by each machine in different time periods and for the number of hours the machines work together. Since the question and the choices include variables, picking numbers is an efficient strategy to answering this question.

Pick numbers for a and b, the number of widgets produced, that divide evenly by the number of hours you're given for each machine. 3 is a good choice for a because that means Machine P would produce 1 widget per hour. 8 is a good choice for b because that means Machine Q would produce 2 widgets per hour. So together the two machines would produce 3 widgets per hour. Choose any small number for c, say 2: in 2 hours the machines would produce 6 widgets. 6 is your target as you replace a with 3, b with 8, and c with 2 in the choices. A quick glance at the choices tells you that $ac = 6$ and $bc = 16$ are used in every choice. Jot them down to reduce the calculations.

Testing **(A)**:

$$\frac{3ac + 4bc}{12} = \frac{3(6) + 4(16)}{12} = \frac{18 + 64}{12} = \frac{82}{12} \neq 6$$

Eliminate.

Testing **(B)**:

$$\frac{4ac + 3bc}{12} = \frac{4(6) + 3(16)}{12} = \frac{24 + 48}{12} = \frac{72}{12} = 6$$

Keep this choice, but when picking numbers, you must eliminate all other choices.

Eliminate **(C)** and **(D)** because they have the same numerator as **(B)**, but different denominators.

Testing **(E)**:

$$\frac{ac + 2bc}{4} = \frac{6 + 2(16)}{4} = \frac{6 + 32}{4} = \frac{38}{4} \neq 6$$

Eliminate. **(B)** is correct.

Alternatively, you could take an algebraic approach. First, find the hourly rate for each machine by dividing the number of widgets by the number of hours needed to produce those widgets.

Machine P's rate of production is $\frac{a}{3}$ per hour and Q's is $\frac{b}{4}$ per hour. Convert both fractions to have a denominator with the LCM, 12, to get the total production per hour: $\left(\frac{4}{4}\right)\frac{a}{3} + \left(\frac{3}{3}\right)\frac{b}{4} = \frac{4a}{12} + \frac{3b}{12} = \frac{4a + 3b}{12}$. Since the machines operate for c hours, multiply the per hour rate by c to get the total production: $c\left(\frac{4a + 3b}{12}\right) = \frac{4ac + 3bc}{12}$. **(B)** is correct.

19. (C)

The question asks for the length of the hypotenuse of right triangle I. The hypotenuse of right triangle II is also one of the legs of right triangle I. Dimensions of some of the sides are provided in terms of the variable y. You also know the difference, in feet, between the perimeters of the two triangles. Use the properties of right triangles to find the side lengths needed, calculate the two perimeters, then use the difference in feet to find the value of y.

Looking at right triangle II, the leg of length $9y$ feet can be expressed as $3 \times (3y$ feet) and the leg of length $12y$ feet is $4 \times (3y$ feet). So right triangle II is a 3-4-5 right triangle with each member of the 3 to 4 to 5 ratio multiplied by $3y$ feet. That means the length of the hypotenuse of right triangle II is $5 \times (3y$ feet) = $15y$ feet.

Now find the length of PQ. Triangle I is a right triangle with one leg of length $8y$ feet and the other leg (the hypotenuse of triangle II) of $15y$ feet. You may have the ratio 8:15:17 memorized, and if so, you know that PQ is $17y$ feet. Alternatively, you can use the Pythagorean theorem: $a^2 + b^2 = c^2$, or $(8y)^2 + (15y)^2 = PQ^2$.

$$PQ^2 = (8y)^2 + (15y)^2$$
$$= 64y^2 + 225y^2$$
$$= (64 + 225)(y^2)$$
$$= 289y^2$$
$$PQ = \sqrt{289y^2} = 17y$$

You now know the lengths of all the sides of triangles I and II.

The perimeter of triangle I is $8y + 15y + 17y = 40y$.

The perimeter of triangle II is $9y + 12y + 15y = 36y$.

The perimeter of triangle I is 16 feet greater than the perimeter of triangle II. So $40y = 36y + 16$, $4y = 16$, and $y = 4$. The length of PQ, in feet, is $17y = 17(4) = 68$. **(C)** is correct.

To confirm your answer, check that $17y$ makes sense for the length of that side. The other two sides of the triangle are $8y$ and $15y$, so that third side must be less than $8y + 15y = 23y$ and more than $15y - 8y = 7y$.

20. (E)

This questions asks for the value of $\frac{x+y}{y}$. Because you have only one equation and two variables, x and y, you won't be able to solve for each variable and then combine them in the expression. Rewrite $\frac{x+y}{y} = \frac{x}{y} + \frac{y}{y} = \frac{x}{y} + 1$ and solve the given equation for $\frac{x}{y}$.

Begin by simplifying the equation $\frac{7x^2 + 72xy + 4y^2}{4x^2 + 12xy + 5y^2} = 4$.

$$7x^2 + 72xy + 4y^2 = 4\left(4x^2 + 12xy + 5y^2\right)$$

$$7x^2 + 72xy + 4y^2 = 16x^2 + 48xy + 20y^2$$

$$-9x^2 + 24xy - 16y^2 = 0$$

$$9x^2 - 24xy + 16y^2 = 0$$

Notice that this is the expansion of the frequently tested quadratic $(a - b)^2 = a^2 - 2ab + b^2$ where $a = 3x$ and $b = 4y$. So, $(3x - 4y)(3x - 4y) = 0$.

Solve the equation $3x - 4y = 0$ for the value of $\frac{x}{y}$:

$$3x - 4y = 0$$

$$3x = 4y$$

$$\frac{3x}{y} = 4$$

$$\frac{x}{y} = \frac{4}{3}$$

Thus, $\frac{x+y}{y} = \frac{x}{y} + 1 = \frac{4}{3} + 1 = \frac{7}{3}$. **(E)** is correct.

Advanced Data Sufficiency Practice Set

1. (A)

This is a Yes/No question. Essentially, the question asks whether $\frac{(40x)^x}{y}$ is an integer. Note that x and y are both even. Also note that because x is even and 40 is an integer, the expression $(40x)^x$ must be even. Finally, note that x is a factor of the base as well as the exponent.

To determine that y divides evenly into $(40x)^x$, you need to know that y has no prime factors that are not found in 40 or x and that it has no prime factor raised to an exponent that is greater than the number of times that prime number is a factor of $(40x)^x$. The prime factors of 40 are $2 \times 2 \times 2 \times 5$.

Statement (1), when rewritten, tells you that $y = 128x$. Taking this statement into account, the question now becomes whether $\frac{(40x)^x}{128x}$ is an integer. Because $(40x)^x = 40x(40x)^{x-1}$ you can factor out $40x$ in the numerator and simplify further:

$$\frac{40x(40x)^{x-1}}{128x} = \frac{5 \times \cancel{2} \times \cancel{2} \times \cancel{2} \times \cancel{x}(40x)^{x-1}}{\cancel{2} \times \cancel{2} \times \cancel{2} \times 2 \times 2 \times 2 \times 2 \times \cancel{x}} =$$

$\frac{5(40x)^{x-1}}{16}$. So, if $5(40x)^{x-1}$ is divisible by 16, then this is an integer. Remember that x is positive and even, so $x \geq 2$. So, $40x$ will be a multiple of 80, which factors to $(2 \times 2 \times 2 \times 2 \times 5)$. That will evenly divide by $16 = (2 \times 2 \times 2 \times 2)$, which means this is indeed an integer. Statement (1) is sufficient. Eliminate **(B)**, **(C)**, and **(E)**.

Statement (2) tells you that y is a multiple of 160 and thus has 2 and 5 as its distinct prime factors. While that may seem to align with the 40 in the numerator, y being a multiple of 160 means that it could be infinitely large and thus potentially too big to be a factor, given that you don't know the value of x. Statement (2) is insufficient. **(A)** is correct.

2. (E)

The question stem gives two equations and asks whether a third algebraic fraction is greater than a constant, making this a Yes/No question. You can simplify the given information by combining the two equations. Note that multiplying them together will make the y cancel out: $\left(\frac{x}{y}\right)\left(\frac{y}{z}\right) = \left(-\frac{1}{a}\right)\left(\frac{b}{3}\right)$ results in $\frac{x}{z} = -\frac{b}{3a}$. The question asks about $\frac{x}{z}$, so if you can find the values of a and b, you will have sufficiency. You will also have sufficiency if you can find the value of $\frac{a}{b}$ or $\frac{b}{a}$. Finally, you will have sufficiency if you can find that, in some other way, there is only one answer to the question regarding $\frac{x}{z}$ and $\frac{1}{2}$.

Statement (1) uses only one of the variables needed, so it is insufficient. Eliminate **(A)** and **(D)**.

Statement (2) also uses only one of the variables needed, so it is insufficient too. Eliminate **(B)**.

Combine the two statements. Neither of the statements is simpler than the other, so begin by factoring either of them. In Statement (1), factoring $a^2 - 2a - 3 = 0$ yields $(a + 1)(a - 3) = 0$, making $a = -1$ or 3. In Statement (2), subtract 1 from both sides, to get $b^2 - 4b + 3 = 0$. Factoring $b^2 - 4b + 3 = 0$ produces $(b - 1)(b - 3) = 0$, making $b = 1$ or $b = 3$. So, the four possible combinations of a and b are:

$a = -1$ and $b = 1$
$a = -1$ and $b = 3$
$a = 3$ and $b = 1$
$a = 3$ and $b = 3$

Use these pairs to determine whether $\frac{x}{z}$ is always greater than $\frac{1}{2}$. Test the first pair, as it is the easiest. If $a = -1$ and $b = 1$, then $\frac{x}{z} = -\frac{b}{3a} = -\frac{1}{3(-1)} = \frac{1}{3}$, which is *not* greater than $\frac{1}{2}$. In this case, the answer to the question is no.

Notice that with both a and b positive, $-\frac{b}{3a}$ will be negative, and the answer will still be no. So stay with $a = -1$. You can expect a greater value for $\frac{x}{z}$ when $b = 3$ than when $b = 1$, so test $b = 3$. If $a = -1$ and $b = 3$, $\frac{x}{z} = -\frac{b}{3a} = -\frac{3}{3(-1)} = 1$. In this case, $\frac{x}{z} > \frac{1}{2}$ and the answer to the question is yes. Because both yes and no answers are possible, **(E)** is correct.

3. (B)

This is a Value question. The question stem contains a diagram with multiple figures, and you need to be able to find a single possible area of the semicircle DPA to have sufficiency. In order to do that, you would need to know the length of diameter AD of the semicircle. AD is also a side of quadrilateral $ABCD$. Because a semicircle has half the area of a circle with the same diameter, knowing the length of AD would allow you to calculate the area of semicircle DPA.

Statement (1) tells you that the area of the quadrilateral $ABCD$ is 140. Using the formula for the area of a trapezoid, Area $= \frac{b_1 + b_2}{2} \times h$, it would appear that you could plug in the information you know from the diagram and Statement (1) (the area, the height, and b_1) to solve for b_2. However you are not given enough information to determine whether sides AD and BC are parallel; therefore, $ABCD$ is not necessarily a trapezoid. Statement (1) is thus insufficient, and you can eliminate **(A)** and **(D)**.

Statement (2) tells you that the length of the line segment whose endpoints are B and D is 25. This line segment, if added to the figure, would be the hypotenuse of right triangle ABD. Since you now know two sides of a right triangle, it would be possible to calculate the length of the third side, AD, by using the Pythagorean theorem. Statement (2) is sufficient. Therefore, **(B)** is correct.

4. (A)

This is a Yes/No question. Unlike some remainder questions for which you can pick numbers, the remainders in the statements would be very tedious and time-consuming to test. Whenever the numbers given are unwieldy, the most efficient way to establish divisibility is to find the prime factors. In this case, 39 breaks down to 3×13, so for x to be divisible by 39, it must be divisible by both 3 and 13.

Statement (1) gives the number 65. Consider that 65 is 5×13; one of the prime factors of 39 is present. For x to be divisible by 13, the remainder itself must be a multiple of 13. The remainder 7 is not a multiple of 13, so it is impossible for x to be divisible by 13 or 39. This makes the answer to the question always no, and Statement (1) is sufficient. Eliminate choices **(B)**, **(C)**, and **(E)**.

In evaluating Statement (2), you can use the same principle. The number 36 is divisible by 3, one of the necessary primes, so the remainder must also be divisible by 3. The remainder 15 is divisible by 3, meaning that x is a multiple of 3. Since you don't know anything else about x, it's entirely possible that x is also divisible by 13, while there are certain values that would make x not divisible by 13. Statement (2) is insufficient.

The correct choice is (A).

5. (A)

This is a Yes/No question. The given information provides a clue about the two numbers having different units digits and tells you that b is a perfect square. Units digits of certain groups of numbers often fall into consistent patterns, and squares certainly fit into that category. The units digits of the squares of 1–10 are {1, 4, 9, 6, 5, 6, 9, 4, 1, 0}, and this pattern will continue, since the units digits of 11–20, 21–30, and so on will be the same as those of 1–10. So a perfect square can only have one of six units digits: 0, 1, 4, 5, 6, or 9. For a to be a perfect square, its units digit must be one of those numbers.

Evaluating Statement (1), you see that the sum of the integers a and b has a units digit of 8. Work your way through the list of possible units digits of squares of integers. Again, that list is 0, 1, 4, 5, 6, and 9. If the units digit of b is 0, then the units digit of a is 8, and 8 is not on the list. If the units digit of b is 1, the units digit of a is 7, and 7 is also not on the list. If the units digit of b is 4, the units digit of a is 4, but this is not permitted because the units digits of a and b must be different. If the units digit of b is 5, the units digit of a is 3, and 3 is not on the list. If the units digit of b is 6, the units digit of a is 2, and 2 is not on the list. If the units digit of b is 9, the units digit of a is 9, but again, the units digits of a and b must be different. It follows that the units digit of a cannot be the units digit of the square of an integer, so a cannot be the square of an integer. The answer to the question is definitively no, and Statement (1) is sufficient. Eliminate (B), (C), and (E).

Statement (2) precludes a from having 1 as its units digit, but it does nothing else, since the only relevant limitation is that the two numbers have different units digits. Statement (2) is insufficient. (A) is correct.

6. (C)

This is a Value question that asks for the value of $8x + y$. Information that allows the calculation of a single value for $8x + y$ is sufficient. Since the question asks about the value of a combination of variables, you don't necessarily need enough information to solve for each variable separately.

Each of the two statements is an equation with the same three variables. Because both statements contain the unknown z, neither statement alone is sufficient to solve for $8x + y$, so you can eliminate (A), (B), and (D).

To combine statements, first simplify the equation in Statement (2):

$$2(x + 3y) - (y + 2z) = -25$$
$$2x + 6y - y - 2z = -25$$
$$2x + 5y - 2z = -25$$

In combination, the two statements provide a system of two equations containing three variables. Since the statements provide only two equations, (E) might be tempting. However, when a question concerns solving a system of equations for an expression rather than a single variable, consider whether combining them will allow you to solve. Multiplying the equation in Statement (1) by 2 results in $6x - 4y + 2z = 20$. Now add the two equations:

$$
\begin{aligned}
6x - 4y + 2z &= 20 \\
+2x + 5y - 2z &= -25 \\
\hline
8x + y &= -5
\end{aligned}
$$

Since both statements together are enough to find a single value for $8x + y$, (C) is correct.

7. (C)

This is a Yes/No question. The question stem tells you that the variables b and c are integers between 10 and 99 inclusive and asks whether $b - c$ is a multiple of 22.

Statement (1) states that the two digits of b are the same, so the value of b must be 11, 22, 33, etc. However, there is no information about c, so Statement (1) by itself is insufficient. Eliminate (A) and (D).

Statement (2) means that $b + c$ is a multiple of 22 (since $b + c = 22x$ and x is an integer). However, the question asks about $b - c$, not $b + c$, so this statement, too, is insufficient. If you were unsure, you could plug in some number pairs to verify that $b - c$ could be a multiple of 22, but need not be. Set $b = 12$ and $c = 10$; $b + c = 22$, which is divisible by 22, but $b - c = 2$, which clearly is not divisible by 22. Now try $b = 11$ and $c = 33$: $b + c = 44$ is divisible by 22, while $b - c = -22$ is divisible by 22 as well. Eliminate **(B)**.

Now combine the statements along with the information in the question stem. Statement (1) says that both digits of b are the same, so b is a multiple of 11. Statement (2) says that $b + c$ is a multiple of 22. Since b is a multiple of 11 and $b + c$ is a multiple of 11, c must also be a multiple of 11. Because b and c are both multiples of 11, $b - c$ is also a multiple of 11. Since $b + c$ is a multiple of 22, $b + c$ is even. This means that both b and c are even or both b and c are odd. In either case, $b - c$ is even; in other words, $b - c$ is a multiple of 2. Since $b - c$ is a multiple of 11 and a multiple of 2, and the integers 2 and 11 have no common factor greater than 1, $b - c$ is a multiple of $2 \times 11 = 22$. The statements taken together are sufficient to answer the question definitively yes. **(C)** is correct.

8. (C)

This is a Value question that asks for the remainder when $x^2 - y^2$ is divided by 8. You are told that x and y are positive integers. Since $y > 8$, the minimum value of y is 9. Since $x > y + 8$, x must be greater than $9 + 8 = 17$. Thus, x is at least 18. Furthermore, you can factor the expression $x^2 - y^2$ to its equivalent $(x + y)(x - y)$.

Statement (1): Since the remainder when $x + y$ is divided by 8 is 7, you can represent $x + y$ as $8m + 7$, where m is an integer. Substituting this into the factored expression, $(8m + 7)(x - y)$ still doesn't tell you enough about $x - y$ to get a definite answer, so Statement (1) is insufficient. Eliminate **(A)** and **(D)**.

Statement (2): This time, you can substitute $8n + 5$ for $x - y$, where n is an integer, but now you don't know enough about $x + y$, so Statement (2) is also insufficient; eliminate **(B)**.

Combining statements, you can write the expression $(8m + 7)(8n + 5)$ as $64mn + 40m + 56n + 35$. Since the first three terms contain the coefficients 64, 40, and 56, respectively, and all of these are multiples of 8, and m and n are integers, each of these terms is evenly divisible by 8. Thus, the remainder resulting from dividing the expression $x^2 - y^2$ by 8 is the remainder when 35 is divided by 8, which is 3. So the statements together are sufficient, and **(C)** is correct.

9. (D)

This Yes/No question asks whether $3^{x+1} + 3(2^y) = 12v$. Using the law of exponents that states $b^a b^c = b^{a+c}$, you can rewrite 3^{x+1} as $(3^x)(3^1) = 3(3^x)$. Replace 3^{x+1} with $3(3^x)$: $3(3^x) + 3(2^y) = 12v$. Factor a 3 out to yield $3^x + 2^y = 4v$. Thus, the question is really asking, "If $x > y > 0$, does $3^x + 2^y = 4v$?"

Statement (1): Rewrite the equation $\frac{3^{2x} - 2^{2y}}{3^x - 2^y} = 4v$ to evaluate it. There is a law of exponents that says that $(b^a)^c = b^{ac}$, so $3^{2x} = (3^x)^2$ and $2^{2y} = (2^y)^2$. Therefore, it follows that $3^{2x} - 2^{2y} = (3^x)^2 - (2^y)^2$. This is one of the classic quadratics: $(3^x + 2^y)(3^x - 2^y)$. So Statement (1) can be written as $\frac{(3^x + 2^y)(3^x - 2^y)}{3^x - 2^y} = 4v$. Cancel the common factor from the numerator and denominator of the fraction to get $3^x + 2^y = 4v$. Since this answers the question you simplified in the stem, Statement (1) is sufficient. Eliminate **(B)**, **(C)**, and **(E)**.

Statement (2): Simplify the statement: $2(3^{x+2}) = 2(3^x)(3^2) = 2(3^x)(9) = 18(3^x)$ and $9(2^{y+1}) = 9(2^y)(2^1) = 18(2^y)$. Thus, the statement can be rewritten $18(3^x) + 18(2^y) = 72v$. Factor 18 out of all terms to yield $3^x + 2^y = 4v$. This answers the question, so Statement (2) is sufficient, and **(D)** is correct.

10. (B)

This is a Value question. The figure shows a right triangle whose hypotenuse is one side of a square. The question asks for the length of one of the legs of the triangle, AB.

Statement (1): The area of right triangle ABE is:

$$\frac{1}{2}(AE)(AB) = \frac{1}{2}(12)(AB) = 6(AB)$$

Since triangle ABE is a right triangle, the Pythagorean theorem says that $(BE)^2 = (AB)^2 + 12^2 = (AB)^2 + 144$. Thus, $BE = \sqrt{(AB)^2 + 144}$. The area of square $BCDE$ is: $(BE)^2 = \sqrt{(AB)^2 + 144} \times \sqrt{(AB)^2 + 144} = (AB)^2 + 144$

Since the ratio of the area of triangle ABE to the area of square $BCDE$ is $\dfrac{6}{25}$, $\dfrac{6(AB)}{(AB)^2 + 144} = \dfrac{6}{25}$. To make calculations easier, factor the 6 out of the two numerators, substitute y for AB, and then solve for y:

$$\frac{y}{y^2 + 144} = \frac{1}{25}$$
$$25y = y^2 + 144$$
$$y^2 - 25y + 144 = 0$$

Factor $y^2 - 25y + 144$: the factors are $(y - 9)(y - 16)$. So $(y - 9)(y - 16) = 0$. Thus, it is possible that the length of AB is either 9 or 16. Because more than one answer to the question is possible, Statement (1) is insufficient. Eliminate (A) and (D).

Statement (2): The perimeter of square $BCDE$ is 80, so the length of one side of the square is $\dfrac{80}{4} = 20$. Because the ratio of AE to AB is 3 to 4, right triangle ABE is a 3-4-5 right triangle. Knowing the ratios of the sides and the length of the hypotenuse, you could calculate the length of side AB. However, since this is a Data Sufficiency question, there is no need to perform the calculations. Statement (2) is sufficient. (For the record, right triangle ABE has side lengths of 12, 16, and 20. AB is the longer leg and equals 16.) (B) is correct.

11. (E)

This Value question involves a geometric sequence in which each term after the first term is r times the previous term. So if the nth term is a_n, where n is an integer and $n \geq 1$, then $a_1 = a$, $a_2 = ar$, $a_3 = ar^2$, $a_4 = ar^3$, and so on. In general, if n is an integer and $n \geq 1$, then the nth term is the product of one factor of a and $n - 1$ factors of r, or $a_n = ar^{n-1}$.

Statement (1): The sum of the first two terms is 16. Thus, $a + ar = 16$. This is one equation with two variables, and there are many possible values for a and r. Statement (1) is insufficient. Eliminate (A) and (D).

Statement (2): This statement says that $a_{18} = 81a_{14}$. You know the following:

$$a_{15} = a_{14}r$$
$$a_{16} = a_{15}r$$
$$a_{17} = a_{16}r$$
$$a_{18} = a_{17}r$$

So $a_{18} = a_{17}r = a_{16}r^2 = a_{15}r^3 = a_{14}r^4$.

Since $a_{18} = 81a_{14}$, $a_{14}r^4 = 81a_{14}$. Thus, $r^4 = 81$. Because $81 = 3^4 = (-3)^4$, $r = 3$ or $r = -3$. This statement provides two values for r and no information about a, so the fourth term cannot be calculated. Statement (2) is insufficient, so eliminate (B).

The statements taken together: From Statement (1), you know that $a + ar = 16$. From Statement (2), you know that $r = 3$ or $r = -3$.

Consider the case where $r = 3$. Substituting 3 for r into the equation $a + ar = 16$ yields $a + a(3) = 16$, $a + 3a = 16$, $4a = 16$, and $a = 4$. In this case, the fourth term is $4(3^3) = 4(27) = 108$. Now consider the case where $r = -3$. Substituting -3 for r into the equation $a + ar = 16$ yields $a + a(-3) = 16$, $a - 3a = 16$, $-2a = 16$, and $a = -8$. With these values of r and a, the fourth term is $(-8)(-3)^3 = (-8)(-27) = 216$. Because there is more than one possible answer to the question, the statements taken together are insufficient, and (E) is correct.

12. (C)

This Value question requires the probability of a single event: membership in club E. A quick glance at the statements tells you the question involves two non-mutually exclusive events: membership in club D and club E. This question is testing the formula that relates those events. Call the probability that the person selected is a member of club D as $P(D)$ and the probability that the person is a member of club E as $P(E)$. The formula that connects the two events is $P(D \text{ or } E) = P(D) + P(E) - P(D \text{ and } E)$. Information that provides either $P(E)$ or the three other terms required will be sufficient.

Statement (1) states that the probability that the person selected is not a member of either club is $\frac{1}{4}$. The probability that an event does not occur is equal to 1 minus the probability that the event does occur, so the probability that the person chosen is a member of at least one of the two clubs—that is, $P(D \text{ or } E)$—is $1 - \frac{1}{4} = \frac{3}{4}$. So $P(D) + P(E) - P(D \text{ and } E) = \frac{3}{4}$. However, without any other information about $P(D)$ or $P(D \text{ and } E)$, you cannot find $P(E)$. Statement (1) is insufficient. Eliminate **(A)** and **(D)**.

Statement (2) tells you the probability that the chosen person is a member of club D and not club E is $\frac{5}{12}$: $P(D \text{ and not } E) = \frac{5}{12}$. Since $P(D) = P(D \text{ and } E) + P(D \text{ and not } E)$, $P(D \text{ and not } E) = P(D) - P(D \text{ and } E)$. Thus, $P(D) - P(D \text{ and } E) = \frac{5}{12}$. But there is no way to find $P(E)$ from this information. Statement (2) is insufficient, and **(B)** can be eliminated.

The statements taken together provide values for three of the four terms in the original equation $P(D \text{ or } E) = P(D) + P(E) - P(D \text{ and } E)$ and are sufficient. **(C)** is correct. Statement (1) provides $P(D \text{ or } E)$ and Statement 2 provides $P(D) - P(D \text{ and } E)$.

13. (D)

This Value question asks for the population of a town in 2005 and provides the percent increases in population from 2005 to 2010 and from 2010 to 2015. Because the percent increases provide relationships among the populations in 2005, 2010, and 2015, any information that enables you to determine the actual population in any one of those years will be sufficient.

Statement (1) provides the population in 2015, and is sufficient. Eliminate **(B)**, **(C)**, and **(E)**. You do not want to do the math, especially without a calculator, but you can derive the equation $1.56(1.75)N = 2.73N = 21{,}840$, where N is the population on January 1, 2005. Then $N = \frac{21{,}840}{2.73}$. This equation produces just one value for N, so Statement (1) is sufficient.

Statement (2) provides an actual number that can be applied to the increase in the population from 2005 to 2010, and is also sufficient. **(D)** is correct. Again, setting up the math is not necessary, but for the record: The increase in

population from 2005 to 2010 can be written as $1.56N - N = 0.56N$. The increase in population from 2010 to 2015 is $2.73N - 1.56N = 1.17N$. Because the increase from 2010 to 2015 was 4,880 greater than the increase from 2005 to 2010, you can derive the equation $1.17N = 0.56N + 4{,}880$. This is one equation with one variable, so you could solve for N, which means that Statement (2) is sufficient.

14. (C)

A definite answer to this Value question requires either the values of x and z or the value of the entire expression $x - 3z$.

Statement (1) is insufficient. The equation $x + 4y = 3$ does not include the variable z. Eliminate **(A)** and **(D)**.

Statement (2) is also insufficient because the value of y is not provided, so there will be different possible values for $x - 3z$ as the value of y changes. Recall that, to calculate definite values for 3 variables, 3 equations are required. Since you have only one equation, Statement (2) is insufficient. Eliminate **(B)**.

To combine the statements, start by simplifying the left side of the equation in Statement (2). Since Statement (1) provides a value for $(x + 4y)$, see if factoring out that expression is helpful:

$$x^2 + 4xy - 3xz - 12yz = x(x + 4y) - 3z(x + 4y)$$
$$= (x + 4y)(x - 3z)$$

Statement (2) is equivalent to $(x + 4y)(x - 3z) = 24$. Statement (1) says that $x + 4y = 3$. Substitute 3 for $x + 4y$ in the equation $(x + 4y)(x - 3z) = 24$ to produce $3(x - 3z) = 24$. Dividing both sides by 3 yields $x - 3z = 8$. The statements together lead to a single possible value of 8 for $x - 3z$. **(C)** is correct.

15. (D)

This Value question asks for the perimeter of the triangle. The radius of the circle will be sufficient because sides OA and OC of triangle OAC are both radii of the circle, so $OA = OC$. Since the triangle is isosceles, $\angle OCA$ must also equal 60°. Because the three angles of a triangle must sum to 180°, the central angle is also 60°—in other words, triangle OAC is equilateral. So each of its three sides is equal to the circle's radius. Once you find the radius, you can find the perimeter of the triangle.

Statement (1) provides the difference between the lengths of the two arcs that together form the circumference of the circle. Because the measure of the central angle $\angle AOC$ is fixed, there is only one circumference that will have a long arc that is exactly 16π greater than the length of the shorter arc. You could calculate that circumference and, from there, find the radius. Statement (1) is sufficient. Eliminate **(B)**, **(C)**, and **(E)**.

Statement (2), which says that the area of triangle OAC is $36\sqrt{2}$, is also sufficient. You know the triangle is equilateral, and there is only one side length, and therefore one radius, that could yield that exact area. **(D)** is correct.

16. (B)

In order for a statement to be sufficient for this Yes/No question, it must specify the relationship between y and -18. It is not necessary to narrow down the exact value of y. Simplify the inequality given in the stem, $3x > 8y$, to get $y < \frac{3}{8}x$.

Statement (1): The possible values of x are limited by the range of this inequality, so examine the endpoints of the range. If $x > -9$, the least value that is permissible for x is -8, since x is an integer. Because y is less than $\frac{3}{8}x$, it follows that $y < -3$. Some values of y could be greater than -18, but there is no lower limit for y, so it could also be less than -18. Statement (1) is already insufficient at this point, so there is no need to evaluate the upper boundary of x and you can eliminate **(A)** and **(D)**. You could have also reached this conclusion by analyzing the upper endpoint of the range. If $x < 20$ and x is an integer, its maximum value is 19. Because y is less than $\frac{3}{8}x$ and must also be an integer, it follows that y can be at most 7, which leaves open the possibility of either yes or no answers.

Statement (2): Simplify the equation by multiplying both sides by 5 to get $5y = x - 42$. Add 42 to both sides and $x = 5y + 42$. Substitute this value for x into the inequality $3x > 8y$:

$$3(5y + 42) > 8y$$
$$15y + 126 > 8y$$
$$7y + 126 > 0$$

$$7y > -126$$
$$y > -18$$

Statement (2) is sufficient to answer definitively yes. Therefore, **(B)** is correct.

17. (A)

This Yes/No question asks if Danny collected *more* than 8 cards on Thursday. The stem is packed with information relating the numbers of cards he collected each day. In particular, the largest number of cards collected on Thursday that would result in a no answer to the question is 8. Additionally, the number of cards collected Monday, Tuesday, and Wednesday is different each day.

Statement (1) says that Danny collected 49 cards on Friday. In order for the answer to be no, the maximum numbers of cards he could collect on the other days are 5, 6, 7, and 8. Totaling up all the days, $5 + 6 + 7 + 8 + 49 = 75$. Collecting 8 cards on Thursday does not enable Danny to collect 76 cards in total given the constraints of the question, so the information in Statement (1) means that Danny must have collected more than 8 cards on Thursday. Statement (1) is sufficient to answer always yes, so eliminate **(B)**, **(C)**, and **(E)**.

Based on Statement (2), if Danny collects 6 cards on one of the first 3 days, the fewest cards he could have collected on those days would be $6 + 2 + 1 = 9$, leaving $76 - 9 = 67$ cards to be collected on Thursday and Friday. Danny could have collected 7 cards on Thursday and 60 on Friday, in which case the answer to the question is no. Alternatively, he could have collected as many as 33 cards on Thursday and 34 on Friday and the answer is yes. Therefore, Statement (2) is insufficient and **(A)** is correct.

18. (A)

This Yes/No question asks about the validity of a complicated equation, so start by simplifying the equation in the question stem. Notice that you can write all three powers with a base of 2, since $4 = 2^2$ and $16 = 2^4$. Substituting these values produces $(2^{5y})((2^2)^{120}) = (2^4)^{20x}$, which simplifies to $(2^{5y})(2^{2 \times 120}) = 2^{4 \times 20x}$, or $(2^{5y})(2^{240}) = 2^{80x}$. This, in turn, can be rewritten as $2^{5y + 240} = 2^{80x}$. Because the bases on both sides of the equation are equal, the exponents must also be equal, so $5y + 240 = 80x$. Remember that $y = x^2$, so you can substitute x^2 for y to yield $5x^2 + 240 = 80x$. Subtracting $80x$ from both sides results in $5x^2 - 80x + 240 = 0$. Divide both sides by 5 to get $x^2 - 16x + 48 = 0$. This factors to $(x - 4)(x - 12) = 0$. So $x - 4 = 0$ or $x - 12 = 0$, and $x = 4$ or $x = 12$. If a statement provides evidence that x always equals either 4 or 12, then the answer to the question is yes and the statement is sufficient. Alternatively, a statement can also be sufficient if it decisively concludes that x is neither of those values, as the answer will always be no.

Statement (1) says that $(4 - x)(12 - x) = 0$, which means that $4 - x = 0$ or $12 - x = 0$. If $4 - x = 0$, then $x = 4$. If $12 - x = 0$, then $x = 12$. Statement (1) is sufficient, as x is always either 4 or 12, meaning the answer to the question is always yes. Eliminate **(B)**, **(C)**, and **(E)**.

Statement (2) says that $(x - 4)(x - 8)(x - 24) = 0$, which means the possible values of x are 4, 8, and 24. If $x = 4$, the answer to the question is yes; if $x = 8$ or 24, the answer to the question is no. Statement (2) is thus insufficient and the correct answer is **(A)**.

19. (B)

This is a Value question. Since the question asks for the total number of students, start by rewriting the part-to-part ratio in the question stem as a part-to-whole ratio. The ratio of seniors to non-seniors is $\frac{7}{5}$, so the ratio of the number of seniors to the total number of students is $\frac{7x}{12x}$ and the ratio of the number of non-seniors to the total number of students is $\frac{5x}{12x}$. If you can find the common multiplier x, you can find the total number of students, and you have sufficiency. To find the common multiplier, you need information about either the number of seniors or the number of non-seniors.

Statement (1) gives you the ratio of the number of students who are seniors who are taking history to the number of students who are not seniors who are taking history. There is no actual number of students given, so it is not possible to find the common multiplier and Statement (1) is insufficient. Eliminate **(A)** and **(D)**.

From Statement (2), you know the proportion of seniors taking history, the proportion of non-seniors taking history, and the difference in number of students between these two groups. Of the $7x$ seniors, $\frac{3}{5}$ are taking history. In other words, $\frac{(7x)(3)}{5} = \frac{21x}{5}$ seniors are taking history. Similarly, $\frac{1}{5}$ of the $5x$ non-seniors are taking history, so $\frac{5x}{5} = x$ non-seniors are taking history. Furthermore, the number of seniors taking history is 208 greater than the number of non-seniors taking history, so you can write an equation to solve for x: $\frac{21x}{5} = x + 208$. This is a single equation in one variable, so you can stop here and declare Statement (2) to be sufficient. **(B)** is the correct answer.

20. (E)

This Yes/No question compares the value of a fraction involving two variables with 3. Since y is positive, you can multiply both sides of the given inequality by y and yield the equivalent Yes/No question "If $y > 0$, is $x < 3y$?"

To evaluate Statement (1), factor $x + y$ out of the left side of the inequality to yield the inequality $(x + y)(x - 4y) < 0$. When the product of two quantities is negative, one of the quantities must be negative and the other quantity must be positive. So either (i) $x + y < 0$ and $x - 4y > 0$, or (ii) $x + y > 0$ and $x - 4y < 0$. (Keep in mind that y is positive.)

In case (i), if $x + y < 0$, then $x < -y$. If $x - 4y > 0$, then $x > 4y$. So in case (i), $x < -y$ and $x > 4y$. Since y is positive, $x < -y$ means that x is less than $-y$, where $-y$ is a negative number. Since y is positive, $x > 4y$ means that x is greater than $4y$, where $4y$ is a positive number. So case (i) requires that x be less than the negative number $-y$ and also requires that x be greater than the positive number $4y$. This is impossible. Move on to case (ii), which is $x + y > 0$ and $x - 4y < 0$. (Again, keep in mind that $y > 0$.) If $x + y > 0$, then $x > -y$. If $x - 4y < 0$, then $x < 4y$. So this time, $x > -y$ and $x < 4y$. Since y is positive, $x > -y$ means that x is greater than the negative number $-y$. Since y is positive, $x < 4y$ means that x is less than the positive number $4y$. So case (ii), $x + y > 0$ and $x - 4y < 0$, is possible. In case (ii), you can conclude that $-y < x < 4y$. Because case (i) is impossible, Statement (1) is equivalent to $-y < x < 4y$. Since y is positive,

$3y < 4y$. You know that $x < 4y$. However, you do not know whether $x < 3y$. More than one answer to the question is possible, so Statement (1) is insufficient. Eliminate (A) and (D).

Statement (2): Simplify the inequality $5(y + 8) < 20y - 3x + 40$.

$$5(y + 8) < 20y - 3x + 40$$
$$5y + 40 < 20y - 3x + 40$$
$$5y < 20y - 3x$$
$$3x < 15y$$
$$x < 5y$$

Statement (2) is equivalent to $x < 5y$. Since y is positive, $3y < 5y$. You know that $x < 5y$. However, you do not know whether $x < 3y$. Statement (2) is insufficient. Eliminate (B).

The statements taken together: Statement (1) is equivalent to $-y < x < 4y$, and Statement (2) is equivalent to $x < 5y$. Because the question requires that y is positive, any x that satisfies the inequality $-y < x < 4y$ must also satisfy the inequality $x < 5y$. Therefore, the statements taken together require that $-y < x < 4y$, which you have already determined to be insufficient. Therefore, (E) is correct.

PART FOUR

GMAT VERBAL REASONING: STRATEGIES, CONTENT, AND PRACTICE

CHAPTER 13

VERBAL REASONING STRATEGY: CRITICAL REASONING QUESTIONS

LEARNING OBJECTIVES

- Describe the format and content of Critical Reasoning questions
- Apply the steps of the Kaplan Method for Critical Reasoning
- Apply various strategic approaches to answer Critical Reasoning questions
- Recognize how the four Core Competencies apply to Critical Reasoning questions

---

You'll see about 10 Critical Reasoning questions among the 36 questions in the Verbal Reasoning section. In order to leave enough time to answer the other 26 questions, you should plan to spend about 2 minutes on each Critical Reasoning question. The Kaplan Method for Critical Reasoning will help you move through these questions confidently and efficiently.

Each question consists of a short paragraph, called the stimulus, and a question stem, which asks you something about the information in the stimulus. There will be five answer choices.

The directions for Critical Reasoning questions are concise. They look like this:

Directions: Select the best of the answer choices given.

As we do throughout this book, we refer to the five answer choices by the letters **(A)**, **(B)**, **(C)**, **(D)**, and **(E)**. As the directions above indicate, you need to select one of the five. Even though the directions tell you to find the "best" answer choice, that doesn't mean there will be a second-best. There won't be a situation where two choices both answer the question and you have to decide which one is better. One answer choice is correct, and the other four are incorrect for demonstrable reasons. This means that you can select the correct answer by identifying it out of the lineup or, equally well, by eliminating the four wrong choices.

Critical Reasoning tests the reasoning skills involved in making arguments, evaluating arguments, and formulating or evaluating a plan of action. No outside knowledge is needed to answer any of these questions; instead, you'll use your reasoning skills to evaluate the information presented to you. Specifically, you will be measured on your ability to do the following:

- **Understand an argument's construction:** Recognize the basic structure of an argument, properly drawn conclusions, underlying assumptions, explanatory hypotheses, or parallels between structurally similar arguments.

- **Evaluate the argument:** Analyze an argument, recognize elements that would strengthen or weaken it, and identify reasoning errors or aspects of the argument's development.

- **Formulate and evaluate a plan of action:** Recognize the relative appropriateness, effectiveness, and efficiency of different plans of action, as well as factors that would strengthen or weaken a proposed plan of action.

Because the analytical task you must perform varies from one Critical Reasoning question to another, learning to identify exactly what the question is asking for is key to success. The first step of the Kaplan Method has you do just that.

The Kaplan Method for Critical Reasoning

Kaplan has studied the approaches of test takers who do well on these questions and distilled their process into a simple four-step Method for Critical Reasoning that anyone can use.

THE KAPLAN METHOD FOR CRITICAL REASONING

- Identify the question type.
- Untangle the stimulus.
- Predict the answer.
- Evaluate the choices.

Step 1: Identify the Question Type

Reading the question stem first is the best way to focus your reading of the stimulus. Determine the question type, and you'll know exactly what you're looking for. The next chapter is devoted to a thorough analysis of each type of Critical Reasoning question, including practice questions for each type. There may be other important information in the question stem as well—possibly the conclusion of the argument or a particular aspect of the stimulus that you will need to focus on.

This step also helps you answer the question that's actually being asked. One of the most disheartening experiences in Critical Reasoning is to understand the author's argument fully but then supply an answer to a question that wasn't asked. For instance, when you're asked to strengthen or weaken an argument, there will almost certainly be a choice that does the opposite of what's asked. Choosing such a wrong choice is less a matter of failing to understand the argument than of failing to remember the task at hand.

Step 2: Untangle the Stimulus

With the question stem in mind, read the stimulus actively, paraphrasing to make sure you understand the construction of the stimulus and hunting for any potential problems. Most Critical Reasoning stimuli contain arguments, but many will not. Depending on the type of question that you identified in step 1, you will look to gather different information from the stimulus.

Step 3: Predict the Answer

Form an idea of what the correct answer should say or do. You must approach the answer choices with at least some idea of what the answer should look like; otherwise, you won't know what you're looking for, and you'll find that some wrong choices seem appealing.

How you form your prediction will vary depending on the question type. For some question types, it can be difficult to form a specific prediction of what the correct answer choice will say, but based on your analysis in steps 1 and 2, you will always know at least what function the correct answer will accomplish. You'll learn more about how to predict answers for different question types in the next chapter.

Step 4: Evaluate the Choices

Attack each answer choice critically. Keep your prediction in mind and see whether the answer choice matches it. If you don't find a "clear winner" among the five choices, read through the ones that you haven't eliminated yet. You know what you *like* about each; now focus on what might be *wrong*.

While evaluating the potential answers, focus on the scope of the stimulus. Most of the wrong choices are wrong because they are irrelevant to the argument's conclusion or, in the case of Inference questions, are unsupported by the stimulus. In other words, the wrong answer choices contain elements that don't match the author's ideas or that go beyond the context provided. However, don't jump to eliminate an answer choice simply because it introduces a new term into discussion. A common error is to think that scope is purely about terminology. It's much more about the relationship of the ideas in the answer choice to the ideas in the stimulus. If your choice contains the right idea, the answer is relevant, regardless of how it's worded. This fact reinforces the importance of using your paraphrasing skills to clearly grasp how the ideas in a stimulus relate to one another.

Applying the Kaplan Method

Following is a typical Critical Reasoning question. Work through the question, trying to apply the Kaplan Method. As you answer the question, think about how you can use what you've learned so far, but also what you still need to learn to approach these kinds of questions. Following the question is an explanation that models how a GMAT expert would use the Kaplan Method and an understanding of argument construction to answer it.

A study of 20 overweight males showed that each study participant experienced significant weight loss after adding SlimDown, an artificial food supplement, to his daily diet. For three months, each participant consumed one SlimDown portion every morning after exercising and then followed his normal diet for the rest of the day. Clearly, all adult males who consume one portion of SlimDown every day for at least three months will lose weight.

Which one of the following is an assumption on which the argument depends?

- ○ The study participants will gain back the weight they lost if they discontinue the SlimDown program.
- ○ No other dietary supplement will have the same effect on overweight males.
- ○ The daily exercise regimen was not responsible for the effects noted in the study.
- ○ Females will not experience similar weight reductions if they adhere to the SlimDown program for three months.
- ○ Overweight males will achieve only partial weight loss if they do not remain on the SlimDown program for a full three months.

Step 1: Identify the Question Type

The mention of an "assumption" in this question stem indicates that the argument in the stimulus is missing a link in the chain of reasoning—some piece of support that the author takes for granted without which the conclusion wouldn't be valid. You will now turn to the stimulus, ready to find that link.

Step 2: Untangle the Stimulus

Sentence 1 introduces a study of 20 males who used a certain food supplement. All 20 lost weight. Sentence 2 describes how they used it: once a day, for three months, after morning exercise. The key word *clearly* usually indicates that a conclusion follows, and that's the case here: in sentence 3, the author predicts that any adult male who has one portion of the product daily for three months will lose weight, too.

Read strategically, looking for shifts between the terms of the evidence and those of the conclusion. What happened to the exercise? It's in the evidence as part of the study regimen but is absent from the conclusion.

You could also look at the argument more abstractly:

A bunch of guys did *A* and *B* and had *X* result. So if another guy does *A*, he'll get *X* result, too.

The argument implies that there could only be one cause for a certain effect even though other causes might, in reality, be possible. This kind of sloppy thinking about causality is a common GMAT pattern that you can use to help form your prediction.

Step 3: Predict the Answer

Because exercise was part of the study but the conclusion doesn't mention exercise, predict something like *The author assumes exercise doesn't matter.*

Step 4: Evaluate the Choices

Judge the answer choices based on how well they fulfill the requirements of your prediction. Only **(C)** even mentions the exercise regimen. Indeed **(C)**, though expressed in different words than your prediction, expresses exactly the same idea. The author indeed assumes that the exercise did not cause the weight loss.

(A) is incorrect because it focuses on what happens if someone stops taking SlimDown, which is irrelevant to whether taking it will lead to weight loss. Similarly, **(B)** is incorrect because the efficacy of other supplements says nothing about whether SlimDown is effective. **(D)** and **(E)** don't help fill in the gap in the argument either; the fact that SlimDown isn't fully effective in certain circumstances doesn't support the idea that it would be effective for men whether or not they exercise.

CONCEPT CHECK

- When tackling a Critical Reasoning problem, what should you read first?

  _____

- Why is step 1—identify the question type—important to success in Critical Reasoning?

  _____

- Before you evaluate the answer choices, you should always _____.

Example answers are in your book's online resources (**kaptest.com/login**).

Next, you'll find in-format Critical Reasoning questions so you can practice using the Kaplan Method.

Practice Set: The Kaplan Method for Critical Reasoning

(Answers and explanations are at the end of the chapter.)

1. Residents of Cordoba County who receive unemployment benefits are allowed to attend courses on job search skills at the local community college at no charge. In addition, the unemployment benefits office offers free assistance with résumé writing. Many retail employees were recently laid off due to the closure of five Boxia Stores locations. Of the affected employees, those who live in Cordoba County will certainly not rely solely on their own resources as they look for new jobs.

    Which of the following is an assumption that is required for the conclusion of the argument?

    O   If an unemployed worker has access to job search resources, the worker will take advantage of those resources.

    O   Retail employees have more difficulty finding new jobs after being laid off than do workers in other occupations.

    O   In Cordoba County, the usual cost for job search skills courses and résumé writing assistance is too great for most people to afford.

    O   When it closed several locations, Boxia Stores laid off some employees who will have difficulty finding new employment if they do not receive assistance.

    O   The job search skills courses at the local community college and the résumé-writing assistance offered at the unemployment benefits office are usually helpful for individuals seeking employment.

2. A business owner noticed that many of her employees exhibited signs of fatigue throughout the workday. To combat this, the business owner has partnered with a local gym to offer employees a discounted rate on annual memberships. The business owner is confident this program will help to lessen employee fatigue, as studies have shown that people who exercise regularly have higher energy levels than people who do not.

    Which of the following, if true, would most seriously call into question the claim that the business owner's plan will reduce fatigue?

    O   Making minor changes to one's diet can boost energy as effectively as can regular exercise.

    O   The discount offered is so small that most employees will not be encouraged to purchase an annual membership.

    O   Employees with higher energy levels are not necessarily more productive at work.

    O   The local gym would have to offer more classes to accommodate the increase in membership.

    O   There is no way to eliminate fatigue altogether.

3. Last month, a group of salespeople from a software firm attended a seminar on persuasive speaking. In the weeks following the seminar, the salespeople who attended the seminar have made more sales, on average, than those who did not attend the seminar. To increase sales, the sales manager plans to send the remaining salespeople to the same seminar next month.

    Which of the following, if true, would most support the prediction that the sales manager's plan will achieve its goal?

    ○   Last month's seminar focused solely on tactics relevant to the work at the particular company.

    ○   Total company sales last month were higher than sales from the month prior to the seminar.

    ○   To prepare for the seminar, the attending salespeople read a book on improving communication skills.

    ○   Over the last month, the company's sales were greater than the sales of its largest competitor.

    ○   Invitations to last month's seminar were not accepted solely by salespeople with above-average sales.

4. Some scientists are researching how to manipulate viruses so as to be useful in nanotechnology applications, particularly in the human body. Since viruses do not engage in metabolic activity to survive and reproduce, they may be durable building blocks for composite materials. Viruses can be altered to serve human purposes through two approaches, chemical modification and genetic engineering. To make a virus into an effective nanotechnological structure, it is necessary to determine how to attach biological interfaces to the surface of the virus's protein coat.

    The discussion above most strongly supports which of the following statements?

    ○   Research into nanotechnology is likely to produce useful applications in the human body.

    ○   Viruses are the best choice to make composite materials on a nanotechnological scale.

    ○   The protein coats of viruses naturally lack biological interfaces.

    ○   Composite materials are of interest primarily due to their potential uses in the human body.

    ○   For their research to be successful, scientists must figure out how to make attachments to the protein coats of viruses.

Step 2: Untangle the Stimulus—A Deep Dive

LEARNING OBJECTIVES

- Draw upon strategic reading skills in order to pay attention to the right details in the stimulus
- Distinguish an argument's evidence from its conclusion
- Predict potential problems with an argument

Untangling the stimulus is a key step in Kaplan's Method for Critical Reasoning. After all, you can't answer a question about the stimulus if you don't know what it says.

Read Strategically

Strategic reading means reading not so much for facts but rather for structure and for the author's point of view. On Critical Reasoning questions, this means using key words to identify the parts of the stimulus that are relevant to answering the question that you read in step 1 and paraphrasing the main ideas.

Is There an Argument?

The first thing you need to determine is whether a stimulus contains an argument. If there is an argument, you'll need to understand its structure, which you'll learn about next. The stimuli for certain question types, such as Explain, Inference, and even Strengthen/Weaken (an argument), may not contain arguments at all. In that case, use your strategic reading skills and knowledge of the question type (you'll learn more about question types in the next chapter) to analyze the stimulus.

For instance, an Explain question will present you with two seemingly contradictory facts, so you'll need to first identify those facts and then think about how both could be true.

The stimulus for an Inference question will likely contain a series of facts with no conclusion; as you read the stimulus, you'll need to think about how the given facts relate to each other and what else must be true based on those facts.

If the stimulus for a Strengthen or Weaken question offers a claim, such as *We should enact Plan X*, but offers no evidence for the claim, you'll need to think about what sort of information would support or undermine the notion that Plan X is a good idea.

Understand the Structure of an Argument

An argument is an author's attempt to convince you of a point. Every GMAT argument is made up of two basic parts:

1. The **conclusion** (the point that the author is trying to make)
2. The **evidence** (the support that the author offers for the conclusion)

Success on argument-based questions hinges on your ability to identify the parts of the argument. There is no general rule about where the conclusion and evidence appear in the argument. The conclusion could be first, followed by the evidence, or it could be the other way around. Or the author could provide some evidence, draw a conclusion, and then provide more evidence for that conclusion. Sometimes the conclusion will even be expressed in the question stem rather than in the stimulus. Consider the following stimulus:

> The Brookdale Public Library will require extensive physical rehabilitation to meet the new building codes passed by the town council. For one thing, the electrical system is inadequate, causing the lights to flicker sporadically. Furthermore, there are too few emergency exits, and those few that exist are poorly marked and sometimes locked.

Suppose that the author of this argument was allowed only one sentence to convey her meaning. If she made the following statement, would she feel satisfied that her main point had been communicated?

> The electrical system [at the Brookdale Public Library] is inadequate, causing the lights to flicker sporadically.

No. Given a single opportunity, she would state the first sentence to convey her real purpose:

> The Brookdale Public Library will require extensive physical rehabilitation . . .

That is the conclusion. If you pressed the author to state her reasons for making that statement, she would then cite the electrical and structural problems with the building. That is the evidence for her conclusion.

But does that mean that a statement like "The electrical system is inadequate" can't be a conclusion? Not necessarily—it's just not the conclusion in this argument. Every idea must be evaluated in the context of the stimulus in which it appears.

Consider this stimulus:

> The electrical wiring at the Brookdale Public Library was installed more than 40 years ago and appears to be corroded in some places [evidence]. An electrician, upon inspection of the system, found a few frayed wires as well as some blown fuses [evidence]. Clearly, the electrical system at the Brookdale Public Library is inadequate [conclusion].

In this argument, the inadequacy of the electrical system is now the author's point, which she supports with evidence.

To succeed in Critical Reasoning, you'll have to be able to determine the function of every sentence. The easiest way to do this is to pick up on logical **key words** to identify conclusion and evidence. Not every Critical Reasoning stimulus will include these key words, but most do. Using them to identify the conclusion and evidence will increase your ability to get the right answer and do so quickly.

- **Evidence key words** include *because*, *for*, *since*, *as a result of*, and *due to*.
- **Conclusion key words** include *therefore*, *hence*, *thus*, *so*, *clearly*, and *consequently*.

Notice, for example, how the "[c]learly" in the argument above provides a strong signal that the last sentence is the conclusion.

Finally, take a look at a way a question might be formatted to put the conclusion in the question stem:

> The electrical wiring at the Brookdale Public Library was installed more than 40 years ago and appears to be corroded in some places [evidence]. An electrician, upon inspection of the system, found a few frayed wires as well as some blown fuses [evidence].
>
> Which of the following, if true, provides the strongest support for a prediction that Brookdale Public Library will replace its electrical system [conclusion]?

The author could have ended the stimulus with the sentence *Therefore, the Brookdale Public Library is likely to replace its electrical system.* Instead, this conclusion, a prediction based on the evidence about the dilapidated state of the wiring and fuses, appears in the question stem. A conclusion that you find in the question stem plays the same role in the argument as a conclusion you find in the stimulus.

Paraphrase the Argument

If you can paraphrase an argument, you must understand the argument well enough to break down potentially complex language into simpler terms. And with that level of understanding, the question becomes much more manageable. Therefore, always paraphrase the author's argument to yourself after reading the stimulus and before proceeding to make a prediction in step 3.

In the first library argument, for instance, there's no advantage to grappling with the full complexity of the author's stated conclusion:

> The Brookdale Public Library will require extensive physical rehabilitation to meet the new building codes passed by the town council.

Instead, paraphrase to reduce this to simpler language and a simpler point: *the library will need fixing up to meet the new codes.*

Similarly, the evidence is pretty bulky:

> For one thing, the electrical system is inadequate, causing the lights to flicker sporadically. Furthermore, there are too few emergency exits, and those few that exist are poorly marked and sometimes locked.

You could paraphrase it like this: *the library's electrical system is bad, and the emergency exits are too few, hard to find, and locked.*

So the whole argument might be said simply as follows: *the library's electrical system is bad, and the emergency exits are too few, hard to find, and locked. Therefore, the library will need fixing up to meet the new codes.*

Often, by the time you begin reading through the answer choices, you run the risk of losing sight of the gist of the stimulus. So restating the argument in your own words will not only help you get the author's point in the first place but also help you hold on to it until you've found the correct answer. Keep in mind that it's the *meaning* of the answer choices that matters. Since Critical Reasoning questions hinge on logic, you will be better able to choose the correct answer if you have paraphrased the ideas in the stimulus; doing so will keep you from overlooking a correct choice that doesn't use the exact wording you might expect.

Hunt for Potential Problems with the Argument

You must read actively, not passively, throughout the GMAT, and Critical Reasoning questions are no exception. Active readers are always attacking the passage, analyzing the text, and forming reactions as they go along. Instead of accepting an argument at face value, they look for potential problems. Active reading will pay huge dividends on Critical Reasoning questions.

The source of nearly every problem in an argument-based Critical Reasoning question is the author's assumption. An assumption is a gap between the evidence and conclusion: something that is unstated but that must be true in order for the conclusion to logically follow from the evidence. The assumption can often be spotted by looking for a shift in scope such that there are mismatched concepts in the evidence and the conclusion. In other words, the conclusion introduces a concept that doesn't exist in the evidence.

Consider the argument about the library again. Seems pretty reasonable at first glance—good lighting and working emergency exits are pretty important for a public building. But the critical reader might think, "Wait a second—the conclusion mentions building codes, but that wasn't mentioned in the evidence. Do the codes apply to flickering lights?"

You'll learn more about how to spot assumptions in the next chapter, which will teach you how to tackle Assumption questions as well as their close cousins, Strengthen and Weaken questions and Evaluate questions.

Reading the stimulus right the first time—with a critical eye and an active mind—will allow you to read it once and move on to the answer choices, staying on pace, getting questions right, and earning a high score.

CONCEPT CHECK

- Why is paraphrasing the stimulus important?

  _____

- What are the two key parts of an argument?

  _____

- What is an assumption?

  _____

- What is meant by "There is a shift in scope between evidence and conclusion"?

  _____

Example answers are in your book's online resources (**kaptest.com/login**).

Common Argument Patterns

The arguments in Critical Reasoning stimuli often follow patterns. When you understand the kind of argument an author is making, you can anticipate what kind of assumptions he is likely to make. Thus, recognizing common argument structures will allow you to analyze stimuli more efficiently, zeroing in on the author's central assumption with speed and accuracy.

Causal Arguments

A causal argument is an assertion that a certain cause produced a certain effect. In other words, X caused Y, X made Y happen, or Y is the result of X. The author's assertion of causality may be explicit (e.g., "The drought led to large-scale crop failures," or "The new city plan is responsible for these underdeveloped downtown blocks") or implicit (e.g., "Since the introduction of the new radiator design, Brand X cars have seen an 8 percent increase in incidents of overheating. Customer dissatisfaction will remain high until we announce a redesign"). Examine the following example of a conclusion that contains a claim of causality:

> Married people have been shown in several important studies to have higher levels of happiness than single people. Therefore, marriage causes happiness.

This argument draws its validity from a stated cause-effect relationship (namely, that marriage causes happiness). A conclusion that *X* caused *Y* relies on certain assumptions: (1) that nothing else—*A*, *B*, *C*, etc.—could have caused *Y*; (2) that *Y* was not the cause of *X*; and (3) that the apparent relationship between *X* and *Y* wasn't just a coincidence. An author who makes any of these assumptions may be confusing correlation and causation.

Causal conclusions often appear in the stimuli of Weaken questions. There are three ways to weaken causal arguments based on the assumptions listed above. Here's the causal argument just introduced:

"Marriage causes happiness."

X = cause (marriage); *Y* = effect (happiness)

Now consider the three ways this argument might be weakened:

Alternative explanation: It wasn't *X* that caused *Y*; it was actually *Z* that caused *Y*.

"Marriage doesn't cause happiness. In fact, financial security (which correlates strongly with marriage) was the real cause of the happiness reported in the surveys."

Causality reversed: It wasn't *X* that caused *Y*; it was actually *Y* that caused *X*.

"Marriage doesn't cause happiness. In fact, people who are already happy are significantly more likely to marry."

Coincidence: It wasn't *X* that caused *Y*; any correlation between *X* and *Y* is a coincidence, since they have no direct relationship.

"Marriage doesn't cause happiness. Other studies that looked at the same group of people over time found that people reported similar levels of happiness before and after getting married. Any seeming correlation between marriage and happiness is coincidental or based on other factors."

When you are asked a Weaken question about a causal argument, you won't be able to predict which of these three alternatives will show up in the correct answer choice, so just predict more generally that the correct answer will follow one of these three patterns.

When you are asked a Strengthen question about a causal argument, predict that the correct answer will either remove one of these alternate explanations from consideration or that it will directly support the causal relationship with further evidence.

CONCEPT CHECK

- Describe what is meant by a "causal argument."

  _____

- What three possibilities should you consider when a GMAT argument uses evidence of a correlation to support a conclusion of causation ($X \to Y$)?

  _____

Example answers are in your book's online resources (**kaptest.com/login**).

See how a GMAT expert uses the Kaplan Method to answer a Critical Reasoning question involving causality.

> For the past year, a network television talk-show host has been making fun of the name of a particular brand of chainsaw, the Tree Toppler. The ridicule is obviously taking its toll: in the past 12 months, sales of the Tree Toppler have declined by 15 percent, while the sales of other chainsaws have increased.
>
> Which of the following, if true, casts the most serious doubt on the conclusion drawn above?
>
> O   The talk-show host who is ridiculing the Tree Toppler name actually owns a Tree Toppler.
>
> O   The number of product complaints from owners of the Tree Toppler has not increased in the past year.
>
> O   The average price of all chainsaws has increased by 10 percent in the past year.
>
> O   The number of stores that sell the Tree Toppler has remained steady for the past year.
>
> O   A year ago, a leading consumer magazine rated the Tree Toppler as "intolerably unsafe."

Step 1: Identify the Question Type

Because this stem asks you to "cast doubt" on the conclusion, this is a Weaken question.

Step 2: Untangle the Stimulus

For the last year, a talk-show host has been ridiculing Tree Toppler chainsaws. Over that time, Tree Toppler sales have fallen while other chainsaws' sales have risen. The author concludes that the talk-show host's jokes must have caused the declining Tree Toppler sales.

Step 3: Predict the Answer

To weaken an argument in which X is claimed to have caused Y, consider whether Y might actually have caused X (i.e., reversal) or whether something else might have caused Y (i.e., alternative cause). In this case, it seems unlikely that the decline in sales caused the on-air ridicule; the host is making fun of the chainsaw's name, not its declining sales. Therefore, the correct answer to this Weaken question will probably offer some alternative explanation for the decline in Tree Toppler sales.

Step 4: Evaluate the Choices

(E) provides that alternative explanation. If a prominent magazine rates a chainsaw as unsafe, that could certainly deter people from purchasing it, and a subsequent decline in sales would be reasonable to expect. **(E)** matches the prediction and is the correct answer.

If you hadn't immediately recognized **(E)** as a match for your prediction, you could still find the right answer by eliminating choices that miss the mark. Whether or not the talk-show host actually owns a Tree Toppler, as **(A)** says, the decline in sales could be caused by the host's on-air ridicule; **(A)** is irrelevant. **(B)** actually strengthens the argument by eliminating a potential alternative explanation for the decline in sales. **(C)** might be tempting, but the argument mentions that sales of other chainsaws have increased, so an increase in the purchase price of *all* chainsaws is not a reasonable alternative explanation. **(D)** also strengthens the argument by eliminating another alternative explanation for the decline in sales (that fewer stores are carrying the Tree Toppler).

Note that relevant alternative explanations for a causal relationship may, at first glance, appear to have no bearing on the argument. But this is precisely because the author failed to recognize that there was an alternative possibility. Focus on the *effect* each answer choice has on the alleged causal relationship. By weakening the causal relationship, the correct answer choice will undermine the logic of the argument.

Representativeness

When GMAT arguments include evidence in the form of surveys, studies, polls, anecdotes, or experiments, a key issue is often the representativeness of the group used as evidence. You may be familiar with the idea of representativeness from a statistics or research methods class. This concept is no different on the GMAT. To be representative, a sample must be large enough, the observations must have been taken over an adequate amount of time, and the population in the evidence cannot be different from the population in the conclusion in some relevant way.

The author of an argument that depends on evidence from a sample group is always assuming that sample is representative. Therefore, if you're asked a question about the author's assumption and notice that the stimulus uses the results of a study, survey, poll, experiment, etc., you can predict that the correct answer will say something to the effect that "the sample was representative."

If you are asked to weaken an argument based on an assumption of representativeness, look for a choice that describes differences between the populations in the evidence and conclusion or that indicates a methodological flaw that casts doubt on the reliability of the data. If you are asked to strengthen such an argument, look for the opposite—a relevant similarity between the populations or an indication of methodological soundness—or simply additional evidence that supports the author's conclusion.

CONCEPT CHECK

- What features would make a sample representative?

_____

An example answer is in your book's online resources (**kaptest.com/login**).

Try using the Kaplan Method for Critical Reasoning to answer a question about an argument based on an assumption of representativeness.

> Candidate A was widely believed to be the favorite in her state's gubernatorial race. Candidate B, the incumbent governor, had figured prominently in a corruption scandal during the previous year. Although he was ultimately never charged with a crime, Candidate B received very negative coverage in local and national media. A poll of registered voters in the state showed that a majority supported Candidate A and would vote for her. In fact, election day exit polls of those who voted showed that most had voted for Candidate A, so she was expected to win. However, once the votes were counted, Candidate B was shown to have won a narrow victory. Clearly, respondents to the polls were not being honest when they claimed to have supported Candidate A.

> The argument above depends on which of the following assumptions?

> ○ It is difficult to predict the degree to which an incumbent candidate's support will be affected by negative media coverage.

> ○ The negative media coverage made supporters of Candidate B reluctant to express their views in public, and so they claimed to support Candidate A when they actually had voted for Candidate B.

> ○ No voter ever changes his or her mind about whom to vote for.

> ○ Candidate B successfully used the fact that he had not been charged with a crime to restore his good image with the voting public.

> ○ The sample of voters surveyed in the exit poll was representative of those who voted in the election.

Step 1: Identify the Question Type

This question directs you to find an assumption on which the argument depends, so this is an Assumption question.

Step 2: Untangle the Stimulus

The argument concludes that respondents to recent election exit polls and preelection polls were not being honest when they claimed to have supported Candidate A for governor. The evidence is that despite a strong showing in these polls, Candidate A still lost the election.

Step 3: Predict the Answer

This conclusion is based in part on the results of two polls, so those polls need to have been conducted with representative samples in order for the conclusion to be valid. After all, what if the polls had both been conducted outside campaign rallies for Candidate A or in Candidate A's hometown? The sample group for the polls needs to be an adequate cross section of the voting population, and since this argument stakes its conclusion on the polls, the author of the argument must be assuming that the sample is indeed representative.

Step 4: Evaluate the Choices

(E) matches the prediction and is the correct answer. If you used the Denial Test (explained in the lesson on Assumption questions in the next chapter) to negate **(E)**, by stating that the poll's sample group was *not* representative, then the author's conclusion that voters must have lied can no longer be valid. If the people who participated in the polls were not representative of the larger voting population, then there would be no particular reason to expect the poll and voting results to be similar.

(A) is not necessary to the argument because the author doesn't base the conclusion on a prediction drawn from the press coverage. Rather, the author bases the conclusion on a prediction drawn from the polling data. **(B)**, if true, would strengthen the argument, but this isn't a Strengthen question; the correct answer to an Assumption question must be something upon which the argument relies. While the argument asserts that people polled lied about whom they voted for, it does not depend on any particular reason why they did so. **(C)** is extreme; the argument's point that the polls' respondents lied is not undone if one or two people simply changed their minds. As for **(D)**, the author doesn't necessarily assume anything about *how* Candidate B was able to eke out a victory.

Plans, Proposals, and Predictions

Once you start identifying plans, proposals, and predictions in Critical Reasoning stimuli, you'll realize that many arguments contain conclusions in these forms. All three have a future orientation and indicate the author's opinion.

Plans and **proposals** are found in conclusions that begin, "Thus, we should . . . "or "It's in the company's best interest to . . . " When a conclusion takes the form of a plan or proposal, the author is likely assuming that the plan or proposal is helpful and practical under the current circumstances. GMAT questions often test whether you realize that the idea may not be helpful or currently practical.

Critical Reasoning stimuli involving plans or proposals generally offer only one reason for the plan or proposal. In other words, "Because of X, we should do Y." Thus, the author of such an argument assumes that the cited reason is the only, or at least the most important, factor to consider. Any answer that introduces an alternative consideration weakens the argument. Any answer that rules out a possible alternative consideration strengthens it.

Think about how you might weaken the following proposal:

> Sam often oversleeps because he reaches over and turns off the alarm before he's fully awake.
> To fix this problem, Sam proposes buying a second alarm clock.

Sam's proposal is inherently flawed because it fails to consider some important factors: Sam might put the second clock right next to the first one and just shut it off, too. Alternatively, Sam might have to plug the second clock in too far from his bed. Then he won't hear it, so it won't be of any help. The point is that there are other factors that Sam should take into account before concluding that an additional alarm clock will work.

There may not be any evidence at all; the author may simply state that the plan will lead to a certain outcome. For example, the stimulus might just contain a proposal that can be paraphrased as "X will lead to increased profits." Even though there's no evidence given to support this outcome, the author is making the general assumption that conditions exist that are conducive to success of the plan. The problem is not that the author is unreasonable in claiming that proposal X would increase profits—it might, in fact, do so. However, the proposal could be weakened by evidence that could undermine its chance of success; for instance, while X may lead to increased revenue, it may also increase costs.

Predictions are no different in Critical Reasoning questions than in real life. They use the future tense: "So-and-so will win the Oscar," "The economy will show modest growth," or "We will not be able to meet the production deadline." No one can travel through time and find evidence in the future, so just like everyone else, GMAT authors base their predictions on past and current trends or situations. To weaken such a conclusion, find an answer choice that says conditions will change. To strengthen it, look for a choice that says, "Future events will unfold as expected."

CONCEPT CHECK

- Any answer that introduces an alternative and competing consideration _____ a plan or proposal. Any answer that rules out a possible alternative consideration _____ it.

- How can you weaken an argument whose conclusion is a plan or proposal?

  _____

- How can you weaken an argument whose conclusion is a prediction?

  _____

Example answers are in your book's online resources (**kaptest.com/login**).

See how the Kaplan Method for Critical Reasoning is used to answer a question about a proposal.

A team of researchers at a university hospital has developed a chemical test that detects breast tumors in the early stages of development. In order to save lives, the researchers want to make the test a routine part of examinations at the hospital. However, a spokesperson for the hospital argued that because virtually all breast tumors are detectable by self-examination, the chemical test would have little impact on the breast cancer death rate and thus should not be implemented.

Which of the following, if true, would most seriously weaken the hospital spokesperson's argument?

○ Fatal breast tumors are often not revealed by self-examination until it is too late for effective treatment.

○ Breast tumors are usually discovered at an earlier stage of development than are lung tumors.

○ Mammograms are currently in wide use as a breast cancer test and cost much less than the chemical test.

○ Because breast cancer affects only a small proportion of the population, the new test would be of no benefit to most people.

○ Most people learn how to check for signs of breast cancer from magazines and not from doctors.

Step 1: Identify the Question Type

The words "would most seriously weaken" in the question stem tell you that this is a Weaken question; additionally, the stem directs you specifically to weaken the hospital spokesperson's argument.

Step 2: Untangle the Stimulus

The spokesperson's proposal is that the new chemical test, which detects tumors in their early stages, would have little impact on the breast cancer death rate, so it should not be used. The evidence, signaled by the word "because," is that virtually all breast tumors are detectable by self-examination. So, the spokesperson is assuming that it doesn't matter whether a tumor is detected by self-examination or by the new test, and that there are no other considerations that would affect the outcomes of this proposal.

Step 3: Predict the Answer

The correct answer will weaken the argument by suggesting some advantage of the new test that would result in a greater impact on the breast cancer death rate than the spokesperson imagines.

Step 4: Evaluate the Choices

(A) matches the prediction and is correct. Self-examination may be able to detect almost all tumors, but if it doesn't detect some of them until it is too late, then the new test, which detects tumors in their early stages, might indeed impact the breast cancer death rate.

(B) makes an irrelevant comparison between breast tumors and lung tumors. The argument is solely about breast tumors. **(C)** is also irrelevant because it brings up a third diagnostic tool and focuses on the costs of the tests. The argument is about the chemical test versus self-examination and is only concerned with the death rate, not costs. **(D)** is irrelevant because it doesn't address whether the new test would impact the death rate of those who *do* get breast cancer. **(E)** has no bearing on the argument, which is about the effect of the new test on the current breast cancer death rate. Even if the way people learn to do self-examination affected the accuracy of the examination (something this choice doesn't even suggest), that would already be reflected in the current death rate.

The Four Core Competencies and Critical Reasoning

Critical Reasoning tests the same four Core Competencies that show up throughout the test.

Critical Thinking

As you read a Critical Reasoning stimulus, you'll use Critical Thinking skills to ask questions about what the author is saying. If an argument is not being made, what facts are offered that are important to the question? If an argument is being made, what evidence is given to support the conclusion, and what gaps has the author left? Answering these questions will help you analyze the argument and efficiently move through the answer choices.

Paraphrasing

Frequently, the authors in Critical Reasoning say pretty simple things in complex ways. If you can't accurately paraphrase a Critical Reasoning stimulus to express it in simpler language in your head, you probably don't understand it well enough to be sure of answering the question about it. In addition to helping you understand the argument, paraphrasing will make it easier to stay focused on the central ideas as you evaluate the answer choices.

Attention to the Right Detail

There can be several details in a Critical Reasoning stimulus, and it can be challenging to keep track of how they relate to each other. You'll need to focus on the details that will distinguish between correct and incorrect choices. Pay attention to the language the author uses to introduce details. Key words such as *therefore* and *thus* indicate where the conclusion is, and words like *since* or *due to* could be used to point out key evidence. Other key words such as *but* or *however* might introduce an important contrast, such as between someone else's opinion and the author's. Reading strategically can help you zero in on the right details.

Pattern Recognition

As you get familiar with Critical Reasoning, you'll notice the same patterns show up over and over, and once you recognize them, you'll be able to analyze the stimulus efficiently. For instance, you'll see causal arguments, in which the author claims that one event happened as the result of another, or predictions, in which the author claims that something will happen in the future based on current conditions. On Test Day, you won't have to figure out such stimuli from scratch; you'll be ahead of the game because you've seen the patterns before.

Answers and Explanations

Practice Set: The Kaplan Method for Critical Reasoning

1. (A)

The question stem asks for an "assumption," so this is an Assumption question. The author claims that certain recently unemployed people will get help finding jobs. The evidence is the two forms of no-cost job search assistance that are offered to people receiving unemployment benefits. While the evidence is about the assistance that is available, the conclusion is an unqualified prediction that people will use that assistance. Thus, the author is assuming that if help is offered, it will be taken. (A) matches the prediction and is correct.

(B) and (D) are both incorrect because it is irrelevant how easy or difficult the job search will be; the argument is only about whether these workers will have assistance in their search. (C) discusses job search services that are not free, but the argument is only about the use of free services. (E) shows that the assistance offered is generally helpful. However, the argument is not about the usefulness of the proffered interventions but about whether the laid-off retail employees will use them. If the workers know the courses and help with résumé writing are helpful, they might be more inclined to use these resources, but there is no way to know whether they have this information or, even if they do, whether some other factor would outweigh this one in their decision making.

2. (B)

This asks for something that would "call into question" the business owner's claim, so it's a Weaken question. The business owner argues that partnering with a local gym to offer employees a discounted membership will help reduce fatigue. As evidence, the owner cites a correlation between exercise and high energy levels. The owner assumes that exercise is what causes people who exercise to have high energy levels. There is another assumption as well. The owner makes a plan based on a prediction, which means the author assumes there are no factors that would affect the predicted outcome of the plan.

To weaken the assumption of causation, it could be shown that the high energy levels in exercisers were caused by something else (e.g., caffeine, protein diets, medication). It could also be shown that the author has misunderstood the direction of causality: perhaps people exercise because they already have more energy, not the other way around. Or perhaps increased exercise and increased energy are both just effects of another variable (e.g., motivation). To show that the author's predicted outcome might not occur, you could find a problem with the plan—something that shows it might not help reduce fatigue. Maybe employees will get the gym membership but not exercise more, or maybe the membership will be unappealing even with the discount. (B) matches the second prediction. It shows how the discount will not encourage people to go to the gym, making it less likely they will feel more energetic.

(A) suggests there are other ways to achieve the same results, but that doesn't mean the owner's plan won't work. (C) is irrelevant. Higher productivity might be a nice side effect, but it's not the owner's stated goal; she is discounting gym memberships to reduce fatigue. (D) is also irrelevant. Any extra burden on the gym has no effect on whether the plan will work. (E) is incorrect because the issue is whether fatigue can be reduced, not whether it can be eradicated completely.

3. (E)

This asks for something that supports a prediction, so it's a Strengthen question. The sales manager's goal is to increase sales by having the salespeople who didn't attend the seminar on persuasive speaking attend the next seminar. The evidence provided is that the salespeople who did attend the last seminar had better sales than did non-attendees. However, this is only a correlation. There could be some other reason for the good performance (e.g., other seminars, better leads, luck). It's also possible the author's logic is backward: perhaps the attendees were already above average. Maybe that's why they were chosen to attend the seminar in the first place, or perhaps more highly motivated people both choose to attend seminars and get more sales. The sales manager assumes these factors did not play an important role in the increased sales and that the seminar was responsible. Predict that the correct answer will eliminate one or more of the alternative causes from consideration. (**E**) is correct; if the attendees weren't already top salespeople, it's at least somewhat more likely that the seminar helped improve their performance.

(**A**) doesn't establish that these tactics actually helped sales—perhaps the salespeople already knew these tactics. Moreover, this choice describes the last seminar, but the argument is about the benefits of attending the next seminar. (**B**) and (**D**) are incorrect because overall sales are irrelevant; what matters is whether the seminar was responsible for the increased sales of people who attended the seminar as compared to those who did not. (**C**) weakens the argument by bringing up a potential alternative explanation. Maybe the book was responsible and not the seminar itself.

4.   (E)

The question stem indicates that you are to consider the stimulus as support, or evidence, for your answer choice. Therefore, this is an Inference question. You might paraphrase the stimulus this way: viruses may be useful in nanotechnology because "composite materials" can be built from them. But viruses can only be useful in this way after people attach stuff to them, using one of two approaches. Because the question stem lacks specific clues, you cannot make a specific prediction. But do have firmly in mind what the stimulus says—and what it doesn't say—as you evaluate the choices. (**E**) connects the idea in the first sentence of the stimulus—scientists are investigating how to make viruses useful in nanotechnology—with the idea in the last sentence, which is that the way to make viruses useful requires figuring out how to attach things to them. This statement is fully supported by the stimulus and is correct.

(**A**) is a distortion; scientists are interested in pursuing this avenue of research, but nothing in the stimulus indicates that useful applications are "likely." (**B**) is extreme; viruses may be a good choice for composite materials, but there is no evidence that they are the "best" choice. (**C**) is not supported. The stimulus says that biological interfaces need to be added to viruses for them to be useful in nanotechnology, but it does not say the viruses have no such interfaces now. (**D**) is a distortion because of the word "primarily." While it is inferable that composite materials have potential uses in the human body, nothing in the stimulus indicates that this is the main reason they are useful.

CRITICAL REASONING QUESTION TYPES

Now that you're familiar with the basic principles of Critical Reasoning and the Kaplan Method, let's take a closer look at the most common types of questions. Certain question types appear again and again on the GMAT, so it pays to understand them beforehand.

Here are the types of Critical Reasoning questions that the GMAT asks:

- Assumption
- Strengthen or Weaken
- Evaluate
- Flaw

- Explain
- Inference
- Bolded Statement

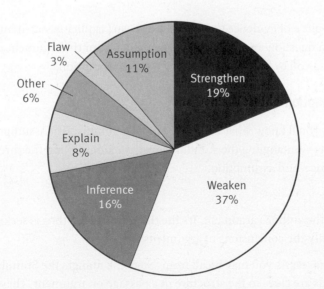

The Approximate Distribution of GMAT Critical Reasoning Questions

You saw many references to arguments in the previous chapter, and indeed analyzing arguments is an important skill for success with Critical Reasoning. Assumption, Strengthen, Weaken, Evaluate, and Flaw questions are all based on arguments. For these five question types, the correct answer will depend on identifying and understanding the argument's conclusion, evidence, and assumption(s).

> **GMAT ARGUMENTS**
>
> - GMAT arguments (given in the stimuli) are usually two to four sentences long.
>
> - GMAT arguments vary in soundness: some are fairly sensible, while others make a big leap from evidence to conclusion.
>
> - To untangle the stimulus, find the conclusion, evidence, and the author's assumption.

Let's examine in depth Kaplan's strategies for the different types of Critical Reasoning questions based on arguments, starting with Assumption questions.

Assumption Questions

LEARNING OBJECTIVES

- Identify Assumption questions by the question stem
- Distinguish between evidence and conclusion in an argument
- Identify assumptions within an argument
- Apply the Kaplan Method for Critical Reasoning to Assumption questions

Assumption questions ask you for a piece of evidence that the author hasn't explicitly stated but is necessary for the argument to be valid. When a question asks you for what's missing from the argument or what the argument depends on, then it's asking you to find the author's necessary assumption.

Untangling the Stimulus for Assumption Questions

By first analyzing the question stem, you'll know what to look for in the stimulus. For Assumption questions—and all questions based on arguments—untangling the stimulus consists of identifying the three parts of a GMAT argument: conclusion, evidence, and assumption.

Conclusion

The conclusion is the main point of the author's argument. It's the thing that the author is seeking to convince you of. There are three ways to identify the conclusions of arguments:

1. **Conclusion key words or phrases:** As you may recall from "Step 2: Untangle the Stimulus—A Deep Dive" in Chapter 13, key words are clues to the structure of a passage or argument. They tell you how the author's ideas relate to one another. Key words and phrases that signal an argument's conclusion include the following: *thus, therefore, so, hence, consequently, in conclusion, clearly, for this reason.*

2. **The one-sentence test:** You can also identify the author's conclusion by asking, "If the author had to boil this entire argument down to one sentence that expresses the main point, which sentence would it be?"

3. **Fact vs. opinion:** The conclusion of the argument is always a reflection of the author's opinion. This opinion can take several forms; it could be the author's plan, proposal, prediction, or value judgment or simply her interpretation or analysis of the evidence. As discussed next, evidence may also be an opinion, but it may also be, and usually is, factual. Therefore, if a statement presents a fact, it is not the conclusion.

Evidence

Evidence is provided to support the conclusion. GMAT arguments usually have little filler, so what isn't the conclusion is typically evidence. Evidence can take the form of data, such as statistics, surveys, polls, or historical facts. Sometimes, however, the evidence is merely a conjecture or an opinion. The best way to identify an argument's evidence is by examining its function within the argument: any material in the stimulus that provides support for the author's conclusion is evidence.

Assumption

All GMAT arguments contain one or more assumptions; identifying the assumptions is an essential step when answering any Critical Reasoning question based on an argument. An assumption is the unstated evidence necessary to make the argument work. It bridges the gap between two pieces of the argument, usually between conclusion and evidence but occasionally between two unconnected pieces of evidence. Without the assumption, the argument falls apart. You can think of it as something the author *must* believe but doesn't directly state.

You can visualize the relationship between the various parts of an argument as follows:

Evidence + Assumption(s) → Conclusion

Predicting the Answer for Assumption Questions

For Assumption questions, your prediction is simply the argument's assumption, which you already identified when you untangled the stimulus during step 2 of the Kaplan Method.

Let's practice the whole process of untangling the stimulus and predicting the answer using this simple stimulus:

> Allyson plays volleyball for Central High School. Therefore, Allyson must be over 6 feet tall.

The conclusion is the second sentence (signaled by the key word "Therefore"), and the evidence is the first. Is there a gap, or assumption, in this argument? Well, who's to say that all high school volleyball players have to be over 6 feet tall? So you can confidently predict that the answer to an Assumption question would say something like this:

> All volleyball players at Central High School are over 6 feet tall.

But what if the assumption doesn't just jump out at you? How can you track it down? One of the most common ways the GMAT uses assumptions is to cover over mismatched concepts between evidence and conclusion. Notice that the argument above starts by talking about playing volleyball and then all of a sudden is talking about being over 6 feet tall. When tackling an Assumption question, look closely at the terms in each part of the argument. Is the scope of the evidence different, even if just slightly, from that of the conclusion?

Consider this seemingly solid argument:

> Candidate A won the presidential election, carrying 40 out of 50 states. Clearly, Candidate A has a strong mandate to push for her legislative agenda.

At first glance, this sounds pretty good. But take a close look at the terms of the argument. The evidence is a win representing a sizable majority of states. The conclusion is about a strong mandate for an agenda. Even if you don't notice the subtle difference between these two things, you could still make a prediction like this: *Candidate A's big victory means she has a mandate for her agenda.* You'd be much more likely to recognize the right answer between these two possibilities:

O No other candidate in the last 24 years has won as many states as did Candidate A.

O Most of the people who voted for Candidate A support her legislative agenda.

The first answer choice doesn't deal with Candidate A's agenda at all. The second one shows a connection between her victory and her agenda, so it must be the right answer.

But what if you still aren't sure that your answer choice is correct? Or what if the assumption is so subtle that you can't predict the answer? In those cases, you can use the Denial Test.

The Denial Test

An assumption must be true in order for the conclusion to follow logically from the evidence. Therefore, in an Assumption question, you can test each answer choice by negating it—in other words, imagining that the information given in the answer choice is false. If this negation makes the author's argument fall apart, then the answer choice is a necessary assumption. If the argument is unaffected, then the choice is wrong. Let's look at what you predicted earlier as the assumption in the volleyball argument:

> All volleyball players at Central High School are over 6 feet tall.

Now let's negate it:

> Some volleyball players at Central High School are not over 6 feet tall.

Would Allyson still have to be over 6 feet tall? Not anymore. That's why that prediction would be a necessary assumption. Keep in mind not to be too extreme when negating answer choices. The denial of *hot* isn't *cold* but rather *not hot*. Similarly, the denial of *all are* isn't *none are* but rather *some aren't*.

Now let's take another look at the answer choices for the question about Candidate A:

O No other candidate in the last 24 years has won as many states as did Candidate A.

O Most of the people who voted for Candidate A support her legislative agenda.

And now we'll negate them:

O Some candidates in the last 24 years have won as many states as did Candidate A.

Could Candidate A still enjoy a strong mandate? Definitely. Just because others in the past were as popular doesn't mean that she doesn't enjoy support for her agenda as well.

O A majority of those who voted for Candidate A do not actually support her legislative agenda.

Now can Candidate A claim a mandate for her agenda? No, she can't. That's why the second choice is the correct answer for this Assumption question.

Give the Denial Test a try on your own using the following argument. Negate each answer choice and then ask, "Can the evidence still lead to the conclusion?"

> I live in the city of Corpus Christi, so I also live in Texas.

The argument assumes which of the following?

- O   Corpus Christi is the only city in Texas.
- O   The only city named Corpus Christi is located in Texas.
- O   If you have not been to Corpus Christi, you have not been to Texas.

The argument here is short and sweet, but it has all the essential elements of any GMAT argument. The conclusion is signaled by the key word *so*: the author lives in Texas. The author's evidence is the claim in the first part of the sentence: he lives in Corpus Christi.

Rather than predict the correct answer right away, let's test the answer choice statements using the Denial Test.

Negation of statement (A): Corpus Christi is not the only city in Texas.

Does that threaten the argument? No. There could be other cities in Texas, and it could still be valid to say that living in Corpus Christi proves that the author lives in Texas. The evidence could still lead to the conclusion, so choice (A) is not the assumption.

Negation of statement (B): There is at least one other city named Corpus Christi that is not located in Texas.

If this is true, does the conclusion still follow logically from the evidence? No. In this case, if there is another town named Corpus Christi located in, say, California or Florida, it would no longer be logically valid to say that the author must live in Texas because he lives in Corpus Christi. Choice (B) is a necessary assumption for the argument.

Negation of statement (C): If you have not been to Corpus Christi, you still could have been to Texas.

Note that when you deny an if/then statement, you should deny the "then" or result portion of the statement. What impact does this negation have on the argument? None. Someone else could visit other cities in Texas, and still it may or may not be valid for the author to say, "I live in Texas because I live in Corpus Christi." Choice (C) is not the necessary assumption.

Argument Analysis Drill

Answers follow.

Now it's time to put all these skills together and practice breaking down some arguments. First find the conclusion, then identify the evidence that supports that conclusion, and finally determine the central assumption(s). Once you've identified the assumption, try the Denial Test to confirm that the assumption you've identified is necessary for the argument to hold:

1. A major car manufacturer produces two editions of its most popular model: the GK and the LK. Since both editions were made available, the manufacturer has sold nearly twice as many GK editions each year as it has LK editions. However, it is likely that the LK edition will outsell the GK edition next year. After all, the GK edition has always sold for significantly less than the LK edition, but the manufacturer is making modifications to the GK edition next year that will raise its selling price to a value exceeding that of the LK edition.

Conclusion:

Evidence:

Assumption(s):

2. Movie studio executive: Last summer, our studio released one of the most popular science fiction movies of the year. This summer, our studio released a critically praised war documentary. Unfortunately, ticket sales for this war documentary were 40 percent lower than that of last year's science fiction movie. Thus, it is clear that movie studios can be more profitable if they do not change the genre of movies they produce.

Conclusion:

Evidence:

Assumption(s):

Argument Analysis Drill: Answers

1. **Conclusion:** The manufacturer will likely sell more LK editions than GK editions next year.

   Evidence: The GK edition will be more expensive next year.

   Assumption: Price is the most significant factor affecting a customer's car-buying decision.

2. **Conclusion:** Movie studios can be more profitable if they choose a movie genre and stick with it.

   Evidence: The war documentary released this year by the executive's studio made less money than the science fiction movie it released last year.

   Assumptions: In this case, the author is taking several things for granted. Lower ticket sales mean the studio made less profit (perhaps the documentary cost much less than the science fiction film to make and was thus more profitable). Another science fiction movie would have performed better than the war documentary this year (perhaps movie receipts were down in general this year, or perhaps another studio offered a great sci-fi film this year and audiences would have ignored a sci-fi movie by this studio). What happened in this situation is representative of what would happen for film studios in general. The lower ticket sales were due to the genre of the film and no other factor (e.g., unpopular or challenging subject matter).

Sample Question Stems

Any wording that suggests that you need to find a missing but vital piece of information indicates an Assumption question. Assumption questions are worded in some of the following ways:

- Which one of the following is assumed by the author?
- The argument depends on the assumption that . . .
- Which one of the following, if added to the passage, would make the conclusion logical?
- The validity of the argument depends on which one of the following?
- The argument presupposes which one of the following?

CONCEPT CHECK

- Fill in the blanks with the elements of an argument: _____ + _____ →
  _____.

- List three ways by which you can identify an argument's conclusion: _____,
  _____, and _____.

- Information, such as data or an opinion, that is explicitly stated in the stimulus and supports the author's conclusion is called _____.

- In an argument, a missing but necessary piece of support for an author's claim is called
  _____.

- For an Assumption question, how does the Denial Test identify the correct answer?

  _____

Example answers are in your book's online resources (**kaptest.com/login**).

Applying the Kaplan Method: Assumption Questions

Now use the Kaplan Method for Critical Reasoning to solve an Assumption question:

> When unemployment rates are high, people with full-time jobs tend to take fewer and shorter vacations. When unemployment rates are low, people tend to vacation more often and go away for longer periods of time. Thus, it can be concluded that full-time workers' perceptions of their own job security influence the frequency and duration of their vacations.
>
> The argument above assumes that
>
> O   the people who take the longest vacations when unemployment rates are low have no fear of losing their jobs
>
> O   travel costs are lower during times of low unemployment
>
> O   most people prefer to work full-time jobs
>
> O   workers' perceptions of their own job security are in some way related to the unemployment rate
>
> O   workers' fears of losing their jobs have increased recently

STEP 1: IDENTIFY THE QUESTION TYPE

The word "assumes" in the question stem is a clear indication of an Assumption question.

STEP 2: UNTANGLE THE STIMULUS

"Thus" signals the argument's conclusion. You could paraphrase it as follows: *how much vacation time full-time workers take depends on how secure they feel in their jobs.* The author's evidence for this conclusion is the relationship between vacations and unemployment. When unemployment is high, workers take fewer and shorter vacations; when unemployment is low, the opposite happens.

CHAPTER 14
CRITICAL REASONING QUESTION TYPES

STEP 3: PREDICT THE ANSWER

To find the key assumption, link the terms in the evidence with the terms in the conclusion. Since the evidence centers on employment levels and vacations, while the conclusion centers on job security and vacations, the two terms that need to be "bridged" are *employment levels* and *job security*. The assumption must address the connection between employment levels and job security.

STEP 4: EVALUATE THE CHOICES

Choice (**D**) matches this prediction, bridging the terms of the evidence with the terms of the conclusion. The Denial Test can help confirm (**D**) as the correct answer; if there were no relationship between workers' perceptions of job security and the unemployment rate, then it would no longer make sense for the author to use evidence about the unemployment rate to support a conclusion about workers' perceptions of job security. (**D**) is an assumption necessary for the argument to hold.

The other choices are all incorrect in some definable way. It's great practice to identify exactly why each wrong choice is wrong. (**A**) is too extreme ("*no* fear of losing their jobs") to be the necessary assumption. (**B**) introduces the idea of travel costs, which have no necessary connection to job security in the conclusion. (**C**) is incorrect because whether those people who work full-time jobs prefer to work them is irrelevant. (**E**) says that workers' perceptions of their job security have deteriorated lately, but that has no necessary connection to the unemployment rate. Remember that the assumption must successfully link the evidence to the conclusion.

Next, you'll find some in-format Assumption questions.

Practice Set: Assumption Questions

(Answers and explanations are at the end of the chapter.)

1. To protect the environment, paper towels in public restrooms should be banned and replaced with hot-air dryers. The use of such dryers would reduce the need to cut down trees to turn into paper towels. Furthermore, since fewer paper towels would be needed, the environmental impact of the emissions from the paper-manufacturing process would be lessened.

    Which of the following is an assumption upon which the above proposal depends?

    O   The operating expenses related to hot-air dryers are no greater than those related to paper towels.

    O   The manufacture and operation of hot-air dryers use fewer natural resources than do the manufacture and use of paper towels.

    O   Hot-air dryers are the only viable alternative to paper towels in public restrooms.

    O   Hot-air dryers are at least as effective at drying the hands as are paper towels.

    O   The operators of public restrooms are willing to replace paper towels with hot-air dryers.

2. A company's health program offers medical coverage for all of its full-time employees. As part of the program, employees can choose from one of three plans, each of which offers a different mix of medical benefits depending on an individual's particular needs. Thus, all full-time employees who take advantage of the company's program are sure to be covered for most, if not all, of their medical needs.

    Which of the following is an assumption on which the argument relies?

    O   Part-time employees can also receive coverage from the company's health program.

    O   None of the three plans costs the company significantly more than the other plans.

    O   There are no full-time employees whose medical needs are mostly uncovered by each of the three available plans.

    O   There is no alternative plan that would cover more medical needs than the plans in the current program.

    O   At least one of the three plans offers dental coverage for full-time employees whose health is impacted by their dental needs.

3. The owner of a local hardware store is concerned that the store's sales will diminish when a competing hardware store opens in the same area next month. However, it is more likely that the existing store's sales will increase. Over the next few months, due to high demand for mixed-use residential and commercial buildings, over three times as many construction projects will be started in the area as were started over the past five years.

The argument above depends on which of the following assumptions?

○ The managers of the new construction projects will purchase an equal amount of material from both hardware stores.

○ The new construction projects will use materials purchased from the existing hardware store.

○ The materials sold at the existing store are higher in quality than those to be sold at the new hardware store.

○ The area revitalization spurred by new mixed-use developments will encourage local residents to improve their own homes.

○ The existing hardware store will lower its prices below those of its competitors to attract new customers.

Strengthen and Weaken Questions

Determining an argument's necessary assumption, as you've just seen, is required to answer an Assumption question. But this skill can also be used to answer two other common types of question: Strengthen and Weaken.

Strengthen and Weaken questions are, as their names imply, all about the strength of the author's position. In the stimulus, the author makes a claim of some sort; for instance, it may be a plan of action, a recommendation, or an explanation for a particular phenomenon. In a Strengthen question, the correct answer is the one that makes the claim more likely to be true, while in a Weaken question, the correct answer makes the claim less likely to be true. It's important to note that the right answers to these questions will not necessarily prove or disprove the claim; they will likely just be evidence for or against the claim.

In many cases, the strength or weakness of the author's claim rests on the validity of her assumption. When the author gives evidence for her claim, use the skills you learned for tackling Assumption questions to find the gap between evidence and conclusion. The answer to many Weaken questions is the one that reveals an author's assumption to be unreasonable or untrue; conversely, the answer to many Strengthen questions provides additional support for the argument by affirming the truth of an assumption.

Sometimes, however, the correct answer might not focus on an assumption made by the author. In a Strengthen question, the right answer may be an independent piece of evidence, that, when added to the author's stated evidence, makes the conclusion more likely to be true. Similarly, the answer to a Weaken question may merely be a fact that casts doubt upon the conclusion.

There may be occasions in which the author presents no evidence at all to back up his claim; he may simply state that his proposed course of action will lead to a certain outcome. In that case, focus on the effect each choice would have on the proposal's likelihood of success. Also helpful in answering these types of questions are the strategies for plans, proposals, and predictions that are discussed in detail in Chapter 7. These strategies are all about how to untangle stimuli that deal with the predicted outcome of future events, so they'll provide some guidance on how to predict the kinds of evidence that will strengthen or weaken the proposal.

Let's return to a stimulus we've seen before and consider it in the context of Strengthen and Weaken questions:

> Allyson plays volleyball for Central High School. Therefore, Allyson must be over 6 feet tall.

Remember which assumption holds this argument together? It is that all volleyball players for Central High are over 6 feet tall. That assumption makes or breaks the argument. So if you're asked to weaken the argument, you'll want to attack that assumption:

> Which one of the following, if true, would most weaken the argument?

Prediction: Not all volleyball players at Central High School are over 6 feet tall.

Correct Answer:

○   Some volleyball players at Central High School are under 6 feet tall.

Notice that we don't have to prove the conclusion wrong, just make it less likely. We've called into doubt the author's basic assumption, thus damaging the argument. Allyson still *could* be over 6 feet tall, but now she doesn't have to be.

What if the question asked you to strengthen the argument? Again, the key would be the necessary assumption:

Which one of the following, if true, would most strengthen the argument?

Prediction: All volleyball players at Central High School are over 6 feet tall.

Correct Answer:

○   No member of the Central High School volleyball team is under 6'2".

Here, by confirming the author's assumption, you've in effect bolstered the argument.

Strengthening and Weakening Arguments Drill

Now it's time to put all these skills together and practice analyzing arguments and identifying possible strengtheners and weakeners. Find the conclusion, evidence (if any), and any assumption(s) that the author may be making for each of the following. Then predict what a correct answer choice might contain for a Strengthen question and for a Weaken question. Answers follow the exercise.

1. Mailing tubes are the safest and most convenient way for people to mail posters and art prints. Over the past six months, post offices and office supply stores throughout the nation have reported a significant increase in the sale of mailing tubes. It is obvious that people are mailing a greater number of posters and art prints.

Conclusion:

Evidence:

Assumption(s):

Predict strengtheners:

Predict weakeners:

2. Last month, a local newspaper published an editorial criticizing a prominent mayoral candidate for refusing to endorse a proposal to renovate the city's primary railroad station. This editorial was ultimately responsible for the candidate's losing the mayoral election. After all, before the editorial was published, the candidate was leading in opinion polls, while after the editorial was published, the candidate's approval ratings dropped sharply.

Conclusion:

Evidence:

Assumption(s):

Predict strengtheners:

Predict weakeners:

3. In the current economic recession in Kelrovia, many companies have chosen to reduce their expenditures in order to avoid bankruptcy. However, one company claims that increasing its research and development budget for its newest smartphone model will lead to increased profits.

Conclusion:

Evidence:

Assumption(s):

Predict strengtheners:

Predict weakeners:

4. According to a recent study, the majority of people in a large city believe that most homeless people are drug addicts who could get jobs if they wanted to work. However, the public is misinformed. The city's Coalition for the Homeless estimates that over 85 percent of the homeless population is moderately to severely mentally ill.

Conclusion:

Evidence:

Assumption(s):

Predict strengtheners:

Predict weakeners:

Strengthening and Weakening Arguments Drill: Answers

1. **Conclusion:** People are mailing more posters and art prints.

   Evidence: The sale of mailing tubes has increased.

   Assumption: The people buying mailing tubes are using them to mail posters and art prints.

   Possible strengthener: When asked about the contents of their packages, almost all customers who use mailing tubes claim they are shipping posters or art prints (or any other evidence that suggests this is how the mailing tubes are being used).

   Possible weakener: Many people have recently started buying mailing tubes in bulk for craft projects at home (or for any reason other than mailing posters and art prints).

2. **Conclusion:** The editorial was responsible for the candidate's loss.

   Evidence: The candidate was leading in polls before the editorial was published, then dropped in popularity afterward.

   Assumption: The change in public opinion was caused by the editorial and not something else.

   Possible strengthener: Most of the city's residents claim that the railroad station renovation is very important to them (or any other reason the editorial would have influenced the election).

   Possible weakener: On the same day the editorial was published, reports were released implicating the candidate in a major tax evasion scandal (or any other reason besides the editorial that people did not vote for the candidate).

3. **Conclusion:** Even in a recession, spending more money on R & D will lead to increased profits for a particular company.

   Evidence: None; there's no support for why the company believes its profits will increase.

   Assumption: Since there's no evidence, there's also no assumption.

   Possible strengthener: The increased budget will allow the company to add features that make the smartphone especially useful to those searching for and applying to new jobs (or any other reason the smartphone will be profitable, especially given the recession).

   Possible weakener: In order to recoup the increased costs of producing the phone, the company will have to sell the smartphone at a price that is unaffordable to most Kelrovians (or any other reason the smartphone will not be profitable, especially given economic conditions).

4. **Conclusion:** The public is misinformed in its belief that the homeless are drug addicts who don't want to work; in other words, homeless people are not drug addicts and/or do want to work.

   Evidence: An estimate from Coalition for the Homeless that says the vast majority of homeless people are mentally ill.

   Assumption: If a homeless person is mentally ill, that individual is not a drug addict who is able to work.

   Possible strengthener: Moderate to severe mental illness makes it impossible to obtain or maintain employment (or any other evidence that connects mental illness to unemployment or that counters other reasons the homeless don't work).

   Possible weakener: The mentally ill are capable of maintaining employment if they want to, or many mentally ill people who could work are also drug addicts.

Sample Stems

The stems associated with these two question types may use the word *weaken* or *strengthen*, or they may use other phrasing. Here's a list of some you can expect to see on Test Day.

Weaken:

- Which one of the following, if true, would most weaken the argument?
- Which one of the following, if true, would most seriously damage the argument?
- Which one of the following, if true, casts the most doubt on the argument?
- Which of the following, if true, would most seriously call into question the plan outlined by the consultant?

Strengthen:

- Which one of the following, if true, would most strengthen the argument?
- Which one of the following, if true, would provide the most support for the conclusion in the argument?
- The argument would be more persuasive if which one of the following were found to be true?

There is some variance in the way these questions are asked. It's common for the question stem to refer explicitly to part of the argument. You might, for example, see something like this:

> Which of the following, if true, casts the most doubt on the author's conclusion that the Brookdale Public Library does not meet the requirements of the new building codes?

A Strengthen question may ask you to fill in the blank at the end of an argument, where the blank is preceded by a key word signaling evidence, such as *since*. As with other Strengthen questions, you must choose the answer that supplies evidence that supports the author's conclusion.

You may also see other slight variations on how Strengthen and Weaken questions are asked; for instance, you may be asked for a choice that would strengthen one conclusion and weaken another one. With such variations, simply pay attention to what effect the answer choice will have on the claims made in the stimulus and use the same strategies to evaluate the choices as you would for a more traditional question.

When you identify the question type during step 1 of the Method, make sure you understand what effect the correct answer will have on the argument. Wrong answers that have the opposite of the desired effect are extremely common on Strengthen and Weaken questions. If you're asked to weaken an argument, watch out for wrong answers that would strengthen it. Asked to strengthen? Be wary of weakeners. Pay close attention to what the question asks so you can avoid this trap.

CONCEPT CHECK

- To answer Strengthen and Weaken questions, what parts of the argument must you identify?

  _____

- How does the correct answer choice affect the author's argument in a Strengthen question? In a Weaken question?

  _____

- What are some common wrong answer types that show up Strengthen and Weaken questions?

  _____

Example answers are in your book's online resources (**kaptest.com/login**).

Applying the Kaplan Method: Strengthen and Weaken Questions

Now let's use the Kaplan Method for Critical Reasoning to solve a Strengthen or Weaken question:

> Due to recent success, Lawton, a contractor, can be more selective than in the past regarding the types of clients he chooses to service. If he restricts his business to commercial clients and only those residential clients requiring $10,000 of work or more, he would cease doing most of the kind of residential work he currently does, which would allow him to earn a higher average profit margin per job.
>
> Which of the following, if true, would most strengthen the conclusion that limiting his service in the manner cited would increase Lawton's average profit margin per job?
>
> O   Lawton's recent success is due primarily to an upsurge in the number of residential clients he services.
>
> O   Lawton's commercial clients would prefer that he focus more of his time and energy on their projects and less on the concerns of his residential clients.
>
> O   Residential work for which Lawton cannot bill more than $10,000 comprises a significant proportion of his low-profit-margin work.
>
> O   Due to the use of a more efficient cost-accounting system, Lawton's average profit margin per job has increased in each of the last three years.
>
> O   Commercial jobs typically take longer to complete than residential jobs.

STEP 1: IDENTIFY THE QUESTION TYPE

In addition to containing the telltale word "strengthen," the question stem helps you by identifying the conclusion. When the GMAT gives you a gift like this, accept it!

STEP 2: UNTANGLE THE STIMULUS

The conclusion has been handed to you by the question stem: by restricting his work to commercial projects and expensive ($10,000+) residential projects, Lawton will increase his average profit margin. The only evidence is the first sentence, which informs you that due to recent success, Lawton can restrict his work to certain clients if he chooses.

STEP 3: PREDICT THE ANSWER

The evidence proves that Lawton can be selective. However, it does not establish that restricting his business will actually improve his profit margin. The author's claim depends on an assumption: inexpensive residential jobs have lower profit margins than do commercial jobs and pricey residential jobs.

STEP 4: EVALUATE THE CHOICES

Choice (C) supports the assumption, thereby strengthening the argument, and is the correct answer.

Wrong answer choices on Strengthen and Weaken questions commonly provide facts that are irrelevant to the argument; since such choices have no direct bearing on the argument, there's no way they could strengthen or weaken it. (A) is incorrect because the source of Lawton's recent success is irrelevant and has no connection to higher profit margins. (B) discusses the preferences of Lawton's commercial clients, which are also irrelevant. (D) credits a new accounting system with an increase in Lawton's profit margin per job. This statement doesn't tell us whether expensive jobs have a higher profit margin than do small residential jobs, so it doesn't help the argument. Furthermore, (D) focuses on past improvements, which have no bearing on whether his future plans will be successful. (E) tells us that commercial jobs will take longer to complete, but the profit margin of the jobs, not their duration, is what matters in this argument.

Next, you'll find some in-format Strengthen and Weaken questions.

Practice Set: Strengthen and Weaken Questions

(Answers and explanations are at the end of the chapter.)

4. Earlier this year, our city's three main reservoirs had unusually low water levels. As a result, city officials initiated a program that encouraged residents to reduce their water usage by 20 percent. Since the program was announced, the water level at all three reservoirs has returned to normal. Our city officials should be applauded for their role in preventing a crisis.

   Which of the following, if true, casts the most doubt on the efficacy of the officials' program?

   O   The current water level in the reservoirs is lower than it was at the same time last year.

   O   Other nearby reservoirs recovered from lower water levels this year, even though those reservoirs provide water to cities that did not enact water restriction policies.

   O   Residents reduced their water usage for lawn maintenance significantly more than they did for washing clothes.

   O   Imposing stiff penalties on residents who did not conserve water would have resulted in even higher water levels in the reservoirs.

   O   Water usage in the city dropped steadily during the first two weeks of the program before leveling off.

5. To attract new visitors, the local zoo is planning to offer new experiences. One proposal involves allowing visitors to assist in feeding the big cats, such as the lions and the tigers. However, unlike the zookeepers, visitors do not spend time interacting with the cats and becoming familiar to them. Enacting this plan would be like inviting people to enter the home of a well-armed stranger without knocking.

   Which of the following statements, if true, would most strengthen the argument?

   O   Visitors have not spent as much time studying the behavior of big cats as the zookeepers have.

   O   Those who would be most interested in opportunities to assist in feeding big cats are already regular visitors and would not bring along new visitors.

   O   Burglars who are attacked by an occupant during a home invasion usually incur serious injuries requiring emergency treatment.

   O   People who visit zoos have less experience interacting with wild animals than do people who do not visit zoos.

   O   Feeding big cats requires entering their habitat, which can only be done safely after previous interaction with the animals.

6. The city of Northtown collects an average of $2.2 million in business taxes per year. Neighboring Southtown collects an average of $1.8 million in business taxes per year. Both cities assess business taxes on net profits. In an attempt to attract new businesses to Southtown, the spokesperson for the chamber of commerce of that city uses these statistics to claim that Southtown provides a lower business tax rate that creates a more favorable environment for businesses than can be found in Northtown.

    Which of the following, if true, would most seriously undermine the spokesperson's argument?

    O   Most tax revenue collected in Northtown comes from business taxes.

    O   Most tax revenue collected in Southtown comes from business taxes.

    O   The net profits generated by Northtown businesses are twice those of Southtown businesses.

    O   Northtown has twice the population of Southtown.

    O   Southtown businesses generate twice as much sales revenue as do Northtown businesses.

7. Public interest law focuses on the legal issues that affect the entire community or involve broad areas of public concern, such as illegal discrimination, environmental protection, child welfare, and domestic violence. A particular nonprofit agency focusing on public interest law is woefully understaffed; many lawyers are urgently needed to continue its important work providing low-cost legal services to residents who are unable to afford a private attorney. In order to fill these vacancies as efficiently as possible, the agency should advertise the jobs to students in this year's graduating class at the local law school to encourage them to enter the field of public interest law.

    Each of the following, if true, weakens the recommendation above EXCEPT:

    O   Positions in corporate law that are advertised at the local law school have higher average salaries than do legal positions at nonprofit agencies.

    O   The local law school maintains an active placement service for its graduates and publicizes job openings in the community to its graduating class.

    O   The open positions at the nonprofit agency require several years of prior experience in the practice of law.

    O   Several lawyers recently left the nonprofit agency because the agency's salaries did not enable the lawyers to make their student loan payments.

    O   The local law school is ranked third highest in the country, and graduates of the school aspire to work for large, highly rated law firms located in major cities.

8. Wunderlich Park has a strict regulation that requires mountain bicyclists to wear helmets. Recently, a group of bicyclists acknowledged that helmets may prevent injuries to the wearer but protested, claiming the park should only regulate activities that may hurt a third party. Hence, the bicyclists argued that they should have the right to refrain from wearing helmets.

Which of the following, if true, most seriously weakens the conclusion in the passage?

O   Ninety percent of bicyclists who use Wunderlich Park prefer to wear a helmet to protect themselves in case of an accident.

O   The repeal of the helmet regulation would lead to an increase in park entrance fees to cover the park's legal expenses associated with personal injury lawsuits.

O   Motorcyclists in a neighboring county are required to wear a helmet while on the road.

O   Parks that require the use of helmets have a lower percentage of bicycle accidents resulting in the death of the cyclist than parks that don't require helmet use.

O   More bicyclists who do not wear helmets are seriously injured in accidents than bicyclists who do wear helmets.

Evaluation Questions

> ## LEARNING OBJECTIVES
>
> - Identify Evaluation questions by the question stem
> - Draw upon the author's evidence and conclusion in order to evaluate the validity of an argument
> - Apply the Kaplan Method for Critical Reasoning to Evaluation questions

An Evaluation question asks you to identify information that would help you assess an argument's strength. The correct answer won't strengthen or weaken the author's reasoning or supply a missing assumption. Instead, the right answer will specify the kind of evidence that would help you judge the validity of the author's argument.

Since the needed information will usually fill a gap in the argument, the correct answer to an Evaluation question typically relates in some way to the assumption. For example, let's say that a stimulus could be paraphrased in the following way: *Because country Y has many business-friendly policies, a recent increase in minimum wage will not affect the willingness of businesses to relocate their operations here.* This argument assumes that the advantages conferred by the country's other policies outweigh the increased labor costs. A Strengthen or Weaken answer choice would likely provide evidence to either support or refute this assumption. An Evaluation answer choice, however, would instead claim that it would be most useful to know *whether factors besides labor costs affect the decisions of certain businesses to relocate their operations to country Y.* If there are no other factors besides labor costs, the argument would be weakened, and if there are other factors, it would be strengthened. Incorrect Evaluation answer choices are generally irrelevant; the information they ask for would have little or no effect on the argument.

Sample Stems

Here are some example question stems that indicate an Evaluation question:

- Which of the following would it be most useful to know in order to evaluate the argument?
- The answer to which of the following questions would be most important in evaluating the proposal?
- To assess the likelihood that the plan will achieve its objective, it would be most useful to determine which of the following?
- To evaluate the author's reasoning, it would be most useful to compare . . .
- Which of the following must be studied in order to evaluate the argument presented above?

CONCEPT CHECK

- Evaluation questions ask you to determine what information would most help to

  _____

- The correct answer choice for an Evaluation question will fill in the gap in logic created by
  _____.

- What feature do incorrect Evaluation answer choices generally have?

  _____

Example answers are in your book's online resources (**kaptest.com/login**).

Applying the Kaplan Method: Evaluation Questions

Now use the Kaplan Method for Critical Reasoning to answer an Evaluation question.

> Committee member: Last week, committee members were encouraged to nominate candidates for the position of committee chairperson. So far, seven members have submitted nominations. That means we can expect contentious lead-up to the election. After all, such contention always occurs before an election whenever there are more than three candidates for any elected position.
>
> Which of the following would be most useful to know in order to evaluate the likelihood of the committee member's prediction?
>
> O Whether any of the nominated members are known for arguing frequently with other members
>
> O Whether a candidate can be nominated by more than one committee member
>
> O Whether any more nominations for chairperson will be made
>
> O Whether members were allowed to nominate themselves for chairperson
>
> O Whether there has ever been contention before an election with only two candidates

STEP 1: IDENTIFY THE QUESTION TYPE

The question asks for something that would be useful "to evaluate" a position. That signals an Evaluation question.

STEP 2: UNTANGLE THE STIMULUS

The committee member predicts that there is likely to be a lot of contention before the upcoming election for committee chairperson. The evidence is that contention occurs any time there are more than three candidates, and seven nominations have already been made.

STEP 3: PREDICT THE ANSWER

There are two assumptions here, both based on the suggestion that contention arises when there are more than three candidates for a position. First, the evidence only says seven *nominations* were made. That doesn't mean those people are actually going to run in the election. Maybe some will decline the nomination, or maybe some will accept but then drop out. Second, there are seven nominations, but that doesn't mean they are for seven different people. Perhaps everyone nominated the same member and that person will run unopposed. So the author is assuming both that the nominated members will be candidates and that more than three people were nominated. The correct answer will question whether either one of these assumptions is valid.

STEP 4: EVALUATE THE CHOICES

(B) is correct, as it questions the assumption about duplicated nominations. If candidates can receive multiple nominations, then the seven nominations need not be for more than three candidates. That would make the argument less convincing. However, if there is no duplication, then there are seven different people nominated, and the argument is strengthened. **(A)** is irrelevant. Contention is said to be based on the number of candidates in the election, not how argumentative those candidates are. **(C)** is irrelevant. There are already seven nominations. If that includes more than three distinct candidates, then it doesn't matter how many more nominations, if any, are made. The prediction is valid either way. **(D)** is irrelevant. The contention is said to be based on the number of candidates, not on who nominated them. **(E)** is irrelevant. The argument is based on the assumption that there will be more than three candidates. It doesn't matter what happens when there are only two candidates.

Next, you'll find some in-format Evaluation questions.

Practice Set: Evaluation Questions

(Answers and explanations are at the end of the chapter.)

9. Soil quality is one of the most important factors affecting the growth of crops. Farmers often look for ways to improve soil conditions in order to increase crop production. One possibility involves the planting of dynamic accumulators—plants, such as comfrey, that may draw up significant quantities of beneficial nutrients from beneath the topsoil. Numerous reports have shown that plants grown in areas alongside dynamic accumulators are healthier and more abundant than those grown in areas without dynamic accumulators.

    The answer to which of the following questions would be most useful in evaluating the claim that planting dynamic accumulators would help farmers increase crop production?

    O   Would tending to dynamic accumulators increase the costs of crop production?

    O   Are there solutions other than planting dynamic accumulators that would be more effective at increasing the farmers' crop production?

    O   Are there plants other than comfrey that would draw up a greater number of nutrients?

    O   Are any of the plants in the reports the types of crops grown by farmers?

    O   Would planting dynamic accumulators provide any additional benefits to farmers other than increased soil quality?

10. A grain-processing company is considering purchasing a catfish farm in an attempt to reduce waste by using the by-products of its grain processing as fish food. Catfish whose diet includes grain by-products have been found to reach marketable size in five months, and restaurants have expressed interest in having a reliable source for catfish.

    The answer to which of the following questions is LEAST directly relevant to the grain-processing company's consideration of whether fish farming is a preferable alternative to discarding grain by-products?

    O   How does the cost of discarding grain by-products compare to the operating costs of a fish farm?

    O   How many pounds of catfish are served by restaurants locally and nationally each year?

    O   Are there government regulations that apply to the production and transportation of fish?

    O   Do catfish require nutrients not supplied by grain by-products?

    O   In how many months do wild catfish reach marketable size?

Flaw Questions

LEARNING OBJECTIVES

- Identify Flaw questions by the question stem
- Predict the manner in which an argument is flawed by identifying conclusion, evidence, and assumptions
- Apply the Kaplan Method for Critical Reasoning to Flaw questions

Flaw questions are similar to Weaken questions, but instead of asking you for some new fact that, if true, would make the argument questionable, Flaw questions ask what's already wrong with the argument. So your prediction should focus on reasoning errors the author makes.

The good news is that the GMAT uses a handful of common flaws over and over. Here are the two general categories of errors in reasoning:

1. Unsupportable shifts between the concepts in the evidence and conclusion
2. Overlooked alternatives

And here are some common patterns that show up:

- Confusing correlation and causation
- Confusing percent and actual value
- Inappropriate analogies (comparing things that aren't comparable)
- Inappropriate conflation/distinction of terms

All of these flaws and any others you find in GMAT Critical Reasoning questions center on the author's assumption, so you should handle them similarly to how you've handled all the other argument-based questions so far: by identifying the conclusion, evidence, and assumption.

Sample Stems

Here are some example question stems that indicate a Flaw question:

- Which of the following is a flaw in the reasoning above?
- The argument above is vulnerable to which of the following criticisms?

CONCEPT CHECK

- Flaw questions ask you to describe what aspect of the author's argument?

  _____

- The three parts of the argument you need to identify to answer a Flaw question are _____, _____, and _____.

- What are some common flaws of Critical Reasoning arguments?

  _____

Example answers are in your book's online resources (**kaptest.com/login**).

Applying the Kaplan Method: Flaw Questions

Now use the Kaplan Method for Critical Reasoning to answer a Flaw question.

> The public service advertising campaign promoting the use of helmets has improved bicycle safety dramatically. Over the past 12 months, the number of serious bicycling injuries has been reduced by nearly 70 percent. Unfortunately, helmet usage has not reduced the number of all types of bike injuries. While serious head trauma has decreased by nearly 85 percent, broken bones now represent 20 percent of all reported bicycling injuries. This is a significant increase from last year's 14 percent.

> The reasoning in the argument is flawed because the argument does which of the following?

- ○ It fails to include information about any types of bicycle injuries other than head trauma and broken bones.

- ○ It implies that the same conclusion can result from two different sets of causes.

- ○ It fails to take into account any possible increase in the number of people riding bicycles over the past 12 months.

- ○ It presumes that an increase in the percentage of injuries involving broken bones precludes a decrease in the actual number of such injuries.

- ○ It ignores the fact that a 70 percent overall decrease in injuries would not allow for an 85 percent decrease in one specific type of injury.

STEP 1: IDENTIFY THE QUESTION TYPE

The question stem alerts you to the idea that this argument is flawed, so Flaw is definitely the question type here.

STEP 2: UNTANGLE THE STIMULUS

The author concludes that the number of broken-bone bicycle injuries has gone up from last year to this year. The evidence for this is that broken bones made up 20% of this year's total bicycle-related injuries but were only 14% of last year's total.

K

STEP 3: PREDICT THE ANSWER

As soon as you see both percentages and numbers mentioned in the stimulus for a Flaw question, check whether the author is confusing the two. A higher percent of a small total can be less than a lower percent of a large total. Since the total number of injuries is much lower this year than last year, 20% of this year's lower total could equal a smaller number than 14% of last year's higher total. The flaw here is the author's assumption that an increase in percentage cannot be consistent with a decrease in actual number.

Step 4: Evaluate the Choices

(D) accurately captures the logical flaw in this argument—confusing percent and actual value.

The fact that the author mentions only two types of injuries, as **(A)** says, is not a flaw in the argument, which concerns only whether or not the number of broken bones has been reduced. Other types of injuries are irrelevant. Since two sets of causes aren't discussed, you can rule out **(B)**. Causation does figure in many GMAT flaws, but not this one. **(C)** might seem tempting, since it does relate to the "percentage versus actual number" issue, but if the total number of bicyclists increased over the past year, the reduction in the number of total injuries would actually be greater. And since a 70% overall decrease in injuries could, in fact, allow for an 85% decrease in one specific type of injury, **(E)** can be ruled out as well.

Next, you'll find some in-format Flaw questions.

Practice Set: Flaw Questions

(Answers and explanations are at the end of the chapter.)

11. The legislature is considering legislation to ban skateboarding on city streets, citing safety concerns. However, a review of public health records reveals that the legislature's concern is misplaced. Each year, many more people are injured while jogging than are injured while skateboarding. So in fact, skateboarding is safer than jogging.

Which of the following indicates a flaw in the reasoning above?

   O   It fails to distinguish professional skateboarders who attempt very dangerous maneuvers from amateurs who are comparatively cautious.

   O   It assumes without warrant that no one who skateboards also jogs.

   O   It fails to consider the number of people who skateboard as compared with the number of people who jog.

   O   It ignores the possibility that other activities cause even more injuries than either skateboarding or jogging.

   O   It fails to address the issue and instead attacks the character of the legislature.

12. Solo concert pianists, by convention, are not permitted to use musical scores during their performances. However, most members of chamber groups and orchestras are permitted to use sheet music during performances and perform well as a result. Therefore, all solo concert pianists should also be allowed to consult their musical scores during performances.

The argument is most vulnerable to criticism on which of these grounds?

   O   It overlooks the possibility that some solo concert pianists prefer performing without consulting musical scores.

   O   It takes for granted that members of a chamber group or orchestra are less skilled than solo musicians and thus have more need for musical scores.

   O   It overlooks the possibility that some solo concert pianists have broken with tradition and used musical scores during their performances.

   O   It takes for granted that a solo concert pianist would use a musical score in the same way as does a member of a chamber group or orchestra.

   O   It overlooks the possibility that performing in an orchestra is difficult despite the ability to use a musical score during the performance.

Explain Questions

Questions based on arguments (Assumption, Strengthen, Weaken, Evaluation, and Flaw) make up over 70 percent of all Critical Reasoning questions, but you will likely run into other question types on Test Day that are not based on arguments.

Explain question stimuli are not argumentative. Rather, they present a seeming discrepancy and ask you to find an explanation for the paradox. Paraphrasing the stimulus in your own simple but accurate words will expose the nature of the apparent contradiction. Once you've identified the discrepancy, look for an answer choice that explains how the apparently contradictory facts in the stimulus could both be true.

It's sometimes difficult to predict exactly what the correct answer will contain, since an apparent contradiction can often be resolved in a number of different ways. On questions for which there could be multiple ways for the test maker to phrase the correct answer, make a prediction of what the right answer will mean or do, not the words it will use.

Sample Stems

Here are some example question stems that indicate an Explain question:

- Which of the following, if true, would best explain the discrepancy between customer satisfaction and sales?
- Which of the following, if true, would best resolve the paradox described above?

CONCEPT CHECK

- Instead of an argument, Explain question stimuli feature _____.

- What does the correct answer to an Explain question do?

  _____

Example answers are in your book's online resources (**kaptest.com/login**).

Applying the Kaplan Method: Explain Questions

Try using the Kaplan Method for Critical Reasoning to answer an Explain question.

> Over an extended period of time, the average seawater temperature in a region of an ocean increased by over 1 degree Celsius. During that same time, the average size of the haddock population in the region decreased by more than 25 percent. This observation led scientists to hypothesize that warmer waters favored smaller fish because their bodies were better adapted to the warmer water. However, long-term laboratory experiments showed no changes in the average size of haddock as water temperatures were increased.
>
> Which of the following best explains the differences between the observations in nature and those in the laboratory experiments?
>
> O   The measurements of fish size in the ocean were made by oceanographers, but the ones in the laboratory were made by biologists.
>
> O   Measurements were made more frequently in the laboratory experiments than in the ocean.
>
> O   A change in marine fishing regulations during the period allowed the use of nets with a more tightly spaced mesh than had previously been permitted.
>
> O   The population of ocean-dwelling predators that feed on smaller haddock increased during the period.
>
> O   The water salinity measured in the laboratory exactly matched that of the ocean.

STEP 1: IDENTIFY THE QUESTION TYPE

The wording of this stem signals that there were differences between observations in the ocean and the results of laboratory experiments. Your task is to seek a possible explanation for the different results.

STEP 2: UNTANGLE THE STIMULUS

When untangling the stimulus, paraphrase the given information and make sure you understand the paradox. The findings described in this stimulus seem contradictory: average haddock size and water temperature were negatively related in the ocean, leading scientists to form a hypothesis as to why this occurred, but there was no correlation between size and temperature in the laboratory.

STEP 3: PREDICT THE ANSWER

There could be many reasons why this happened, so you cannot predict the exact answer here. But no matter how the right answer is phrased, it will concern a difference between the real-world and laboratory environments that is relevant to fish size.

STEP 4: EVALUATE THE CHOICES

If the spacing of the mesh in fishing nets decreased, that means that relatively large fish that used to be able to escape the nets are now going to be caught and thus be taken out of the general population of haddock. This phenomenon would reduce the average size of the population of fish in the ocean. **(C)** is correct.

Remember that for an answer choice to be correct, it must relate logically to the seeming contradiction in the stimulus. The incorrect choices here fail to resolve the paradox. The idea that if different kinds of scientists make the measurements, the results would be different requires an assumption that one or the other group is unlikely to report accurate results, so **(A)** does not explain the discrepancy. The frequency of the measurements, per **(B)**, would not have any effect on the end results in either environment. If there were more predators of smaller haddock in the ocean, as in **(D)**, one would expect the average size of fish there to *increase*. This is the opposite of what was observed, so it certainly does not explain the discrepancy. **(E)** describes a variable that was the same in both the ocean and the laboratory, so it cannot explain the different outcomes.

Next, you'll find some in-format Explain questions.

Practice Set: Explain Questions

(Answers and explanations are at the end of the chapter.)

13. Sales of yoga mats from Daniel's yoga studio this year were double those of last year. However, average enrollment per class at Daniel's studio decreased from the prior year, despite Daniel's studio being the only yoga studio in town.

    Which of the following, if true, most helps to explain the discrepancy in sales?

    ○   Daniel offered a greater variety of yoga mats for sale than he had offered the previous year.

    ○   The prices of yoga mats in Daniel's studio increased from the previous year.

    ○   Daniel began to teach additional styles of yoga this year, increasing the number of classes offered and attracting new students.

    ○   Daniel increased the cost of each of his yoga classes from the previous year.

    ○   Daniel's studio requires that an individual bring his or her own yoga mat to each of the classes.

14. A certain town's pizza shop initiated an advertising campaign to bring in new customers and increase sales in December. The advertising campaign consisted of sending emails that promoted a two-for-one deal on sheet pizzas. Even though the pizza shop sent out thousands of these email advertisements, sales remained about the same in December as they had been in previous months.

    Which of the following, if true, most helps to explain the apparent discrepancy between the volume of advertisements and the volume of sales?

    ○   The emails did not list every type of pizza on the pizza shop's menu.

    ○   In December, a new coffee shop opened in the same neighborhood as the pizza shop.

    ○   Not every resident in the pizza shop's delivery area had an email address.

    ○   The pizza shop had email addresses only for customers who were members of its rewards club, which offers members weekly specials.

    ○   The other two pizza shops in town specialize in gourmet pizzas, which are more expensive on average than items on this pizza shop's menu.

CHAPTER 14
CRITICAL REASONING QUESTION TYPES

Inference Questions

LEARNING OBJECTIVES

- Identify Inference questions by the question stem
- Explain what an inference is on the GMAT and draw valid inferences from an argument
- Apply the Kaplan Method for Critical Reasoning to Inference questions

A question type common to both Critical Reasoning and Reading Comprehension is the Inference question. The process of inferring is a matter of considering one or more statements as evidence and then drawing a conclusion from them. A valid inference is something that must be true if the statements in the stimulus are true—not *might* be true, not *probably* is true, but *must* be true.

Think of an inference as a conclusion that you draw based on the information, or evidence, given. It is your job on these questions to choose the inference that requires no assumption whatsoever; the correct answer will follow directly from the stimulus. But the answer to an Inference question is just as likely to be drawn from only one or two details as it is to take into account the stimulus as a whole. For this reason, you often cannot predict the correct answer with precision. Nevertheless, you can make a general prediction: since the answer *must* be true based on the facts in the stimulus, a mental paraphrase of those facts will arm you to evaluate the answer choices. Then eliminate choices one by one, ruling out options that don't match the facts as you've paraphrased them. Once you've eliminated four choices, the one that remains must be correct.

Here's a somewhat expanded version of the volleyball team argument:

> Allyson plays volleyball for Central High School, despite the team's rule against participation by nonstudents. Therefore, Allyson must be over 6 feet tall.

Incorrect answer:

> O   Allyson is the best player on the Central High School volleyball team.

Certainly Allyson *might* be the best player on the team. It's tempting to think that this would *probably* be true—otherwise the team would not risk whatever penalties violating the rule might entail. But *must* it be true? No. Allyson could be pretty good but not the best. Or perhaps the coach owed Allyson's dad a favor. You have no support for the idea that she's the best on the team, so you need to eliminate a choice that includes this idea.

Valid inference:

> O   Allyson is not a student at Central High School.

Clearly, if Allyson plays volleyball *despite* the team's rule against participation by nonstudents, she must not be a student. Otherwise, she wouldn't be playing despite the rule; she'd be playing in accordance with the rule.

Note that this inference is not a necessary assumption of the argument because the conclusion about Allyson's height doesn't depend on it. So be careful: unlike an assumption, an inference need not have anything to do with the author's conclusion. In fact, many Inference stimuli don't have conclusions at all—they consist not of arguments but of a series of facts. Make sure you are prepared for Inference questions, as they require a different approach than do other Critical Reasoning questions. Remember, everything that you need will be contained in the stimulus, so focus on the information as it's presented and avoid answers that twist the facts (or make up new ones).

Sample Stems

Inference questions probably have the most varied wording of all the Critical Reasoning question stems. Some question stems denote inference fairly obviously, while others are more subtle. The bottom line is that if a question asks you to take the stimulus as fact and find something based on it, then you're looking at an Inference question. Here's a sample of various Inference question stems that you may see on your test:

- Which one of the following can be inferred from the argument above?
- Which one of the following is implied by the argument above?
- If all the statements above are true, which one of the following must also be true?
- The statements above, if true, best support the argument that _____.
- Which of the following is the conclusion toward which the author is probably moving?
- The statements above best support which of the following conclusions?

CONCEPT CHECK

- On the GMAT, what are the characteristics of a valid inference?

  _____

- How are Inference questions different from Assumption, Strengthen/Weaken, and Evaluate questions?

  _____

- The correct answer for an Inference question is one that must be _____.

Example answers are in your book's online resources (**kaptest.com/login**).

Applying the Kaplan Method: Inference Questions

Use the Kaplan Method for Critical Reasoning to answer an Inference question.

> A new electronic security system will allow only a single person at a time to pass through a secure door. A computer decides whether or not to unlock a secure door on the basis of visual clues, which it uses to identify people with proper clearance. The shape of the head, the shape and color of the eyes, the shape and color of the lips, and other characteristics of a person's head and face are analyzed to determine his or her identity. Only if the person trying to open a secure door has the required clearance will the door unlock. Because this new system never fails, an unauthorized person can never enter a secure door equipped with the system.
>
> If the statements above are true, which of the following conclusions can be most properly drawn?

- ○ The new system is sure to be enormously successful and revolutionize the entire security industry.
- ○ The new system can differentiate between people who are seeking to open a secure door and people passing by a secure door.
- ○ No two people have any facial features that are identical, for example, identical lips.
- ○ High costs will not make the new security system economically unviable.
- ○ The new computer system is able to identify slight facial differences between people who look very similar, such as identical twins.

STEP 1: IDENTIFY THE QUESTION TYPE

Since the stem asks you to accept the statements as true and draw a conclusion on the basis of them, this is an Inference question.

STEP 2: UNTANGLE THE STIMULUS

When untangling the stimulus of an Inference question, briefly paraphrase the important facts to ensure you understand them. The stimulus tells you that a new electronic security system is completely fail-safe and will never allow an unauthorized person through a door equipped with the system. The system allows an authorized person to enter solely on the basis of the person's appearance and facial features.

STEP 3: PREDICT THE ANSWER

An inference is something that must be true, not just something that could or might be true. Hold your mental paraphrase of the facts presented in the stimulus firmly in mind and measure the answer choices against them.

STEP 4: EVALUATE THE CHOICES

The correct inference is (**E**): if one twin is authorized and the other isn't, the system must be able to tell them apart, because the stimulus states that the security system never fails. This is the answer choice that is unequivocally supported by the stimulus.

(**A**) is unsupported. There is no evidence of how the security industry is going to respond to the new system, so you can't say that this statement must be true based on what the stimulus states. (**B**) also doesn't need to be true. The new system doesn't need to differentiate between people passing by the door and people trying to enter, so long as it lets authorized people in and keeps unauthorized people out. (**C**) is extreme. According to the stimulus, the security system examines multiple facial features to determine identity. You don't know that any *one* feature cannot be the same. All you know is that *all* of the features can't be the same. As for (**D**), the stimulus only discusses the likelihood that unauthorized people will be able to get past the security system and through a secure door; there is no support for a statement about costs.

Next, you'll find some in-format Inference questions.

Practice Set: Inference Questions

(Answers and explanations are at the end of the chapter.)

15. Hyperkalemia occurs when the body contains an excessive amount of potassium. In severe circumstances, hyperkalemia can lead to abnormal heart rhythms. Lowering potassium levels is essential to treating those who suffer from hyperkalemia. However, patients with severe hyperkalemia are initially given an injection of calcium, even though calcium does not lower the body's potassium levels. Instead, the calcium protects the heart from the negative effects of excess potassium. Patients are then given doses of a medicine, such as insulin or albuterol, that helps reduce potassium levels.

    The information given, if true, most strongly supports which of the following?

    O   If an injection of calcium is not given first, medicines such as insulin or albuterol could exacerbate the conditions of severe hyperkalemia.

    O   Patients with mild to moderate hyperkalemia are not given calcium to protect their heart.

    O   Patients given calcium injections cannot be given insulin until the calcium has provided its full effect.

    O   Not all treatments for hyperkalemia are intended to address the root cause of the condition.

    O   Patients cannot reduce their potassium levels without a sufficient intake of calcium.

16. A local department store hires college students for one month every spring to audit its unsold inventory. It costs the department store 20 percent less to pay wages to students than it would cost to hire outside auditors from a temporary service. Even after factoring in the costs of training and insuring the students against work-related injury, the department store spends less money by hiring its own auditors than it would by hiring auditors from the temporary service.

    The statements above, if true, best support which of the following assertions?

    O   The amount spent on insurance for college-student auditors is more than 20 percent of the cost of paying the college students' basic wages.

    O   It takes 20 percent less time for the college students to audit the unsold inventory than it does for the outside auditors.

    O   The department store pays its college-student auditors 20 percent less than the temporary service pays its auditors.

    O   By hiring college students, the department store will cause 20 percent of the auditors at the temporary service to lose their jobs.

    O   The cost of training its own college-student auditors is less than 20 percent of the cost of hiring auditors from the temporary service.

Bolded Statement Questions

LEARNING OBJECTIVES

- Identify Bolded Statement questions by the question stem
- Classify in general terms the role a given statement serves in an argument
- Apply the Kaplan Method for Critical Reasoning to Bolded Statement questions

Bolded Statement questions are usually based on stimuli that contain arguments, but the way you will analyze these arguments is different from what you have learned for other argument-based questions. Bolded Statement questions focus more on the structure than the substance of the stimulus.

A Bolded Statement question asks for the role that specific text plays in an argument. The relevant sentence or sentences are, as the name implies, written in bold font. There are usually two bolded statements in the stimulus, but you may see questions with only one bolded statement. The answers to these questions will be abstract, using language such as "The first provides a counterexample to an opinion, while the second reaffirms that opinion by dismissing the counterexample." This technical language can make these questions seem intimidating.

If you do see any of these questions on Test Day, remind yourself that Bolded Statement questions test the same core skill as much of the rest of the Critical Reasoning section: the ability to identify the evidence and the conclusion of an argument.

One caution: Unlike most GMAT stimuli, Bolded Statement questions often contain multiple arguments. Make sure that you note not only which parts of the argument are evidence and which are conclusions but also which evidence is connected to which conclusion. In addition, use key words in the stimulus to identify which conclusion (if any) the author agrees with. Once you've done so, you should be able to make a prediction about the role of the bolded statement or statements.

Then, if there are two bolded statements in the stimulus, use the format of Bolded Statement answer choices to your advantage. As you'll see in the practice questions in this lesson, the choices for this question type always state the role of the first statement, followed by the role of the second statement. First evaluate the choices against your prediction for just one of the statements. To do this, you need to read only half of each choice, the part related to the statement you're working with. You can probably eliminate two or three choices because they don't match your prediction for that statement. Then finish up by reading the other half of the remaining choices, comparing them to your prediction for the role of the other statement.

Sample Stem

Bolded Statement question stems refer directly to the part(s) of the argument in bold type, so these stems are among the easiest to identify. A Bolded Statement question stem will look something like this:

- The portions of the argument in boldface play which of the following roles?

CONCEPT CHECK

- How does the ability to identify the argument, evidence, and conclusion apply to Bolded Statement questions?

An example answer is in your book's online resources (**kaptest.com/login**).

Applying the Kaplan Method: Bolded Statement Questions

Practice using the Kaplan Method for Critical Reasoning to solve a Bolded Statement question:

Auto manufacturer: For the past three years, the Micro has been our best-selling car. This year, however, sales of the Micro have been down for two consecutive quarters. Therefore, we are going to make certain features, like leather seats and a rear view camera, standard on the Micro, rather than require buyers to pay extra for them. **This will make the Micro more attractive to buyers, thus stimulating sales.**

Auto dealer: Most people who buy the Micro do so because of its low cost. **Adding new standard features will raise the base price of the Micro**, costing us sales.

In the argument above, the two statements in **bold** play which of the following roles?

- ○ The first is a conclusion; the second suggests that this conclusion is based on evidence that is irrelevant to the issue at hand.
- ○ The first presents a hypothesis; the second casts doubt on the evidence on which that hypothesis is based.
- ○ The first provides a conclusion; the second weakens the assumption on which that conclusion relies.
- ○ The first offers evidence that is disproved by the second.
- ○ The first presents a conclusion; the second supports the conclusion but offers a different interpretation of how it will impact the speakers' business.

STEP 1: IDENTIFY THE QUESTION TYPE

This stem offers standard language for a Bolded Statement question—it asks you to determine the roles played in the arguments by each of the boldface statements.

STEP 2: UNTANGLE THE STIMULUS

The stimulus is organized as a dialogue. This is a rare stimulus format, but it does occasionally turn up on the GMAT. Here, the manufacturer has devised a solution to revive flagging sales of the Micro: to make certain features standard that used to cost buyers extra. The auto dealer, on the other hand, posits that adding new standard features will increase the price of the Micro, thereby hurting sales.

STEP 3: PREDICT THE ANSWER

Predict the answer by identifying the function of each of the bolded statements within the context of the argument-counterargument structure. The first bolded statement is a prediction that serves as the auto manufacturer's conclusion: adding more standard features to the Micro will stimulate sales. The manufacturer's conclusion relies on one of two assumptions: either that the added features will not result in an increase to the Micro's base price or that car buyers interested in the Micro are willing and able to pay more for a version of the car with added features. However, as the auto dealer states, people who buy the Micro do so primarily because of its low price. Because the addition of more standard features will result in an increase in price, the manufacturer's proposal will actually lower sales. The second bolded statement, therefore, weakens the manufacturer's prediction by challenging one of its underlying assumptions.

STEP 4: EVALUATE THE CHOICES

Only **(C)** matches this analysis of the arguments and is correct. **(A)** begins correctly, but the second bolded statement does not challenge any of the manufacturer's evidence (that the Micro was the best-selling model for three years, that sales of the Micro have been down for two quarters, and that the company is planning to add new standard features to the Micro). **(B)** can also be eliminated for this reason. **(D)** is incorrect because the first bolded statement is not the manufacturer's evidence but her conclusion. **(E)** might also have appealed to you, since the auto dealer does offer a different point of view on how these new standard features will affect sales of the Micro. However, the dealer's point of view is actually the opposite of the manufacturer's conclusion, so saying that the second statement "supports the conclusion" of the first is incorrect.

Next, you'll find some in-format Bolded Statement questions.

Practice Set: Bolded Statement Questions

(Answers and explanations are at the end of the chapter.)

17. The use of fingerprint analysis to identify criminal suspects dates back to the late 1800s, although the theory behind the technique existed long before it was actually used in practice. **In fact, the hypothetical possibility was so intriguing to Mark Twain that he used fingerprint identification as a plot device in his quasi-memoir** *Life on the Mississippi* **nearly a decade before fingerprints were used to solve a crime in real life.** Since then, fingerprint analysis has become a standard law enforcement technique for real and fictional detectives alike. Yet, despite its widespread use, the practice has never been subjected to rigorous scientific study, and some of the assumptions that underpin its use—such as the notion that each person has a unique set of fingerprints—may not be accurate. **The time has come for the legal community to acknowledge that fingerprint analysis is an unsubstantiated forensic science and to advocate for more research in the field.**

    In the argument given, the two portions in boldface play which of the following roles?

    O   The first is a detail that supports the author's main idea, and the second raises a contrary opinion.

    O   The first is a detail that supports one opinion, and the second is a contrary opinion held by the author.

    O   The first introduces an opinion, and the second contradicts that opinion.

    O   The first is a detail that supports the author's main idea, and the second is additional evidence for the author's main idea.

    O   The first is a detail that supports a claim made in the argument, and the second is the author's main point.

18. Historian: It is often claimed that in many ancient societies, spices were used to disguise the taste of spoiled meat. This claim should, however, be evaluated in its full economic context. **In the early days of the Roman Empire, a pound of ginger could cost as much as 5,000 times the average daily wage.** Surely, anyone who could afford such a luxury would simply buy fresh meat rather than attempt to hide the unpleasant flavors of rotten meat.

    In the above argument, the statement in **boldface** plays which of the following roles?

    O   It is data in support of a claim that the historian is attempting to refute.

    O   It is evidence that supports the historian's conclusion.

    O   It is the conclusion of the historian's argument.

    O   It is a claim that the historian is attempting to refute.

    O   It is data whose accuracy the historian questions.

Critical Reasoning Question Type Identification Drill

Identifying the question type during step 1 of the Kaplan Method for Critical Reasoning puts you in control of the entire process that follows: what to read for in the stimulus, how to frame your prediction, and how to evaluate answer choices. This exercise will help you practice identifying the key words that signal the question type. Note that often the stem in actual questions will be more detailed than the examples below and will reference parts of the stimulus.

For the questions that follow, analyze key words in the question stem and determine what task the question is setting you. Based on this analysis, choose the correct question type from the list of choices.

1. Which of the following, if true, provides the best support for the author's position?

   ○   Assumption
   ○   Explain
   ○   Inference
   ○   Strengthen
   ○   Weaken

2. Which of the following is an assumption upon which the argument is based?

   ○   Assumption
   ○   Evaluate
   ○   Explain
   ○   Inference
   ○   Strengthen

3. Which of the following, if true, most seriously calls into question the author's conclusion?

   ○   Assumption
   ○   Explain
   ○   Flaw
   ○   Inference
   ○   Weaken

4. If the above statements are true, they provide the best support for which of the following?

   ○   Assumption
   ○   Explain
   ○   Inference
   ○   Strengthen
   ○   Weaken

5. Which of the following points out a serious shortcoming in the author's argument?

   ○   Evaluation
   ○   Explain
   ○   Flaw
   ○   Inference
   ○   Weaken

6. Which of the following would be most useful to investigate for the purpose of determining the validity of XXXXXXX?

   ○   Assumption
   ○   Evaluation
   ○   Explain
   ○   Strengthen
   ○   Weaken

7. Each of the following, if true, casts doubt upon the author's argument EXCEPT

   ○   Explain
   ○   Flaw
   ○   Inference
   ○   Strengthen
   ○   Weaken

8. Which of the following, if true, best explains the seeming contradiction described by the author?

   ○   Bolded Statement
   ○   Evaluation
   ○   Explain
   ○   Strengthen
   ○   Weaken

9. The portions of the argument in boldface play which of the following roles?

   O   Bolded Statement

   O   Evaluation

   O   Explain

   O   Inference

   O   Strengthen

10. Which of the following, if true, provides the strongest grounds for the author's prediction that XXXXXXX will occur?

   O   Assumption

   O   Evaluate

   O   Explain

   O   Inference

   O   Strengthen

11. The argument is most vulnerable to which of the following criticisms?

   O   Evaluation

   O   Explain

   O   Flaw

   O   Inference

   O   Weaken

12. In order for the author's conclusion to be correct, which of the following statements must be true?

   O   Assumption

   O   Explain

   O   Inference

   O   Strengthen

   O   Weaken

13. Which of the following, if true, increases the likelihood that the author's conclusion is correct?

   O   Explain

   O   Flaw

   O   Inference

   O   Strengthen

   O   Weaken

14. If the above statements are true, then which of the following must also be true?

   O   Assumption

   O   Evaluate

   O   Inference

   O   Strengthen

   O   Weaken

15. Which of the following, if true, contributes most strongly to the point of view of those critical of the author's position?

   O   Evaluation

   O   Explain

   O   Flaw

   O   Inference

   O   Weaken

16. Which of the following, if true, most helps to justify the author's opinion?

   O   Assumption

   O   Evaluation

   O   Explain

   O   Inference

   O   Strengthen

Question Type Identification Drill: Answers

1. (D)

When the stem asks for what supports the conclusion, you are dealing with a Strengthen question.

2. (A)

Often, an Assumption question will actually use the word "assumption" in the stem.

3. (E)

Any outside information (as indicated by "if true") that "calls into question" the conclusion would certainly weaken that conclusion. This is a Weaken question.

4. (C)

Notice that "if . . . true" in this stem refers to the stimulus. Although "support" is frequently associated with a Strengthen question, in this case the question asks which of the choices is supported by the stimulus, meaning which can be inferred. So this is an Inference question.

5. (C)

The question points you toward identifying a "shortcoming" in the argument as it currently exists, rather than bringing in outside information to weaken it, so you are looking for an error in the reasoning that supports the conclusion. This is a Flaw question.

6. (B)

The phrase "most useful to investigate" means that you are looking for something that would be helpful in evaluating the argument. Thus, this is an Evaluation question.

7. (E)

The words "cast doubt" mean that this is a Weaken question. However, since the question uses EXCEPT, you are looking for the choice that either does not affect the conclusion or actually strengthens it.

8. (C)

As is often the case, the word "explains" in the stem tells you that this is an Explain question.

9. (A)

Boldface questions will be directly identified as such, since they refer to the parts of the stem that are in boldface.

10. (E)

Since the stem mentions the author's "prediction," the prediction is the author's conclusion. You're asked for the "strongest grounds" for that conclusion, so this is a Strengthen question.

11. (C)

If the argument is "vulnerable" to criticism, that means that there can be some truth to the criticism and the argument is thus flawed. This is a Flaw question.

12. (A)

For a conclusion to be correct, the underlying assumption must be valid. Therefore, this is an Assumption question.

13. (D)

If a statement "increases the likelihood" that the conclusion is correct, then it strengthens the argument. This is a Strengthen question.

14. (C)

This is an Inference question. The stem starts by telling you that the stimulus is true and requires you to use that as the basis to determine which of the choices must be true.

15. (E)

If a statement strengthens the argument of those who oppose the author, then it makes the author's opinion less strong. This is a Weaken question.

16. (E)

If a statement helps to "justify" the author's opinion, then it makes the argument stronger. This is a Strengthen question.

Congratulations on completing the Question Type Identification Exercise! As you've seen in this chapter, different types of Critical Reasoning questions ask you to approach the stimulus and answer choices differently. By executing step 1 of the Kaplan Method for Critical Reasoning—by understanding the specific task each question is asking you to perform—you will put yourself in a good position to be successful with these questions and earn a strong Verbal score.

Following are the answers and explanations for the practice sets in this chapter.

Answers and Explanations

Practice Set: Assumption Questions

1. (B)

The author recommends that hot-air dryers replace paper towels in restrooms. As evidence, the author cites the adverse environmental effects of paper towels. However, the author includes no information about the environmental impact of hot-air dryers. The author is therefore assuming that hot-air dryers will have less environmental impact than do paper towels, so for this Assumption question, predict that the correct answer will state this idea in some fashion. **(B)** is correct, as it favorably compares the environmental impact of hot-air dryers to that of paper towels.

The argument is about environmental impact, making the comparison of operating expenses in **(A)** and effectiveness in **(D)** irrelevant. **(C)** is incorrect because it's not necessary for hot-air dryers to be the only alternative to paper towels for dryers to be the better alternative. **(E)** is incorrect because the author's conclusion is that paper towels *should* be banned, not that they *will* be banned; even if the ban can't be enacted, it could still be a good idea.

2. (C)

The author concludes that all full-time employees who sign up for the company's insurance program will have most of their medical needs covered. As evidence, the author cites the fact that employees can choose one of three plans. The author therefore assumes that at least one of the three plans will provide each employee with complete coverage and, moreover, that every employee will choose a plan that does so. Predict that the correct answer to this Assumption question will provide some link between the availability of three plans and the coverage of all medical needs. **(C)** matches this prediction. This is easier to see if you reword the double-negative phrasing: "There are no full-time employees whose medical needs are mostly uncovered by [each plan]" becomes "Every full-time employee's medical needs are mostly covered by [each plan]."

(A) is incorrect; the argument is about full-time employees, so the coverage available for part-time employees is irrelevant. **(B)** is also irrelevant; the argument is about whether employees will have coverage, not how much it costs the company. **(D)** is incorrect because the argument asserts only that the plans provide complete coverage for this company's employees; even if other plans exist that cover more, these three plans could provide these employees with ample coverage. **(E)** is incorrect. The argument does not claim that *everything* is covered, only that *most* medical needs are covered. Moreover, there is no evidence that any of these employees suffer ill health due to dental needs, so they could have complete coverage without dental insurance.

3. (B)

The author is making the claim that, contrary to expectations, the local hardware store will likely see an increase in sales. The author's evidence is the increasing number of construction projects in the area. For this Assumption question, therefore, predict that the correct answer will establish a necessary link between an increase in construction projects and an increase in sales at this hardware store. **(B)** matches this prediction, as it states that the construction materials will be purchased from the local hardware store.

(A) is incorrect because how much the construction managers buy from the other hardware store doesn't matter, as long as they buy enough from this hardware store to cause its total sales to increase. **(C)** and **(E)** are incorrect because there is no necessary connection between either the quality of materials or the price of materials and increased sales. No information is provided in these statements or in the stimulus about how construction managers decide where to buy materials. **(D)** is incorrect because it does not establish a connection between the home improvements and the purchase of materials from this local hardware store.

Practice Set: Strengthen and Weaken Questions

4. (B)

The author concludes that the officials' water usage reduction program was effective. The evidence is that water levels were unusually low earlier, the city instituted a conservation plan, and that water levels have since returned to normal. To cast doubt on this argument, as required by this Weaken question, first identify the author's central assumption. The author assumes a causal relationship between the city's water reduction plan and the restoration of normal water levels in the reservoir. On the GMAT, causal assumptions are commonly weakened by providing an alternative explanation for the observation; in this case, it's that the restoration of water levels was due to something other than the officials' program. **(B)** suggests exactly this: if water levels recovered in cities that did not enact water usage reduction programs, then it's likely that some other factor (say, increased rainfall throughout the area) is responsible.

(A) is incorrect because the program could have been effective this year even if water levels were higher last year. After all, the goal was to help water levels recover this year, and that did indeed happen. **(C)** and **(E)** are incorrect because both provide evidence that water usage was reduced, which is consistent with the efficacy of the program. The comparisons that each choice introduces, between water usage activities in **(C)** and between time frames in **(E)**, are irrelevant to the overall argument. **(D)** is incorrect because the program could still have been effective even if other programs would have been even more effective.

5. (E)

The author concludes that the zoo's proposal, if adopted, would expose visitors to grave danger, as expressed through a clever analogy. As evidence, the author explains that the animals would not have gotten to know the new people delivering their food. To move from the animals' lack of familiarity with these people to the animals' aggression toward them, the author must assume both that familiarity is the reason the big cats do not attack their zookeeper handlers and that they would

not be prevented from attacking their new visitors. For this Strengthen question, look for a choice that speaks to one or both of these assumptions. **(E)** states that the visitors would have to enter the cats' habitat and emphasizes the need to build familiarity before safely interacting with the animals.

(A) states that visitors are not as knowledgeable as the zookeepers. However, the argument hinges on how well the cats know the people feeding them, not the other way around. In addition, the argument depends only on whether a sufficient threshold of familiarity is met, not on whether the cats are as familiar with the visitors as they are with the zookeepers. Moreover, this statement provides no evidence that visitors—well-informed or not—would be in any danger, as the author concludes. **(B)** is incorrect because it speaks to the effectiveness of the proposal and has no effect on the author's conclusion, which is about the safety of visitors. **(C)** is incorrect because it attempts to strengthen the author's analogy instead of the argument's assumption. **(D)** is incorrect because it introduces a comparison between zoo visitors and non-visitors. The comparison described in the stem is between the visitors and the zookeepers.

6. (C)

The Southtown spokesperson uses statistics about tax revenues to claim that Southtown has a lower business tax rate than does Northtown. This Weaken question asks you to "undermine" the spokesperson's reasoning. The statistics provided show that Northtown collects more money in business taxes per year than does Southtown. However, this doesn't mean that Southtown has a lower tax *rate*. It is possible that the business tax rate in Northtown is lower than that of Southtown, yet Northtown collects more taxes overall because it has more businesses or its businesses are more profitable than those in Southtown. Therefore, a good prediction would be that Southtown has less business profits to tax or a higher rate of taxation. **(C)** matches the prediction and is correct. If Northtown has twice the business profits but collects less than twice the tax revenue of Southtown, then Northtown must have a lower business tax rate.

Eliminate (A) and (B); the argument is only about the impact of business taxes, so whether a smaller or larger proportion of all taxes are business taxes has nothing to do with tax rates and is irrelevant to the conclusion. (D) is also irrelevant. The size of the population does not necessarily correlate with the amount of business taxes collected. (E) does not undermine the claim because according to the stimulus, business taxes are not assessed on sales but on net profits.

7.   (A)

The key word "should" in the final sentence indicates the author's conclusion: the author recommends that the agency advertise its job vacancies to the local law school's graduating class and, further, states that this is the most efficient way to staff these jobs. The author supports this recommendation with information on public interest law and the claim that "many lawyers are urgently needed" to fill open positions at a nonprofit agency that specializes in such law. For this Weaken EXCEPT question, look for a choice that either strengthens or has no effect on the author's recommendation. (A) fails to weaken the recommendation because the author gives no reason to believe that the local law school graduates are motivated entirely by money. As long as enough of the graduates are content to settle for a lower salary, perhaps with the added motivation of serving the public interest, a targeted ad campaign could still be the most effective way to staff the open positions.

(B) points out that the local law school is already providing information about open positions to its graduating class, making it less likely that the advertising will have any effect. (C) weakens the argument by suggesting that the graduating students would not be qualified to fill the positions at the agency. (D) states that several of the agency's vacancies are due to lawyers leaving the agency because of low pay, making it more likely that salaries, not advertising, are the issue. (E) makes it less likely that the agency's advertising will find a receptive audience.

8.   (B)

The argument's conclusion is presented in the final sentence, introduced by the key word "hence": the bicyclists claim that they shouldn't have to wear helmets in the park. Their reasoning is based on the idea that the park should not restrict an activity that doesn't harm others. The correct answer, therefore, will show how not wearing a helmet actually does harm someone else. The correct answer, (B), does just that, stating that not requiring cyclists to wear helmets would inflict financial harm on all park users.

(A) discusses cyclists' preferences, but the argument about whether to require helmet use has to do with whether others would be harmed, not with a personal preference. The 10% of cyclists who would stop wearing helmets if doing so were no longer required could cause harm to others. (C) discusses a law in a different city about motorcyclists and is therefore irrelevant to this argument about Wunderlich Park. (D) and (E) both give good reasons to wear a helmet, but they suggest that only the cyclist is at risk, not someone else.

Practice Set: Evaluation Questions

9.   (D)

For this Evaluate question, you need to identify information that would help evaluate the claim in the question stem—that planting certain species of plants, called dynamic accumulators, would be beneficial to farmers' crops. The author bases this claim on the fact that dynamic accumulators have been shown to be beneficial to plants growing nearby. The evidence is about unspecified plants, while the conclusion is about crops grown by farmers, so predict that the correct answer will focus on similarity between the plants that have benefited from the accumulators and the crops that farmers grow. Answering the question in (D) would provide information about the similarity of the plants. If the answer is yes, the reports support the claim. If the answer is no, the reports do not support the claim.

(A) and (E) are irrelevant; all that matters is whether the use of dynamic accumulators increases crop production, not whether it's more expensive or whether it has other benefits. (B) is irrelevant because the effectiveness of other solutions has no bearing on whether this particular solution would be effective. (C) focuses too specifically on comfrey, which is just one example of a dynamic accumulator. Determining whether there are better dynamic accumulators than comfrey wouldn't help determine whether dynamic accumulators in general are helpful for crop growth.

10. (E)

The question stem tells you what to evaluate: whether this company's fish-farming plan would be better than simply discarding its by-products. Since this is an Evaluate EXCEPT question, the four incorrect choices will help evaluate that claim; they will focus on the advantages and disadvantages of the proposed plan. The correct choice will be a question whose answer would not shed light on the effectiveness of this company's proposal. (E) is that choice; the answer to this question could help you determine whether a plan involving wild catfish would be feasible, but it would do nothing to evaluate the specified claim, which involves farmed catfish.

(A) focuses on the costs of the new plan; knowing whether the fish farm would cost more than current operations would help determine whether it would be a good idea. Similarly, (B) would help the company determine whether there is a demand for the product it is thinking of selling. (C) and (D) both ask questions about potential problems with the new business plan: whether government regulations would make the plan more difficult to implement and whether the grain company would need to buy other foods or supplements, making the project more expensive.

Practice Set: Flaw Questions

11. (C)

The author argues that skateboarding should not be banned, based on the evidence that more joggers than skaters are injured each year. This Flaw question asks you to find the problem with the author's reasoning. The author uses as evidence total numbers of injuries but draws a conclusion about the relative risk of each activity. However, say there were 100 skateboarders and 1,000 joggers. If 75 percent of skateboarders and only 10 percent of joggers were injured each year, then skateboarding would be more dangerous, even though there would be fewer skateboarding injuries. Predict that the author fails to consider the relative numbers of skateboarders and joggers. (C) is correct; it points out that the author isn't considering how many people participate in each activity.

(A) and (D) are irrelevant comparisons. What matters is the proportion of people who are injured in the two activities; whether those injuries are suffered by professionals or amateurs is irrelevant, as is whether there are other, more dangerous activities. (B) is incorrect because the author does not, in fact, assume this. Nothing in the argument excludes the possibility that everyone who skateboards also jogs; the argument is based on the number of injuries that occur during each activity. The author also never attacks anyone's character, so (E) is incorrect.

12. (D)

The author concludes that all solo concert pianists should be allowed to consult their musical scores while performing. This conclusion is supported by the evidence that most members of chamber groups and orchestras use sheet music and perform well as a result. Correctly identifying the argument's vulnerability, as required by this Flaw question, involves finding the flaw in the author's argument. In this case, the author assumes that solo pianists and chamber group/orchestra members use the same skill set or that they have similar requirements during a performance. Predict that the author is making a faulty assumption about the similarities between the solo pianist and the group members. (D) is correct because it acknowledges that the author takes for granted that soloists and chamber group/orchestra members use scores in the same way.

(A) is incorrect because it doesn't matter to the argument whether solo concert pianists prefer using musical scores; the author's argument states that they should be allowed to use them because they would perform better if they did. (B) may be tempting because it outlines a specific situation that could be used as an example to refute the author's assumption. However, a difference in ability is not a necessary component of the author's assumption, so this choice is ultimately incorrect. (C) is incorrect because the fact that certain musicians currently break the rules doesn't necessarily have any bearing on whether the rules should be changed for everyone. (E) is incorrect because the author's argument hinges on an unfounded comparison between soloists and orchestra members, but this choice only discusses one aspect of playing in an orchestra.

Practice Set: Explain Questions

13. (C)

As is typical with Explain questions, the stimulus here presents a paradox, or, in this case, a "discrepancy in sales." The question stem provides the following information: (1) Daniel's yoga mat sales doubled from last year, (2) Daniel's average yoga class size decreased from last year, and (3) Daniel has the only yoga studio in town. The correct answer will reconcile the seeming contradiction between (1) and (2), higher mat sales and smaller class size. (C) does this. If Daniel is teaching a greater number of classes, he could have more students in total than before, even if the average class size decreased. A greater number of new students could understandably result in a doubling of mat sales from the previous year, so the apparent contradiction is resolved.

(A) ignores the fact that class size is smaller and gives no reason to believe that a greater variety of mats would lead current students to buy more mats. (B) actually deepens the mystery, as one would expect higher mat prices to lead to lower mat sales, not higher sales. (D) might explain why class size is smaller but not why mat sales are up. (E) might be relevant if it described a new requirement, but there is no indication that this requirement was instituted this year.

14. (D)

This Explain question asks you to find a reason why a certain pizza shop saw no increase in sales despite emailing an enticing deal to thousands of people. The correct answer will provide a reason why these advertisements had no impact on sales. (D) provides just such a reason. If the people who were offered the two-for-one deal were already members of the rewards club, then the promotion wouldn't attract new customers. And, if those members are already offered weekly specials, then the deal is unlikely to motivate them to buy more pizza.

(A) is incorrect because the deal is only for sheet pizzas. Even if other pizza types aren't listed in the email, the deal could still have enticed people to buy more sheet pizzas. (B) offers no reason why opening a coffee shop would impact a pizza shop's sales. (C) is incorrect because, even if some potential customers don't have an email address, the deal was sent out to thousands of people who *do* have an email address. This choice doesn't explain why those people didn't seem to take advantage of the deal. While (E) explains why customers who prefer a higher-end pizza might buy their pizza elsewhere and customers on a budget would prefer this shop, it does nothing to explain why a special deal on sheet pizza wouldn't appeal to the customers who want less expensive pizza.

Practice Set: Inference Questions

15. (D)

What identifies this as an Inference question is that the information in the stimulus "most strongly supports" the correct answer choice. The stimulus describes the medical condition of hyperkalemia. Paraphrasing, you can summarize the known facts as follows: hyperkalemia is treated with medicines that reduce potassium levels, but patients with severe hyperkalemia are first given calcium to protect their hearts from the excess potassium. The correct answer will state something that must be true based on the statements in the stimulus. (D) does that. Calcium is one of the treatments given for severe hyperkalemia, yet calcium does not address the root cause of hyperkalemia, which is excess potassium.

(A) is incorrect because the stimulus never indicates that any medicine can make the conditions of severe hyperkalemia worse. (B) is incorrect because the fact that people with severe hyperkalemia *are* given calcium doesn't mean people with mild to moderate hyperkalemia are *not* given calcium. The stimulus leaves open the possibility that at least some of those people are also given calcium. (C) can be rejected because there is nothing in the stimulus about waiting for calcium to have its full effect before insulin is given. (E) tries to connect calcium to the reduction of potassium, but the stimulus explicitly states that calcium does *not* lower potassium levels.

16. (E)

This is an Inference question, as the given statements will support the correct answer choice. The stimulus compares the cost of hiring college students to the cost of hiring outside auditors for a one-month task. The store pays students 20% less than it would pay a service to provide outside auditors. By hiring students, the store also has to pay for training and insurance. However, the store still spends less money overall when hiring students. So, that implies that the training and insurance are not expensive enough to exceed the 20% savings in wages. That makes (E) the correct answer.

(A) is incorrect because the stimulus effectively puts an upper limit on non-wage expenses (less than 20% of total pay), not a lower limit. (B) is incorrect because the stimulus only discusses money. There's no indication how much time it takes anyone to do their work. (C) is incorrect because students are paid 20% less than what the *store* would pay the service that provides outside auditors. However, there's no indication of how much the temporary service pays its auditors; it could be less than the total amount the service receives. (D) is incorrect because there's no suggestion that anyone will lose their jobs. The outside auditors could still work elsewhere.

Practice Set: Bolded Statement Questions

17. (E)

The stimulus opens with a series of facts about fingerprint analysis, both in life and in popular culture. The first bolded statement is an example to support the claim made in the previous sentence that the theory of fingerprint identification predates its actual use. The key word "Yet" signals an important shift: the second bolded statement is a recommendation made by the author. Because the rest of the stimulus builds toward this recommendation, it is the author's main point. (E) describes these roles and is correct.

(A) and (B) incorrectly state that the second statement is "contrary" to the author's main idea, when in fact the opposite is true; additionally, (B) incorrectly states that the first statement is supporting an opinion, not a factual claim. Similarly, (C) claims that the first statement is an opinion, but it's actually a supporting detail, and that the second statement "contradicts" the opinion, but there is no conflict between them. Finally, (D) is incorrect because it asserts that the second statement is evidence, but it is actually the author's main point or conclusion.

18. (B)

The stimulus opens with a claim that spices were often used to cover up the flavor of spoiled meat. This statement is immediately followed by the author's contrasting recommendation that the preceding opinion is properly evaluated. The bolded statement then provides data that relates to the extremely high cost of ginger in ancient Rome. In the final sentence, the author posits that anyone who could afford the luxury of ginger would just buy unspoiled meat. Since the bolded statement is historical economic data, predict an answer that identifies the bolded statement as evidence for the author's proposal. (B) matches the prediction and is correct.

(A) is incorrect because the bolded statement is data for the author's claim, not for the claim that the author is attempting to refute. (There is no evidence in the stimulus to support the claim that appears in the first sentence.) (C) mischaracterizes the statement as the historian's conclusion rather than as evidence, and (D) mischaracterizes the statement as someone else's claim. (E) asserts that the historian questions the accuracy of the data in the bolded statement. Since the historian uses this evidence to support her conclusion, the historian does not doubt its veracity.

CHAPTER 15

CRITICAL REASONING QUESTIONS: PUTTING IT ALL TOGETHER

LEARNING OBJECTIVES

- Recognize immediately the format of a Critical Reasoning question and apply the Kaplan Method for Critical Reasoning
- Determine quickly a question's type and consider nuances to the Kaplan Method for Critical Reasoning that will be helpful for the specific question type
- Evaluate your performance on Critical Reasoning questions

This quiz is designed to give you practice with a mix of Critical Reasoning question types, just like the mix of CR questions you'll see on Test Day. Take this quiz after you have studied the different Critical Reasoning question types and common stimulus patterns and practiced applying the Kaplan Method for Critical Reasoning to them.

How to Take This Quiz

By the time you take this quiz, you are hopefully well on your way to mastery of Critical Reasoning, so set a timer. Give yourself 2 minutes per question. So if you do all 10 questions at once, set the timer for 20 minutes; if you decide to do fewer questions than that in one sitting, set the timer accordingly.

Make sure to use the steps of the Kaplan Method on every question. Students are often tempted to skip step 1 and not bother identifying the question type. They get some questions right without doing this task, so they reason that it's not important. But they would get even more questions right if they were crystal clear about the task before reading the stimulus. Students are also prone to skip step 3, making a prediction, finding it easier to look in the answer choices for ideas about what might be the right answer. By leaning on the test to do their thinking for them, however, they risk falling for cleverly worded wrong-answer traps.

Furthermore, remember that on Test Day, you can't take notes on the computer screen or skip forward and back between questions. So challenge yourself now not to take notes in this book (use separate scratch paper or an erasable noteboard) and to do the questions in order.

After you've finished the quiz and are reviewing the explanations, make sure you not only can explain why the right answer is correct but also can articulate why each wrong answer is incorrect. Being able to clearly identify why wrong choices are wrong will help you avoid picking them.

In addition, if you missed a question, understand *why* you missed it. There is always a reason! The Kaplan Method can be a useful checklist to diagnose where you went wrong.

- Did you misunderstand the task set by the question stem?
- Did you misunderstand a key pattern or detail of the stimulus?
- Was your prediction off base or too specific (or too general), or did you omit making a prediction?
- Were you tempted by a choice that did not actually match your prediction, perhaps because you could have read more carefully or because you fell for a common wrong-answer trap?

If you know why you missed a question, you can avoid making that error again.

Above all, be patient and forgiving with yourself. Practice for the GMAT is not about judging yourself. It's about making mistakes so you can learn from them and improve your score.

Critical Reasoning Quiz

(Answers and explanations are at the end of the chapter.)

1. To avoid the appearance of conflicts of interest, the board of a major U.S. stock exchange is considering a new policy that would ban former top executives of the exchange from taking positions at publicly traded companies for a period of two years after leaving the stock exchange. Critics of the plan say the policy is unfair because it would likely prevent former top executives of the exchange from earning a decent living.

   Which of the following statements, if true, would most strengthen the prediction made by the critics of the proposed company policy?

   ○ The labor union that represents most of the stock exchange's employees has made public statements that threaten a strike if the policy is not adopted.

   ○ Former employees of the exchange most often work for publicly traded companies after leaving the exchange.

   ○ Low-level managers at the exchange have an average tenure of 13 years, one of the longest in the industry.

   ○ Low-level managers at the exchange most often leave their jobs for positions with the state or federal government.

   ○ Former top executives of the exchange have a particular set of skills such that they are usually able to find work only with publicly traded companies.

2. The increase in taxes on cigarettes next month will not limit the use of addictive tobacco products to the extent that health advocates hope. Many cigarette smokers will shift their spending to cigars and chewing tobacco when the law takes effect.

   Which of the following, if true, would most strongly weaken the argument above?

   ○ Cigars and chewing tobacco can satisfy the nicotine cravings of most cigarette smokers.

   ○ The taste, smell, and texture of cigars and chewing tobacco are sufficiently different from those of cigarettes to deter cigarette smokers from using them.

   ○ Many health advocates themselves use tobacco products.

   ○ The government might also impose significant taxes on cigars and chewing tobacco over the course of two years.

   ○ Cigars and chewing tobacco are often more expensive than cigarettes.

3. The percentage of local businesses with more than 10 employees is higher in Grandview City than in any other city in the state. However, the percentage of local businesses with 15 employees or more is higher in Lakeshore City, which is in the same state, than in any other city in the state.

   If the statements above are true, then which of the following must also be true?

   O   The percentage of local businesses with more than 18 employees is higher in Lakeshore City than in any other city in the state.

   O   The state has more local businesses with more than 10 employees than any other state in the country.

   O   The number of local businesses with 15 or more employees is greater in Lakeshore City than in Grandview City.

   O   Some local businesses in Grandview City have 11 to 14 employees.

   O   The average number of employees per business is higher in Lakeshore City than in Grandview City.

4. The Ministry of Tourism in country X began an expensive television advertising campaign in country Y two years ago. Since that time, the number of visitors to country X from country Y has increased by more than 8 percent. Clearly, the Ministry of Tourism's campaign is responsible for the increase.

   Which of the following, if true, would most weaken the argument above?

   O   The advertisements sponsored by the Ministry of Tourism in country X were panned by the country Y media for lack of imagination.

   O   A devaluation of the currency in country X two years ago made travel there more affordable for residents of country Y.

   O   Increasing political turmoil in country X will lead to a decrease in visitors from country Y next year.

   O   The number of visitors from country Y to country Z increased by more than 8 percent over the past two years.

   O   Over the past two years, the advertisement campaign launched by the Ministry of Tourism in country X cost more money than residents of country Y spent traveling in country X.

5. A corporation's recent financial report indicates that customers in its Quarx stores, which play upbeat music through an in-store audio system, spend on average 25 percent more per shopping trip than customers in its Cubix stores, which advertise specials over the audio system. Clearly, hearing music has a greater impact than hearing advertisements on how much money customers spend when shopping.

   Which of the following, if true, would most strengthen the argument above?

   O A study conducted by a psychologist found that hearing music makes shoppers feel financially secure, so they are more likely to make impulse purchases.

   O Customers who hear advertisements for things they dislike form a negative association between their shopping experience and what they heard, making them less likely to return to the store where they heard the advertisement.

   O Stores that play music tend to carry products that are essential to daily life, while those that advertise specials often stock unessential, fun items that the stores hope consumers will decide to buy on a whim if offered a special price.

   O An economist who studied consumer shopping habits found that about half the population likes to listen to music while shopping, while the other half reports either disliking music or not noticing that music is playing.

   O According to a recent sociological study, customers say that hearing specials announced while they are shopping is irritating, but they often take advantage of the discounts offered in those announcements.

6. Cable television executive: **Our service and reliability have increased dramatically over the past year.** Our customer service line is receiving 30 percent fewer reports of interrupted service, and the number of subscribers canceling their accounts is barely half of what it was last year.

   Cable television customer: That doesn't mean your service and reliability have improved. **It's possible that customers don't bother to call your customer service line to report problems because they never get any assistance when they do.** And the drop-off in the number of canceled accounts could reflect the fact that nearly all of your dissatisfied customers have already canceled their accounts.

   In the argument above, the two portions in boldface play which of the following roles?

   O The first is evidence designed to lead to a conclusion; the second offers further evidence in support of that conclusion.

   O The first is evidence designed to lead to a conclusion; the second offers evidence designed to cast doubt on that conclusion.

   O The first is a conclusion; the second offers evidence in support of that conclusion.

   O The first is a conclusion; the second offers evidence designed to cast doubt on that conclusion.

   O The first is a conclusion; the second is an alternative conclusion based on the same evidence.

7. Opponents of the laws prohibiting the use of nonprescription narcotic drugs in Leffingwell argue that in a free society, people should have the right to take risks as long as the risks do not harm others who have not elected to take such risks. These opponents conclude that people should have the legal right to make the decision whether or not to use narcotic drugs.

    Which of the following is an assumption required by the argument?

    ○   Some narcotic drugs have been shown to have medicinal qualities.

    ○   There are laws in Leffingwell that govern the use of prescription drugs.

    ○   People who use nonprescription narcotic drugs are no more likely to perpetuate a violent crime when under the influence of these drugs than when not under the influence.

    ○   People who use certain types of narcotic drugs are no more likely to die of an overdose than of natural causes.

    ○   The rate of drug overdoses is lower in countries that do not have laws governing the use of narcotic drugs than in Leffingwell.

8. In a survey of undergraduates, two-fifths admitted to having cheated on an exam at least once during their education. However, the survey may underestimate the proportion of undergraduates who have cheated because _____.

    Which of the following best completes the passage above?

    ○   some undergraduates who have cheated at least once might have claimed on the survey never to have cheated

    ○   some undergraduates who have never cheated might have claimed on the survey to have cheated

    ○   some undergraduates who claimed on the survey to have cheated at least once may have cheated on multiple occasions throughout their education

    ○   some undergraduates who claimed on the survey to have cheated at least once may have been answering honestly

    ○   some students who are not undergraduates have probably cheated at least once during their education

9. During the last 18 years, the number of people who live or work in the Dry River Valley, which is prone to flash flooding, has continually increased, as has traffic on local roads and bridges. However, the number of people caught in flash floods has decreased, even though the annual number of floods has increased slightly.

    Which of the following, if true, best explains the decrease described above?

    O   Flash floods are more likely to happen in the first hour of a rainstorm than afterward.

    O   Flash floods killed some people in the Dry River Valley in every one of the last 18 years.

    O   Better meteorological technology has improved local authorities' ability to predict when and where flash floods will occur.

    O   Many people work in the Dry River Valley but live elsewhere.

    O   A law that went into effect 18 years ago mandated that all new homes built in the valley be built on raised foundations, making those homes much less susceptible to flood damage.

10. Colleges in Tycho City have failed to prepare their students for the business world. A recent study revealed that the majority of college graduates in Tycho City could not write a simple business letter.

    Which of the following, if true, would provide additional evidence in support of the claim above?

    O   A majority of students attending colleges in Tycho City are business majors.

    O   The state college in neighboring Twyla Township has recently improved its business program by adding courses in business writing.

    O   Most Tycho City college graduates move outside the Tycho City area after they graduate.

    O   Most Tycho City college students live in on-campus dormitories.

    O   The majority of college graduates living in Tycho City received their college degrees from institutions located in Tycho City.

Answers and Explanations

Critical Reasoning Quiz

1. (E)

You're looking to strengthen the argument here—specifically the prediction made by the critics of a policy. A new policy would ban former top executives of a stock exchange from working for certain companies for two years after leaving the exchange. Critics of the policy contend that the policy will prevent the executives from earning a good living. To strengthen the prediction, look for an answer choice that makes it more likely that the former executives can't earn a decent living. **(E)** is correct; it states that these executives can usually find work only at publicly traded companies, which would mean a ban on working at such companies would hurt their ability to make a living.

Whether or not the union strikes has no bearing on the effect the new policy would have on the former executives if enacted; thus, **(A)** is incorrect. **(B)** simply states that most former employees of the exchange work for publicly traded companies; it does not tell you that they could not make a decent living elsewhere if need be. Further, this choice is about employees in general, not necessarily the top executives that are the subject of the prediction. **(C)** and **(D)** refer to low-level managers, and the prediction only discusses top executives; thus, both choices are irrelevant and incorrect.

2. (B)

The words "weaken the argument" in the question stem indicate that this is a Weaken question. The author's conclusion is the prediction that many cigarette smokers will shift their spending from cigarettes to cigars and chewing tobacco. The correct answer will weaken the argument by suggesting some reason why cigarette smokers *won't* switch, despite the evidence that taxes on cigarettes will increase next month. **(B)** does this and is therefore correct. Cigarette smokers might be unhappy with the higher taxes on cigarettes, but if they are deterred by the other tobacco products' taste, smell, and texture, they are less likely to switch to them.

(A) strengthens the prediction. If cigars and chewing tobacco can satisfy cigarette smokers' nicotine cravings, then it is *more* likely that smokers will switch to them instead of paying more for cigarettes. **(C)** is incorrect because the personal habits of health advocates have no bearing on the author's prediction. **(D)** is irrelevant, because the author's prediction only concerns how cigarette smokers will respond to a tax increase that will occur next month, not what might happen in the next two years. **(E)** might have been tempting, because you wouldn't expect cigarette smokers to switch to more expensive products. However, "often" doesn't mean *always*, and the price difference might be insignificant. Also, perhaps these products won't be more expensive once the cigarette tax is increased.

3. (D)

The correct answer must be true based on the given statements, making this an Inference question. The stimulus provides data about the local businesses in two cities, Grandview and Lakeshore. Grandview has the highest percentage of businesses with more than 10 employees (or 11+ employees), so Grandview's percentage of 11+ businesses must be higher than Lakeshore's. These businesses also include all of the businesses with 15+ employees but, for that subset, Lakeshore has the highest percentage. So, Grandview's percentage of 15+ businesses must be lower. That means Grandview's percentage of 11+ businesses is higher than its percentage of 15+ businesses, which means at least some of its 11+ businesses do not have 15+ employees. In other words, some of Grandview's businesses must have 11–14 employees. **(D)** is correct.

(A) is incorrect because there's no indication how many or what percentage of Lakeshore's 15+ businesses, if any, have 18+ employees. **(B)** is incorrect because no data is given about any other state for comparison. **(C)** confuses numbers and percentages. Lakeshore might have a higher percentage, but not necessarily a higher number (e.g., 50% of 10 businesses is a smaller number than 25% of 100 businesses). **(E)** is incorrect because the statistics are only about minimum sizes. Grandview could have a smaller percentage of 15+ businesses, but those businesses could have substantially more employees than any business in Lakeview, giving Grandview a larger overall average.

4.   (B)

This is a Weaken question, as indicated by the wording "would most weaken the argument above." The conclusion, signaled by "clearly," is that country X's advertising campaign is responsible for the increase in visitors from country Y to country X. The evidence is that since the ad campaign began running, the number of visitors from country Y to country X has gone up by more than 8%. You may have recognized the classic causality argument pattern here: the author notes a correlation between two things, in this case the ad campaign and the increase in visitors, and then concludes that one of the things caused the other. A weakener will suggest an alternative explanation for the correlation. This is exactly what **(B)** does, making it correct. More visitors might have come from country Y because it became more affordable for them to travel to country X, not because the ad campaign enticed them to visit.

(A) is incorrect because even if the advertisements lacked imagination, they still could have spurred the increase in visitors. **(C)** is irrelevant because it concerns the future, whereas the argument is concerned only with what has caused the increase in the past two years. **(D)** is incorrect because travel from Y to Z is irrelevant to the argument about travel from Y to X. This choice might have been tempting if you thought it suggested the alternative explanation that people in country Y are simply traveling more than they used to, regardless of destination. But it doesn't indicate what motivated the visits to country Z and thus has no bearing on the argument. **(E)** deals with the cost-effectiveness of the ad campaign. This is irrelevant to the argument, which concerns only whether the ad campaign caused the increased tourism.

5.   (A)

The words "most strengthen the argument above" in the question stem make this a Strengthen question. The author's conclusion, indicated by "clearly," is that hearing music has a greater impact than hearing advertisements on how much money customers spend when shopping. The evidence offered is a financial report on two chains of stores. According to the report, Quarx stores play music on their audio systems and saw customers spend

25% more per trip, on average, than did customers at Cubix stores, which advertise specials on their audio systems. The author is assuming there was no other factor that accounted for the difference in spending between the store chains. The correct answer will either make it *more* likely that hearing music causes customers to spend more or that hearing about specials makes customers spend less, or will make it *less* likely that some other factor was what led to the spending difference. **(A)** does the former and is therefore correct. While it doesn't address the effects of hearing advertised specials, it does strengthen the link between hearing music and then spending more money. It therefore makes the author's explanation more likely to be correct.

(B) is irrelevant, as it focuses on whether customers will return to the store. The argument is concerned only with how much the customers spend when they are actually in the store and hear the ads. **(C)** has no effect on the argument because it doesn't link the information about product types to how much money customers spend. **(D)** also has no effect on the argument because it doesn't relate the economist's findings to money spent per shopping trip. **(E)** is the opposite of what is needed. It suggests that customers who hear about specials end up spending more than they originally planned. While it doesn't address the effects of hearing music, it still makes the author's explanation that music has a greater impact a little less likely to be true.

6.   (D)

The cable television executive uses evidence of fewer customer complaints and cancellations to conclude that the cable company's service has improved over the past year. Therefore, the first bolded statement is the cable executive's conclusion. The second bolded statement is evidence from the customer that would support a contradictory conclusion. According to the customer, there may be fewer cancellations because all the dissatisfied customers have already canceled their accounts; the decreased number of complaints indicates that frustrated customers have simply given up. Predict that the correct choice will reflect this structure. **(D)** is correct; the second statement is evidence used to question the validity of the conclusion in the first.

Since the first bolded statement represents the executive's conclusion, you can eliminate (A) and (B), which characterize this statement as evidence. The customer clearly disagrees with the executive, so you can eliminate (C). (E) may be tempting; the second statement does provide an alternate explanation of some of the evidence, but the second statement is not a conclusion, merely a possible interpretation of evidence.

7.   (C)

As in all argument-based questions, you need to find the conclusion and evidence; because this is an Assumption question, the correct answer will connect these two. The conclusion is the last sentence: the use of nonprescription narcotic drugs should be everyone's personal decision. The evidence is that people have the right to take risks as long as taking those risks doesn't hurt anyone besides themselves. The opponents of the laws assume that nonprescription narcotics pose risks only to the people who use them. Look for a choice that paraphrases this assumption. (C) does the job; this choice is more specific than the prediction, but it is certainly one thing that the author assumes. If people are no more likely to commit violent crimes while under the influence of drugs, then others are less likely to be at risk from drug users.

(A) is incorrect because it introduces the idea of medicinal qualities, which is irrelevant to the argument. The author focuses on the harm caused by drug-using behavior, not potential benefits. The prescription drugs in (B) are likewise unrelated to the argument, which is concerned only with nonprescription drugs. While (D) does establish that certain drugs may not cause overdoses, this information has no bearing on the argument since it concerns a risk to the user of the drug, not a threat to others. Finally, (E) is an irrelevant comparison. The overdose rate in other countries without such laws has no bearing on the argument because overdose rates indicate only personal risk, not others' danger.

8.   (A)

Here, you have a question that asks you to complete the final sentence of a brief argument. The word before the blank is "because," an evidence key word; since the missing information is evidence that would support the

author's point of view, this question is a Strengthen question. The author's conclusion is that the survey may have underestimated the proportion of undergraduates who cheated. You know from the first sentence that two-fifths of the students *reported* having cheated at least once. The one correct answer will provide a reason to think that there are additional, unreported cheaters among the undergraduate population. (A) is a match for the prediction and is correct: some undergrads may have cheated but lied about it on the survey.

(B) is the opposite of what is needed because it offers a reason why the survey might *overestimate* the proportion of undergrads cheating. (C) is incorrect because it refers to multiple cases of cheating per student, but the survey measures the proportion of students who have cheated at least once, which would already include students who cheated multiple times. (D) gives a reason why the survey might be accurate, which is not what you want. (E) introduces students who are not undergraduates, which is not the focus of the survey, and is thus incorrect.

9.   (C)

This is an Explain question; your task is to resolve the seemingly disparate pieces of information in order to explain the atypical result. The stimulus tells you about two increases—the number of people and the number of flash floods—in the Dry River Valley. The key word "however" signals the seeming discrepancy: despite those increases, the number of people caught in flash floods has gone down. The correct answer will reconcile these two facts. (C) gives you the explanation you need and is correct: more accurate advance notice of floods allows local authorities to better prevent people from getting caught in the flooding.

While (A) may be true of flash flooding in general, it doesn't describe any difference between the floods now and those 18 years ago. (B) is incorrect since it is irrelevant to the argument, which deals with people *caught* in the floods, not people killed by them. (D) fails to provide any new information; you already know from the stimulus that there are commuters. Furthermore, it doesn't explain the fact that fewer people are caught in flash floods even as the number of floods increases, as there's no reason to think that flash floods somehow selectively avoid commuters. **(E)** is also irrelevant because the argument does not focus on property damage.

10. (E)

To "provide additional evidence in support" of an argument is to strengthen it, so this is a Strengthen question. The argument concludes that colleges in Tycho City don't do a good job of preparing their graduates for the business world, because the majority of college grads living in Tycho City couldn't write a simple business letter. The evidence is based on "college graduates in Tycho City," while the conclusion refers to the supposed failings of "colleges in Tycho City." For the conclusion to hold, it must be true that the college graduates in the study are alumni of colleges in Tycho City. Look for an answer that bolsters that assumption. **(E)** demonstrates

that the majority of people in the sample studied are actually alumni of colleges in Tycho City; therefore, it is correct.

(A) is incorrect, while the argument concerns whether students are prepared for the business world, what subject students major in has no direct bearing on this; even if graduates majored in business, the fact remains that they cannot write a simple business letter. **(B)** is irrelevant. What some other college is doing does not affect an argument about the effectiveness of Tycho City college programs. **(C)** weakens the argument. If most Tycho City college graduates leave the Tycho City area after graduation, then it is unlikely that a study of graduates in Tycho City is representative of graduates of Tycho City colleges. Finally, **(D)** is irrelevant, since where the students live has no effect on whether or not they're adequately prepared for the business world.

CHAPTER 16

VERBAL REASONING STRATEGY: READING COMPREHENSION QUESTIONS

> **LEARNING OBJECTIVES**
>
> - Describe the characteristics of the Reading Comprehension format and the subject matter of Reading Comprehension passages
> - Apply the steps of the Kaplan Method for Reading Comprehension
> - Recognize how the four Core Competencies apply to Reading Comprehension questions

On the GMAT Verbal section, you will likely see four Reading Comp passages with three or four questions on each, for a total of approximately 13 or 14 questions. Plan to take no longer than 4 minutes to read and make notes on the passage and a little less than 1.5 minutes to answer each question.

You will see only one question at a time on the screen, and you will have to answer each question before you can see the next question. The passage will appear on the left side of the screen and will remain there until you've answered all of the questions that relate to it. That's important, because it means you don't have to study the passage to learn the material, the way you might have studied a textbook in school. You'll be able to research details when you need them. If the text is longer than the available space, you'll be given a scroll bar to move through it.

The directions for Reading Comprehension questions look like this:

> **Directions:** The questions in this group are based on the content of a passage. After reading the passage, choose the best answer to each question. Base your answers only on what is stated or implied in the text.

The passages you'll see on the GMAT will concern an area of business, social science, biological science, or physical science. As the directions indicate, you are not expected to be familiar with any topic beforehand—all the information you need is contained in the text in front of you. In fact, if you happen to have some previous knowledge about a given topic, it is important that you not let that knowledge affect your answers. The passages will have the tone and content that one might expect from scholarly research or serious journalism.

Reading Comprehension is designed to assess your critical reading skills. Among other things, it tests whether you can do the following:

- Summarize the main idea of a passage
- Understand logical relationships between facts and concepts
- Make inferences based on information in a text
- Analyze the logical structure of a passage
- Deduce the author's tone and attitude about a topic from the text

In this chapter, you will learn strategic approaches to help you read and research the text efficiently, given the kinds of questions the GMAT will ask about it.

The Kaplan Method for Reading Comprehension

Many test takers read the entire passage closely from beginning to end, taking detailed notes and making sure that they understand everything, and then try to answer the questions from memory. Or, conscious of the passage of precious minutes on the clock, they rush through the passage so quickly, they know little more about it when they're done than before they read it. Neither of these approaches is very effective.

The best test takers know that the GMAT requires a different approach to reading from the reading you do every day. After all, most people read to learn something or to pass the time pleasantly. Neither of these goals has much to do with the GMAT. On Test Day, you have a very specific goal—to get as many right answers as you can. So your reading needs to be tailored to that goal. There are really only two things a Reading Comp question can ask you about: the "big picture" of the passage or its "little details."

Since the passage is right there on the screen, you don't need to worry much about the little details as you read. In fact, doing so may hinder your ability to answer questions, as you'll soon see. Your main goal as you read is to prepare yourself to get the big-picture questions right, while leaving yourself as much time as possible to research the answers to the little-detail questions.

You will attack the passages and questions critically in an aggressive, energetic, and goal-oriented way. Working this way pays off because it's the kind of pragmatic and efficient approach that the GMAT rewards— the same type of approach that business schools like their students to take when faced with an intellectual challenge.

To help this strategic approach become second nature, Kaplan has developed a Method that you can use to attack each and every Reading Comp passage and question.

> **THE KAPLAN METHOD FOR READING COMPREHENSION**
>
> **STEP 1** Read the passage strategically.
>
> **STEP 2** Analyze the question stem.
>
> **STEP 3** Research the relevant text.
>
> **STEP 4** Make a prediction.
>
> **STEP 5** Evaluate the answer choices.

Step 1: Read the Passage Strategically

Like most sophisticated writing, the prose you will see on the GMAT doesn't lay out the *why* and *how* of a passage up front. After all, if the ideas were plainly outlined, the test makers couldn't ask probing questions about them. So to set up the questions—to test how you think about the prose you read—the GMAT uses passages in which authors convey their reasons for writing through implication and challenge you to extract them.

This is why it's essential to start by reading the passage strategically, staying on the lookout for structural key words and phrases. With this strategic analysis as a guide, you should construct a passage map—a brief summary of each paragraph and its function in the passage's structure. You should also note the author's topic, scope, and purpose. Start by identifying the broad topic. Then hunt for scope, getting a sense of where the passage is going, what the author is going to focus on, and what role the first paragraph is playing. As you finish reading each paragraph, jot down a short note about its structure and the role it plays in the passage. When you finish reading the passage, double-check that you got the topic and scope right (sometimes passages can take unexpected turns) and note the author's overall purpose.

The **topic** is the big, broad subject matter of the passage. Almost always, it will be right there in the first sentence. There's no need to obsess over exactly how you word the topic; you just want a general idea of what the author is writing about so the passage gets easier to understand.

The **scope** is the narrow part of the topic that the author focuses on. If the author expresses his own opinion, then the thing he has an opinion about is the scope. Your statement of the scope should be as narrow as possible while still reflecting the passage as a whole. Your scope statement should also answer the question "What about this topic interests the author?" Identifying the scope is crucial because many incorrect choices are unsupported by the facts the author has actually chosen to provide. Remember that even though the first paragraph usually narrows the topic down to the scope, there probably won't be a "topic sentence" in the traditional sense.

The **purpose** is what the author is seeking to accomplish by writing the passage. You'll serve yourself well by picking an active verb for the purpose. Doing so helps not only by setting you up to find the right answer—many choices contain active verbs—but also by forcing you to consider the author's opinion. Here are some verbs that describe the purpose of a neutral author: *describe, explain, compare*. Here are some verbs for an author with an opinion: *advocate, argue, rebut, analyze*.

After you finish reading, your **passage map** should contain a few words or phrases summarizing the role of each paragraph and a short statement for each of the topic, scope, and purpose.

Take no more than 4 minutes to read and write your passage map. After all, you get points for answering questions, not for creating detailed passage maps. The more time you can spend working on the questions, the better your score will be. But creating a passage map and identifying the topic, scope, and purpose will prepare you to handle those questions efficiently and accurately.

It generally works best to create your passage map paragraph by paragraph. Don't write while you're reading, since you'll be tempted to write too much. But it's also not a good idea to wait until you've read the whole passage before writing anything, since it will be more difficult for you to recall what you've read. Analyze the structure as you read and take a few moments after you finish each paragraph to summarize the main points. Include details that are provided as evidence only when key words indicate their importance. A few words of paraphrase is generally enough to summarize a paragraph. Don't waste time trying to write out entire sentences or even words when they are long; use fragments, symbols, and abbreviations.

Step 2: Analyze the Question Stem

Only once you have read the passage strategically and jotted down your passage map should you read the first question stem. The second step of the Kaplan Method is to identify the question type; the most common question types are Global, Detail, Inference, and Logic. The next chapter will cover each of these question types in detail. For now, know that for each question, you will ask, "What should I do on this question?" Because different questions set you different tasks, if you approach every question the same way, you'll be likely to choose wrong answers instead of right ones.

Here are some guidelines for identifying each of the main question types:

- **Global.** These question stems contain language that refers to the passage as a whole, such as "primary purpose," "main idea," or "appropriate title for the passage."
- **Detail.** These question stems contain language such as "according to the author," "the passage states explicitly," or "is mentioned in the passage."
- **Inference.** These question stems contain language such as "most likely agree," "suggests," or "implies."
- **Logic.** These question stems ask for the purpose of a detail or paragraph and contain language such as "in order to," "purpose of the second paragraph," or "for which of the following reasons."

In addition to identifying the question type, be sure to focus on *exactly* what the question is asking. Let's say you see this question:

> The passage states which of the following about the uses of fixed nitrogen?

Don't look for what the passage says about "nitrogen" in general. Don't even look for "fixed nitrogen" alone. Look for a discussion of how fixed nitrogen is *used*.

Step 3: Research the Relevant Text

Treat the GMAT like an open-book test, knowing you can return to the passage as needed—and then do invest the time to research the text for particulars rather than rely on memory. However, for many questions, you are likely to find the answers simply by checking your passage map. Here is how you should focus your research for each question type:

- **Global.** The answer will deal with the passage as a whole, so review the topic, scope, and purpose you noted in your passage map.
- **Detail.** Use the specific reference in the question stem to direct your research in the text.
- **Inference.** For questions that include specific references, research the passage based on the clues in the question stem. You may need to research different parts of the passage as you evaluate each answer choice.
- **Logic.** Refer to your passage map for the author's overall purpose as well as the purpose of the relevant paragraph. If the question stem cites a specific detail, keep in mind the function of the paragraph it's in but also re-read the cited text to understand how the author uses the given detail.

Step 4: Make a Prediction

Predicting the answer before you look at the choices one of the most powerful strategies you can use to increase your efficiency and accuracy. Making a prediction allows you to know what you're looking for before you consider the choices. Doing so will help the right answer jump off the screen at you. It will also help you avoid incorrect choices that might otherwise be tempting. Here is how you should form your prediction for each question type:

- **Global.** Use the topic, scope, and purpose that you noted as the basis of your prediction.
- **Detail.** Predict an answer based on what the context tells you about the detail.
- **Inference.** Since the correct answer *must* be true based on the passage, a mental paraphrase of the author's relevant statements will serve as your prediction.
- **Logic.** Predict an answer that focuses on *why* the paragraph or detail was used, not on *what* it says.

Step 5: Evaluate the Answer Choices

Hunt for the choice that matches your prediction. If only one matches, it's the correct answer.

If you don't find a match for your prediction, if more than one choice seems to fit your prediction, or if you had difficulty forming a prediction, then you'll need to evaluate each choice, looking for errors. If you can prove four choices wrong, then you can confidently select the one that remains, even if you aren't completely sure what you think about it. This is the beauty of a multiple-choice test—knowing how to eliminate four choices you can find fault with enables you to answer correctly.

Here are some common characteristics of incorrect choices to look out for:

- **Global.** Choices that misrepresent the scope or purpose of the passage and answers that focus too heavily on details from one part of the passage
- **Detail.** Choices that distort the context or focus on the wrong details entirely
- **Inference.** Choices that include extreme language or exaggerations of the author's statements, distortions of the passage's meaning, or the opposite of the author's idea
- **Logic.** Choices that get the specifics right but the purpose wrong

Look out for "half-right/half-wrong" choices, which are fine at the beginning but then take a wrong turn; it's important to read all the way through a choice before selecting it. Some choices may be tempting because they have the correct details and the right scope, but they have a *not*, a *doesn't*, or some other twist that flips their meanings to the opposite of what the question asks for.

CONCEPT CHECK

- What should your notes from step 1 of the Kaplan Method—read the passage strategically—include?

  _____

- How does step 2 of the Kaplan Method—analyze the question stem—help you answer Reading Comprehension questions efficiently?

  _____

- How does step 3 of the Kaplan Method—research the relevant text—help you answer Reading Comprehension questions efficiently?

  _____

- How does step 4 of the Kaplan Method—make a prediction—help you answer Reading Comprehension questions efficiently?

  _____

Example answers are in your book's online resources (**kaptest.com/login**).

Applying the Kaplan Method for Reading Comprehension

Now try to apply the Kaplan Method to an actual GMAT-length passage and a couple of its questions. Read the passage strategically and practice making a passage map. Then compare your map to the example map following the passage. Did you capture the gist of the text in your notes? If not, or if you found it challenging to complete in under 4 minutes, that's OK! We'll be discussing passage mapping in detail in the next section, and you'll have plenty more chances to practice with passages here in the book and in your online resources.

Then, try your hand at the questions. Again, don't worry if you're not quite sure how to identify the question types; we will cover those thoroughly in the next chapter. Concentrate on analyzing what the question asks of you and using the Kaplan Method to take the most efficient path from question to correct answer. Ask yourself whether your reading of the passage prepared you well to research the answers to the questions. Compare your step-by-step approach to that of a GMAT expert in the explanations that follow each question.

Many historians consider the Marshall Plan one of the United States' major foreign policy successes of the last century. Behrman argues that the financial support provided by the United States was largely responsible for the recovery of the participating European economies after the Second World War. He
5   credits the "multiplier effect" with generating four to six additional dollars of European production for each Marshall Plan dollar distributed. Farmers, shopkeepers, and manufacturers would purchase equipment and materials through their national banks, which would then submit a request for Marshall Plan funds. Upon approval, the U.S. supplier would be paid from the Marshall
10   Plan, and the national bank would retain the local currency, which could be used for infrastructure repair and other national recovery efforts.

However, other scholars are more critical. Although Ferguson concedes Behrman's economic analysis, he disputes Behrman's claim that the Marshall Plan was crucial to Europe's recovery by outlining the many other programs
15   and policies that were already in place. Ferguson identifies the political impact of the Marshall Plan as the most significant result; the citizens of Western Europe saw the United States as assisting them through the difficult process of economic restoration and strengthened their connections with their transatlantic ally. LaFeber and other revisionist historians are even more
20   critical, describing the Marshall Plan as economic imperialism, a way to bind Western Europe's economy to that of the United States and to assist the recovery of U.S. industry, which had to return to producing domestic needs after several years of manufacturing armaments and military supplies, rather than as a mechanism for the restoration of the Western European national
25   economies.

Step 1: Read the Passage Strategically

Here's an example of how the passage should be analyzed. The passage is presented as seen through the lens of strategic reading. On the left is the text as you might read it, with key words and important points in bold. On the right is what you might be thinking as you read.

PASSAGE	ANALYSIS
Many historians consider the Marshall Plan one of the United States' **major** foreign policy successes of the last century.	Here's an opinion (and opinions are heavily tested). The prevailing view is that the Marshall Plan was a success. When an opinion is presented as being held by "many" people, expect that another point of view is coming up.

PASSAGE	ANALYSIS
Behrman argues that the financial support provided by the United States was **largely** responsible for the recovery of the participating European economies after the Second World War. He **credits** the "multiplier effect" with generating four to six additional dollars of European production for each Marshall Plan dollar distributed. Farmers, shopkeepers, and manufacturers would purchase equipment and materials through their national banks, which would then submit a request for Marshall Plan funds. Upon approval, the U.S. supplier would be paid from the Marshall Plan, and the national bank would retain the local currency, which could be used for infrastructure repair and other national recovery efforts.	Behrman is one of the "many historians" who are in favor of the Marshall Plan. His evidence that the plan was a success is detailed here. Behrman thinks that the economic "multiplier effect" was important. Read the details quickly, note the location, and come back and read carefully only if needed for a question.
However, other scholars are more critical. **Although Ferguson concedes Behrman's** economic analysis, he disputes Behrman's claim that the Marshall Plan was crucial to Europe's recovery by outlining the many other programs and policies that were already in place. **Ferguson identifies** the political impact of the Marshall Plan as the **most significant** result; the citizens of Western Europe saw the United States as assisting them through the difficult process of economic restoration and strengthened their connections with their transatlantic ally. **LaFeber** and other revisionist historians are **even more critical**, describing the Marshall Plan as economic imperialism, a way to bind Western Europe's economy to that of the United States and to assist the recovery of U.S. industry, which had to return to producing domestic needs after several years of manufacturing armaments and military supplies, **rather than** as a mechanism for the restoration of the Western European national economies.	Here's the other opinion, as expected. "Other scholars" disagree. Ferguson is one of these "others." Ferguson thinks Behrman has the economics right, but he disagrees with Behrman's conclusion. Ferguson says that the political effect is most important. Ferguson's explanation; again, there's no need to grasp the details now. Wait until you need them for a question. LaFeber, another of these "other" historians, is "even more critical." Note the gist of his reasoning (the plan was intended to benefit the U.S., not Europe). Note that the author never expresses an opinion as to which historian's analysis is most likely to be correct.

Your passage map would look something like this:

> ¶1: Many hists think MP success, e.g., B: economic "mult effect"
>
> ¶2: F: B econ is right, but MP not crucial, good relations most imp. LaF: MP for US, not Eur
>
> Topic: Marshall Plan
>
> Scope: Historians' views of success of MP
>
> Purpose: Describe three historians' views

This isn't the only way to word the passage map, of course. Anything along these lines would work—so long as you note that there are three historians' opinions and that the author doesn't prefer one over the others. After analyzing the passage, you are well prepared to apply steps 2–5 to the questions.

1. The passage suggests that Ferguson would be most likely to agree with which of the following claims about the "multiplier effect" (line 5)?

   ○ It was unlikely to have generated the returns for the European national economies that Behrman claims.

   ○ It may have been helpful to the European national economies, but it was not the most important outcome of the Marshall Plan.

   ○ It was the most controversial aspect of the Marshall Plan, generating intense resistance from those countries that chose not to participate.

   ○ It was a crucial part of the Marshall Plan, being substantially responsible for the recovery of participating Western European economies.

   ○ It was designed primarily to assist the recovery of industry in the United States, despite its benefits to Western European national economies.

Step 2: Analyze the Question Stem

The key word "suggests" identifies this as an Inference question. The correct answer will be fully supported by information in the passage about Ferguson's point of view on the "multiplier effect."

Step 3: Research the Relevant Text

The additional context clue "multiplier effect" and the line number in the question direct your research to the first paragraph. The first words of the second sentence identify the description of the "multiplier effect" that follows as that of Behrman, not Ferguson. Skim this section to refresh your memory of the "multiplier effect." The passage map locates Ferguson's opinion in the beginning of the second paragraph, so re-read that section as well, specifically looking for Ferguson's view of Behrman's discussion of the "multiplier effect."

Step 4: Make a Prediction

Behrman describes the "multiplier effect" as the mechanism by which each dollar of distributed Marshall Plan funds resulted in an additional four to six dollars made available for use by the European national banks. Lines 12–13 state "Ferguson concedes Behrman's economic analysis," but Ferguson goes on to dispute Behrman's conclusion. Predict that the correct answer will include "the multiplier effect is valid,"

"Behrman's conclusion is incorrect," or both. Notice that, once you clearly understand the relationship of the two historians' views, a detailed understanding of the mechanism of the "multiplier effect" is unnecessary.

Step 5: Evaluate the Answer Choices

(B) matches both concepts in the prediction and is correct. (A) is a distortion of Ferguson's view. Ferguson agrees with Behrman's economic analysis, but not Behrman's assessment of the impact of the "multiplier effect." (C) is not mentioned in the passage and is incorrect. Be careful if you happen to know that some nonparticipating countries were hostile to the Marshall Plan; the text only discusses the United States and the participating Western European countries. (D) and (E) are misused details from the passage that answer the wrong question. (D) is Behrman's view, and (E) is LaFeber's view; neither is Ferguson's.

2. Which of the following statements best describes the function of the last sentence in the passage?

    ○ It provides evidence that might undermine the viewpoint of the historians mentioned in the first sentence.

    ○ It resolves the conflict over the efficacy of the Marshall Plan introduced in the first paragraph.

    ○ It clarifies some of the reasons the Marshall Plan is generally considered to have been a success.

    ○ It qualifies a claim made earlier in the passage about return earned on each dollar spent by the Marshall Plan.

    ○ It supports a claim made earlier in the passage about the importance of the Marshall Plan to the economic recovery of Western Europe.

Step 2: Analyze the Question Stem

The phrase "best describes the function . . ." identifies this as a Logic question. The correct answer to a Logic question will explain how or why the author uses a feature of the passage, not the content of the feature. The context clue "last sentence in the passage" identifies the feature.

Step 3: Research the Relevant Text

Always begin the research for a Logic question with the purpose of the passage; then predict the relationship of the specified feature to the author's purpose. From the passage map, the author's purpose is to "describe three historians' views" of the Marshall Plan. The final sentence is one of those views, that of LaFeber, who is described as critical of the motives of the United States in offering the Marshall Plan; he believes the Marshall Plan was primarily intended to bind the U.S. and European economies and to revitalize industry in the United States. Consult the passage map to refresh your memory of the opinions of the other two historians: "Behrman is firmly in the "Marshall Plan was a success" camp, and Ferguson is somewhere in the middle.

Step 4: Make a Prediction

A good prediction would be *to describe a historian's view that is critical of the Marshall Plan.*

Step 5: Evaluate the Answer Choices

(A) matches the prediction and is correct. The "many" historians in the first sentence believe the Marshall Plan was a major foreign policy success. LaFeber's view undermines this idea by pointing out the possibility that the intended benefit of the Marshall Plan devolved to the United States, not Europe. **(B)** is not discussed in the passage and is incorrect. The author simply presents the differing views of the historians and does not "resolve" them. **(C)** and **(E)** are the opposite of what you're looking for. In the last sentence, LaFeber is challenging, not supporting, the idea that the Marshall Plan was a foreign-policy success. **(D)** is a misused detail from the text. The passage discusses the "multiplier effect" that impacted the return on the dollars spent on the Marshall Plan, but LaFeber's view on the "multiplier effect" is not mentioned.

Practice Set: The Kaplan Method for Reading Comprehension

(Answers and explanations are at the end of the chapter.)

Questions 1–4 are based on the following passage.

Bog bodies, most of them dating from between 500 BCE and 100 CE, have been found across northwestern Europe. They are remarkably well preserved in many cases, sometimes down to wrinkles and scars on their leathery, reddish-brown skin. They have not been kept intact in the same way as Egyptian
5   mummies, deliberately embalmed through painstaking human technique, but have likely been perpetuated by an accident that archaeologists who study the Iron Age might call a happy one.

The wetlands in which the bodies are found are exclusively sphagnum moss bogs. These exist in temperate climes where the winter and early spring
10   weather is cold, leaving the water in the bogs below 40°F during those months, and the bogs are all near sources of salt water. Together these elements create the perfect environment for the preservation of skin and internal organs.

The biochemistry of preservation in bogs has several components. Both the cold temperatures and dense peat from the moss, which constitutes a mostly
15   anaerobic environment, prevent significant bacterial growth in the water. As layers of moss die and deteriorate in the water, they create humic acid, also known as bog acid; the acidic environment further inhibits bacteria. Interestingly, this acid often erodes the bones of bog bodies, leaving only the skin and organs, in a process quite the opposite of that which acts upon
20   bodies outside of bogs. The dead layers of moss also release sphagnan, a carbohydrate that attaches itself to the skin of the bodies, preventing rot and water damage.

Besides bodies, bogs have also preserved books, boats, and even bread and "bog butter"—a waxy dairy- or meat-based substance sometimes found stored
25   in barrels in the bogs. These barrels likely served as the equivalent of Iron Age refrigerators, preserving food when buried in the bog. Much can be learned about our ancestors from the Iron Age and even earlier due to the unique ability of sphagnum moss bogs to preserve so thoroughly that which has fallen into them: scholars have studied such diverse features of early human life as
30   medical conditions like arthritis and parasitic infection, diet, and how far from home people traveled. The bogs offer a fascinating window into the past.

1. According to the passage, all of the following conditions are conducive to the preservation of bog bodies EXCEPT

   ○ long winters

   ○ low air temperatures

   ○ proximity to salt water

   ○ cool water

   ○ sphagnum moss

2. The primary purpose of the passage is to

   ○ explain the ways in which bog bodies are different from other preserved bodies, such as mummies

   ○ challenge the position that the preservation of bodies in bogs is probably the result of intentional effort

   ○ discuss the characteristics of sphagnum moss bogs that allow bodies to be found in a condition that permits unique study

   ○ argue that scholars would not understand significant aspects of human life during the Iron Age had bog bodies not been discovered

   ○ analyze the differences between sphagnum moss bogs and the types of environments in which bodies decay

3. In the context of the passage as a whole, the third paragraph serves primarily to

   ○ evaluate the relative importance of the elements discussed in the second paragraph

   ○ provide support for an argument presented in the fourth paragraph about the significance of the subject of the passage

   ○ outline the creation of the environment that produces the effect that is the topic of the passage

   ○ elaborate on the mechanisms underlying an effect achieved by elements introduced in the second paragraph

   ○ explain the prominence of a particular academic discipline in the study of the topic of the passage

4. According to the passage, bacterial growth is inhibited by all of the following EXCEPT

   ○ an anaerobic environment

   ○ the presence of sphagnum moss

   ○ breakdown of layers of dead moss

   ○ cold water temperature

   ○ release of sphagnan from dead moss

Questions 5–8 are based on the following passage.

Women around the world graduate from college at higher rates than men. However, women's participation in the workforce, especially in the ranks of senior management, continues to lag far behind that of men. Research into marriages between men and women indicates that, as women marry and start families, their earnings and opportunities for promotion decrease. While the difficulties that women encounter as they attempt to balance work and family life are frequently discussed, and are beginning to be addressed by employers, it is interesting to note that the difficulties faced by working married men are seldom raised.

Scott Coltrane, a researcher at the University of Oregon who has studied marriages between men and women, has found that, while the earnings of women tend to go down with each additional child, the earnings of married men not only exceed those of both unmarried men and divorced men but also tend to go up with each additional child. One reason for this disparity may be that, as the size of the family grows, men rely on women to manage most of the responsibilities of housekeeping and child raising. While within the past few decades men have assumed a greater share of household responsibilities, in the United States, women still spend nearly twice as much time as men do in caring for children and the home. The time diaries of highly educated dual-income male-female U.S. couples show that men enjoy three and a half times the leisure time as their female partners do.

If married men earn higher salaries and have more leisure time than their female counterparts do, what difficulties do these working men face? Research indicates three possible problems. First, the perceived responsibility of providing for a family drives men to work more hours and strive for promotion. Many men report feeling dissatisfied because the level of performance that is required to earn promotions and higher salaries prevents them from spending time with their families. Second, these demands on men also contribute to higher levels of marital discord. In a 2008 survey, 60 percent of U.S. fathers reported work-family conflicts, compared to 47 percent of mothers.

The pressure to be perceived as a good provider contributes to the third reason that married men may struggle. While women's decisions to use family leave benefits, move to part-time employment, or leave the workforce to care for children are seen as valuable contributions to family life and, by extension, society, men's decisions to do the same are frequently viewed by their employers as signs of weakness. Studies suggest that men who take advantage of paternity leave policies are viewed as weak or inadequate by both women and men. Research conducted in Australia found that men's requests to work flexibly were denied at twice the rate of those of women.

5. The author of the passage is primarily concerned with

    O   advocating changes in employers' practices regarding female employees with children

    O   examining some of the reasons that married men may experience problems related to their employment

    O   describing the psychological consequences for men of earning high salaries

    O   taking issue with those who believe that women should not earn more than men

    O   analyzing the indirect effects of discrimination against women on married men

6. The passage provides information in support of which of the following assertions about married men who work?

    O   The ability to provide for their families is the most important aspect of employment for married men.

    O   Married men in high-status positions are easily able to integrate their careers and family lives.

    O   Married men who achieve greater earnings while having a larger family are more satisfied on average than their wives.

    O   The perceived demands on men to earn enough income to support a family may have harmful effects on family life.

    O   As married men achieve higher earnings, they are able to take more time off from work to spend with their families.

7. The author of the passage discusses Coltrane's research primarily in order to

    O   illustrate the benefits that employers extend to their married male employees

    O   identify a benefit of work that married men experience that is accompanied by some potential costs

    O   defend the family leave policies and flexible work schedules that some employers offer

    O   modify the prevailing view that women experience disadvantages in the workplace after marrying and having children

    O   point out several ways in which women experience discrimination in the workplace

8. According to the passage, married men generally receive higher salaries and have a better chance of being promoted than do single men because

    O   employers consider married men to be more diligent and responsible than single men

    O   married men have usually accrued more experience than have single men

    O   married men may be able to rely on their spouses to address child care and household responsibilities

    O   higher pay typically corresponds with greater job security and enhanced benefits

    O   employers recognize the difficulties of providing for a larger number of children and seek to ease this burden

Step 1: Read the Passage Strategically—A Deep Dive

LEARNING OBJECTIVES

- Draw upon strategic reading skills to identify the passage's topic and scope, the author's overall purpose in writing, and the central ideas of each paragraph
- Use key words to map the structure of a passage
- Distinguish between significant ideas and minor details in passages

As we mentioned in the previous section, the only reason you're reading GMAT passages is to quickly answer as many questions correctly as you can. Because of this goal, the way you'll read strategically for the GMAT will be very different from the way you read other materials for other purposes. "Strategic reading" breaks down into four basic tasks.

Look for the Topic and Scope of the Passage

Think of the topic as the big idea that the entire passage will relate to in one way or another. Almost always, the topic will be right there in the first sentence. It will be something broad, far too big to discuss in the 150–350 words of most GMAT passages. Here's an example of how a passage might begin:

> The great migration of European intellectuals to the United States in the second quarter of the twentieth century prompted a transmutation in the character of Western social thought.

What's the topic? The "migration of European intellectuals to the United States in the second quarter of the twentieth century." Don't worry about how exactly to word it in your notes. You just need to get a good idea of what the passage is talking about so you have a focus to your reading. You might jot down something like this:

Euro ints → US

Only you need to understand your notes.

Now consider scope. Think of scope as a narrowing of the topic. You're looking for the idea on which the author focuses for the length of a GMAT passage. If the topic is the "migration of European intellectuals to the United States in the second quarter of the twentieth century," then perhaps the scope will be *some of the effects of that migration upon Western social thought*. It may be even more specific: *one aspect of Western social thought affected by the migration*. Or perhaps the passage compares two different migrations or contrasts two different effects. Look for clues in the text that tell you on what specific subject(s) the author intends to focus.

Finding the scope is critically important to doing well on Reading Comp. Many incorrect choices are wrong because the information that would be needed to support them is simply not present in the passage. It's highly unlikely that there will be a topic sentence that lays out plainly what the author intends to write about—but the first paragraph probably will give some indication of the focus of the rest of the passage.

Some passages are only one paragraph long. In these cases, the topic can still appear in the first sentence. The passage will probably (but not necessarily) narrow in scope somewhere in the first third of the paragraph, as the author doesn't have much text to work with and needs to get down to business quickly.

Get the Gist of Each Paragraph and Its Structural Role in the Passage

The paragraph is the main structural unit of any passage. At first, you don't yet know the topic or scope, so you have to read the first paragraph pretty closely. But once you get a sense of where the passage is going, all you need to do is understand what role each new paragraph plays. Ask yourself the following:

- Why did the author include this paragraph?
- What's discussed here that's different from the content of the paragraph before?
- What bearing does this paragraph have on the author's main idea?
- What role do the details play?

As you encounter details in the passage, don't ask, "What does this mean?" but rather, "Why is it here?" Many GMAT passages try to swamp you with tedious, dense, and sometimes confusing details. Consider this paragraph:

> The Burgess Shale yielded a surprisingly varied array of fossils. Early chordates were very rare, but there were prodigious numbers of complex forms not seen since. *Hallucigenia*, so named for a structure so bizarre that scientists did not know which was the dorsal and which the ventral side, had fourteen legs. *Opabinia* had five eyes and a long proboscis. This amazing diversity led Gould to believe that it was highly unlikely that the eventual success of chordates was a predictable outcome.

This is pretty dense stuff. But if you don't worry about understanding all of the science jargon and instead focus on the gist of the paragraph and *why* the details are there, things get easier. The first sentence isn't that bad:

> The Burgess Shale yielded a surprisingly varied array of fossils.

A quick paraphrase is that the "Burgess Shale," whatever that is, had a lot of different kinds of fossils. The passage continues:

> Early chordates were very rare, but there were prodigious numbers of complex forms not seen since. *Hallucigenia*, so named for a structure so bizarre that scientists did not know which was the dorsal and which the ventral side, had fourteen legs. *Opabinia* had five eyes and a long proboscis.

When you read this part of the passage strategically, asking what its purpose is in context, you see that this is just a list of the different kinds of fossils and some facts about them. There were not a lot of "chordates," whatever they are, but there was lots of other stuff.

> This amazing diversity led Gould to believe that it was highly unlikely that the eventual success of chordates was a predictable outcome.

The emphasis key word "amazing" should draw your attention. Also, "Gould . . . believe[s]" something—when someone has an opinion about something, that is always worth noting. This sentence tells you *why* those intimidatingly dense details are in the passage: they are the facts that led Gould to a belief—namely that the rise of "chordates" couldn't have been predicted. You might jot down something like this:

Evidence for G's belief—chordate success not predictable

Notice that you don't have to know what any of these scientific terms mean in order to understand why the author brings them up. Taking apart every paragraph like this allows you to create a map of the passage's overall structure. We'll call this a *passage map* from here on. Making a passage map will give you a sense of mastery over the passage, even when it deals with a subject you don't know anything about, and it will leave you with a grasp of the big picture of the passage that is essential for answering GMAT questions.

To break down paragraphs and understand the structural function of each part, look for key words, or structural words or phrases that link ideas to one another. Key words can help you distinguish the important things (such as opinions) from the unimportant (such as supporting examples) and to understand why the author wrote each sentence.

Types of key words:

- **Contrast** key words such as *but*, *however*, *nevertheless*, and *on the other hand* tell you that a change or disagreement is coming. They are generally signals to read more carefully, recalling the previous idea and identifying how the new point relates to that idea.

- **Continuation** key words such as *moreover*, *also*, and *furthermore* tell you that the author is continuing on the same track or general idea. These are good opportunities to read more quickly—what's coming is more of the same.

- **Logic** key words, which are also very important in Critical Reasoning stimuli, alert you to an author's reasoning. **Evidence** key words let you know that something is being offered in support of a particular idea. The specifics of the support are usually unimportant for the first big-picture read, but you do want to know what the idea is. Examples of evidence key words are *since*, *because*, and *as*. **Conclusion** key words such as *therefore* and *hence* are usually *not* associated with the author's main point in Reading Comp. Rather, they indicate that the next phrase is a logical consequence of the sentence(s) that came before.

- **Emphasis** and **Opinion** key words can be subtler than those in the other categories, but these are perhaps the most important key words of all. Emphasis key words are used when the author wants to call attention to a specific point. Examples include *very*, *important*, and *critical*. Opinion key words point to the ideas in a passage; these opinions are frequently the focus of GMAT questions. Be sure to distinguish between the author's opinions and those of others. Others' opinions are easier to spot and will be triggered by words such as *believe*, *theory*, or *hypothesis*. The author's opinion is more likely to reveal itself in words that imply a value judgment, such as *valid* or *unsupported*. (If the passage expresses something in the first person, such as *I disagree*, that's also a clear sign.) Key words with an emotional charge such as *fortunately*, *sadly*, *brilliant*, *flawed*, *beneficial*, and *dead end* also signal the author's tone and attitude.

- **Illustration** key words let you know that what follows is an example of a broader point. One example, of course, is *example*. *For instance* is another favorite in GMAT passages. If you understand the purpose of the example, this is another opportunity to note the location of the example and to speed up your reading. If you do not understand the author's point yet, read the example more carefully to help you do so.

- **Sequence/Timing** is a broader category of key words. These are any words that delineate lists or groupings. *First*, *second*, and *third* are obvious examples. But you could also get a chronological sequence (*17th century*, *18th century*, and *today*). Science passages may discuss complicated experimental procedures or observed phenomena using sequence key words (*at a high temperature* and *at a low temperature*, for example).

As you might have guessed, reading the passage strategically doesn't mean simply going on a scavenger hunt for key words. Rather, it means using those key words to identify the important parts of the passage—its opinions and structure—so you can focus on them and not on little details. Key words also help you predict the function of the text that follows. Let's see how this works by taking a look at a simple example. Say you saw a passage with the following structure on Test Day. What kinds of details can you anticipate would fill each of the blanks?

Kelley is eagerly awaiting the release of the new season of her favorite show because

_____. Furthermore, _____. Moreover,

_____. However, _____.

You learn about Kelley's attitude toward the upcoming release through the words "eagerly" and "favorite," which are emphasis key words. After "because" (a logic key word) will be a reason that Kelley enjoys the show. After "[f]urthermore" and "[m]oreover" (continuation key words) will be additional reasons or elaborations of the reason in the first sentence. After "[h]owever," you'll read about some drawback or counterexample that undermines the previous string of good things about the show. You can't predict the exact details that fill the blanks, but you can predict the tone and purpose of the details. Reading this way is valuable because the GMAT test makers are more likely to ask you why the author put the details in, not what's true about them.

Reading for key words seems straightforward when the passage deals with subject matter that's familiar or easy to understand. But what if you were to see the following passage about a less familiar topic? How can you decode the structure of the following paragraph?

Quantum-enabled communication systems—communication systems based on the

principles of quantum mechanics—are theoretically impervious to hacking because

_____. Furthermore, _____

Moreover, _____. However, _____.

Here, the emphasis key phrase "impervious to hacking" lets you know why the author cares about quantum-enabled communication systems: they're tough to undermine. The details that would fill these blanks are probably dense and intimidating for the non-physicist, but the strategic reader will still be able to understand the passage well enough to answer GMAT questions correctly. Notice that the structure is identical to that of the paragraph about Kelley, so the details that fill the blanks will serve the same purpose as those you predicted previously. You can anticipate what they will be and why the author is including them. Reading strategically allows you to take control of the passage; you will know where the author is going and what the GMAT will consider important, even if you know nothing about the subject matter of the passage.

Look for Opinions, Theories, and Points of View—Especially the Author's

An important part of strategic reading is distinguishing between factual assertions and opinions or interpretations. It's the opinions and interpretations that Reading Comp questions are most often based on, so you should pay the most attention to them. Let's say you come upon a paragraph that reads:

> The coral polyps secrete calcareous exoskeletons, which cement themselves into an underlayer of rock, while the algae deposit still more calcium carbonate, which reacts with sea salt to create an even tougher limestone layer. All of this accounts for the amazing renewability of the coral reefs despite the endless erosion caused by wave activity.

In a sense, this is just like the Burgess Shale paragraph; it begins with a lot of scientific jargon and later tells you why that jargon is there. In this case, it explains how coral reefs renew themselves. But notice a big difference—the author doesn't tell you how someone else interprets these facts. She could have written "scientists believe that these polyps account for . . . ," but she didn't. This is the author's own interpretation.

It's important to differentiate between the author's own voice and other people's opinions. GMAT authors may disagree with other people, but they won't contradict themselves. So the author of the Burgess Shale passage might well disagree with Gould in the next paragraph, but the author of the Coral Reef passage definitely thinks that coral polyps and algae are responsible for the renewability of coral reefs.

Spotting opinions and theories also helps you to accomplish the goal of reading for structure. Once you spot an idea, you can step back from the barrage of words and dissect the passage critically, asking, "Why is the author citing this opinion? Where's the support for this idea? Does the author agree or disagree?"

Consider how you would read the following paragraph strategically:

> Abraham Lincoln is traditionally viewed as an advocate of freedom because he issued the Emancipation Proclamation and championed the Thirteenth Amendment, which ended legal slavery in the United States. And indeed this achievement cannot be denied. But he also set uncomfortable precedents for the curtailing of civil liberties.

A strategic reader will zero in on the passage's key words and analyze what each reveals about the structure of the passage and the author's point of view. Here, the key word "traditionally" lets you know how people usually think about Lincoln. You might already anticipate that the author is setting up a contrast between the traditional view and his own. Sure enough, the key word "but" makes the contrast clear: the author asserts that despite his other accomplishments, Lincoln in fact restricted civil liberties. And the word "uncomfortable" is an opinion key word indicating that the author is not pleased with Lincoln because of it. However, the author already tempered his criticism with the phrase "this achievement cannot be denied," meaning that he won't go so far as to say that Lincoln was an enemy of freedom.

At this point, the strategic reader can anticipate where the passage's structure will lead. Given how this opening paragraph ends, you can predict that the author will spend at least one paragraph describing these "uncomfortable precedents" and how they restricted civil liberties. It might even be possible, since he uses the word "precedents," that he goes on to describe how later governments or leaders used Lincoln's actions as justification for their own restrictions.

This is the power of predictive, strategic reading: by using key words to anticipate where the author is heading, you will not only stay more engaged as you read, but you'll also develop a better understanding of the structure of the passage and the author's point of view—the very things that pay off in a higher GMAT score.

Put together, the passage's structure and the opinions and theories it contains will lead you to understand the author's primary purpose in writing the passage. This is critical, as most GMAT passages have a question that directly asks for that purpose. For the Lincoln passage, you might get a question like this:

> Which of the following best represents the main idea of the passage?
>
> ○ The Emancipation Proclamation had both positive and negative effects.
>
> ○ Lincoln's presidency laid the groundwork for future restrictions of personal freedoms.
>
> ○ The traditional image of Lincoln as a national hero must be overturned.
>
> ○ Lincoln used military pressure to influence state legislatures.
>
> ○ Abraham Lincoln was an advocate of freedom.

Just from a strategic reading of the first few sentences, you could eliminate (A) as a distortion of the first and third sentences, (C) as too extreme because of the "cannot be denied" phrase, (D) as irrelevant—either too narrow or just not present in the passage at all, and (E) as missing the author's big point—that Lincoln helped restrict civil liberties. And just like that, you can choose (B) as the correct answer and increase your score.

Don't Obsess over Details

On the GMAT, you'll need to read only for short-term—as opposed to long-term—retention. Once you answer the questions about a certain passage, that passage is over and done with. You're promptly free to forget everything about it.

What's more, there's no need to memorize—or even fully comprehend—details. You *do* need to know why they are there so that you can answer big-picture questions, but you can always go back and re-read them in greater depth if you're asked a question that hinges on a detail. And you'll find that if you have a good sense of the passage's scope and structure, the ideas and opinions in the passage, and the author's purpose, then you'll have little problem navigating through the text as the need arises.

Furthermore, you can even hurt your score by reading the details too closely. Here's how:

- **Wasted time.** Remember, there will usually be only three or four questions per passage. The test makers can't possibly ask you about all the little details. So don't waste your valuable time by focusing on minutiae you will likely not need to know. If you do, you won't have nearly enough time to deal with the questions.

- **Tempting wrong answers.** Attempting to read and understand fully every last detail can cause your mind to jumble all the details—relevant and irrelevant alike—together in a confusing mess. Since most of the incorrect choices in GMAT Reading Comp are simply distortions of details from the passage, they will sound familiar and therefore be tempting to uncritical readers. The strategic reader doesn't give those details undue importance and thus isn't tempted by the choices that focus on them. Instead, he takes advantage of the open-book nature of the test to research specific details only when asked.

- **Losing the big picture.** It's very easy to miss the forest for the trees. If you get too drawn into the small stuff, you can pass right by the emphasis and opinion key words that you'll need to understand the author's main purpose.

Here's a great tip for cutting through confusing, detail-laden sentences: focus on the subjects and verbs first, throwing away modifying phrases, and don't worry about fancy terminology. Let's revisit some dense text from before:

> The coral polyps secrete calcareous exoskeletons, which cement themselves into an underlayer of rock, while the algae deposit still more calcium carbonate, which reacts with sea salt to create an even tougher limestone layer. All of this accounts for the amazing renewability of the coral reefs despite the endless erosion caused by wave activity.

Now look at what happens if you paraphrase these sentences, distilling them to main subjects and verbs, ignoring modifiers, and not worrying about words you don't understand:

> Coral polyps (whatever they are) secrete something . . . and algae deposit something. This accounts for the amazing renewability of the coral reefs.

The structure of this paragraph has suddenly become a lot more transparent. Now the bulkiness of that first sentence won't slow you down, so you can understand its role in the big picture.

Now try using key words to predict the passage on your own.

Key Words Drill

Use the key words in the following excerpts to answer the questions. Answers follow the drill.

1. For decades, commercial agricultural operations have relied on monoculture to provide the United States with ample food resources . . .

   If this were the opening sentence of a passage, what would likely be the focus of the passage?

   _____

2. Though some human resource experts question the policy's effect on employee morale, it remains the only option if the sector is to remain profitable.

   Based on this excerpt, what is the author's attitude toward the policy?

   _____

3. Some early manufacturing processes remain elusive. For instance, ancient celestial globes used for navigation were perfectly cast metal spheres that have yet to be duplicated by modern processes.

   What is the author's purpose in mentioning the ancient celestial globes?

   _____

Key Words Drill: Answers

1. *Evidence showing that commercial agriculture may not be able to rely on monoculture in the future.* A passage that opens by mentioning a traditional or past belief ("[f]or decades") will usually go on to outline recent discoveries or rethinking that undermines or contradicts that belief.

2. *Approval.* With the contrast word "[t]hough," the author indicates a belief that the negative consequences of not implementing the policy (the loss of the sector's profitability) override the human resource experts' concerns.

3. *To illustrate an assertion.* Introduced with "[f]or instance," this detail is an example supporting the claim that some early manufacturing processes are still elusive. Don't expect celestial globes to be a major focus of the passage.

Now, try to use these principles to analyze a passage similar to one you may see on Test Day. Unlike passages you'll see on Test Day, the following text has been formatted to approximate the way a strategic reader might see it—important key words and phrases are in bold, the main ideas are in normal type, and the supporting details are grayed out. Take a moment to read only the bold and regular text: identify what the key words tell you about the structure, take notes that paraphrase the crucial text, and practice predicting what the grayed-out portions contain.

The Federal Aviation Administration, commonly known as the FAA, is the government agency tasked with regulating civil aviation in the United States. One of the FAA's **more prominent** functions is to regulate the safety of the airline industry, which it does by creating and enforcing rules that govern

5   the manufacture and operation of commercial aircraft. **However**, the FAA is also charged with a number of other responsibilities, including a mandate to promote civil aviation. Many of the FAA's **critics have argued** that this role is directly incompatible with the agency's primary duty to regulate safety and have called on Congress to redefine the FAA's mission to exclude the duty to

10   promote civil aviation from the agency's list of responsibilities.

The critics' concern is that the safety of the airline industry cannot be adequately regulated by the same agency that is supposed to promote the industry as a whole. **According to the critics**, if a safety issue were to arise, the FAA would have to weigh the potential harm that the airline industry would

15   suffer due to increased regulation against the benefits of remedying the safety concern, which might lead to inaction by the FAA. **For example**, several leading safety advocates have recommended that the FAA prohibit the practice of allowing infants under two years old to fly as "lap children" and instead require a separate seat for all passengers regardless of age. **Because** many parents

20   would opt out of flying if they were required to purchase separate tickets for their young children, the advocates' recommendation would, if adopted, lead to a decline in airline ticket sales. The failure of the FAA to act on this proposal is, **to many critics**, a sign that the agency is more concerned with the potential loss of revenue to the airline industry than the potential loss of a young

25   child's life.

The critics' claim is not entirely without merit, as it is common for the FAA to consider potential financial consequences when contemplating a new regulation. **However, the critics fundamentally misunderstand** the role that this cost-benefit analysis plays in the agency's decision-making process.

30   If the FAA enacts regulations that make plane tickets prohibitively expensive, people will instead travel by car, statistically a much more dangerous mode of transportation than flying. **Thus**, when the FAA declines to revise its "lap child" policy, it does so not to protect the airline industry's revenues but to reduce the risks associated with travel for children and their parents. **Moreover**,

35   there is a built-in safeguard to prevent the FAA from protecting revenues at the expense of travelers' safety: if the FAA failed to act on a significant safety concern, the public would lose confidence in airline travel, causing harm to the industry itself. **Ultimately**, the FAA's duty to promote commercial aviation serves to reinforce its safety mission rather than undermine it.

This passage starts with a neutral, factual tone as it describes the major functions of the FAA. The contrast key word "[h]owever" in line 5 offers the first indication of a potential conflict within the FAA's list of responsibilities, and the next sentence offers an opinion related to it: some believe that two of the FAA's missions—regulating safety and promoting civil aviation—are incompatible. Note that the author attributes this viewpoint to the "critics," so you don't yet know whether the author agrees with it. As you continue to read the passage, be on the lookout for key words that indicate the author's opinion.

On Test Day, you would take some brief notes about the main idea of the first paragraph before moving on:

¶1: Critics: FAA has incompatible duties of safety and promotion

At the beginning of the next paragraph, the phrase "critics' concern" indicates that the author will now provide further information about the critics' point of view. Since you already know the critics' core position from the first paragraph, you don't need to get too invested in the additional explanation here. Read the second paragraph briskly and jot down a quick note before moving on:

¶2: Explanation of critics' position; example

In the third paragraph, the author finally gives her opinion. While the author says that the critics claim has some "merit," the use "[h]owever" and "fundamentally misunderstand" in the second sentence indicates that the author essentially disagrees with the critics' position. Indeed, the rest of the paragraph explains why the author believes that the FAA's responsibilities are not incompatible. Again, you don't need to worry about the details; just focus on the broad strokes in your notes:

¶3: Author: FAA's duties are not incompatible

Just from this quick analysis, notice how much you already understand about the structure of the passage and the author's point of view. You effectively know what the grayed-out parts of the passage accomplish, even though you can't recite the details they contain. You are now in a strong position to approach the questions that accompany this passage, knowing that you can always return to the passage to clarify your understanding of any relevant details. Let's look at this first question:

1. Which of the following best describes the author's main idea?

    O   The FAA's mandate to promote civil aviation is fundamentally incompatible with its duty to regulate the safety of commercial airline travel.

    O   The FAA is the government agency that oversees commercial aviation within the United States.

    O   In response to the critics' claim that the FAA has incompatible mandates, Congress should remove the duty to promote civil aviation from the FAA's list of responsibilities.

    O   Despite claims to the contrary, the FAA's duty to promote civil aviation is not incompatible with its responsibility to regulate airline safety.

    O   The FAA's decision to continue the practice of allowing lap children will ultimately save lives.

This question asks for the author's main idea. Fortunately, you already have information about the author's position in your notes, so there's no need to go back to the passage itself to answer this question. In the third paragraph, the author rebuts the critics' claim and asserts that the FAA's duties are not fundamentally incompatible. **(D)** matches this prediction and is correct.

If you weren't sure about the answer, you could eliminate incorrect answer choices by finding the specific faults they contain. **(A)** is the critics' position, not the author's, so it cannot be correct. **(B)** is incorrect because the author's main idea is not to describe the FAA but to give her opinion about whether or not the FAA has incompatible responsibilities. **(C)** is incorrect because this is a belief held by some of the critics, not by the author. Finally, while the author would agree with the statement in **(E)**, it is included as an example that supports the author's reasoning, not as the author's main idea.

Take a look at one more question about this passage:

2. The author refers to the "cost-benefit analysis" (see line 29) undertaken by the FAA most likely in order to

    O   summarize the primary responsibilities of the FAA

    O   explain the rationale that underpins a policy decision made by the FAA

    O   question the ability of the FAA to balance two competing obligations

    O   criticize a policy decision made by the FAA

    O   defend the FAA's ability to successfully manage its list of responsibilities

This question asks why the author discusses the FAA's "cost-benefit analysis," and the line reference places this quoted text in the third paragraph. Once again, this question does not require any additional research beyond the notes you've already taken. According to your notes, the third paragraph introduces and explains the author's position, which is that the FAA's duties are not incompatible. Because this is a defense of the FAA against the critics who claim that the agency is incapable of managing its competing responsibilities, **(E)** is correct.

(A) is incorrect because the author's summary of the FAA's responsibilities is in the first paragraph, not the third. **(B)** is incorrect because the author's primary concern in the third paragraph is to defend the FAA, not merely to explain a lone policy decision. While the author offers a justification for the FAA's position on lap children, she does so in order to support her broader point, which is that the agency is able to balance its responsibilities. **(C)** and **(D)** are incorrect because the author does not "question" or "criticize" the FAA in the third paragraph. Those characterizations are more closely aligned with the critics, whose opinions are discussed in the first and second paragraphs.

CONCEPT CHECK

- How could contrast key words affect your reading strategy?

  _____

- How could emphasis and opinion key words affect your reading strategy?

  _____

- How could continuation key words affect your reading strategy?

  _____

- How could illustration key words affect your reading strategy?

  _____

Example answers are in your book's online resources (**kaptest.com/login**).

The Four Core Competencies and Reading Comprehension

Because of its format—you read material and answer questions about it—Reading Comprehension lulls many students into turning off their analytical thought processes. As this chapter has shown, however, GMAT Reading Comp requires you to think very analytically about passages and the questions about them. Therefore, as they are throughout the GMAT, the four Core Competencies are being tested.

Critical Thinking

Reading actively is key to Reading Comp success. As you read, interrogate the text. Ask why the author is including certain details and what the author's choice of key words implies about how the ideas in the passage are related. Asking these questions as you read will prepare you to answer the questions the GMAT asks.

Pattern Recognition

Since the GMAT constructs Reading Comprehension passages in similar ways and asks questions that conform to predictable types, you can learn to anticipate how authors will express their ideas and what the GMAT test makers will ask you about a passage. The more you focus on passage structure as you read, and the more familiar you become with the question types and common wrong answer patterns, the stronger your Pattern Recognition skills will become.

Attention to the Right Detail

Reading Comp passages are typically filled with more details than you could reasonably memorize—and more, in fact, than you will ever need to answer the questions. Since time is limited, you must prioritize the information you assimilate from the passage, focusing on the big picture. However, using key words to identify particularly important details—such as evidence that supports the opinion of the author or someone else—and noting their location in your passage map will allow you to efficiently research those details as needed.

Paraphrasing

Practice Paraphrasing constantly as you read, both to keep yourself engaged and to make sure you understand what's being discussed. You should hone this skill as you practice GMAT Reading Comp, but you can also use and improve this skill as you read for work, for school, or to catch up on the news. Developing this habit will make taking notes much easier, since you'll have already distilled and summarized the most important information in your head. You'll streamline your paraphrasing even further as you condense your analysis into your passage map.

Answers and Explanations

"Bog Bodies" Passage: Questions 1–4

Step 1: Read the Passage Strategically

On the left, we've shown how key words help to identify the major elements of the passage and its structure and what you could skim over. On the right, we've shown what you might be thinking as you read the passage strategically.

PASSAGE	ANALYSIS
Bog bodies, most of them dating from between 500 BCE and 100 CE, have been found across northwestern Europe. They are **remarkably** well preserved in many cases, sometimes down to wrinkles and scars on their leathery, reddish-brown skin. They have **not** been kept intact in the same way as Egyptian mummies, deliberately embalmed through painstaking human technique, **but** have likely been perpetuated by an accident that archaeologists who study the Iron Age might call a happy one.	This introduces the topic of the passage: bog bodies are preserved, probably accidentally.
The wetlands in which the bodies are found are **exclusively** sphagnum moss bogs. These exist in temperate climes where the winter and early spring weather is cold, leaving the water in the bogs below 40°F during those months, and the bogs are all near sources of salt water. **Together** these elements create the **perfect environment** for the preservation of skin and internal organs.	This paragraph provides details on the conditions that promote preservation in the bogs where bodies are found.
The biochemistry of preservation in bogs has **several components**. Both the cold temperatures and dense peat from the moss, which constitutes a mostly anaerobic environment, prevent significant bacterial growth in the water. As layers of moss die and deteriorate in the water, they create humic acid, also known as bog acid; the acidic environment **further** inhibits bacteria. **Interestingly**, this acid often erodes the bones of bog bodies, leaving only the skin and organs, in a process quite the opposite of that which acts upon bodies outside of bogs. The dead layers of moss **also** release sphagnan, a carbohydrate that attaches itself to the skin of the bodies, preventing rot and water damage.	Here, you'll find scientific details on how chemical processes in the bog interact with bodies to preserve them. Skim them for now and come back to read in depth if needed for a question.

PASSAGE	ANALYSIS
Besides bodies, bogs have **also** preserved books, boats, and even bread and "bog butter"—waxy dairy- or meat-based substances sometimes found stored in barrels in the bogs. These barrels likely served as the equivalent of Iron Age refrigerators, preserving food when buried in the bog. **Much can be learned** about our ancestors from the Iron Age and even earlier due to the unique ability of sphagnum moss bogs to preserve so thoroughly that which has fallen into them: scholars have studied such diverse features of early human life as medical conditions like arthritis and parasitic infection, diet, and how far from home people traveled. The bogs offer a fascinating window into the past.	This paragraph describes the scholarly value of bog bodies and artifacts.

Passage Map

Here is an example of the notes that you might have made as you read:

¶1: Bog bodies = accidentally preserved?

¶2: Conditions of bogs

¶3: Biochemistry that allows preservation

¶4: Other things preserved; value for learning

Topic: Bog bodies

Scope: How sphagnum moss bogs preserve ⎯⎯⎯↑

Purpose: Describe and explain ⎯⎯⎯↑

1.   (A)

The phrase "According to the passage" indicates that this is a Detail question, but "EXCEPT" means that the four incorrect choices will be supported by the passage, while the correct answer will not be. The second paragraph describes "the perfect environment" for preserving bodies. Review that section and eliminate choices that are discussed: sphagnum moss, cold temperatures, cool water, and nearby salt water. Although the winter weather is described as cold, the length of the season is not mentioned, making **(A)** is correct.

Since **(B)**, **(C)**, **(D)**, and **(E)** are mentioned in the passage as contributing to "the perfect environment" for preserving bodies, they are incorrect.

2.   (C)

The phrase "primary purpose" means this Global question is asking for the reason the author wrote the passage. As you concluded your strategic reading of the passage, you likely summarized the author's topic, scope, and purpose. The purpose of the passage is to explain how bog bodies and other artifacts are preserved in sphagnum moss and why these items are important. **(C)** matches this summation.

While the author suggests a difference between bog bodies and mummies, contrasting bog bodies with other remains is mentioned only in passing, so **(A)** is incorrect. The author does not "challenge" any position; **(B)** is incorrect. Although the last paragraph describes some important insights into ancient societies made from bog artifacts, the text only describes these as "fascinating" and the author primarily focuses on other issues in the rest of the passage. **(D)** is also incorrect. The passage explains what is distinct about sphagnum moss bogs but never goes into detail about other environments, so analyzing differences between them, as in **(E)**, cannot be the primary purpose.

3.   (D)

The phrase "serves primarily to" indicates that this is a Logic question asking how or why the author included a part of the passage. For this question, you need to determine the purpose of the third paragraph. Review your passage map or paragraph notes and predict that the third paragraph contributes to the author's overall purpose of describing bog bodies by outlining the biochemical processes that preserve items buried in sphagnum bogs. This matches **(D)**; the "mechanisms" are the biochemical processes, and the "effect achieved by elements introduced in the second paragraph" is the preservation due to the unique conditions of the bogs that are described in paragraph 2.

The author doesn't indicate that some factors described in paragraph 2 are more important than others, so **(A)** is incorrect. The author does say in the last paragraph that bog bodies are important, but the third paragraph does not provide support for this assertion; eliminate **(B)**. **(C)** is also incorrect; "the environment that produces the effect that is the topic" refers to the bog, but this paragraph describes how the bog works on bodies, not how the bog is formed. **(E)** distorts the author's use of "biochemistry"; the role of this paragraph is not to explain the importance of biochemistry as a science but to explain how certain bogs preserve bodies using biological molecules.

4.   (E)

The phrase "According to the passage" indicates that this is a Detail question, but "EXCEPT" means that the four incorrect choices will be supported by the passage, while the correct answer will not be. The first two sentences of the third paragraph describe the conditions that "prevent significant bacterial growth in the water." Review that section and eliminate choices that are discussed: cold temperatures, peat from sphagnum moss, the anaerobic environment, and humic acid from decaying moss. **(E)** is mentioned as "preventing rot and water damage," not inhibiting bacterial growth, and is correct.

(A), **(B)**, **(C)**, and **(D)** all match relevant details in the passage and are incorrect.

"Working Married Men" Passage: Questions 5–8

Step 1: Read the Passage Strategically

On the left, we've shown how key words help to identify the major elements of the passage and its structure and what you could skim over. On the right, we've shown what you might be thinking as you read the passage strategically.

PASSAGE	ANALYSIS
Women around the world graduate from college at higher rates than men. **However**, women's participation in the workforce, especially in the ranks of senior management, continues to lag far behind that of men. **Research** into marriages between men and women **indicates** that, as women marry and start families, their earnings and opportunities for promotion decrease. **While** the difficulties that women encounter as they attempt to balance work and family life are frequently discussed, and are beginning to be addressed by employers, **it is interesting to note** that the difficulties faced by working married men are seldom raised.	The passage starts by introducing the difficulties faced by working women, but the contrast key word "[h]owever" introduces the actual topic of the passage: the difficulties faced by working married men.
Scott Coltrane, a researcher at the University of Oregon who has studied marriages between men and women, has found that, **while** the earnings of women tend to go down with each additional child, the earnings of married men **not only** exceed those of both unmarried men and divorced men **but also** tend to go up with each additional child. **One reason** for this disparity may be that, as the size of the family grows, men rely on women to manage most of the responsibilities of housekeeping and child raising. While within the past few decades men have assumed a greater share of household responsibilities, in the United States, women still spend nearly twice as much time as men do in caring for children and the home. The time diaries of highly educated dual-income male-female U.S. couples show that men enjoy three and a half times the leisure time as their female partners do.	Married men earn more with additional children. One reason is provided. The rest of the paragraph expands on that reason.

PASSAGE	ANALYSIS
If married men earn higher salaries and have more leisure time than their female counterparts do, what difficulties do these working men face? Research indicates **three possible problems**. **First**, the perceived responsibility of providing for a family drives men to work more hours and strive for promotion. Many men report feeling dissatisfied because the level of performance that is required to earn promotions and higher salaries prevents them from spending time with their families. **Second**, these demands on men also contribute to higher levels of marital discord. In a 2008 survey, 60 percent of U.S. fathers reported work-family conflicts, compared to 47 percent of mothers.	The opening question signals a return to the topic introduced in the first paragraph. Three reasons married men are struggling will be discussed. First reason: married men work harder and longer to provide for their families, so they lose family time. Second reason: more marital problems.
The pressure to be perceived as a good provider contributes to the **third reason** that married men may struggle. **While** women's decisions to use family leave benefits, move to part-time employment, or leave the workforce to care for children are seen as valuable contributions to family life and, by extension, society, men's decisions to do the same are frequently viewed by their employers as signs of weakness. Studies suggest that men who take advantage of paternity leave policies are viewed as weak or inadequate by both women and men. Research conducted in Australia found that men's requests to work flexibly were denied at twice the rate of those of women.	Third reason: men's decisions to limit work are not valued like those of women.

Passage Map

Here is an example of the notes that you might have made as you read:

¶1: Married men (MM) face difficulties in the workplace

¶2: Research: MM earn more, have more leisure

¶3: MM work harder and longer to support families, experience more marital discord

¶4: MM don't get same flexibility in workplace

Topic: Working married men

Scope: Difficulties faced by ⎯⎯⎯⎯⎯↑

Purpose: Explain the reasons behind ⎯⎯⎯⎯⎯↑

5.   (B)

The phrase "primarily concerned with" means this Global question is asking for the main idea of the passage. You'll be well positioned to answer such questions when you conclude your strategic reading of the passage with a summary of the author's topic, scope, and purpose. Matching the purpose—to explain the difficulties faced by married men in the workplace—to the choices yields (**B**), the correct answer.

A quick vertical scan, where you look at only the first words of the choices, shows that (**A**) and (**D**) are incorrect; the passage does not advocate or take issue with anything. (**C**) misstates the main idea of the passage. The focus of the text is on the issues that are faced by working married men, not only those who earn high salaries. (**E**) is not discussed in the passage; the text does not attribute the difficulties of married men to discrimination against women.

6.   (D)

This Inference question asks you to identify the statement supported by the passage; strictly compare each to the text, keeping the author's overall purpose in mind. Start your research in the third and fourth paragraphs, which provide many details on working married men. (**D**), the correct answer, is supported by the latter half of the third paragraph. There you find that men "work more hours and strive for promotion" because they perceive a responsibility to provide for their families. The last two sentences of the paragraph outline the toll these efforts may take on family life.

(**A**) goes beyond what is stated in the passage and is incorrect; the passage never indicates that providing for their families is the *most* important aspect of employment for married men. (**B**) is the opposite of what the passage states. The third and fourth paragraphs discuss the difficulties faced by working married men. (**C**) is an irrelevant comparison; the satisfaction levels of working women are not discussed. (**E**) contradicts the passage; one of the complaints of married men outlined in the fourth sentence of paragraph 3 is that their job responsibilities prevent them from spending time with their families.

7.   (B)

As indicated by the phrase "in order to," this is a Logic question. Your task is to identify why the author discussed Coltrane's research. Coltrane is introduced in paragraph 2, so look at your passage map for that paragraph or review the relevant text. According to paragraph 2, Coltrane found that married men tend to earn more than other men and earn more as they have more children. This benefit comes with costs, however, as detailed in the third and fourth paragraphs. The author is primarily interested in "the difficulties faced by married men," so predict that Coltrane's research is used to highlight these difficulties. (**B**) is correct because it accurately identifies how the author uses the research: to focus on the downsides of something commonly regarded as an advantage.

While (**A**) captures the beneficial aspect, it ignores the broader context of the passage, which is to discuss the overlooked difficulties that married working men face. (**C**) is incorrect because the author does not offer policy recommendations in the passage; the author is examining a problem but not offering solutions. (**D**) is incorrect because the author is not denying that married women face problems in the workplace but rather is interested in showing that married men also face their own problems. (**E**) is incorrect because Coltrane's research concerns working men, not working women.

8.   (C)

The phrase "According to the passage" indicates the answer to this Detail question will provide the reason, stated in the text, that married men may have higher salaries and better chances of promotion than single men. Your passage map or paragraph notes should indicate that the second paragraph opens with a discussion of the higher salaries earned by married men. The text states, "One reason . . . may be that, as the size of the family grows, men rely on women to manage most of the responsibilities of housekeeping and child raising." (**C**) summarizes this idea.

The remaining choices may be plausible in everyday life, but none of them are mentioned in the passage, so they are all incorrect.

CHAPTER 17

READING COMPREHENSION QUESTION TYPES

LEARNING OBJECTIVES

- Recognize the different Reading Comprehension question types
- Identify the question type based on the question stem
- Apply the Kaplan Method for Reading Comprehension to questions of all types

---

Though you might be inclined to classify Reading Comp according to the kinds of passages that appear—business, social science, biological science, or physical science—you can read all passages in essentially the same way, employing the same strategic reading techniques for each. It's more valuable to focus on the different types of questions the GMAT asks about the passages.

The four main question types on GMAT Reading Comp are Global, Detail, Inference, and Logic. Let's walk through each of these question types in turn, focusing on what they ask and how you can approach them most effectively.

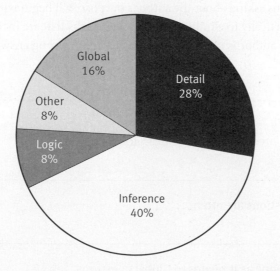

The Approximate Distribution of GMAT Reading Comprehension Questions

Global Questions

Any question that explicitly asks you to consider the passage as a whole is a Global question. Here are some examples:

- Which of the following best expresses the main idea of the passage?
- The author's primary purpose is to . . .
- Which of the following best describes the organization of the passage?
- Which of the following would be an appropriate title for this passage?

The correct answer will be consistent with the passage's topic, scope, purpose, and structure. If you've jotted these down (and you should!), then it will take well under a minute to select the right answer. That's significantly under the average time per Reading Comprehension question, giving you more time for questions that require more research.

Most wrong answers will either get the scope wrong (too narrow or too broad) or misrepresent the author's point of view. Be wary of Global answer choices that are based on details from the first or last paragraph. These are designed to take advantage of test takers who read the first paragraph carefully and then lose focus, or who rush through the passage and remember only the last bit. Mapping the passage and noting the topic, scope, and purpose will make it easy to avoid these wrong answers.

Often, answer choices to Global questions asking about the author's purpose will begin with verbs; in this case, the most efficient approach is to scan vertically to eliminate choices with verbs that are inconsistent with the author's purpose. For example, when an author is neutral on a topic, common wrong answers use verbs that indicate an opinionated stance.

CONCEPT CHECK

1. How does a passage map let you predict the answer to a Global question?

   _____

2. Incorrect choices for Global questions are often . . .

   _____

3. Describe the vertical scan technique as it relates to Global questions.

   _____

Example answers are in your book's online resources (**kaptest.com/login**).

Detail Questions

> **LEARNING OBJECTIVES**
>
> * Identify Detail questions by the question stem
> * Use content clues and your passage map to locate relevant details for answering Detail questions
> * Articulate strategies for eliminating wrong answer choices in Detail questions

Detail questions ask you to identify what the passage explicitly says. Here are some sample Detail question stems:

* According to the passage, which of the following is true of X?
* The author states that . . .
* The author mentions which of the following in support of X?

It would be impossible to keep track of all of the details in a passage as you read through it. Fortunately, Detail question stems will always give you clues about where to look to find the information you need. Many Detail stems include specific words or phrases that you can easily locate in the passage. A sentence or phrase might even be highlighted in the passage. Using these clues, you can selectively re-read parts of the passage to quickly zero in on the answer—a more efficient approach than trying to memorize a lot of details you won't even be asked about.

So locating the detail that the GMAT is asking about is usually not much of a challenge. What, then, are these questions testing? They are testing whether you understand that detail *in the context of the passage*. The best strategic approach, then, is to read not only the sentence that the question stem sends you to but also the sentences before and after it. Consider the following question stem:

> According to the passage, which of the following is true of the guinea pigs discussed in the highlighted portion of the passage?

Let's say that the highlighted portion of the passage goes like this:

> . . . a greater percentage of the guinea pigs that lived in the crowded, indoor, heated area survived than did the guinea pigs in the outdoor cages.

If you don't read for context, you might think that something like this could be the right answer choice:

> O   Guinea pigs survive better indoors.

But what if you read the full context, starting one sentence before?

> Until recently, scientists had no evidence to support the hypothesis that low temperature alone, and not other factors such as people crowding indoors, is responsible for the greater incidence and severity of influenza in the late fall and early winter. Last year, however, researchers uncovered several experiment logs from a research facility whose population of guinea pigs suffered an influenza outbreak in the winter of 1945; these logs documented that a greater percentage of the guinea pigs that lived in the crowded, indoor, heated area survived than did the guinea pigs in the outdoor cages.

Now you could identify this as the right answer:

○   Researchers discovered that some guinea pigs survived better indoors than outdoors during a flu outbreak.

By reading not just the highlighted portion of the passage but the information before it, you realize that it's not necessarily true that guinea pigs always survive better indoors; only a specific subset did. By understanding the information *in context*, you will choose the correct answer.

Pay attention to key words as you research Detail questions. They tell you how the idea referenced by the question stem relates to the ideas around it. Here, the "no evidence" and "however" form the support for the right answer.

CONCEPT CHECK

1.   Where will you find all the information needed to answer a Detail question?

    _____

2.   How could an answer choice that accurately reflects an idea from the passage be the incorrect choice for a Detail question?

    _____

Example answers are in your book's online resources (**kaptest.com/login**).

Inference Questions

LEARNING OBJECTIVES

- Identify Inference questions by the question stem
- Explain what an inference is in the context of Reading Comprehension
- Articulate strategies for assessing which answer choices are supported by the passage and eliminating wrong answers, using your passage map and your understanding of the author's opinions

Reading Comprehension Inference questions, like Critical Reasoning Inference questions, ask you to find something that must be true based on the passage but that is not mentioned explicitly in the passage. Often, for example, a correct answer will logically associate two ideas from different paragraphs. All the information in the answer is in the passage, but you need to connect a few dots to recognize it.

Here are some sample Inference question stems:

- Which of the following is suggested about X?
- Which of the following can be most reasonably inferred from the passage?
- The author would most likely agree that . . .

Inference questions come in two types. The first uses key phrases or highlighting to refer to a specific part of the passage. To answer this kind of question, find the relevant detail in the passage and consider it in the context of the surrounding material. Then make a flexible prediction about what the correct answer will state.

Consider the following Inference question, asking about the guinea pigs discussed in the lesson on Detail questions:

> Which of the following is implied about the guinea pigs mentioned in the highlighted portion of the passage?

Just like last time, you want to review the context around the highlighted portion. Doing so, you'll find that "until recently," there was "no evidence" that temperature affected the flu; "however," last year records were discovered about guinea pigs with flu. The logical inference is not explicitly stated, but if you put the information from the two sentences together, you can predict that the answer will be something like this:

○   Their deaths provided new evidence that influenza may be more dangerous in lower temperatures.

Other Inference questions make no specific references, instead asking what can be inferred from the passage as a whole or what opinion the author might hold. Valid inferences can be drawn from anything in the passage, from big-picture issues like the author's opinion to any of the little details. But you will probably be able to eliminate a few answers quickly because they contradict the big picture.

Then you'll investigate the remaining answers choice by choice, looking to put each answer in one of three categories—(1) proved right, (2) proved wrong, or (3) not proved right but not proved wrong either. It's distinguishing between the second and third categories that will lead to success on Inference questions. Don't throw away an answer because you aren't sure about it or "don't like it."

If you can't find material in the passage that proves an answer choice wrong, don't eliminate it. Since the correct answer to an Inference question is something that *must* be true based on the passage, you can often find your way to the correct answer by eliminating the four choices that *could* be false.

CONCEPT CHECK

- Correct answers to Inference questions must _____.
- Unlike the answers to Detail questions, the answer to an Inference question is not _____.

Example answers are in your book's online resources (**kaptest.com/login**).

Logic Questions

Logic questions ask why the author does something—why the author cites a source, includes a certain detail, puts one paragraph before another, and so forth. Logic questions ask not for the purpose of the passage as a whole but for the purpose of a part of the passage. As a result, any answer choice that focuses on the content of a detail will be incorrect.

Here are some sample Logic question stems:

- The author mentions X most probably in order to . . .
- Which of the following best describes the relationship of the second paragraph to the rest of the passage?
- What is the primary purpose of the third paragraph?

Most Logic questions can be answered correctly from your passage map—your written summary of each paragraph and the passage's overall topic, scope, and purpose. If the question references a detail, as does the first sample question stem above, then review the context in which that detail appears—just as you would for any Detail or Inference question that references a specific detail.

"Other" Questions

> **LEARNING OBJECTIVES**
>
> * Identify questions that do not fall into one of the major categories of Reading Comprehension question types
> * Use your passage map; the author's topic, scope, and purpose; and your ability to draw inferences to answer any question posed

A small number of Reading Comprehension questions will not fall neatly into the four main categories described so far. Nonetheless, these questions tend to test reasoning skills you'll be familiar with from practicing Critical Reasoning questions or from real life.

"Critical Reasoning" Questions

Occasionally in Reading Comp, you will be asked a question phrased the same way as one of the common Critical Reasoning question types, such as an Assumption, Strengthen, Weaken, or Evaluate. These questions refer to arguments—the author's or someone else's—just as they do in Critical Reasoning.

Research the portion of the passage that includes the argument referenced by the question stem. Just as you would in Critical Reasoning, identify the conclusion and relevant evidence; then use the central assumption to form a prediction for the right answer.

Parallelism Questions

These questions ask you to apply the ideas in a passage through analogy to a new situation. For example, a passage might describe a chain of economic events that are related causally, such as reduced customer spending leading to a slowdown of industrial production, which in turn leads to the elimination of industrial jobs. A Parallelism question might then ask you the following:

> Which of the following situations is most comparable to the economic scenario described in the passage?

Don't look for a choice that deals with the same subject matter as the passage, as such choices are usually wrong. Instead, look for a logically similar scenario, in this case a chain of causally connected events. In this example, the correct choice might describe water pollution from a factory causing the death of a certain type of algae, which in turn causes a decline in the fish population that relied on that type of algae as its primary food source.

Application Questions

Application questions ask you to identify an example or application of something described in the passage. For instance, if the passage describes a process for realigning a company's management structure, an Application question could give you five answer choices, each of which describes the structure of a given company. Only the correct choice will accurately reflect the result of the process described in the passage. Whereas Parallelism questions ask you to identify an analogous logical situation (irrespective of subject matter), Application questions ask you to apply information or ideas directly, within the same subject area.

Both Parallelism and Application questions mirror the kind of reasoning often required in business, where a manager needs to use experience and information acquired elsewhere to a new problem.

Reading Comprehension Question Type Identification Drill

Identifying the question type during step 2 of the Kaplan Method for Reading Comprehension is a chance for you to put yourself in control of the entire process that follows: how to research, what to predict, and, thus, how to evaluate answer choices.

In this exercise, analyze key words in the question stem to determine what the question is asking you to do. Then choose the correct question type from the list of choices.

1. The passage implies which of the following about XXXXXXX?

   O Global
   O Detail
   O Inference
   O Logic
   O Other

2. According to the passage, each of the following is true of XXXXXXX EXCEPT

   O Global
   O Detail
   O Inference
   O Logic
   O Other

3. The author mentions XXXXXXX in order to

   O Global
   O Detail
   O Inference
   O Logic
   O Other

4. The author's primary objective in the passage is to

   O Global
   O Detail
   O Inference
   O Logic
   O Other

5. The author makes which of the following statements concerning XXXXXXX?

   O Global
   O Detail
   O Inference
   O Logic
   O Other

6. An appropriate title for the passage would be

   O Global
   O Detail
   O Inference
   O Logic
   O Other

7. Which of the following statements about XXXXXXX can be inferred from the passage?

   O Global
   O Detail
   O Inference
   O Logic
   O Other

8. Which of the following, if true, would most weaken the theory proposed by XXXXXXX?

   O Global
   O Detail
   O Inference
   O Logic
   O Other

9. Which of the following best states the central idea of the passage?

   ○ Global
   ○ Detail
   ○ Inference
   ○ Logic
   ○ Other

10. Which of the following situations is most comparable to XXXXXXX as it is presented in the passage?

   ○ Global
   ○ Detail
   ○ Inference
   ○ Logic
   ○ Other

11. The passage provides support for which of the following assertions about XXXXXXX?

   ○ Global
   ○ Detail
   ○ Inference
   ○ Logic
   ○ Other

12. The author indicates explicitly that which of the following has been XXXXXXX?

   ○ Global
   ○ Detail
   ○ Inference
   ○ Logic
   ○ Other

13. The author would most likely agree with which of the following?

   ○ Global
   ○ Detail
   ○ Inference
   ○ Logic
   ○ Other

14. The author refers to XXXXXXX most probably in order to

   ○ Global
   ○ Detail
   ○ Inference
   ○ Logic
   ○ Other

15. Which of the following represents the clearest application of XXXXXXX's theory as described in the passage?

   ○ Global
   ○ Detail
   ○ Inference
   ○ Logic
   ○ Other

16. The passage is primarily concerned with

   ○ Global
   ○ Detail
   ○ Inference
   ○ Logic
   ○ Other

Question Type Identification Drill: Answers and Explanations

1. C

When you see "implies" or "suggests," know that you're facing an Inference question.

2. B

When you see direct, categorical language like "according to the passage," know that you're facing a Detail question.

3. D

The phrase "in order to" means that this is a Logic question. Logic questions deal with the author's motivations. If a question asks you why the author includes a paragraph, brings up a detail, or cites a source, know that you are facing a Logic question.

4. A

The phrase "primary objective" means that this is a Global question.

5. B

The phrase "makes which of the following statements" signals that this is a Detail question.

6. A

The phrase "title for the passage" means that you must base your answer on the whole passage, so this is a Global question.

7. C

The word "inferred" means that this is an Inference question.

8. E (Weaken)

The word "weaken" means that this is a Weaken question, common in Critical Reasoning but one of the rarer question types in Reading Comp.

9. A

The phrase "central idea of the passage" means that this is a Global question.

10. E (Parallelism)

The phrase "most comparable to" means that this is a Parallelism question.

11. C

The phrase "passage provides support for" means that this is an Inference question.

12. B

The phrase "indicates explicitly" means that this is a Detail question.

13. C

The phrase "most likely agree" signals an Inference question.

14. D

The phrase "in order to" means that this is a Logic question.

15. E (Application)

The phrase "represents the clearest application of" means that this is an Application question. Application questions ask you to find the answer choice that is most consistent with a description, theory, or process described in the passage.

16. A

The phrase "passage is primarily concerned with" means that this is a Global question.

CHAPTER 18

READING COMPREHENSION QUESTIONS: PUTTING IT ALL TOGETHER

LEARNING OBJECTIVES

- Recognize immediately the format of Reading Comprehension passages and questions and call upon strategies for approaching them
- Determine quickly a question's type and apply nuances to the Kaplan Method for Reading Comprehension to research the passage, predict the correct answer, and eliminate wrong answers
- Evaluate your performance on Reading Comprehension questions

This quiz is designed to give you practice with a mix of Reading Comprehension passages and question types, just like the mix of passage sets you'll see on Test Day. Take this quiz after you have studied the different types of questions the test maker asks and practiced applying the Kaplan Method for Reading Comprehension, including the strategic reading that the test rewards.

How to Take This Quiz

By the time you take this quiz, you are hopefully well on your way to mastery of Reading Comprehension, so set a timer. Give yourself 3–4 minutes per passage and 1 minute 15 seconds per question. So if you do all six passages and 30 questions in this set at once, set the timer for 58 minutes; if you decide to do fewer passage sets than that in one sitting, set the timer accordingly.

Make sure to use the steps of the Kaplan Method on every question. Students are often tempted to give step 1 short shrift, reading through the passage quickly so they can get to the questions. While you certainly want to read *efficiently*, investing the time in taking some summary notes will ensure you absorb the main points the author is making, the location of key examples, the structure of the passage, and any opinions expressed—all material you're likely to see questions on. Students are also prone to skip step 4, making a prediction, finding it easier to search the choices for an answer that "sounds right." However, you're much more likely to find the answer you want—the correct answer—if you know what you're looking for before you look for it.

Note that the GMAT will typically give you three or four questions per passage, drawing those questions adaptively from a larger pool of up to six to eight questions. (The computer considers both your current score level and the distribution of question types you've seen so far.) For several passages on this quiz, we've given you more than four questions so that you can see the full range of questions the GMAT might ask about a given passage. But remember that on Test Day, you'll probably see only three or four.

Furthermore, remember that on Test Day, you can't mark up the passage on screen or skip forward and back between questions. So challenge yourself now not to take notes in this book (use separate scratch paper, an onscreen whiteboard, or an erasable notepad like the one you'd use at a testing center) and to do the questions in order.

After you've finished the quiz and are reviewing the explanations, make sure you not only can explain why the right answer is correct but also can articulate why each wrong answer is incorrect. Being able to clearly identify why wrong choices are wrong will help you avoid picking them.

In addition, if you missed a question, understand *why* you missed it. There is always a reason! The Kaplan Method can be a useful checklist to diagnose where you went wrong.

- After reading the passage, had you mapped it well enough to avoid extensive re-reading as you answered the questions?
- Did you identify the task set by the question?
- Were you able to efficiently research the context clue in the question stem either in your passage map or the passage itself?
- Was your prediction off base or too specific (or too general), or did you omit making a prediction?
- Were you tempted by a choice that did not actually match your prediction, perhaps because you could have read more carefully or because you fell for a common wrong-answer trap?

If you know why you missed a question, you can avoid making that error again.

Above all, avoid judging yourself. The only evaluation of your skill that actually matters is the one on Test Day. So if you make mistakes, resolve to learn from them and improve your score.

Reading Comprehension Quiz

(Answers and explanations are at the end of the chapter.)

Questions 1–3 refer to the following passage.

It is believed that half or more of the languages spoken on Earth will be extinct within a century. The United Nations Educational, Scientific, and Cultural Organization (UNESCO), which monitors endangered languages, says that "with each vanishing language, an irreplaceable element of human
5   thought in its multiform variations is lost forever." As the world becomes more interconnected, many languages, as well as the culture captured within them, may be lost.

There is a strong link between language and cultural identity. In nineteenth-century Japan, attempts to assimilate the Ainu people into Japanese culture
10   included banning their language; some indigenous languages in both North America and Australia suffered the same fate. Many of those languages are lost or dying. With loss of language comes loss of links to the past and feelings of belonging to a community, which research has linked to mental health. One study of Aboriginal communities found that youth suicide rates dropped
15   to almost zero when the residents had conversational knowledge of native languages.

One problem endangered languages face is lack of official recognition. Residents of a country are expected to know its official language or languages, but many countries do little to recognize minority regional languages. Take
20   Basque, a language spoken in both Spain and France. In France, only French is recognized as an official language. In Spain, the constitution allows for regional recognition of official languages besides Spanish, so in Basque-speaking parts of the country, both Spanish and Basque are official languages. It is not surprising, therefore, that UNESCO cites Basque as "vulnerable" in Spain but
25   "critically endangered" in France.

Consider, in contrast, the case of Finnish. This tongue is not endangered, even though Finland was ruled from the Middle Ages until 1917 by first Sweden and then Russia and, during this period, Swedish was used as the language of administration and government. In 1919, a newly independent Finland
30   constitutionally adopted both Finnish and Swedish as official languages, legally recognizing its native language as important to its burgeoning national identity. As of 2013, Finnish was spoken by 89 percent of the population of Finland.

In order to preserve languages that will otherwise be lost, linguists have proposed creating a database of endangered languages. But how would an
35   academic repository serve the often marginalized groups that speak such languages? While directed toward a noble goal, this project would fail to address the issue of language's critical role in preserving a sense of cultural identity.

1. According to the passage, Basque is more endangered in France than in Spain because

   ○ France has suppressed Basque in order to maintain a French cultural identity

   ○ there are more Basque speakers in Spain than in France

   ○ Basque has no governmental recognition as an official language in France

   ○ multiple languages are recognized as official throughout Spain

   ○ Basque-speaking regions in Spain have developed a separate cultural identity

2. Which of the following statements, if true, would support the assertion that Finnish was "important to [Finland's] burgeoning national identity" (line 31)?

   ○ Speaking Finnish after 1919 became a point of pride for those in Finland, whereas it previously had often been a source of shame.

   ○ Both Swedish and Finnish were taught in Finnish schools after 1919, just as they had been before the new constitution was adopted.

   ○ Finland adopted a new flag and national anthem after the new constitution was approved in 1919.

   ○ Some people in Finland continued to use Swedish as their preferred language even after Finnish was adopted as an official language.

   ○ Those who worked to modernize Finnish in the late nineteenth century so it would achieve broader acceptance favored the western dialect over the eastern.

3. Which of the following statements most clearly exemplifies the aspect of language extinction that UNESCO considers problematic?

   ○ As one of the world's oldest languages, Basque is worth preserving as a living historical artifact as well as a modern spoken language.

   ○ Because scholars have been unable to translate the Linear A script, the intellectual capital of the culture that produced it remains inaccessible.

   ○ Because Socrates did not leave behind any written works, his ideas have been preserved only through secondhand sources.

   ○ Most linguists term Korean a "language isolate" because it is not known to be related to any other languages.

   ○ Because it has no equivalent word in many languages, "serendipity" is a particularly difficult term to translate.

Questions 4–6 refer to the following passage.

Unlike vaccinations for polio, measles, mumps, and many other virus-borne diseases, which yield lifetime protection with one vaccination or a short series of vaccinations, vaccinations combating the influenza virus must be administered annually, and even then they may not be fully successful in
5   preventing illness. The reason for this striking difference is the ability of the influenza virus to evolve quickly. The antigens, the parts of the influenza virus recognized by the human body, include two important surface proteins, hemagglutinin and neuraminidase. Hemagglutinin is involved in the invasion of a cell within the human body, and neuraminidase assists in the release of
10   new viruses from the cell after the viruses are replicated. As hemagglutinin is copied, it is not replicated exactly, so the human immune system does not recognize the mutation as the same protein it has encountered before and does not inaugurate the immune response. In this process, called antigenic drift, the known strains of influenza are recognized and effectively combated, but,
15   unchallenged by the immune system, mutated viruses are able to reproduce freely and, thus, form a new strain of influenza.

Researchers in immune therapy are working on a variety of innovations to improve influenza vaccinations such as faster methods of production of vaccines and improvements to existing vaccines to strengthen the immune
20   response of the human body. By far the most intriguing of these efforts are researchers' attempts to produce vaccines that would target the evolutionarily conserved areas of the influenza virus. The stem that attaches hemagglutinin to the virus, the neuraminidase protein, and M2—a protein found in the membrane of the influenza virus—all appear to be nearly identical across
25   virus strains and seem to evolve slowly. While much work remains to be done, a vaccine targeting one of these may be the key to a one-time immunization protocol that would provide efficacious protection against most influenza strains.

4. The primary purpose of the passage is to

    O   explain the process by which the influenza virus mutates quickly, thus making the development of a single vaccination impossible

    O   identify the action of hemagglutinin within the influenza virus that causes the virus to evolve rapidly

    O   compare and contrast the influenza virus with the viruses that cause polio, measles, mumps, and other virus-borne diseases

    O   discuss the reason influenza vaccinations are administered annually and recent innovations in research that may address this anomaly

    O   describe the mechanism of antigenic drift and how this process affects the human immune system

5. It can be inferred from the passage that the author believes which of the following to be true about a vaccine that could provide permanent protection against influenza with a single immunization protocol?

    O   Research into such a vaccine is promising, and the vaccine will be available soon if tests are completed successfully.

    O   The vaccine could affect neuraminidase or other areas of the virus that do not mutate rapidly.

    O   Such a vaccine cannot be effective because hemagglutinin antigens evolve too quickly.

    O   The vaccine will most likely target hemagglutinin antigens because their rapid mutation makes them susceptible to the defenses of the human immune system.

    O   The vaccine will have a similar mechanism to that of the vaccines now administered for polio, measles, mumps, and other virus-borne diseases.

6. According to the passage, each of the following is true of the influenza virus EXCEPT:

    O   The evolution of hemagglutinin on the surface of the virus can prevent the human immune system from recognizing and attacking the virus.

    O   Some of the surface proteins on the influenza virus have different functions.

    O   Antigenic drift prevents the immune system from recognizing some influenza viruses.

    O   Annual immunization is not always effective protection against the influenza virus.

    O   The influenza virus is remarkable in its ability to mutate more rapidly than any other known virus.

Questions 7–12 refer to the following passage.

Responding to the negative, one-dimensional representation of African
Americans in the Hollywood films of the 1970s, the women of Delta Sigma
Theta, an African American service sorority, embarked on an ambitious project
to produce a feature film that would challenge these stereotypes. Filmmaker
5 S. Torriano Berry recounts in his documentary on the sorority's efforts how,
unfortunately, what could have been a historic project with the power to
transform the U.S. entertainment industry failed due to the sorority's reliance
on the major movie studios' traditional marketing and distribution system.

Lillian Benbow, the president of Delta Sigma Theta, and the sorority's Arts
10 and Letters committee headed the effort to raise money for the production of
the film, *Countdown at Kusini*, from donations. While most of the funds were
contributed by the thousands of sorority members across the United States,
African American entertainment luminaries not only supported the project
financially but also donated their talent and expertise. However, after arriving
15 on location in Nigeria, the producers found that lack of qualified technicians,
editors, film crews, equipment, and cinematic support services within the
country meant that unexpected costs quickly added up, drastically exceeding
the initial budget.

Even with the cost overruns, the movie could have paid for itself and perhaps
20 even turned a modest profit if the sorority's initial marketing proposal had
been followed. When preparing the budget, Delta Sigma Theta expected to use
a four-wall marketing plan, in which the sorority's extensive membership would
rent local theaters across the country, then sell tickets to other members,
friends, and family. Additional screenings would be held as demand warranted.
25 As one of the oldest and most extensive service sororities, Delta Sigma Theta
had enough members in enough cities to at least recoup production costs.
However, a major Hollywood film company became aware of the project and
approached the sorority with an offer to distribute the film. Buoyed by the
interest of the mainstream media, the sorority believed that the film company's
30 expertise in marketing and distribution would lead to broader exposure and
greater opportunities for success. Unfortunately, when the film was released
through traditional channels, without any coordination with the local chapters
of the sorority, it quickly failed.

Despite the film's commercial failure, the project is remarkable for its
35 prescience, providing an early example of crowdfunding and media activism.
Delta Sigma Theta took active steps to counter the limited range of stereotypes
of African Americans in Hollywood films, and it funded these efforts through
numerous small contributions. Moreover, the film's ultimate impact may not be
only historical but also tangible in the modern Nigerian film industry, second
40 in size only to that of India. When *Countdown at Kusini* was produced, there

was no filmmaking infrastructure in Nigeria. While some of the production equipment was brought back to the United States, much was left behind, as well as the newly developed expertise of the local technicians, editors, actors, and production staff who were trained on the film. One of the most intriguing

45   questions surrounding *Countdown at Kusini* may be that of its effect on the nascent Nigerian film industry.

7.   The primary purpose of the passage is to

    O   criticize Hollywood's depictions of African Americans in the films of the 1970s

    O   compare and contrast the presentations of African Americans in *Countdown at Kusini* with those found in Hollywood films

    O   explain how *Countdown at Kusini* transformed the film industry, particularly in Nigeria

    O   chronicle the reasons for the production of *Countdown at Kusini* and the film's significance

    O   describe the technical difficulties encountered in the production of *Countdown at Kusini* and how they were overcome

8.   The author's reference to a "four-wall marketing plan" in line 22 serves primarily to

    O   explain the factors that contributed to the successful release of the film

    O   illustrate the characteristics of a traditional Hollywood film release

    O   contrast the original marketing strategy with the one that subsequently failed

    O   indicate the reasons the sorority's plan proved to be unworkable

    O   demonstrate why the film was unlikely to recover its production costs

9.   According to the passage, the sorority agreed to the Hollywood film company's marketing plan for which of the following reasons?

    O   The sorority believed that cost overruns in the production of the film demanded higher sales in order for the film to recover those costs.

    O   The sorority determined the four-wall marketing plan would not be feasible.

    O   The sorority thought that, since the Hollywood film company had more resources and experience, the film company's plan would be more effective.

    O   The sorority members were not able to rent sufficient theaters to ensure the success of the four-wall marketing strategy.

    O   The sorority members were concentrated in a limited number of geographic locations and needed the broader distribution channels the company was able to provide.

10. Which of the following best describes the purpose of the fourth paragraph of the passage?

    ○ To explain several significant aspects of the film that indicate its historic importance

    ○ To provide further evidence of the failure of the film's marketing strategy

    ○ To present a comprehensive analysis of the effects of the Hollywood film company's marketing plan

    ○ To contrast the commercial failure of the film with the exceptional effort of the producers

    ○ To introduce facts that contradict S. Torriano Berry's opinion of the film's significance

11. The passage suggests that many of the members of Delta Sigma Theta responded to the 1970s Hollywood films featuring African Americans in which of the following ways?

    ○ They appreciated the employment opportunities offered by the introduction of major films with primarily African American actors.

    ○ They accepted the limited portrayal of African American characters as a first step toward broader media exposure.

    ○ They organized campaigns across the country protesting the limited range of stereotypical depictions of African American life in Hollywood films.

    ○ They mobilized their financial resources and organizational skills in an effort to present an alternative image of African Americans.

    ○ They became aware of the many advantages of mainstream media exposure to challenge negative stereotypes.

12. It can be inferred from the passage that which of the following is one of the reasons *Countdown at Kusini* is considered a historic African American film?

    ○ *Countdown at Kusini* is the first recorded instance of crowdfunding.

    ○ *Countdown at Kusini* introduced Hollywood studios to the marketing of privately produced films.

    ○ *Countdown at Kusini* was the first commercially successful film to present a more realistic portrayal of African Americans.

    ○ *Countdown at Kusini* was successful as an educational film despite its commercial failure.

    ○ *Countdown at Kusini* may have been instrumental in the establishment of the Nigerian film industry.

Questions 13–18 refer to the following passage.

A one-child policy was implemented in China in 1979, and for nearly 40 years, until the policy was amended to allow two children in 2015, some Han Chinese families could legally have only one child. This rule was implemented in an attempt to slow continued growth of a population that had almost doubled
5   since 1949. The Chinese government claimed that the policy prevented 400 million births, though some have suggested that the decline may be at least partly due to economic reasons, not legal ones.

One result of the policy seems to be the birth and survival of significantly more boys than girls. One study found that China had 33 million more boys than
10   girls under the age of 20, and it is believed that by 2030, 25 percent of Chinese men in their late 30s will never have been married. Research has shown that an excess of men of marriageable age is linked to higher rates of psychological problems, as it creates a marginalized underclass, and history would suggest such situations may correlate with increased aggression and violence, both
15   inside and outside a country's borders.

Economist Amartya Sen wrote in 1990 of the phenomenon of "missing women" in population data, noting that in China, "the survival prospects of female children clearly have been unfavorably affected by restrictions on the size of the family." In a society that has traditionally strongly favored sons, it has been
20   suggested that sex-specific pregnancy terminations and infanticide account for the discrepancy in numbers. But others have countered this argument, believing that disease might better explain the phenomenon, either by making women more likely to give birth to male children or by making it more likely that female children will die prenatally or when very young. For at least some
25   of the missing girls, however, a less sinister explanation may prove the correct one: parents who already had a child, or who wanted to be able to have another in an attempt to have a son, simply never registered their daughters with government officials. A recent study found evidence that as many as 25 million girls were not registered at birth, some of them officially "existing"
30   only many years later and others perhaps never officially existing at all.

13. The primary purpose of the passage is to

   O criticize the accepted explanation for missing girls in China since the implementation of the one-child policy

   O show why the expected population decline in China due to the one-child policy was not due to a decrease in the number of males

   O demonstrate how China's one-child policy has influenced past and future birth rates

   O explore the phenomenon of missing girls in China during the years of the one-child policy

   O argue that the expected population decline in China due to the one-child policy was due entirely to a decrease in the number of women

14. According to the passage, which of the following is true of societies in which there are not enough female partners for men of marriageable age?

   O They occurred historically but are not known to occur in the modern day.

   O They may be at increased risk of international conflict.

   O They are more likely to develop when a significant proportion of the population is psychologically damaged.

   O They are not known to have occurred prior to the modern day.

   O They can result in the disappearance of women from official records.

15. The last paragraph in the passage serves primarily to

   O present multiple potential explanations for a phenomenon described in the second paragraph

   O offer a critique of explanations put forward for the outcome of the policy in which the author is primarily interested

   O demonstrate that the least sinister explanation of a troubling phenomenon is the correct one

   O explain fully the phenomenon described in the second paragraph

   O outline why social attitudes may explain the result of the policy that is the topic of the passage

16. According to the passage, each of the following is a possible reason for missing girls in China EXCEPT:

    O   Disease may cause more boys to be born than girls.

    O   The one-child policy does not require girls to be registered.

    O   Disease may cause more girls to die prenatally than boys.

    O   Infanticide of female children occurs because families prefer sons.

    O   Some girls are not registered so that parents can have another child.

17. Based on information in the passage, which of the following outcomes would have been most likely to occur if a Han Chinese family had a baby daughter prior to 2015?

    O   The parents are eventually pleased to have had a daughter, because there are so many marriageable men.

    O   Because the daughter may succumb to disease, the parents have another child in hopes of having a son.

    O   The parents appeal to the authorities to approve an exception to the number of children allowed.

    O   Because a pregnancy is more likely to result in a son than a daughter, the parents have another child.

    O   The parents fail to officially register the daughter, and they have another child.

18. The author mentions a "marginalized underclass" (line 13) most likely in order to

    O   show one potential societal risk of the one-child policy

    O   give an example of why there are more men than women in China

    O   demonstrate that men are inherently more violent than women

    O   argue that widespread poverty may cause people to value boys more than girls

    O   illustrate the effect of the one-child policy on average family income

Questions 19–24 refer to the following passage.

Generally, interspecific matings represent an evolutionary dead end, producing sterile offspring, if any at all. For some species of birds, however, such pairings may indeed bring evolutionary advantages to the participants. In the case of the female collared flycatchers of Gotland, three distinct factors may work to
5 make interspecific pairings with pied flycatcher males reproductively beneficial.

In many instances, female collared flycatchers nest with male pied flycatchers while continuing to mate with other collared flycatchers, in effect parasitizing the pied flycatchers, who invest in rearing and fledging any offspring. Often, more than half of the offspring raised by interspecific flycatcher pairs are, in
10 fact, not hybrids. Furthermore, an estimated 65 percent of the hybrid offspring of the resident pied flycatcher male are male. Because hybrid females are sterile and males are not, this male bias minimizes the primary disadvantage of interspecific matings: sterile offspring. Habitat specialization may be a third mechanism: these pairings tend to occur in the late spring when the coniferous
15 woods favored by the pied flycatcher provide a greater availability of food than the deciduous woods where the collared flycatchers tend to live. Together, these factors form a mechanism to improve substantially the reproductive success of female collared flycatchers beyond what would be expected of interspecific mating with pied flycatcher males.

20 Although all three of these mechanisms appear to act in concert to form a single elaborate mechanism specifically evolved to circumvent the usual disadvantages of interspecific mating, studies have shown similar motivations for the behavior of female collared flycatchers mating within the species. According to Professor Sievert Rohwer, collared flycatcher females will choose
25 to nest with subordinate collared flycatcher males that inhabit good territory because collared flycatcher females must pair-bond in order to be successful in raising offspring. To engender the best offspring, however, the females will continue to copulate with higher-quality collared males with whom they are not paired. Thus, females seem to be nesting with males of any species with the best territories available at the time, but they will continue to mate with more
30 attractive males outside of their pair bonds.

A highly unusual behavior, interspecific mating seems to provide certain reproductive advantages to the collared flycatcher female. However, it remains unclear whether the mating behavior of female collared flycatchers evolved to circumvent the usual problems with interspecific mating or whether the
35 behavior is simply an extension of how female collared flycatchers behave when mating within their own species.

19. The author's primary purpose is to

    ○ criticize the basis of a scientific theory

    ○ defend a hypothesis concerning birds' mating behaviors

    ○ point out the need for further study of female collared flycatchers

    ○ describe the interspecific mating behavior of female collared flycatchers and possible explanations for it

    ○ defend an unpopular view of a natural phenomenon

20. According to the passage, female collared flycatchers' mating with male pied flycatchers could be explained by any of the following reasons EXCEPT:

    ○ Food is more available in pied flycatcher territories during the mating season.

    ○ Male pied flycatchers can help raise offspring successfully, even if the offspring are not theirs.

    ○ Male pied flycatchers sire more female offspring than do collared flycatcher males, increasing the reproductive success of the female collared flycatcher.

    ○ Females are known to nest with subordinate males while pursuing extra-pair matings with higher-quality males.

    ○ Females enjoy greater reproductive success by pair-bonding with an inferior male than by not pair-bonding at all.

21. The bias toward male offspring resulting from the mating of collared flycatcher females and pied flycatcher males is presented as evidence that

    ○ collared flycatcher females that mate with pied flycatcher males have more dominant male offspring

    ○ the offspring from extra-pair matings with collared flycatcher males are more frequently male

    ○ female flycatchers are not deterred from interspecific pairing by the likelihood of sterile hybrid offspring

    ○ males are produced to reduce interspecific inbreeding in future generations

    ○ interspecific breeding is normal in all varieties of flycatchers

22. It can be inferred from the passage that one of the circumstances that helps to promote the success of collared flycatchers is that

   O female flycatchers use strategies to procure sufficient nourishment when raising broods

   O collared flycatcher pairs are capable of producing broods that are 50 percent male

   O flycatchers generally mate for life

   O males do not vary in the benefits they provide to their offspring

   O over half of all females engage in extra-pair matings

23. Professor Rohwer would most likely agree with which of the following statements?

   O All traits related to particular functions have evolved only for those particular functions.

   O Flycatchers represent the best population for studies of bird-mating behavior.

   O Behaviors may appear functional even under conditions other than those under which the behaviors evolved.

   O Evolution has played no role in shaping the behavior of interspecifically paired flycatchers.

   O Hybridization is generally beneficial for species that can produce fertile hybrid offspring.

24. The mating behavior of female collared flycatchers paired with subordinate male flycatchers is offered as

   O an unwarranted assumption behind the adaptive explanation of interspecific matings

   O an alternative explanation for pair matings of collared females with pied males

   O evidence supporting the hypothesis of adaption for interspecific breeding

   O a discredited mainstream explanation for why hybridization is a dead end for most species

   O proof in support of the theory that collared and pied flycatchers are separate species

Questions 25–30 refer to the following passage.

Rainbows have long been a part of religion and mythology in cultures around the globe, appearing as bridges between the heavens and the earth, as messages from the gods, or as weapons wielded by divine powers. Some cultures have viewed rainbows themselves as deities, or even as demonic

5   beings from which to hide children. But in the early fourteenth century, Theodoric of Freiburg, a German friar, and Kamal al-Din al-Farisi, a Persian scientist, independently turned a scientific eye to the study of rainbows.

Theodoric and al-Farisi were thousands of miles apart, but both had studied Ibn al-Haytham's *Book of Optics*. Each concluded that a rainbow's appearance is

10   the result of sunlight refracting and reflecting through water droplets left after a rainfall. They conducted experiments to provide support for their conclusions, successfully re-creating the conditions necessary to make a rainbow appear; al-Farisi used a sphere and a camera obscura, while Theodoric used flasks and globes.

15   Both scholars were, as modern physics has shown, correct in their assessments. When light hits a water droplet, the water causes the light's speed to decrease. Furthermore, the light refracts—or changes direction—upon entering the droplet, and some of the light reflects off the back of the droplet, refracting again as it exits. The angle of refraction depends on the wavelength

20   of the light; thus, refraction "breaks" white light into multiple wavelengths—a phenomenon called dispersion—which appear as different colors.

But for a rainbow to fill the sky with color, more is needed. A single droplet of water will disperse the entire visible light spectrum, with each wavelength leaving at a different angle, but it alone cannot create a rainbow. Only a little

25   of the light from a particular droplet reaches the eye of the human observer, striking the eye from a particular angle. For the observer to perceive the rainbow's characteristic banded arc of different colors, a multitude of droplets suspended in the air, refracting and dispersing light, are needed, with the shorter wavelengths and shallower angles of indigo and violet appearing to the

30   observer at the bottom and the longer wavelengths and steeper angles of red and orange appearing at the top.

25.   The author mentions the angle at which light leaves water droplets (lines 22–23) primarily in order to

      ○   describe how refraction causes light to disperse as it leaves a water droplet

      ○   show that indigo and violet appear at the bottom of rainbows because those colors have shallower angles

      ○   illustrate that a change in the angle of light changes the wavelength of the light

      ○   explain that the human eye perceives a rainbow only when light is refracted from multiple points

      ○   introduce evidence that may help solve a long-standing mystery about the physics of refraction

26.   Based on the passage, it can be inferred that the rainbow's middle colors of yellow, green, and blue

      ○   are not broken into separate bands by the dispersion of light leaving a droplet of water

      ○   have longer wavelengths than do the red and orange light at the top of the rainbow

      ○   have wavelengths that all strike the eye of a human observer at the same angle

      ○   have wavelengths that are refracted at shallower angles than the wavelengths of indigo and violet light

      ○   have wavelengths that are shorter than those of red and orange light and longer than those of indigo and violet light

27.   According to the passage, the refraction of light upon entering and leaving a water droplet

      ○   changes the angle at which light leaves the water droplet, thereby altering the light's wavelength

      ○   causes the light to be reflected and thus intensify, becoming more visible to the human observer

      ○   disperses white light, allowing it to be seen as its different component colors

      ○   causes the light to slow and thus more readily disperse according to its different wavelengths

      ○   alters the light's wavelengths so they fall within the visible spectrum

28. The primary purpose of the passage is to

    ○   explain why rainbows are a relatively rare phenomenon

    ○   describe traditional and scientific explanations for the appearance of rainbows

    ○   raise doubts about a historical explanation for the appearance of rainbows

    ○   explore the reasons that the refraction of light causes it to appear as different colors

    ○   examine the physics underlying the appearance of rainbows to the human observer

29. It can be inferred that the author of the passage would most likely agree with which of the following statements about the study of rainbows?

    ○   Scientific experiments performed hundreds of years ago sometimes provided accurate results.

    ○   Cultures that associate rainbows with divinity do not approve of scientific inquiry into the nature of rainbows.

    ○   The experiments of Theodoric and al-Farisi established that refraction of light occurs in water droplets but did not examine larger volumes of water.

    ○   In societies in which the results of scientific studies of rainbows are widely accepted, rainbows are no longer associated with spiritual meaning.

    ○   Studies such as Theodoric's and al-Farisi's now have no value because modern science has shown them to be simplistic.

30. The primary function of the second paragraph is to

    ○   discuss a challenge to the conception of rainbows as a religious symbol

    ○   evaluate two historical methods for observing rainbows

    ○   describe the difficulties early scholars overcame in their attempts to understand rainbows

    ○   support the idea that medieval science is similar in value to modern science

    ○   outline historical attempts to understand the scientific basis of rainbows

Answers and explanations follow on the next page. ▶ ▶ ▶

Answers and Explanations

"Endangered Languages" Passage: Questions 1–3

Step 1: Read the Passage Strategically

On the left, we've shown how key words help you to identify the major elements of the passage and its structure and what you could skim over. On the right, we've shown what you might be thinking as you read the passage strategically.

PASSAGE	ANALYSIS
It is believed that half or more of the **languages** spoken on Earth will be extinct within a century. The United Nations Educational, Scientific, and Cultural Organization (UNESCO), which monitors endangered languages, says that "with each vanishing language, an irreplaceable element of human thought in its multiform variations is lost forever." As the world becomes more interconnected, many languages, as well as the **culture** captured within them, may be **lost**.	Topic: many languages/cultures are in danger of extinction.
There is a **strong link** between **language** and **cultural identity**. In nineteenth-century Japan, attempts to assimilate the Ainu people into Japanese culture included banning their language; some indigenous languages in both North America and Australia suffered the same fate. Many of those languages are lost or dying. **With** loss of language comes loss of links to the past and feelings of belonging to a community, which research has linked to mental health. **One study** of Aboriginal communities found that youth suicide rates dropped to almost zero when the residents had conversational knowledge of native languages.	Language and identity are linked. There are examples given.

PASSAGE	ANALYSIS
One problem endangered languages face is lack of official recognition. Residents of a country are expected to know its official language or languages, **but** many countries do little to recognize minority regional languages. **Take Basque**, a language spoken in both Spain and France. In France, only French is recognized as an official language. In Spain, the constitution allows for regional recognition of official languages besides Spanish, so in Basque-speaking parts of the country, both Spanish and Basque are official languages. It is not surprising, **therefore**, that UNESCO cites Basque as "vulnerable" in Spain but "critically endangered" in France.	This paragraph identifies one problem: lack of official recognition for regional language; Basque is given as an example.
Consider, **in contrast**, the case of Finnish. This tongue is not endangered, **even though** Finland was ruled from the Middle Ages until 1917 by first Sweden and then Russia and, during this period, Swedish was used as the language of administration and government. In 1919, a newly independent Finland constitutionally adopted **both** Finnish and Swedish as official languages, legally recognizing its native language as **important** to its burgeoning national identity. As of 2013, Finnish was spoken by 89 percent of the population of Finland.	A contrast from the problem described in the previous paragraph. A language's connection to national identity can help it survive; Finnish is an example.
In order to preserve languages that will otherwise be lost, linguists have **proposed** creating a database of endangered languages. **But** how would an academic repository serve the often marginalized groups that speak such languages? **While** directed toward a noble goal, this project would **fail** to address the issue of language's **critical** role in preserving a sense of cultural identity.	One proposed solution: saving endangered languages in a database. But it wouldn't help those who will lose their native tongue/cultural identity.

Passage Map

¶1: Languages/culture endangered

¶2: Language = cultural identity

¶3: Official/not official; ex: Basque in Fr & Sp

¶4: Finnish; made official

¶5: Database won't preserve cultural identity

Topic: Language and cultural identity

Scope: Preservation of both

Purpose: Explain importance and problems & argue against one solution

1. (C)

This Detail question directs you to use evidence from the passage to identify why Basque is more endangered in France than in Spain. Using your passage notes, or re-reading as needed, will bring you to paragraph 3, which says that "lack of official recognition" impacts a language's survival. It goes on to note that "In France, only French is recognized." Therefore, predict that Basque's endangerment stems from a lack of recognition. (C) matches the prediction and is correct.

While France does not recognize Basque as an official language, nothing in the passage suggests that Basque has been actively suppressed there, eliminating (A). Nothing is said of how many speakers of Basque are in each country, so (B) can be eliminated. (D) and (E) may or may not be true, but neither is a reason why, according to the passage, Basque is more endangered in France than in Spain.

2. (A)

The phrase "support the assertion" indicates that this is a Strengthen question. Research the line referenced, reading the entire sentence for context. The author states that Finland acknowledged that Finnish was key to its national identity in 1919, when adopting its new constitution and making Finnish an official language. Predict an answer that shows that the use of Finnish was associated with a revitalization of national pride. (A) is correct because it describes a key change in feelings about Finnish in 1919, from negative to positive.

(B) and (D) are incorrect because they are examples of the continuation of the status quo after Finnish was adopted, so neither supports the assertion that the language was important to developing nationalism. Eliminate (C): this choice supports the idea that national symbols, not the Finnish language, may have expressed or promoted nationhood. If anything, (E) would be a weakener, as it implies cultural divisions within Finland instead of national unity.

3. (B)

This Application question asks you to evaluate an idea that is not in the passage in terms of how well it reflects an idea that is in the passage. UNESCO's assertion about the dangers of language loss appears in the first paragraph and can be paraphrased as *When a language is lost, the ideas it expresses are also lost.* Such a paraphrase would make a good prediction for this question. (B) matches the prediction, because the inability to translate the script results in an inability to access its "intellectual capital," that is, the ideas from the culture that used Linear A.

(A) may be tempting because it mentions the loss of Basque, a concern of the author. However, this choice speaks only about the value of the language itself, not about the value of the ideas it communicates. (C) is a counterexample to UNESCO's concern; though there is no way to read the thoughts of Socrates in his own words, his ideas are preserved in the writings of others, diminishing the importance of whether his original language has survived. (D) and (E) are incorrect because they are not relevant to the loss of a language or its ideas; both Korean and the English word "serendipity" are alive and well.

"Influenza Vaccination" Passage: Questions 4–6

Step 1: Read the Passage Strategically

On the left, we've shown how key words help you to identify the major elements of the passage and its structure and what you could skim over. On the right, we've shown what you might be thinking as you read the passage strategically.

PASSAGE	ANALYSIS
Unlike vaccinations for polio, measles, mumps, and many other virus-borne diseases, which yield lifetime protection with one vaccination or a short series of vaccinations, vaccinations combating the influenza virus **must** be administered annually, and **even then** they may not be fully successful in preventing illness.	Comparison between vaccinations for many virus-borne diseases and . . .
The reason for this **striking** difference is the ability of the influenza virus to **evolve quickly**. The antigens, the parts of the influenza virus recognized by the human body, include two important surface proteins, hemagglutinin and neuraminidase. Hemagglutinin is involved in the invasion of a cell within the human body, and neuraminidase assists in the release of new viruses from the cell after the viruses are replicated. As hemagglutinin is copied, it is not replicated exactly, so the human immune system does not recognize the mutation as the same protein it has encountered before and does not inaugurate the immune response. In this process, called antigenic drift, the known strains of influenza are recognized and effectively combated, but, unchallenged by the immune system, mutated viruses are able to reproduce freely and, thus, form a new strain of influenza.	. . . vaccinations for influenza. You have to get flu shot every year, and it may not work. The passage will discuss the reason for this, and here it is: flu evolves rapidly. And this is the mechanism for how it does it. Skim these details, and if you need these details for a question, come back and read this more carefully.

PASSAGE	ANALYSIS
Researchers in immune therapy are working on a variety of **innovations** to improve influenza vaccinations such as faster methods of production of vaccines and improvements to existing vaccines to strengthen the immune response of the human body. By far the **most intriguing** of these efforts are researchers' attempts to produce vaccines that would target the evolutionarily conserved areas of the influenza virus. The stem that attaches hemagglutinin to the virus, the neuraminidase protein, and M2—a protein found in the membrane of the influenza virus—all appear to be nearly identical across virus strains and seem to evolve slowly. **While** much work remains to be done, a vaccine targeting one of these **may be the key** to a one-time immunization protocol that would provide efficacious protection against most influenza strains.	The second paragraph is about new ways to improve flu shots: (1) make them faster, (2) make them stronger. But the author really likes option (3): new vaccines that would work differently. How new vaccines might work—again, speed up and re-read this section if you need it to answer a question. Nothing final yet, but may be possible.

Passage Map

¶1: Influenza vs. other virus-borne diseases. Flu vaccines annual, not 100% effective

    Reason: flu mutates quickly

¶2: New flu vaccine possibilities:

    (1) make faster

    (2) make stronger

    (3) new mechanism, au favorite, promising, but not yet

Topic: Influenza vaccination

Scope: Problem w/existing flu vaccinations

Purpose: To explain why flu vaccinations have to be given annually and discuss possible improvements

4. (D)

The phrase "primary purpose" indicates this Global question is asking you to identify why the author wrote the passage. As you concluded your strategic reading of the passage, you likely summarized the author's topic, scope, and purpose. A purpose along the lines of "to explain why flu vaccinations have to be given annually and discuss possible improvements" yields (**D**), the correct answer.

(**A**) is half-right, half-wrong. The passage does explain why the influenza virus mutates rapidly, but then goes on to identify new approaches that may make a single vaccination possible. (**B**) is too narrow; the author discusses errors in replication of hemagglutinin, but then uses this information to explain why new influenza vaccines must be developed. (**C**) is also too narrow; the author only mentions these diseases in the first sentence. (**E**) is a distortion of information in the passage. While the process of antigenic drift is discussed, the text only states that the mutated viruses produced are not recognized by the immune system; the effect of these viruses on the immune system is not described.

5.   (B)

The word "inferred" indicates that the answer to this Inference question will be fully supported by the text. The question asks about permanent protection with a single vaccine, so direct your research to the second paragraph. Within that paragraph, the emphasis phrase "By far the most intriguing" identifies the characteristics of possible new vaccines: they may target neuraminidase, M2, the stem of hemagglutinin, or other surface proteins that are "nearly identical . . . and evolve slowly." (B) paraphrases this description and is correct.

(A) is extreme. The last sentence of the passage states "much work remains to be done" and does not describe the vaccine as available "soon." (C) is a distortion of information presented in the text. Hemagglutinin does evolve quickly, but this is a reason the new vaccine will likely target other areas of the virus, not a reason why the new vaccine would be ineffective. (D) is the opposite of what's needed. The rapid evolution of hemagglutinin makes it less, not more, likely to be identified and targeted by the immune system. (E) is not mentioned in the passage. The two types of vaccines would both be administered once and provide similar protection, but no comparison is made between the mechanisms of how the different vaccines would work.

6.   (E)

The phrase "according to the passage" identifies this as a Detail question, and "EXCEPT" means the four incorrect choices will be stated in the passage while the correct answer will either contradict or not be mentioned in the passage. The details of the influenza virus are found in the first paragraph: it mutates rapidly, quickly rendering vaccines obsolete. The text never identifies influenza as the virus that evolves *most* rapidly but only as a virus that evolves faster than the viruses that cause measles, mumps, and polio; (E) is extreme and correct.

(A) is found in the fifth sentence of the first paragraph. (B) is stated in the fourth sentence of the first paragraph where hemagglutinin and neuraminidase are identified as two proteins that serve different functions in the replication of the virus. (C) is found in the last sentence of the first paragraph, and (D) is stated in the first sentence of the first paragraph. Since they are all supported by the passage, these choices are incorrect.

"Countdown at Kusini" Passage: Questions 7–12
Step 1: Read the Passage Strategically

On the left, the bolded key words indicate the major elements and the structure of the passage. On the right is a sample mental narrative of an expert GMAT test taker to show what you might be thinking as you read the passage strategically.

PASSAGE	ANALYSIS
Responding to the **negative, one-dimensional** representation of African Americans in the Hollywood films of the 1970s, the women of Delta Sigma Theta, an African American service sorority, embarked on an **ambitious** project to produce a feature film that would challenge these stereotypes. Filmmaker **S. Torriano Berry** recounts in his documentary on the sorority's efforts how, **unfortunately**, what could have been a historic project with the power to transform the U.S. entertainment industry failed **due to** the sorority's reliance on the major movie studios' traditional marketing and distribution system.	The topic is going to be a response to images the author considers "negative." "Ambitious" has a positive connotation. The author approves of the sorority's effort. Berry thinks project was important ("historic") and its failure unfortunate. Project failed because traditional marketing was used.
Lillian Benbow, the president of Delta Sigma Theta and the sorority's Arts and Letters committee, headed the effort to raise money for the production of the film *Countdown at Kusini* from donations. **While** most of the funds were contributed by the thousands of sorority members across the United States, African American entertainment luminaries **not only** supported the project financially **but also** donated their talent and expertise. **However**, after arriving on location in Nigeria, the producers found that a lack of qualified technicians, editors, film crews, equipment, and cinematic support services within the country meant that unexpected costs quickly added up, **drastically** exceeding the initial budget.	How they raised the money. *Countdown at Kusini* is the topic! "Most" money from many small donations, but some stars helped. But costs were much higher than expected.

PASSAGE	ANALYSIS
Even with the cost overruns, the movie could have paid for itself and perhaps even turned a modest profit **if** the sorority's initial marketing proposal had been followed. When preparing the budget, Delta Sigma Theta expected to use a four-wall marketing plan, in which the sorority's extensive membership would rent local theaters across the country, then sell tickets to other members, friends, and family. Additional screenings would be held as demand warranted. As one of the oldest and most extensive service sororities, Delta Sigma Theta had enough members in enough cities to at least recoup production costs. **However**, a major Hollywood film company became aware of the project and approached the sorority with an offer to distribute the film. **Buoyed** by the interest of the mainstream media, the sorority **believed** that the film company's expertise in marketing and distribution would lead to broader exposure and greater opportunities for success. **Unfortunately**, when the film was released through traditional channels, without any coordination with the local chapters of the sorority, it quickly failed.	The movie could have broken even, if the initial was followed. Expect to find details on this plan in the rest of the paragraph. Ah! Initial plan was "4-wall" marketing. Explanation of 4-wall marketing. Read this quickly; if there's a question about it, come back here to research the answer. But wooed by Hollywood. Sorority changed its mind. Film failed because no local support.

PASSAGE	ANALYSIS
Despite the film's commercial failure, the project is **remarkable** for its prescience, providing an early **example** of crowdfunding and media activism. Delta Sigma Theta took active steps to counter the limited range of stereotypes of African Americans in Hollywood films, and it funded these efforts through numerous small contributions. **Moreover**, the film's ultimate impact may **not be only** historical **but also** tangible in the modern Nigerian film industry, second in size only to that of India. When *Countdown at Kusini* was produced, there was no filmmaking infrastructure in Nigeria. **While** some of the production equipment was brought back to the United States, much was left behind, as well as the newly developed expertise of the local technicians, editors, actors, and production staff who were trained on the film. One of the **most intriguing questions** surrounding *Countdown at Kusini* may be that of its effect on the nascent Nigerian film industry.	Author's point of view on the film is positive. Reasons: forerunner of crowdfunding, media activism It benefitted the Nigerian film industry. *CAK* may have started Nigerian film industry.

Passage Map

¶1: Film CAK, ambitious, historic, but failed commercially

¶2: How funded

¶3: Marketing: sorority (4-wall) vs. H'wood, H'wood fails

¶4: Reasons film is still notable

Topic: CAK (Countdown at Kusini)

Scope: How/why made, impact

Purpose: Describe the production, marketing, and importance of CAK

7. (D)

The phrase "primary purpose" indicates this Global question is asking for the reason the author wrote the

passage. As you concluded your strategic reading of the passage, you noted the topic, scope, and purpose. Use the purpose—to describe the production, marketing, and importance of *Countdown at Kusini*—as your prediction. **(D)** restates this purpose, and is correct.

(A) is extreme. While the text mentions these depictions and describes the film as responding to them, criticizing Hollywood's portrayal of African Americans is not the purpose of the passage. Similarly, **(B)** exaggerates the importance of that detail in the passage. The author's purpose is broader than simply comparing the presentations of African Americans in the two types of film. **(C)** also distorts information in the text. Although the movie did transform the Nigerian movie industry, the film industry overall was not affected. In the first paragraph, the author laments the failure of the film to transform the U.S. entertainment industry. **(E)** is too narrow to encompass the entire passage. While the production difficulties are a detail discussed in the passage, this choice ignores the author's focus on the historic significance of the film.

8.   (C)

The phrase "serves primarily to" indicates this Logic question asks how or why the author used a specific piece of information—"a four-wall marketing plan"—to develop the main idea of the passage. The third paragraph describes four-wall marketing as the sorority's original plan. This paragraph goes on to discuss why the sorority adopted Hollywood's methods instead, methods that ultimately failed. Predict that the correct answer will say that the author included the details of the paragraph in order to show a marketing approach that might have worked but wasn't used. (C) matches the prediction and is correct.

(A) contradicts the text. The passage explains that the movie was a commercial failure. (B) also contradicts the passage. Four-wall marketing was the sorority's proposed marketing plan, not the traditional Hollywood approach. (D) is not mentioned in the passage. The sorority did not implement the four-wall strategy, so reasons why it failed are not addressed. (E) is another contradiction. Although the film did not recover its production costs, the four-wall marketing plan was presented as the way the movie might have been able to break even.

9.   (C)

The phrase "According to the passage" signals a Detail question whose correct answer will explicitly state the reason the sorority agreed to the film company's marketing plan. Your passage map or paragraph notes should focus your research on the third paragraph where the marketing plans are discussed. Skim the first part of the paragraph describing the sorority's plan and slow down when the contrast key word "However" introduces the Hollywood film company's plan. The next sentence provides the answer: "the sorority believed that the film company's expertise in marketing and distribution would lead to broader exposure and greater opportunities for success." (C) restates this information and is correct.

(A) is a faulty use of an accurate detail from the passage. The first sentence of the third paragraph indicates that the sorority believed it would recover even the increased costs with their original marketing plan, so these costs were not the reason why it switched to the Hollywood film company's plan. (B) contradicts the passage. The first sentence of the third paragraph indicates that the four-wall marketing plan would likely have been successful. (D) is not mentioned in the passage; the text never discusses the members' inability to acquire sufficient theaters. (E) is another contradiction. The fourth sentence of paragraph 3 states that the sorority "had enough members in enough cities to at least recoup production costs."

10.   (A)

This question asks for the purpose of the fourth paragraph, making it a Logic question. Review your paragraph notes and predict how the fourth paragraph contributes to the author's purpose: it provides the reasons the film is still notable, despite its commercial failure. (A) restates this prediction and is correct.

(B) is incorrect because the contrast key word "Despite" at the start of the paragraph indicates a change of direction from the discussion of the film's commercial failure. (C) is extreme. The passage simply indicates that the marketing plan failed and does not provide a "comprehensive analysis." (D) is incorrect because the "exceptional effort of the producers" is never discussed in the text. (E) contradicts the passage. The last sentence of the first paragraph says that Berry believed the film could have been a powerful, "historic project" and described the film's failure as unfortunate. The fourth paragraph supports Berry's opinion, not contradicts it.

11.   (D)

The word "suggests" makes this an Inference question. The response of the sorority members to the 1970s Hollywood films featuring African Americans will be found in the passage, but is likely not mentioned explicitly. In the first paragraph, the author describes the sorority's response as an "ambitious" and "historic" feature film that addressed "negative, one-dimensional . . . stereotypes." (D) paraphrases this prediction and is correct.

The remaining choices may be true but are not mentioned in the passage. Specifically, "employment opportunities," (**A**), and "broader media exposure," (**B**), are never discussed. (**C**) is a distortion. While the sorority had members across the country, the only "campaign" mentioned is the production and marketing plan for the film. (**E**)'s use of mainstream media to challenge stereotypes is also never mentioned.

12. (E)

The word "inferred" identifies this as an Inference question, and "one of the reasons *Countdown at Kusini* is considered a historic African American film" directs you to the fourth paragraph where the significance of the film is discussed. There, three impacts are found. Predict *crowdfunding*, *media activism*, and *effect on the nascent Nigerian film industry* alone or in any combination. (**E**) correctly describes the film's impact on the Nigerian film industry and is correct.

(**A**) is extreme. The film is identified as an early example of crowdfunding, but not necessarily as the first. (**B**) is not mentioned in the passage, as a connection between *Countdown at Kusini* and other privately produced films is not discussed. (**C**) contradicts the passage. The film was a commercial failure, not a success. (**D**) is incorrect because the educational aspect of the film is not mentioned in the text.

"One-Child Policy" Passage: Questions 13–18

Step 1: Read the Passage Strategically

On the left, we've shown how key words help you to identify the major elements of the passage and its structure and what you could skim over. On the right, we've shown what you might be thinking as you read the passage strategically.

PASSAGE	ANALYSIS
A **one-child policy** was implemented in **China** in 1979, and for nearly 40 years, until the policy was amended to allow two children in 2015, some Han Chinese families could legally have only one child. This rule was implemented in **an attempt** to slow continued growth of a population that had almost doubled since 1949. The Chinese government **claimed** that the policy prevented 400 million births, **though** some have suggested that the decline may be at least partly due to economic reasons, **not** legal ones.	The first sentence announces the topic: the one-child policy in China. "Claimed" is a flag that there may be a dispute, and "though" signals another point of view or evidence to the contrary. Government claims one thing; "some" claim another explanation.
One result of the policy **seems** to be the birth and survival of significantly more boys than girls. **One study found** that China had 33 million more boys than girls under the age of 20, and it is believed that by 2030, 25 percent of Chinese men in their late 30s will never have been married. **Research has shown** that an excess of men of marriageable age is linked to higher rates of psychological problems, as it creates a marginalized underclass, **and history would suggest** such situations may correlate with increased aggression and violence, both inside and outside a country's borders.	A result of the one-child policy: more boys born/ survive than girls. Research links this to psychological problems. History shows excess male population correlates with increased violence, but this seems more speculative.

PASSAGE	ANALYSIS

Economist Amartya Sen wrote in 1990 of the phenomenon of "**missing women**" in population data, noting that in China, "the survival prospects of female children clearly have been unfavorably affected by restrictions on the size of the family." In a society that has traditionally strongly favored sons, it has been **suggested** that sex-specific pregnancy terminations and infanticide account for the discrepancy in numbers. **But** others have **countered** this argument, believing that disease might better explain the phenomenon, either by making women more likely to give birth to male children or by making it more likely that female children will die prenatally or when very young. **For at least some** of the missing girls, however, a **less sinister** explanation may prove the correct one: parents who already had a child, or who wanted to be able to have another in an attempt to have a son, simply never registered their daughters with government officials. **A recent study** found evidence that as many as 25 million girls were not registered at birth, some of them officially "existing" only many years later and others perhaps never officially existing at all.

There are "missing women." Some believe this is due to deliberate actions.

"Others" believe there is a natural explanation.

Third possible explanation: not registering with government officials, per a recent study.

Author takes no stance on any of the theories.

Passage Map

¶1: China's one-child policy

¶2: Result of policy: more boys born/survive than girls; potential negative results

¶3: Three theories about why: deliberate (prefer son), natural (disease), lack of government registration

Topic: China's one-child policy

Scope: Result of the policy = missing girls?

Purpose: Examine one apparent result of the one-child policy and three potential explanations for it

13. (D)

The phrase "primary purpose" indicates that this is a Global question. You need to find the answer that describes the passage as a whole, so look to your passage map's "purpose." For example, you might have said there that the author is examining a result of the one-child policy and three theories explaining this outcome. The correct answer, (D), reflects this summary.

Because the author is not criticizing any of the explanations, (A) is incorrect. While the start of the second paragraph states that more males than females are born and survive, the author does not even consider the argument that the decline in population growth is due to a decrease in males; (B) is incorrect. (C) is incorrect because the author does not mention future birth rates. (E) is extreme: the author discusses the decrease in the number of women at length but does not suggest that this decrease is "entirely" responsible for the decline in population growth.

14. (B)

"According to the passage" indicates a Detail question; the correct answer will be a result of the gender imbalance mentioned in the passage. Your passage map should show that the second paragraph discusses some of the outcomes of the policy, so research the answer there. The author states that a higher ratio of males to females of marriageable age is "linked to higher rates of psychological problems" and "increased aggression and violence,

both inside and outside a country's borders." (B) matches the second claim; its qualified language ("may be") corresponds to that of the passage.

Because the author discusses a potential modern-day example, the claim in (A) that gender imbalance happened only in the past makes this choice incorrect. You can also eliminate (D) because the author mentions possible historical occurrences as well as the modern example. (C) confuses cause and effect: the passage indicates that psychological damage occurs as a result of the imbalance, not that the imbalance develops due to psychological damage. (E) is incorrect because the gender imbalance does not lead to the disappearance of women from official records; rather, the author suggests that this disappearance might contribute to the perception of a more extreme gender imbalance than actually exists.

15. (A)

"Serves primarily to" indicates that this is a Logic question, asking for the purpose of the final paragraph. A strong passage map would indicate that the last paragraph discusses theories about why there are fewer females than males in China. Predict that the final paragraph provides explanations without evaluating their merit. (A) correctly matches the prediction. The verb "present" matches the author's neutral tone. The "phenomenon described in the second paragraph" is that, in China, the number of boys born and surviving seems to exceed the number of girls.

Because the author does not evaluate the various explanations, there is no "critique," so (B) is incorrect. Although the author describes the last explanation as "less sinister," the text does not imply that it is the correct one, so (C) is incorrect. You can eliminate (D) because the final paragraph only presents several explanations offered by other people; it does not "explain fully" the missing girls' absence. Even though (E) paraphrases one of the explanations offered in the final paragraph, the author gives equal consideration to a couple of others as well, so (E) is incorrect.

16. (B)

"According to the passage" indicates that this is a Detail question. The "EXCEPT" means that each incorrect answer will be found in the passage, while the correct answer will not. In this case, you cannot easily predict the correct answer; however, you can predict the incorrect ones because they will be stated in the text. The author lists the possible reasons in the third paragraph: societal preference for boys, disease, or parents' failure to register girls' births. Eliminate choices that reflect these possibilities, and you are left with (**B**).

Choices (**A**) and (**C**) match the disease explanation, (**D**) fits the reasoning that concerns societal preferences, and (**E**) restates the suggestion about a failure to register the births of females.

17. (E)

This Application question asks you to find the answer to a hypothetical situation based on the text's information. The author introduces the Han in the first paragraph, mentioning that before 2015, some were allowed to have only one child. The remainder of the passage discusses various consequences of the law, and actions that parents might take are mentioned in the third paragraph. The correct answer, (**E**), is supported in the final paragraph, where the author suggests that some parents failed to register girls in order to have another child.

The text does not say that parents of girls change their feelings about their children over time, so (**A**) is unsupported. While the passage cites disease as a possible reason for a smaller number of female children, (**B**) is incorrect because the author does not suggest that the

possibility of a girl's death leads parents to have a second child. Because the author does not mention the possibility of an appeal, you can eliminate (**C**). The text never states that boys are more likely to result from pregnancy than girls, so (**D**) can also be eliminated.

18. (A)

The phrase "in order to" indicates that this is a Logic question. Specifically, the question asks why the author mentions a "marginalized underclass." To make a prediction, first research the relevant text. The preceding line states, "Research has shown that an excess of men of marriageable age is linked to higher rates of psychological problems, as it creates a marginalized underclass . . ." Predict that the author uses the phrase as part of the evidence for the one-child policy's potential negative impact, which matches (**A**).

Although the passage mentions that more boys are born and survive than girls, the author actually says that the existence of a "marginalized underclass" is a result of the demographic imbalance between males and females; (**B**) is incorrect. The passage states that violence may arise if there are significantly more marriageable men than women, not that men are innately more violent, so (**C**) is a distortion. (**D**) is incorrect because the author is not making an argument, nor does the text indicate that attitudes toward boys and girls are caused by poverty. (**E**) is incorrect because the author never discusses "average family income" or other economic statistics.

"Flycatchers" Passage: Questions 19–24

Step 1: Read the Passage Strategically

On the left, we've shown how key words help you to identify the major elements of the passage and its structure and what you could skim over. On the right, we've shown what you might be thinking as you read the passage strategically.

PASSAGE	ANALYSIS
Generally, interspecific matings represent an evolutionary **dead end**, producing sterile offspring, if any at all. For some species of birds, **however**, such pairings may indeed bring evolutionary advantages to the participants. **In the case of** the female collared flycatchers of Gotland, **three distinct factors** may work to make interspecific pairings with pied flycatcher males reproductively **beneficial**.	"Generally" implies that there will be an exception. Usually, interspecific mating doesn't work. The female collared flycatcher is the exception. You're going to see three reasons why.
In many instances, female collared flycatchers nest with male pied flycatchers while continuing to mate with other collared flycatchers, in effect parasitizing the pied flycatchers, who invest in rearing and fledging any offspring. **Often**, more than half of the offspring raised by interspecific flycatcher pairs are, **in fact**, not hybrids. **Furthermore**, an estimated 65 percent of the hybrid offspring of the resident pied flycatcher male are male. **Because** hybrid females are sterile and males are not, this male bias minimizes the primary disadvantage of interspecific matings: sterile offspring. Habitat specialization may be **a third mechanism**: these pairings tend to occur in the late spring when the coniferous woods favored by the pied flycatcher provide a greater availability of food than the deciduous woods where the collared flycatchers tend to live. **Together**, these factors form a mechanism to **improve substantially** the reproductive success of female collared flycatchers beyond what would be expected of interspecific mating with pied flycatcher males.	Why interspecific mating works for female collared flycatchers: 1. They get pied flycatchers to raise their collared flycatcher offspring. 2. The offspring aren't all sterile. 3. Pied flycatchers live where the food is. These factors seem to work together.

PASSAGE	ANALYSIS
Although all three of these mechanisms appear to act in concert to form a single elaborate mechanism specifically evolved to circumvent the usual disadvantages of interspecific mating, **studies have shown similar motivations** for the behavior of female collared flycatchers mating within the species. **According to** Professor Sievert Rohwer, collared flycatcher females will choose to nest with subordinate collared flycatcher males that inhabit good territory **because** collared flycatcher females must pair-bond in order to be successful in raising offspring. To engender the best offspring, **however**, the females will continue to copulate with higher-quality collared males with whom they are not paired. **Thus**, females **seem to** be nesting with males of any species with the best territories available at the time, **but they will** continue to mate with more attractive males outside of their pair bonds.	"Although . . . similar motivations": female collared flycatchers act the same way when mating with male collared flycatchers. Pair with males that have good nests; mate with others, too.
A **highly unusual** behavior, interspecific mating **seems to provide** certain reproductive **advantages** to the collared flycatcher female. **However**, it **remains unclear** whether the mating behavior of female collared flycatchers evolved to circumvent the usual problems with interspecific mating or whether the behavior is simply an extension of how female collared flycatchers behave when mating within their own species.	The author is wrapping up. "However" shows the central unanswered question: did female collared flycatchers evolve this way because of interspecific mating or just because they act this way generally?

Passage Map

¶1: Interspecific mating—usually evolutionary dead end/sterile offspring; FCF is exception

¶2: 3 advantages of interspecific mating for FCF

¶3: FCF nests/mates same way intraspecifically, too. Same advantages

¶4: Question—did FCF evolve this way for interspecific mating or just in general?

Topic: Interspecific mating—female collared flycatcher exception

Scope: FCF's interspecific and intraspecific mating behaviors and their evolutionary advantages

Purpose: Describe FCF's mating/nesting behavior and pose an unanswered question about its origins

19. (D)

"Primary purpose" signals that this is a Global question. Consult your passage map. One possible statement of the author's purpose would be to describe the mating behavior of the female collared flycatcher and pose explanations for it. The final paragraph summarizes two possible explanations for the behavior: it evolved to resolve some of the problems of interspecific mating, or it's simply an extension of intraspecific mating behavior. (D) summarizes the author's purpose and is correct.

(A) is incorrect because the author never takes a stand on either explanation and so does not "criticize" anything. Similarly, (B) and (E) are incorrect because the author does not "defend" anything. The author never calls for further research, so (C) is incorrect.

20. (C)

"According to the passage" is an indication that this is a Detail question. However, EXCEPT means that the four incorrect choices will give possible explanations for the female's behavior. The correct answer may contradict the text or not be mentioned in the passage. Here, predict what the wrong answers will state; the four incorrect choices will all be cited in the text and will give possible

explanations for the female collared flycatcher's unusual mating behavior. The passage says that pied males that mate with collared females father more males than females. Thus, (C) directly contradicts paragraph 2, making (C) the correct answer.

The female collared flycatcher's nesting and mating behaviors are explained in the second paragraph. The coniferous forests where the pied flycatchers live are indeed richer in food late in the season, as (A) suggests. Females may use the pied males for their help in rearing young—including those sired by other males—as (B) says. While the question asks specifically about explanations for the interspecific mating behaviors, the third paragraph notes that the motivations for intraspecific mating behaviors are similar. (D) and (E) are both supported by this paragraph.

21. (C)

The language "is presented as evidence that" indicates that this is a Logic question that asks why the author included a detail. This stem tells you that the detail at issue—the predominance of male offspring from male pied and female collared flycatcher mates—is presented as evidence. The reference to the offspring of male pied and female collared flycatcher mates leads you to paragraph 2. You're told that the male offspring are not sterile, thus minimizing a typical downside to interspecies mating. Therefore, you can predict that the correct answer will tell you that the male offspring bias is evidence that a typical disadvantage—sterile offspring—of interspecies mating is not present when female collared flycatchers and male pied flycatchers mate. (C) matches the prediction and is correct.

(A) is not mentioned in the passage; the dominance of offspring is not discussed. (B) is a distortion; it is the interspecific hybrids, not pure collared flycatchers, that show a male bias in their offspring. (D) is incorrect because no argument is ever made about future generations of interspecific breeding. And (E) is incorrect because the passage does not comment on the regularity of interspecific breeding by any bird other than the female collared flycatcher.

22. (A)

The word "inferred" means that this Inference question is asking for something that, based on information in the passage, must be true about the conditions that help flycatchers succeed as a species. However, the answer is probably not stated explicitly in the passage. The second paragraph points out that the greater abundance of food in pied flycatcher habitats late in the mating season is a mechanism that makes interspecies pairings reproductively beneficial. If nourishment was not relevant to the success of raising offspring, it would not be a mechanism that aids the success of flycatchers. (A) is true based on the passage.

All four incorrect answers are either unsupported by the passage or contradict the passage. (B) is not mentioned—the percentage of male offspring is discussed only in relation to interspecific pairs. Mating for life is never mentioned either, so (C) is incorrect. The fact that females *do* choose males on the basis of reproductive benefits makes (D) incorrect; it contradicts what the passage implies. Lastly, you have no basis for knowing the proportion of females that engage in extra-pair matings, so (E) is unsupported.

23. (C)

This is an Inference question, as signaled by the phrase "most likely agree with." The key is to spot that it is Professor Rohwer's opinion from which you are drawing your inference. His opinion is discussed in the third paragraph, where the passage demonstrates the similarities between the female collared flycatcher's interspecies and intraspecies mating behavior. Professor Rohwer's point is that pair-bonding is essential to the female collared flycatcher's success in rearing young. The functional behavior is the female's continued mating with more attractive males outside of her pair-bond. As the fourth paragraph describes, this behavior may have evolved to include interspecific matings after it began as an intraspecific behavior to strengthen the species. The implication is that the female collared flycatcher will nest with one male and mate with others regardless of whether she is engaged in intra- or interspecies mating, which supports (C) as the correct answer.

(A) and (D) include the phrases "all traits" and "played no role," respectively, which makes them too extreme based on the information in the text. Because Rohwer's view involves female collared flycatcher pair-bonding with one male while continuing to mate with others, (B) and (E) are unsupported, as Rohwer's views, if any, on the content of these two choices are not described.

24. (B)

"Is offered as" means this Logic question is asking you why the author mentions a specific fact. The female collared flycatchers that pair with subordinate males are mentioned in the third paragraph. The third paragraph is about the female collared flycatcher's intraspecies nesting and mating behaviors. The fact highlighted by the author is that the female collared flycatcher behaves similarly when mating with male collared flycatchers as when mating with pied males. The author's point is that the female collared flycatcher's behavior may not have evolved exclusively in support of interspecies mating. You can anticipate that the correct answer will address that point. This prediction leads to (B).

Stated evidence can never be an assumption, which by definition is unstated, so (A) is incorrect. The evidence in question does not support the adaptive explanation for interspecies breeding—in fact, it does just the opposite—so (C) is incorrect. This evidence is also not an explanation for why hybridization is a dead end. Indeed, it is not a dead end for collared flycatchers. Thus, (D) is incorrect. Lastly, that the collared and pied flycatchers are separate species is a given in the passage, and nowhere does the author feel it necessary to establish this fact. (E) is incorrect.

"Rainbows" Passage: Questions 25–30

Step 1: Read the Passage Strategically

On the left, we've shown how key words help you to identify the major elements of the passage and its structure and what you could skim over. On the right, we've shown what you might be thinking as you read the passage strategically.

PASSAGE	ANALYSIS
Rainbows have long been a part of religion and mythology in cultures around the globe, appearing as bridges between the heavens and the earth, as messages from the gods, or as weapons wielded by divine powers. Some cultures have viewed rainbows themselves as deities, or even as demonic beings from which to hide children. **But** in the early fourteenth century, Theodoric of Freiburg, a German friar, and Kamal al-Din al-Farisi, a Persian scientist, independently turned a **scientific** eye to the study of rainbows.	The topic of the passage is rainbows. Presence in religion/mythology. "But" signals shift of focus: scientific study.
Theodoric and al-Farisi were thousands of miles apart, **but both** had studied Ibn al-Haytham's *Book of Optics*. **Each** concluded that a rainbow's appearance is the result of sunlight refracting and reflecting through water droplets left after a rainfall. They conducted experiments to provide **support for their conclusions**, successfully re-creating the conditions necessary to make a rainbow appear; al-Farisi used a sphere and a camera obscura, while Theodoric used flasks and globes.	14th-c studies: very far apart, but both men reached same conclusion about rainbows; both were able to re-create a rainbow in experiments.

PASSAGE	ANALYSIS
Both scholars were, as **modern physics** has shown, **correct** in their assessments. When light hits a water droplet, the water causes the light's speed to decrease. Furthermore, the light **refracts**—or changes direction—upon entering the droplet, and some of the light reflects off the back of the droplet, **refracting again** as it exits. The angle of refraction depends on the wavelength of the light; thus, refraction "breaks" white light into multiple wavelengths—a phenomenon called **dispersion**—which appear as different colors.	Jumps to modern knowledge. Refraction = light waves change direction. Dispersion = light breaks into separate wavelengths (colors).
But for a rainbow to fill the sky with color, **more** is needed. A **single droplet** of water will disperse the entire visible light spectrum, with each wavelength leaving at a different angle, **but** it alone cannot create a rainbow. **Only** a little of the light from a particular droplet reaches the eye of the human observer, striking the eye **from a particular angle**. For the observer to perceive the rainbow's characteristic banded arc of different colors, a **multitude of droplets** suspended in the air, refracting and dispersing light, are **needed**, with the shorter wavelengths and shallower angles of indigo and violet appearing to the observer at the bottom and the longer wavelengths and steeper angles of red and orange appearing at the top.	Just refraction and dispersion aren't enough; angle also important. Rainbow = many drops refracting/reflecting light.

Passage Map

¶1: Rainbows in religion/myth & 14th-c. science

¶2: Medieval studies of rainbows by Theodoric/al-Farisi—different methods, same conclusion

¶3: Physics of rainbows confirms T & al-F's thinking; refraction/dispersion

¶4: More physics of rainbows (angle of observation); many droplets needed for rainbow

Topic: Rainbows

Scope: Explanations of rainbows in myth & science

Purpose: To describe supernatural and scientific explanations of rainbows

25. (D)

The phrase "primarily in order to" means this Logic question asks why the author included information about the angle of light leaving water droplets. The cited lines are in the last paragraph. First consult your passage map to review the main point of the paragraph: to explain why lots of droplets are needed for someone to see a rainbow. Then review the text, including a little above and below the cited lines. The author says that light emerges from a droplet at various angles, but light from that droplet only strikes the human eye at one angle, and this is why light from many droplets is needed for a rainbow to appear. Predict that the correct answer will associate the information about angles with the way a rainbow is perceived by the human observer. **(D)** matches the prediction and is correct.

(A) relates to the discussion of refraction in the third paragraph, and dispersion of light is associated with the angles at which light leaves the water droplet. However, the author does not mention the angle of light in the fourth paragraph to describe refraction. **(B)** is found later in the fourth paragraph. The author says that different angles of light are associated with different colors of the rainbow, but showing this to be true is not why the author discusses the angle of light in the cited lines. **(C)** misstates information in the passage; light's wavelength affects its angle of refraction, not the other

way around. As for **(E)**, based on the passage, refraction is well understood, but even if it weren't, nothing in the passage implies that the angle of light is the key to understanding refraction.

26. (E)

This Inference question asks what you can reasonably conclude, based on the passage, about the three middle colors of the rainbow. The middle colors of yellow, green, and blue are not directly mentioned in the passage, but what colors *are* mentioned? The final sentence says that red and orange have the longest wavelengths and refract at the sharpest angles, and they appear at the top of the rainbow; by contrast, indigo and violet have the shortest wavelengths and refract at the shallowest angles, and they appear at the bottom of the rainbow. Based on this research, you can infer that the colors in the middle of the rainbow are also in the middle when it comes to wavelengths and angles of refraction. The correct answer should include one or both of these ideas. **(E)** matches the prediction and is correct.

(A) is not supported by the passage, which never indicates that some colors' wavelengths do not disperse. **(B)** contradicts the passage: the longer wavelengths are associated with higher positions on the rainbow, so the middle colors cannot have longer wavelengths than do red or orange. **(C)** also contradicts what the passage implies, which is that light of different colors refracts at different angles. **(D)** is another contradiction. The passage indicates that shallower angles are associated with lower positions on the rainbow, so the middle colors cannot have shallower angles than do indigo and violet.

27. (C)

The phrase "According to the passage" indicates this is a Detail question. Here you are asked for something the passage says about refraction. Refraction is defined in the third paragraph as the changing of direction of a light wave upon entering or leaving a droplet of water. How much the light changes direction depends on its wavelength. White light consists of different wavelengths, so it is broken up, or dispersed, by refraction, and light at different wavelengths is seen as different colors. Predict that the correct answer will include one or more of these facts. **(C)** paraphrases the last sentence of the third paragraph and is correct.

(A) is half right, but it says that refraction changes the light's wavelength. In fact, the light's wavelength affects the angle of refraction, so **(A)** can be eliminated. Some light is reflected in the droplet, and while this allows the light to be refracted a second time, the reflection is not caused by refraction, nor is anything said about "intensifying" the light. Eliminate **(B)**. As for **(D)**, the light wave does slow down when it hits a water droplet, and this is also when refraction occurs, but it's not said whether one causes the other. And finally, while refraction separates light according to its wavelengths, nothing is said about wavelengths being altered. Eliminate **(E)**.

28. (B)

This is a Global question, asking for the primary purpose of the passage as a whole. As you completed your strategic reading you summarized the topic, scope, and purpose. Match the purpose—to describe various explanations for rainbows—to the choices. **(B)** matches the prediction and is correct.

Whether or not rainbows are rare, let alone why they might be, is not mentioned in the passage, so **(A)** is incorrect. **(C)** contradicts the text, as the author confirms that the two historical explanations discussed are borne out by modern physics. **(D)** can be eliminated because this is merely a detail from the passage; the author is interested in explaining rainbows, not the refraction of light. Finally, **(E)** only addresses the last two paragraphs and is not the purpose of the passage as a whole.

29. (A)

This is an Inference question, asking for the statement with which the author would "most likely agree" about the study of rainbows. Since most of the passage is about the study of rainbows, review the passage map to have the structure of the passage fresh in your mind as you review the answer choices. Plan to research each choice as needed to accept or eliminate it. **(A)** is supported by the passage and is correct. Fourteenth-century science is first mentioned in the first paragraph and elaborated on in the second. Then, at the beginning of the third

paragraph, the author says that modern physics has shown the findings of Theodoric and al-Farisi to be accurate. Thus, the author would agree that some experiments performed hundreds of years ago produced accurate results.

(B) can be researched in the first paragraph, where such cultures are discussed. While the author discusses these cultures' nonscientific beliefs about rainbows, the author never discusses their stance toward scientific studies. **(C)** is not supported. The passage only discusses these researchers' work with water droplets, so whether they studied larger volumes of water is unknown. **(D)** is similar to **(B)** in that the author never implies that a scientific understanding of rainbows voids a belief in their spiritual significance. **(E)** contradicts the text. The author specifically mentions the accuracy of Theodoric and al-Farisi's work, thereby implying its value.

30. (E)

Since it asks for the "primary function of the second paragraph," this Logic question asks why the author included the paragraph. Review the passage map: the second paragraph is concerned with "medieval studies of rainbows by Theodoric/al-Farisi—different methods, same conclusion." Predict that the author uses the second paragraph to introduce the scientific study of rainbows. **(E)** matches the prediction and is correct.

(A) is extreme. The author indicates that Theodoric's and al-Farisi's approaches differed from a religious or mythological view, but the passage never goes so far as to imply they challenged the use of rainbows as a symbol in their religions. For **(B)**, the author does evaluate the two scholars' methods in a general way but at the beginning of the third paragraph, which states that the researchers' findings agree with those of modern physics. This is not the function of the second paragraph, so eliminate this choice. Nothing is said about any difficulties Theodoric or al-Farisi may have faced, so **(C)** can be eliminated. **(D)** is extreme. While the author indicates that in this case, findings from the fourteenth century agree with those of modern physicists, the passage in no way implies that medieval science as a whole is similar in value to modern science.

CHAPTER 19

VERBAL REASONING STRATEGY: SENTENCE CORRECTION QUESTIONS

LEARNING OBJECTIVES

- Describe the format and content of Sentence Correction questions
- Apply the steps of the Kaplan Method for Sentence Correction
- Recognize how the four Core Competencies apply to Sentence Correction questions

---

The GMAT Verbal Reasoning section includes about 13 Sentence Correction questions among the 36 total questions. You need enough time to answer the other questions on the Verbal section, which involve more reading than does Sentence Correction. Therefore, we recommend that you spend about 1 minute on each Sentence Correction question. Kaplan's Method for Sentence Correction helps you to work efficiently, moving quickly but without feeling rushed.

The directions for Sentence Correction questions look like this:

> **Directions:** Each Sentence Correction question presents a sentence, part or all of which is underlined. Below each sentence, you will find five ways to phrase the underlined portion. The first answer choice repeats the original version, while the other four choices are different. If the original seems best, choose the first answer choice. If not, choose one of the revisions.
>
> In choosing an answer, follow the norms of standard written English: grammar, word choice, and sentence construction. Choose the answer that produces the most effective sentence, aiming to eliminate awkwardness, ambiguity, redundancy, and grammatical error.

As noted in the directions, the first choice, which we label (**A**) for ease of reference, always repeats the underlined portion of the sentence as written. Thus, after you've read the sentence, you don't need to spend time reading (**A**).

As always on the GMAT, there is only one correct answer; each of the four incorrect choices contains some error of grammar, usage, or style. Spotting these errors and eliminating the four incorrect choices—reading only as much as necessary to spot an error—is often a more efficient way to land on the right answer than reading through all five choices trying to figure out which one "sounds" best. This is especially true for more difficult questions, in which the correct answer may be worded a bit oddly but be free of actual errors.

Sentence Correction tests your command of standard written English—the rather formal language that is used in textbooks and scholarly periodicals. It's the language that's used to convey complex information precisely, as opposed to the casual language that we use for everyday communication. The good news is that you do *not* need to know every grammar rule for these questions. Errors involving certain rules show up repeatedly on the GMAT. The next chapter teaches you what you need to know about these rules. Focus on learning these commonly tested rules and practice spotting errors in their application, and you'll be well prepared for Sentence Correction questions.

The Kaplan Method for Sentence Correction

Kaplan has studied the approach taken by test takers who ace Sentence Correction questions. Based on their approach, we've developed a simple, step-by-step Method that anyone can use to be successful. Through regular practice, you will be an expert by Test Day.

> **THE KAPLAN METHOD FOR SENTENCE CORRECTION**
>
> **STEP 1** Read the original sentence carefully, looking for errors.
>
> **STEP 2** Scan and group the answer choices.
>
> **STEP 3** Eliminate choices until only one remains.

Step 1: Read the Original Sentence Carefully, Looking for Errors

As you read the sentence, stay alert for the GMAT-tested grammar and usage errors. If you spot an error, eliminate (**A**) immediately but keep reading, because there may be more than one error that the correct choice needs to fix.

If you don't spot an error the first time through, or if you're not sure whether something is wrong, a quick vertical scan of the beginnings and ends of the answer choices will give you a strong clue about what sorts of grammatical issues the question is testing. This information will help you focus on these issues and possibly spot an error, or realize there is no error, in the sentence. If the choices don't vary with regard to a certain part of the sentence, then that part can't possibly be an error.

But don't spend too long here. After your initial analysis of the sentence, re-reading it over and over is not likely to yield further insights—especially because there may not be an error at all! Instead, move to step 2.

Step 2: Scan and Group the Answer Choices

Instead of wasting time reading each answer choice individually, quickly scan and compare the answers with one other. If you spotted an error in step 1, sort the answer choices into two groups: those that do not fix the error (which you can eliminate) and those that appear to fix it.

If you *didn't* spot an error, try to zero in on a grammatical or stylistic difference that splits the answer choices into distinct groups. This will let you identify one of the issues that the question is testing. Once you know what is being tested, you can apply your knowledge of English grammar to determine which group is correct—thereby eliminating multiple answers at once.

Step 3: Eliminate Choices Until Only One Remains

If more than one choice remains, go back to step 2 and scan again to find another difference. Then eliminate accordingly. Repeat this process until only one choice remains. Finally, before heading to the next question, read your choice back into the sentence and make sure the entire sentence makes sense. By doing this, you'll make sure that all elements in the underlined portion match up with the non-underlined text.

Important pacing tip: If more than one choice remains after you have eliminated all of the answers that you are sure are wrong, just go with your best guess. If you don't know the rule by Test Day, you probably won't successfully teach it to yourself while taking the exam. You'll get a much higher score by investing that time in other questions.

Apply the Method

Below is a typical Sentence Correction question for you to try. As you answer the question, note the features of its format and the rules it's testing. Also consider what you do and don't already know about how to solve. The explanation that follows the question demonstrates how a GMAT expert uses Kaplan's three-step Method for Sentence Correction and certain grammar knowledge to solve this question efficiently.

> Several years ago, a leading packaged food manufacturer, seeking to appeal to consumers who increasingly favor fresh foods, <u>has acquired a company that specializes in freezing produce immediately after harvest as a subsidiary</u>.

- ○ has acquired a company that specializes in freezing produce immediately after harvest as a subsidiary
- ○ has acquired as a subsidiary a company that specializes in freezing produce immediately after harvest
- ○ acquired like a subsidiary a company that specializes in freezing produce immediately after harvest
- ○ acquired as a subsidiary a company that specializes in freezing produce immediately after harvest
- ○ acquired as a subsidiary a company specializing immediately after harvest in the freezing of produce

Step 1: Read the Original Sentence Carefully, Looking for Errors

The underlined portion begins with the verb "has acquired." This is the present perfect verb tense, which is used to describe an action that began in the past and is still occurring. In this case, the acquisition of the subsidiary happened entirely in the past—"Several years ago"—so this verb tense is incorrect. Eliminate choice **(A)**, which repeats the underlined portion as written.

Step 2: Scan and Group the Answer Choices

A quick vertical scan of the beginnings of the choices shows a 3-2 split between "has acquired" and "acquired." If you hadn't spotted the verb error when reading the original sentence in step 1, the fact that the choices differ by verb tense would be a signal to double-check whether the tense used in the sentence is correct, essentially returning to step 1.

Step 3: Eliminate Choices Until Only One Remains

In addition to (A), eliminate (B) for using the wrong verb tense. Note that you don't need to read past the first couple of words of (B) to eliminate it.

Now compare the remaining choices. (C) begins with "acquired like a subsidiary," while (D) and (E) begin with "acquired as a subsidiary." With "like," (C) seems to be saying that the acquired company is similar to a subsidiary but not actually a subsidiary, which does not make sense. This word choice introduces a comparison that the author is not trying to make. Eliminate (C).

Read (D) and (E) in parallel to spot how they are different. (E) moves "immediately after harvest" after "specializing," but "immediately after harvest" logically describes when the company freezes produce. Also, "in the freezing of produce" is an unnecessarily wordy way of saying "in freezing produce." Eliminate (E).

That leaves only (D). Read this answer back into the sentence to confirm there are no errors: "Several years ago, a leading packaged food manufacturer, seeking to appeal to consumers who increasingly favor fresh foods, <u>acquired as a subsidiary a company that specializes in freezing produce immediately after harvest.</u>"

CONCEPT CHECK

- You should spend about _____ minute(s) on each Sentence Correction question.

- What does choice (A) always represent, and about how often is (A) correct?

  _____

- How does step 2 of the Kaplan Method—scan and group the answer choices—help you answer Sentence Correction questions efficiently?

  _____

- Why is it important to read your answer back into the sentence before moving to the next question?

  _____

Example answers are in your book's online resources (**kaptest.com/login**).

Next, you'll find in-format questions so you can practice applying the Kaplan Method for Sentence Correction.

Practice Set: The Kaplan Method for Sentence Correction

(Answers and explanations are at the end of the chapter.)

1. Although an open letter from several self-described experts in attendance at the International Symposium on Unexplained Phenomena in Deep Space Studies were written stating that the newly discovered interstellar object is an alien space probe, most astronomers who have studied the object closely agree that it is a comet.

    ○ Although an open letter from several self-described experts in attendance at the International Symposium on Unexplained Phenomena in Deep Space Studies were written

    ○ An open letter from several self-described experts in attendance at the International Symposium on Unexplained Phenomena in Deep Space Studies were written

    ○ An open letter from several self-described experts in attendance at the International Symposium on Unexplained Phenomena in Deep Space Studies was written

    ○ Although several self-described experts in attendance at the International Symposium on Unexplained Phenomena in Deep Space has written an open letter

    ○ Although several self-described experts in attendance at the International Symposium on Unexplained Phenomena in Deep Space have written an open letter

2. The green flash, an atmospheric refractive phenomenon whereby the top edge of a setting sun will momentarily turn green, rarely is seen by the naked eye, primarily on account of requiring that specific favorable conditions to occur.

    ○ on account of requiring that

    ○ on account of their requiring

    ○ because they require

    ○ because it requires

    ○ because of requiring that

3. The new hummingbird species, which was discovered only recently, had been categorized as critically endangered due to its habitat's being limited and the low estimated size of its population.

    ○ had been categorized as critically endangered due to its habitat's being limited

    ○ had been categorized as critically endangered because it has a limited habitat

    ○ has been categorized as critically endangered because it has limited its habitat

    ○ has been categorized as critically endangered because of its limited habitat

    ○ will be categorized as critically endangered due to its limiting its habitat

4. Fitness experts say that the weighted barbell squat or the weighted hip thrust, each part of a family of training maneuvers called compound movements, <u>is one of the best exercises for isolating and building the gluteal muscles</u>.

- ○ is one of the best exercises for isolating and building the gluteal muscles
- ○ are among the best exercises to isolate and for building the gluteal muscles
- ○ is one of the best exercises for isolating and to build the gluteal muscles
- ○ are among the best exercises for isolating and building the gluteal muscles
- ○ is one of the best exercises to isolate and for building the gluteal muscles

5. Although <u>they contain many repeated themes and depict multiple characters with strikingly similar traits</u>, the anthology consists of stories written by a diverse group of authors representing several different genres.

- ○ they contain many repeated themes and depict multiple characters with strikingly similar traits
- ○ they contain many themes repeatedly and depict multiple characters with similar traits strikingly
- ○ it contains many repeated themes and depicts multiple characters with strikingly similar traits
- ○ it contains many repeated themes and characters that depict multiple strikingly similar traits
- ○ it contains many themes repeatedly that depict multiple characters with strikingly similar traits

The Four Core Competencies and Sentence Correction

Sentence Correction questions may look different from all the other questions on the GMAT—after all, no other question type tests your ability to apply the rules of English grammar and usage. However, these questions test the same four Core Competencies that show up throughout the test. Sentence Correction just puts its own twist on them.

Critical Thinking

Trying to evaluate every sentence and answer choice for every possible error the GMAT tests would be too time-consuming. Instead of reading uncritically, hoping that errors jump out at you, you'll use your critical thinking skills and knowledge of commonly tested rules to zero in on the places where errors are most likely. This application of critical thinking will make it easier to pay attention to the right details.

Paraphrasing

One way in which the GMAT tries to make some Sentence Correction questions difficult is by making the sentences long or complex. Mentally erasing lengthy descriptive phrases and clauses can help you see the "bones" of the sentence and check for fundamental errors, such as subject-verb agreement. Paraphrasing a sentence describing multiple actions can help you identify their relative time frames and check for verb tense errors.

Pattern Recognition

The Sentence Correction format itself follows a pattern: the first choice, (A), is always an exact duplicate of the underlined portion of the original sentence. (A) is correct about 20 percent of the time—it's correct just as often as any other choice. Therefore, if you feel confident that there are no errors in the sentence, you should confidently choose (A).

The rest of the choices, too, are often patterned, with the same error showing up in more than one. The Kaplan Method for Sentence Correction takes advantage of this feature by having you scan and group choices that are the same in some way. Then, if more than one choice has the same error, you can eliminate all those choices without reading them further.

Certain patterns in the sentences provide valuable clues to where errors might be. For example, the test makers don't insert the underlining at random; the first and last part of the underlined portion of the sentence are usually worth particular scrutiny, as they are often likely places for a GMAT-tested error. Furthermore, when the underlined portion is lengthy, scanning the beginnings and ends of answer choices for such errors is usually easier than trying to scan through the middles of the choices.

In addition, certain patterns of sentence construction and answer choices are suggestive of certain types of errors. You'll learn more about these patterns in the next chapter, which discusses each error type in detail, but here are a few examples to prime your thinking.

- If all or part of a list is underlined, parallelism in the list items is definitely worth checking.
- If there's an extended amount of descriptive information in the middle of the sentence, check whether that information is separating two related grammatical elements, such as a subject and verb that must agree.
- If the sentence begins with a modifying phrase followed by a comma, check that the next element is the thing that the phrase describes; there may be a modification error.

- When each choice is a significantly rearranged restatement of the underlined portion, the GMAT may well be testing your ability to spot the correct placement of modifying phrases.
- If a single word or phrase is underlined, it's likely that idiomatic usage is being tested.

Practice will help you become familiar with these patterns and many more, and you'll be able to attack Sentence Correction with confidence.

Attention to the Right Detail

After (**A**), the other choices rewrite the underlined portion of the sentence in different ways. It's not unusual for a choice to fix all the errors in the original sentence but introduce a new error. Therefore, it is important to read all the way through the choice you pick, paying attention to every word, to make sure it really is correct. Reading your choice back into the sentence before moving to the next question will serve as a final check that there are no errors in your selection.

An opportunity that many students overlook is in their analysis of the original sentence. It's natural to look only for errors, since finding an error allows you to eliminate (**A**) and begin the search for a choice that fixes the error. As you improve your mastery of Sentence Correction, however, try to read also for points in the sentence that are correct but where a GMAT-tested error is possible. As noted above, one or more answer choices may well introduce an error where the original sentence is correct, and pre-identifying these likely trouble spots will prepare you to spot the new errors when they crop up.

Finally, although you can only change the underlined portion of the sentence, errors may reach beyond the underlined portion and involve elements in the non-underlined portion. For example, the underlined portion may include a verb that must agree with its non-underlined subject. For this reason, read the entire sentence carefully to identify any essential connections of grammar, usage, and logic between the underlined and non-underlined text.

Answers and Explanations

Practice Set: The Kaplan Method for Sentence Correction

1. (E)

The subject of the underlined portion is "open letter," a singular noun. That does not agree with the plural verb "were." Eliminate (A).

(E) is correct because it changes the subject to the plural "self-described experts," which agrees with the new plural verb "have." (B) is incorrect because it continues to use the plural "were" with the singular subject "open letter." Also, it eliminates "although" at the beginning, making the opening clause independent; that creates a run-on sentence with the second clause, which is also independent. (C) also improperly eliminates "although" and is thus incorrect, even though it correctly changes the verb. (D) is incorrect because, while it changes the subject to the plural "self-described experts," it also changes the verb to the singular "has."

Although several self-described experts in attendance at the International Symposium on Unexplained Phenomena in Deep Space Studies have written an open letter stating that the newly discovered interstellar object is an alien space probe, most astronomers who have studied the object closely agree that it is a comet.

2. (D)

By ending with the word "that," the underlined portion creates the incorrect idiom *requiring that X to occur*. The phrase should use *that* (*requiring that X occurs*) or an infinitive verb (*requiring X to occur*), but not both. Because the infinitive ("to occur") is not underlined, it cannot be removed, so the correct answer needs to remove "that" instead. Eliminate (A).

(D) is correct because it eliminates "that" and changes the awkward "on account of requiring" to the simpler "because it requires." (B) and (C) are incorrect because they use plural pronouns ("their" and "they") to refer to a singular subject ("green flash"). (E) is incorrect because, like the original, it ends with "that," reproducing the incorrect *that X to occur* idiom. Read your choice back into the sentence:

The green flash, an atmospheric refractive phenomenon whereby the top edge of a setting sun will momentarily turn green, rarely is seen by the naked eye, primarily because it requires specific favorable conditions to occur.

3. (D)

The underlined portion starts with the past perfect verb "had been." The past perfect tense implies that this action occurred before the other past action in this sentence. However, the other past action is that the bird was "discovered only recently." It's illogical to suggest the bird was categorized as endangered before it was even discovered, so "had been" needs to change so that the categorizing logically occurs after the discovery. Further, there is a compound construction, *due to X and Y*, in which X and Y must be in parallel form. The underlined portion includes the verb phrase "habitat's being limited" that fails to parallel the corresponding element, "size." To be parallel, the two items joined by the "and" should both be nouns or both be verbs. Because "size" cannot be changed, the underlined portion should end in a noun. Eliminate (A).

(D) is correct. Changing "had been" to "has been" makes the categorization occur in the present, after the bird's discovery. This choice also changes the phrase "its habitat's being limited" to "its limited habitat," which better parallels "the low estimated size." Though it also changes "due to" to "because of," these phrases have equivalent meaning and usage. (B) is incorrect because it continues to use "had been." (C) and (E) are both incorrect because they end with verbs ("limited" and "limiting"), which are not parallel to the noun "size." They also illogically state that the bird limits its own habitat. Read your choice back into the sentence:

The new hummingbird species, which was discovered only recently, has been categorized as critically endangered because of its limited habitat and the low estimated size of its population.

4.   (A)

The underlined verb "is" is singular. The subject of the verb is the two exercises, connected by the conjunction "or." Because the compound subject is connected by "or" and the last noun in the subject ("weighted hip thrust") is singular, the subject takes a singular verb, and "is one of" is correct. The rest of the sentence proceeds logically and without error. In the last phrase, two -*ing* words, "isolating" and "building," connected by "and" have proper parallel structure. **(A)** is correct.

Since "is" is the correct verb, eliminate **(B)** and **(D)**. Of the remaining choices, **(C)** and **(E)** do not use a parallel structure in the phrase at the end, using "for isolating and to build" and "to isolate and for building," respectively.

5.   (C)

The underlined modifying text begins with the pronoun "they," which refers to the noun being modified: "the anthology." Even though the anthology consists of multiple stories, the opening phrase refers to the singular "anthology" and should thus use "it," not "they." Eliminate **(A)**.

(C) is correct because it resolves the pronoun error and uses the correct verbs with the new singular pronoun: "it contains . . . and depicts." **(B)** is incorrect, as it begins with "they." **(D)** and **(E)** are incorrect because the anthology is intended to be the subject that depicts something. **(D)** says that it is the "characters that depict" and **(E)** says it is the "themes . . . that depict." Check your answer by reading it back into the sentence:

Although it contains many repeated themes and depicts multiple characters with strikingly similar traits, the anthology consists of stories written by a diverse group of authors representing several different genres.

CHAPTER 20

SENTENCE CORRECTION: GRAMMAR AND USAGE REVIEW

LEARNING OBJECTIVES

- Describe the commonly tested areas of grammar and usage on the GMAT
- Identify commonly tested grammar and usage errors in a sentence
- Apply the Kaplan Method for Sentence Correction to sentences with a variety of grammar and usage errors or no error

Doing well on Sentence Correction questions begins with knowing how to approach them and then learning the errors that appear most frequently. Test takers who learn the most commonly tested patterns on GMAT Sentence Correction will be able to answer these questions confidently and efficiently. In this section, you'll learn about the seven most commonly tested areas of grammar and usage:

1. Verbs
2. Pronouns
3. Modification
4. Parallel Structure
5. Comparisons
6. Usage/Idioms
7. Clauses and Connectors

Keep in mind that many questions, particularly those of higher difficulty, will test multiple issues. Many questions involve more than one error. Using the Kaplan Method for Sentence Correction will give you an efficient way to focus on one error at a time. With both knowledge of these commonly tested areas and mastery of the Kaplan Method, you'll be able to handle even the toughest Sentence Correction questions.

Verbs

> **LEARNING OBJECTIVES**
>
> - Explain what it means for the subject and verb to agree in a sentence
> - Use logic and sequence of events to determine the proper tense for each verb in a sentence
> - Apply the Kaplan Method for Sentence Correction to sentences that may have subject-verb agreement or verb tense errors

The GMAT tests verbs in two ways: does the verb agree with its subject, and is the verb in the correct tense?

Subject-Verb Agreement

A sentence is defined as an independent sequence of words that contains a subject and a verb. Verbs must agree with their subjects. Singular subjects have singular verbs, and plural subjects have plural verbs. Look out for the following patterns that may indicate a subject-verb agreement issue:

- Long modifying phrases or clauses following the subject
- Phrases and clauses in commas between the subject and the verb
- Subjects joined by *either/or* and *neither/nor*
- Sentences in which the verb precedes the subject
- Collective nouns, such as *majority, committee, audience, team, group, flock,* and *family,* especially when preceded by *the* and followed by a prepositional phrase containing a plural noun (*the group of legislators*)
  - Collective nouns take a singular verb when the members of the collective act as a unit (*the flock of geese is flying south*) or are uncountable (*a lot of water was spilled*).
  - When the members of the collective act as individuals, the collective noun takes a plural verb (*a majority of voters mail their ballots; a number of solutions are possible*).

Subject-Verb Agreement Drill

Correct each of the following subject-verb errors. Answers follow the drill.

1. The depletion of natural resources, in addition to the rapid increase in utilization of these resources, have encouraged many nations to conserve energy.

2. There is, without a doubt, many good reasons to exercise.

3. Among the many problems plaguing suburbanites is the ubiquity of shopping malls, the increasing cost of gasoline, and the unavailability of mortgages.

4. The neighbors told police investigators that neither Annette nor her brother are capable of telling the truth.

5. The assembly of delegates intend to scrutinize the governor's policy decisions.

Subject-Verb Agreement Drill: Answers

1. "Depletion" is the subject. Correct by changing "have" to *has* or by changing "in addition to" to *and*.

2. There *are* many good reasons. A good strategy for checking subject-verb agreement is to ignore, temporarily, any parts of the sentence that are set off by commas.

3. If the sentence ended at "malls," "is" would be correct. But because there is more than one problem listed, *are* is the correct verb here.

4. "Neither Annette nor her brother *is* capable." In *or/nor* constructions, the verb agrees with the subject it is closer to. So if this read *Neither Annette nor her friends*, then *are* would be called for.

5. Even though "delegates" is plural, the subject of the sentence, "assembly," is a singular noun referring collectively to the group. "Assembly" therefore takes a singular verb: "The assembly *intends* to scrutinize."

Verb Tense

A verb tense indicates the order in which separate actions or events occur. Deciding which verb tense is appropriate in a given situation isn't just a matter of grammar; it's also a question of logic. Many GMAT sentences are long and complicated, involving or implying several different actions. The correct tenses make the sequence of events clear.

To determine whether the verbs in a sentence are in the proper tenses, pick one event as a standard and measure every other event against it. Ask yourself whether the other events are supposed to have happened before the standard event took place, after it took place, or while it took place. Those aren't mutually exclusive options, by the way: it is possible in English to have one action start before a second action and continue during that second action.

A frequent GMAT verb error is the inappropriate use of *-ing* forms: *I am going, I was going, I had been going,* and so on. As far as the GMAT is concerned, the only reason to use an *-ing* form along with helper verbs is to emphasize that an action is continuing or that two actions are occurring simultaneously. To remember this rule, think of the word *during* and its *-ing* ending. Unless a complicated tense is required by the sentence, pick a simpler tense—one that doesn't use the *-ing* form.

Most Commonly Tested Verb Tenses

- **Simple present**—*I am*—Used for an action happening now, with no contextual information about when it started, or for an action or state of being that is always true.

- **Simple past**—*I was*—Used for an action that happened at a specified time in the past.

- **Simple future**—*I will*—Used for an action that will happen in the future.

- **Past perfect**—*I had been*—Used for an action that happened *before* another past action (e.g., *I had been on the subway for 30 minutes before I realized that I was going the wrong direction*).

- **Present perfect**—*I have been*—Used for an action that started in the past but is still continuing now (e.g., *I have been on the subway for two hours now, and I still don't know where I'm going!*) or for past events that happened at an unspecified time (e.g., *He has read* Don Quixote *seven times*).

There are other verb tenses in the English language, but these are the ones that are tested most often on the GMAT.

Verb Tense Drill

Correct the verb tenses in each sentence. Answers follow the drill.

1. The criminal escaped from custody and is believed to flee the country.
2. Some archaeologists believe that the Minoans of 3,700 years ago had practiced a religion that involved human sacrifice.
3. If the experiment works, it will be representing a quantum leap forward for pharmaceutical chemistry.
4. He had seen that movie recently, so he doesn't want to see it tonight.
5. By the time she retires, she will save enough money to allow her to live comfortably.
6. She already closed the door behind her when it occurred to her that she wasn't able to get back in later.

Verb Tense Drill: Answers

1. "The criminal escaped" correctly uses simple past tense to refer to an event that happened at a specific time. The believing happens now, so simple present "is believed" is correct. However, the fleeing happened at an unknown and unspecified time in the past, so the present perfect should be used: . . . *is believed to have fled the country.*

2. Here, there's no indication the Minoans practiced human sacrifice for a while and then did something else. So use the simple past *practiced* instead of the past perfect "had practiced."

3. The experiment won't "be representing" a quantum leap; it will *represent* a quantum leap.

4. "Had" plus a past tense verb is used to indicate which of two things that went on in the past occurred earlier. That's not necessary in this sentence. *He saw that movie recently, so he doesn't want to see it tonight.* (*He had seen the movie recently, so he didn't want to see it tonight* also works, although it changes the meaning of the sentence to indicate that the desire happened earlier tonight instead of happening now.)

5. Here, we're indicating an action that began in the past but will end in the future. Think of it this way: at some future time, what will have happened? *She will have saved enough money.*

6. "Closed," "occurred," and "wasn't able to get back in" are all in the simple past tense. But you need to indicate that she first closed the door and then something occurred to her—namely, that she wouldn't be able to do something in the future. *She had already closed the door behind her when it occurred to her that she wouldn't be able to get back in later.*

CONCEPT CHECK

1. The GMAT commonly tests which two types of grammar rules involving verbs?

   _____

2. What are some indicators that a Sentence Correction question may be testing subject-verb agreement?

   _____

3. What action must a sentence express to correctly include a verb with "had"?

   _____

4. What action must a sentence express to correctly include a verb with "have"?

   _____

Example answers are in your book's online resources (**kaptest.com/login**).

Applying the Kaplan Method: Verbs

Now use the Kaplan Method to answer a Sentence Correction question dealing with verbs.

> The governor's approval ratings <u>has been extremely high until</u> a series of corruption scandals rocked his administration last year.

- ○ has been extremely high until
- ○ have been extremely high until
- ○ had been extremely high until
- ○ were extremely high as
- ○ had been extremely high as

Step 1: Read the Original Sentence Carefully, Looking for Errors

Whenever a sentence contains an underlined verb, make sure that it agrees with its subject and is in the correct tense. Here, the underlined portion contains a singular verb, "has been," that disagrees with the plural subject, "ratings." The verb is also in the wrong tense—"has been" indicates that the ratings are still high, but the sentence contradicts that. You can eliminate choice (**A**) immediately.

Step 2: Scan and Group the Answer Choices

Now it's time to look for a split in the answer choices. You see that the choices begin with many different verb forms: two "had been," one "were," one "have been," and one "has been." That's not a very helpful split. If you don't find a split at the beginnings of the answer choices, look for a split at the ends. Answer choices (**A**), (**B**), and (**C**) end with "until," whereas (**D**) and (**E**) end with "as"; this is a 3-2 split.

Step 3: Eliminate Choices Until Only One Remains

You eliminated (**A**) because the subject, "ratings," is plural, so the singular verb, "has been," cannot be correct. But verb tense is also at issue here. The correct verb tense is "had been extremely high," because the past perfect tense is used to indicate that something had already happened in the past before something else happened in the past. Here, the governor's ratings *had been* high, until scandals "rocked" his administration. This eliminates (**B**) and (**D**). And (**E**) can be eliminated, since changing the preposition from "until" to "as" loses the sense that the scandals occurred before, and led to, the reversal in the governor's approval ratings. For the record, note that (**D**) also contains this error. This leaves (**C**) as the only flawless answer. Read this choice back into the sentence to confirm:

The governor's approval ratings <u>had been extremely high until</u> a series of corruption scandals rocked his administration last year.

Next, you'll find some in-format questions involving verb issues.

Practice Set: Verbs

(Answers and explanations are at the end of the chapter.)

1. The string section, which included more than 30 violinists and violists as well as more than a dozen cellists and bassists, <u>were justly praised for the tremendous passion they invoked</u> in last night's performance of Stravinsky's *Rite of Spring*.

    ○ were justly praised for the tremendous passion they invoked

    ○ were justly praised for invoking their tremendous passion

    ○ were justly praised for the passion they were tremendous in invoking

    ○ was justly praised for invoking tremendous passion

    ○ was justly praised for the tremendous passion they invoked

2. Galileo Galilei <u>had discovered four moons orbiting Jupiter, including Ganymede, the largest moon in the solar system</u>, by the time Christiaan Huygens discovered Titan, the largest moon of Saturn, in 1655.

    ○ had discovered four moons orbiting Jupiter, including Ganymede, the largest moon in the solar system

    ○ had discovered four moons orbiting Jupiter, which includes Ganymede, being the largest moon in the solar system

    ○ will have discovered four moons, including Ganymede, orbiting Jupiter, which is the largest moon in the solar system

    ○ will have discovered four moons orbiting Jupiter, the largest moon in the solar system including Ganymede

    ○ has discovered four moons orbiting Jupiter, with the largest moon in the solar system being Ganymede

3. While Thomas Edison is often credited with inventing the incandescent light bulb, historians note that <u>several people have designed and created similar light bulbs before Edison received his patent</u>.

    ○ several people have designed and created similar light bulbs before Edison received his patent

    ○ several people having designed and created similar light bulbs before Edison receiving his patent

    ○ several people had designed and created similar light bulbs before Edison received his patent

    ○ similar light bulbs had been designed and created by several people before Edison receives his patent

    ○ similar light bulbs having been designed and created by several people before Edison received his patent

4. Discovered by a French soldier in 1799, the Rosetta Stone was inscribed with three distinct scripts in two languages, Egyptian and Greek, <u>and were instrumental in helping scholars decipher the hieroglyphs used by ancient Egyptians</u>.

   ○ and were instrumental in helping scholars decipher the hieroglyphs used by ancient Egyptians

   ○ instrumental in helping scholars decipher the hieroglyphs being used by ancient Egyptians

   ○ which was instrumental in helping scholars decipher the hieroglyphs the ancient Egyptians have used

   ○ and was instrumental in helping scholars decipher the hieroglyphs used by ancient Egyptians

   ○ and was instrumental in its deciphering of ancient Egyptian hieroglyphs, which helped scholars

Advanced Practice Set: Verbs

5. Companies need to ensure that the language in all of their financial reports <u>are reviewed carefully by a team of legal experts</u> since any errors can lead to serious problems for employees as well as shareholders and other investors.

   ○ are reviewed carefully by a team of legal experts

   ○ being reviewed by a careful team of legal experts

   ○ is reviewed carefully by a team of legal experts

   ○ was reviewed carefully by a legal team of experts

   ○ were reviewed by a legal team of experts carefully

6. While the skeleton of a typical human adult <u>will contain 206 bones, that of a newborn human baby usually has approximately 270, some of which fused together as the baby's body grew</u>.

   ○ will contain 206 bones, that of a newborn human baby usually has approximately 270, some of which fused together as the baby's body grew

   ○ contains 206 bones, that of a newborn human baby usually has approximately 270, some of which fuse together as the baby's body grows

   ○ contained 206 bones, that of a newborn human baby usually will have approximately 270, some of which fuse together as the baby's body grows

   ○ contains 206 bones, that of a newborn human baby usually has approximately 270, some of which fused together as the baby's body grew

   ○ will contain 206 bones, that of a newborn human baby usually has approximately 270, some of which fuse together as the baby's body grows

7. Scotland enjoys a robust tourism industry centered around the so-called Loch Ness monster; however, evidence that tends to support the existence of the monster, such as grainy photographs that purport to show the creature, <u>is outweighed by the evidence that supported</u> the idea that there is no such monster.

    O   is outweighed by the evidence that supported

    O   are outweighed by the evidence that supports

    O   are outweighed by evidence that supports

    O   is outweighed by evidence for supporting

    O   is outweighed by evidence that supports

Pronouns

> **LEARNING OBJECTIVES**
>
> - Define *pronoun* and describe what it means for a pronoun to be ambiguous
> - Describe how pronouns must agree with their antecedents
> - Apply the Kaplan Method for Sentence Correction to sentences that may have ambiguous pronouns or pronoun-antecedent agreement errors

Pronoun errors are one of the most common Sentence Correction issues on the GMAT. Luckily, the GMAT doesn't test every kind of pronoun error. Common errors fall into two categories: reference and agreement.

Pronoun Reference

Pronoun reference errors mean that a given pronoun does not refer to—or stand for—a specific noun or pronoun in the sentence (its antecedent). The pronouns that cause the most trouble on the GMAT are *it*, *its*, *they*, *their*, *them*, *who*, *whom*, *which*, and *that*. Be aware that these *are* pronouns and therefore need antecedents.

A common pattern is to use *which* or *that* to refer to an action that is not represented in the sentence as a noun. Take this sentence, for example: *The executive spoke eloquently at the annual meeting, which won the executive much praise.* The author means to say that the executive's eloquent speech earned praise, but what the author has actually said is that the annual meeting won the executive praise. Just because what the author means to say is obvious does not mean the author has actually said that.

Another reference error to be on the alert for is the use of *which* or *that* to refer to a person. People are represented by *who* or *whom*. Here's an example: *The journalist <u>that/who</u> spoke at the symposium answered many questions after her speech.* The correct pronoun is *who*.

Pronoun Agreement

For pronoun agreement errors, it's a question of numbers: perhaps a pronoun that refers to a singular noun is not in singular form, or a pronoun that refers to a plural noun is not in plural form.

As usual, the GMAT presents camouflaged examples of these two mistakes. Whenever you see a pronoun in the underlined portion of a sentence, look out for the following:

- Pronouns the test maker likes to misuse, such as *it, they, that*, and *which*.
- Pronouns that don't agree in number with their antecedents

Pronoun Reference and Agreement Drill

Correct the following common pronoun reference and agreement errors. Answers follow the drill.

1. Beatrix Potter's stories depict animals in an unsentimental and humorous manner, and she illustrated them with delicate watercolor paintings.
2. There is no known cure for certain forms of hepatitis; they hope, though, that a cure will be found soon.
3. If the partners cannot resolve their differences, the courts may have to do it.

4. In order to boost their name recognition, the Green Party sent canvassers to a busy shopping mall.

5. It is now recognized that the dangers of nuclear war are much graver than that of conventional warfare.

Pronoun Reference and Agreement Drill: Answers

1. "She" is clearly intended to refer to *Beatrix Potter*, but notice that the proper noun *Beatrix Potter* doesn't appear anywhere in this sentence; a pronoun cannot refer to a modifier, even a possessive modifier such as "Beatrix Potter's." There's a second problem as well: it's not clear whether the "them" that are illustrated are the stories or the animals. Here's a rewrite that solves all the problems: *Beatrix Potter not only wrote stories that depicted animals in an unsentimental and humorous manner, but also illustrated each story with delicate watercolor paintings.*

2. It's unclear what "they" refers to. The only plural noun is "forms," but it can't be the "forms of hepatitis" that are hoping for a cure. It must be *scientists* or some other group of people: *scientists hope to find a cure soon.*

3. "It" is the unclear pronoun here. There's no singular noun in the sentence for "it" to refer to. The main clause should read: . . . *the courts may have to do so.*

4. A pronoun or possessive should match the form of the noun it refers to. Use *its* and not "their" in place of the Green Party, because *party*, like *audience*, is a singular noun that stands for a collective group: *In order to boost its name recognition, the Green Party . . .*

5. "Dangers" is plural, so the pronoun "that" should be plural as well: . . . *than those of conventional warfare.*

CONCEPT CHECK

1. What are the two ways in which the GMAT tests pronouns?

   _____

2. How do you recognize a pronoun reference error?

   _____

3. How do you recognize a pronoun agreement error?

   _____

4. Describe the correct usage of the pronouns *which* and *that*.

   _____

Example answers are in your book's online resources (**kaptest.com/login**).

Applying the Kaplan Method: Pronouns

Now use the Kaplan Method to answer a Sentence Correction question dealing with pronouns.

Despite <u>the platform of the opposition party supporting the measure, they keep</u> voting against campaign finance reform in Congress.

- ○ the platform of the opposition party supporting the measure, they keep
- ○ the opposition party's platform supporting the measure, they keep
- ○ the opposition party's platform which supports the measure, it keeps
- ○ support of the measure being in the opposition party's platform, it keeps
- ○ the opposition party's platform supporting the measure, party members keep

Step 1: Read the Original Sentence Carefully, Looking for Errors

Pattern Recognition and Attention to the Right Detail are essential to spotting pronoun issues in Sentence Correction. Here, you should be paying attention to the word "they" in the underlined portion of the sentence. Colloquially, it's common to use "they" as a nebulous pronoun with no clear antecedent. On the GMAT, though, such usage is always wrong. In this sentence, it isn't clear who "they" refers to, so you know that's an issue that needs to be fixed by the correct answer.

Step 2: Scan and Group the Answer Choices

The beginnings of the answer choices don't yield much in the way of splits, but the ends definitely do: (**A**) and (**B**) end with "they," (**C**) and (**D**) end with "it," and (**E**) dispenses with pronouns entirely. You have a 2-2-1 split.

Step 3: Eliminate Choices Until Only One Remains

The pronoun use here is wrong, because the sentence does not contain an antecedent plural noun to which "they" could refer. So (**A**) and (**B**) are incorrect. (**C**) and (**D**) contain the singular pronoun "it"—but once again, the pronoun reference is confusing and wrong. It's not the *party platform* that keeps voting against the measure, as these choices imply. Both (**C**) and (**D**) can be eliminated. Only (**E**), which avoids faulty pronoun reference and makes it clear that "party members" keep voting against the measure, makes sense and is the correct answer.

Next, you'll find some in-format questions dealing with pronouns.

Practice Set: Pronouns

(Answers and explanations are at the end of the chapter.)

8. A major pharmaceutical company, in cooperation with an international public health organization and the medical research departments of two large universities, <u>is expected to announce tomorrow that it will transfer the</u> rights to manufacture a number of tuberculosis drugs to several smaller companies.

    O   is expected to announce tomorrow that it will transfer the

    O   are expected to announce tomorrow that they will transfer their

    O   are expected to announce tomorrow that they will transfer the

    O   is expected to announce tomorrow that they will transfer the

    O   is expected to announce tomorrow that there would be a transfer of the

9. Film critics often cite the example of Nicolas Cage's winning the Academy Award for Best Actor as a reason that <u>they should not automatically classify actors as elite for winning them</u>.

    O   they should not automatically classify actors as elite for winning them

    O   it should not automatically classify actors having won them as elite

    O   it should not automatically classify actors as elite for winning them

    O   actors should not automatically be classified as elite for winning an Academy Award

    O   actors should not be classified as automatically elite for winning an Academy Award

10. <u>As one step in its plan to engender greater goodwill in the community, town council members organized a series of public meetings when</u> residents could air grievances about the opacity of decision making, a tendency to award contracts to cronies, and a failure to follow through on promised reforms.

    O   As one step in its plan to engender greater goodwill in the community, town council members organized a series of public meetings when

    O   As one step in their plan to engender greater goodwill in the community, town council members organized a series of public meetings at which

    O   As one step in their plan to engender greater goodwill in the community, a series of public meetings were organized by town council members when

    O   Town council members, organizing a series of public meetings as one step in their plan to engender greater goodwill in the community, when

    O   Town council members, as one step in its plan to engender greater goodwill in the community, organized a series of public meetings at which

Advanced Practice Set: Pronouns

11. The visiting lecturer presented some lesser-known facts about snowflakes: for example, <u>they are not white, all have exactly six sides, they do not all have a unique pattern, and they—along with ice—constitutes</u> about 75 percent of Earth's freshwater.

    O   they are not white, all have exactly six sides, they do not all have a unique pattern, and they—along with ice—constitutes

    O   it is not white, all snowflakes have exactly six sides, not all snowflakes have a unique pattern, and snow—along with ice—constitute

    O   it is not white, it has exactly six sides, not all of it has a unique pattern, and it—along with ice—constitutes

    O   they are not white, all have exactly six sides, not all have a unique pattern, and they—along with ice—constitute

    O   they are not white, all has exactly six sides, not all has a unique pattern, and it—along with ice—constitutes

12. The defense attorneys wanted to interview the jurors following the guilty verdict, but a gag order issued by the judge prohibited <u>them from discussing the trial even after it had concluded</u>.

    ○ them from discussing the trial even after it had concluded

    ○ the jurors from discussing the trial even after it is concluded

    ○ them from discussing the trial even after it is concluded

    ○ the jurors from discussing the trial even after it had concluded

    ○ the jurors to discuss the trial even after it had concluded

13. One often-referenced online dictionary defines *nut* as "a hard-shelled dry fruit or seed with a separable rind or shell and interior kernel," indicating that <u>it does not include almonds, cashews, peanuts, pistachios, or walnuts</u>.

    ○ it does not include almonds, cashews, peanuts, pistachios, or walnuts

    ○ this definition does not include almonds, cashews, peanuts, pistachios, and walnuts

    ○ almonds, cashews, peanuts, pistachios, and walnuts are not included as examples of them

    ○ almonds, cashews, peanuts, pistachios, and walnuts are not included in it

    ○ they do not include almonds, cashews, peanuts, pistachios, or walnuts

Modification

> **LEARNING OBJECTIVES**
>
> - Define *modifier* and differentiate between adjectives and adverbs
> - Identify where in a sentence a modifier should be found, relative to the concept it is modifying
> - Apply the Kaplan Method for Sentence Correction to sentences that may have modification errors

A modifier is a word, phrase, or clause that describes another part of the sentence. It should be placed as close as possible to whatever it is modifying. Adjectives modify nouns; adverbs modify verbs, adjectives, or other adverbs. Modifiers describe the word that they are right next to. (The only exception is the case of two modifiers; one has to be first.) The GMAT often creates modification errors by making a modifier appear to describe a word that it actually doesn't. Use Pattern Recognition to help you spot modification errors on the GMAT.

Modifiers and Their Placement

The most common GMAT modification error occurs when there is a long modifier at the beginning of the sentence. It should modify the subject of the sentence but may not do so properly. Another common modification error occurs when a long modifier appears in the middle or at the end of a sentence. Often, such a modifier on the GMAT will logically describe something elsewhere in the sentence, but grammatically a modifying phrase must modify the word that comes immediately before or after it. The result of a misplaced modifier is a nonsensical sentence. Also look out for the following:

- Sentences beginning or ending with descriptive phrases
- Clauses beginning with *that* or *which* because these function as modifiers

Modification Drill

In each of the following sentences, first identify what each clause or phrase is modifying. Then, fix each error you find. Answers follow the drill.

1. Upon landing at the airport, the hotel sent a limousine to pick us up.
2. Based on the most current data available, the company made plans to diversify its holdings.
3. Small and taciturn, Joan Didion's presence often goes unnoticed by those she will later write about.
4. I took several lessons to learn how to play tennis without getting the ball over the net even once.
5. The house overlooked the lake, which was set back from the shore.

Modification Drill: Answers

1. The sentence seems to be saying that the *hotel* landed at the airport. Your common sense will tell you that "[u]pon landing at the airport" really intends to modify the unnamed *we*, instead. So you could say, *Upon landing at the airport, we were met by a limousine the hotel had sent.*

2. As written, it sounds as though the company was based on current data. "Based on the most current data available" modifies the subject "company." Obviously, though, what was based on the data were the "plans," not the company. *Based on the most current data available, plans were made to diversify the company's holdings.* Another option is to change the wording so the introductory phrase *does* describe either the "company" or the action "made plans": *Using the most current data available, the company made plans . . .*

3. It's Joan Didion—not her presence—who is small and taciturn. *Small and taciturn, Joan Didion often goes unnoticed . . .*

4. As written, "without getting the ball over the net" is describing "how to play tennis." The intended meaning is much more likely to be *I took many tennis lessons before I could get the ball over the net even once.*

5. The misplaced modifying clause produces an absurd image: a lake that's set back from its own shore. Of course, the "which" clause should follow "[t]he house": *The house, which was set back from the shore, overlooked the lake.*

CONCEPT CHECK

1. What is a modifier?

   _____

2. Where must a modifier be located?

   _____

3. What must a modifying phrase at the start of a sentence do?

   _____

4. Clauses that begin with *that* or *which* are often _____.

Example answers are in your book's online resources (**kaptest.com/login**).

Applying the Kaplan Method: Modification

Now use the Kaplan Method to answer a Sentence Correction question that involves modification.

> Subjects tend to be vividly but disturbingly portrayed in Egon Schiele's portraits, often his closest friends and relatives.

○ Subjects tend to be vividly but disturbingly portrayed in Egon Schiele's portraits, often his closest friends and relatives.

○ Subjects tend to be vividly but disturbingly portrayed in Egon Schiele's portraits, who were often his closest friends and relatives.

○ Subjects of Egon Schiele's portraits, often his closest friends and relatives, tend to be vividly but disturbingly portrayed.

○ In Egon Schiele's portraits, the subjects, often his closest friends and relatives, tend to be vividly but disturbingly portrayed.

○ Vividly but disturbingly, the subjects portrayed in Egon Schiele's portraits tended to be his closest friends and relatives.

Step 1: Read the Original Sentence Carefully, Looking for Errors

The entire sentence is underlined, but just systematically look for commonly tested errors as you normally would. In this case, the error is a misplaced modifier at the end of the sentence. The modifier is the final phrase set off by a comma, "often his closest friends and relatives." This phrase should refer to "subjects," but it's placed right next to "portraits." Always ask yourself when you see a modifier, "What should this word or phrase refer to? Is it as close to that word or phrase as possible?"

Step 2: Scan and Group the Answer Choices

In these choices, the modifying phrase appears in several different positions. Any choice placing it far from the word it modifies—"subjects"—should be eliminated. In (B), the modifying clause "who were often his closest friends and relatives" seems to refer to "portraits" rather than "subjects." Choice (B) retains the same problem as (A), so you can eliminate it. Choice (D) places the modifier immediately after "subjects," so this is likely to be your answer.

Step 3: Eliminate Choices Until Only One Remains

In (C), "subjects of Egon Schiele's portraits" seems to be one syntactical unit, so the phrase "often his closest friends and relatives" appears correctly to modify "subjects," even though it is not directly adjacent to "subjects." However, (C) is wrong because it is unclear whether "tend to be vividly but disturbingly portrayed" refers to how these subjects are displayed in the portraits or elsewhere; perhaps biographers of Schiele depict them in this manner.

(E) is incorrect because the adverbial phrase "Vividly but disturbingly" appears to refer to the verb "tended" rather than to the adjective "portrayed," making it seem as if the subjects' tendency to be Egon's friends is what's vivid and disturbing. Only (D) properly addresses this misplaced modifier problem; it is therefore your correct answer. Moreover, (D), unlike (C), makes it clear that the vivid but disturbing portrayal is in the portraits themselves.

Next, you'll find some in-format questions involving modification issues.

Practice Set: Modification

(Answers and explanations are at the end of the chapter.)

14. Despite being called one of the founding members of the Impressionist movement, <u>Edgar Degas's</u> <u>paintings often depicted interior scenes as opposed to the landscapes depicted by most other</u> <u>Impressionists, and he publicly rejected the label</u>.

   ○ Edgar Degas's paintings often depicted interior scenes as opposed to the landscapes depicted by most other Impressionists, and he publicly rejected the label

   ○ Edgar Degas's paintings were unlike most other Impressionists in that they often depicted interior scenes as opposed to landscapes, and he publicly rejected the label

   ○ Edgar Degas publicly rejected the label and often depicted interior scenes in his paintings instead of landscapes, which were unlike most other Impressionists

   ○ Edgar Degas publicly rejected the label and, unlike most other Impressionists, often depicted interior scenes in his paintings instead of landscapes

   ○ the interior scenes depicted by Edgar Degas, who rejected the label, were unlike the landscapes depicted by most other Impressionists

15. The superb lyrebird is known for <u>the producing of elaborate songs, including astounding mimicry</u> <u>of other birds and even non-bird animals such as dingoes, which it often uses as part of a complex</u> <u>courtship ritual</u>.

   ○ the producing of elaborate songs, including astounding mimicry of other birds and even non-bird animals such as dingoes, which it often uses as part of a complex courtship ritual

   ○ producing elaborate songs, which are often used as part of a complex courtship ritual and can include astounding mimicry of other birds and even non-bird animals such as dingoes

   ○ their elaborate songs, which can include both astounding mimicry of other birds and even non-bird animals such as dingoes, and also is used as part of a complex courtship ritual

   ○ its elaborate songs and astounding mimicry of both other birds as well as non-bird animals such as dingoes, which are often used as part of a complex courtship ritual

   ○ the elaborate songs, which they produce, often being used as a part of a complex courtship ritual, including an astounding mimicry of other birds and even non-bird animals such as dingoes

16. Believing in 1958 that Alaska and Hawaii would soon become U.S. states, <u>high school student Bob Heft, for a history class project, designed a flag with 50 stars; approved by President Eisenhower, that design became the new American flag</u>.

  ○ high school student Bob Heft, for a history class project, designed a flag with 50 stars; approved by President Eisenhower, that design became the new American flag

  ○ for a history class project, high school student Bob Heft designed a flag with 50 stars, approved by President Eisenhower, that design became the new American flag

  ○ the new American flag, designed by high school student Bob Heft with 50 stars for a history class project, was approved by President Eisenhower

  ○ high school student Bob Heft, for a history class project, designed a flag with 50 stars; approved by President Eisenhower, the new American flag was what that design became

  ○ for a history class project, high school student Bob Heft designed a flag with 50 stars; approved by President Eisenhower, the new American flag was what that design became

17. Consisting of surreal, nightmarish dreamscapes, <u>H. R. Giger created artwork that often inspires feelings of unease and dread in those who view it, and these reactions are why it was</u> chosen as the basis for the design of the title creature in the 1979 horror movie *Alien*.

  ○ H. R. Giger created artwork that often inspires feelings of unease and dread in those who view it, and these reactions are why it was

  ○ the artwork of H. R. Giger often inspires feelings of unease and dread in those who view it, and these reactions are why it is

  ○ H. R. Giger created artwork that often inspired feelings of unease and dread in those who view it, and these reactions are why it is

  ○ the artwork of H. R. Giger often inspires feelings of unease and dread in those who view it, and these reactions are why it was

  ○ the artwork of H. R. Giger often inspired feelings of unease and dread in those who view it, and these reactions are why it was

Advanced Practice Set: Modification

18. The recently discovered planet Kepler-90i was found via machine learning, a form of artificial intelligence in which <u>the identification of planets learned by computers is done from data by finding in the Kepler telescope instances of recorded signals from planets</u> beyond our solar system, known as exoplanets.

   O   the identification of planets learned by computers is done from data by finding in the Kepler telescope instances of recorded signals from planets

   O   computers learn to identify planets by finding in the Kepler telescope instances of recorded signals from planets

   O   computers learn to identify planets by finding in data from the Kepler telescope instances of the planet's recorded signals from

   O   computers learn to identify planets by finding in data from the Kepler telescope instances of recorded signals from planets

   O   the identification of planets is learned by computers by finding in data from the Kepler telescope instances of recorded signals from planets

19. <u>Closely interrelated concepts, a change in macroeconomic policy tends to affect numerous microeconomic transactions, and the accumulation of microeconomic decisions typically influences the focus of macroeconomic studies, so</u> any economics curriculum requires considerable study of both macroeconomic and microeconomic concepts.

   O   Closely interrelated concepts, a change in macroeconomic policy tends to affect numerous microeconomic transactions, and the accumulation of microeconomic decisions typically influences the focus of macroeconomic studies, so

   O   A change in macroeconomic policy tends to affect microeconomic transactions numerously, and the accumulation of microeconomic decisions influences the focus of macroeconomic studies typically; since the concepts of macroeconomics and microeconomics are related closely,

   O   A change in macroeconomic policy tends to affect numerous microeconomic transactions, and the accumulation of microeconomic decisions typically influences the focus of macroeconomic studies as a closely related concept, so

   O   A change in macroeconomic policy tends to affect numerous microeconomic transactions, and the accumulation of microeconomic decisions typically influences the focus of macroeconomic studies; given these closely related concepts,

   O   A change in macroeconomic policy tends to affect numerous microeconomic transactions, and the accumulation of microeconomic decisions typically influences the focus of macroeconomic studies; since the concepts of macroeconomics and microeconomics are closely related,

20. Noting <u>the fact that the three students were arguing while they were writing a joint science report over the proper use of semicolons, their discussion was interrupted by the teacher</u> to give them a quick lesson on punctuation.

    ○   the fact that the three students were arguing while they were writing a joint science report over the proper use of semicolons, their discussion was interrupted by the teacher

    ○   that the three students were arguing while they were writing a joint science report over the proper use of semicolons, their discussion was interrupted by the teacher

    ○   that the three students were arguing over the proper use of semicolons while they were writing a joint science report, the teacher interrupted their discussion

    ○   the fact that the three students were arguing over the proper use of semicolons while they were writing a joint science report, the teacher interrupted their discussion

    ○   that the three students were arguing over the proper use of semicolons while writing a joint science report, the teacher interrupted their discussion

Parallelism

> **LEARNING OBJECTIVES**
>
> - Define *parallelism* and recognize grammatical structures that require parallelism
> - Apply the Kaplan Method for Sentence Correction to sentences that may have non-parallel constructions

The basic concept behind parallelism is pretty simple: ideas with the same importance and function—nouns, verbs, phrases, or whatever—should be expressed in the same grammatical form. There are two types of constructions that test parallel structure on the GMAT:

1. Lists of items or a series of events
2. Two-part constructions such as *from X to Y, both X and Y, either X or Y, prefer X to Y, not only X but also Y,* and *as much X as Y*

Parallel Construction

Prepositions, articles, and auxiliaries can begin a list without needing to be repeated throughout. But if they are repeated, they must be in every element of the list.

- Correct: "Will you travel by plane, car, or boat?"
- Also correct: "Will you travel by plane, by car, or by boat?"
- Incorrect: "Will you travel by plane, car, or by boat?"

Analogies, similes, and other comparisons all require parallel structure.

- He was as brazen as his brother was diffident.
- Seeing her smile was like feeling the warmth of the sun.

Parallelism Drill

For each of the following sentences, put parallel items into the same form. Answers follow the drill.

1. The city's decay stems from governmental mismanagement, increasing unemployment, and many businesses are relocating.
2. Tourists' images of France range from cosmopolitan to the pastoral.
3. Excited about visiting New York, Jasmine minded neither riding the subways nor to cope with the crowded sidewalks.
4. To visualize success is not the same as achieving it.
5. I remember my aunt making her own dandelion wine and that she played the fiddle.
6. In my favorite Armenian restaurant, the menu is fascinating and the entrées exquisite.

Parallelism Drill: Answers

1. "[M]any businesses are relocating" should be written as *business relocation* to parallel "governmental mismanagement" and "increasing unemployment."

2. If you say "the pastoral," you have to say *the cosmopolitan*. Or you could say . . . *from cosmopolitan to pastoral*.

3. To parallel "riding," you need *coping*—not "to cope."

4. "To visualize" should be *visualizing* to parallel "achieving." Alternately, "achieving" could be written as *to achieve* to be in parallel with "[t]o visualize."

5. Change "my aunt making" to *that my aunt made* to be parallel with "that she played." Another possibility is to change "that she played" to *playing* to match "making."

6. "[T]he menu" is singular, but "entrées" is plural, so you must say *are exquisite* to parallel the phrase "is fascinating."

CONCEPT CHECK

1. What does parallel structure mean?

   _____

2. What are two types of grammatical constructions that require parallel structure?

   _____

3. What are some words and phrases that can signal parallel structure?

   _____

4. If a preposition, article, or auxiliary is used in a list, it can appear before _____ or before _____ in the list.

Example answers are in your book's online resources (**kaptest.com/login**).

Applying the Kaplan Method: Parallelism

Now use the Kaplan Method to answer a Sentence Correction question that involves parallelism.

Pablo Picasso's genius is only fully revealed when one considers the various facets of his work as they developed through many artistic phases, beginning with his Red <u>period, continuing through his Blue period, and finishing with his period of Cubism.</u>

- ○ period, continuing through his Blue period, and finishing with his period of Cubism
- ○ period, continuing through his Blue period, and finishing with his Cubist period
- ○ period, and continuing through his Blue period and his Cubist period
- ○ period phase, his Blue period phase, and his phase of Cubism
- ○ period, his Blue period, and his period of Cubism

Step 1: Read the Original Sentence Carefully, Looking for Errors

The original sentence contains a list, so check for parallel structure. Because the first two items in the list contain "Red period" and "Blue period," the third item in the list should follow the adjective-noun pattern and contain "Cubist period." Instead, this sentence ends with "period of Cubism," breaking the pattern and making choice (**A**) incorrect.

Step 2: Scan and Group the Answer Choices

Choices (**B**) and (**C**) end with "his Cubist period," while (**A**) and (**E**) reference "his period of Cubism" and (**D**) ends with the similar construction "his phase of Cubism." You have a 3-2 split.

Step 3: Eliminate Choices Until Only One Remains

You've established that (**A**) is incorrect, so eliminate (**D**) and (**E**) as well. This leaves only (**B**) and (**C**) with the correct parallel construction "Cubist period." The list should also contain the parallel phrases "beginning . . . continuing . . . and finishing." (**C**) is wrong because it drops "finishing," thereby altering the meaning and violating parallel structure. Only (**B**) exhibits parallel structure throughout the list. Read it back into the sentence to confirm there are no errors:

Pablo Picasso's genius is only fully revealed when one considers the various facets of his work as they developed through many artistic phases, beginning with his <u>Red period, continuing through his Blue period, and finishing with his Cubist period.</u>

Next, you'll find some in-format questions dealing with parallelism.

Practice Set: Parallelism

(Answers and explanations are at the end of the chapter.)

21. Although carotene and xanthophyll are present in leaves throughout the year, these pigments are not usually visible until <u>the days shorten, temperature drops, and the breaking down of the chlorophyll in the leaves reveals</u> the yellow and orange colors.

    O the days shorten, temperature drops, and the breaking down of the chlorophyll in the leaves reveals

    O the days shorten, the temperature drops, and the chlorophyll breakdown in the leaves is to reveal

    O the days shorten, the temperature drops, and the chlorophyll in the leaves breaks down, revealing

    O the days are shorter, the temperature is lower, and less chlorophyll in the leaves due to breakdown reveals

    O the days shorten, the temperature drops, and chlorophyll breaks down, revealing in the leaves

22. By conducting a national study of opioid abuse on college campuses, researchers hope to determine where students purchase opioids, how frequently students abuse opioids on average, and <u>which college stressors most commonly contribute to opioid abuse among students</u>.

    O which college stressors most commonly contribute to opioid abuse among students

    O which are the college stressors common to students who are likely to be turning to opioid abuse

    O the common stressors of college that are likely to contribute to opioid abuse among students

    O the stressors of college common among students who turn to opioid abuse

    O the types of college stressors that are common to students who are likely to turn to opioid abuse

23. Although deciding the outcome of an election by chance may seem antiquated, <u>a toss of a coin, playing a round of poker, and drawing straws are all methods that have been used</u> in recent decades to determine the winner of a deadlocked election somewhere in the United States.

    O a toss of a coin, playing a round of poker, and drawing straws are all methods that have been used

    O the tossing of a coin, playing a round of poker, and drawing straws are all methods that have been used

    O tossing a coin, playing a round of poker, and drawing straws are all methods that would have been used

    O a toss of a coin, playing a round of poker, and drawing straws are all methods that had been used

    O tossing a coin, playing a round of poker, and drawing straws are all methods that have been used

Advanced Practice Set: Parallelism

24. According to one nutrition consultant, healthy adults should not hesitate to consume eggs, since this food contains six grams of high-quality protein, all nine essential amino acids, <u>vitamins B12 and D, and is a source of various other nutrients</u>.

    ○ vitamins B12 and D, and is a source of various other nutrients

    ○ vitamins B12 and D, and including various other nutrients

    ○ vitamins B12 and D, and various other nutrients are included

    ○ and vitamins B12 and D and is a source of various other nutrients

    ○ the vitamins B12 and D, and provides various other nutrients

25. *In Cold Blood* <u>is not only often considered</u> Truman Capote's most popular novel but also the first "nonfiction novel," a literary genre that uses techniques of fictional storytelling to depict actual people and events.

    ○ is not only often considered

    ○ is as often not only considered

    ○ is often considered not only

    ○ not only is often considered to be

    ○ not only is considered as often

26. The self-portraits of Frida Kahlo can be considered both introspective explorations of a psyche that ranged free, unbounded by historical notions of cultural identity and <u>feminine, as well as subverting</u> traditional European portraiture.

    ○ feminine, as well as subverting

    ○ being feminine, and subverted

    ○ that was feminine, and subversions of

    ○ the femininity, as well as subverted

    ○ femininity, and subversions of

Comparisons

> **LEARNING OBJECTIVES**
>
> - Identify faulty comparisons involving comparison words, modifying phrases, and parallelism
> - Apply the Kaplan Method for Sentence Correction to sentences that may have illogical or malformed comparisons

Faulty comparisons account for a significant number of errors in GMAT Sentence Correction questions. Most relate to the simple idea that you can't compare apples to oranges. You must compare things that are not only grammatically similar but also logically similar. You can't logically compare, say, a person to a quality or an item to a group. You have to compare one individual to another, one quality to another, one group to another, and so on.

Three Kinds of Comparison Errors

Read the sentence with an attention to details like these:

- Key comparison words such as *like*, *as*, *compared to*, *less than*, *more than*, *other than*, *that of*, and *those of* may be used incorrectly.
- Long modifying phrases between compared elements can make it difficult to spot comparison errors. Mentally "delete" the modifying phrase so you can more easily check the compared elements.
- Compared items must be parallel in terms of construction.
  - Incorrect: I took advice from my mentor but not coworkers.
  - Correct: I took advice from my mentor but not from my coworkers.

Comparisons Drill

Fix the comparisons in the sentences below. Answers follow the drill.

1. Like a black bear that I once saw in the Buenos Aires Zoo, the Central Park Zoo polar bear's personality strikes me as being highly charismatic.
2. The article questioned the popularity of jazz compared to classical music.
3. The challenger weighed 20 pounds less than that of the defender.
4. The Boston office contributes less to total national sales than any other U.S. branch.
5. The host paid more attention to his celebrity guest than the others.

K

Comparisons Drill: Answers

1. "Like" creates a comparison, and you can compare only similar things. Here, you have to compare bears to bears or personalities to personalities. *Like a black bear I once saw in the Buenos Aires Zoo, the Central Park Zoo polar bear strikes me as being highly charismatic.*

2. *The article questioned the popularity of jazz compared to* that *of classical music.*

3. *The challenger weighed 20 pounds less than the defender did,* or *The challenger's weight was 20 pounds less than that of the defender.*

4. There are two ways to read this sentence as it's written. We could be comparing the Boston office's contribution to national sales and other branches' contributions, but we also could be comparing the Boston office's contribution to national sales and the Boston office's contribution to those other branches. The former comparison is more logical, so we clarify: *. . . than any other U.S. branch* does.

5. A similar problem—you need to repeat the verb after "than" (*than* he *paid to the others*) or refer to the verb by placing *to* after "than" (*than to the others*).

CONCEPT CHECK

1. What are some words and phrases that signal comparisons?

   _____

2. To be correct, comparisons must be both _____ and _____.

Example answers are in your book's online resources (**kaptest.com/login**).

Applying the Kaplan Method: Comparisons

Apply the Kaplan Method to a Sentence Correction question that involves comparison.

Like most other marsupial species and all other kangaroo species, the diet of the swamp wallaby consists of leaves and other sorts of vegetation.

- O   Like most other marsupial species and all other kangaroo species, the diet of the swamp wallaby consists
- O   Like those of most other marsupial species and all other kangaroo species, the diets of the swamp wallaby consists
- O   Just like the diet of most other marsupial species and all other kangaroo species, the diet of the swamp wallaby consists
- O   Similar to the diets of most other marsupial species and all other kangaroo species, the swamp wallabies have a diet which consists
- O   Like most other marsupial species and all other kangaroo species, the swamp wallaby has a diet consisting

Step 1: Read the Original Sentence Carefully, Looking for Errors

This sentence begins with the word "[l]ike," which signals that you have a comparison to check. Look at the items being compared and make sure they are comparable. In the original sentence, "species" are compared to a "diet." That's an incorrect comparison.

Step 2: Scan and Group the Answer Choices

All the answer choices contain "[l]ike" or "[s]imilar to," so they all contain comparisons. As you examine each choice, check whether it makes a proper comparison.

Step 3: Eliminate Choices Until Only One Remains

The incorrect comparison in the original sentence means that you can eliminate (**A**). Aside from sounding awkward, (**B**) contains a subject/verb agreement problem—the plural noun "diets" takes the singular verb "consists," which is incorrect. (**C**) should be eliminated because in the introductory phrase "diet" should be plural; also, there's no reason to use "[j]ust like" rather than "[l]ike." In addition, "[l]ike" is preferable to "[s]imilar to" in (**D**), which also incorrectly compares "diets" to "wallabies." Only (**E**) correctly compares the swamp wallaby to other species. Read this choice back into the sentence to confirm it is correct:

Like most other marsupial species and all other kangaroo species, the swamp wallaby has a diet consisting of leaves and other sorts of vegetation.

Next, you'll find some in-format questions involving comparisons.

Practice Set: Comparisons

(Answers and explanations are at the end of the chapter.)

27. As an example of the seeming paradoxes encountered by the student of the natural world, consider the largest animal on Earth, the blue whale: while the blue whale's body is indeed larger than <u>the sperm whale, the sperm whale's brain is actually larger than the blue whale</u>.

    ○ the sperm whale, the sperm whale's brain is actually larger than the blue whale

    ○ that of the sperm whale, the sperm whale's brain is actually larger than that of the blue whale

    ○ that of the sperm whale, the sperm whale's brain is actually larger than the blue whale

    ○ the sperm whale, its brain is actually larger than the blue whale

    ○ that of the sperm whale, the brain of the sperm whale is actually larger

28. <u>No less significant than</u> international pressures are the constraints that domestic culture and ideology impose on decision making by national political figures.

    ○ No less significant than

    ○ The things that are just as significant as

    ○ Just like the significant

    ○ Not lesser than the significance of

    ○ What are as significant as

29. Establishing goals for a nonprofit organization is often different <u>than setting</u> goals for a profit-making enterprise because the stakeholders of the former may be more varied.

    ○ than setting

    ○ than the setting of

    ○ from

    ○ from setting

    ○ from the setting of

Advanced Practice Set: Comparisons

30. Reducing the population of Japanese beetles is done <u>most easily by applying pesticides to turf-dwelling young larvae in late summer than applications</u> to mature larvae in spring or adult beetles at any time of year.

    ○ most easily by applying pesticides to turf-dwelling young larvae in late summer than applications

    ○ most easily by the application of pesticides to turf-dwelling young larvae in late summer than that

    ○ more easily by applying pesticides to turf-dwelling young larvae in late summer than

    ○ easier through the application of pesticides to turf-dwelling young larvae in late summer than

    ○ more easily by applying pesticides to turf-dwelling young larvae in late summer rather than applying

31. With an elaborate menu featuring innovative dishes from a variety of world cuisines as well as <u>serving its signature breakfast fare, Penelope's Pancake Palace, an established downtown eatery, offers a more diverse selection of food than does any</u> restaurant in the city.

    ○ serving its signature breakfast fare, Penelope's Pancake Palace, an established downtown eatery, offers a more diverse selection of food than does any

    ○ its signature breakfast fare, Penelope's Pancake Palace, an eatery established downtown, offers a more diverse selection of food than does any

    ○ with serving its signature breakfast fare, Penelope's Pancake Palace, an established downtown eatery, offers a more diverse selection of food than does any other

    ○ its signature breakfast fare, Penelope's Pancake Palace, an established downtown eatery, offers a more diverse selection of food than does any other

    ○ its signature breakfast fare, Penelope's Pancake Palace, an established downtown eatery, offers more of a diverse selection of food as any other

32. The United States' trade deficit with China rose in 2003 to $123 billion, <u>which was 17 percent more than the previous year</u> and more than ten times the U.S.-China trade deficit in 1998.

    ○ which was 17 percent more than the previous year

    ○ which was 17 percent higher than it was the previous year

    ○ 17 percent higher than the previous year's figure was

    ○ an amount that was 17 percent more than the previous year was

    ○ an amount that was 17 percent higher than the previous year's figure

Usage and Idioms

The principle of **usage** concerns the "right" way to use words to say things as determined by users of English over time. There is no overarching grammar rule that applies across situations; each word or phrase is governed by its own rule.

Idioms are combinations of words that together have a meaning distinct from the definition of each word. For example, at the supermarket, you *pick up some bread* and *pick out a kind of frozen pizza*. The meanings of *pick up* and *pick out* are not much related to the meanings of *up* and *out*.

How to Recognize Errors Involving Usage and Idioms

Usage and idioms are likely to show up on a handful of Sentence Correction questions. If you have had consistent exposure to "standard" written English, as generally defined in academic and journalistic circles, then you will be able to trust your ear to tell you what sounds right, and what sounds wrong, in a sentence. For example, if someone were to say, "I am aware about these problems, because I saw the newscast yesterday," you'd likely pick up on the error right away. The correct idiom is "aware *of*," not "aware *about*."

Even so, issues of usage and idiom frequently involve small, seemingly unimportant words, like prepositions, so it is easy to overlook these errors if you don't keep alert for them—especially under time pressure as on the GMAT. Therefore, Attention to the Right Detail is important for success on questions involving usage and idioms.

If you have not had long-standing exposure to the formal written English tested on the GMAT, then you won't be able to trust your ear as much. In this case, you'll definitely want to learn the commonly tested words and phrases that appear in this chapter and in your online resources. Making flashcards with these words and phrases can help. You might pattern your flashcards after the exercises in this section, putting a sentence with a blank in it on the front of the card and the correct word or phrase to fill in the blank on the back.

Common Errors of Usage and Idioms

When answering Sentence Correction questions on the GMAT, look out for the following:

- Prepositions (*to*, *from*, *at*, *over*, etc.) in the underlined portion of the sentence. Their usage is often dictated by idiomatic rules.

- Verbs whose idiomatic usage you've seen frequently tested. Common examples are *prefer*, *credit*, and *regard*.

- Comparisons that aren't expressed with the correct combination of words. One example is *as many X as Y*. It would be incorrect to say, for example, *You know as many idioms than you need*.

See the Usage and Idioms drills later in this section for practice with these and other constructions in which errors often lurk.

Also keep a lookout for sentences that use more words than necessary, as well as those that seem to bury the important idea behind less important wording. The GMAT prefers active voice and a clear, direct style. That said, sometimes the correct answer on the test will not be the way you would write the sentence but will be the only grammatically correct choice: grammar is a more important criterion than style when it comes to choosing correct answers. Nonetheless, sentences that demonstrate any of the following are unlikely to be correct:

- Unnecessary passive voice: *The letter was written by John* is not wrong, but better is *John wrote the letter*.

- Unnecessary wordiness and redundancy. For example, the word *because* is better than the phrase *in view of the fact that*.

- Awkward, choppy, or clunky phrasing: if you can trust your "ear," use it to identify sentences and phrases that simply don't read well.

Finally, here's a specific tip: be alert for verbs that trigger the subjunctive mood. The subjunctive mood is called for in two situations:

1. **Orders and recommendations:** With verbs such as *order*, *demand*, *insist*, *recommend*, *ask*, *suggest*, etc. or sentences that indicate a request or requirement, what follows the verb should be *that*, a new subject, and the infinitive form of a verb but without the *to*. Examples:

   - He *asked* that the door *be* left open.

   - She *suggests* that her clients *read* all documents carefully.

   - It is *important* that applicants *pass* a background check.

2. **Hypothetical situations:** When contemplating hypothetical or contrary-to-fact situations in the present, use *were* (singular and plural) and *would*. For such situations in the past, change the verb tense accordingly. Examples:

   - If I *were* rich, I *would* quit my job.

   - If only I *were* there with you, I *would* be happy.

   - If James *had been* in charge, he *would* not have allowed excess expenditures.

Usage and Idioms Drill, Part I

Fill in the blank with the correct word or phrase that completes the idiom correctly in the sentence. In some cases, the correct idiom may not require any additional words. Answers follow the drill.

1. He modestly *attributed* his business's success _____ good luck.

2. My dictionary *defines* "idiom" _____ the usual way in which the words of a particular language are joined together.

3. Alexander Graham Bell is *credited* _____ inventing the telephone.

4. Some people with color-blindness cannot *distinguish* red _____ green.

5. Other people with color-blindness cannot *distinguish* _____ yellow _____ blue.

6. Although his story seems incredible, I *believe* it _____ the truth.

7. She is *regarded* _____ an expert on public health policy.

8. He is *considered* _____ a close friend of the president.

9. I like to *contrast* my plaid pants _____ a lovely paisley jacket.

10. According to Aristotle, contentment is *different* _____ happiness.

11. The oldest rocks on Earth are *estimated* _____ 4.6 billion years old.

12. Louisiana's legal system is *modeled* _____ the Napoleonic code.

13. I don't mean for my comments to be *perceived* _____ criticism.

14. Cigarette ads *aimed* _____ children have been banned by the FDA.

15. The mass extinction of dinosaurs has been *linked* _____ a large meteor impact.

16. Don't *worry* _____ all the idioms that might appear on the GMAT. Just learn the ones you come across between now and Test Day.

Usage and Idioms Drill, Part II

Fill in the blank with the correct word or phrase that completes the idiom correctly in the sentence. In some cases, choose the option that correctly completes the idiom. Answers follow the drill.

1. I sold more glasses of lemonade _____ my neighbor sold.

2. She sold as many glasses of lemonade _____ she could.

3. The bigger they come, _____ they fall, or so it is said.

4. According to my diet, I can have either cake <u>or/and</u> ice cream, but not both.

5. Given my choice, I would have both cake _____ ice cream.

6. I must decide between one _____ the other.

7. Neither the coach _____ the players <u>was/were</u> happy with the team's performance.

8. I couldn't decide <u>if/whether</u> he was kidding or not.

9. <u>Between/Among</u> the three candidates, he has the <u>more/most</u> impressive record.

10. There are <u>less/fewer</u> students in class today than there were yesterday.

11. However, the <u>amount/number</u> of students enrolled in this class has increased.

12. People are forbidden <u>from entering/to enter</u> the park at night.

13. The ruling prohibits the defendant <u>from discussing/to discuss</u> the case.

14. Most politicians do not want to be seen associating <u>with/among</u> convicted felons.

15. We should treat others <u>as/like</u> we would want them to treat us.

16. I would prefer a salty treat <u>like/such</u> as potato chips <u>over/to</u> a candy bar.

17. The annual meeting was a situation <u>where/in which</u> the leadership team needed to use its influence.

18. My great-grandmother was born <u>sometime/somewhere</u> around 1880.

19. Scores on the GMAT range from 200 _____ 800.

20. Most local residents view the monument _____ an eyesore.

21. In the United States, there is less opposition _____ the use of genetically modified foods than in Europe.

22. Stress can lower one's resistance _____ cold and flu viruses.

23. The rise in inflation has become so significant _____ constitute a threat to the economic recovery.

24. The actress's performance was so poignant _____ the entire audience was moved to tears.

25. Just try _____ do as well as you can on the test.

Usage and Idioms Drill, Part I: Answers

1. He modestly *attributed* his business's success *to* good luck.

2. My dictionary *defines* "idiom" *as* the usual way in which the words of a particular language are joined together.

3. Alexander Graham Bell is *credited* *with* inventing the telephone.

4. Some color-blind people cannot *distinguish* red *from* green.

5. Other color-blind people cannot *distinguish* *between* yellow *and* blue.

6. Although his story seems incredible, I *believe* it *to be* the truth.

7. She is *regarded* *as* an expert on public health policy.

8. He is *considered* a close friend of the president. *[This blank takes nothing.]*

9. I like to *contrast* my plaid pants *with* a lovely paisley jacket.

10. According to Aristotle, contentment is *different* *from* happiness.

11. The oldest rocks on Earth are *estimated* *to be* 4.6 billion years old.

12. Louisiana's legal system is *modeled* *after* the Napoleonic code.

13. I don't mean for my comments to be *perceived* *as* criticism.

14. Cigarette ads *aimed* *at* children have been banned by the FDA.

15. The mass extinction of dinosaurs has been *linked* *to* a large meteor impact.

16. Don't *worry* *about* all the idioms that might appear on the GMAT. Just learn the ones you come across between now and Test Day.

Usage and Idioms Drill, Part II: Answers

1. I sold more glasses of lemonade ***than*** my neighbor sold.

2. She sold as many glasses of lemonade ***as*** she could.

3. The bigger they come, ***the harder*** they fall, or so it is said.

4. According to my diet, I can have either cake ***or*** ice cream, but not both.

5. Given my choice, I would have both cake ***and*** ice cream.

6. I must decide between one ***and*** the other.

7. Neither the coach ***nor*** the players ***were*** happy with the team's performance.

8. I couldn't decide ***whether*** he was kidding or not.

9. ***Among*** the three candidates, he has the ***most*** impressive record.

10. There are ***fewer*** students in class today than there were yesterday.

11. However, the ***number*** of students enrolled in this class has increased.

12. People are forbidden ***to enter*** the park at night.

13. The ruling prohibits the defendant ***from discussing*** the case.

14. Most politicians do not want to be seen associating ***with*** convicted felons.

15. We should treat others ***as*** we would want them to treat us.

16. I would prefer a salty treat ***such as*** potato chips ***to*** a candy bar.

17. The annual meeting was a situation ***in which*** the leadership team needed to use its influence.

18. My great-grandmother was born ***sometime*** around 1880.

19. Scores on the GMAT range from 200 ***to*** 800.

20. Most local residents view the monument ***as*** an eyesore.

21. In the United States, there is less opposition ***to*** the use of genetically modified foods than in Europe.

22. Stress can lower one's resistance ***to*** cold and flu viruses.

23. The rise in inflation has become so significant ***as to*** constitute a threat to the economic recovery.

24. The actress's performance was so poignant ***that*** the entire audience was moved to tears.

25. Just try ***to*** do as well as you can on the test.

CONCEPT CHECK

1. What do usage issues on the GMAT involve?

   _____

2. What do idiom issues on the GMAT involve?

   _____

3. What are some issues of style that are likely to be incorrect?

   _____

4. What are two situations that trigger the subjunctive?

   _____

Example answers are in your book's online resources (**kaptest.com/login**).

Applying the Kaplan Method: Usage and Idioms

Now use the Kaplan Method on a Sentence Correction question dealing with usage and idioms.

> Growth in the industry is at an all-time low, with <u>less than 68,000 people employed and</u> <u>fewer</u> opportunity in the field than there has been during any of the past ten years.

- ○ less than 68,000 people employed and fewer
- ○ fewer than 68,000 people employed and fewer
- ○ lesser than 68,000 people employed and fewer
- ○ fewer than 68,000 people employed and less
- ○ less than 68,000 people employed, and there is less

Step 1: Read the Original Sentence Carefully, Looking for Errors

Notice that the underlined portion of the sentence contains the words "less" and "fewer." On the GMAT, "less" can refer only to non-countable items, such as soup or confidence. "Fewer" must refer to countable items, such as chairs or peanuts. In this sentence, since "people" can be counted, there are "fewer" people, and since "opportunity" cannot be counted, there is "less" opportunity.

Step 2: Scan and Group the Answer Choices

Even if that didn't occur to you as the issue in the sentence, you should note that some of the choices use "less" (or "lesser") and others use "fewer" and group accordingly into a 3-2 split. This step should prompt you to think about the associated usage rule.

Step 3: Eliminate Choices Until Only One Remains

Eliminate choice (**A**) because the original sentence misuses "less" and "fewer." Choices (**C**) and (**E**) make similar errors. Choice (**C**)'s "lesser than" would be unidiomatic in any context. In addition to using "less" in front of "people," (**E**) breaks off "opportunity in the field" into a new independent clause, adding unnecessary extra words and an awkward repetition of "there." Choice (**B**) uses "fewer" correctly to refer to the people but also uses it to refer to the uncountable "opportunity," so eliminate this choice. That leaves (**D**), which is correct: it uses "fewer" to describe the countable noun "people" and "less" to describe "opportunity." Read (**D**) back into the original sentence:

Growth in the industry is at an all-time low, with <u>fewer than 68,000 people employed and less</u> opportunity in the field than there has been during any of the past ten years.

Next, you'll find some in-format questions involving usage and idioms.

Practice Set: Usage and Idioms

(Answers and explanations are at the end of the chapter.)

33. In addition to winning the Nobel Prize in Physics for his accomplishments in quantum electrodynamics, Richard Feynman worked on both the Manhattan Project in Los Alamos <u>as well as the Rogers Commission, which investigated</u> the space shuttle *Challenger* disaster in 1986.

    ○   as well as the Rogers Commission, which investigated

    ○   and also on the Rogers Commission that investigated

    ○   and on the Rogers Commission, which investigated

    ○   and the Rogers Commission, which is investigating

    ○   and the Rogers Commission, which investigated

34. To boost the nation's economy, it is <u>at least as important for businesses to focus</u> on developing worker productivity than it is for them to hire new employees.

    ○   at least as important for businesses to focus

    ○   at least as important for businesses focusing

    ○   no less important for businesses to focus

    ○   no less important that businesses focusing

    ○   as important, if not more important, for businesses to focus

35. The "Mpemba effect" refers to the observation that, under some conditions, hot water can freeze <u>more quickly in comparison to cold water; the researchers who investigated this effect also observed that cold water can sometimes heat more quickly in relation to warm water</u> and named that phenomenon the "inverse Mpemba effect."

    ○   more quickly in comparison to cold water; the researchers who investigated this effect also observed that cold water can sometimes heat more quickly in relation to warm water

    ○   faster; the researchers who investigated this effect also observed that cold water can sometimes heat faster

    ○   more quickly than cold water; the researchers who investigated this effect also observed that cold water would sometimes heat more quickly than warm water

    ○   faster than cold water; the researchers who investigated this effect also observed that cold water can sometimes heat faster than warm water

    ○   faster than cold water; the researchers who investigated this effect also observed that the opposite is sometimes true

Advanced Practice Set: Usage and Idioms

36. The entrepreneurs credited the website that helped owners of small businesses find suppliers <u>to keep their new enterprise viable when cash flow was neither ample or steady</u>.

   - ○   to keep their new enterprise viable when cash flow was neither ample or steady
   - ○   toward keeping their new enterprise viable at a time when cash flow was not ample or steady
   - ○   with keeping their new enterprise viable when cash flow was neither ample nor steady
   - ○   to keeping their new enterprise viable when cash flow was neither ample nor steady
   - ○   with keeping their new enterprise viable when there was neither ample or steady cash flow

37. All volunteers who wish to be judges of the annual county fair baking competition are required, regardless of whether or not they have prior experience, <u>for taking a food handler course</u>.

   - ○   for taking a food handler course
   - ○   for making sure a food handler course is taken
   - ○   to take a food handler course
   - ○   to have taken of a food handler course
   - ○   of taking a food handler course

38. The United States <u>would achieve a 10 percent reduction in gasoline consumption if Congress will raise</u> fuel economy standards to 31.3 miles per gallon for passenger cars and to 24.5 miles per gallon for light trucks.

   - ○   would achieve a 10 percent reduction in gasoline consumption if Congress will raise
   - ○   will achieve a 10 percent reduction in gasoline consumption if Congress were to raise
   - ○   will have achieved a 10 percent reduction in gasoline consumption if Congress will raise
   - ○   would achieve a 10 percent reduction in gasoline consumption if Congress were to raise
   - ○   would achieve a 10 percent reduction in gasoline consumption if Congress were raising

Clauses and Connectors

> **LEARNING OBJECTIVES**
>
> - Explain the ways in which clauses are often joined incorrectly in Sentence Correction questions
> - Apply the Kaplan Method for Sentence Correction to sentences whose parts may be connected incorrectly

The GMAT uses compound and complex sentences to test your knowledge of clauses and connectors. Recall that a clause is a group of words that contains a subject and a verb. When the underlined portion of a sentence includes a junction between ideas, make sure the ideas are joined correctly.

How to Recognize Errors Involving Clauses and Connectors

Typically, clauses should be connected by a single connecting word or phrase (*because, although, even though, as, but*, etc.). The exception is two independent clauses that are joined by a semicolon; the relationship between their ideas may or may not be indicated by a key word. Be alert for choices that omit any connector. At the same time, avoid choices that result in the use of two connectors that indicate the same relationship between the same two ideas; the sentence only needs one.

Furthermore, the connector used should make sense given the logical relationship between the clauses. If you have not already done so, review the discussion of key words in "Step 1: Read the Passage Strategically" in Chapter 16. Contrast, continuation, and logic (evidence, conclusion) key words are particularly apt to be a source of error on Sentence Correction questions. Wrong answer choices may change connector words in a way that changes the meaning of the sentence from what the author intended or that produces an illogical meaning.

Clauses and Connectors Drill

For each of the following sentences, correct the error related to clauses and connectors. Answers follow the drill.

1. Although the vice president ordered all employees to work through the weekend, but some employees went home.

2. Many citizens agree that austerity measures are necessary, few are happy about the ones that have been enacted.

3. Several new restaurants have recently opened next to Carlotta's Bistro on Main Street, and also a yoga studio has opened in the same building as Carlotta's too.

4. As a result of the raging wildfire, many residents were forcibly evacuated, so the fire is still out of control.

5. Since the manager is competent, nonetheless she has been promoted repeatedly.

Clauses and Connectors Drill: Answers

1. "Although" establishes a contrast between clauses, and so does "but." Only one of these words should be in the sentence.

2. The two clauses in this sentence need to be related by a connector: *Many citizens agree that austerity measures are necessary, although few are happy about the ones that have been enacted.*

3. The "and" is sufficient to connect the clause about the new restaurants to the clause about the yoga studio. The words "also" and "too" are unnecessary and should be omitted.

4. This sentence starts out with a logical cause-and-effect sequence, but then "so" indicates the fire is out of control because the residents were evacuated. This does not make sense, especially since the sentence has already said the residents were evacuated because of the fire. The word "so" should be replaced by "and" or some other logical connector.

5. "Since" indicates a reason why something happened. It's logical to say that the manager has been promoted because of her competence. The contrast key word "nonetheless" is at odds with the logical relationship between these clauses and should be deleted.

CONCEPT CHECK

1. What is a clause?

   _____ .

2. What should you do to determine the correct connector between two clauses?

   _____

Example answers are in your book's online resources (**kaptest.com/login**).

Applying the Kaplan Method: Clauses and Connectors

Try using the Kaplan Method on a Sentence Correction question dealing with clauses and connectors.

<u>More and more couples wait before trying to start</u> a family, the average age of first-time parents is increasing.

- ○ More and more couples wait before trying to start
- ○ As more and more couples wait before trying to start
- ○ As more and more couples wait before trying and starting
- ○ Although more and more couples wait before trying to start
- ○ Being that more and more couples are waiting before trying to start

Step 1: Read the Original Sentence Carefully, Looking for Errors

This sentence contains two complete clauses, each with its own subject and verb. The subject of "wait" is "couples," and the subject of "is increasing" is "age." Two complete clauses should be joined with a conjunction, but this sentence has no conjunction and is thus a run-on. The correct answer will provide the sentence with a conjunction. Moreover, the logical relationship between clauses is one of cause and effect. The delay in starting a family in the first clause logically leads to an increase in the average age. So look for a choice that establishes that relationship. Finally, note that the junction between the clauses is not underlined, so the connector word cannot go there; it will have to place the first clause into the correct relationship with the second.

Step 2: Scan and Group the Answer Choices

Choices (**B**) and (**C**) introduce "[a]s" at the beginning of the sentence. Choice (**D**) substitutes "[a]lthough," and (**E**) uses "[b]eing that."

Step 3: Eliminate Choices Until Only One Remains

Eliminate (**A**) for omitting a connecting word. "Being that" is a weak, awkward construction, and on the GMAT an answer choice containing it will be wrong; eliminate (**E**). Choice (**D**) adds the conjunction "[a]lthough," which indicates a contrast and therefore doesn't make logical sense. (**B**) and (**C**) both start with "[a]s," meaning "because," which does make logical sense as a conjunction for this sentence. (**C**) changes "trying to start" to "trying and starting," which is idiomatically incorrect. The correct answer is (**B**), which adds an appropriate conjunction and does not create any new errors. Read (**B**) back into the sentence to confirm:

<u>As more and more couples wait before trying to start</u> a family, the average age of first-time parents is increasing.

Next, you'll find some in-format questions dealing with clauses and connectors.

Practice Set: Clauses and Connectors

(Answers and explanations are at the end of the chapter.)

39. <u>Due to countries in a monetary union having to issue debt in a joint currency over which they lack full control, therefore</u> investors become nervous about the financial health of a country, that nation may not be able to finance its debt at the same rate enjoyed by its neighbors and thus will experience the liquidity crisis that investors fear.

   O   Due to countries in a monetary union having to issue debt in a joint currency over which they lack full control, therefore

   O   It is because countries in a monetary union have to issue debt in a joint currency they do not fully control, as

   O   Because countries in a monetary union must issue debt in a joint currency over which they lack full control, if

   O   Countries that are in a monetary union have to issue debt in a joint currency over which they lack full control, causing

   O   In a monetary union, countries have to issue debt in a joint currency over which they fully lack control, so

40. Kererū pigeons, of the species *Hemiphaga novaeseelandiae*, <u>can become intoxicated when they eat fermented fruit from the forest floor and, if they consume enough, may</u> fall from the trees where they roost.

   O   can become intoxicated when they eat fermented fruit from the forest floor and, if they consume enough, may

   O   can become intoxicated when they eat fermented fruit from the forest floor but, if they consume enough, may

   O   becoming intoxicated if they were to eat fermented fruit from the forest floor if they were to consume enough, and may

   O   can become intoxicated when it eats fermented fruit from the forest floor and, if it consumes enough, may

   O   can become intoxicated when they eat fermented fruit from the forest floor and, if they consume enough, then they may

41. Science fiction has been described as the genre that, by addressing the future, <u>that it concerns ideas of large scope rather than the ephemeral thoughts</u> and emotions of individuals.

   O   that it concerns ideas of large scope rather than the ephemeral thoughts

   O   that concerns ideas of large scope instead of the ephemeral thoughts

   O   concerns ideas of large scope rather than the ephemeral thoughts

   O   so concerns ideas of large scope instead of the ephemeral thinking

   O   it concerns ideas of large scope but not the ephemeral thoughts

Advanced Practice Set: Clauses and Connectors

42. Although staff at one fast-food chain, in an effort to encourage children to eat healthier, proposed that the company create a <u>vegetable taste</u> like bubblegum, the company's chief executive officer ultimately reported that children who had tried the food expressed confusion about its flavor.

    O   vegetable taste

    O   vegetable tastes

    O   taste for a vegetable

    O   vegetable that has a taste

    O   vegetable that tastes

43. During the latter stages of the insurrection, the revolution's leaders resorted to ever more violent means, including public execution of members of the upper class, <u>to establish their authority, and they suppressed</u> dissent ruthlessly.

    O   to establish their authority, and they suppressed

    O   that established their authority, and it suppressed

    O   of establishing their authority and to suppress

    O   to establish their authority, and they were suppressing

    O   so that their authority was established, and it suppressed

44. <u>Either stocks or bonds have advantages: stocks can increase in value and give investors more income over time, while bonds can not only provide predictable income but also are guarantees of</u> the return of investors' principal.

    O   Either stocks or bonds have advantages: stocks can increase in value and give investors more income over time, while bonds can not only provide predictable income but also are guarantees of

    O   Both stocks and bonds have advantages: stocks can increase in value and give investors more income over time, while bonds can not only provide predictable income but also guarantee

    O   Both stocks have advantages and so do bonds: stocks can increase in value and give investors more income over time, while bonds not only can provide predictable income but also guarantee

    O   Advantages are to be had from either stocks or from bonds: stocks can increase in value and give investors more income over time, while bonds can not only provide predictable income but also guarantee

    O   Both stocks and bonds have advantages: stocks can increase in value and give investors more income over time, while bonds can not only provide predictable income but also can guarantee

Answers and explanations follow on the next page. ▶ ▶ ▶

Answers and Explanations

Practice Set: Verbs

1. (D)

The underlined portion begins with the plural verb phrase "were justly praised." While there are many individual musicians, the recipient of the praise is the "string section," a singular noun. This creates a subject-verb agreement error. Eliminate **(A)**.

(D) is correct because it fixes the subject-verb agreement error by changing "were justly praised" to "was justly praised." **(B)** and **(C)** both contain the same subject-verb agreement error as **(A)**. **(E)** is incorrect because although the verb has been corrected, the plural pronoun "they" is still used to refer to the singular "string section." Read your choice back into the sentence to confirm:

The string section, which included more than 30 violinists and violists as well as more than a dozen cellists and bassists, <u>was justly praised for invoking tremendous passion</u> in last night's performance of Stravinsky's *Rite of Spring.*

2. (A)

The underlined portion begins with "had discovered," which is the past perfect tense. This tense is correctly used for past actions that happened prior to another action in the past. In this sentence, the discovery of Titan happened in 1655, and Galileo's discovery happened before that, as conveyed by the phrase "by the time." Furthermore, the modifying phrase describing Ganymede as being the largest moon in the solar system is correctly placed next to "Ganymede." There are no errors in the sentence, so **(A)** is correct.

(B) uses the correct verb tense, but it is incorrect for adding "which" after "Jupiter," making it seem as though Jupiter itself includes Ganymede, and for adding the unnecessary verb "being" after "Ganymede." **(C)** and **(D)** are incorrect because they use the future perfect tense for something that has already happened. **(E)** incorrectly uses present perfect tense for a discovery that happened over 300 years ago.

3. (C)

The underlined clause begins with the subject "several people" and the present perfect verb phrase "have designed." However, the act of designing occurred in the past and finished before another past event happened (Edison's receipt of his patent). Thus, the correct answer will contain the past perfect "had designed." Eliminate **(A)**.

(C) is correct because it fixes the verb tense error and introduces no other errors. **(B)** and **(E)** change the verb to "having" and "having been," respectively, eliminating the main verb and rendering the sentence incomplete. **(D)** is incorrect because it uses the present tense verb "receives," despite the fact that the rest of the sentence puts all actions in the past. Read your choice back into the sentence:

While Thomas Edison is often credited with inventing the incandescent light bulb, historians note that <u>several people had designed and created similar light bulbs before Edison received his patent</u>.

4. (D)

The verb in the underlined portion is "were," a plural verb that does not match the singular subject "the Rosetta Stone." The author needs to use the singular verb "was" in order to have subject-verb agreement. Eliminate **(A)**.

(D) is correct because it uses the singular tense "was" without changing the meaning of the rest of the sentence. **(B)** eliminates the verb altogether, resulting in a misplaced modifier that changes the sentence's meaning. **(C)** similarly creates a misplaced modifier that shifts the focus of the sentence from the stone to the Greek language. **(E)** is incorrect because the choice makes it sound like the Rosetta Stone itself was actively working to decipher hieroglyphs. Read your choice back into the sentence to confirm:

Discovered by a French soldier in 1799, the Rosetta Stone was inscribed with three distinct scripts in two languages, Egyptian and Greek, <u>and was instrumental in helping scholars decipher the hieroglyphs used by ancient Egyptians</u>.

Advanced Practice Set: Verbs

5. (C)

The underlined portion begins with the plural verb "are reviewed." The subject of this verb, however, is "the language," which is singular. Note that the subject cannot be "financial reports," since that is the object of the preposition "of" and the object of a preposition is never the subject. Eliminate (A).

(C) is correct because it properly uses the singular verb "is reviewed" and introduces no new errors. (B) is incorrect because it uses the present participle "being," creating a fragment. Also, the change from "reviewed carefully" to "a careful team" alters the meaning of the sentence. (D) is incorrect because it uses the past tense "was reviewed," which is inconsistent with the present tense used in the rest of the sentence. (E) is incorrect because it uses the past tense plural "were reviewed," which is inconsistent with the other verb tenses and with the singular subject. Check your answer by reading it back into the sentence:

Companies need to ensure that the language in all of their financial reports is reviewed carefully by a team of legal experts since any errors can lead to serious problems for employees as well as shareholders and other investors.

6. (B)

A vertical scan of the beginnings of the choices shows a mix of future, present, and past tense, so verb tense is at issue in this question. Since the author is discussing the number of bones in the human body—a fact that was, is, and will be true—the present tense is needed. Eliminate (A) with its future tense "will."

(B) properly uses the present tense verb "contains" and continues using the present tense in the latter phrases, which continue to discuss facts about bones. (C) uses the past tense "contained," and (E) repeats the error of the original with "will contain." Eliminate (D), which incorrectly uses the past tense verbs "fused" and "grew." Read your choice back into the sentence to confirm:

While the skeleton of a typical human adult contains 206 bones, that of a newborn human baby usually has

approximately 270, some of which fuse together as the baby's body grows.

7. (E)

The underlined portion starts with the singular verb "is," and a scan of the answer choices shows a choice between "is" and the plural "are." The thing that "is outweighed by the evidence" is other "evidence." Therefore, this singular verb is correct. However, there's also a comparison between the evidence for and against the existence of the Loch Ness monster. The first part of the comparison, "evidence that tends," is not underlined and so cannot be changed. The second, "evidence that supported," is also about evidence that exists in the present and so should also be in the present tense. Eliminate (A).

(E) is the only choice that corrects both issues. (B) and (C) incorrectly use "evidence . . . are." (D) introduces a parallelism error: "evidence that tends" is now compared with "evidence for supporting." To confirm your choice, read the sentence with (E) plugged in:

Scotland enjoys a robust tourism industry centered around the so-called Loch Ness monster; however, evidence that tends to support the existence of the monster, such as grainy photographs that purport to show the creature, is outweighed by evidence that supports the idea that there is no such monster.

Practice Set: Pronouns

8. (A)

The underlined portion begins with the verb "is." The subject of the verb is "company"; none of the information between commas about other organizations the company is cooperating with affects the fact that the subject is singular. Therefore, "is" is correct. The underlined portion also contains the singular pronoun "it," which is also correct to refer to the "company." The sentence is correct as written, making the answer (A).

Eliminate (B) and (C) on the basis of the first word, the plural verb "are." (D) uses the plural pronoun "they," but it is the singular pharmaceutical company that is transferring rights to manufacture certain drugs. (E) removes the subject of the dependent clause altogether, creating ambiguity around who will be transferring the rights; the original sentence is clear on this point. By using "would," (E) also introduces the idea that some condition must be met for the rights to be transferred, but that idea is not present in the sentence.

9.   (D)

The underlined portion contains two pronouns: "they" and "them." The plural pronoun "they" works well because it refers to the plural subject "critics." However, "them" is also a plural pronoun but inappropriately refers to the singular "Academy Award for Best Actor." Eliminate (A).

(D) is correct, replacing the problematic pronoun with a direct reference to "an Academy Award." (B) and (C) are incorrect because they still end with "them" in reference to a single award. (E) is incorrect because "automatically" should modify "classified," not "elite." To confirm, read the correct choice back into the sentence:

Film critics often cite the example of Nicolas Cage's winning the Academy Award for Best Actor as a reason that <u>actors should not automatically be classified as elite for winning an Academy Award</u>.

10.   (B)

The opening phrase in the underlined portion contains the singular pronoun "its." However, the pronoun refers to a plural <u>noun</u>: "town council members." Either "its" should be changed to *their* or "town council members" should be changed to *town council*. The underlined portion also ends with "when," which should be used only in reference to a time, not an event or a venue such as "public meetings." Eliminate (A).

(B) is correct, changing the singular "its" to the plural "their" and changing "when" to the more appropriate "at which." (C) and (D) are incorrect for, among other things, continuing to use "when" instead of "at which." (C) also pairs the singular "series" with the plural verb "were organized." By changing "organized" to "organizing," (D) also loses its main verb and becomes a fragment. (E) is incorrect because it continues to use the singular "its" to refer to the plural subject "members." To confirm the correct answer, read it back into the original sentence:

<u>As one step in their plan to engender greater goodwill in the community, town council members organized a series of public meetings at which</u> residents could air grievances about the opacity of decision making, a tendency to award contracts to cronies, and a failure to follow through on promised reforms.

Advanced Practice Set: Pronouns

11.   (D)

The underlined phrase refers to "snowflakes," a plural noun. The use of "they" is therefore appropriate. However, at the very end, the singular verb "constitutes" is used. Don't be misled by the modifying phrase about ice. The singular verb "constitutes" does not agree with its plural subject "they." Eliminate (A).

(D) is correct. It retains the plural nouns and pronouns ("they" and "all"), and it correctly changes the verb at the end to the plural "constitute." (B) and (C) are incorrect because they change the pronoun to "it," which does not properly represent the plural "snowflakes." (E) is incorrect for changing the final pronoun to "it" and for containing the incorrect phrase "all has" instead of the proper "all have." Read your choice back into the sentence:

The visiting lecturer presented some lesser-known facts about snowflakes: for example, <u>they are not white, all have exactly six sides, not all have a unique pattern, and they—along with ice—constitute</u> about 75 percent of Earth's freshwater.

12.   (D)

The underlined portion starts with the pronoun "them," which ambiguously refers to either the "defense attorneys" or the "jurors" earlier in the sentence. Logically, the pronoun should refer to the jurors, so the correct answer should eliminate the ambiguous pronoun. Eliminate (A).

(D) is correct because it eliminates the ambiguous pronoun and replaces it with "the jurors," while using the correct idiomatic expression "prohibited the jurors from discussing." This choice also correctly uses the past perfect tense at the end of the underlined portion. (B) changes the verb phrase at the end to a present tense form ("is concluded"). **(C)** is incorrect because it does not eliminate the ambiguous pronoun "them." **(E)** is incorrect because it reads "prohibited the jurors to discuss" instead of the idiomatically correct "prohibited the jurors from discussing." Plug your choice back into the sentence to confirm it reads correctly:

The defense attorneys wanted to interview the jurors following the guilty verdict, but a gag order issued by the judge prohibited <u>the jurors from discussing the trial even after it had concluded</u>.

13. (B)

The underlined portion begins with the pronoun "it," which does not clearly refer back to any particular noun in the sentence. If anything, it seems to refer to the subject, which is a dictionary. However, it's not logical to describe a dictionary as including almonds, cashews, etc. Eliminate **(A)**.

(B) is correct. By substituting the noun "definition" for the pronoun, it clearly expresses the idea that the listed items do not fit the category of nuts. **(C)** and **(E)** are incorrect because they use the pronoun "them" or "they," respectively, without having a plural noun the pronoun could logically represent. **(D)** is incorrect for the same reason as the original: the pronoun "it," now placed at the end of the sentence, has no clear antecedent. Read your choice back into the sentence:

One often-referenced online dictionary defines *nut* as "a hard-shelled dry fruit or seed with a separable rind or shell and interior kernel," indicating that <u>it does not include almonds, cashews, peanuts, pistachios, or walnuts</u>.

Practice Set: Modification

14. (D)

The underlined portion comes immediately after an opening modifying phrase. That opening phrase describes Edgar Degas, not his paintings. Therefore, the subject after the comma should be Degas himself, not his paintings. Eliminate **(A)**.

(D) is correct, fixing the modification error and correctly making Degas the subject of the sentence. **(B)** and

(E) are incorrect because they start with "Edgar Degas's paintings" and "the interior scenes," respectively, neither of which is described by the opening phrase. **(C)** fixes the modification issue at the beginning but introduces a different error. The pronoun "which" refers to "landscapes," which are then illogically compared to other Impressionists. It's Degas himself, not his landscapes, who was unlike other Impressionists. Read your choice back into the sentence:

Despite being called one of the founding members of the Impressionist movement, <u>Edgar Degas publicly rejected the label and, unlike most other Impressionists, often depicted interior scenes in his paintings instead of landscapes</u>.

15. (B)

The underlined portion begins with incorrect phrasing: the noun form of "to produce" is "production," not "the producing of." Eliminate **(A)**. In addition, the last modifying phrase begins with "which," which seems to refer to "dingoes," but dingoes are unlikely elements of a courtship ritual. This phrase needs to follow "songs."

(B), the correct answer, starts with a simple verb phrase ("producing elaborate songs"), and the modifying phrase beginning with "which" refers to the songs. The modifying phrase includes a clear compound action presented in parallel form: the songs "are . . . used" in the ritual and "can include" mimicry. Eliminate **(C)** for starting with the pronoun "their" to refer to the singular noun "lyrebird." In **(D)**, "which" still refers to "dingoes." **(E)** can be eliminated for using the plural pronoun "they" to refer to the singular "lyrebird. As a final test, read **(B)** back into the original sentence:

The superb lyrebird is known for <u>producing elaborate songs, which are often used as part of a complex courtship ritual and can include astounding mimicry of other birds and even non-bird animals such as dingoes</u>.

16. (A)

The non-underlined part of the sentence is a modifying phrase describing what someone believed; "high school student Bob Heft" is that person, so the underlined portion starts off correctly. The next modifying phrase is "for a history class project," an adverbial phrase saying why Bob designed the flag, and it is properly positioned next to the verb it modifies. After the semicolon, the next complete thought also begins with an introductory modifying phrase, "approved by President Eisenhower," which is correctly followed by the thing Eisenhower approved, "that design." The sentence contains no errors of grammar or logic, and (**A**) is correct.

By replacing the semicolon with a comma, (**B**) creates a run-on. The two independent clauses must be connected with either a semicolon or a coordinating conjunction. Eliminate (**C**) for beginning with "the new American flag;" the flag is not capable of "believing" anything. (**D**) and (**E**) begin correctly, but these choices not only end in passive voice with "the new American flag was what that design became" but also introduce a modification error in the second clause. President Eisenhower approved the flag *design*, not "the new American flag." Eliminate (**D**) and (**E**).

17. (D)

The opening clause of the sentence is a modifying phrase, so what comes after the comma must be the noun that phrase modifies. The modifier describes something that consists of "dreamscapes," but the underlined segment begins with the name of a person, H. R. Giger. Instead, it should begin with Giger's artwork. Eliminate (**A**).

(**D**) corrects the modification error and properly uses the past tense verb "was" at the end of the underlined portion, making this choice the correct one. With the present tense "is" at the end, (**B**) introduces a verb tense error. Since the verb is used to describe an event that happened in the past (artwork used in a 1979 movie), the past tense is appropriate. (**C**) not only contains the initial modification error but also incorrectly changes the verb at the end of the underlined segment to the present tense. (**E**) incorrectly pairs the past tense verb "inspired" with the present tense verb "view." Since the actions occur in the same time frame, the verb tenses should match. Confirm (**D**) by reading it into the sentence:

Consisting of surreal, nightmarish dreamscapes, <u>the artwork of H. R. Giger often inspires feelings of unease and dread in those who view it, and these reactions are</u>

<u>why it was</u> chosen as the basis for the design of the title creature in the 1979 horror movie *Alien.*

Advanced Practice Set: Modification

18. (D)

In the original sentence, the start of the underlined portion "the identification of planets learned by computers" is ambiguous. The intention of the sentence is that computers can learn to *identify* planets, but the sentence could be read as saying the computers are learning the planets. Moreover, the sentence states that computers found instances of recorded signals "*in* the telescope," which is illogical. A telescope is used to make observations and gather data, and it's in these data that the computer could find signals from planets. Eliminate (**A**).

(**D**) addresses both issues and is correct. In addition, (**D**) properly places the modifier "known as exoplanets" close to "planets," the word it is modifying. (**B**) still has the computers finding signals in the telescope; eliminate. When read in context with what follows the underlined portion, (**C**) introduces another modification error: the "signals from beyond our solar system" are not "known as exoplanets." (**E**) corrects the errors, but it uses the passive construction "learned by computers." Active voice is preferred on the GMAT, and (**D**) has the subject "computers" directly performing the verb "learn." Confirm (**D**) is correct by reading it back into the sentence:

The recently discovered planet Kepler-90i was found via machine learning, a form of artificial intelligence in which <u>computers learn to identify planets by finding in data from the Kepler telescope instances of recorded signals from planets</u> beyond our solar system, known as exoplanets.

19. (E)

The underlined text before the first comma is a modifying phrase, so check whether it appropriately modifies whatever comes right after that comma: "Closely interrelated concepts, a change" involves an illogical modification of "a change" by "closely interrelated concepts." Eliminate (**A**). Continue reading and identify the "closely interrelated concepts" to assist in evaluating the remaining choices. The last non-underlined phrase tells you those concepts are macroeconomics and microeconomics.

(E) correctly modifies the two concepts and logically connects with the non-underlined portion. The opening clause properly and logically introduces the relationship between the two fields of study. This choice is correct. **(B)** correctly modifies the two concepts, but it introduces a modification error with "affect microeconomic transactions numerously." The adverb "numerously" cannot be used to modify "affect"; eliminate this choice. **(C)** illogically says "accumulation . . . and focus" are the related concepts; eliminate. **(D)** does not make it clear which are the "closely related concepts": it seems to be connecting "a change" and "an accumulation," not microeconomics and macroeconomics. Confirm your choice by reading **(E)** back into the sentence:

A change in macroeconomic policy tends to affect numerous microeconomic transactions, and the accumulation of microeconomic decisions typically influences the focus of macroeconomic studies; since the concepts of macroeconomics and microeconomics are closely related, any economics curriculum requires considerable study of both macroeconomic and microeconomic concepts.

20. (C)

The sentence starts with a modifying phrase ("Noting the fact that . . . "), so the noun that this phrase is intended to modify must appear immediately after the comma. In this case, the teacher is the one who is noting something, so it is incorrect for the clause after the comma to start with "their discussion." Eliminate **(A)**.

Correct choice **(C)** fixes the modification issue and is more concise by eliminating "the fact that" in favor of just "that." **(B)** contains the same initial modifier error as **(A)**, and it makes it seem as though the science report was on the topic of semicolon usage; eliminate it. **(D)** is correct but includes the unnecessarily wordy phrase "the fact that"; eliminate this choice. **(E)** seems more concise, but by deleting "they were," this choice introduces a new ambiguity: was the teacher "Noting . . . while writing" or the students "arguing . . . while writing"? Eliminate **(E)**. Read **(C)** into the sentence to confirm:

Noting that the three students were arguing over the proper use of semicolons while they were writing a joint science report, the teacher interrupted their discussion to give them a quick lesson on punctuation.

Practice Set: Parallelism

21. (C)

The underlined portion contains a list, the items of which are not in parallel form. The first two items of the list are in the same noun-verb form ("days shorten," "temperature drops"), while the third item is not ("breaking down of the . . . "). Additionally, the first and third items begin with "the," while the second does not. Eliminate **(A)**.

(C) is correct because each item uses the same basic noun-verb form ("days shorten," "temperature drops," "chlorophyll . . . breaks down"), and the definite article "the" appears before each item. **(B)** fixes the problem with "the," but the verb in the third item, "is to reveal," is not parallel with "shorten" and "drops" from the first two items. **(D)** changes the form of all three items, but the third item is still not parallel with the first two. **(E)** fails to fix the problem with "the," using "the" to introduce the first two items but not the third. Check your answer by reading it into the sentence:

Although carotene and xanthophyll are present in leaves throughout the year, these pigments are not usually visible until the days shorten, the temperature drops, and the chlorophyll in the leaves breaks down, revealing the yellow and orange colors.

22. (A)

Because the underlined portion is an element in a list, determine whether that list has a parallel structure. The list is "where students . . . how frequently students . . . and which college stressors . . . " As written, the list has parallel structure, with each item beginning with a word—"where," "how," and "which"—that could begin a question (an interrogative adverb, if you're curious) followed by a noun—"students," "students," and "college stressors," respectively. Other elements worth checking are the modifying words "most commonly" before the verb "contribute" and the idiomatic usage of "contribute to." All are used properly, and **(A)** is correct.

(B) incorrectly follows "which" with the verb "are." This choice adds a verb to one item in the list, violating parallel structure. **(C)**, **(D)**, and **(E)** incorrectly begin with nouns. These choices all break the parallel structure of the list.

23. (E)

The underlined portion begins with a list of three items, all of which must exhibit parallel structure. However, the first item is a noun phrase ("a toss of a coin"), while the other two items are gerund (-*ing*) phrases ("playing a round of poker" and "drawing straws"). Eliminate **(A)**.

(E) is correct because it changes the first item in the list to "tossing a coin," which matches the form of the other items in the list. **(B)** changes the first item in the list, but that item is still not parallel to the other two. The word "the" is unique to this item, as is the use of a prepositional phrase ("tossing *of a* coin"). **(C)** is incorrect because it adds "would" to the verb at the end of the underlined portion, making the sentence sound hypothetical even though the described methods of deciding an election have actually been used "in recent decades." **(D)** has the same parallelism problem as the original sentence and introduces a verb tense error. Confirm **(E)** by reading it back into the sentence:

Although deciding the outcome of an election by chance may seem antiquated, tossing a coin, playing a round of poker, and drawing straws are all methods that have been used in recent decades to determine the winner of a deadlocked election somewhere in the United States.

Advanced Practice Set: Parallelism

24. (D)

The underlined text includes part of a list, so examine its elements for parallelism. The first items in the list are nouns, the "grams" of protein and the "amino acids," so each succeeding item must also be a noun. While "vitamins" works well in the list, "is a source" is verb clause. Since **(A)** contains a parallelism error, it can be eliminated.

(D) is correct because it introduces the conjunction "and" before "vitamins" to indicate the final item in the list. Since "vitamins B12 and D" now ends the list, what follows, connected by another "and," is the second part of a compound verb (the clause is now "since this food *contains* [list] and *is* a source"). **(B)** is incorrect because the final element of the list is a verb phrase ("including various other nutrients") instead of a noun. **(C)** and **(E)** contain similar parallelism errors as they do not complete the list with a noun. Read your choice back into the sentence:

According to one nutrition consultant, healthy adults should not hesitate to consume eggs, since this food contains six grams of high-quality protein, all nine essential amino acids, and vitamins B12 and D and is a source of various other nutrients.

25. (C)

The underlined portion contains the phrase "not only," which is part of the idiomatic conjunction *not only X . . . but also Y.* The elements that follow both "not only" and "but also" must be in parallel form. In the non-underlined portion of the sentence, "but also" is followed by a noun, so look for a noun to also follow "not only." Eliminate **(A)** because the element that follows "not only" is the verb "considered," which in turn is modified by the adverb "often."

(C) is correct because shifting the position of "not only" now means this conjunction is followed by the noun "novel," preceded by a modifying phrase. The conjunction's structure is now "not only . . . novel but also . . . novel." **(B)** is incorrect because "not only" is again followed by the verb "considered." **(D)** and **(E)** are both incorrect because the element that follows "not only" is the verb "is considered."

Read your choice back into the sentence:

In Cold Blood is often considered not only Truman Capote's most popular novel but also the first "nonfiction novel," a literary genre that uses techniques of fictional storytelling to depict actual people and events.

26. (E)

The construction "*both* introspective explorations . . ." needs to be completed by *and* to be idiomatically correct, and the *and* must be followed by a noun that is parallel with "explorations." Thus, "as well as" is incorrect, and so is "subverting." Moreover, the two halves of the phrase "of cultural identity and feminine" should be in parallel form, but since "identity" is a noun and "feminine" is an adjective, this phrase is incorrect as written. Eliminate (**A**).

(**E**) replaces "as well as" with "and." This choice also correctly uses the noun "subversions" after "and," making the *both X and Y* construction parallel. Furthermore, "femininity" is parallel with "cultural identity." (**B**) is incorrect because it uses the verb "subverted" instead of a noun, and "being feminine" is not parallel with "cultural identity." (**C**) is incorrect because "that was feminine" is not parallel with the first half of the phrase "of cultural identity." (**D**) is incorrect since it contains "as well as" instead of "and." Read your choice back into the sentence:

The self-portraits of Frida Kahlo can be considered both introspective explorations of a psyche that ranged free, unbounded by historical notions of cultural identity and <u>femininity, and subversions of</u> traditional European portraiture.

Practice Set: Comparisons

27. (B)

The underlined text both follows from and includes the comparison phrase "larger than," so check that the two comparisons are both logical and in parallel form. The first comparison is between the blue whale's *body* and the sperm *whale* and is thus not logical. Similarly, the second comparison, as written, states that the brain of the sperm whale is actually larger than the largest animal—another illogical comparison. Eliminate (**A**).

(**B**) is correct. By including "that of" in both comparisons, this choice logically compares the blue whale's body to "that of the sperm whale" and the sperm whale's brain to "that of the blue whale." Eliminate (**C**) because it resolves the first comparison error but not the second one. (**D**) commits the same error in the first comparison

as the original sentence. Moreover, the pronoun "its" would have to represent "blue whale's body," so the sentence says in effect that the blue whale's body's brain is larger than the blue whale—an impossibility. (**E**) is incorrect because the omission of *than X* from the second comparison leaves the comparison unclear; the implication is that the sperm whale's brain is larger than the blue whale's body, which is larger than the sperm whale's body. Read (**B**) back into the sentence:

As an example of the seeming paradoxes encountered by the student of the natural world, consider the largest animal on Earth, the blue whale: while the blue whale's body is indeed larger than <u>that of the sperm whale, the sperm whale's brain is actually larger than that of the blue whale</u>.

28. (A)

The original sentence makes a comparison between "international pressures" and "constraints," two elements that are both logically comparable and parallel, so (**A**) is correct. When confronted with an unusual sentence construction, rearranging the sentence to fit a more typical format can make it easier to evaluate the different choices: "The constraints that . . . are no less significant than international pressures."

Eliminate (**B**) as it unnecessarily adds "the things" to refer to "the constraints." Eliminate (**C**) because it changes the meaning of the sentence by leaving out the idea that the constraints are equally significant. (**D**) is incorrect as it introduces an illogical comparison between "significance" and "constraints." (**E**) is incorrect for a similar reason as (**B**), since it unnecessarily adds the pronoun "what" to refer to "the constraints."

29. (D)

The underlined portion incorrectly uses the word "than" to contrast two nouns. In this sentence, the *-ing* words "establishing" and "setting" are verb forms that function as nouns here, so the comparison needs to use *from*, not "than." Eliminate (**A**)

(**D**) is correct because it uses the phrase "different from" to contrast "establishing" and "setting." (**B**) is incorrect because it repeats the mistake found in the original sentence and introduces a further issue by making the comparison unparallel. **(C)** is incorrect because it eliminates "setting," creating a nonparallel contrast between the gerund "establishing" and the simple noun "goals." Like **(B)**, **(E)** violates parallelism by contrasting "establishing" with "the setting of." Confirm **(D)** by reading it back into the sentence:

Establishing goals for a nonprofit organization is often different <u>from setting</u> goals for a profit-making enterprise because the stakeholders of the former may be more varied.

Advanced Practice Set: Comparisons

30. (C)

This sentence compares ways of reducing a population of insects. The comparison is created with the words "most easily . . . than" in the underlined portion. The correct construct for a comparison, however, is *more . . . than*, not *most . . . than*. Note that the comparison also contains a parallelism error, since "applying pesticides" is not in the same form as "applications." For both reasons, eliminate **(A)**.

(C) changes "most" to "more" and fixes the parallelism error, making it correct. **(B)** fails to change "most" to "more." **(D)** uses an adjective, "easier," to modify the verb phrase "is done." The correct way to modify the verb phrase is with an adverb or adverb phrase, such as "more easily." **(E)** is incorrect because one thing is done *more easily than* another, not *more easily rather than* another. Read **(C)** back into the sentence to confirm that it is correct:

Reducing the population of Japanese beetles is done <u>more easily by applying pesticides to turf-dwelling young larvae in late summer than</u> to mature larvae in spring or adult beetles at any time of year.

31. (D)

The underlined portion contains the comparison "more . . . than does any restaurant." Since Penelope's Pancake Palace is itself a restaurant in the city, the comparison as written claims in part that Penelope's offers a more diverse selection of food than does Penelope's. This is an illogical comparison, so eliminate **(A)**. Note that the sentence also contains a parallelism

error centered on the words "as well as." If read "with an elaborate menu . . . as well as serving . . . ," the sentence joins a noun ("menu") with an *-ing* verb ("serving"). If read "with an elaborate menu featuring . . . as well as serving . . . ," the sentence is illogical, as menus don't serve food.

(D) is correct because it fixes the comparison error by changing "any restaurant" to "any other restaurant," thereby excluding Penelope's from the second part of the comparison. It also corrects the parallelism error by joining two nouns with "as well as" ("menu . . . as well as . . . breakfast fare"). **(B)** is incorrect because it repeats the same comparison error from the original sentence. **(C)** corrects the comparison error but retains the parallelism error. **(E)** is incorrect because a comparison started with the word "more" needs to be completed with the word "than." The proper construction is *more . . . than*, not *more . . . as*, as this choice is worded. Read **(D)** back into the sentence to confirm that it is correct:

With an elaborate menu featuring innovative dishes from a variety of world cuisines as well <u>as its signature breakfast fare, Penelope's Pancake Palace, an established downtown eatery, offers a more diverse selection of food than does any other</u> restaurant in the city.

32. (E)

Because the relative pronoun "which" refers to the noun that immediately precedes the comma, **(A)** is incorrect as it illogically compares a sum of money, "$123 billion," to "the previous year."

(E) is correct since "an amount" and "the previous year's figure," are both quantifiable values and are therefore logically comparable. Because "which" refers to "123 billion," **(B)** seems to say, nonsensically, that $123 billion is 17 percent higher than $123 billion was the previous year. **(C)** is incorrect because the use of the verb "was" is not only unnecessary but is also not parallel with the last part of the sentence, which does not use the verb. **(D)** fails to fix the illogical comparison; because it compares "an amount" to "the previous year," it is incorrect.

Read your selection back into the sentence to confirm:

The United States' trade deficit with China rose in 2003 to $123 billion, <u>an amount that was 17 percent higher than the previous year's figure</u> and more than ten times the U.S.-China trade deficit in 1998.

Practice Set: Usage and Idioms

33. (E)

The first words of the underlined portion, "as well as," are connected to the word "both" earlier in the sentence to form "both . . . as well as." The correct idiom is *both . . . and*. Eliminate (A).

(E) uses the correct idiomatic form "both the Manhattan Project . . . and the Rogers Commission" and is therefore correct. (B) makes the correct change from "as well as" to "and" but adds the word "also," which is redundant. It also changes "which" to "that," implying that there was more than one Rogers Commission and the author is referring to this one in particular. (C) is incorrect because it adds the word "on." The word "on" appears earlier in the sentence before the *both . . . and* idiom, but the idiom requires that the items *after* the words *both* and *and* be in parallel form. Here, "the Manhattan Project" is not parallel to "on the Rogers Commission." (D) corrects the idiom, but it changes the past tense "investigated" to the present tense "is investigating," which is inappropriate for describing work that was done in the past. Read (E) back into the sentence to confirm that it is correct:

In addition to winning the Nobel Prize in Physics for his accomplishments in quantum electrodynamics, Richard Feynman worked on both the Manhattan Project in Los Alamos <u>and the Rogers Commission, which investigated</u> the space shuttle *Challenger* disaster in 1986.

34. (C)

The underlined portion begins with the words "at least as," which should be paired idiomatically with *as* (*at least as X as Y*). However, they are incorrectly paired with "than" ("at least as . . . than"), so eliminate (A). Note that "than" appears in the unchangeable non-underlined portion of the sentence, so "at least as" must be changed to something that correctly connects to "than."

(C) is correct, as it changes "at least as" to "no less," which does pair with "than" (e.g., *I am no less interested in pizza than in ice cream*). (B) is incorrect because it contains the same idiom error ("at least as . . . than") as the original sentence. (D) correctly changes "at least as" to "no less," but it also changes "for businesses to focus," which states the first important action that businesses need to take, to "that businesses focusing," which would describe which businesses the author is referring to. It leaves the sentence without an active verb telling what these businesses need to do. (E) is incorrect because "as important" still needs to be paired with "as," not "than." Read (C) back into the sentence to confirm that it is correct:

To boost the nation's economy, it is <u>no less important for businesses to focus</u> on developing worker productivity than it is for them to hire new employees.

35. (D)

The underlined text does not contain any errors of grammar or meaning, so look for stylistic issues. A quick glance at the choices tells you "faster than" is a more concise way to say "more quickly in comparison to." Eliminate (A).

(D) is concise and forms the comparisons properly; this is the correct answer. (B) is the most concise, but it is incorrect because it fails to complete the comparison between hot water and cold water. (C) unnecessarily introduces "would." (E) makes the meaning of the original sentence ambiguous; "the opposite is true" could mean that maybe hot water doesn't freeze faster than cold water. Eliminate (E). Read (D) back into the sentence to confirm:

The "Mpemba effect" refers to observation that, under some conditions, hot water can <u>freeze faster than cold water; the researchers who investigated this effect also observed that cold water can sometimes heat faster than warm water</u> and named that phenomenon the "inverse Mpemba effect."

Advanced Practice Set: Usage and Idioms

36. (C)

The verb "credited" in the non-underlined portion must be accompanied by either *to* or *with*. Use *to* to focus on a cause, and use *with* to focus on a result. For example, you would *credit a high score to your good study habits* but *credit your good study habits with your earning a high score*. In this question, the entrepreneurs are crediting the website *with* helping their business succeed, so "to" is incorrect. In addition, the correct phrase is *neither . . . nor*, not "neither . . . or" as written here. Eliminate (A).

(C) uses the expression "credited . . . with" and uses "neither . . . nor" properly; this is the correct answer. Eliminate (B) for the idiomatically incorrect "credited . . . toward." Although (D)'s "credited . . . to" is a properly structured idiom, in this sentence the viability of the business is the result, not the cause, of using the website. The intention of the sentence requires "credited . . . with"; eliminate. (E) uses the proper idiom with "credited" but retains the "neither . . . or" construction. Read (C) back into the sentence to confirm:

The entrepreneurs credited the website that helped owners of small businesses find suppliers <u>with keeping their new enterprise viable when cash flow was neither ample nor steady</u>.

37. (C)

When analyzing this sentence, it is helpful to mentally delete the supplemental information between commas. The word "for" at the beginning of the underlined portion is part of the phrase "required . . . for taking." However, saying *X is required for Y* suggests that you need X in order to have Y. That doesn't logically work in this sentence. To make it clear that the volunteers must take the course, the sentence should read *required . . . to take*. Eliminate (A).

Correct choice (C) replaces "for" with "to" and "taking" with "take." Eliminate (B); it uses "for" instead of "to" and suggests that it doesn't matter who takes the training, as long as it's taken. (D) properly uses "to" but unnecessarily puts the action in the past, and the word "of" is idiomatically incorrect. (E) changes "for" to

"of," which is still incorrect. Read the correct choice back into the sentence:

All volunteers who wish to be judges for the annual county fair baking competition are required, regardless of whether or not they have prior experience, <u>to take a food handler course</u>.

38. (D)

The word "if" in the underlined part of this sentence signals a hypothetical situation, so you must use "were" and "would." "Would achieve" is correct, but "will raise" is not. Rule out (A).

(D) correctly uses both "would achieve" and "if Congress were to raise." (B) and (C) are incorrect because "will achieve" should be "would achieve." (E)'s "if Congress were raising," incorrectly shifts the verb to present tense; the reduction in gasoline consumption depends on a future action. Confirm (D) by reading it back into the sentence:

The United States <u>would achieve a 10 percent reduction in gasoline consumption if Congress were to raise</u> fuel economy standards to 31.3 miles per gallon for passenger cars and to 24.5 miles per gallon for light trucks.

Practice Set: Clauses and Connectors

39. (C)

"Due to . . . therefore" is a redundant way to indicate cause and effect. Also, no logical or grammatical connection is established between the clause starting "therefore" and the one starting "that nation." (A) is incorrect.

In (C), the connecting word "because" establishes the first clause as stating a cause, and the connecting word "if" establishes the second clause as a condition. Using these logical connectors with the first two clauses sets up the clause starting with "that nation . . . " as the main clause. (C) is correct. (B) uses "as" after the comma; this word can mean either "because" or "while," but either way, it fails to logically connect these clauses. When you read (D) back into the sentence, you get "causing investors become nervous"; the correct phrasing is "causing investors *to* become nervous." (E) also fails when read back into sentence. The "so" at the end sets up the second clause as an independent clause that ends with "country," and then, without a further connector, the final clause "that . . . fear" makes the sentence a run-on. Confirm that (C) is correct by reading it back into the sentence:

Because countries in a monetary union must issue debt in a joint currency over which they lack full control, if investors become nervous about the financial health of a country, that nation may not be able to finance its debt at the same rate enjoyed by its neighbors and thus will experience the liquidity crisis that investors fear.

40. (A)

The underlined text begins with the main verb of the clause; "can become" is used appropriately with the subject, "pigeons." Later in the sentence, the conditional clause "if they consume enough" is placed appropriately, and the plural pronoun "they" clearly refers to the "pigeons." The compound predicate "can become . . . and . . . may fall" is parallel, and both verbs are in the correct simple present tense to describe actions that are generally true. The conjunction "and" expresses the correct relationship between the two actions. (A) is correct.

(B) replaces the conjunction "and" with "but." This is incorrect because the fact that the pigeons become intoxicated and the fact that sometimes they fall out of the trees should be joined by a continuation word, not a contrast word. With "becoming . . . and may," (C) is not parallel and loses the main verb of the sentence. (D) replaces the plural pronoun "they" with the singular "it," which doesn't correctly refer to the "pigeons." In (E), the "then they" is redundant.

41. (C)

The clause starting "that it concerns ideas" and continuing to the end of the sentence describes the genre of science fiction. Since the non-underlined part of the sentence before the comma already has a "that," there is no need for another "that" after the comma or for the pronoun "it." (A) is incorrect.

(C) eliminates both redundant pronouns and uses proper parallel structure to compare "ideas . . . rather than . . . thoughts and emotions." This is the correct answer. Eliminate (B) and (E) for starting with "that" and "it," respectively. (D) uses "so" improperly and

changes "thoughts" to "thinking," which is not parallel with "ideas" or "emotions." Confirm (C) by reading it back into the sentence:

Science fiction has been described as the genre that, by addressing the future, concerns ideas of large scope rather than the ephemeral thoughts and emotions of individuals.

Advanced Practice Set: Clauses and Connectors

42. (E)

Read the entirety of the sentence to understand that the vegetable in the underlined text is, in this context, a food being created to taste like bubblegum. However, as written, the sentence inappropriately makes "vegetable" the subject that tastes something and not a food with a certain taste. The confusion is due to a connector error—the author doesn't establish the correct relationship between the two underlined words. Furthermore, the underlined text contains a subject-verb agreement issue, because "vegetable" is a singular subject while "taste" is a plural verb. Eliminate (A).

(E) is correct. This choice establishes the proper relationship between the two underlined words and corrects the subject-verb disagreement. (B) corrects the subject-verb agreement error but does not fix the connection problem. (C) is incorrect because it introduces an unspecified flavor that is being created for a vegetable that is "like bubblegum." Eliminate (D); even though it fixes the errors, (E) is more concise. Read the correct choice back into the sentence:

Although staff at one fast-food chain, in an effort to encourage children to eat healthier, proposed that the company create a vegetable that tastes like bubblegum, the company's chief executive officer ultimately reported that children who had tried the food expressed confusion about its flavor.

43. (A)

The revolution's leaders committed violent acts for the purpose of establishing their authority—"to establish their authority"—and they also suppressed dissent. The infinitive form "to establish" is correct, the plural pronouns "their" and "they" correctly refer to "leaders," and "suppressed" is in the correct past tense to be parallel with "resorted" in the first clause. The various elements of the sentence are logically connected to convey the intended meaning, and there are no errors. **(A)** is correct.

The pronoun "it" in **(B)** is both ambiguous and the incorrect number; "it" could refer to either "leaders" or "means," but both of these nouns are plural. Eliminate **(B)**. In **(C)**, "resorted" and "to suppress" are not parallel. In **(D)**, "were suppressing" is a progressive tense that would be appropriate only to discuss an action that was ongoing when another action occurred; in this case, the suppression happened in the same time frame as the resorting to violence. **(E)** has multiple issues: "so that their authority was established" is wordy and unnecessarily passive, and "it" refers to the plural "leaders."

44. (B)

The underlined text contains two issues. "Either . . . or" means one of the items in the pair, but not both, is the topic of the sentence, so the first clause before the colon indicates that either stocks or bonds, but not both, has advantages. However, what follows the colon describes advantages of both types of investments. Therefore, the "either . . . or" conjunction is an illogical connector. The construction "not only . . . but also" requires that what follows each part be in parallel form. Here, the author has written "not only provide . . . but also are guarantees of," which is not parallel. Eliminate **(A)**.

(B) addresses both issues and is correct. It properly opens with "Both . . . and" and uses parallel structure for "not only provide . . . but also guarantee." **(C)**'s "Both stocks have advantages and so do bonds" interrupts the structure of the plural subject ("stocks and bonds") with the verb ("have advantages"), so this choice is incorrect. Eliminate **(D)** for also using "either . . . or." **(E)** has "bonds *can not only provide* predictable income *but also can guarantee*"; because "can" appears before the "not only . . . but also" construction, that word applies to both "provide" and "guarantee" and should not be repeated. Read **(B)** into the sentence to confirm it's correct:

Both stocks and bonds have advantages: stocks can increase in value and give investors more income over time, while bonds can not only provide predictable income but also guarantee the return of investors' principal.

CHAPTER 21

SENTENCE CORRECTION QUESTIONS: PUTTING IT ALL TOGETHER

LEARNING OBJECTIVES

- Recognize immediately the format of a Sentence Correction question and apply the Kaplan Method for Sentence Correction
- Determine quickly which grammatical issues are in play in the original sentence and the answer choices and eliminate wrong choices
- Evaluate your performance on Sentence Correction questions

This quiz is designed to give you practice with a mix of Sentence Correction questions, just like the variety of Sentence Correction questions you'll see on Test Day. Take this quiz after you have studied the different types of grammar and usage issues that show up in Sentence Correction and practiced applying the Kaplan Method for Sentence Correction.

How to Take This Quiz

By the time you take this quiz, you are hopefully well on your way to mastery of Sentence Correction, so set a timer. Give yourself 1 minute per question. So if you do all 15 questions in this set at once, set the timer for 15 minutes; if you decide to do fewer questions than that in one sitting, set the timer accordingly.

Make sure to use the steps of the Kaplan Method on every question. Students are often drawn into reading through the original sentence and all the choices from beginning to end, giving every word and phrase equal weight. Instead, use a mental checklist of GMAT-tested errors, based on the errors taught in the previous chapter, to focus your reading on potential problems with the sentence.

Furthermore, remember that on Test Day, you can't skip forward and back between questions, so challenge yourself to do the questions in order.

After you've finished the quiz and are reviewing the explanations, make sure you can explain why each wrong answer is incorrect. Being able to clearly identify the errors of grammar and usage in the four wrong choices will help you avoid picking them.

In addition, if you missed a question, understand *why* you missed it. There is always a reason! The Kaplan Method can be a useful checklist to diagnose where you went wrong.

- Were you unable to identify the error in the original sentence or recognize that there was no error?

- Did you have difficulty scanning the answer choices and grouping them in a meaningful way?

- When seeking to eliminate choices, did you have to rely on what "sounded wrong" rather than being able to point to an error that definitely made the choice wrong?

If you know why you missed a question, you can avoid making that error again.

Above all, be patient with yourself. If you make a mistake, feeling bad about it will not improve your score. Just learn from it and make a plan to address whatever skill or knowledge you still need through more study and practice.

Sentence Correction Quiz

(Answers and explanations are at the end of the chapter.)

1. <u>The private companies that managed airport screening during the twentieth century</u> allowed travelers to bring a considerable variety of items through the security checkpoint, did not focus as much on travelers' physical or behavioral characteristics as on security risk factors, and did not maintain terrorism watch lists.

   ○ The private companies that managed airport screening during the twentieth century

   ○ Managing airport screening during the twentieth century, there were private companies that

   ○ Private companies during the twentieth century, which managed airport screening,

   ○ During the twentieth century, the airport screening that was managed by private companies

   ○ Private companies managed airport screening during the twentieth century, which

2. While the *deus ex machina*, a plot device involving a sudden and unlikely resolution to a seemingly unsolvable problem, has often been ridiculed for being contrived and unartistic, <u>they have, on occasion, been used effectively, according to some critics</u>.

   ○ they have, on occasion, been used effectively, according to some critics

   ○ they have occasionally been used effectively, according to some critics

   ○ it occasionally, according to some critics, has been used effectively

   ○ according to some critics, and effectively, as it has been occasionally used

   ○ it has, according to some critics, occasionally being used effectively

3. Inspired by the circumstances he witnessed and documented during the Polish-Soviet War of 1920, Isaac Babel wrote *Red Cavalry*, a short story collection that is filled, as <u>are many of Babel's writings, of</u> brutal and often horrific depictions of war.

   ○ are many of Babel's writings, of

   ○ are many of Babel's writings, with

   ○ Babel did in many of his writings, of

   ○ many of Babel's writings did, with

   ○ was done in many of Babel's writings, of

4. Many scholars dismiss the view that Hephaestus, son of Zeus and god of fire, is to Greek mythology <u>just like Thor, son of Odin and god of thunder, is to</u> Norse mythology, despite observations that both deities are typically depicted wielding a hammer.

    O   just like Thor, son of Odin and god of thunder, is to

    O   the same as Thor, son of Odin and god of thunder, relates to

    O   what Thor, son of Odin and god of thunder, is to

    O   as Thor, son of Odin and god of thunder, is part of

    O   the way that Thor is, as son of Odin and god of thunder, to

5. In a many crossword puzzles, the black boxes are placed to make the grid diagonally symmetric, and each empty box gets filled with a single letter that is <u>part of both an across word, which is entered horizontally, and of a down word, which is</u> entered vertically.

    O   part of both an across word, which is entered horizontally, and of a down word, which is

    O   part of both an across word, which is entered horizontally, and a down word, which is

    O   part of both an across word entered horizontally and of a down word

    O   both part of an across word entered horizontally and of a down word

    O   both part of an across word entered horizontally as well as a down word

6. Brand management in the personal care industry, <u>like any industry, is the art of defining consumer perceptions of the utility and value promised by the product line</u> and the personality projected by the company.

    O   like any industry, is the art of defining consumer perceptions of the utility and value promised by the product line

    O   similar to how any industry does it, is the art of defining consumer perceptions of the utility and value promised by the product line

    O   like brand management in any industry, is the artistic defining of consumer perceptions of the product line's promises of utility and value

    O   as in any industry, is artfully defining consumer perceptions of the utility and value promised by the product line

    O   as in any industry, is the art of defining consumer perceptions of the utility and value promised by the product line

7.   The principal residence of French royalty from 1682 to 1789, the Palace of Versailles is now one of the most frequently visited historic monuments in Europe and is often celebrated for its impressive Baroque architecture, the extravagant decor in such rooms as the Hall of Mirrors, and the elaborate and expansive gardens that surround the palace.

   ○   architecture, the extravagant decor in such rooms as the Hall of Mirrors, and the

   ○   architecture, for the extravagant decor in such rooms as the Hall of Mirrors, and it has

   ○   architecture, the extravagant decor in such rooms as the Hall of Mirrors, and for having

   ○   architecture and extravagant decor in such rooms as the Hall of Mirrors, also having

   ○   architecture as well as for having extravagant decor in such rooms as the Hall of Mirrors, and the

8.   Like some humans, some adult cats lack a sufficient quantity of the enzyme lactase to digest milk; as a result of drinking it, such cats become sick, as evidenced by their vomiting or excreting diarrhea or gas.

   ○   it, such cats become sick, as evidenced by their

   ○   milk, such cats become sick, as evidenced by its

   ○   milk, such cats become sick, as evidenced by those cats'

   ○   it, they become sick, as evidenced by their

   ○   milk, such cats become sick, as evidenced by their

9.   The rise of alternative funding opportunities, such as microlending, crowdfunding, and peer-to-peer lending, have enabled many small entrepreneurs to rapidly grow successful companies specializing in products that are of interest only to niche markets.

   ○   have enabled many small entrepreneurs to rapidly grow successful companies specializing in products that are of interest only to niche markets

   ○   have enabled many small entrepreneurs to rapidly grow successful companies only specializing in products that are of interest to niche markets

   ○   has enabled many small entrepreneurs to rapidly grow successful companies specializing in products that are of interest only to niche markets

   ○   has enabled many small entrepreneurs to rapidly grow only successful companies specializing in products that are of interest to niche markets

   ○   has enabled many small entrepreneurs to grow successful companies specializing rapidly in products that are of interest only to niche markets

10. Despite rising interest rates, real estate sales in the neighborhood this summer were <u>5 percent higher than they were last summer</u>.

    ○   5 percent higher than they were last summer

    ○   5 percent higher than last summer

    ○   5 percent more than last summer was

    ○   higher than 5 percent last summer

    ○   more than 5 percent higher last summer

Answers and explanations follow on the next page. ▶ ▶ ▶

Answers and Explanations

Sentence Correction Quiz

1. (A)

The underlined text "that managed airport screening" appropriately modifies "private companies," describing which private companies are being discussed. Then "during the twentieth century" correctly modifies "managed airport screening," describing when this action occurred. The verb "managed" is correctly in the simple past tense, and there are no other issues. **(A)** is correct.

In **(B)**, the passive construction "there were" leaves unclear what was managing airport screening. This sentence loses the original's clear, direct connection between the private companies and their function. **(C)** makes it sound as though either all private companies in the twentieth century managed airport screening or the twentieth century managed airport screening. Either reading is illogical. **(D)** opts for the less preferred passive voice and, in the process, changes the meaning of the sentence to say that the airport screening itself did various things. However, as the original sentence makes clear, the *companies* that ran the screening set various policies. Finally, **(E)** says that the twentieth century performed the list of actions; eliminate **(E)**.

2. (C)

The underlined portion opens with the pronoun "they," so check to see which word the pronoun refers to. The opening modifying phrase is talking about "the *deus ex machina*," defined as "a plot device," so the pronoun should be the singular "it." Also note that the non-underlined verb "has" requires a singular subject. Eliminate **(A)**.

(C) properly opens with "it" and proceeds logically and correctly; "it occasionally . . . has been used" employs the correct verb tense, the modifying phrase "according to some critics" immediately precedes the critics' opinion, and "effectively" properly describes how the plot device "has been used." **(C)** is the correct answer. **(B)** and **(D)** can be eliminated because they do not follow the opening modifying phrase with a noun or a pronoun that refers to *deus ex machina*. **(E)** fails to provide an

active verb to connect with "has," leaving the sentence incomplete. Its phrase "occasionally being used effectively" illogically becomes a modifier of "critics." Confirm **(C)** by reading it back into the original sentence:

While the *deus ex machina*, a plot device involving a sudden and unlikely resolution to a seemingly unsolvable problem, has often been ridiculed for being contrived and unartistic, it occasionally, according to some critics, has been used effectively.

3. (B)

The underlined portion contains the plural verb "are," which agrees with "Babel's writings." The word "as" indicates a comparison, which is logically drawn (the one book is filled in the same way as other writings are). However, the last word of the underlined portion is "of," which is connected to the verb "filled." That's idiomatically incorrect. A book is filled *with* certain details, not filled *of* those details. Eliminate **(A)**.

(B) changes only the final word and is correct. **(C)** and **(E)** can be eliminated for using "filled . . . of." **(D)** changes the modifying phrase to make it sound as if Babel's writings *did* something, but the writings didn't fill themselves; eliminate **(D)**. To confirm **(B)**, read it back into the original sentence:

Inspired by the circumstances he witnessed and documented during the Polish-Soviet War of 1920, Isaac Babel wrote *Red Cavalry*, a short story collection that is filled, as are many of Babel's writings, with brutal and often horrific depictions of war.

4. (C)

The underlined portion begins with "just like," which indicates a comparison. Before that, the sentence uses the structure *A is to B* (Hephaestus is to Greek mythology). However, the construct *A is to B just like C is to D* is not idiomatically correct. Eliminate **(A)** and look for a choice that joins the two ideas idiomatically and does not introduce any other errors.

(C) uses the proper idiomatic and parallel construction "Hephaestus . . . is to Greek mythology what Thor . . . is to Norse mythology" and is correct. **(B)**, **(D)**, and **(E)**

can all be eliminated for using incorrect idioms. To confirm, read (**C**) back into the original sentence:

Many scholars dismiss the view that Hephaestus, son of Zeus and god of fire, is to Greek mythology <u>what Thor, son of Odin and god of thunder, is to</u> Norse mythology, despite observations that both deities are typically depicted wielding a hammer.

5. (B)

The underlined portion contains the word "both." When listing two items, the word "both" should be paired with the word "and" (*both X and Y*), and the two items should be presented in parallel form. The word "and" is used properly, but "of both an across word . . . and *of* a down word" is not parallel. The "of" should not be repeated since it appears before "both" and therefore applies to both items. Eliminate (**A**).

(**B**) corrects the issue, does not introduce any other errors, and is the answer. (**C**) repeats the error of (**A**), so eliminate (**C**). (**D**) and (**E**) move the phrase "part of" to after the word "both." That would be fine, if there were still parallelism. To be correct, the rest of the sentence would have to read: *both part of X and part of Y*. However, (**D**) leaves out the second "part," and (**E**) also leaves out the second "part of" while replacing "and" with "as well as." As a final step, read (**B**) back into the original sentence:

In many crossword puzzles, the black boxes are placed to make the grid diagonally symmetric, and each empty box gets filled with a single letter that is <u>part of both an across word, which is entered horizontally, and a down word, which is</u> entered vertically.

6. (E)

The word "like" that begins the underlined portion of the sentence indicates that the sentence is comparing two things. Comparisons must be logical and parallel. Here, "brand management" should logically be compared to some kind of management, but instead it is compared to "any industry." Eliminate (**A**).

(**E**) correctly compares brand management *in* one industry (personal care) to brand management *in* any industry. The remainder of the sentence proceeds

logically and without introducing new errors. (**E**) is correct. (**B**) substitutes "similar to how" for "like." In addition to being wordier, this choice still doesn't compare "management" to management, so it's incorrect. (**C**) starts with "like" as (**A**) does, but it solves the comparison problem by inserting the term "brand management" into the second part of the comparison. However, when one thing "is" another, the two things must be expressed in parallel form, and "brand management . . . is the artistic defining" is not parallel. "Brand management" needs to be paired with another noun, not an *-ing* verb form. (**D**) repeats the same parallelism error with "Brand management . . . is artfully defining." Read (**E**) back into the sentence to confirm:

Brand management in the personal care industry, <u>as in any industry, is the art of defining consumer perceptions of the utility and value promised by the product line</u> and the personality projected by the company.

7. (A)

In the underlined portion, the sentence is listing features of the Palace of Versailles. When items are listed, they should be in parallel form. In this case, there are three features: architecture, decor, and gardens. Each is described with a noun phrase, so everything is consistent. (**A**) is correct.

(**B**) and (**C**) both keep the list format of the original sentence. However, (**B**) adds "for" and "it has," creating a *for X . . . , for Y . . . , and it has Z* structure that is not parallel. Similarly, (**C**) adds "for having" to the end, creating a non-parallel *for X . . . , Y . . . , and for having Z* structure. (**D**) leaves the final item in the list dangling at the end with the verb "having," which has no clear subject. By linking the first two items of the list with "as well as," (**E**) ends the list with "the Hall of Mirrors." Then when it starts the last part of the sentence with "and the . . . ," it creates a whole new clause that fails to include an active verb.

8. (E)

The underlined text begins with the ambiguous pronoun "it," which could refer to either "lactase" or "milk." Read on for other issues to watch for in the choices. The last underlined word is another pronoun, "their." This clearly refers to "cats" and is correct. Eliminate (**A**).

(**E**) replaces "it" with "milk," clarifying the pronoun, and retains the correct "their" at the end. This is the correct answer. (**B**) and (**C**) also add "milk," but (**B**) inappropriately refers to the plural "cats" with the singular pronoun "its." (**C**) adds "those cats'," but since the text that immediately follows the semicolon refers to "such cats" becoming sick, this phrase is unnecessarily repetitive. (**D**) contains the same ambiguous pronoun "it" as (**A**); eliminate. Read (**E**) into the sentence to confirm that it is correct:

Like some humans, some adult cats lack a sufficient quantity of the enzyme lactase to digest milk; as a result of drinking <u>milk, such cats become sick, as evidenced by their</u> vomiting or excreting diarrhea or gas.

9. (C)

The underlined portion begins with the plural verb phrase "have enabled," but the subject of that verb phrase is the singular "rise" at the beginning of the sentence. Singular subjects require singular verbs, so eliminate (**A**).

(**C**) is correct because it uses the singular verb phrase "has enabled" and introduces no new errors. (**B**) fails to correct the original subject-verb error. (**D**) fixes the subject-verb error but changes the meaning of the sentence by placing "only" before "successful companies." This makes it sound like the entrepreneurs start nothing but successful companies, while the original sentence says that there are some start-ups that are successful even though their products have limited markets. (**E**) is incorrect because it changes the meaning of the sentence by moving "rapidly" to describe the rate of specialization instead of the rate of growth. Read (**C**) back into the sentence to confirm that it is correct:

The rise of alternative funding opportunities, such as microlending, crowdfunding, and peer-to-peer lending, <u>has enabled many small entrepreneurs to rapidly grow successful companies specializing in products that are of interest only to niche markets.</u>

10. (A)

The words "higher than" in the underlined portion form a comparison between this summer's sales and last summer's sales. The pronoun "they" refers to the sales, so the compared items are logical and parallel. (**A**) is correct.

(**B**) compares this summer's sales to last summer itself, which makes no sense. (**C**) makes the same illogical comparison between this summer's sales and last summer, rather than to last summer's sales. (**D**) suggests that this summer's sales also existed last summer somehow, which is impossible. (**E**) also suggests, illogically, that this summer's increase occurred last summer.

CHAPTER 22

VERBAL REASONING: PUTTING IT ALL TOGETHER—ADVANCED PRACTICE

In this chapter, you'll find a 28-question practice set consisting entirely of questions most test takers find challenging. The practice set contains a mix of Critical Reasoning, Reading Comprehension, and Sentence Correction questions. Following the practice set, you'll find complete explanations for every question.

How to Use This Practice Set

Use this question set to hone your Critical Thinking skills if you are aiming for a very high GMAT score. If you are not yet comfortable with the practice questions in the preceding chapters of this book, then continue to review the Critical Reasoning, Reading Comprehension, and Sentence Correction topics presented there until you are able to find the correct answers to most of those practice questions. Then you'll be ready to tackle the tougher questions here.

If you are ready to do so, set a timer, giving yourself 1 minute for each Sentence Correction question and 2 minutes for each Critical Reasoning question. For Reading Comprehension, give yourself 3–4 minutes per passage and 1 minute 15 seconds per question. If you decide to do the entire set in one sitting, put 50 minutes on the timer.

As always, be sure to *review the explanation* to every question you do in this chapter. Noting a different way to work through a question, even if you got that question right, is a powerful way to enhance your Critical Thinking skills—and it's ultimately those skills that you will be relying on in order to achieve a very high score on Test Day.

Ready to crank up the level on your Verbal score? Then turn the page and begin work!

Advanced Verbal Practice Set

(Answers and explanations are at the end of the chapter.)

1. Our architecture schools must be doing something wrong. Almost monthly we hear of domes and walkways collapsing in public places, causing serious injuries. In their pursuit of some dubious aesthetic, architects design buildings that sway, crumble, and even shed windows into our cities' streets. This kind of incompetence will disappear only when the curricula of our architecture schools devote less time to so-called artistic considerations and more time to the basics of good design.

   Which of the following, if true, would most seriously weaken the author's claim?

   O All architecture students are given training in basic physics and mechanics.

   O Most of the problems with modern buildings stem from poor construction rather than poor design.

   O Less than 50 percent of the curriculum at most architecture schools is devoted to aesthetics.

   O Most buildings maintain their structural integrity well past their projected life expectancies.

   O Architects study as long and as intensively as most other professionals.

2. In recent years, many advertisements have won awards for their artistic quality. But since advertising must serve as a marketing tool, advertising executives must exercise their craft with an eye to the effectiveness of their advertisement. For this reason, advertising is not art.

   The argument above depends on which of the following assumptions?

   O Some advertisements are made to be displayed solely as art.

   O Some advertising executives are more concerned than others with the effectiveness of their product.

   O Advertising executives ought to be more concerned than they currently are with the artistic dimension of advertising.

   O Something is not "art" if its creator must be concerned with its practical effect.

   O Artists are not concerned with the monetary value of their work.

3. Studies have shown that the number of books read in elementary school is correlated with later academic success. In the past year, local elementary students have read an average of 10 fewer books than the nationwide elementary student average of 35 books per year, while 90 percent of those local students report playing sports at least twice a week. If these students participated less in sports, they would read more books.

    Which of the following, if true, would most effectively weaken the argument?

    O   A nationwide survey of middle school students determined that if given a choice between reading a book and playing a sport, most of these students would choose reading a book.

    O   Participating in sports in elementary school has been shown to be as highly correlated as reading books to later academic success.

    O   The attention spans of elementary school students do not allow these children to read for as long as older students and adults are expected to read.

    O   The local elementary school is in a rural area in which there is no bookstore or public library and internet service is unreliable.

    O   Some local elementary school students who used to enjoy reading have said they no longer choose to read books, preferring to play sports at least twice a week.

4. Attempts to blame the mayor's policies for the growing inequality of wages are misguided. The sharp growth in the gap in earnings between college and high school graduates in this city during the past decade resulted from overall technological trends that favored the skills of more educated workers. The mayor's response to this problem cannot be criticized, as it would hardly be reasonable to expect him to attempt to slow the forces of technology.

    Which of the following, if true, casts the most serious doubt on the conclusion drawn in the last sentence above?

    O   The mayor could have initiated policies that would have made it easier for less-educated workers to receive the education necessary for better-paying jobs.

    O   Rather than cutting the education budget, the mayor could have increased the amount of staff and funding devoted to locating employment for graduating high school seniors.

    O   The mayor could have attempted to generate more demand for products from industries that paid high blue-collar wages.

    O   Instead of reducing the tax rate on the wealthiest earners, the mayor could have ensured that they shouldered a greater share of the total tax burden.

    O   The mayor could have attempted to protect the earnings of city workers by instituting policies designed to reduce competition from foreign industries.

5. Loneliness is commonly reported in populations of older adults. A study of older adults found that those who owned dogs reported feeling less lonely than those who did not own dogs. Clearly, an older person who adopts a pet will be less likely to suffer feelings of loneliness than an older person without a pet.

Which of the following, if true, would most strengthen the argument above?

○ Owning a pet has been linked to several health benefits, including lower blood pressure.

○ Some people feel that cats do not engage socially with their owners as much as dogs do.

○ The number of older adults who own pets is projected to rise in the coming years.

○ A large percentage of older dog owners report taking their dogs for walks and to dog parks.

○ Pets other than dogs provide the same benefits of companionship as do dogs.

6. A social worker surveyed 200 women, each of whom had recently given birth to her first child. Half of the women surveyed had chosen to give birth in a hospital or obstetrics clinic; the other half had chosen to give birth at home under the care of certified midwives. Of the 100 births that occurred at home, only 5 presented substantial complications, whereas 17 of the hospital births presented substantial complications. The social worker concluded from the survey that the home is actually a safer environment in which to give birth than a hospital or clinic.

Which of the following, if true, most seriously calls the social worker's conclusion into question?

○ Women who give birth in hospitals and clinics often have shorter periods of labor than do women who give birth at home.

○ Many obstetricians discourage patients from giving birth at home.

○ All of the women in the study who had been diagnosed as having a high possibility of delivery complications elected to give birth in a hospital.

○ Women who give birth at home tend to experience less stress during labor than women who deliver in hospitals.

○ Pregnant doctors prefer giving birth in a hospital.

7.   It appears that the number of people employed by a typical American software firm decreased in the 1980s and 1990s. This trend is borne out by two studies, conducted 20 years apart. In a large 1980 sample of randomly chosen American software firms, the median size of the firms' workforce populations was 65. When those same firms were studied again in 2000, the median size was 57.

Which of the following points to the most serious logical flaw in the reasoning above?

○   The studies do not address other industries in which American firms experienced a decrease in the median number of employees during the 1980s and 1990s.

○   The studies ignore the extent to which software firms in the 1980s and 1990s increasingly relied on subcontractors to write code.

○   The studies focused on the number of employees, but there are many ways of judging a firm's size, such as revenues and profits.

○   The data in the studies refer only to companies that existed in 1980.

○   The median number of employees is not as sound a measure of the number of employees employed in an industry as is the mean number of employees, which accounts for the vast size of the few large firms that dominate most industries.

8.   A team of pediatricians recently announced that pet birds are more likely to bite children under age 13 than people of any other age group. The team's finding was based on a study showing that the majority of all bird bites requiring medical attention involved children under 13. The study also found that the birds most likely to bite are cockatiels and parakeets.

Which of the following, if true, would most weaken the pediatricians' conclusion that birds are more likely to bite children under age 13 than people of any other age group?

○   More than half of bird bites not requiring medical attention, which exceed the number requiring such attention, involve people aged 13 and older.

○   The majority of bird bites resulting in the death of the bitten person involve people aged 65 and older.

○   Many serious bird bites affecting children under age 13 are inflicted by birds other than cockatiels and parakeets.

○   Most bird bites in children under age 13 that require medical attention are far less serious than they initially appear.

○   Most parents can learn to treat bird bites effectively if they avail themselves of a small amount of medical information.

9. Several people have died while canoeing during high water on a nearby river in recent years. The local police have proposed a ban on canoeing when the river reaches flood stage. Opponents of the ban argue that the government should prohibit an activity only if it harms people other than those who willingly participate in the activity. They therefore conclude that the proposed ban on high-water canoeing is unwarranted.

    Which of the following, if true, most seriously weakens the opponents' conclusion?

    O   Sailboats are not allowed on a nearby lake when winds exceed 50 miles per hour.

    O   Several other local governments have imposed similar bans on other rivers.

    O   Several police officers have been seriously injured while trying to rescue canoeists who were stranded on the river while attempting to canoe during high water.

    O   More canoeists drown while canoeing rivers at normal water levels than while canoeing rivers at high water levels.

    O   Statistics provided by the U.S. National Park Service show that fewer people drown on rivers with high-water canoeing bans than on rivers without such bans.

10. The Internal Revenue Service (IRS) has a mandate to operate more efficiently. However, if taxpayers did not have a respectful fear of the IRS, the timely collection of taxes could not be maintained. For the last 10 years, polls have shown that most American taxpayers fear the fines and late fees that can follow an IRS audit.

    The statements above, if true, would best serve as an argument that

    O   most American taxpayers are not concerned with receiving tax credits or refunds

    O   those American taxpayers who comply voluntarily with the tax laws do not fear the potential consequences of an audit

    O   projecting a friendlier public image would likely be counterproductive for the IRS

    O   more American taxpayers fear the IRS today than feared it 10 years ago

    O   collecting delinquent taxes costs the IRS more than does collecting taxes on time

11. Occupational safety advocate: Logging is one of the most dangerous occupations in the United States. A company has developed a chainsaw that it claims will instantly shut off if there is kickback of the chain, which studies have shown to be the most common cause of chainsaw injuries. The logging industry should adopt this new chainsaw as standard equipment in order to prevent most of the logging-related deaths that occur each year.

Which of the following statements, if true, most seriously weakens the occupational safety advocate's argument?

○ Loggers are sometimes killed by problems with chainsaws other than the kickback of the chain.

○ Injuries from falling trees cause the vast majority of deaths in the logging industry.

○ The new chainsaw is inexpensive and easy to learn how to use.

○ There are other, equally safe chainsaws available, but the logging industry has not adopted them.

○ The chainsaw manufacturer's claims about its product are supported by a study conducted by a government agency.

12. According to a recent study, advertisements in medical journals often contain misleading information about the effectiveness and safety of new prescription drugs. The medical researchers who wrote the study concluded that the advertisements could result in doctors' prescribing inappropriate drugs to their patients.

The researchers' conclusion would be most strengthened if which of the following were true?

○ Advertisements for new prescription drugs are an important source of revenue for medical journals.

○ Editors of medical journals are often unable to evaluate the claims made in advertisements for new prescription drugs.

○ The Food and Drug Administration, the government agency responsible for drug regulation, reviews advertisements for new drugs only after the ads have already been printed.

○ Advertisements for new prescription drugs are typically less accurate than medical journal articles evaluating those same drugs.

○ Doctors rely on the advertisements as a source of information about new prescription drugs.

13. One problem with labor unions today is that their top staffs often consist of college-trained lawyers, economists, and labor relations experts who cannot understand the concerns of real workers. One goal of union reform movements should be to build staffs out of workers who have come up from the ranks of the industry involved.

The argument above depends primarily upon which one of the following assumptions?

O   Higher education lessens people's identification with their class background.

O   Union staffs should include more people with firsthand industrial supervisory experience.

O   Some people who have worked in a given industry can understand the concerns of workers in that industry.

O   Most labor unions today do not fairly represent workers' interests.

O   A goal of union reform movements should be to make unions more democratic.

Questions 14–16 refer to the following passage.

First commercially available in 1978, video optical discs were technologically more advanced than video cassettes—they offered better picture quality without degradation over time—yet video cassettes and recorders were far more successful commercially, at least in part because relatively few movies

5   were ever released on optical discs. As this example illustrates, superior technology is no guarantee of success in the home audio and video market.

In home audio, vinyl records were the dominant format until the 1970s, when audio cassette tapes were introduced. Cassette tapes offered no better sound quality than vinyl records (in fact, some believed they offered lower quality),

10   yet this format became widely successful for reasons having little to do with technical advancements in sound quality. Cassettes were more portable than records, and the ability to record from records onto cassettes made the two formats complementary. In addition to buying prerecorded records and tapes, consumers could now make copies of vinyl records and listen to them outside

15   the home. Thus, cassette tape sales grew even as vinyl remained a popular format.

The rise of audio compact discs (CDs) was quite different. Introduced in 1983, CDs clearly offered higher sound quality than records or cassettes, yet they were not an immediate success. However, CDs were persistently and

20   aggressively marketed by the industry, and by the 1990s they had become the most popular audio format. The dominant position of CDs was further cemented later in the 1990s by the advent of new technology that allowed consumers to create their own CDs at home—thus combining one of the best features of audio cassettes with the higher sound quality of CDs.

25   In home video, after the failure of optical discs, video cassettes remained the dominant format until the advent of digital video discs (DVDs). Introduced in North America in 1997, DVDs quickly gained widespread popularity. These

discs were based on a technology similar to that of optical discs and offered several clear advantages over video cassettes, including better picture quality
30 and better search features. Yet perhaps the real key to their rapid rise was the fact that manufacturers quickly made many titles available on DVD. This combination of better technology and smart marketing helped the DVD avoid the fate of the optical disc.

14. The passage is primarily concerned with which of the following?

O   Contrasting the success of DVDs with the failure of optical discs

O   Describing the crucial role played by technology in the home audio and video market

O   Questioning the wisdom of introducing new audio or video formats

O   Illustrating that there is more than one path to success in the home audio and video market

O   Proving that good marketing is the only way to guarantee success in the home audio and video market

15. The author's statement "the ability to record from records onto cassettes made the two formats complementary" in lines 12–13 serves primarily to

O   illustrate why vinyl records were popular when they first launched

O   explain why two formats of sound recording could be successful at the same time

O   demonstrate why optical discs did not find the same success as cassette tapes

O   indicate the main marketing feature of cassette tapes

O   contrast the success of cassette tapes to that of CDs

16. Based on the passage, which of the following strategies is least likely to produce a successful media format?

O   Releasing titles sparingly until consumer tastes are determined

O   Aggressively marketing a brand-new format

O   Innovating to deliver a higher-quality audiovisual experience

O   Creating a new format based on an earlier technology

O   Introducing a product that works with existing products

Questions 17–21 refer to the following passage.

Parfleche, the widely adopted French name for rawhide items fashioned by the Native Americans of the Great Plains, has especially come to mean an envelope-shaped container used to store clothes, food, and personal items. These wallets or bags, depending on the size, served not only as a practical and durable

5   storage solution but also as a decorative object of spiritual significance. Among certain tribes, notably the Cheyenne, *parfleches* were decorated by the women's painting society, whose members among the Cheyenne were known as the Selected Ones. Although similar in economic and social importance to craft guilds in medieval and Renaissance Western Europe, the painting society also

10   had a spiritual or religious nature. The shamanistic society required application for admission and held its members to high artistic and moral standards. The society further established its importance by defining aspects of Cheyenne wealth and status.

Painting on rawhide was fraught with challenges. If painting was attempted

15   while the prepared hide was too moist, the applied paint bled, but if the hide was too dry, the skin did not absorb the pigments. This restricted the time frame in which painting could best be completed, which meant that designs had to be visualized fully before the work started. Moreover, every aspect of creating a *parfleche* was a sacred act. Each design element, for instance, was

20   a syntagma—a linguistic or visual unit intended to convey meaning—freighted with symbolic referents. For example, diamond shapes represented the grasshopper, an abundant grass eater itself symbolic of the bison, the sacred source of food, shelter, tools, and clothing. The tools used were also symbolic: the shape of the "flesher" used to prepare the hide represented lightning

25   bolts—emblematic of the masculine essence of spirit. The flesher removed the flesh from the hide, transforming it into a spiritual container that would hold earthly matter (the people's material goods).

Even the position of the *parfleche* in the lodge held symbolic significance. It was stored beneath the bed of older women, not only because they were

30   careful guardians, but also because they were closer to Grandmother Earth, from whose union with the lightning spirit the animals and plants of the middle world came to provide food and shelter. The symbolism of every aspect of the *parfleche,* therefore, from the interpretable design work on its outside to its storage place within the lodge, reflects the Cheyenne belief in a universe

35   created through a complementary blending of the masculine spirit and the feminine physical matter.

17. According to the passage, one reason there was a limited time frame in which to paint a prepared rawhide was that

   O   the pigments dried quickly and thus had to be applied with speed to avoid cracking

   O   if the hide was too dry, it absorbed too much paint

   O   if the hide was too moist, the paint bled

   O   if the hide was too moist, it rejected the pigments

   O   the designs had to be fully visualized before painting was started

18. The main purpose of the passage is to

   O   describe a tool used among Native Americans of the Great Plains when working with rawhide

   O   rebut a commonly held view about the symbolism of the *parfleche* for certain Native Americans

   O   analyze the social roles and spiritual worldview of the Cheyenne

   O   propose a new method for analyzing the use of symbolism in Native American art

   O   discuss the spiritual and symbolic importance of a rawhide container and its decorations to certain Native American tribes

19. According to the author, the Cheyenne women's painting society was unlike Western European guilds of the Middle Ages and the Renaissance in that

   O   application for membership was required

   O   the group had significant economic standing in the community

   O   the group had significant social standing in the community

   O   the women's painting society was religious in nature

   O   the society had an influence on social standing and material valuation

20. You can most reasonably conclude that the Cheyenne designation of the women who painted *parfleches* as "Selected Ones" (line 8) reflects

    ○   the high status some women enjoyed as artists in Cheyenne culture

    ○   the shamanistic spiritual origins of the women's painting society

    ○   the notion that artists were chosen by the gods to perform their tasks

    ○   the austere and frugal code of conduct of the women's painting society

    ○   a woman's skill in using rawhide tools such as the "flesher"

21. The author describes the symbolic meanings of the diamond shape most likely in order to

    ○   indicate how precious the completed *parfleche* was to its owner

    ○   imply that the grasshopper was held superior to the bison in Cheyenne religion

    ○   illustrate the visual complexity of the abstract forms used in creating a *parfleche*

    ○   provide an example of the many layers of symbolism involved in creating a *parfleche*

    ○   demonstrate the relationship between the symbolic shapes of the tools and the abstract designs used in creating a *parfleche*

22. Although her X-ray photographs <u>had laid the foundation for describing the structure of DNA, Rosalind Franklin, an accomplished chemist, did not receive the Nobel prize when it was awarded for this achievement</u> in 1962.

    ○   had laid the foundation for describing the structure of DNA, Rosalind Franklin, an accomplished chemist, did not receive the Nobel prize when it was awarded for this achievement

    ○   had laid the foundation for its description, the structure of DNA did not result in accomplished chemist Rosalind Franklin receiving the Nobel prize awarded for it

    ○   of the structure of DNA had laid the foundation for their description, the accomplished chemist Rosalind Franklin was not awarded the Nobel prize for this achievement

    ○   were the foundation for describing the structure of DNA, the Nobel prize was not awarded to accomplished chemist Rosalind Franklin for it

    ○   were an achievement by Rosalind Franklin, an accomplished chemist, it did not receive the Nobel prize for laying the foundation for describing the structure of DNA

23. The European Union announced that cod and mackerel are the only fish that <u>exceeds their new requirements for dioxin level and that they allow</u> fisheries to catch.

○ exceeds their new requirements for dioxin level and that they allow

○ exceed its new requirements for dioxin level and that they allow

○ exceeds its new requirements for dioxin level and that it allows

○ exceed its new requirements for dioxin level and that it allows

○ exceed their new requirements for dioxin level and that they allow

24. Completed in 1951 and designated a National Historic Landmark in 2006, <u>the International Style of architecture is prominently exemplified by the Farnsworth House, which was designed by Ludwig Mies van der Rohe.</u>

○ the International Style of architecture is prominently exemplified by the Farnsworth House, which was designed by Ludwig Mies van der Rohe

○ Ludwig Mies van der Rohe designed the Farnsworth House, a prominent example for the International Style of architecture

○ Ludwig Mies van der Rohe has designed the Farnsworth House, a prominent example of the International Style of architecture

○ the Farnsworth House was designed by Ludwig Mies van der Rohe and serves as a prominent example of the International Style of architecture

○ the Farnsworth House was prominently exemplified by the International Style of architecture, which was designed by Ludwig Mies van der Rohe

25. On the Scottish island of Uist, conservationists have spent many years working on plans <u>for trapping European hedgehogs, which are</u> an invasive species in Uist and have been blamed for reducing the population of several wading birds, and relocate them to the mainland.

○ for trapping European hedgehogs, which are

○ for the trapping of European hedgehogs, which are

○ to trap European hedgehogs, which are

○ to trap European hedgehogs, being

○ to trap European hedgehogs.

26. <u>In 2017, completing the journey in six less days than was previously done, the record for sailing around the world alone was broken by French sailor François Gabart.</u>

    ○ In 2017, completing the journey in six less days than was previously done, the record for sailing around the world alone was broken by French sailor François Gabart.

    ○ In 2017, completing the journey in six fewer days than the previous record holder, French sailor François Gabart broke the record for sailing around the world alone.

    ○ Completing the journey in six fewer days than the previous record, the record for sailing around the world alone was broken by French sailor François Gabart in 2017.

    ○ Completing the journey in six fewer days than was previously done, the record for sailing around the world alone in 2017 was broken by French sailor François Gabart.

    ○ In 2017, completing the journey in six less days than the previous record, French sailor François Gabart broke the record for sailing around the world alone.

27. Since 2007, the Department of Defense has maintained a program designed to investigate unidentified flying objects, <u>despite the views of many scientists who considered</u> that these phenomena will be found to have natural explanations.

    ○ despite the views of many scientists who considered

    ○ despite the views of many scientists who consider

    ○ despite the views of many scientists believe

    ○ despite the views of many scientists who believe

    ○ although scientists believed

28. Nina Simone, <u>whose distinctive technique is credited as to her early classical training, is known to be famous for</u> her renditions of blues, jazz, and folk compositions as well as for her impassioned civil rights activism.

    ○ whose distinctive technique is credited as to her early classical training, is known to be famous for

    ○ who is credited to her early classical training on account of her technique, is famously known as

    ○ who had a distinctive technique that is credited with her early classical training, is known for

    ○ credited with a distinctive technique due to her early classical training, is known for

    ○ whose distinctive technique is credited to her early classical training, is known for

Answers and explanations follow on the next page. ▶ ▶ ▶

Answers and Explanations

Advanced Verbal Practice Set

1.   (B)

The author is claiming that the myriad of problems affecting the buildings will only cease when architecture schools modify their curricula to favor the fundamentals of good design, instead of artistic considerations. To correctly answer this Weaken question, first identify the author's central assumption. Here, the author is assuming that the listed problems are caused by architecture schools' curricula. The correct answer will weaken the causal relationship. **(B)** does just that, as it states that the problems are caused by poor construction rather than by architects' poor designs.

(A) is incorrect because one can study physics and mechanics yet lack an understanding of design. **(C)** is irrelevant because the author's assumption does not depend on what percentage of the curriculum is devoted to aesthetics. Even if less than 50 percent of the curriculum is devoted to aesthetics, the author may still consider this excessive. **(D)** is incorrect because the fact that "most" buildings do not collapse does not negate the fact that some are falling down and causing the "serious injuries" that are the inspiration for the author's complaint. **(E)** is incorrect because the author is concerned that architects are not spending enough time learning the fundamentals of good design, a concern that is not affected by how much they study in relation to other professions.

2.   (D)

To answer this Assumption question, identify the author's conclusion and evidence and consider the gap the author has left between them. The key phrase "For this reason" indicates the conclusion: advertising isn't art. The evidence is that the executives making the advertisements need to take into account whether the ads work or not. Therefore, the author assumes that if the effectiveness of a creative product is an important consideration, that product is not art. **(D)** matches this prediction.

(A) describes the intent of some creators of advertisements, but why some people make ads has no bearing on whether they actually are art. **(B)** is an irrelevant comparison; the argument does not depend on there being variation in executives' interest in the effectiveness of the ads. **(C)** lies completely outside the argument; the author is neither making nor assuming this value judgment about what executives "ought to" do. If you use the Denial Test on **(E)** and say that *Artists are concerned with the monetary value of their work*, that statement has no effect on the argument, since artists in general could be concerned with making work that fetches a good price and advertisements could still not qualify as art.

3.   (D)

The author's conclusion is that if the local elementary students were to devote less time to sports, then they would read a greater number of books. The author's evidence is that the local elementary school students read significantly fewer books than does the average elementary school student while nearly all local students play sports. To weaken this argument, as required by this Weaken question, first find the author's primary assumption: the author is assuming a causal relationship between reading less and participation in sports. Predict that the correct choice will undermine this causal relationship by providing an alternative explanation for the lower average number of books read by the local elementary school students. **(D)** is correct because it provides an alternative explanation: that the local elementary school students may not be reading much because it is difficult to get books in their particular area.

(A) is incorrect because middle school students are not relevant to the author's argument. **(B)** is incorrect because the author's argument is about why children aren't reading, not the best way they can succeed academically. **(C)** is incorrect because it provides an irrelevant comparison between elementary students and older students and adults. **(E)** actually strengthens the author's assumption that participation in sports is impacting the number of books read by local students.

4. (A)

The author is concluding that there is nothing that the mayor could have done differently to combat the growing wage gap. The supporting evidence is that it is not reasonable to expect the mayor to be able to fight modern trends in the employment landscape. Since you need to cast doubt on the conclusion drawn in the last sentence, this is a Weaken question, and you must first identify the author's main assumption. Here, the author assumes there was little the mayor could have done to address the problem of wage inequality. So, predict that the correct answer will provide evidence that this assumption is mistaken. **(A)** is correct because it does exactly that: it shows that he could have helped less-educated workers gain the skills required in order to not be left behind by the new technological realities.

(B) is incorrect because a high school graduate who gains employment with the help of dedicated staff may still be paid a significantly lower wage than a more skilled college graduate: this would not address the problem of wage inequality. **(C)** is incorrect because the demand for products would not necessarily lead to an increase in high paying jobs in the mayor's city. While it may contribute to job creation elsewhere, the argument is limited to the mayor's city. **(D)** may be tempting because it states a potential solution to financial inequality. However, since the author's argument is concerned specifically about wage inequality, which is quite distinct from taxation, this choice is ultimately incorrect. **(E)** is incorrect because it sidesteps the issue in question altogether. The author does not imply that the wage inequality is caused by foreign competition.

5. (E)

The argument's conclusion is that an older person who adopts a pet will be less likely to suffer feelings of loneliness than an older person without a pet. The supporting evidence comes from a study that shows that older adults who own dogs reported feeling less lonely than older people who don't own dogs. Here, the author is assuming that the findings about dog ownership are representative of pet ownership as a whole. To correctly answer this Strengthen question, predict that the correct choice will provide information that makes this assumption more likely to be true. **(E)** is correct because it

supports the idea that the benefits of dog ownership are similar to the benefits provided by the ownership of other kinds of pets.

(A) is incorrect because it fails to address the author's specific claim about loneliness, even though it introduces additional benefits of pet ownership. **(B)** actually weakens the argument because it shows that what is true of dogs may not be true of other types of pets (in this case, cats). **(C)** is incorrect because a predicted increase in pet ownership says nothing about what benefits they may provide. **(D)** is incorrect because it only references dogs and thus does not support the author's conclusion about all types of pets. It also fails to show clearly that ownership of dogs, or any other pet, alleviates loneliness; elderly people could take their dog on outings without interacting with other humans.

6. (C)

The argument's conclusion is that giving birth at home is safer than giving birth in a hospital or clinic. This conclusion is supported by the evidence presented in the survey: that the women giving birth in a home setting experienced significantly fewer complications than did the women giving birth in a hospital or clinical setting. The social worker's assumption is that the lower number of complications is indicative of a safer environment. To correctly answer this Weaken question, look for a choice that would provide information undermining the social worker's assumption. One way to think about this argument is from the perspective of representativeness: the author's assumption holds true only if there are no relevant differences between the two groups of women from the survey, other than the location in which they give birth. Another way to think about the argument is from the perspective of causality: the author's assumption would be weakened if there were some other reason, besides the setting of the births, for the different rates of complications. **(C)** is correct because it says that women who are more likely to experience complications during labor chose to give birth in the hospital. Thus, the survey's data about each group suffers from a significant selection bias and cannot be held to be representative of all pregnant women. Moreover, the risk of complications determined birth setting, rather than the other way around.

(A) is incorrect because nothing in the stimulus suggests that a longer labor is associated with an increased likelihood of complications. (B) and (E) are incorrect because the obstetricians' opinions and the pregnant doctors' preferences may be based on factors other than safety. (D) is incorrect because the information presented could potentially strengthen the social worker's conclusion, rather than weaken it.

7. (D)

The question asks for a "logical flaw in the reasoning," making this a Flaw question. The argument concludes that the typical American software firm employs fewer people in the 2000s than it did in the 1980s and 1990s. The evidence comes from two studies: one in 1980, which surveyed a random sample of software firms, and one in 2000, which surveyed the same firms. However, while those firms may have comprised a good representative sample in 1980, there's no indication that those companies still represent the typical software firm in 2000. Also, the 2000 survey ignores any software firms that may have arisen in that 20-year period. (D) is correct, pointing out the flaw of relying on potentially unrepresentative data.

(A) is incorrect because the argument is only about software firms, not industries in general. (B) is incorrect because the argument is about the number of employees, not who's doing the work. (C) is incorrect because the argument is not about judging a firm's size. It's only about employment numbers. (E) is not a problem here. Even if mean is a better measure than median, that doesn't imply that using the median is poor or mistaken.

8. (A)

On occasion, the GMAT provides some guidance by restating the conclusion in the question stem. This is one such occasion; the pediatricians conclude that birds are more likely to bite children under the age of 13 than people of any other age group. The evidence is a study that states the majority of all bird bites that required medical attention involved children under the age of 13. To correctly answer this Weaken question, first determine the assumption upon which the argument depends. The author assumes that bird bites that require medical attention are representative of all bird bites.

To weaken this argument, find a choice that essentially says, "Bites that require medical attention are *not* representative of bites in general." (A) matches the prediction, stating that most bird bites don't require medical attention, and of those that don't, more than half are suffered by people *over* the age of 13.

(B) is incorrect because the number of lethal bird bites is not relevant to the author's argument. It would be possible for all bird bite fatalities to be among the elderly but for a majority of bird bites in general to occur among children. (C) is incorrect because the species of birds are only mentioned as a secondary conclusion in the stimulus; they are not relevant to the pediatricians' conclusion addressed by the question, which is concerned only with bird bites in general. (D) is incorrect because the argument deals with the likelihood that a bird will bite someone, not with the likelihood that the bite is serious. (E) commits a similar error by dealing with treatment; this argument is only concerned with the relative frequency of bird bites occurring in the first place and not with the treatment plans for bites that have already occurred.

9. (C)

The question stem asks you to weaken the conclusion of the opponents of the ban. The ban's opponents conclude that the government should not ban high-water canoeing, based on the evidence that the government shouldn't ban an activity that poses no risk to people who don't voluntarily participate. Predict that the correct choice will show some way in which high-water canoeing may injure those who are not willingly participating. (C) offers such a reason: police officers, who did not consent to expose themselves to the dangers of canoeing in high water, were harmed as a result of such canoeing.

(A) is incorrect because sailing on a lake during high wind is irrelevant to canoeing on a river during high water. Even though, as (B) says, other governments may have also enacted the bans, those bans could be unreasonable; the opponents might still have a valid argument. Therefore, (B) is also irrelevant. (D) offers an irrelevant comparison: that more canoeists drown while the river is at normal levels may simply be due to the fact that there are more canoeists at that time to begin with. (E) might be tempting because it seems to provide a reason why the ban on high-water canoeing is a good idea. However, the opponents are not concerned with the deaths of the canoeists themselves, and (E) doesn't give an example of non-canoeists harmed by the canoeing.

10. (C)

The stimulus provides statements that will support the claim in the correct answer, making this an Inference question. According to the stimulus, the IRS strives for efficiency. However, that goal would be threatened if people didn't fear the IRS, and that fear has existed for the last 10 years. So, to avoid any loss of efficiency, it's logical to conclude that the IRS should maintain its fear-inducing reputation. Thus, as (C) says, trying to change to something friendlier and less fear-inducing could be problematic. That's the correct answer.

(A) introduces the idea of credits and refunds. Although the stimulus says most taxpayers are concerned about late fees and penalties, this does not mean they aren't also interested in credits and refunds. (B) is not supported. It's possible that people who comply with the law *do* fear audits (as most people do), and that's why they comply. (D) is not supported. The stimulus only provides an overall statistic for the last 10 years. No change in any direction is stated or implied. (E) is an irrelevant comparison. The stimulus speaks to whether or not taxes can be collected on time but says nothing about the costs of tax collection.

11. (B)

The word "weakens" in the question stem tells you that this is a Weaken question. The conclusion is the proposal that the logging industry adopt a new chainsaw to prevent most of the "logging-related deaths" each year. The evidence is that the chainsaw shuts off when there is kickback, the most common cause of "chainsaw injuries." Notice the mismatch between chainsaw injuries and logging deaths. The advocate assumes that most of the logging-related deaths are the result of kickback-induced injuries. A weakener will attack this connection. (B) does this. If most deaths are caused by falling trees, and not by injuries from chainsaw kickback, then adopting

the new chainsaw will not prevent most logging-related deaths.

(A) is incorrect because the word "sometimes" could translate to a very small percentage of deaths. Kickback might still cause "most" of the logging-related deaths each year. (C) might be relevant to the new chainsaw's adoption rate, but it doesn't relate to whether the proposed course of action would prevent most of the deaths. (D) is irrelevant, as the argument is about what would happen if the industry were to adopt the new chainsaw in particular. The existence of other safe chainsaws has no bearing on this. (E) is incorrect because it doesn't address the link between kickback and the majority of logging-related deaths. The manufacturer's claims pertain only to preventing kickback.

12. (E)

The phrase "most strengthened" tells you that this is a Strengthen question. The researchers' argument concludes with a prediction: doctors will prescribe inappropriate drugs to their patients. This is based on the evidence that ads in medical journals often are not entirely accurate about the effectiveness and safety of these drugs. To strengthen this argument, you want a choice that gives a reason why the prediction will come to pass. Doctors would be more likely to prescribe these inappropriate drugs if they actually base decisions on the inaccurate ads. (E) points this out and is correct.

(A) tells you why the journals might carry the ads, but it doesn't strengthen the idea that doctors will use them to make inappropriate prescriptions. (B) and (C) could each explain why the ads are published despite the inaccurate and misleading information contained in them, but like (A), they do not show how the ads lead to inappropriate prescriptions. (D) makes an irrelevant comparison between the accuracy of ads and that of articles.

13. (C)

This is an Assumption question. The author argues that unions should get more "workers who have come up through the ranks" into leadership because the lawyers and experts don't understand what real workers worry about. So, the author is assuming that, unlike the college-trained experts, "workers who have come up through the ranks" can understand the concerns of the "real workers." Scanning the choices, the one that matches this prediction is (**C**).

(**A**) may explain why the experts seem to be out of touch, but it doesn't fill the gap between the evidence and conclusion. (**B**) is the exact opposite of the author's point; she thinks union staffs should feature workers, not supervisors. (**C**) goes too far; the author talks about a problem that "often" exists with unions, but this choice talks about "most" unions. (**E**) is irrelevant; the argument has nothing to do with whether unions are democratic.

Passage Map for Questions 14–16

¶1: Optical discs technologically advanced, but failed because few movies available

¶2: tapes: not better than vinyl, but succeeded because of portability and ability to make copies

¶3: CDs: more advanced, but not successful until aggressive marketing campaign

¶4: DVDs: similar advantages as optical discs, but succeeded due to movie availability

Topic: Media formats

Scope: Their successes and failures

Purpose: Explain the various reasons that different media formats succeeded or failed

14. (D)

The phrase "The passage is primarily concerned . . . " indicates this is a Global question asking for the topic and scope of the passage. In your passage map, you should have summarized the topic as something like "A/V technologies" and the scope as something like "various factors that have led to their commercial success." This summary is a good prediction, and (**D**) is a match.

(**A**) focuses only on the fourth paragraph; the contrasting fates of DVDs and optical disks are only one example the author uses to tell a larger story. (**B**) accurately summarizes the details used in the passage but again misses the author's overall point. (**C**) misconstrues the author's argument. The author cites examples of new

formats that have been successful; the examples of new technologies that have not been successful show only that a new format is not sufficient for success. With the word "only," (**E**) is extreme. In the third paragraph, the author states that a big marketing effort helped CDs become popular, but the author cites a number of other reasons, such as quality and portability, that these products—including, in their later years, CDs—have seen success.

15. (B)

The phrase "serves primarily to" indicates this Logic question asks how or why the author uses a quoted phrase to develop the main idea of the passage. The phrase is found in the second paragraph, so research your passage map for the purpose of that paragraph and re-read the text that includes the quoted words. Paragraph 2 describes the commercial success of audio cassette tapes. The two sentences after the cited detail describe its significance: " . . . consumers could now make copies of vinyl records and listen to them outside the home. Thus, cassette tape sales grew *even as* vinyl remained a popular format." In other words, the "complementary" nature of the formats meant that, instead of just competing with one another, they helped each other be popular. (**B**) matches that prediction.

Although records were dominant when cassette tapes were launched, the author never talks about the launch of vinyl records; eliminate (**A**). The author does not discuss optical discs, in (**C**), in the second paragraph, and the quoted text does not explain anything about the discs. While the compatibility of records and cassettes promoted the success of both, the author never mentions that it was featured in the marketing for cassettes or, indeed, mentions marketing in paragraph 2 at all, so (**D**) is incorrect. (**E**), like (**C**), is incorrect because CDs are not mentioned in the paragraph and the quoted statement does not concern them.

16. (A)

The phrase "based on the passage" indicates an Inference question. Reading further, you see that you're being asked to infer which of five listed strategies have no support in the passage for being successful. The strategies may not be explicitly discussed in the text, but the passage will provide enough information to deduce which one likely wouldn't work. The first and fourth paragraphs both mention that the optical disc probably failed because not enough titles were available. That's evidence for the idea that a slow release of titles might lead to failure, making **(A)** correct.

(B) is mentioned in paragraph 3 as a reason CDs succeeded, and **(E)** is mentioned in paragraph 2 as a reason cassettes succeeded. Eliminate both choices. Higher-quality audio and/or video, **(C)**, is mentioned in paragraph 1 as a feature that didn't help video optical discs and in the last paragraph as a feature that may have had little to do with the success of DVDs. However, the failure of optical discs was not due to their higher quality, and higher quality didn't hurt DVDs. **(C)** is incorrect. In the last paragraph, the passage notes that DVDs, a successful product, "were based on a technology similar to that of optical discs," so basing a product on an earlier technology is not likely to be a factor that leads to failure; eliminate **(D)**.

Passage Map for Questions 17–21

¶1: Intro to the parfleche and the people who created it

¶2: The process and symbolism involved in making the parfleche

¶3: The parfleche as a symbol of the Cheyenne worldview

Topic: The parfleche

Scope: The spiritual significance of the production, decoration, and use of the parfleche

Purpose: To explain the cultural and spiritual significance of the parfleche to the Plains peoples

17. (C)

As indicated by the phrase "According to the passage," this is a Detail question. It asks you to find in the passage an explanation for why a prepared rawhide had to be painted in a short time. How *parfleches* were made is described in paragraph 2, so review that paragraph to find an answer to the question. The third sentence

contains the key concept from the question, "restricted the time frame," but the pronoun "This" at the start of the sentence points you to the previous sentence. Match the choices to the two reasons provided in the second sentence. **(C)** is correct because it restates the first reason.

(A) is incorrect because the author never mentions the pigments drying quickly or the paint cracking. **(B)** incorrectly describes the result of dry rawhide; the passage says a too-dry hide would not absorb the pigments, not that it would absorb too much paint. **(D)** incorrectly describes the result of a moist hide; according to the passage, the paint would bleed on these hides. **(E)** is the result of the limited time frame, not a reason for it.

18. (E)

The phrase "main purpose" means this Global question is asking for the reason the author wrote the passage. As you concluded your strategic reading of the passage, you summarized the author's topic, scope, and purpose. This author describes the cultural significance and construction of the *parfleche*, so predict a purpose similar to "to explain" or "to describe" the importance of the *parfleche*. **(E)** is correct, because the *parfleche* is a decorated rawhide container and the verb "discuss" matches the tone of the passage.

Although a tool used to make a *parfleche* is described in paragraph 2, **(A)** is incorrect because the tool is mentioned merely as an example of one of the symbolic aspects of the *parfleche*. The author did not write the passage to describe the tool. The verb "rebut" makes **(B)** incorrect because the author does not present an argument. **(C)** may be tempting because the author does examine Cheyenne society and spirituality through the lens of the *parfleche*, but the focus of the passage is on the *parfleche* and this choice does not mention it. The passage describes some of the symbolism involved with the *parfleche*, but no new method is proposed for analyzing the symbolism in Native American art; **(D)** is also incorrect.

19. (D)

"According to the passage" identifies this as a Detail question. The correct answer will paraphrase the comparison between the Cheyenne women's painting societies and the Western European guilds that the author makes in the passage. The fourth sentence of paragraph 1 introduces the comparison: the Cheyenne women's painting societies were "similar in their economic and social importance to craft guilds," but "also had a spiritual or religious nature." The question asks about a difference between the two groups, so predict that the correct answer will include the spiritual or religious dimension; **(D)** matches this prediction.

Although **(A)** is mentioned in the text as a characteristic of Cheyenne women's painting societies, applying for membership is not discussed with respect to the European guilds, so this choice is incorrect. Because the first part of the fourth sentence of paragraph 1 describes **(B)**, **(C)**, and **(E)** as similarities with, not differences from, the European craft guilds, these choices are also incorrect.

20. (A)

The phrase "most reasonably conclude" indicates that the answer to this Inference question will be fully supported by passage. Start to research at the line mentioned in the question, that states that "the Selected Ones" were members of the women's painting societies. The following sentences describe characteristics of these societies. They had a "spiritual or religious nature," "held [their] members to high artistic and moral standards," and were important in "defining aspects of Cheyenne wealth and status." Predict that these painters were carefully chosen and well respected. **(A)** matches this prediction and is correct.

(B) is incorrect because, although the painting societies are described as "shamanistic," the origins of the societies are never discussed. Although the *parfleche* decorators were known as "the Selected Ones," the passage never states that the gods chose the women, so **(C)** is incorrect. The text mentions "high . . . moral standards" but does not specify what those were in Cheyenne society; austerity and frugality may not have been involved. **(D)** is incorrect. The importance of the "flesher" is discussed in paragraph 2, but this tool is never connected directly to the "Selected Ones," so **(E)** is incorrect.

21. (D)

As indicated by the phrase "in order to," this is a Logic question. You're asked to identify why the author described the symbolism involved with the diamond shape. The symbolism of various aspects of the *parfleche* is described in paragraph 3, so refer to your passage map or re-read the paragraph. The opening sentences of paragraph 3 state "every aspect of creating a *parfleche* was a sacred act. Each design element . . . was . . . freighted with symbolic referents." Immediately following this sentence, the diamond shape is noted as the first example of one of these design elements. Predict that the author mentions the diamond to illustrate how shapes conveyed a spiritual or symbolic meaning. **(D)** matches this prediction and is correct.

The ownership of the *parfleche* is never discussed; **(A)** is incorrect. **(B)** is incorrect because the author never compares the importance of either the symbols or the creatures the symbols represent. The individual symbols are described, but not the "visual complexity" of the design; **(C)** is incorrect. Although both the symbolism of the shape of the flesher and some of the abstract designs are discussed, the text never draws a relationship between them; **(E)** is incorrect.

22. (A)

The verb "had laid" is in the past perfect tense used to describe a past action completed before another action in the past. The past perfect is correct here, since Franklin's photographs "laid the foundation" before the scientist won the Nobel prize in 1962. The only pronoun in the sentence, "it," unambiguously represents "the Nobel Prize." Finally, the overall structure of the sentence is logical: her photographs laid a foundation for a scientific discovery, but Franklin did not win a prize for the discovery. There are no errors, so **(A)** is correct.

In **(B)**, the final "it" seems to refer to "the structure of DNA," but describing the DNA earned the prize; the structure itself didn't earn anything. In **(C)**, the plural pronoun "their" could refer only to the plural noun "photographs," but the photographs were not being described. It's hard to know what the "it" at the end of **(D)** might refer to. And the "it" in **(E)** would refer to the "photographs," but "it" is singular and "photographs" is plural; moreover, Franklin (not her photographs) would have been awarded the Nobel.

23. (D)

In this sentence, it is the European Union that has requirements and allows fisheries to catch certain fish. Therefore, both underlined pronouns, "their" and "they," refer to the European Union, which is a singular noun. The sentence should use "its" and "it," respectively. Once "they" is corrected to "it," the verb that follows should be the singular "allows." Also, the first underlined verb, "exceeds," must agree with "fish." The singular and plural forms of "fish" are spelled the same way, but in this case, the author is discussing two types of fish, so the noun is plural. The verb should therefore be "exceed." Eliminate (A).

Choice (D) correctly uses the plural "exceed" and the singular pronouns "it" and "its," and this is the correct answer. A vertical scan of the first word of each choice allows you to eliminate (C) for continuing to use the singular verb "exceeds." A vertical scan of the second word eliminates (E) for retaining the plural pronoun "their." (B) continues to use the plural pronoun "they." Read your choice back into the sentence to confirm:

The European Union announced that cod and mackerel are the only fish that exceed its new requirements for dioxin level and that it allows fisheries to catch.

24. (D)

The underlined portion is preceded by a modifying phrase. An opening modifier should be followed immediately by the person or object being modified. The underlined portion begins with "the International Style of architecture." However, the style wasn't completed and designated a landmark—the Farnsworth House was. The underlined phrase should begin with "the Farnsworth House." Eliminate (A).

(D) properly opens with "the Farnsworth House" and proceeds logically. This is the correct answer. (B) and (C) can be eliminated for putting the wrong subject immediately after the opening modifier. (E) provides the right noun after the opening modifier, but "was . . . exemplified by" illogically suggests that the architectural style is an example of the house. Furthermore, this

version indicates that Mies van der Rohe designed the architectural style instead of the house. To confirm (D) is correct, read it back into the original sentence:

Completed in 1951 and designated a National Historic Landmark in 2006, the Farnsworth House was designed by Ludwig Mies van der Rohe and serves as a prominent example of the International Style of architecture.

25. (C)

The underlined portion begins with "for trapping European hedgehogs," which is the first of two actions that are part of the conservationists' plans. The second action comes at the end of the sentence: "relocate them." However, "for trapping" and "relocate" are not parallel. Furthermore, the phrase "plans for trapping" is incorrect. Idiomatically, it's proper to say *plans to do something* instead of *plans for doing something*. Eliminate (A).

(C) uses "to trap," which properly creates the parallel construction "plans to trap . . . and relocate." The comma and "which" properly introduce the supplemental information describing the hedgehogs. (C) is correct. Eliminate (B) for using "for trapping." (D) changes "which are" to "being." This creates the phrase "being . . . and have been blamed," which is not parallel. And (E) removes the verb altogether, creating the phrase "an invasive species . . . and have been blamed," which is not parallel. Read (C) back into the original sentence to confirm:

On the Scottish island of Uist, conservationists have spent many years working on plans to trap European hedgehogs, which are an invasive species in Uist and have been blamed for reducing the population of several wading birds, and relocate them to the mainland.

26. (B)

Because days are countable, the sentence should state that the journey was completed in six *fewer* days. Eliminate (A). Also, consider that the sentence describes an accomplishment of "French sailor François Gabart," and this passive construction is not preferred on the GMAT. Be alert for a choice that fixes the usage error and potentially recasts the sentence in active voice.

(B) correctly uses "fewer days." It also uses the preferred active voice, with "Gabart broke the record." This choice is correct. **(C)** and **(D)** introduce modification errors; the modifying phrases at the start of these choices describe Gabart, but the phrases are immediately followed by "the record." By using "less days," **(E)** has the same error as the original.

27. (D)

The phrases "since 2007" and "has maintained" indicate that the program mentioned is still continuing. Thus, the past tense "considered" at the end of the underlined portion is incorrect. Additionally, following "considered" with a clause starting with "that" is unidiomatic usage in this sentence; correct phrasing would be *scientists who consider these phenomena to have natural explanations.* For both of these reasons, eliminate **(A)**.

(D) is correct because it replaces "who considered" with "who believe," which is in the present tense and, unlike *consider*, is properly paired with "that" in this sentence. **(B)** is incorrect because although it does change "considered" to the present tense "consider," it still pairs "consider" with "that." **(C)** incorrectly drops the word "who" to read "the views . . . believe." This makes no sense. The views don't believe; the scientists believe. **(E)** is incorrect because "believed," like the original sentence's "considered," is past tense. Read **(D)** back into the sentence to confirm that it is correct:

Since 2007, the Department of Defense has maintained a program designed to investigate unidentified flying objects, despite the views of many scientists who believe that these phenomena will be found to have natural explanations.

28. (E)

The underlined portion of the sentence contains the unidiomatic "credited as to." It also includes the redundant "known to be famous for." Eliminate **(A)**.

(E) is correct. It uses the proper idiom for when a quality of a person is being attributed to a source: "credited to." It also fixes the redundancy error by changing "known to be famous for" to the succinct "known for." **(B)** says that Simone herself is "credited to" her training, which makes no sense. It also says Simone is "known as" her musical renditions, which is equally illogical. **(C)** is incorrect because "credited with" gives credit for her classical training to her technique, when the relationship is actually the other way around. **(D)** distorts the meaning of the sentence by saying that the reason Simone is *given credit* for her distinctive technique is that she received classical training. Read **(E)** back into the sentence to make sure it is correct:

Nina Simone, whose distinctive technique is credited to her early classical training, is known for her renditions of blues, jazz, and folk compositions as well as for her impassioned civil rights activism.

PART FIVE

INTEGRATED REASONING AND ANALYTICAL WRITING: STRATEGY AND PRACTICE

CHAPTER 23

INTEGRATED REASONING

> **LEARNING OBJECTIVES**
>
> - Describe important attributes of the Integrated Reasoning section including format, question types, timing, and scoring
> - Explain how the user interface in Integrated Reasoning differs from that used on other GMAT sections
> - Apply Critical Thinking skills to approach systematically a variety of tasks on the Integrated Reasoning section

Integrated Reasoning questions are designed to resemble the types of problems you will encounter in business school and in your business and management career. These questions focus on your ability to solve complex problems using data from multiple sources in a variety of formats.

There are 12 items in the Integrated Reasoning section, nearly all of which include multiple parts. For example, a single graph, discussion, or chart will be used as the basis for several parts of one question, and each question may measure a different skill set.

You have 30 minutes to answer the questions, and although IR is not adaptive, you may only move forward through the section. This means that pacing is very important. If you are uncertain how to approach a question or simply feel it will take too much time, you should guess and go on to make sure you get to all the items. However, since you won't be able to go back to earlier questions if you have extra time at the end, there's no point in working too quickly; you should invest time in the questions you know you can get right.

The Integrated Reasoning section does not contribute to the total 200–800 GMAT score. Instead, it's scored on its own scale from 1 to 8, in whole-point increments. Since there are 12 items on the IR section, there is not a one-to-one correspondence between the number of items you get right and your score on the section. This is at least in part due to the presence of some unscored experimental items. Since you will not know which items are experimental, treat every item as though it counts.

While a few items in the IR section are traditional multiple-choice questions, most items require two or three selections. There is no partial credit. Thus, getting two questions right and one question wrong on a three-part Table Analysis or Multi-Source Reasoning item is exactly the same as getting all three questions wrong.

Integrated Reasoning Question Formats and Content

In the Integrated Reasoning section, you will analyze different types of data (presented in graphs, tables, and passages, among other formats), synthesize data in verbal and graphical formats, and evaluate outcomes and trade-offs. Some of the data are presented in interactive formats, such as spreadsheets. You may need to sort data within columns to determine the answer or click on multiple tabbed pages to view additional information.

The Integrated Reasoning section consists of four item types:

1. **Graphics Interpretation** items contain two statements that must be completed using drop-down menus. The statements pertain to a graph, scatter plot, or other visual information format.

2. **Multi-Source Reasoning** items provide given information in the form of text, charts, or tables spread across two or three tabbed pages. Some of the items are traditional five-answer multiple-choice, while others consist of three true/false–style statements that must all be answered correctly in order to receive credit for the item.

3. **Table Analysis** items present information in the form of a sortable spreadsheet. Table Analysis items feature the same true/false question format seen in Multi-Source Reasoning questions.

4. **Two-Part Analysis** items start out like ordinary Quant or Verbal questions, but instead of selecting one answer from five choices, you must select answers to two related questions from a common pool of five or six choices. Unless the item specifies that the two answers are different, they aren't necessarily on different rows but can be the same.

In this chapter, you will find two to three examples of each type of item. You can practice with additional Integrated Reasoning questions, complete with answers and explanations, in your online resources. Practicing online is recommended because the Integrated Reasoning section looks different from the rest of the GMAT. There's a distinct way to interact with each question type, and you'll have access to an onscreen calculator.

Integrated Reasoning User Interface

As noted, you will see question formats on the IR section other than standard multiple-choice. Sometimes you will select your answer from drop-down menus or true/false options. You will also need to navigate through spreadsheets and tabbed pages. The spreadsheets for Table Analysis items can be sorted using a drop-down menu; as you practice, pay close attention to how the drop-down menu operates and make sure to consider all your sorting options.

You have the use of an onscreen calculator for the Integrated Reasoning section *only*. You are not allowed to use your own calculator. The calculator performs basic functions and can be accessed by clicking an icon on the screen. A calculator screen will then pop up over the question. The calculator looks like this:

Use caution when using the calculator. You run the risk of entering information incorrectly, resulting in a wrong answer. Moreover, rounding and estimation are often much faster than the time-consuming process of entering large numbers. Use the calculator only when necessary.

Because the questions in the Integrated Reasoning section vary greatly in form and content, flexibility will be key to success. Fortunately, since IR questions draw on many of the same skills you need for the Verbal and Quantitative sections, thorough practice with GMAT questions of all types will have you well prepared by Test Day.

CONCEPT CHECK

- You will have _____ minutes to answer _____ questions on the Integrated Reasoning section.

- How does your Integrated Reasoning score relate to your overall GMAT score?

  _____

- What are the four question types that appear on the Integrated Reasoning section?

  _____

Example answers are in your book's online resources (**kaptest.com/login**).

The Kaplan Method for Integrated Reasoning

LEARNING OBJECTIVES

- Explain the purpose of each step of the Kaplan Method for Integrated Reasoning
- Apply the steps of the Kaplan Method for Integrated Reasoning

Now that you've read about the format of the IR section and its four question types, it's time to learn how to approach these questions strategically. Kaplan has developed a Method for Integrated Reasoning that you can use flexibly to solve each question in this section. Approaching these questions methodically is important, given the tight time constraints you'll be working under.

THE KAPLAN METHOD FOR INTEGRATED REASONING

STEP 1 Analyze the information.

STEP 2 Approach strategically.

Step 1: Analyze the Information

All items on the IR section have this in common: they will present you with information you need to analyze before you can approach answering the question(s). In Graphics Interpretation items, this information is presented in some sort of graph. In Table Analysis, it's given to you in a sortable mini spreadsheet. In Multi-Source Reasoning, you'll get two or three tabs of information, often a mix of text, tables, and/or graphs. And in Two-Part Analysis, you'll be given anything from a paragraph expressing an argument to a geometry figure.

In all cases, it will be critical to get the gist of this information so you don't attempt questions without all the useful facts. When a good amount of data is presented, as in a graph, in a table, or on tabs, noting where to find various details will be important so you can research them efficiently if and when you need them.

Step 2: Approach Strategically

Since time is of the essence on the IR section, you don't want to do any work you don't have to. While a strategic approach takes many forms on these diverse questions, you'll always want to do three things:

1. Zero in on the exact information you need to answer the question.

2. Use the strategies you employ on the Quantitative and Verbal sections to get to the answer efficiently. These strategies include passage mapping, estimation, predicting, backsolving, and elimination of incorrect choices based on your understanding of the scenario before doing any hard work.

3. Don't be afraid to guess and go. Very few students can complete all 12 items in the IR section in the 30 minutes given. If you can quickly ascertain that a certain item does not match well to your skill set, guess on the question(s) and move on. This guessing approach will ensure that you get to all of the items that you can get right with enough time to solve.

The Integrated Reasoning Item Types

LEARNING OBJECTIVES

- Distinguish among the four types of Integrated Reasoning questions
- Describe what it means to "get the gist" of the information—whether presented in text, graphs, and/or tables—given in each question type

Graphics Interpretation

Graphics Interpretation items test your ability to interpret and analyze data presented visually in graphs or graphical images. For each item, you will see a graph with accompanying text and two questions.

As with a Reading Comprehension passage, you do not need to absorb every bit of information on the graph to answer the questions. What you *do* need to do is get the gist of the graph and what it contains so that you can efficiently find the information you need. You will then read the question stem, view the answer choices, and use the information in the graph to select the correct answer.

Graphics Interpretation items feature many different types of graphs, including line graphs, scatter plots, Venn diagrams, and even geological timelines. All graphics are accompanied by two incomplete sentences. Test takers must use a drop-down menu to select a word or phrase that completes the sentence according to the information presented in the graphic. There is no partial credit. The drop-down menus in this chapter are represented in multiple-choice format for ease of reading.

Let's take a look at some Graphics Interpretation items.

Eruptions of the Old Faithful Geyser, Yellowstone National Park

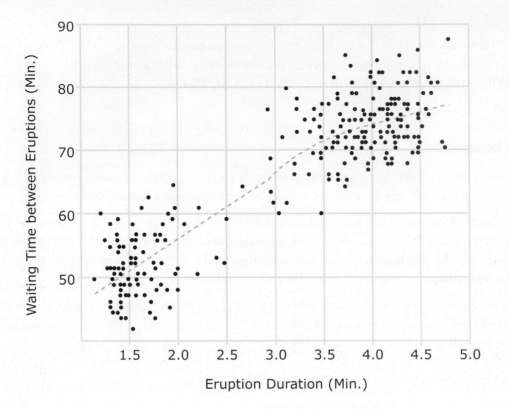

The graph above is a scatter plot with each point representing the duration of an eruption of Old Faithful, a geyser in Yellowstone National Park, and the time in minutes until the following eruption occurred. The dotted line represents a regression line. For each blank, select the answer choice that correctly completes the statement according to the information in the graph.

1a. The graph suggests that Old Faithful has _____ of eruption.

    O   one type

    O   two distinct types

    O   more than two distinct types

1b. For an eruption of less than two minutes, the maximum recorded wait time is _____ the minimum recorded wait time of an eruption of more than four minutes.

    O   greater than

    O   equal to

    O   less than

Step 1: Analyze the Information

Your first step with an item of this type should be to read the text that accompanies the graph. You may see only a single sentence, or you may see (as in this case) a full paragraph. This text is important. Although most Graphics Interpretation questions can be answered without reference to the text, reading will give you an overview of the information the graph contains and how it is presented. On Test Day, taking a moment to paraphrase the written information will improve your understanding of the image, speeding up your analysis and reducing your chances of committing a careless error.

Here, the paragraph tells you that the graph shows the behavior of a single geyser, Old Faithful. The graph presents two types of information: how long the eruptions of Old Faithful last and how long it then takes before the next eruption happens. Each point on the graph represents an eruption.

Next, look at the graph itself. Get a bird's-eye view of the graph by reading the title and the labels of the axes and notice how the information from the paragraph is represented in the graph. Here, you'll notice that the duration, or length, of the eruption is measured against the waiting time that follows it before the next eruption. Now look at the units of measurement that correspond to each axis and determine whether the scales are similar. In this case, both axes are measured in minutes, but the scales are very different: the x-axis is measured in 0.5-minute increments, while the y-axis is measured in 10-minute increments. Furthermore, the x-axis starts at 1.0 and ends at 5.0, while the y-axis starts at 40 and goes to 90.

The final step before answering the questions is to look at the data to see if they fall into a general pattern. On this scatter plot, most of the data points separate into two distinct groups. With a pattern this clear, you can anticipate that this observation will be key to answering one or more of the accompanying questions. Making these observations before analyzing the questions will help you answer each question more effectively.

Step 2: Approach Strategically

Question 1a: Begin by paraphrasing the question for yourself: does Old Faithful have one, two, or more than two distinct types of eruption? As you noticed before, the data points separate themselves into two main clusters. There are a few stray data points scattered outside these clusters, but their number is not significant. Therefore, you can infer from the graph that Old Faithful has two types of eruptions, **(B)**.

Question 1b: For this question, you need to examine the data in the graph more closely. This statement contains a comparison between two data points: the maximum wait time for an eruption that lasts less than two minutes and the minimum wait time for an eruption that lasts more than four minutes. Note that you're asked to compare the wait times of these two points—that's their height along the y-axis. So this question asks you to find these two points and compare their heights. The first point is the highest point to the left of the two-minute line on the x-axis, which looks to be just below 65 on the y-axis. Now find the second point, the lowest point to the right of the four-minute line on the x-axis. The lowest point to the right of that line appears to be just below the 70-minute mark on the y-axis. The first point is therefore lower than the second, so you would choose "less than," **(C)**.

We've discussed how, before attacking any Graphics Interpretation question, you need to understand what the graph contains and how it is constructed. You can then target your research to answer each question correctly and efficiently. Try using these techniques on the next set of questions.

Study of Adults' Sleep Habits

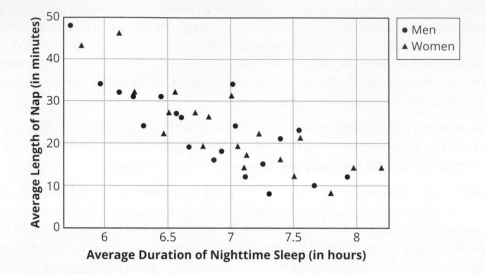

As part of a study on the napping habits of adults, several scientists asked 40 individuals who nap frequently—20 men and 20 women—to record the duration of their naps for one month. These individuals were also asked to record the amount of sleep they get at night. For the purpose of the study, the accepted ideal nap length was set at 10 to 20 minutes per nap. This length has been shown to help combat fatigue and make one feel more alert. The chart above shows the average nap duration and average nighttime sleep length for each of the individuals.

For each statement, select the option from the drop-down menu that completes the statement as accurately as possible according to the information provided.

2a.   Of the women whose average nap length was in the accepted ideal range, the greatest number received an average of _____ hours of nighttime sleep.

   O   between 6 and 6.5

   O   between 6.5 and 7

   O   between 7 and 7.5

   O   between 7.5 and 8

2b.   Of the men in the survey, _____. of them napped, on average, for more than 30 minutes.

   O   25%

   O   30%

   O   55%

   O   60%

Step 1: Analyze the Information

The graph provided is a scatter plot. The text provides context for the graph. According to the text, each point on the chart represents an individual in a study, and each point provides the average nap length and average nighttime sleep length for that person over one month. In addition, the text states that the accepted ideal nap length, for the purpose of the study, is 10 to 20 minutes.

The graph's legend tells you that the men are represented by circles and the women are represented by triangles. It can be noted that both groups have a negative correlation—as nighttime sleep length increases, nap duration tends to drop. In addition, consider the note that the ideal nap length is 10 to 20 minutes. Most people in this chart are taking longer naps than this. Everyone in that range is getting at least 6.5 hours of nighttime sleep, with most such people getting at least 7 hours of nighttime sleep.

Step 2: Approach Strategically

Question 2a: The question asks for the amount of nighttime sleep being achieved by the most women getting an ideal nap length. From the descriptive text, the ideal length is between 10 and 20 minutes. The choices provide ranges of nighttime sleep length. Use those to find which range contains the most triangles with nap times between 10 and 20 minutes. There are no such triangles between 6 and 6.5 hours of nighttime sleep. There's only one between 6.5 and 7 hours. There are four between 7 and 7.5 hours. And there are only three between 7.5 and 8 hours. So, it's the nighttime sleep range of 7 to 7.5 hours that contains the most women getting the ideal nap length. That makes (**C**) correct.

Question 2b: This question asks how many men had an average nap length of over 30 minutes. The men are represented by circles. Above the 30-minute line there are six circles. However, the choices are not in numbers but in percentages. According to the descriptive text, there are 20 men in total. So the percentage would be $\frac{6}{20} \times 100\% = 30\%$. That makes (**B**) correct. This could also have been estimated to save calculation and eliminate the wrong choices. Knowing that 25% would be one-fourth, or 5 out of 20, helps eliminate the first choice. And 6 out of 20 is certainly less than half, which eliminates the remaining choices.

Computer Algorithm

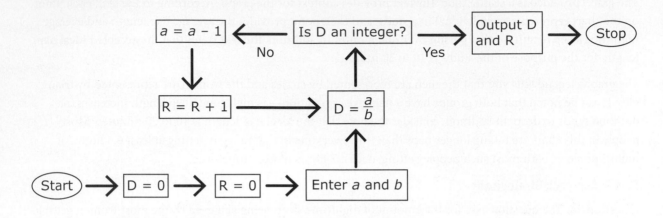

The flowchart represents a computer algorithm that takes two positive integers as the input and is intended to return two integers as the output. Each process is symbolized by an equation, such as $a = a - 1$. In this particular process, 1 is subtracted from the current value of the variable a, and the difference then becomes the value of a. For example, if the value of a is 5 before the process $a = a - 1$ is completed, then the value of a will be 4 after the process is completed. Algorithms that are incorrectly formed may sometimes get stuck in an infinite loop. An infinite loop is a sequence of instructions that never terminates. Complete the following statements by making selections from the drop-down menus in accordance with the algorithm represented by the flowchart.

3a. If 58 and 11 are entered as the values for a and b, respectively, then one of the outputs of the function will be _____.

O $D = 0$

O $D = 4$

O $D = 55$

O $R = 3$

O $R = 4$

3b. The algorithm will get stuck in an infinite loop

O   if $a > b$

O   if $a = b$

O   if $a < b$

O   never

Step 1: Analyze the Information

Paraphrase what the algorithm does. First, D is set to $\frac{a}{b}$. Then, if D is an integer, the algorithm outputs D and R and stops. If D is not an integer, then a is decreased by 1 and R is increased by 1, and the process repeats. Thus, the loop will keep repeating until $\frac{a}{b}$ is an integer, at which point it will output the value of D (which is $\frac{a}{b}$) and R (which is the number of times the algorithm divided a by b and didn't get an integer).

If you try a few examples, you might notice that the outputs of this algorithm are the integer part (D) and the remainder (R) when a is divided by b. R also acts as a "counter" of the number of times the algorithm loops before stopping. For example, given $a = 13$ and $b = 5$, the outputs are D = 2 and R = 3, because $\frac{13}{5}$ equals 2 with a remainder of 3, and the algorithm will loop three times before it stops.

Step 2: Approach Strategically

Question 3a: The first time through the loop, D will be set to $\frac{58}{11}$, a will be set to $58 - 1 = 57$, and R will be set to $0 + 1 = 1$. The second time through the loop, D will be set to $\frac{57}{11}$, a will be set to $57 - 1 = 56$, and R will be set to $1 + 1 = 2$. The third time through the loop, D will be set to $\frac{56}{11}$, a will be set to $56 - 1 = 55$, and R will be set to $2 + 1 = 3$. On the fourth time through the loop, D will be set to $\frac{55}{11} = 5$, which is an integer, so the algorithm will stop and the values of a and R will not be changed. Thus, the outputs are D = 5 and R = 3. D = 5 is not present among the selections, but R = 3 is. The correct answer is **(D)**.

Question 3b: If $a > b$, then you've already seen that the algorithm will stop. If $a = b$, then the algorithm will also stop, because a number divided by itself always equals 1 with a remainder of 0. If $a < b$, it may seem that the algorithm will get stuck because D will keep getting set to a fraction. For example, if $a = 9$ and $b = 10$, D will get set to $\frac{9}{10}$, then $\frac{8}{10}$, then $\frac{7}{10}$, and so on. However, a will eventually be reduced to 0, at which point $\frac{a}{b}$ will equal 0 (which is an integer) and the algorithm will stop. Thus, no matter the values of a and b, the algorithm's termination condition is always triggered. This means that it will never not stop, which is **(D)**.

Multi-Source Reasoning

As its name suggests, Multi-Source Reasoning tests your ability to synthesize information from multiple sources to answer questions. The information will be presented on two or three tabbed pages. You will have to click through the tabs to find the information you need. The data can be in the form of text, graphs, or tables.

The information on the tabs may seem overwhelming, so approach it similarly to how you approach Reading Comprehension passages. Get the gist of what the tabs contain and take brief notes highlighting the main points of each tab. Don't try to absorb all of the information, but make sure you scan all of the information on each tab so that you'll know where to find it when you answer the questions.

The tabbed pages are on the left side of the screen, and the questions appear one at a time on the right. You can get hands-on experience with tabbed pages in your online resources. Take a few minutes to become familiar with the navigation of this section. Doing so will save you valuable time when answering the questions.

Some of the items about the tabbed information will be in the standard multiple-choice format that you're familiar with from the Verbal and Quantitative sections. Others, called multiple dichotomous choice items, will require you to evaluate three statements or questions individually; you'll usually be choosing whether statements are true or false or whether the answer to a question is yes or no. There is no partial credit.

| Stainless Steel | Table #1 | Table #2 |

Stainless Steel Categories

Stainless steels are alloys of iron and carbon that also contain a minimum of 10.5% chromium and various amounts of other alloying materials, which may include molybdenum, manganese, and nickel, among others. Stainless steels are designated with three-digit SAE numbers generally ranging from the 200s to the 600s, sometimes followed by a single letter. The three most common categories of stainless steel are described below, and examples of seven specific varieties from within these three categories are listed in the tables that follow.

Ferritic steels contain 12.5%–17% chromium, less than 0.1% carbon, and up to 1% nickel. Ferritic steels are magnetic and can be strengthened by cold working but cannot be heat treated. They are commonly used in automotive exhaust systems, agricultural equipment, and high-heat applications such as furnaces and boilers.

Austenitic steels contain 16%–26% chromium, not more than 0.8% carbon, and 6%–15% nickel. They are nonmagnetic and are not heat treatable. Austenitic steels are the most common type of stainless steel globally, and they are commonly used in food-processing equipment, piping, and kitchen utensils.

Martensitic steels contain 10.5%–17% chromium, up to 1.2% carbon, and not more than 0.4% nickel. They are magnetic and heat treatable. Martensitic steels are commonly used in knives, cutting tools, and dental and surgical equipment.

| Stainless Steel | Table #1 | Table #2 |

Partial Composition of Various Stainless Steels

SAE NUMBER	CHROMIUM %	CARBON %	NICKEL %
304	18.0–20.0	0.08	8.0–10.5
309S	22.0–24.0	0.08	12.0–15.0
316	16.0–18.0	0.08	10.0–14.0
321	17.0–19.0	0.08	9.0–12.0
409	10.5–11.75	0.08	0.50
410	11.5–13.5	0.15	0.75
430	16.0–18.0	0.20	0.75

| Stainless Steel | Table #1 | Table #2 |

Select Physical Properties of Various Stainless Steels

SAE NUMBER	DENSITY (KG/M³)	ROCKWELL HARDNESS	HEAT TREATABLE	MAGNETIC
304	7,900	90	No	No
309S	7,950	85	No	No
316	8,000	95	No	No
321	7,900	95	No	No
409	7,800	75	No	Yes
410	7,850	80	Yes	Yes
430	7,800	89	No	Yes

4. Consider each of the following statements. Indicate *Yes* if the given information supports the statement. Otherwise, indicate *No*.

Yes	No	
O	O	All of the listed stainless steels with a carbon content of 0.08% are Austenitic.
O	O	A stainless steel among those listed with a Rockwell hardness of at least 85 must be either Austenitic or Ferritic.
O	O	Of the steels listed, the average density of Austenitic steels is greater than the average density of Ferritic steels.

5. Based on the information in the passage and tables, the stainless steel with the highest ratio of carbon to nickel has which of the following hardness ratings?

   O   80

   O   85

   O   89

   O   90

   O   95

Step 1: Analyze the Information

You approached Graphics Interpretation by first getting a general sense of how the graph works. Similarly, you need to know what is on each tabbed page before you begin answering Multi-Source Reasoning questions. Take brief notes on the content of each tab as you examine it.

In the first tab, you find a definition of stainless steel and data about three classes of stainless steel, including certain physical properties of each, such as whether it is magnetic or heat treatable, and their common uses.

On the second tab, you are given a table detailing the chromium, carbon, and nickel content ranges of seven different stainless steels, listed by their SAE numbers. Note that the content ranges are listed as percentages.

Switch to the third tab to view another table. This one shows physical properties of each of the same seven steels, including density, hardness, and whether the steel is magnetic or heat treatable.

Step 2: Approach Strategically

Question 4a: The text in Tab 1 indicates that Austenitic steels contain 16%–26% chromium, not more than 0.8% carbon, and 6%–15% nickel. These steels are also neither magnetic nor heat treatable.

The question restricts itself to steels that are 0.08% carbon, so find those steels in Tab 2. They are SAE 304 through SAE 409. Of these, SAE 409 has less than 16% chromium and only 0.5% nickel. Therefore, it is not Austenitic. Alternatively, you could check Tab 3 for the magnetic and heat-treatable characteristics. Here, you'll see that SAE 409 is magnetic and therefore not Austenitic. The answer is No.

Question 4b: Because this specifies a hardness of 85 or above, begin by examining the table in Tab 3; all of the SAE 300-series steels and SAE 430 have a hardness of 85 or higher. Next, return to the text in Tab 1 to determine what constitutes Ferritic steel: it is magnetic but not heat treatable. You've already determined from the previous question that an Austenitic steel is neither. Put another way, any steel in the table that is not heat treatable is either Austenitic or Ferritic. According to the table in Tab 3, none of the SAE 300-series steels is heat treatable and neither is SAE 430, so the answer is Yes.

Question 4c: From the first two questions in this set, you've determined from the information in the text and the table in Tab 3 that all of the SAE 300-series steels are Austenitic. You've also determined that SAE 409 and SAE 430 are Ferritic. A glance at Tab 3 will confirm that SAE 410, being both magnetic and heat treatable, is neither Austenitic nor Ferritic. Rather than doing complex calculations, notice that the two Ferritic steels, SAE 409 and SAE 430, each have a density of 7,800, while all of the Austenitic steels are above 7,850. Thus, you can conclude that the Austenitic steels have a higher average density, so the answer is Yes.

Question 5: Because this question asks for a ratio of carbon to nickel, think of carbon as the numerator of a fraction and nickel as the denominator. The highest ratio will be the fraction with the largest numerator relative to the denominator. Therefore, you can quickly eliminate all of the SAE 300-series steels, since their denominators are many times greater than any of the SAE 400-series steels while their numerators are less than or equal to those of the 400 series. Now use estimation to compare SAE 409 to SAE 410: 0.08 over 0.50 is less than 0.15 over 0.75, since 0.15 is nearly twice 0.08 but 0.75 is considerably less than twice 0.50. What about SAE 430? Since it has a bigger numerator than SAE 410 but the same denominator, it must have the highest ratio. Now find its hardness rating in the table in Tab 3: 89. Therefore, **(C)** is correct.

You've learned from working through this set of Multi-Source Reasoning items that it's crucial to get the gist of each tabbed page and take brief notes highlighting the main points before attempting to answer any questions. Now apply these techniques to the next set of Multi-Source Reasoning items.

| Email #1 | Email #2 | Email #3 |

*Email from **project manager** to financial officer*

August 3, 9:43 a.m.

Did all three bids arrive on time last night? We need to minimize delays on construction, so if the contractors have submitted their estimates and our research team has compiled reports on the contractors' histories, we should make a decision on which firm to hire by the end of the day.

| Email #1 | Email #2 | Email #3 |

*Email from **financial officer** in response to the project manager's August 3, 9:43 a.m. email*

August 3, 10:12 a.m.

Appaloosa Construction sent us a bid of $1.35 million. Its bid is the highest of the three, but its track record is spotless; none of the past 10 major projects it has worked on has gone over budget by more than 4 percent. Breton Construction did manage to underbid them—its representative claims that it can do the project for $1.25 million. However, in the past two years, Breton oversaw two different projects that went over budget by a full 25 percent. If our project were to exceed Breton's estimate by a comparable percentage, we would run out of funds before completion. Finally, Campolina Construction presented a $1.1 million plan, and its track record is as good as Appaloosa's. Unfortunately, although Appaloosa and Breton can both start tomorrow, Campolina would be unable to begin work until August 25, so we cannot accept Campolina's low bid.

| Email #1 | Email #2 | Email #3 |

*Email from **project manager** in response to the financial officer's August 3, 10:12 a.m. email*

August 3, 10:38 a.m.

Even though Breton's work could potentially cost less than either of the other two, that savings does not justify the risk of being unable to complete the project. But as far as Campolina is concerned, you're not considering the actual cost of a delay. It's true that we are losing money at a constant rate each day we don't start building. But even after factoring in the losses of waiting until August 25, the estimated cost of working with Campolina still ends up $50,000 below Appaloosa's bid.

6. Consider each of the following statements. Does the information in the three emails support the inferences as stated? Choose *Yes* if the statement can be accurately inferred; otherwise, choose *No*.

Yes   No

○   ○   In making their decision, the project manager and the financial officer considered how much time the contractors would spend on construction.

○   ○   The project manager and the financial officer disagree about the best choice of contractors for completing the project.

○   ○   The project manager is willing to wait a few days before deciding on Campolina's bid.

7. The amount of money lost each day that construction is delayed is closest to

○ $2,500

○ $10,000

○ $20,000

○ $55,000

○ $65,000

Step 1: Analyze the Information

First, look through the tabbed pages and notice the basics: you have three emails, sent minutes apart, between a project manager and a financial officer. Use your Reading Comprehension Passage Mapping skills to create a brief synopsis of each email in your scratchwork:

Email #1—project manager to financial officer:

- Asking about the bids
- Start construction as soon as possible
- Make a decision by the end of the day

Email #2—financial officer to project manager:

- Appaloosa—$1.35 million—great track record
- Breton—$1.25 million—usually over budget—would run out of funds before completion
- Campolina—$1.1 million—can't begin work until August 25—can't accept

Think strategically here: although the financial officer never draws an explicit conclusion about which company should be hired, his opinion is clear. Breton could cause the company to run out of money for the project, and Campolina's delayed start date is unacceptable, so the financial officer must be in favor of Appaloosa.

Email #3—project manager to financial officer:

- Breton—not worth the risk
- Reminder about the cost of delay
- Campolina is still cheaper, even with the delay

It is not necessary to jot down all of the figures and calculations from the email. Just as with Reading Comprehension, if you need the details, they will be there for you to refer to later.

Step 2: Approach Strategically

Question 6: Notice that you have another set of yes/no questions. As always, you'll want to read the introductory sentences very carefully. Your task is to consider whether the inferences in the questions are supported by the information in the three emails. Critical Reasoning skills will help you here; you must use *only* the evidence in the three emails to determine your answers.

Question 6a: Read carefully here. Time is discussed, but it is discussed in reference to when the construction can begin, not how long it will take. There isn't any mention of the length of construction in your notes, and if you glance through the three emails, there isn't any information there either. The answer is No.

Question 6b: This question asks whether the project manager and financial officer disagree about who would be the best contractor. The answer to this question, as seen in your notes on the emails, is Yes. The project manager thinks Campolina is the best choice, and the financial officer is in favor of Appaloosa.

Question 6c: Here, the question asks whether the project manager is willing to wait a few days to decide. Glance at your notes to find relevant key words: "decision" is mentioned in the first email, and "delay," or waiting, is mentioned in the third. Going to the first email, you see that the project manager wants to reach a decision by the end of the day. This seems to contradict the inference given in the question, but don't stop just yet. Check the third email to see whether the project manager changed her mind. In the third email, the project manager discusses waiting, stating that it might be acceptable to wait to begin construction with Campolina—but there is nothing in this email about waiting to make a decision. Thus, you cannot infer that the project manager is willing to wait a few days, and the answer here is No.

Question 7: By now, you can expect that you'll need to find information in multiple emails to answer this question. Looking at your notes, you see that the delay costs are discussed in the third email. The email states that a constant amount is lost every day that construction is delayed. From the second email, you find that the other two companies can start the next day, August 4, but Campolina can't start until August 25, a delay of 21 days. Next, use the information given to determine how much money is lost in those 21 days.

The third email says that even with the delay, Campolina would cost $50,000 less than Appaloosa's $1.35 million bid, or $1.3 million. That means the cost caused by the delay would be $1.3 million – $1.1 million, or $200,000. To determine the cost per day, calculate $\frac{\$200,000}{21} \approx \$9,524$. However, since the question asks for the number that's "closest to" the amount lost per day, you can save time by estimating. Round 21 to 20 and calculate much more easily that $200,000 divided by 20 is $10,000, or (**B**).

Table Analysis

Table Analysis items measure your ability to interpret and analyze information presented in a sortable table similar to a spreadsheet. You will see a table, a paragraph of text that describes it, and one set of the same three-part multiple dichotomous choice items you saw for Multi-Source Reasoning (i.e., yes/no, true/false, etc.).

Directly above the table, you will see a Sort button that, when clicked, opens a drop-down menu of options that correspond to the column headers in the table. When you select a category from the drop-down menu, the entire chart will be sorted based on the category you select. If the information in that column is numerical, it will be sorted from lowest to highest. If the information in that column is text, it will be sorted in alphabetical order. While working through the questions in this book, decide how you would sort the information before answering each question. To gain experience sorting tables in the test interface, use the questions in your online resources.

Read the text that accompanies the table first to get an overview of the table's content. Then look at the table itself, paying special attention to the column headings. Now let's look at some Table Analysis items.

Total Fall Enrollment in Private Degree-Granting Institutions: 2018

Sort By [Select... | ▼]

| | | UNDERGRADUATE | | | | POSTBACCALAUREATE | | |
| | | 4-YEAR | | 2-YEAR | | | | |
	Total	Not-for-profit	For-profit	Not-for-profit	For-profit	Total	Not-for-profit	For-profit
Alabama	58,558	23,229	34,000	0	1,329	7,343	4,128	3,215
Arizona	291,869	3,539	275,530	0	12,800	81,066	4,507	76,559
California	264,775	136,304	76,356	2,375	49,740	147,979	129,522	18,457
Colorado	69,460	18,375	40,733	165	10,187	20,507	13,586	6,921
District of Columbia	71,465	37,967	33,498	0	0	49,061	36,575	12,486
Florida	206,477	106,089	79,732	152	20,504	56,629	48,067	8,562
Georgia	76,356	47,701	23,670	1,057	3,928	23,757	17,940	5,817
Illinois	200,263	134,075	56,676	1,126	8,386	98,568	86,235	12,333
Indiana	88,896	68,677	13,020	495	6,704	16,110	15,652	458
Iowa	113,385	45,397	67,601	151	236	16,487	10,919	5,568
Massachusetts	173,897	166,873	2,800	1,737	2,487	97,339	97,203	136
Michigan	101,252	93,562	4,649	0	3,041	23,507	22,870	637
Minnesota	78,855	50,793	25,723	106	2,233	75,567	21,232	54,335
Missouri	117,735	95,299	12,510	2,275	7,651	49,937	49,298	639
New York	390,435	341,205	24,241	6,575	18,414	168,531	166,449	2,082
North Carolina	75,228	68,524	4,635	572	1,497	18,773	18,039	734
Ohio	146,395	107,277	7,044	1,272	30,802	31,669	30,621	1,048
Pennsylvania	251,369	195,359	17,783	7,492	30,735	83,943	83,372	571
Tennessee	75,283	54,023	8,373	278	12,609	18,187	17,097	1,090
Texas	127,359	92,495	12,935	867	21,062	36,657	33,996	2,661
Virginia	90,439	59,959	24,416	0	6,064	27,236	24,789	2,447

The table above gives the 2018 enrollment in private degree-granting institutions for the 20 states with the highest total enrollment, as well as for the District of Columbia. These statistics do not include state-funded and federally funded public institutions. The data include both for-profit and not-for-profit institutions; enrollment for both of these categories is provided in addition to the total enrollment.

8. Consider the following statements about enrollment in the 21 locations shown in the table. For each statement, indicate whether the statement is *True* or *False*, based on the information provided in the table.

True	False	
○	○	The state with the largest number of students enrolled in for-profit four-year undergraduate programs has the smallest number of students enrolled in not-for-profit four-year undergraduate programs.
○	○	The state with the median number of students enrolled in not-for-profit four-year undergraduate programs also has the median number of students enrolled in not-for-profit two-year undergraduate programs.
○	○	More than half of the students enrolled in degree-granting programs in Minnesota attend for-profit schools.

Step 1: Analyze the Information

As with Graphics Interpretation items, your first step should be to read the text accompanying the table. Here, the text explains that the table shows the private school enrollment numbers for various states, as well as for the District of Columbia, in 2018. It also tells you that the table distinguishes between for-profit and not-for-profit institutions.

Next, look at the table itself and read the column headings. The private institutions are split into two main categories, undergraduate and postbaccalaureate, which are further broken down into for-profit and not-for-profit schools. The undergraduate schools are also divided into two- and four-year programs. Total enrollment numbers for undergraduate and postbaccalaureate programs are also provided. This is a lot of information, and you will need to pay attention to how it is organized in order to answer the questions.

Step 2: Approach Strategically

Question 8a: Many Table Analysis questions ask you to compare pieces of information. Take each question one piece at a time. For this question, you first need to find the state with the largest enrollment in for-profit four-year undergraduate schools. Look at your table and find the column that contains that information. Here, it's easy to see that Arizona has the highest enrollment, with 275,530 students. If you weren't able to see that at a glance, you could sort the table by the for-profit four-year undergraduate column. Now that you have the first piece of information, it's time to find the second. You now know that you're looking for information about Arizona. Sort the table by the not-for-profit four-year undergraduate column, and you'll see that Arizona is by far the lowest, at 3,539 students. Arizona, the state with the largest for-profit four-year undergraduate enrollment, does in fact have the smallest not-for-profit four-year undergraduate enrollment, so the answer is True.

Question 8b: Here, you are asked again to compare two pieces of information. By now, you should be zeroing in on the key words in the statement that will tell you how to sort the table. In this case, you are looking for the "not-for-profit four-year undergraduate" column and the "not-for-profit two-year undergraduate" column. Also notice the key word "median," which appears twice. You need to sort two columns and compare the median numbers. The median number of each set will appear exactly in the middle of the set when all the terms are placed in ascending or descending order. You won't be able to eyeball the median number, so get ready to use the Sort function. First, sort by not-for-profit four-year undergraduate institutions:

Sort By [Undergraduate 4-year Not-for-profit | ▼]

| | | UNDERGRADUATE | | | | POSTBACCALAUREATE | | |
| | | 4-YEAR | | 2-YEAR | | | | |
	Total	Not-for-profit	For-profit	Not-for-profit	For-profit	Total	Not-for-profit	For-profit
Arizona	291,869	3,539	275,530	0	12,800	81,066	4,507	76,559
Colorado	69,460	18,375	40,733	165	10,187	20,507	13,586	6,921
Alabama	58,558	23,229	34,000	0	1,329	7,343	4,128	3,215
District of Columbia	71,465	37,967	33,498	0	0	49,061	36,575	12,486
Iowa	113,385	45,397	67,601	151	236	16,487	10,919	5,568
Georgia	76,356	47,701	23,670	1,057	3,928	23,757	17,940	5,817
Minnesota	78,855	50,793	25,723	106	2,233	75,567	21,232	54,335
Tennessee	75,283	54,023	8,373	278	12,609	18,187	17,097	1,090
Virginia	90,439	59,959	24,416	0	6,064	27,236	24,789	2,447
North Carolina	75,228	68,524	4,635	572	1,497	18,773	18,039	734
Indiana	88,896	68,677	13,020	495	6,704	16,110	15,652	458
Texas	127,359	92,495	12,935	867	21,062	36,657	33,996	2,661
Michigan	101,252	93,562	4,649	0	3,041	23,507	22,870	637
Missouri	117,735	95,299	12,510	2,275	7,651	49,937	49,298	639
Florida	206,477	106,089	79,732	152	20,504	56,629	48,067	8,562
Ohio	146,395	107,277	7,044	1,272	30,802	31,669	30,621	1,048
Illinois	200,263	134,075	56,676	1,126	8,386	98,568	86,235	12,333
California	264,775	136,304	76,356	2,375	49,740	147,979	129,522	18,457
Massachusetts	173,897	166,873	2,800	1,737	2,487	97,339	97,203	136
Pennsylvania	251,369	195,359	17,783	7,492	30,735	83,943	83,372	571
New York	390,435	341,205	24,241	6,575	18,414	168,531	166,449	2,082

There are 21 locations in this table, so you will be looking for the 11th state. To calculate which line you're looking for in a table with an odd number of lines, you can always use the following formula:

$$\text{Median} = \frac{\text{Total} - 1}{2} + 1.$$

In this example, $\frac{21 - 1}{2} + 1 = 10 + 1 = 11$. According to the sorted chart, the 11th state is Indiana. Once you know to focus on Indiana, sort the table by not-for-profit two-year undergraduate institutions:

Sort By [Undergraduate 2-year Not-for-profit | ▾]

| | Total | UNDERGRADUATE | | | | Total | POSTBACCALAUREATE | |
| | | 4-YEAR | | 2-YEAR | | | | |
		Not-for-profit	For-profit	Not-for-profit	For-profit		Not-for-profit	For-profit
Arizona	291,869	3,539	275,530	0	12,800	81,066	4,507	76,559
Michigan	101,252	93,562	4,649	0	3,041	23,507	22,870	637
Virginia	90,439	59,959	24,416	0	6,064	27,236	24,789	2,447
District of Columbia	71,465	37,967	33,498	0	0	49,061	36,575	12,486
Alabama	58,558	23,229	34,000	0	1,329	7,343	4,128	3,215
Minnesota	78,855	50,793	25,723	106	2,233	75,567	21,232	54,335
Iowa	113,385	45,397	67,601	151	236	16,487	10,919	5,568
Florida	206,477	106,089	79,732	152	20,504	56,629	48,067	8,562
Colorado	69,460	18,375	40,733	165	10,187	20,507	13,586	6,921
Tennessee	75,283	54,023	8,373	278	12,609	18,187	17,097	1,090
Indiana	88,896	68,677	13,020	495	6,704	16,110	15,652	458
North Carolina	75,228	68,524	4,635	572	1,497	18,773	18,039	734
Texas	127,359	92,495	12,935	867	21,062	36,657	33,996	2,661
Georgia	76,356	47,701	23,670	1,057	3,928	23,757	17,940	5,817
Illinois	200,263	134,075	56,676	1,126	8,386	98,568	86,235	12,333
Ohio	146,395	107,277	7,044	1,272	30,802	31,669	30,621	1,048
Massachusetts	173,897	166,873	2,800	1,737	2,487	97,339	97,203	136
Missouri	117,735	95,299	12,510	2,275	7,651	49,937	49,298	639
California	264,775	136,304	76,356	2,375	49,740	147,979	129,522	18,457
New York	390,435	341,205	24,241	6,575	18,414	168,531	166,449	2,082
Pennsylvania	251,369	195,359	17,783	7,492	30,735	83,943	83,372	571

Again, Indiana is the median (the 11th state), so the answer to this question is True.

Question 8c: For this question, you'll be looking for information about Minnesota. Specifically, you'll need to find the number of students in that state who attend for-profit schools and then determine whether that number is more than half of Minnesota's total enrollment.

Approach strategically here—rather than add all the numbers, do some comparisons. In the four-year undergraduate programs, there are approximately 25,000 more students in not-for-profit schools. Look next at the two-year undergraduate enrollments. These numbers are probably too low to significantly affect the total, so turn your attention to the postbaccalaureate column: here, there are approximately 33,000 more students enrolled in for-profit schools. Because 33,000 is significantly higher than 25,000, you know that there are more students enrolled in the for-profit schools, making the answer to this question True.

Of course, if you have time to check your work, you can use the on-screen calculator:

For-profit: $25{,}723 + 2{,}233 + 54{,}335 = 82{,}291$

Not-for-profit: $50{,}793 + 106 + 21{,}232 = 72{,}131$

More than half the enrollments in Minnesota are in for-profit institutions, confirming our answer of True.

Remember, for success in Table Analysis, you need to understand what information the table contains and how it is organized before attacking the questions. Pay close attention to the column headings and use the Sort function when a vertical scan of a column is not practical, especially when finding the median. Apply this strategic approach to the next set of Table Analysis questions.

U.S. Coastal Counties Most Frequently Hit by Hurricanes: 1960–2008

Sort By [Select... ▼]

COASTLINE REGION	STATE	COUNTY	NUMBER OF HURRICANES	PERCENT CHANGE IN POPULATION, 1960–2008
Gulf of Mexico	Florida	Monroe County	15	50.8
Gulf of Mexico	Louisiana	Lafourche Parish	14	67.2
Atlantic	North Carolina	Carteret County	14	104.3
Atlantic	North Carolina	Dare County	13	465.9
Atlantic	North Carolina	Hyde County	13	10.1
Gulf of Mexico	Louisiana	Jefferson Parish	12	108.9
Atlantic	Florida	Palm Beach County	12	454.7
Atlantic	Florida	Miami-Dade County	11	156.5
Gulf of Mexico	Louisiana	St. Bernard Parish	11	17.2
Gulf of Mexico	Louisiana	Cameron Parish	11	4.8
Gulf of Mexico	Louisiana	Terrebonne Parish	11	78.7

The table presents data on the 11 U.S. coastal counties that were hit by the most hurricanes between 1960 and 2008. It also lists the percent change in population for each county during the same time period. Positive percentages represent population growth.

9. Consider the following statements. For each statement, evaluate whether that statement is *True* or *False*, according to the information in the table.

True	False	
○	○	The median number of hurricanes in the Florida counties was higher than the median number of hurricanes in each of the other states' counties.
○	○	The counties listed in the table that experienced the three greatest percent changes in population during the period are all part of the coastline region whose listed counties had the greater range in number of hurricanes during the same period.
○	○	The Gulf of Mexico coastline region experienced fewer hurricanes per county listed in the table, on average, than did the Atlantic coastline region.

Step 1: Analyze the Information

This table has fewer columns than the previous one did, but don't assume that means you're in for an easy time—the questions might compensate for the graph's simplicity. They may require more thought, more math, or both. Begin as always by reading the paragraph of text that accompanies the table. It tells you that the table provides data about hurricane occurrences in U.S. coastal counties during a specific time period.

Now look at the table itself. Note that the first three columns provide geographical data and move from more general to more specific as you go from left to right. There are only two coastline regions, but they include three states, which in turn contain a total of 11 counties. The last two columns contain numerical data. Glance at the numbers in the columns to get a feel for the ranges and to see whether there are any obvious outliers. The numbers in the Hurricanes column don't vary much, but the numbers in the Percent population change column, while all positive (signifying population growth), vary widely.

Step 2: Approach Strategically

Question 9a: This statement deals with the median number of hurricanes in each state's counties. Since it compares Florida to the other states, you want to sort by State, not by County. That will allow you to see each state's counties grouped together vertically, which will make it easier to find the median for each state:

Sort By [State   ▾]

COASTLINE REGION	STATE	COUNTY	NUMBER OF HURRICANES	PERCENT CHANGE IN POPULATION, 1960–2008
Gulf of Mexico	Florida	Monroe County	15	50.8
Atlantic	Florida	Palm Beach County	12	454.7
Atlantic	Florida	Miami-Dade County	11	156.5
Gulf of Mexico	Louisiana	Lafourche Parish	14	67.2
Gulf of Mexico	Louisiana	Jefferson Parish	12	108.9
Gulf of Mexico	Louisiana	St. Bernard Parish	11	17.2
Gulf of Mexico	Louisiana	Cameron Parish	11	4.8
Gulf of Mexico	Louisiana	Terrebonne Parish	11	78.7
Atlantic	North Carolina	Carteret County	14	104.3
Atlantic	North Carolina	Dare County	13	465.9
Atlantic	North Carolina	Hyde County	13	10.1

There are three counties in Florida: Monroe, Palm Beach, and Miami-Dade. There were 15, 12, and 11 hurricanes in those counties, respectively. Thus, the median number of hurricanes for Florida's counties was 12. Louisiana has five counties, so the median number of hurricanes will be the third one when they are listed in numerical order. Louisiana's five counties (Lafourche Parish, Jefferson Parish, St. Bernard Parish, Cameron Parish, and Terrebonne Parish) had 14, 12, 11, 11, and 11 hurricanes, respectively. Thus the median for Louisiana was 11. North Carolina's three counties (Carteret, Dare, and Hyde) had 14, 13, and 13 hurricanes, respectively, for a median of 13. Since Florida's median of 12 is lower than North Carolina's median of 13, Florida's median was not higher than the median in each of the other states' counties, and the answer is False.

Question 9b: Take a moment to think about where to begin here, because this statement relates population change, counties, *and* coastline regions. You need to figure out which counties experienced the greatest percent change in population and which coastline region had the greater range in number of hurricanes. You can work on either one first. If you start with the population growth, you can scan down the Percent change in population column and look for the three largest numbers. If you find it hard to keep track of them this way, sort the table on that column:

Sort By [Percent change in population... | ▼]

COASTLINE REGION	STATE	COUNTY	NUMBER OF HURRICANES	PERCENT CHANGE IN POPULATION, 1960–2008
Gulf of Mexico	Louisiana	Cameron Parish	11	4.8
Atlantic	North Carolina	Hyde County	13	10.1
Gulf of Mexico	Louisiana	St. Bernard Parish	11	17.2
Gulf of Mexico	Florida	Monroe County	15	50.8
Gulf of Mexico	Louisiana	Lafourche Parish	14	67.2
Gulf of Mexico	Louisiana	Terrebonne Parish	11	78.7
Atlantic	North Carolina	Carteret County	14	104.3
Gulf of Mexico	Louisiana	Jefferson Parish	12	108.9
Atlantic	Florida	Miami-Dade County	11	156.5
Atlantic	Florida	Palm Beach County	12	454.7
Atlantic	North Carolina	Dare County	13	465.9

The last three rows represent the counties with the greatest percent change in population: Miami-Dade County, at 156.5%, Palm Beach County, at 454.7%, and Dare County, at 465.9%. Now glance at the Coastline region column to see that all three of these counties are in the Atlantic coastline region. The question that remains is whether the counties in the Atlantic coastline region had a greater range in number of hurricanes than did the counties in the Gulf of Mexico region. Sort the table, this time on the Coastline region column:

Sort By [Coastline region...   ▼]

COASTLINE REGION	STATE	COUNTY	NUMBER OF HURRICANES	PERCENT CHANGE IN POPULATION, 1960–2008
Atlantic	North Carolina	Dare County	13	465.9
Atlantic	Florida	Palm Beach County	12	454.7
Atlantic	Florida	Miami-Dade County	11	156.5
Atlantic	North Carolina	Carteret County	14	104.3
Atlantic	North Carolina	Hyde County	13	10.1
Gulf of Mexico	Louisiana	Jefferson Parish	12	108.9
Gulf of Mexico	Louisiana	Terrebonne Parish	11	78.7
Gulf of Mexico	Louisiana	Lafourche Parish	14	67.2
Gulf of Mexico	Florida	Monroe County	15	50.8
Gulf of Mexico	Louisiana	St. Bernard Parish	11	17.2
Gulf of Mexico	Louisiana	Cameron Parish	11	4.8

In the Atlantic coastline region, Carteret County in North Carolina experienced the greatest number of hurricanes, at 14. Miami-Dade County in Florida experienced the smallest number of hurricanes, at 11. Thus, the range for counties in the Atlantic region was $14 - 11 = 3$. In the Gulf of Mexico region, Monroe County in Florida experienced the greatest number of hurricanes, at 15. Three counties in the region experienced 11 hurricanes, the smallest number for the region. The range for counties in the Gulf of Mexico region was therefore $15 - 11 = 4$. Since the counties with the three greatest percent changes in population were part of the Atlantic coastline region, which had a smaller range than did the Gulf of Mexico coastline region, the answer is False.

Question 9c: Since this statement compares the Gulf of Mexico coastline region to the Atlantic coastline region, sort the table again by coastline region (see the sorted table above in the explanation for Question 9b). The statement asks about the number of hurricanes per county, on average, so you'll have to calculate the average for each coastline region.

Add the number of hurricanes for the Atlantic coastline region to get $13 + 12 + 11 + 14 + 13 = 63$. There are five counties in the Atlantic coastline region, so the average number of hurricanes per county was $\frac{63}{5}$. You can simplify this to $12\frac{3}{5}$ or use the calculator to get $63 \div 5 = 12.6$. For the Gulf of Mexico coastline region, there were a total of $12 + 11 + 14 + 15 + 11 + 11 = 74$ hurricanes. There are six counties in that coastline region, so the average number of hurricanes per county was $\frac{74}{6}$. Simplify this to $12\frac{1}{3}$ or use the calculator to get $74 \div 6 = 12.3333$. Since $12.3333 < 12.6$ (or $12\frac{1}{3} < 12\frac{3}{5}$), the Gulf of Mexico coastline region did indeed experience fewer hurricanes per county, on average, than did the Atlantic coastline region, so the answer is True.

Branch Manager Performance Reviews

Sort By [Select... ▼]

MANAGER	EMPLOYEE SATISFACTION RATING (%)	YEARLY SALES (THOUSANDS OF DOLLARS)	PERCENT CHANGE IN SALES OVER PREVIOUS YEAR	UNDERGROUND PARKING	FREE SHIPPING	SIZE OF SALES FORCE
L. Jenkins	32.3	58.4	+5.3	no	no	5
P. Parsons	44.4	92.0	−7.8	yes	yes	11
A. Yangzou	65.7	105.2	−1.2	no	yes	10
D. Xin	55.7	85.1	+10.8	yes	yes	15
M. Stover	18.0	116.9	+15.5	no	yes	12
Z. Szymes	50.1	64.7	+4.8	no	no	8
T. Emerald	64.2	77.4	+0.3	yes	no	11
O. McDonough	75.5	79.6	+31.2	no	yes	8
K. Eriksson	46.9	58.9	−20.0	no	no	13
B. Stripley	48.7	101.7	−9.4	yes	yes	16

A small furniture store chain conducted performance reviews of its 10 branch managers. The managers' performance in several metrics over the last year has been compiled in the table. The table also lists some relevant features of each manager's branch.

10. For each of the following statements, select *True* if the statement can be verified to be true based on the given information. Otherwise, select *False*.

True	False	
○	○	A majority of the managers who oversaw an increase in sales over the previous year have an employee satisfaction rating higher than the median.
○	○	There is a positive correlation between the size of a branch's sales force and that branch's change in year-over-year sales.
○	○	The branch that had the highest sales in the previous year has underground parking.

Step 1: Analyze the Information

For each of 10 branch managers, three measures of job performance are given, as well as three features of their stores.

Step 2: Approach Strategically

Question 10a: Sort the data by employee satisfaction rating to quickly find the median; it's about 49%. Six managers saw positive sales growth. Of these, four have an employee rating above 49%—Emerald, Xin, Szymes, and McDonough—and two have an employee rating below 49%—Jenkins and Stover. Four out of six is a majority. The correct answer is True.

Question 10b: The second statement asserts that as the size of a branch's sales force increases, so too does its change in year-over-year sales. This is untrue: the three smallest branches saw positive growth, while the two biggest branches saw negative growth. There is in fact no correlation between sales force and change in sales, and the second statement is False.

Question 10c: For the third statement, locate the branch that had the highest sales in the previous year. Start by looking at the branches with the highest sales this year and use the percent change to estimate last year's sales. While Stover's branch had the highest sales this year, because they were up 15.5% over the previous year, Stover's sales in the previous year were under $100,000. The branch with the highest sales the previous year was Stripley's. Its $101,700 in sales this year with a 9.4% decrease over the previous year puts the previous year's sales at around $112,000. Stripley's branch does have underground parking, so this statement is True.

Two-Part Analysis

Simply put, Two-Part Analysis items have solutions in two parts. Two-Part Analysis items consist of a few lines of text and instructions to select choices in a table based on the given information. These items may test quantitative or verbal skills.

Solving an algebraic Two-Part Analysis usually necessitates setting up an algebraic equation with two variables. You'll want to begin by first reading the text and identifying the two quantities, which may be provided or may need to be assigned variables. Then, you'll create one or more equations that relate the two values or variables. Once you've set up your equations, you can simplify them and look for a match (if the answer choices are algebraic equations or expressions) or start plugging in answer choices from the table until you find two corresponding values that work together.

Verbal Two-Part Analysis questions draw on many of the same logical reasoning skills, such as drawing supported inferences and finding assumptions, that you use on the Verbal section of the GMAT. For example, after reading about a type of dwelling used by a certain species of animal, you might identify from among the choices a characteristic that must be true of all dwellings of that type and a characteristic that can never be true. Alternatively, you might be asked to strengthen and weaken an author's argument.

All this will make much more sense with concrete examples, so let's take a look at some questions to see how Two-Part Analysis items work.

11. At University X, there are 146 students who are taking economics and 97 students who are taking history.

In the table below, pick two numbers that are consistent with the information that is given. In the first column, select the row that shows the number of students at University X who are taking at least one of economics and history, and in the second column, select the row that shows the number of students at University X who are taking both economics and history.

TAKING AT LEAST ONE OF ECONOMICS AND HISTORY	TAKING BOTH ECONOMICS AND HISTORY	POSSIBLE ANSWERS
O	O	78
O	O	83
O	O	104
O	O	154
O	O	160
O	O	164

Step 1: Analyze the Information

The text in Two-Part Analysis items is likely to be brief, so read it thoroughly before doing anything else. Here, you are given information about students at University X: the number of students who are taking economics, 146, and the number of students who are taking history, 97. The question asks you to find two numbers: the number of students taking at least one of these two subjects and the number of students taking both.

Step 2: Approach Strategically

Start by solving for the number of students taking at least one subject. The most efficient way to determine this number is to think critically. If you add together the numbers of students taking each subject, you get $146 + 97 = 243$. However, you know from the question stem and the column header that some students are taking both; if you rely on simple addition, you end up counting those students twice. Instead, set up an equation that relates the number of students in *at least* one subject, a, to the number of students in *both*, b.

Initial formula:	# in at least one = # in Group 1 + # in Group 2 − # in both
Fill in what you know:	$a = 146 + 97 - b$
Simplify:	$a = 243 - b$

Before you start plugging in the answer choices to find two values that satisfy this equation, think critically: Which number will be bigger? In this case, it has to be a. With that in mind, move to the answer choices.

Because your equation is $a = 243 - b$, start by plugging b into the equation to determine if there is a corresponding value for a in the chart. b must be the smaller of the two numbers, so start testing at the top of the column with $b = 78$. Your equation is now $a = 243 - 78 = 165$. Do you see 165 in the possible answer choices? Nope. The closest they get is 164, so this is not the correct answer. Once you know that 78 is not a possible answer for b, move on to 83. Plugging it into the formula, you have $a = 243 - 83 = 160$. Do you see 160 among the possible answer choices? Yes. This question format always has a single solution, so you don't need to test any further answer choices. You have your answer: $a = 160$ and $b = 83$.

Before submitting your answers, make sure that you enter each of your choices in the correct column. It would be unfortunate to do all of the work correctly, get the correct answers, and then not receive credit simply because you selected the numbers in the opposite columns. Look back at your scratchwork and remember that a represents the number of students in at least one subject and b represents the number of students in both subjects. You can now be sure that 160 belongs in the first column and 83 belongs in the second column.

Take what you've learned about solving for unknowns by using the given information to set up an equation and apply it to the next Two-Part Analysis question.

12. When Car P travels at a constant speed of x miles per hour for 84 minutes, and Car Q travels at an average speed of y miles per hour for 168 minutes, Car P travels 21 miles more than Car Q.

   In the table below, select a value for x and a value for y that together are consistent with the given information. In the first column, select the row that corresponds to the value of x, and in the second column, select the row that corresponds to the value of y.

VALUE OF X	VALUE OF Y	POSSIBLE ANSWERS
O	O	8
O	O	14
O	O	17
O	O	29
O	O	42
O	O	49

Step 1: Analyze the Information

When reading the information, remember that your goal is to use it to create an equation that relates the two unknowns, x and y. The text gives information about two cars and states one definitive relationship between them: Car P travels 21 more miles than Car Q. That is enough to indicate that your equation will focus on distance traveled. Go back to the beginning of the question stem to determine what you can about the distance the two cars travel.

Step 2: Approach Strategically

Since the time traveled is given in terms of minutes, and speed is given in terms of miles per hour, you need to convert to get all of the times expressed in the same units.

$$\text{Car P time traveled} = 84 \text{ minutes} \times \frac{1 \text{ hour}}{60 \text{ minutes}} = 1.4 \text{ hours}$$

$$\text{Car Q time traveled} = 168 \text{ minutes} \times \frac{1 \text{ hour}}{60 \text{ minutes}} = 2.8 \text{ hours}$$

Since Distance = Speed × Time, the distance each car traveled, in terms of x and y, is as follows:

$$\text{Car P distance traveled} = \frac{x \text{ miles}}{\text{hour}} \times 1.4 \text{ hours} = 1.4x \text{ miles}$$

$$\text{Car Q distance traveled} = \frac{y \text{ miles}}{\text{hour}} \times 2.8 \text{ hours} = 2.8y \text{ miles}$$

Once you have determined the distance traveled by each car, use the information that Car P travels 21 miles farther to set up the following equation: $1.4x = 2.8y + 21$. Before moving to the answer choices, be sure to get one variable entirely by itself. In this case, you can divide both sides by 1.4 to get $x = 2y + 15$. You can now plug possible values for y into this equation to see what value for x would result.

To simplify the process of plugging in answer choices, first determine which value is going to be bigger. Since all of the answer choices are positive (as they would have to be, since they represent the speed a car travels), you know that x must be greater than y. This makes sense when you think about the logic of the problem, which specifies that Car P travels a greater distance than Car Q in a shorter amount of time.

Use the possible answer choices to start testing for y. As before, since you are starting with the smaller value, y, you will start plugging in numbers from the top of the list and work down. Start with $y = 8$. Substituting into the equation, you get $x = 2(8) + 15 = 31$. Since 31 is not an option in the table, you know that 8 is not the value of y. Next, try $y = 14$. In this case, the calculation would be $x = 2(14) + 15 = 43$. Again, 43 is not one of the available choices, so keep going. If $y = 17$, then $x = 2(17) + 15 = 49$. Since 49 is among the answer choices, it must be the value for x. Again, be very careful when filling in the answer choices. Your answers are $x = 49$ and $y = 17$.

Now that you are familiar with the basic format and structure of Two-Part Analysis items, try your hand at the following item, which focuses on your reasoning skills rather than on math.

13. A father is planning to knit a striped hat and a checkered blanket for his newborn son. Each of these items will consist of four distinct colors of yarn. Since the hat and blanket are part of a matching set, they must share at least two colors. Each color of yarn is available in three types: one made with cotton fiber, one made with wool fiber, and one made with acrylic fiber. The cotton and wool yarns are made from natural fibers, while the acrylic yarn is from a synthetic fiber. Due to cost concerns, each item can contain no more than two colors of yarn in natural fibers; the other colors will be synthetic. All of the yarn of the same color in each item will be made of the same kind of fiber. He has already chosen the following styles of yarn for each item.

Hat:

Green wool

Yellow wool

Blue acrylic

Blanket:

Red acrylic

Gray cotton

Blue acrylic

Select a style of yarn that could be used in exactly one of the items, but not both. Then select a style of yarn that can be used in neither the hat nor the blanket. Make only two selections, one in each column.

EITHER THE HAT OR BLANKET, BUT NOT BOTH	NEITHER HAT NOR BLANKET	POSSIBLE YARN STYLES
○	○	Brown acrylic
○	○	Orange acrylic
○	○	Gray acrylic
○	○	White acrylic
○	○	Red cotton
○	○	Black acrylic

Step 1: Analyze the Information

You have two items to be knitted; each will be made of four kinds of yarn, and the knitter has already decided on three of them for each project. Paraphrase the rules that govern selecting the fourth type of yarn: each item must have four different colors, each can have only two colors at most in natural fiber, and the two items must share two colors.

Step 2: Approach Strategically

Use the GMAT Core Competency of Attention to the Right Detail as you consider the rules governing each item. The hat already has two types of yarn made of natural fiber, so the fourth color there must be acrylic. The blanket only has one type of yarn with natural fibers, so its fourth color could be either natural (cotton or wool) or acrylic. The items already share one color, so at least one color picked to finish the items must be the same as another color in the other item in order for there to be two shared colors. On Test Day, you'd quickly paraphrase this info on your notepad.

Keep the rules in mind as you evaluate the choices. For the first column, you want to pick a style of yarn that would work for either item individually but not work for both, and for the second column, you want to pick one that can't be used in either. You already noted that an acrylic yarn would work in either item. Gray acrylic would be permissible for the hat but not for the blanket, since that item already has gray wool yarn. Thus, gray acrylic is the answer for the first column. If the fourth color in each item were brown, orange, white, or black, then each would have four distinct colors and two shared colors. So brown, orange, white, or black acrylic yarn could be used in both items, which means they're incorrect for both columns. Red cotton can't be used for the hat since it already has two wool yarns, and it can't be used for the blanket since it already has red acrylic yarn; this is the right answer for the second column.

Pay close attention to the column headings when filling in the answer choices. The correct answer for the first column is gray acrylic, and the correct answer for the second column is red cotton.

14. State A currently allows casino gambling while State B does not. The legislature of State B is considering a proposal under which a limited number of casino licenses would be granted within the state in order to compete with State A for gambling revenue. Given the fact that a great many citizens of State B currently visit casinos in State A, the legislature of State B would be foolish not to enact this proposal.

In the table below, select one statement that would *strengthen* the proposal and another that would *weaken* it. Make exactly two selections, one in each column.

WOULD STRENGTHEN PROPOSAL	WOULD WEAKEN PROPOSAL	POSSIBLE STATEMENTS
○	○	Some other states that have granted casino licenses have subsequently experienced an overall increase in revenue.
○	○	The residents of State B who currently visit casinos in State A travel to State A primarily to visit a nature preserve that serves as a major tourist attraction.
○	○	Currently, more State A residents than State B residents undertake international travel.
○	○	Before State A offered casinos, those residents of State B who wanted to visit casinos had to travel nearly twice as far in order to do so.
○	○	Most residents of State B who traveled to State A within the past year made the trip primarily to visit casinos.
○	○	Over the past five years, the gambling revenue that State A has taken in has more than offset the associated infrastructure costs associated with gambling tourism.

Step 1: Analyze the Information

In order to strengthen or weaken an argument, start by finding the conclusion, evidence, and assumption—exactly as you would do when attacking Strengthen or Weaken questions in Critical Reasoning. The author's conclusion is that State B should adopt the proposal to grant casino licenses. The evidence is that residents of State B currently visit casinos in State A. The author assumes that those same State B residents would visit casinos in State B if they had the opportunity to do so rather than visit the casinos in State A.

Step 2: Approach Strategically

To strengthen the argument, look for a statement that supports the assumption that State B residents would stay home if there were casinos in State B rather than travel to State A. The fifth statement does so very well: "Most residents of State B who traveled to State A within the past year made the trip primarily to visit casinos." If State B residents are traveling to State A specifically to visit casinos, they might well save themselves the trip if there were casinos in State B.

To weaken the argument, look for a statement that undercuts the assumption—that is, find a statement that makes it less likely that residents of State B would visit casinos within their own state if given the opportunity to do so. That's the second statement: "The residents of State B who currently visit casinos in State A travel to State A primarily to visit a nature preserve that serves as a major tourist attraction." If State B residents are traveling to State A in order to visit a nature preserve, then they are not traveling specifically in order to visit casinos, and perhaps their casino visits are not all that important to them. They will likely continue to travel to State A (and perhaps continue to visit the casinos there as part of their visit), but there is no reason to believe that they might make separate trips to visit casinos within State B.

The correct answers are "Most residents of State B who traveled to State A within the past year made the trip primarily to visit casinos" to strengthen the proposal and "The residents of State B who currently visit casinos in State A travel to State A primarily to visit a nature preserve that serves as a major tourist attraction" to weaken the proposal.

Note that the first choice is incorrect because even if some states did see increased revenue from casino gambling, there may be more states that did not, or that even saw revenue decreases. The third and fourth choices are wrong because international travel and what happened before State A offered casinos both have no bearing on the argument. Finally, the last choice is wrong because the argument is about revenue only; infrastructure costs have no impact.

As you've seen from the examples in this chapter, Integrated Reasoning questions measure many of the same skills that you use for the Quantitative and Verbal sections of the test, such as paraphrasing information, finding key words, determining whether an inference is supported, and using estimation instead of calculation. Regular review of the questions in this chapter, as well as those found in the quizzes and practice tests in your online resources, will help you get the best score you possibly can on Integrated Reasoning.

ANALYTICAL WRITING ASSESSMENT

The Analytical Writing Assessment (AWA) is either the first task or the last task on the GMAT, depending on which section order you choose. When the section begins, you will be presented with the Analysis of an Argument essay assignment. You will have 30 minutes to complete it.

You'll type your essay into a simple word processing program. It allows you to do only the following basic functions:

- Insert text
- Delete text
- Cut and paste
- Undo the previous action
- Scroll up and down on the screen

Spell-check and grammar-check functions are not available in the program, so you will have to check those things carefully yourself. (As you practice writing essays, turn off your word processor's or internet browser's spell- and grammar-check functions.) One or two spelling errors or a few minor grammatical errors will not lower your score. But many spelling errors can hurt your score, as can grammar errors that are serious enough to obscure your intended meaning.

Your task for the Argument essay is always the same: to assess the logic and use of evidence in an argument. It doesn't matter whether you agree or disagree with the argument's conclusion. Rather, you need to explain the ways in which the author has failed to fully support that conclusion.

Thirty minutes is not enough time to produce the same kind of essay you've written for college classes. Nor is it enough time to do a lot of trial and error as you type. It is, however, enough time to write a "strong first draft" if you plan carefully, and that's what the essay graders are looking for. The Kaplan Method for Analytical Writing is a proven approach for producing a solid essay in the allotted time.

How the AWA Is Scored

LEARNING OBJECTIVES

- Outline the process by which the Analytical Writing Assessment is scored by human and computer raters
- Describe characteristics of essays that score in each of the score bands

Your essays will be graded on a scale from 0 to 6 (highest). You'll receive one score, which will be an average of the scores that you receive from each of the two graders, rounded up to the nearest half point. This score does not contribute to your overall 200–800 score, nor is it combined with any other subscore. Business schools receive not only your score but also the text of your essay. Some schools compare your writing in your application's personal statement to your writing on the AWA to confirm that your application essay was plausibly written by you and not someone else.

Your essay will be graded by a human grader as well as a computerized essay grader (the IntelliMetric™ system). The two grade completely independently of each other—IntelliMetric™ isn't told the human's score, nor is the human told the computer's. If the two scores are identical, then that's your score. If the scores differ by one point, those scores are averaged. If they differ by more than one point, a second human will grade the essay to resolve any differences, but this is rarely necessary.

IntelliMetric's™ grading algorithm was designed using 400 officially graded essays for each prompt. That's a huge sample of responses, so don't worry about whether IntelliMetric™ will understand your ideas—it's highly likely that someone out of those 400 responses made a similar point.

Before you begin to write, outline your essay. Good organization always counts, but with a computer grader, it's more important than ever. Use transitional phrases like *first*, *therefore*, *since*, and *for example* so that the computer can recognize structured analysis. The length of your essay is not a factor, as neither the computer nor the human rater counts the number of words in your response. The paragraphs in the body of your essay should develop your ideas in some depth and so should be at least several sentences long. However, the quality of your thinking and writing is much more important than the quantity of words.

Furthermore, computers are not good judges of humor or creativity. The human judges don't reward those either. The standard is business writing, and you shouldn't be making overly witty or irreverent remarks in, say, an email to a CEO.

Though IntelliMetric™ doesn't grade spelling per se, it could give you a lower score if it can't understand you or thinks you used the wrong words.

Here's what your essay will be graded on:

- **Structure.** Does your essay have good paragraph unity, organization, and flow?
- **Evidence.** It's not enough simply to assert good points. Do you develop them well? How strong are the examples you provide?
- **Depth of logic.** Do you take apart the argument and analyze its major weaknesses effectively?
- **Style.** The GMAC calls this "control of the elements of standard written English." How well do you express your ideas?

Now let's take a more in-depth look at the scoring scale so you get a sense of what to aim for. This rubric shows how the GMAC will grade your essay based on the four categories of Structure, Evidence, Depth of Logic, and Style.

	1 SERIOUSLY DEFICIENT	2 SUBSTANTIALLY FLAWED	3 INADEQUATE	4 SATISFACTORY	5 GOOD	6 EXCELLENT
Structure	Lacks length and organization; *does not adhere* to topic.	Lacks length and organization; *unclear understanding* of topic.	Lacks length enough for real analysis; *strays from topic* or is partially unfocused.	Has *good basic organization* and sufficient paragraphing.	Has *well-developed paragraphs* and structure; stays on topic.	Has well-developed paragraphs and structure; *paragraphing works with examples*.
Evidence	Provides *few, if any, examples* to back up claims.	Provides *very sparse examples* to back up claims.	Provides *insufficient examples* to back up claims.	Provides *sufficient examples* to back up claims.	Provides *strong examples* to back up claims.	Provides *very strong examples* to back up claims.
Depth of Logic	Shows *very little understanding of the argument* and gives no analysis of/ takes no position on it.	Presents the writer's views, but *fails to give any analytical critique*.	Analyzes somewhat, but *fails to show some key parts of the argument*.	Shows key parts of the argument adequately with *some analysis*.	Shows key parts of the argument and *analyzes them thoughtfully*.	Shows key parts of the argument and *analyzes them with great clarity*.
Style	Has *severe and persistent errors* in sentence structure and use of language; meaning is lost.	*Frequently uses language incorrectly*, and sentence structure, grammar, and usage errors inhibit meaning.	*Uses language imprecisely* and is deficient in variety; some major errors or a number of small errors.	*Controls language adequately*, including syntax and diction; a few flaws.	*Controls language with clarity*, including variety of syntax and diction; may have a flaw here and there.	*Controls language extremely well*, including variety of syntax and diction; may have a small flaw here and there.

GMAC will grade your essay holistically based on the above rubric to arrive at your final score:

- **6: Excellent.** Essays that earn the top score must be insightful, well supported by evidence, logically organized, and skillfully written. A 6 essay need not be perfect, just very good.

- **5: Good.** A 5 essay is well written and well supported but may not be as compellingly argued as a 6. There may also be more frequent or more serious writing errors than in a 6.

- **4: Satisfactory.** The important elements of the argument are addressed but not explained robustly. The organization is good, and the evidence provided is adequate. The writing may have some flaws but is generally acceptable.

- **3: Inadequate.** A 3 response misses important elements of the argument, offers little or no evidence to support its ideas, and doesn't clearly express its meaning.

- **2: Substantially Flawed.** An essay scoring a 2 has some serious problems. It may not use any examples whatsoever or support its ideas in any way. Its writing will have many errors that interfere with the meaning of the sentences.

- **1: Seriously Deficient.** These essays are rare. A 1 score is reserved for essays that provide little or no evidence of the ability to analyze an argument or to develop ideas in any way. A 1 essay will have so many writing errors that the essay may be unintelligible.

- **0: No Score.** A score of 0 signifies an attempt to avoid addressing the prompt at all, either by writing only random or repeating characters or by copying the prompt. You could also score a 0 by not writing in English or by addressing a completely different topic.

- **NR: Blank.** This speaks for itself. This is what you get if you write no essay at all. Some schools will not consider your GMAT score if your essay receives an NR.

CONCEPT CHECK

- You will have _____ minutes to write your essay.

- A satisfactory score on the AWA is _____.

- How does your score on the Analytical Writing Assessment relate to your overall GMAT score?

  _____

- What are the four dimensions that the graders evaluate when assigning a score to your essay?

  _____

Example answers are in your book's online resources (**kaptest.com/login**).

The Kaplan Method for Analytical Writing

LEARNING OBJECTIVES

- Explain the purpose of each step of the Kaplan Method for Analytical Writing
- Apply the steps of the Kaplan Method for Analytical Writing

You have a limited amount of time to show the business school admissions officers that you can think logically and express yourself in clearly written English. They don't care how many syllables you can cram into a sentence or how fancy your phrases are. They care that you make sense. Whatever you do, don't hide beneath a lot of hefty words and abstract language. Make sure that everything you say is clearly written and relevant to the topic. Get in there, state your main points, back them up, and get out. The Kaplan Method for Analytical Writing—along with Kaplan's recommendations for how much time you should devote to each step of the Method—will help you produce the best essay you're capable of writing in 30 minutes.

THE KAPLAN METHOD FOR ANALYTICAL WRITING

STEP 1   Take apart the argument.

STEP 2   Identify the points you will make.

STEP 3   Organize using Kaplan's essay template.

STEP 4   Write your essay.

STEP 5   Proofread your work.

Step 1: Take Apart the Argument

- Read through the prompt to identify the author's conclusion and the evidence used to support it.
- This is exactly the same as analyzing the stimulus for an argument-based Critical Reasoning question on the Verbal section.
- You can take about 2 minutes on this step.

Step 2: Identify the Points You Will Make

- Identify at least two important gaps (assumptions) between the evidence and the conclusion.
- Think of how you'll explain or illustrate those gaps. For example, are there circumstances under which the author's assumptions would not hold true? Also, think about how the author could remedy those weaknesses.
- This part of the Kaplan Method is very much like predicting the answer to a Critical Reasoning Strengthen or Weaken question.
- Step 2 should take about 5 minutes.

Step 3: Organize Using Kaplan's Essay Template

- Organize your thinking from step 2 according to Kaplan's essay template (below).
- Cross out any thinking that is incomplete, combine points that are closely related, and number the remaining points, giving the number 1 to the point you can write the strongest paragraph about. Leading with your best ideas ensures that you'll discuss them before time runs out.
- The organization process should take less than 1 minute.

Step 4: Write Your Essay

- Still following the template, type out your ideas using clear, concise, direct prose.
- Using the same kinds of key words that help you understand Reading Comprehension passage structure will help your grader understand your essay.
- Plan to spend no more than 20 minutes typing your essay. The thinking and organizing you did in steps 1, 2, and 3 will mean that 20 minutes is plenty of time.

Step 5: Proofread Your Work

- Fix any spelling, usage, or grammar errors you spot. Also, add key words as needed to improve the flow of ideas.
- This step is similar to Sentence Correction; you should follow the same rules of formal academic English that are tested in the Verbal section.
- Don't add any new ideas or change the structure of your essay. There just isn't time.
- Save 2 minutes for this step.

ORGANIZING THE ARGUMENT ESSAY: THE KAPLAN TEMPLATE

PARAGRAPH 1:

Show that you understand the argument by putting it in your own words.

PARAGRAPH 2:

Point out one flawed assumption in the author's reasoning; explain why it is questionable.

PARAGRAPH 3:

Identify another source of the author's faulty reasoning; explain why it is questionable.

ADDITIONAL PARAGRAPHS AS APPROPRIATE:

Continue to bring in points of fault in the argument, as time permits.

SECOND-TO-LAST PARAGRAPH:

Describe evidence that would—if it were provided—strengthen the argument.

LAST PARAGRAPH:

Conclude that without such evidence, you're not persuaded.

Applying the Kaplan Method for Analytical Writing

Screen 1: General Instructions

The general instructions for the Argument essay will look like this:

Analytical Writing Assessment Instructions
Analysis of an Argument Essay

Time: 30 Minutes

In this part of the test, you will be asked to write a critical analysis of the argument in the prompt. You are not being asked to give your own views on the topic.

COMPOSING YOUR ESSAY: Before you begin to type, take a little time to look at the argument and plan your essay. Make sure your ideas are organized and clearly stated. Leave some time to read over your essay and make any changes you think are necessary. You will have 30 minutes to write your essay.

ESSAY ASSESSMENT: Qualified graders with varied backgrounds, including experience in business subject areas, will assess the overall quality of your analysis and composition. They will look at how well you:

- Identify key elements of the argument and examine them
- Arrange your analysis of the argument presented
- Give appropriate examples and reasons for support
- Master the components of written English

The instructions on Screen 1 tell you to read the argument, plan your essay before writing it, and leave a little time at the end for review. Sound familiar? The Kaplan Method mirrors these steps. While the prompts for the essay vary, the general directions are always the same. Become familiar with the essay directions now so you don't waste valuable time reading them on Test Day.

Screen 2: Specific Prompt

The next screen you go to will contain the specific essay prompt.

Read the argument and the directions that follow it, and write down any ideas that will be helpful in mapping out your essay. Begin writing your essay in the box at the bottom of this screen.

The following appeared as part of a business plan created by a management consultant hired by Comfy Food Restaurant:

"After adding several vegetarian entrees to its dinner menu late last year, Comfy Food experienced a 21 percent increase in the average number of entrees ordered each evening. Furthermore, restaurant reviewers have viewed menu innovations at other dining establishments favorably, writing positive reviews. Therefore, Comfy Food should continue to expand the vegetarian offerings on its menu by replacing several meat entrees with salads, as well as adding meatless appetizers and side dish options. Doing so will allow Comfy Food to gain a competitive advantage over other local restaurants and increase its profits."

> Consider how logical you find this argument. In your essay, be sure to discuss the line of reasoning and the use of evidence in the argument. For example, you may need to consider what questionable assumptions underlie the thinking and what alternative explanations or counterpoints might weaken the conclusion. You may also discuss what types of evidence would strengthen or refute the argument, what changes in the argument would make it more logically sound, and what, if anything, would help you better evaluate its conclusion.

The only part of Screen 2 that will change is the specific prompt, which is in quotation marks. The instructions above and below it will stay the same. Again, practicing with these directions now will mean that you won't waste time reading them on Test Day.

The Stimulus

Analysis of an Argument topics will probably remind you of certain Critical Reasoning questions, in particular Strengthen/Weaken and Evaluate questions. Just as in these Critical Reasoning questions, the writer tries to persuade you of something—her conclusion—by citing some evidence. So look for these two basic components of an argument: a conclusion and supporting evidence. Furthermore, just as in Critical Reasoning, be on the lookout for assumptions—the ways the writer makes the leap from evidence to conclusion. These can often be found in mismatched terms between the evidence and conclusion and in possibilities the author has overlooked.

The Question Stem

The question stem instructs you to decide how convincing you find the argument, explain why, and discuss what might improve the argument. Note that there is a right answer here: the argument *always* has some problems. You want to focus your efforts on finding them, explaining them, and fixing them.

Exactly what are you being asked to do here? Paraphrase the following sentences of the question stem.

> Consider how logical you find this argument. In your essay, be sure to discuss the line of reasoning and the use of evidence in the argument.

Translation: Critique the argument. Discuss the ways in which it is not convincing. How and why might the evidence not fully support the conclusion?

> For example, you may need to consider what questionable assumptions underlie the thinking and what alternative explanations or counterpoints might weaken the conclusion. You may also discuss what types of evidence would strengthen or refute the argument, what changes in the argument would make it more logically sound, and what, if anything, would help you better evaluate its conclusion.

Translation: Spot weak links in the argument and offer constructive modifications that would strengthen them.

Let's use the Kaplan Method for Analytical Writing on the Analysis of an Argument topic we saw before:

> The following appeared as part of a business plan created by a management consultant hired by Comfy Food Restaurant:

"After adding several vegetarian entrees to its dinner menu late last year, Comfy Food experienced a 21 percent increase in the average number of entrees ordered each evening. Furthermore, restaurant reviewers have viewed menu innovations at other dining establishments favorably, writing positive reviews. Therefore, Comfy Food should continue to expand the vegetarian offerings on its menu by replacing several meat entrees with salads, as well as adding meatless appetizers and side dish options. Doing so will allow Comfy Food to gain a competitive advantage over other local restaurants and increase its profits."

Step 1: Take Apart the Argument

First, identify the conclusion—the point the argument is trying to make. Here, the conclusion is the recommendation in the third sentence:

Comfy Food should continue to expand the vegetarian offerings on its menu by replacing several meat entrees with salads, as well as adding meatless appetizers and side dish options.

Next, identify the evidence—the basis for the conclusion. Here, several pieces of evidence are provided. You might jot them on your notepad like this:

- Fact: Adding veggie dinner entrees → more entrees ordered
- Fact: Other restaurants changed menus → good reviews
- Opinion: More desirable entrees + good reviews will make this restaurant more competitive relative to other restaurants
- Opinion: Attracting more customers from other restaurants will lead to greater profits

Finally, paraphrase the argument as a whole in your own words: *Comfy Foods should increase its selection of vegetarian items because doing so will be good for business.*

If you aren't able to put the argument in your own words, you don't yet understand it well enough to analyze it sufficiently. Don't rush this step; you can afford a full 2 minutes if you need it.

Step 2: Identify the Points You Will Make

Now that you've found the conclusion and evidence, think about what assumptions the author makes. What's wrong with her reasoning? What important questions does she leave unaddressed? Here are some key assumptions this author makes:

- Because adding vegetarian entrees boosted entree ordering before, adding more salads to the menu will have the same effect.
- Because other restaurants' menu changes got good reviews, Comfy Food's planned menu change will get good reviews.
- Diners who don't currently eat (or eat often) at Comfy Food will eat there (more often) in response to salads and good reviews.
- The markup on the new menu items won't be so much less than the markup on the items they are replacing that profits could go down, even if volume goes up.

You also will need to explain how these assumptions could be false or how the questions reveal weaknesses in the author's argument. Add counterexamples and reasoning to your notes. The following notes are written out so they can be easily understood by readers of this book, but on Test Day, no one needs to understand your notes but you. So use just enough words to remind yourself of your ideas, and abbreviate wherever possible.

- Because adding vegetarian entrees coincided with entree ordering before, adding more salads to the menu will have the same effect.
  ◦ The increase in entree orders may have been due to some other factor and not the menu change.
  ◦ The "vegetarian entrees" in the evidence weren't necessarily "salads," so there's no support for adding salads specifically to the menu. Perhaps diners who eat at Comfy Foods like hearty bean-and-rice casseroles.
  ◦ There's no evidence that adding vegetarian appetizers and side dishes will influence customer behavior; the evidence is only about entrees.
  ◦ Perhaps the restaurant is already providing all the vegetarian items that patrons want, so adding yet more items will do nothing for sales.
- Because other restaurants' menu changes got good reviews, Comfy Food's planned menu change will get good reviews.
  ◦ The other restaurants may have made completely different menu changes, such as to include more locally sourced, organic ingredients or to offer different cuisines. Reviewers may not look favorably upon Comfy Food's changes.
- Diners who don't currently eat (or eat often) at Comfy Food will eat there (more often) in response to salads and good reviews.
  ◦ The author provides evidence that people ordered more entrees when the menu was changed last year, but that doesn't necessarily mean more people visited this restaurant instead of another one. Maybe diners substituted entrees for other orders.
  ◦ The author offers no evidence that potential customers respond to reviews. Maybe people tend to keep going to the restaurants they're already familiar with rather than trying someplace they've read about in a review.
- The markup on the new menu items won't be so much less than the markup on the items they are replacing that profits could go down, even if volume goes up.
  ◦ Even if changing the menu attracts more customers and they order more food, that's no guarantee that the restaurant will be more profitable. If the difference between what dishes cost to make and what the restaurant can charge decreases, selling more food might result in less profit.

Then think about evidence that would make the argument stronger or more logically sound:

- Evidence, such as a customer survey, confirming that local diners want salads and meatless appetizers and side dishes
- The same survey could provide data about why diners visit one restaurant over another
- Evidence, such as from conversations with restaurant critics or research into dining trends, that the proposed menu changes will garner positive reviews
- Evidence in the form of financial projections that shows an increase in customer orders, given the new mix of menu items and their markups, will in fact result in increased profits

Step 3: Organize Using Kaplan's Essay Template

Look over the notes you've jotted down. Select the strongest point to be first, the next-strongest to be second, and so on. Two criteria determine whether a point is strong. One is how well you can explain it. If, for example, you aren't sure how to explain potential inertia in customer behavior, you should use that idea last—if at all. The other is how seriously the weakness undermines the argument's persuasiveness. If customers have no interest in salads, for example, the argument is in serious trouble.

Then decide how you'll arrange your points. Follow the Kaplan template. You can just number the ideas you've already brainstormed. Here's one way someone might organize this essay. Note that this person has reorganized the order of ideas from the notes above, and she's divided up the third idea—about what drives customer behavior—combining parts of it with two other ideas instead of writing about it in a separate paragraph.

¶ Restate argument and assert that it relies too heavily on assumptions

¶ Assump: increased orders = profits

¶ Assump: reviews will be positive & reviews drive customer behavior

¶ Assump: demand for salads, etc. & menu choices drive customer behavior

¶ Evidence that would strengthen argument

¶ Conclude

Remember, you may not have time to use all your points. Leaving your weakest for last means that if you run short on time, you'll leave out your weakest point instead of your best.

Here's another tip: If you're concerned about running out of time, write a strong concluding sentence that restates your thesis (that in the absence of further evidence, the argument is not persuasive) right after you write your introductory paragraph. After all, you know how your essay will end. Then spend the available time filling in the middle with body paragraphs, without the pressure of needing to leave time to write a clear conclusion.

Step 4: Write Your Essay

Begin typing your essay now. Keep in mind the principles of sound writing discussed earlier.

Keep your writing simple and clear. Choose words that you know how to use well. Avoid the temptation to make your writing "sound smarter" with overly complicated sentences or vocabulary that feels awkward.

Keep your eye on the clock and make sure that you don't run out of time to proofread. If you need to, leave out your last point or two. Just make sure that you include at least two main points.

> The business consultant recommends that Comfy Foods Restaurant change its menu, specifically by replacing some meat entrees with salads and adding other vegetarian options. This strategy will, according to the consultant, give the restaurant an advantage over other area restaurants and be more profitable. Certainly this argument would be compelling if it were credible. However, the argument relies on unsupported assumptions and is therefore unconvincing.

The consultant supports this proposal in part by stating that it will increase the restaurant's profits. Even if the plan works as intended and Comfy Foods enjoys greater market share and more customers, profits may not follow. A higher volume of food orders will result in higher profits only if the total margin is greater. If these new items cost more to make than the old items, or if the restaurant cannot charge as much for them, or some combination of the two, even greater sales may not lead to greater profits. Unless data are provided to address this issue, the restaurant's management cannot be sure that this alleged benefit of the plan will come to pass.

Moreover, it is far from certain that customers will respond positively to changes in the menu. The consultant implies that reviewers will write positive reviews after the changes, because they have written positive reviews about changes to the menus at other restaurants. However, no information is provided about what those changes were. Perhaps those restaurants shifted to using more locally sourced, organic ingredients, or perhaps they incorporated items from diverse cuisines into their offerings. Even if those restaurants did begin serving more vegetarian food, maybe they prepared the food in an exceptionally delicious manner and that is what reviewers responded to—not the change to the menu itself. Finally, there is no evidence that restaurant patrons act on what they read in reviews. They may continue to visit the establishments they know and love, no matter how enticing a review may be. Without knowing more about what factors influence reviews and how reviews influence customer behavior, management should be skeptical of the effects of this plan.

In addition, the consultant assumes that the restaurant's experience with adding a few unspecified vegetarian entrees to the menu supports the specific recommendation to add salads and non-entree dishes. First, there is no evidence that adding the new entrees actually increased sales of entrees, other than the fact that the two events happened at the same time. Perhaps entree sales would have gone up for some other reason, regardless of the menu change. Second, maybe Comfy Foods customers like hearty bean-and-rice casseroles and will be uninterested in salads. Finally, there is no evidence to support the idea that vegetarian side dishes and appetizers will be well received. Indeed, since the restaurant has already expanded its vegetarian offerings, perhaps customer demand for this food is already being satisfied and further offerings will have no effect.

Comfy Foods management should ask the consultant to provide more data to support her assumptions. A survey of local residents could confirm what people who dine out want to see on restaurant menus and how they decide to visit one restaurant over another. Conversations with restaurant critics or research into dining trends would give more insight into whether the proposed menu changes would garner the positive reviews that the consultant anticipates. A detailed breakdown of costs and prices of current and proposed menu items, at different volumes, would help management determine whether changing the menu would increase profits.

Unfortunately, because the consultant has not provided these types of evidence, management should not rely on her plan to improve the business.

Step 5: Proofread Your Work

Save a few minutes to go back over your essay and catch any obvious errors or opportunities for improvement. The best way to improve your writing and proofreading skills is practice. When you practice responding to AWA prompts, do so on a computer—but to mimic test conditions, don't use the automatic spell-check or grammar-check. You can turn off these functions in your browser or word processor settings.

Write practice essays using the prompts at the end of this chapter or those provided by the test maker at **mba.com**. The pool of prompts provided by the test maker contains the actual prompts from which the GMAT will select your essay topic on Test Day.

Step 4: Write Your Essay—A Deep Dive

LEARNING OBJECTIVE

- Evaluate whether your writing has a logical structure; demonstrates control of language; and is concise, forceful, and correct

You aren't being evaluated solely on the strength of your ideas. Your score will also depend on how well you express them. If your writing style isn't clear, your ideas won't come across, no matter how brilliant they are.

Use a Logical Structure

Good essays have a straightforward, linear structure. Of course, people rarely think in a straightforward, linear way—especially under time pressure. That's why it's important to plan your response before you begin typing. If you type *while* planning, your essay will likely loop back on itself, contain redundancies, or fail to follow through on what it sets up. It's confusing to the reader when an essay keeps jumping back and forth between the different weaknesses of an argument. Discuss one point fully and then address the next. Don't write another paragraph about a topic you've already discussed.

Maintaining paragraph unity will help keep your essay as a whole organized. Paragraph unity means that each paragraph discusses one thing and all the discussion of that one thing happens in that paragraph. Let's say the argument you're analyzing proposes a new idea for a business and you're discussing various reasons why the proposed idea might not work. You'd likely use the first paragraph in the body of your essay to address one reason. Your next paragraph should move on to another reason. If, in the middle of that next paragraph, you began to explain more about the first reason, you'd be violating paragraph unity.

In addition, develop a consistent flow of ideas. If your introductory paragraph says that you will explain why a proposed fast-food franchise might be unpopular with demographic groups with disposable income, you need to make sure that you actually discuss this. If your essay instead gives reasons why the population as a whole will prefer cooking at home to eating out in the coming decade, the body of the essay won't flow from its introductory paragraph.

Similarly, avoid suddenly expanding the scope of the essay in the last sentence. It's not unusual, after you've had a chance to think and write about a topic for nearly 30 minutes, to suddenly have a pretty great idea about it. It can be tempting to try to shoehorn that great idea into the end of your essay. Resist the temptation, however, as you will leave the reader with a final impression of disorganization.

Demonstrate Control of Language

Your writing must follow the same general rules of standard written English that are tested by Sentence Correction questions. If you're not confident of your mastery of grammar, review the Sentence Correction chapters of this book.

In addition to using correct grammar, your essay should employ correct diction. *Diction* means word choice. Do you use the words *affect* and *effect* correctly? What about *its* and *it's*; *there*, *their*, and *they're*; *precede* and *proceed*; *principal* and *principle*; and *whose* and *who's*? In addition to avoiding errors of usage, you will need to use language precisely and convey the formal, professional tone expected of academic and business writing.

It's also important to demonstrate a command of syntax. *Syntax* refers to sentence structure. Do you construct your sentences so that your ideas are clear and understandable? Do you vary the length and structure of your sentences?

Keep Things Simple

Perhaps the single most important piece of advice to bear in mind when writing a GMAT essay is to keep everything simple. This rule applies to word choice, sentence structure, and organization. If you get distracted by how to use or spell an unusual word, you may lose time and confidence. The more complicated your sentences are, the more likely they'll be plagued by errors. The more complex your organization becomes, the harder it will be for graders to follow your points.

Keep in mind that simple does not mean *simplistic*. A clear, straightforward approach can still be sophisticated and convey perceptive insights.

GMAT Style Checklist

On the GMAT, there are three rules of thumb for successful writing: be concise, be forceful, and be correct. Following these rules is a sure way to improve your writing style—and your score. Let's look at each one in more depth.

Be Concise

- Cut out words, phrases, and sentences that don't add any information or serve a necessary purpose.
- Watch out for repetitive phrases such as "critically important" or "absolutely essential."
- Don't use conjunctions to join sentences that would be more effective as separate sentences.
- Don't use needless qualifiers such as "really" or "kind of."

Here are some examples:

> **Wordy:** The agency is not prepared to undertake expansion at this point in time.
>
> **Concise:** The agency is not ready to expand.
>
> **Redundant:** All of these problems have combined together to create a serious crisis.
>
> **Concise:** Combined, these problems create a crisis.
>
> **Too many qualifiers:** Ferrara seems to be sort of a slow worker.
>
> **Concise:** Ferrara works slowly.

Be Forceful

- Don't refer to yourself needlessly. Avoid phrases such as "in my personal opinion," "I agree," or "I think." Since you are writing the essay, opinions you express are assumed to be yours.

- Avoid jargon and pompous language; it won't impress anybody. For example, "a waste of time and money" is better than "a pointless expenditure of temporal and financial resources."

- Avoid using the passive voice. Whenever possible, write in active voice, which means placing verbs after their subjects.

- Avoid clichés and overused terms or phrases (for example, "beyond the shadow of a doubt").

- Don't be vague. Avoid generalizations and abstractions when more specific words and examples would be clearer.

- Sentences that begin with "there is" or "there are" are inherently weak. For example, "There are several ways in which this sentence is awkward" should be rewritten as "This sentence is awkward in several ways."

- Don't be monotonous; vary sentence length and style.

- Use transitions to connect sentences and make your essay easy to follow.

Here are some examples:

> **Needlessly references self:** Although I am no expert, privacy should be given a high value by companies.

> **Speaks confidently:** Companies should value privacy highly.

> **Uses passive voice:** The survey was conducted over a holiday weekend, when many people are not at home.

> **Uses active voice:** The market research firm conducted the survey over a holiday weekend, when many people are not at home.

> **Opens weakly:** It would be of no use to develop a new technology without reducing demand for the old technology.

> **Opens strongly:** The government cannot effectively support the development of a new technology without reducing demand for the old technology.

Be Correct

Observe the rules of standard written English. The most important rules are covered in the chapter in this book on Sentence Correction grammar and usage.

Here are some examples:

> **Subject and verb disagree:** The CEO, along with her associates, expect the sustainable energy proposal to pass.

> **Subject and verb agree:** The CEO, along with her associates, expects the sustainable energy proposal to pass.

> **Uses faulty modification:** Having worked in publishing for 10 years, Stokely's résumé shows that he is well qualified.

Uses correct modification: Stokely, who has worked in publishing for 10 years, appears from his résumé to be well qualified.

Uses pronouns incorrectly: A retirement community offers more activities than a private dwelling does, but it is cheaper.

Uses pronouns correctly: A retirement community offers more activities than a private dwelling does, but a private dwelling is cheaper.

Has unparallel structure: The consultant can teach clients how to brainstorm, how to make decisions, and evaluate business results and deal with setbacks.

Has parallel structure: The consultant can teach clients how to brainstorm, make decisions, evaluate business results, and deal with setbacks.

Is a fragment: Investing in real estate can be lucrative. After one has established oneself in the business world, however.

Is a complete sentence: Investing in real estate can be lucrative, but only after one has established oneself in the business world.

Is a run-on: Antonio has impressive exercise physiology credentials, however, because Madison has been with the gym since 2015, Madison is probably more skilled with the gym's weight-lifting equipment.

Is a correct sentence: Antonio has impressive exercise physiology credentials. However, because Madison has been with the gym since 2015, Madison is probably more skilled with the gym's weight-lifting equipment.

CONCEPT CHECK

- How can you give your essay a logical structure?

  _____

- What does correct diction mean?

  _____

- What does good syntax mean?

  _____

- What is a very convenient resource to use to improve your grammar?

  _____

Example answers are in your book's online resources (**kaptest.com/login**).

Practice Essays

Directions: Write an essay on each of the topics below. Allow yourself 30 minutes to complete each essay. Practice writing under timed conditions so that you get a feel for how much you can afford to write while leaving enough time to proofread.

Essay 1

The following appeared in a memo from the regional manager of Luxe Spa, a chain of high-end salons.

"Over 75 percent of households in Parksboro have Jacuzzi bathtubs. In addition, the average family income in Parksboro is 50 percent higher than the national average, and a local store reports record-high sales of the most costly brands of hair and body care products. With so much being spent on personal care, Parksboro will be a profitable location for a new Luxe Spa—a salon that offers premium services at prices that are above average."

Consider how logical you find this argument. In your essay, be sure to discuss the line of reasoning and the use of evidence in the argument. For example, you may need to consider what questionable assumptions underlie the thinking and what alternative explanations or counterpoints might weaken the conclusion. You may also discuss what types of evidence would strengthen or refute the argument, what changes in the argument would make it more logically sound, and what, if anything, would help you better evaluate its conclusion.

After writing your essay, compare it to the sample response that follows.

Student Response (as written, including original errors)

Though it might seem at first glance that the regional manager of Luxe Spa has good reasons for suggesting that Parksboro would be a profitable location for a new spa, a closer examination of the arguments presented reveals numerous examples of leaps of faith, poor reasoning, and ill-defined terminology. In order to better support her claim, the manager would need to show a correlation between the figures she cites in reference to Parksboro's residents and a willingness to spend money at a spa with high prices.

The manager quotes specific statistics about the percentage of residents with Jacuzzis and the average income in Parksboro. She then uses these figures as evidence to support her argument. However, neither of these statistics as presented does much to bolster her claim. Just because 75 percent of homes have Jacuzzis doesn't mean those homeowners are more likely to go to a pricey spa. For instance, the presence of Jacuzzis in their houses may indicate a preference for pampering themselves at home. Parksboro could also be a planned development in the suburbs where all the houses are designed with Jacuzzis. If this is the case, than the mere ownership of a certain kind of bathtub should hardly be taken as a clear indication of a person's inclination to go to a spa. In addition, the fact that Parksboro's average family income is 50 percent higher than the national average is not enough on its own to predict the success or failure of a spa in the region. Parksboro may have a very small population, for instance, or a small number of wealthy people counterbalanced by a number of medium- to low-income families. We simply cannot tell from the information provided.

In addition, the failure of the manager to provide the national average family income for comparison makes it unclear if earning 50 percent more would allow for a luxurious lifestyle or not.

The mention of a local store's record-high sales of expensive personal care items similarly provides scant evidence to support the manager's assertions. We are given no indication of what constitutes "record-high" sales for this particular store or what "most costly" means in this context. Perhaps this store usually sells very few personal care products and had one unusual month. Even if this one store sold a high volume of hair- and body-care products, it may not be representative of the Parksboro market as a whole. And perhaps "most costly" refers only to the most costly brands available in Parksboro, not to the most costly brands nationwide. The manager needs to provide much more specific information about residents' spending habits in order to provide compelling evidence that personal care ranks high among their priorities.

To make the case that Parksboro would be a profitable location for Luxe Spa, the regional manager should try to show that people there have a surplus of income and a tendency to spend it on indulging in spa treatments. Although an attempt is made to make this very argument, the lack of supporting information provided weakens rather than strengthens the memo. Information such as whether there are other high-end spas in the area and the presence of tourism in the town could also have been introduced as reinforcement. As it stands, Luxe Spa would be ill-advised to open a location in Parksboro based solely on the evidence provided here.

Analysis

Structure: The use of the Kaplan template is evident here. In the first paragraph, the writer demonstrates his understanding of the argument and gives a summary of its flaws. Each paragraph that follows elaborates on one flaw in the author's reasoning. The final paragraph introduces evidence that, if provided, would strengthen the argument.

Evidence: The evidence is strong. The writer develops his points by providing examples to explain why the author's reasoning is questionable. Some minor flaws are evident, as in the second paragraph, when the writer misses an opportunity to point out that a small population might not be enough to support a spa.

Depth of Logic: Once again, the organization of the essay enhances its depth of logic. The writer takes apart the argument methodically and provides clear analysis of each part.

Style: The writing style is smooth and controlled, and grammar and syntax errors are minimal to nonexistent.

This essay would score a 6. The writer makes a very strong showing in all four categories of the grading rubric.

Essay 2

The following appeared in a document released by a community's arts bureau:

"In a recent county survey, 20 percent more county residents indicated that they watch TV programs dedicated to the arts than was reported eight years ago. The number of visitors to our county's museums and galleries over the past eight years has gone up by a comparable proportion. Now that the commercial funding public TV relies on is facing severe cuts, which will consequently limit arts programming, it is likely that attendance at our county's art museums will also go down. Therefore, public funds that are currently dedicated to the arts should be partially shifted to public television."

Consider how logical you find this argument. In your essay, be sure to discuss the line of reasoning and the use of evidence in the argument. For example, you may need to consider what questionable assumptions underlie the thinking and what alternative explanations or counterpoints might weaken the conclusion. You may also discuss what types of evidence would strengthen or refute the argument, what changes in the argument would make it more logically sound, and what, if anything, would help you better evaluate its conclusion.

After writing your essay, compare it to the sample response that follows.

Student Response (as written, including original errors)

In a time of threatened scarcity of funding, a community arts organization is asking to shift public arts funds partly to public television. The organization cites a recent survey of county residents that shows a 20 percent self-reported increase in arts TV-watching over the last eight years concomitant with a similar, documented increase in local museum and art gallery attendance. This earnest plea is understandable, but the underlying rationale for shifting funding is flawed and lacks sufficient substantiation.

First, the author may be confusing correlation with causation. Does the survey—even if we accept its findings as valid—really indicate that people went to museums as a result of seeing arts programming on television? Its quite possible that there are alternate reasons for the increase in attendance at museums, such as partnerships with schools, discount programs for senior citizens, introduction of IMAX theaters, or popular traveling exhibits. Alternatively, people may be watching more arts programming on television as a direct result of being lured into museum attendance for reasons that have nothing to do with television.

A second reason to be hesitant to adopt the recommended funding shift is that it assumes that there are only two viable sources of funding for public television: commercial and public. Before it resorts to diverting public funds from other arts organizations, public television has the option to pursue direct fundraising from viewers; these newly enthusiastic television arts program viewers may be delighted to support such programming directly. Public television has a unique opportunity to reach its audience in a way that is more elusive to smaller art museums. It is potentially in a superior position to recover from reduced corporate funding without needing to rely more heavily on public funds.

Conversely, it is possible that the author knows more than he has shared about a connection between public television watching and local museum attendance. For instance, there may have been some specific partnerships in the last eight years between local museums and local public television stations, including specific programming designed to tie in with current museum exhibitions. The recent survey to which the author alluded may have referenced direct ties between the television programming and museum attendance. Such data would make it more likely that increasing the public funding for public television would also directly benefit local museums.

Until more information is provided to us, however, we cannot accept the authors' argument for a shift in public funds to local public television as a way to support local art museums.

Analysis

Structure: This essay is very well organized. The essayist's use of transitions is particularly strong here, as she leads the reader through the points of fault in the argument and describes evidence that could potentially strengthen the argument.

Evidence: The essayist provides multiple strong examples that strengthen her major points.

Depth of Logic: The essayist accurately identifies the assumptions inherent in the argument and develops her points by proposing plausible alternative explanations for the evidence the argument's author cites.

Style: The essayist has a few problems with misplaced apostrophes; otherwise, the grammar and syntax are strong.

This essay would score a 6. It is an excellent example of how following the Kaplan template will help you organize your ideas into a convincing essay. After the introduction, two paragraphs develop and support the author's two main points, followed by a paragraph describing how the argument could be strengthened and a clear conclusion.

PART SIX

TEST DAY

CHAPTER 25

TAKE CONTROL OF TEST DAY

LEARNING OBJECTIVES
- Make a study schedule to take you from now to Test Day
- Articulate methods for staying confident, building stamina, and keeping your stress under control

In the earlier parts of this book, we looked at the content covered on the various sections of the GMAT. We also discussed the test expertise you'll need to move through those sections. Now we turn to the often overlooked topic of test mentality—that is, how to get into peak mental condition for the GMAT.

Mental Conditioning

Your frame of mind has a lot to do with the level of success you achieve. Here's what's involved in developing your best mindset for the GMAT.

Test Awareness

To do your best on the GMAT, you must always keep in mind that the test is unlike other tests that you've taken in terms of both the content and the scoring system. If you took a test in high school or college and got a quarter of the questions wrong, you'd probably receive a pretty lousy grade. But due to the adaptive nature of the GMAT, missing only a quarter of the questions would give you a very high score. The test is designed to push test takers to their limits, so people rarely get every question right. In fact, you can get a handful of questions wrong and still score in the 99th percentile.

In other words, don't let what you consider to be a subpar performance on a handful of questions ruin your performance on the rest. A couple of missed questions won't, by themselves, spoil your score. But if you allow the frustration of those questions to unnerve you, you could end up compromising your performance on other questions or on the section as a whole. Missing a few points won't ruin your score, but losing your head will.

The test is designed to find your limits, so it should feel challenging. If you feel you've done poorly on a section, don't worry—you may have done just fine. Keep in mind that the questions that you are likely to struggle on most will be the hardest ones—the ones that hurt your score *least* if you miss them. To reach your highest potential score, you must remain calm and focused. Simply do your best on each question, and once a question or section is over, forget about it and move on.

Moreover, don't try to guess which questions are unscored (experimental questions). This kind of speculation has gotten countless test takers into trouble. They have a hunch that a certain question is one that doesn't count and then don't take it seriously. You cannot know which questions are experimental, so treat each one as if it counts. That way, you're covered no matter what. Likewise, don't worry if a question you get seems "too easy." This doesn't necessarily mean that you're doing poorly; it might be experimental. Or it might happen to align well with your individual strengths. Or perhaps you are just well prepared, have great strategies, and are beating the test! Do your best, get it right, and move on with confidence.

Stamina

The GMAT is a grueling experience, and some test takers simply run out of gas when they reach the final questions. To avoid this, you must prepare by taking full-length practice tests (not skipping over any sections) so that on Test Day, the several hours of testing will seem like a breeze—or at least not a hurricane.

Your online resources include full-length CATs for just this purpose. If you finish the tests included with this book, a further option is to download the test maker's GMAT® Official Starter Kit software, which contains two full-length exams and is available free from **mba.com**. One drawback to the software is that it does not include explanations, so you will want to rely on your Kaplan materials, which include thorough explanations, for the bulk of your study. However, the test maker's CATs should give you a good indication of your score range.

Confidence

Confidence in your ability leads to quick, sure answers and a sense of poise that translates into more points. Confidence builds on itself, but unfortunately, so does self-doubt. If you lack confidence, you end up reading sentences and answer choices two, three, or four times until you confuse yourself and get off track. Or you begin to solve a math problem one way, worry that your approach won't work and jump to a different approach, and then go back to your first approach, wasting time without making progress. This uncertainty ruins your timing, perpetuating a downward spiral.

If you cultivate a positive GMAT mindset, however, you'll gear your practice toward taking control of the test. And when you have achieved that goal—armed with the techniques and strategies explained in this book—you'll be ready to face the GMAT with supreme confidence.

Positive Attitude

Those who approach the GMAT as an obstacle and who rail against the necessity of taking it usually don't fare as well as those who see the GMAT as an opportunity. Those who look forward to doing battle with the GMAT—or, at least, who enjoy the opportunity to distinguish themselves from the rest of the applicant pack—tend to score better than do those who resent or dread it.

Take our word for it: developing a positive attitude is a proven test-taking technique. Here are a few steps you can take to make sure you develop the right GMAT attitude:

- Look at the GMAT as a challenge but try not to obsess over it; you certainly don't want to psych yourself out of the game.

- Remember that, yes, the GMAT is obviously important, but contrary to popular belief, this one test will not single-handedly determine the outcome of your life—or even of your business school admissions.

- Try to have fun with the test. Learning how to match your wits against those of the test maker can be a very satisfying experience, and the critical thinking skills you'll acquire will benefit you in business school, as well as in your future career.

- Remember that you're more prepared than most people. You've trained with Kaplan. You have the tools you need, plus the ability to use those tools.

Stress Management

The countdown has begun. Your date with the test is looming on the horizon. Anxiety is on the rise. You have butterflies in your stomach, and your thinking is getting cloudy. Maybe you think you won't be ready. Maybe you already know your stuff, but you're going into panic mode anyway. Don't worry! It's possible to tame that anxiety and stress—before *and* during the test.

Remember, some stress is normal and good. Anxiety is a motivation to study. The adrenaline that gets pumped into your bloodstream when you're stressed helps you stay alert and think more clearly. But if you feel that the tension is so great that it's preventing you from using your study time effectively, here are some things you can do to get it under control.

Take Control

Lack of control is a prime cause of stress. Research shows that if you don't have a sense of control over what's happening in your life, you can easily end up feeling helpless and hopeless. Try to identify the sources of the stress you feel. Which ones can you do something about? Can you find ways to reduce the stress you're feeling from any of these sources?

Make a Study Schedule

Often, the mere realization that you're procrastinating on your GMAT study can cause stress. To help you gain control over your preparation process, make study appointments with yourself on your calendar—and then keep these appointments with yourself! Without setting aside time to study for the GMAT, it's easy to keep putting it off due to looming work deadlines, business school applications, or other commitments on your calendar. The hardest part of studying is getting started, so get started soon and start small. Even committing to working on five problems a day will produce a pleasant feeling of accomplishment and momentum, leading you to be able to make longer and longer commitments to your Test Day success.

Focus on Your Strengths

Make a list of areas of strength you have that will help you do well on the test. We all have strengths, and recognizing your own is like having reserves of solid gold in the bank. You'll be able to draw on your reserves as you need them, helping you solve difficult questions, maintain confidence, and keep test stress and anxiety at a distance. And every time you recognize a new area of strength, solve a challenging problem, or score well on a practice test, congratulate yourself—you'll only increase your reserves.

Imagine Yourself Succeeding

Close your eyes and imagine yourself in a relaxing situation. Breathe easily and naturally. Now think of a real-life situation in which you did well on an assignment. Focus on this success. Now turn your thoughts to the GMAT and keep your thoughts and feelings in line with that successful experience. Don't make comparisons between them; just imagine yourself taking the upcoming test with the same feelings of confidence and relaxed control.

Set Realistic Goals

Facing your problem areas gives you some distinct advantages. What do you want to accomplish in the study time remaining? Make a list of realistic goals. You can't help feeling more confident when you know you're actively improving your chances of earning a higher GMAT score.

Exercise Regularly

Whether it's jogging, yoga, push-ups, or a pickup basketball game, physical exercise will stimulate your mind and body and improve your ability to think and concentrate. A surprising number of test takers fall out of the habit of regular exercise, ironically because they're spending so much time prepping for the exam. A little physical exertion will help you to keep your mind and body in sync and to sleep better at night.

Eat Well

Good nutrition will help you focus and think clearly. Eat plenty of fruits and vegetables; low-fat protein such as fish, skinless poultry, beans, and legumes; and whole grains such as brown rice, whole-wheat bread, and pastas. Don't eat a lot of sugary and high-fat snacks or salty foods. Note that on Test Day, you can't bring food or drink into the testing room. But you can keep a healthy snack in your locker to recharge you between sections.

Sleep Well

Every GMAT problem requires careful critical thinking. Unfortunately, that's the first mental skill to go away when you are sleep deprived. Get a full night's sleep as often as you can during your preparation, especially as Test Day approaches.

Keep Breathing

Conscious attention to breathing is an excellent way to manage stress while you're taking the test. Many folks who get into trouble during the GMAT take shallow breaths; they breathe using only their upper chests and shoulder muscles and may even hold their breath for long periods of time. Conversely, test takers who breathe deeply in a slow, relaxed manner are likely to be in better control during the session.

Stretch

If you find yourself getting spaced out or burned out as you're studying or taking the test, stop for a brief moment and stretch. Even though you'll be pausing for a moment, it's a moment well spent. Stretching will help to refresh you and refocus your thoughts.

Stress Management Quiz

Don't be alarmed: this is not a GMAT quiz. It is important to your score, though. Imagine that there are two people with equal GMAT knowledge, skill, and practice. Why might one still outperform the other? The biggest difference will likely be that one manages stress and anxiety better than the other.

This quiz is a chance to reinforce and expand upon the ideas and advice you've read so far in this chapter. Have fun with it and think about how to apply your insights to your own life and study schedule.

1. What is Test Day stress?

    O   A feeling of anxiety felt only by those aiming for a top score

    O   Any factor, physical or psychological, that impedes my performance on the GMAT

    O   A consequence of poor preparation

    O   A constant fear of not getting into my first-choice school

    O   Something that only poor test takers experience

2. It is most helpful to my Test Day success when my friends and family

    O   push me to study more

    O   tell me how much more I have to learn

    O   compete with me over test scores

    O   have positive attitudes about my ability to achieve my best score and help me get my mind off the test whenever I am not studying

    O   care little about my performance and prevent me from getting sufficient time to prep

3. In the weeks leading up to the exam, how can I reduce stress?

    O   List my weaknesses and create a study schedule to overcome them, one topic at a time

    O   Get some exercise

    O   Limit self-deprecating humor and keep a positive attitude

    O   Get sufficient sleep

    O   All of the above

4. In the final days before my exam, I should worry about all of the topics that I still have trouble with or haven't hit, rather than congratulate myself on how far I've come.

   O True
   O False

5. The night before the exam, what can I do to reduce stress?

   O Try to learn topics that I have not mastered yet
   O Go to my local bar with my friends, drink a few pitchers of beer, and try to get my mind off the exam
   O Briefly review the topics that I mastered but haven't looked at in a while and get a good night's sleep
   O Stay up all night, memorizing the grammar and math concepts
   O Panic

6. On Test Day, what can I do to reduce stress?

   O Make sure I know the testing protocols and logistics
   O Eat a nutritious meal
   O Dress in comfortable clothes
   O Expect to undergo a rigorous security screening before the test begins
   O All of the above

7. During the exam, if I don't know how to answer a question and I begin to panic, I should

    O   keep re-reading the question until I determine the correct approach, no matter how long it takes

    O   bite my fingernails and moan

    O   keep breathing, take a moment to get my bearings, and determine whether I should take a strategic guess or give the question another minute or two

    O   remind myself that if I miss the question, I will not get into business school, I will fail in life, and I will be forced to live with my parents forever

    O   choose an answer choice that I haven't chosen much so far in that section

8. During the GMAT, I should avoid worrying about questions that I have already answered.

    O   True

    O   False

9. What should I do next to make sure that I am prepared to overcome the natural stress that comes with taking an important test?

    O   Understand that anxiety is a sign of weakness and suppress it ruthlessly

    O   Take control of my preparation by following a study schedule and cultivating a positive attitude

    O   Forget about Test Day stress until Test Day and then figure out how to deal with it

    O   Decide not to take the GMAT

    O   Nothing—this exercise has taught me all I need to know about Test Day stress management

The Week Before Test Day

Is it starting to feel like your whole life is a buildup to the GMAT? You've known about it for years, you've worried about it for months, and now you've spent at least a few weeks in solid preparation for it. As Test Day approaches, you may find your anxiety is on the rise. You shouldn't worry. After the preparation you've received from this book, you're in good shape for the test. To calm any jitters you may have, though, let's go over a few strategies for the days leading up to the test.

In the week or so leading up to Test Day, you should do the following:

- If you'll be going to a testing center to take your exam, pay it a visit. Sometimes seeing the actual room where your test will be administered and taking notice of little things—such as the kind of desk you'll be working on, whether there are lockers for you to store belongings, etc.—may help to calm your nerves. And if you've never been to the testing center, visiting beforehand is a good way to ensure that you don't get lost on Test Day. If you can go on the same day of the week and at the same time of day as your actual test, so much the better; you'll be able to scope out traffic patterns and parking. Remember, you must be on time—the computers at the testing centers are booked all day long.

- Practice working on test material, preferably a full-length test, at the same time of day that your test is scheduled for as if it were the real Test Day.

- Practice using the test interface by taking the tutorial at **mba.com/tutorial**. If you'll be taking the test on your own device, find the online whiteboard practice at **mba.com** and try out the different tools until you feel comfortable.

- Time yourself while practicing so you don't feel as though you are rushing on Test Day.

- Evaluate where you stand. Then make your strengths a focus of your studying this week. If you've been trying to get a handle on untangling long word math problems or identify misplaced modifiers in Sentence Correction for weeks or months and these questions are still challenging, you're unlikely to get the hang of them in the next few days. Your strengths, on the other hand, are where you'll rack up a lot of points. Focusing on your strengths is also a great way to build your confidence—and confidence really matters to your score.

The Day Before Test Day

This advice might seem counterintuitive, but try to avoid intensive studying the day before the test. There's little you can do to improve your score at this late date, and you may just wind up exhausting yourself and burning out. Our advice is to review a few key concepts, get together everything you'll need for Test Day (acceptable photo identification, the names of schools to which you'd like to send your GMAT scores, directions to the testing center if you will not be taking the test at home, a healthy snack for the break), and then take the night off entirely. Maybe binge watch a few episodes of a show you haven't been able to keep up with because you've been studying for the GMAT.

On Test Day

Test Day should contain no surprises. Test takers who feel in control of the events leading up to the test take that confidence with them into the testing center.

Give yourself plenty of time: leave early for the testing center or make sure your test space at home is set up and your internet is working. Read something to warm up your brain; you don't want the GMAT to be the first written material your brain tries to assimilate that day. If traveling to a testing center, leave yourself enough time for traffic or mass transit delays. Dress in comfortable clothing.

You will feel most prepared and confident if you have an understanding of how the logistics of Test Day will play out. Taking the full-length practice CATs in your online resources and those from **mba.com** will help you get the feel for the GMAT itself, but certain events are unique to the actual test experience. Check the test maker's website at **mba.com** for the most up-to-date information on Test Day logistics and be ready to follow the online or in-person proctor's instructions.

Here are some strategic reminders to help guide your work on Test Day:

- Read each question stem carefully and re-read it before making your final selection.

- Don't get bogged down in the middle of any section. You may find later questions more to your liking. So don't panic. Eliminate answer choices, guess, and move on.

- Don't fall behind early. Even if you get most of the first 10 questions right, you'll wind up rushing yourself into enough errors that you cancel out your early success. Keep a steady pace throughout the test and finish each section strong, avoiding the penalty for not completing all the questions.

- Don't bother trying to figure out which questions are unscored. It can't help you, and you might very well be wrong. Instead, just resolve to do your best on every question.

- Confidence is key. Accentuate the positives and don't dwell on the negatives. Your attitude and outlook are crucial to your performance on Test Day.

- During the exam, try not to speculate about how you're scoring. Imagine an athlete who's focusing on the crowd's cheers and the sportswriters and the upcoming contract negotiations during the game: there's no surer way to be distracted and perform poorly. Instead, focus on the question-by-question task of picking an answer choice. The correct answer is there. You don't have to come up with it; it's sitting right there in front of you!

What should you do if you . . .

- **Start to lose confidence?** If questions seem to be getting hard, don't lose confidence; since the GMAT is adaptive, it is practically guaranteed to feel like a struggle—for everyone! Trust in your preparation and in the skills and strategies you have practiced.

- **Start to lose concentration?** If you lose your concentration, pause, take a deep breath, exhale, and go back to the test. This will help you refocus and settle back in.

- **Have a problem with your equipment?** Alert the proctor, following the instructions you've been given in case a problem arises.

After Test Day, you should . . .

- Congratulate yourself for all the hard work you've put in. Make sure you celebrate afterward—and start thinking about all of the great times you'll be having at the business school of your choice!

- Plan your approach to business school applications, including references and essays.

- Look for your Official Score Report to be posted online.